CONTEMPORARY MANAGEMENT OF METASTATIC COLORECTAL CANCER

CONTEMPORARY MANAGEMENT OF METASTATIC COLORECTAL CANCER

A Precision Medicine Approach

Edited by

Aslam Ejaz, MD, MPH

Department of Surgery, The Ohio State University Wexner Medical Center, The James Comprehensive Cancer Center, Columbus, OH, USA

Timothy M. Pawlik, MD, MPH, MTS, PhD

Department of Surgery, The Ohio State University Wexner Medical Center, The James Comprehensive Cancer Center, Columbus, OH, USA

Academic Press is an imprint of Elsevier
125 London Wall, London EC2Y 5AS, United Kingdom
525 B Street, Suite 1650, San Diego, CA 92101, United States
50 Hampshire Street, 5th Floor, Cambridge, MA 02139, United States
The Boulevard, Langford Lane, Kidlington, Oxford OX5 1GB, United Kingdom

Notices

Knowledge and best practice in this field are constantly changing. As new research and experience broaden our understanding, changes in research methods, professional practices, or medical treatment may become necessary.

Practitioners and researchers must always rely on their own experience and knowledge in evaluating and using any information, methods, compounds, or experiments described herein. In using such information or methods they should be mindful of their own safety and the safety of others, including parties for whom they have a professional responsibility.

To the fullest extent of the law, neither the Publisher nor the authors, contributors, or editors, assume any liability for any injury and/or damage to persons or property as a matter of products liability, negligence or otherwise, or from any use or operation of any methods, products, instructions, or ideas contained in the material herein.

ISBN: 978-0-323-91706-3

For Information on all Academic Press publications visit our website at https://www.elsevier.com/books-and-journals

Publisher: Stacy Masucci
Acquisitions Editor: Rafael E. Teixeira
Editorial Project Manager: Sam W. Young
Production Project Manager: Sreejith Viswanathan
Cover Designer: Greg Harris

Typeset by Aptara, New Delhi, India

We dedicate this book to our families for their constant support and to our patients for their courage and conviction in their fight against cancer.

Contents

4. Use of molecular markers and other personalized factors in treatment decisions for metastatic colorectal cancer 65

Alex B. Blair, MD, Laura L. Tenner, MD, MPH and Bradley N. Reames, MD, MS, FACS

5. Role of Neoadjuvant therapy in the treatment of patients with colorectal liver metastases 81

Jeremy Sharib, MD, Bryan Clary, MD and Michael E Lidsky, MD

6. Management of the disappeared colorectal liver metastasis 99

Sidra Bonner and Hari Nathan

7. Approach to small liver remnant – strategies to increase resectability 109

Flavio Rocha (G), MD, FACS, FSSO and Kimberly Washington, MD, FACS

8. Two-stage versus ALPPS for large intrahepatic burden of colorectal liver metastasis 123

Victoria Ardiles, MD, PhD, Martin de Santibañes, MD, PhD and Eduardo de Santibañes, MD, PhD

9. Synchronous colorectal liver metastasis – simultaneous vs. staged approach 139

Colin M. Court and Alice C. Wei

10. Minimally invasive approaches to colorectal liver metastases 153

Ahmad Hamad, MD, Timothy M. Pawlik, MD, MPH, MTS, PhD and Aslam Ejaz, MD, MPH

11. Hepatic resection of colorectal liver metastasis in the presence of extrahepatic disease 165

Rachel V. Guest and Rowan Parks

12. Locoregional approaches to colorectal liver metastasis – ablation 179

Jian Zheng and David A. Geller

13. Locoregional approaches to colorectal liver metastasis – intra-arterial 191

David G. Brauer and Michael I D'Angelica

14. Locoregional approaches to colorectal liver metastasis – Radiation options 211

Colin S. Hill, Eugene J. Koay and Joseph M. Herman

Contributors

Victoria Ardiles, MD, PhD Coordinator Surgical Department, Liver Transplant Unit. Hospital Italiano de Buenos Aires. Buenos Aires, Argentina

Azarakhsh Baghdadi, MD, MAS Department of Radiology and Radiological Science, Johns Hopkins Hospital, Baltimore, MD, USA

Kimberly Bertens Department of Surgery, Liver and Pancreas Unit, The Ottawa Hospital, University of Ottawa, 501 Smyth Rd, CCW 1667, Ottawa, ON, K1H 8L6, Canada

Alex B. Blair, MD Department of Surgery, Johns Hopkins Hospital, Baltimore, MD, USA

Sidra Bonner Department of Surgery, University of Michigan, Ann Arbor, MI

David G. Brauer Memorial Sloan Kettering Cancer Center, New York, NY, United States

Pnina Brodt Department of Medicine, Faculty of Medicine, McGill University, Montreal, Québec, QC, H3A 1A1, Canada; Department of Surgery, Montreal, QC, H4A 3J1; Medicine and Oncology, Montreal, QC, H4A 3J1; McGill University and the Cancer Program of the Research Institute of the McGill University Health Center, Montreal, QC, H4A 3J1

Callisia N Clarke, MD, MS Assistant Professor of Surgery, Division of Surgical Oncology, 8701, W. Watertown Plank Road, Milwaukee, WI, 53226

Bryan Clary, MD University of California San Diego, Department of Surgery, USA

Colin M. Court Department of Surgery, Memorial Sloan Kettering Cancer Center, New York, New York, United States of America

Michael I D'Angelica Memorial Sloan Kettering Cancer Center, New York, NY, United States

Eduardo De Santibañes, MD, PhD Honorary Chaiman General Surgery Service. Hospital Italiano de Buenos Aires. Buenos Aires, Argentina

Martin De Santibañes, MD, PhD General Surgery Service and Liver Transplant Unit. Hospital Italiano de Buenos Aires. Buenos Aires, Argentina

Monica M. Dua, MD Department of Surgery, Stanford University School of Medicine, Palo Alto, CA, USA

Aslam Ejaz, MD, MPH Department of Surgery, The Ohio State University Wexner Medical Center, The James Comprehensive Cancer Center, Columbus, OH, USA

Gilton Marques Fonseca Servico de Cirurgia do Figado, Departamento de Gastroenterologia, Hospital das Clinicas HCFMUSP, Faculdade de Medicina Universidade de Sao Paulo

David A. Geller Complex General Surgical Oncology Fellow, Department of Surgery, University of Pittsburgh Medical Center, Pittsburgh, PA

Rachel V Guest Department of Clinical Surgery, University of Edinburgh, Edinburgh, United Kingdom

Ahmad Hamad, MD Department of Surgery, The Ohio State University Wexner Medical Center, The James Comprehensive Cancer Center, Columbus, OH, USA

Joseph M. Herman Department of Radiation Medicine, Zucker School of Medicine at Hofstra/Northwell, Lake Success, New York, United States

Paulo Herman Servico de Cirurgia do Figado, Departamento de Gastroenterologia, Hospital das Clinicas HCFMUSP, Faculdade de Medicina Universidade de Sao Paulo

Colin S. Hill Department of Radiation Oncology & Molecular Radiation Sciences, Johns Hopkins University School of Medicine, Baltimore, MD, United States

Fabian Johnston, MD Division of Surgical Oncology, Department of Surgery, Johns Hopkins Hospital, Baltimore, MD, USA

Ihab R. Kamel, MD, PhD Department of Radiology and Radiological Science, Johns Hopkins Hospital, Baltimore, MD, USA

Eugene J. Koay Department of GI Radiation Oncology, The University of Texas MD Anderson Cancer Center, Houston, TX, United States

Kimberly Kopecky, MD Division of Surgical Oncology, Department of Surgery, Johns Hopkins Hospital, Baltimore, MD, USA

Jaime Arthur Pirolla Kruger Servico de Cirurgia do Figado, Departamento de Gastroenterologia, Hospital das Clinicas HCFMUSP, Faculdade de Medicina Universidade de Sao Paulo

Michael E Lidsky, MD Duke University Medical Center, Department of Surgery, Division of Surgical Oncology, USA

Elizabeth Y. Liu, BA Department of Radiology and Radiological Science, Johns Hopkins Hospital, Baltimore, MD, USA

Ashish Manne, MBBS The Ohio State University, Internal Medicine Department, Medical Oncology Division, Columbus, OH, United States

Guillaume Martel Department of Surgery, Liver and Pancreas Unit, The Ottawa Hospital, University of Ottawa, 501 Smyth Rd, CCW 1667, Ottawa, ON, K1H 8L6, Canada

Raja R. Narayan, MD Department of Surgery, Stanford University School of Medicine, Palo Alto, CA, USA

Hari Nathan Department of Surgery, University of Michigan, Ann Arbor, MI

Anne Noonan, MBBCh The Ohio State University, Internal Medicine Department, Medical Oncology Division, Columbus, OH, United States

Hanna Nyström Department of Surgical and Perioperative Sciences, Surgery, Umeå University, Sweden; Wallenberg Centre for Molecular Medicine, Umeå University, Sweden

Rowan Parks Department of Clinical Surgery, University of Edinburgh, Edinburgh, United Kingdom

Timothy M. Pawlik, MD, MPH, MTS, PhD Department of Surgery, The Ohio State University Wexner Medical Center, The James Comprehensive Cancer Center, Columbus, OH, USA

Shannon Radomski, MD Department of Surgery, Johns Hopkins Hospital, Baltimore, MD, USA

Bradley N. Reames, MD, MS, FACS Division of Surgical Oncology, Department of Surgery, University of Nebraska Medical Center, Omaha, NE, USA

Flavio Rocha (G), MD, FACS, FSSO Division of Surgical Oncology, Knight Cancer Institute, Oregon Health and Science University, Portland, OR, United States

Jeremy Sharib, MD Duke University Medical Center, Department of Surgery, Division of Surgical Oncology, USA

Peter M. Siegel Goodman Cancer Institute, McGill University, Montreal, Québec, QC, H3A 1A3, Canada; Department of Medicine, Faculty of Medicine, McGill University, Montreal, Québec, QC, H3A 1A1, Canada

Laura L. Tenner, MD, MPH Division of Medical Oncology, Department of Internal Medicine, University of Nebraska Medical Center, Omaha, NE, USA

Erin P Ward, MD Medical College of Wisconsin, CGSO Fellow, Surgical Oncology, Milwaukee, WI, United States

Kimberly Washington, MD, FACS Division of Surgical Oncology, Knight Cancer Institute, Oregon Health and Science University, Portland, OR, United States

Alice C. Wei Department of Surgery, Memorial Sloan Kettering Cancer Center, New York, New York, United States of America

Jian Zheng Complex General Surgical Oncology Fellow, Department of Surgery, University of Pittsburgh Medical Center, Pittsburgh, PA

Preface

Hepatic Colorectal Metastases: A Story of Potential Cure for a Stage Four Cancer

Colorectal carcinoma is the third most common cancer in humans. Yearly, over 2 million people worldwide will be diagnosed with this cancer. Nearly a million people will die of colorectal cancer this year. The liver is the most frequent site of hematogenous metastases from colorectal cancer, and the site most responsible for death from this common cancer (Stewart et al., 2018).

Until the late 20th century, metastatic colorectal cancer was thought to be uniformly fatal. Then, observation in autopsy studies and in radiologic studies using CAT scanners invented in the 1970s that metastatic disease can be isolated to the liver encouraged early pioneers to resect liver metastases. Bold pioneers such as Joseph Fortner, Kevin Hughes, James Foster, and Martin Adson performed and reported data to establish such liver resections of metastatic disease as rational practice (Hughes et al., 1988).

By the end of the 20th century, resection of hepatic colorectal metastases was an established field. We knew from the work of Joseph Fortner, with actual 25-year follow-up, that surgical resection alone can result in cure in 25% of patients (Fortner and Fong, 2009). We knew from the work of many including the famed trialist Bernard Nordlinger (Nordlinger et al., 1996) that liver resection at major centers is safe, with mortality less than 5%, and result in 5-year survival of greater than 40 months. The progress in chemotherapy was also remarkable. In 1996, Henri Bismuth reported that 15% of nonresectable cases could be converted to resectable with chemotherapy and result in long-term survival and potential cure (Bismuth et al., 1996).

The progress in the first quarter of the 21st century has also been notable. The current status of the field is well summarized in the current book edited by Dr. Pawlik and Dr. Ejaz. They have included chapters on our current scientific knowledge of epidemiology, molecular pathogenesis, tumor microenvironment, and promising therapeutic targets including immunotherapy. Radiologic and molecular staging have been summarized as relevant for patient selection, surgical planning, and long-term follow-up. Treatment options of resection, ablation, regional chemotherapy, radiation therapy, and minimally invasive approaches are discussed in the context of optimizing patient outcome. Included are also important methods of making more patients eligible for resection by portal vein embolization, two-stage resections, and ALPPS. A number of important special topics are discussed including disappearing metastases, management of synchronous metastasis, and management of recurrences. This is a comprehensive handbook for this field intended for all levels and all disciplines of medical professionals treating patients with metastatic colorectal cancer.

It is gratifying for all of us who have spent a lifetime treating this disease that patients with this stage 4 disease are now provided with an opportunity to survive their disease and live full lives. However, it must be noted that less than 10% of patients with hepatic colorectal metastases are offered liver resection, when 30-50% are eligible (Raoof et al., 2020). As we go forward, the biggest challenge remains to educate all physicians and oncologist surgical resection is the standard of care. Works such as this book by Pawlik and Ejaz will be important for such educational efforts. It is also sobering that access to lifesaving liver surgery is determined by ethnicity (Thornblade et al., 2020) and health insurance coverage (Raoof et al., 2021).

The progress in treatment of patients with metastatic colorectal cancer has been remarkable. Over 50% of patients are now 5-year survivors, and over one-third cured. Now, it is our job not only to continue the great scientific and clinical progress, but also to make social progress to ensure more eligible patients are offered and receive such treatment, regardless of race, ethnicity, or economic resources.

Yuman Fong
Sangiacomo Chair and Chairman
Department of Surgery
City of Hope Medical Center

References

Bismuth, H., et al. (1996). Resection of nonresectable liver metastases from colorectal cancer after neoadjuvant chemotherapy. *Ann. Surg., 224*(4), 509–520.

Fortner, J. G., & Fong, Y. (2009). Twenty-five-year follow-up for liver resection: the personal series of Dr. Joseph G. Fortner. *Ann. Surg., 250*(6), 908–913.

Hughes, K. S., et al. (1988). Resection of the liver for colorectal carcinoma metastases. A multi-institutional study of long-term survivors. *Dis. Colon. Rectum., 31*, 1–4.

Nordlinger, B., et al. (1996). Surgical resection of colorectal carcinoma metastases to the liver. A prognostic scoring system to improve case selection, based on 1568 patients. Association Francaise de Chirurgie. *Cancer, 77*(7), 1254–1262.

Raoof, M., et al. (2020). Systematic failure to operate on colorectal cancer liver metastases in California. *Cancer Med., 9*(17), 6256–6267.

Raoof, M., Jacobson, G., & Fong, Y. (2021). Medicare advantage networks and access to high-volume cancer surgery hospitals. *Ann. Surg., 274*(4), e315–e319.

Stewart, C. L., et al. (2018). Cytoreduction for colorectal metastases: liver, lung, peritoneum, lymph nodes, bone, brain. When does it palliate, prolong survival, and potentially cure? *Curr. Probl. Surg., 55*(9), 330–379.

Thornblade, L. W., et al. (2020). Association of race/ethnicity with overall survival among patients with colorectal liver metastasis. *JAMA Netw. Open, 3*(9), e2016019.

CHAPTER

1

Epidemiology and risk factors for metastatic colorectal disease

Erin P Ward, MD[a] *and Callisia N Clarke, MD, MS*[b]

[a] **Medical College of Wisconsin, CGSO Fellow, Surgical Oncology, Milwaukee, WI, United States** [b] **Assistant Professor of Surgery, Division of Surgical Oncology, 8701, W. Watertown Plank Road, Milwaukee, WI, 53226**

Colorectal cancer incidence and survival

In the United States, colorectal cancer (CRC) is the third leading cause of cancer-related deaths for both women and men. It accounts for 7.9 percent of all new cancer diagnoses each year and 8.7 percent of all cancer deaths (Siegel et al., 2020). The majority of patients diagnosed with CRC are over the age of 50; however, 12 percent of all new CRC cases are diagnosed in patients younger than 50 (Siegel et al., 2020). Although improved screening efforts have led to an overall decrease in incidence in CRC diagnoses since 2000, incidence in young adults under the age of 50 has increased since the 1990s. By 2030, current projections of CRC incidence predict that while the overall rates will decrease, rates of CRC in those between age 35–49 will increase by 27 percent for colon cancer and 46 percent for rectal and rectosigmoid cancer (Bailey et al., 2015).

The American Cancer Society (ACS) estimates the lifetime risk of CRC to be 1 in 23 for men and 1 in 25 for women (American Cancer Society: About Colorectal Cancer., 2021). The Surveillance, Epidemiology, and End Results (SEER) Program data shows that at the time of diagnosis, 38 percent of patients have localized disease, 35 percent have regional disease, 21 percent have distant disease and 7 percent are unstaged. Overall, the rates of localized CRC have decreased since 2007, likely attributable to increased surveillance with colonoscopies and other screening modalities including fecal occult blood tests. For all patients, the annual incidence of localized disease has dropped by 4.2 percent from 2007 to 2016.

The 5-year survival for all patients with CRC is 64.7 percent. When broken down by stage, the 5-year survival for localized disease is 91 percent, 72 percent for regional disease and 15 percent for distant disease. For distant disease, the 5-year survival for patients varies based on age and race. The 5-year survival for patients under 50 with distant disease is 23 percent

Contemporary Management of Metastatic Colorectal Cancer: A Precision Medicine Approach
DOI: https://doi.org/10.1016/B978-0-323-91706-3.00014-X

TABLE 1.1 Modifiable and non-modifiable risk factors for colorectal cancer.

Risk Factors for Colorectal Cancer			
Risk Factor		**Protective**	
Modifiable	**Non-Modifiable**	**Modifiable**	**Non-Modifiable**
Low Physical Activity	Family History of CRC or advanced Polyps	High fiber foods	Gender, Female
Processed Meats	Polyposis syndromes (FAP, MAP, etc.)	Wholegrains	
Red Meat	Lynch Syndrome (HNPCC)	Avoiding Smoking	
Excess body fat	Older Age	Avoiding Alcohol	
"Westernized" diet	Race, Black		

FAP, MAP, HNPCC

compared to 11 percent for those over 65. The 5-year survival for distant disease in black patients is 12 percent compared to 25 percent for white patients (including Hispanics).

Risk factors for colorectal cancer

Environmental/Diet and Lifestyle

The majority of CRCs are sporadic; only a small subset are related to germline mutations or found in the setting of a significant family history (Jasperson, Tuohy, Neklason, and Burt, 2010). Variation in CRC risks across the globe and the observation that younger generations are at increased risk of CRC in westernized countries has further solidified the influence of environmental exposures. Significant research has gone into identifying and trying to quantify the environmental and lifestyle-based risk factors associated with CRC. Global studies document a 45-fold difference in age-standardized incidence for CRC across the world (Keum and Giovannucci, 2019; "Cancer Fact Sheets — Colorectal Cancer", 2018). The lowest rates of CRC are observed in Gambia and other non-industrialized countries, while the highest rates are observed in westernized countries. Over time, rates of CRC within a country are found to increase as a country industrializes and begins to adopt a "westernized diet and lifestyle" (Arnold et al., 2017). Migration studies also document that over time, an individual's risk of cancer will shift towards their host country's risk profile for CRC (Mousavi, Fallah, Sundquist, and Hemminki, 2012). For example, men who migrate to Sweden from "low risk" countries are observed to have increased trends of CRC compared to their home countries' population. The global variations in CRC incidence and migration studies support that variations in diet, environment and lifestyle play a significant role in CRC risk.

Some specific environmental risk factors for CRC have been well established and include smoking, alcohol, diets heavy in processed meats and diets low in fiber (Table 1.1).

Smoking increases the risks of both colorectal adenomas and serrated polyps (Figueiredo et al., 2015). Large observation studies show that increased rates of CRC are observed with more pack-years (Liang, Chen, and Giovannucci, 2009). Recent studies suggest that smoking disproportionally increases rates of rectal and proximal CRC and is associated with BRAF-mutant cancers, but only weakly associated with microsatellite instable (MSI)-high tumors.

Similarly, alcohol consumption is a well-established risk factor for CRC, and recent pooled studies have shown that even light alcohol intake is associated with an increased risk of developing CRC (Choi, Myung, and Lee, 2018).

A diet low in fiber, fruits, and vegetables and high in processed meats, sugary beverages, and refined grains, i.e. a westernized diet, is correlated with higher rates of CRC. It has proven difficult to tease out exactly all that contributes to the increased risk of CRC in a westernized diet. It is likely that several aspects of this diet contribute to the higher incidence of CRC. Studies consistently find that diets high in processed and red meat are associated with increased risks of CRC. A recent meta-analysis of 111 studies including 400 patients reported a 12 percent increase in CRC incidence for each 100 g of red and processed meat intake (Vieira et al., 2017). The authors also found that increased intake of whole grains was overall protective against CRC. Currently, the American Institute for Cancer Research (AICR) recommends a diet low in processed and red meats and high in whole grains containing fiber to reduce the risk of developing CRC.

Multiple studies have demonstrated that obesity and reduced physical activity are associated with increased risk of CRC (Keum and Giovannucci, 2019). Excess body fat, most commonly measured with BMI and waist circumference, are consistently found to be associated with CRC (Dong et al., 2017; Harriss et al., 2009). Sedentary behavior including prolonged sitting or TV watching is also associated with increased risk of CRC (Ma, Yao, Sun, Dai, and Zhou, 2017). Most of the studies validating obesity and low physical activity to be risk factors for CRC have been completed in populations over 50. The increasing burden of young-onset CRC within industrialized countries, like the US, has prompted renewed interest in trying to define the influence of obesity and physical activity on rates of early-onset CRC. Recently, two studies were published using the Nurses' Health Study II, a long-term prospective cohort study of nurses, enrolled between the ages of 25 to 42, to evaluate the impact of obesity and sedentary lifestyle on early-onset CRC (before the age of 50). Liu et al. found that both a higher BMI at age 18 and greater weight gain during the study period contributed to higher rates of early-onset CRC (Liu et al., 2019). The second study observed that increased sedentary activity, primarily estimated by self-reported hours watching TV per week, correlated with higher rates of early-onset CRC (Nguyen et al., 2018). These and other studies support the recommendations from the ACS and other cancer societies that increased physical activity and a healthy weight are important for reducing the risk of CRC.

Polyps

The majority of CRC arise from a benign precursor polyp. As such, a significant personal or family history of high-risk polyps puts patients at increased risk for colorectal cancer. There are several types of polyps, some of which are non-neoplastic (hyperplastic, mucosal, inflammatory and harmatomatous polyps). The remainder, adenomatous polyps and serrated polyps, have malignant potential. The vast majority of sporadic CRCs develop from adenomatous polyps. In the United States, it is estimated that about 1/3 of adults will have a polyp by age 50 (Reinhart et al., 2013). The majority of these, however, will not progress to CRC. Polyps that are > 1 cm, have villous histology or high-grade dysplasia have an increased propensity to progress to CRC. Although less common, serrated polyps are thought to be precursors for up to 10–15 percent of sporadic CRCs.

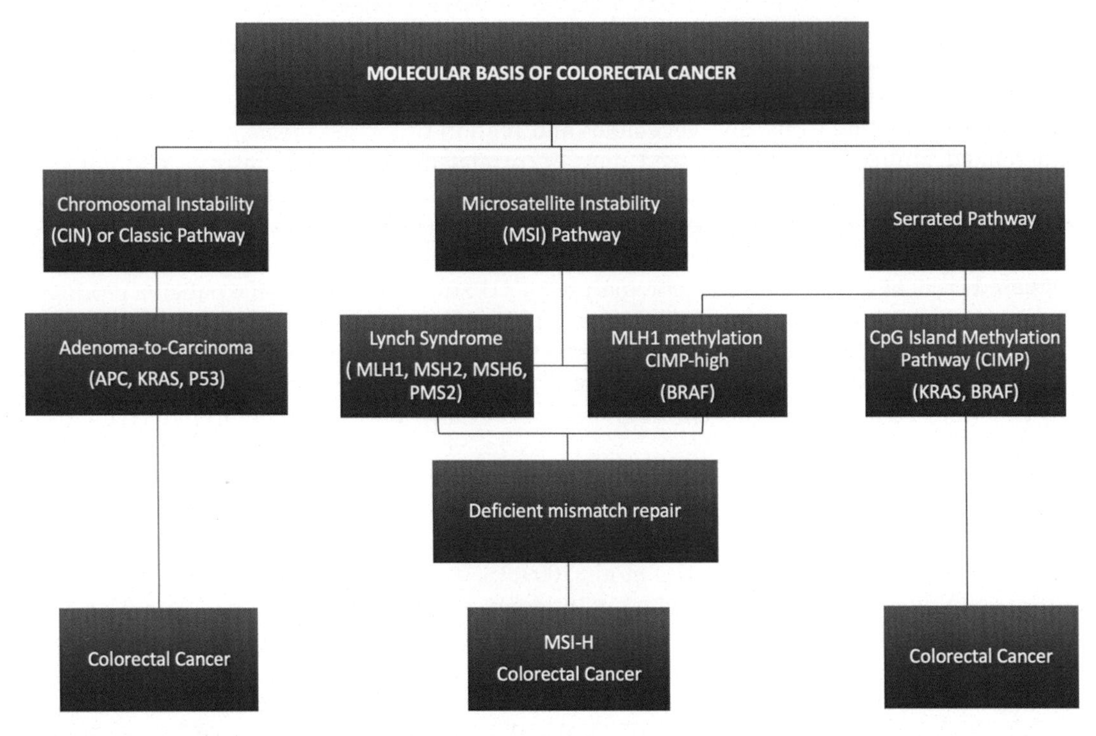

FIGURE 1.1 Three molecular pathways for colorectal carcinogenesis. There are three molecular pathways proposed for colorectal carcinogenesis, the chromosomal instable (CIN) or classic pathway, the micro-satellite instability (MIS) pathway and the serrated pathway.

There are three molecular pathways proposed for colorectal carcinogenesis, two of which revolve around the neoplastic progression of polyps (Fig. 1.1). The classic pathway describes progression of normal cells to adenomas and ultimately to carcinomas over an extended period (Adenoma-Carcinoma sequence). This is predominately associated with development of chromosomal instable (CIN) tumors and accounts for 85–90 percent of all sporadic CRC (Malki et al., 2021; Keum and Giovannucci, 2019). It is typically associated with an early APC gene mutation, an activation of KRAS or BRAF oncogenes which promote growth, and subsequent mutations that leads progression to carcinoma. The CpG island methylator phenotype (CIMP)/serrated pathway accounts for about 10–15 percent of sporadic CRCs (Malki et al., 2021). Many genes are silenced secondary to these alterations in the methylation of promoter regions of genes and overall hypomethylation. These tumors have often have early BRAFV600E mutations which lead to the activation of the MAPK pathway and formation of hyperplastic polyps (Clarke and Kopetz, 2015). The third pathway is the MSI-high pathway. This is the prominent cancer pathway for patients with Lynch Syndrome and constitutes over 95 percent of associated cancers. MSI is rarely found outside of Lynch Syndrome and is driven by the loss of DNA mismatch repair genes that ultimately leads to altered DNA sequences.

Overall, about 8–25 percent of polyps that harbor invasive carcinoma will metastasize to regional lymph nodes. Polyps that are poorly differentiated, have vascular or lymphatic invasion, have invasion into the submucosa or have positive resection margins are at increased risk to have disease that spreads to the regional lymph nodes. Polyps that are unable to be removed with a 1–2 mm margin are also at higher risk for metastatic spread to regional lymph nodes. Given the propensity for cancer to develop from polyps, all polyps that are found during screening should be removed via colonoscopy when possible, and all patients who are found to have a polyp via sigmoidoscopy need a completion colonoscopy to rule out other polyps. For polyps that cannot be removed via colonoscopy or have high risk features for invasive carcinoma, surgery should be recommended. The exact type of surgical intervention will depend on the location of the polyp but should include regional lymphadenectomy to allow for adequate staging.

Hereditary risk factors

The hereditary component of CRC is estimated at 35–40 percent, with 25 percent of CRCs related to a family history without a clear syndrome and about 5 percent attributed by hereditary cancer syndromes (Graff et al., 2017; Jasperson et al., 2010). The most common hereditary cancer syndromes include Hereditary Non-Polyposis Colorectal Cancer (HNPCC, Lynch syndrome), familial adenomatous polyposis (FAP) and MUTYH-associated polyposis (MAP). The most common inherited CRC syndrome is Lynch syndrome, which accounts for about 2–4 percent of all colorectal cancers (Keum and Giovannucci, 2019). For patients under age 50 years at the time of CRC diagnosis, it is estimated that 16 percent have a hereditary syndrome and 8 percent have Lynch syndrome (Pearlman et al., 2017). Patients with Lynch syndrome are at risk for several other cancers, including endometrium, ovary, stomach, small bowel, hepatobiliary tract, pancreas, ureter, and renal pelvis cancers (Win et al., 2012). The genetic mutations that lead to Lynch syndrome are in DNA mismatch repair genes hMLH1, hMSH2, hMSH6 and hPMS2. These patients have a 5–85 percent lifetime risk of developing CRC. Although these patients are more likely to be diagnosed at a younger age, around 45, they are more likely to have better survival. They also have increased rates of right-sided CRC and metachronous or synchronous tumors. A significant proportion of patients with Lynch are not diagnosed; thus, a high index of suspicion is needed even in the setting of no significant family history. The Amsterdam criteria can be used to help identify high-risk families and individuals (Umar et al., 2004).

The second most common inherited colorectal cancer syndrome is FAP and accounts for about 1 percent of CRCs (Talseth-Palmer, 2017). FAP is secondary to a germ line mutation in the APC gene, which results in a truncated APC protein. It is inherited in an autosomal dominant fashion with a 90 percent inheritance. These patients develop thousands of polyps throughout the gastrointestinal tract, with the majority in the colon. Without prophylactic colectomy, CRC will develop in all affected patients with FAP by the third or fourth decade. These patients are also at risk for other extracolonic cancers including duodenal adenomas and carcinomas, desmoid tumors, thyroid cancer, and mandibular osteomas. Early screening is necessary for effected individuals and should start around age 10 to 12.

There are additional polyposis syndromes that increase patients' risk of CRC. These include MAP, which is associated with a mutation in the MUTYH gene and is inherited in a recessive manner (Talseth-Palmer, 2017). This accounts for less than 1 percent of CRC, but patients with MAP have an estimated 43–100 percent lifetime risk of CRC. Other polyposis syndromes with an increased CRC risk include serrated polyposis syndrome, Peutz-Jeghers syndrome and juvenile polyposis syndrome. These are all rare syndromes that account for less than 1 percent of CRC incidence together.

Patients with a history of inflammatory bowel disorders have an increased risk of CRC. Specifically, those with chronic ulcerative colitis have a risk for CRC 30 times higher than the general population. Chronic inflammation in the setting of ulcerative colitis is associated with a 0.5 to 1 percent increased risk of cancer. The tumors that do arise in these settings tend to have early mutations in p53 and are less often associated with mutations in KRAS or APC genes. The cancer also tends to more often be multiple, broadly infiltrating and poorly differentiated. The risk of cancer seems to be directly related to the duration and amount of inflammation, and surveillance is recommended to start 8 years after diagnosis to identify cancer or high grade dysplasia early.

Beyond family history, other non-modifiable risk factors for CRC include race, age, and sex. Overall, male patients have a higher risk for CRC than females; the theories behind this include that women tend to have relatively less visceral fat and benefit from overall protective nature of estrogen against CRC. In addition, men have potentially increased exposure to environmental factors, including alcohol, smoking and poor diets, and are less likely to pursue screening. In the US, population studies show that African Americans have a 11 percent higher incidence of CRC than white Americans, while Asian Americans have the lowest risk of CRC. The reasons behind these discrepancies are likely multi-factorial and based on environmental exposures, access to care issues and reduced screening (Augustus and Ellis, 2018; Siegel et al., 2020). In general, CRC is a disease of older patients; although, as alluded to before, the rates of CRC are decreasing in the over-50 population, whereas the risk of CRC (and rectal cancer in particular) continues to rise in the less-than-50 population. Recent trends suggest that by the year 2030, the rates of rectal cancer will increase by 124 percent for patients aged 20–34 and by 90 percent for colon cancer (Bailey et al., 2015). These trends have promoted a change in the screening recommendations by the major institutions.

Screening guidelines

Beyond a healthy diet, physical activity, and avoiding alcohol and tobacco, appropriate screening remains critical for reducing CRC incidence and morbidity. Up until 2018, all of the major organizations recommended starting CRC screening for average-risk patients at age 50. The increasing rates of CRC diagnosis among patients under 50 prompted the ACS to reduce the recommended age of initial screening from 50 to 45 in 2018 (Wolf et al., 2018). This recommendation was made after an extensive review of the potential risks and benefits of earlier screening. Age 45 was chosen because approximately half of patients diagnosed before age 50 are between the age of 45 and 49, and most of these patients are considered of average risk. In 2018, the U.S. Preventive Services Task Force (USPSTF) reviewed the same evidence and simulation models used to guide the ACS recommendations, but it was not until 2021 that the UPSTF changed the initial screening age from 50 to 45 (Force, n.d.). The UPSTF cites that models from the Cancer Intervention and Surveillance Modeling Network support

TABLE 1.2 Screening guidelines for colorectal cancer screening guidelines for average-risk and higher-risk populations.

	Age of first screening	Type of screening	Frequency of screening
Average Risk	Age 45	a) Colonoscopy	a) Every 10 years
		b) Sigmoidoscopy	b) Every 5 years
		c) CT colonography	c) Every 5 years
		d) DNA-FIT	d) Every 1–3 years
		e) Flexible sigmoidoscopy + FIT	e) Flexible sigmoidoscopy every 10 years, FIT every year
FAP	Age 12	Colonoscopy	Every year until colectomy
Lynch Syndrome	Ages 20–25 or 2–5 years before youngest family member age at diagnosis with CRC	Colonoscopy	Every 1–2 years
IBD	8 years after diagnosis	Colonoscopy	Every 1–3 years
Family Hx of CRC			
First Degree Relative (FDR)	Age 40 or 10 years before youngest FDR	Colonoscopy	Every 5 years
≥ 2 SDR	Age 40		
Family Hx of Advanced Polyp			
Advanced adenoma in FDR ≥ 60			
Advanced adenoma in FDR < 60 or 2 FDRs	Age 40	Colonoscopy	Every 10 years
	Age 40 or 10 years before dx in FDR	Colonoscopy	Every 5 years

FAP, MAP, HNPCC

the notion that beginning screening at 45 will lead to an increase in life years gained and a decrease in cancer cases and deaths from CRC. Current UPSTF screening guidelines describe several accepted screening regimens. These include a colonoscopy every 10 years, flexible sigmoidoscopy every 5 years or a stool-based study every 1 year for average risk patients; the alternative methods are outlined in Table 1.2.

For patients with higher-than-average risk for CRC, screening is recommended to start before age 45. The US Multi-Society Task Force of Colorectal Cancer and National Comprehensive Cancer Network outline recommendations for patients with a family history of cancer or advanced adenomas (Provenzale et al., 2020; Rex et al., 2017). Overall, all patients with first or second degree relatives with a diagnosis of either CRC or an advanced adenoma before age 60 are recommended to start screening at least by age 40. Patients with a first degree relative with CRC or advanced adenoma are to start screening 10 years earlier than the age of diagnosis in the first degree relative with a colonoscopy and then to repeat a colonoscopy every 5 years. Patients with FAP, Lynch or IBD have disease-specific recommendations for screening. Patients with FAP are to start screening at age 10–12 with an annual colonoscopy until colectomy. Lynch patients are to start screening with a colonoscopy every 1–2 years starting at age 20–25, unless a family member was diagnosed before age 25; then, they are to start screening 5 years younger than that family member's age at diagnosis. Patients with IBD are to start screening with colonoscopy every 1–3 years, 8 years after their IBD diagnosis.

Metastatic CRC epidemiology

Current data supports that about 15−20 percent of patients will present with metastatic disease at time of diagnosis (Adam et al., 2015; Elferink, de Jong, Klaase, Siemerink, and de Wilt, 2015; Siegel et al., 2020). The annual incidence of Stage IV disease has decreased by 1.1 percent, although rates of Stage IV disease at presentation varies by age and race. Overall, the survival for those who have distant disease is 14 percent at 5 years, and studies show that the survival for patients with lung- or liver-only metastases is improving over time (Siegel et al., 2020; van der Geest et al., 2015).

Risk factors for presenting with late-stage disease include age less than 50 years (young patients) at the time of diagnosis (Andrew et al., 2018). In young patients, the annual incidence of distant CRC has increased by 2.5 percent from 2012 to 2016. About 26 percent of patients under 50 years present with advanced disease, compared to just 23 percent of patients between 50 and 64 years and 19 percent of patients over age 65 years. There are likely multiple contributing factors to the higher rates of advanced CRC in the early-onset population. The majority of these patients fall outside of standard screening recommendations, and the majority (86 percent) of early-onset CRCs are not diagnosed until symptoms from the disease develop (Dozois et al., 2008). Studies also show that these patients are slower to present for evaluation and often experience diagnostic delays, as their symptoms are more likely to be attributed to other benign disease processes such as hemorrhoids (Scott, Rangel, Osler, and Hyman, 2016; You, Lee, Deschner, and Shibata, 2020).

Race, gender and location of primary tumor also seem to influence the incidence of metastatic disease at diagnosis. Black patients are more likely to be diagnosed with stage IV CRC compared to non-Hispanic Whites: 25 percent vs. 20 percent (Siegel et al., 2020). Lower rates of CRC screening and advanced symptoms at diagnosis are also believed to contribute to these disparities. However, the overall incidence and later stage at diagnosis for CRC is higher at any age in Black patients, suggesting other underlying biological drivers (Augustus and Ellis, 2018). In the Netherlands, male patients have also been found to be more likely to present with distant disease than women (van der Geest et al., 2015). In addition, patients with colon cancer are at increased risk to present with advanced disease compared to those with rectal cancer. This is likely secondary to the earlier symptoms associated with rectal cancer.

Specific metastatic site epidemiology and risk factors

The liver is the most common site for distant metastasis, followed by the peritoneum and lungs (van der Geest et al., 2015). About 15–25 percent of patients will develop liver metastasis within 5 years of diagnosis (Engstrand, Nilsson, Strömberg, Jonas, and Freedman, 2018;

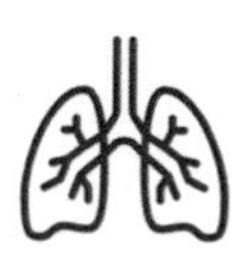

FIGURE 1.2 Risk factors for lung, liver and peritoneal colorectal metastases. The primary location of the tumor, the mutation burden and the cell subtype are associated with different patterns of metastatic colorectal cancer.

Manfredi et al., 2006). Patients with synchronous liver metastases have worse outcomes than those patients that have metachronous liver metastases (Adam et al., 2015). About 20–30 percent of patients with liver metastases present with resectable disease, and those treated with a curative operation have up to a 50 percent 5-year survival. While the ability to resect liver metastasis contributes significantly to improved survival, tumor biology and response to systemic therapy also play a critical role. Recently BRAF mutations have been found to be associated with worse outcomes in patients with liver CRC metastasis (Clarke and Kopetz, 2015; Pikoulis et al., 2016).

Up to 8 percent of patients with CRC will present with synchronous peritoneal disease, although the true incidence is likely underestimated; detection with current cross-sectional imaging is limited to identification of only larger metastatic deposits (Kranenburg, Speeten, and Hingh, 2021). Approximately 19 percent of patients will develop peritoneal metastasis (PM) during the course of their disease, and up to 80 percent of patients with CRC will have PM at the time of autopsy (Koppe, Boerman, Oyen, and Bleichrodt, 2006; Kranenburg et al., 2021). Patients with isolated PMs have overall worse prognoses compared to those with other isolated single-organ metastases (Kranenburg et al., 2021; Franko et al., 2016). Patients with T4 tumors, node-positive disease, proximal colon cancers, BRAF mutation, mucinous or signet histology or a CMS4 molecular subtype are more likely to develop PM during their cancer course (Fig. 1.2) (Kranenburg et al., 2021; Ubink et al., 2018).

PMs occur in up to 5–15 percent of patient with CRC, and patients with KRAS mutations have a higher risk of lung metastases (László et al., 2021; Pereira et al., 2015). Overall lung metastases have better overall survival and slower growth than liver metastases (Li et al., 2019). Currently, the NCCN guidelines support metastectomy if R0 resection is possible, the primary tumor is resectable, and no extra thoracic metastases are present (with an exception for resectable liver metastases). Only a subset of patients, around 20–30 percent, will be candidates for resection. Overall, the rates of metastectomies are increasing. A systematic review found patients have worse survival after a metastectomy when multiple pulmonary metastases were present, thoracic lymph nodes were involved and when the preoperative carcinoembryonic antigen level was elevated (Gonzalez et al., 2013). Overall the 5-year survival rate for pulmonary metastasectomy ranges from 27–68 percent (Gonzalez et al., 2013). Recently, however, the randomized control study Pulmonary Metastasectomy in Colorectal Cancer called into question the survival benefit of pulmonary metastasectomy for these patients; patients without metastectomies had a 3.8-year overall survival, comparable to those who had their pulmonary metastases removed (3.5-year) (Milosevic et al., 2020).

Predicting metastatic behavior through classification

Predicting Metastatic Behavior through Classification Given the biologic heterogeneity of CRC, significant study is underway to better predict the metastatic potential and pattern of CRC spread. Pathologic driver mutations in genes such as BRAF and KRAS, location of primary tumor, and molecular subtypes offer critical prognostic and predictive insight and inform patterns of metastasis (Clarke and Kopetz, 2015; Guinney et al., 2015; Prasanna et al., 2018; Tran et al., 2011). Several studies have demonstrated that primary tumor location affects the pattern and likelihood of metastatic disease (Brouwer et al., 2020; Prasanna et al., 2018). Synchronous lung metastases are more commonly diagnosed in patients with rectal cancer than those with right-sided or leftsided colon cancer. However, patients with colon cancer are more likely to have peritoneum-based metastasis at the time of diagnosis compared to those with rectal cancer: 6 percent vs. 1.7 percent (Brouwer et al., 2020; van der Geest et al., 2015). For both colon and rectal cancer, liver metastases are the most common site of metastases, but patients with colon cancer have a higher rate of liver metastasis (Brouwer et al., 2020). Patients with rectal cancer are at higher risk for the development of brain and bone metastasis (Prasanna et al., 2017).

Studies have also found that the location of the primary tumor influences the survival outcomes for patients with metastatic CRC. Specifically, multiple studies have found that metastatic, right-sided cancers have worse outcomes than metastatic, left-sided CRCs (Brouwer et al., 2020; Holch, Ricard, Stintzing, Modest, and Heinemann, 2017; Loupakis et al., 2015). This is due multiple factors, including variation in molecular drivers between right-sided and left-sided tumors (ie. KRAS, BRAF etc.) resulting in poor response to systemic therapy, higher rates of signet cell pathology and the observed differences in metastatic patterns in right-sided primary CRC in particular (Guinney et al., 2015; Lee, Menter, and Kopetz, 2017; Prasanna et al., 2018).

The presence of mutations in KRAS and BRAF also affect the outcomes for patients with metastatic CRC. About 10 percent of CRCs have a BRAF mutation, while 40 percent of CRCs have a KRAS mutation (Testa, Pelosi, and Castelli, 2018). Pooled metanalysis of

TABLE 1.3 Description of the 4 unique molecular subtypes of CRC: CMS1, CMS2, CMS3 and CMS4.

Subtype	CRC incidence	Driver gene/pathway	Phenotype and Prognosis
CMS1	14 percent	Hypermutation	Right-side tumors
MSI Immune		MSI – high	Older age at diagnosis
		CIMP – high	Females
		BRAF mutated	Intermediate survival
		Immune activation/expression	Worse survival after relapse
CMS2	37 percent	High CIN	Left-side tumors
Canonical		MSS	Better survival
		WNT/MYC pathway activation	
		TP53 mutated	
		EGFR amplification/overexpression	
CMS3	13 percent	CIN-low	Intermediate survival
Metabolic		Metabolic derangement	
		KRAS mutated	
		PIK3CA mutated	
		IGFBP2 overexpression	
CMS4	23 percent	CIN-high	Stromal infiltration
Mesenchymal		TGF-beta activation	Younger age at diagnosis
		NOTCH3/VEGFR2 overexpression	Worse relapse-free and overall survival

randomized trials show that patients with metastatic CRC with either a KRAS or BRAF mutation have inferior overall survival (Modest et al., 2016). This holds true for patients who undergo liver metastectomy with intent for cure (Testa et al., 2018). The presence of a BRAF mutation is associated with higher rates of brain and peritoneal metastases and less lung and liver metastases. Conversely, KRAS mutations are associated with more lung-only and brain metastases (Clarke and Kopetz, 2015; Prasanna et al., 2017; Yaeger et al., 2015).

To further classify and stratify CRC, the Colorectal Cancer Subtyping Consortium identified and described 4 unique molecular subtypes of CRC based on gene expression: CMS1, CMS2, CMS3 and CMS4 (Table 1.3).

(Guinney et al., 2015; Thanki, Nicholls, and Gajjar, 2017) CMS1, also called the microsatellite instability immune subtype, accounts for 14 percent of CRCs and consists of hypermutated, microsatellite unstable tumors with a strong immune activation. CMS2, also called canonical, accounts for 37 percent of tumors and is epithelial with chromosomal instability and marked WNT and MYC activation. The CMS3, or metabolic subtype, accounts for 13 percent of tumors and is epithelial with metabolic dysregulation. Finally, the CMS4, or mesenchymal, tumors account for 23 percent of CRC and have prominent TGF-B activation, stromal invasion, and angiogenesis. These subtypes are associated with different mutations, locations (distal vs. proximal) and response to treatments. Although initially described for early-stage CRC patients, recent studies have evaluated how the CMS subtype influences outcomes and predicts response to chemotherapy for patients with metastatic CRC (Mooi et al., 2018; Stintzing et al., 2019). These studies suggest that CMS may predict prognosis and the therapeutic impact of standard available chemotherapy for metastatic CRC (Hoorn, Sommeijer, and Vermeulen, 2021; Okita et al., 2018).

Summary

In summary, several risk factors that predispose to CRC diagnosis have been identified, including advancing age, western diets, obesity, sedentary lifestyle, Black race, personal history of adenomatous polyps and family history of colon cancer. These risk factors have synergistic effects and appear to directly influence the likely risk of CRC development and metastasis. While the overall incidence of CRC is decreasing due to effective screening and removal of pre-malignant lesions, there is an alarming trend of increasing CRC diagnoses in young Americans with ages less than 50 years. Young patients not only face increasing rates of CRC development but also are likely to present with advanced disease and distant metastasis at the time of diagnosis. Minimizing delays in diagnosis, by including CRC in the differential diagnosis for young patients presenting with common complaints, and strict adherence to new screening guidelines will help mitigate this trend as research continues to better understand the epidemiologic drivers of this disease. Better insight into the molecular drivers of CRC metastasis is needed to inform treatment stratification in patients with CRC liver metastasis and increase the proportion of metastatic CRCs considered candidates for hepatectomy.

References

Adam, R., de Gramont, A., Figueras, J., Kokudo, N., Kunstlinger, F., Loyer, E., et al. (2015). Managing synchronous liver metastases from colorectal cancer: a multidisciplinary international consensus. *Cancer Treatment Reviews*, 41(9), 729–741. https://doi.org/10.1016/j.ctrv.2015.06.006.

American Cancer Society: About Colorectal Cancer (2021). https://www.cancer.org/cancer/colon-rectal-cancer/about.html

Andrew, A. S., Parker, S., Anderson, J. C., Rees, J. R., Robinson, C., Riddle, B., et al. (2018). Risk Factors for Diagnosis of Colorectal Cancer at a Late Stage: a Population-Based Study. *Journal of General Internal Medicine*, 33(12), 2100–2105. https://doi.org/10.1007/s11606-018-4648-7.

Arnold, M., Sierra, M. S., Laversanne, M., Soerjomataram, I., Jemal, A., & Bray, F. (2017). Global patterns and trends in colorectal cancer incidence and mortality. *Gut*, 66(4), 683–691. https://doi.org/10.1136/gutjnl-2015-310912.

Augustus, G. J., & Ellis, N. A. (2018). Colorectal Cancer Disparity in African Americans: risk Factors and Carcinogenic Mechanisms. *American Journal of Pathology*, 188(2), 291–303. https://doi.org/10.1016/j.ajpath.2017.07.023.

Bailey, C. E., Hu, C. Y., You, Y. N., Bednarski, B. K., Rodriguez-Bigas, M. A., Skibber, J. M., et al. (2015). Increasing disparities in the age-related incidences of colon and rectal cancers in the United States, 1975-2010. *JAMA Surgery*, 150(1), 17–22. https://doi.org/10.1001/jamasurg.2014.1756.

Brouwer, N. P. M., van der Kruijssen, D. E. W., Hugen, N., de Hingh, I. H. J. T., Nagtegaal, I. D., Verhoeven, R. H. A., et al. (2020). The Impact of Primary Tumor Location in Synchronous Metastatic Colorectal Cancer: differences in Metastatic Sites and Survival. *Annals of Surgical Oncology*, 27(5), 1580–1588. https://doi.org/10.1245/s10434-019-08100-5.

Cancer Fact Sheets — Colorectal Cancer (2018). International Agency for Research on Cancer. Globocan.

Choi, Y. J., Myung, S. K., & Lee, J. H. (2018). Light alcohol drinking and risk of cancer: a meta-analysis of cohort studies. *Cancer Research and Treatment*, 50(2), 474–487. https://doi.org/10.4143/crt.2017.094.

Clarke, C. N., & Kopetz, E. S. (2015). BRAF mutant colorectal cancer as a distinct subset of colorectal cancer: clinical characteristics, clinical behavior, and response to targeted therapies. *J Gastrointest Oncol*, 6(6), 660–667. https://doi.org/10.3978/j.issn.2078-6891.2015.077.

Dong, Y., Zhou, J., Zhu, Y., Luo, L., He, T., Hu, H., et al. (2017). Abdominal obesity and colorectal cancer risk: systematic review and meta-analysis of prospective studies. *Bioscience Reports*, 37 (6), 1–12. https://doi.org/10.1042/BSR20170945.

Dozois, E. J., Boardman, L. A., Suwanthanma, W., Limburg, P. J., Cima, R. R., Bakken, J. L., et al. (2008). Young-onset colorectal cancer in patients with no known genetic predisposition: can we increase early recognition and improve outcome? *Medicine*, 87(5), 259–263. https://doi.org/10.1097/MD.0b013e3181881354.

Elferink, M. A. G., de Jong, K. P., Klaase, J. M., Siemerink, E. J., & de Wilt, J. H. W. (2015). Metachronous metastases from colorectal cancer: a population-based study in North-East Netherlands. *International Journal of Colorectal Disease*, 30(2), 205–212. https://doi.org/10.1007/s00384-014-2085-6.

Engstrand, J., Nilsson, H., Strömberg, C., Jonas, E., & Freedman, J. (2018). Colorectal cancer liver metastases - a population-based study on incidence, management and survival. *Bmc Cancer [Electronic Resource]*, 18(1), 78–89. https://doi.org/10.1186/s12885-017-3925-x.

Figueiredo, J. C., Crockett, S. D., Snover, D. C., Morris, C. B., McKeown-Eyssen, G., Sandler, R. S., et al. (2015). Smoking-associated risks of conventional adenomas and serrated polyps in the colorectum. *Cancer Causes & Control*, 26(3), 377–386. https://doi.org/10.1007/s10552-014-0513-0.

Force, U. (n.d.). Screening for Colorectal Cancer: US Preventive Services Task Force Recommendation Statement. Jama, *325*, 1965–1977.

Franko, J., Shi, Q., Meyers, J. P., Maughan, T. S., Adams, R. A., Seymour, M. T., et al. (2016). Prognosis of patients with peritoneal metastatic colorectal cancer given systemic therapy: an analysis of individual patient data from prospective randomised trials from the Analysis and Research in Cancers of the Digestive System (ARCAD) database. *The Lancet Oncology*, 17(12), 1709–1719. https://doi.org/10.1016/S1470-2045(16)30500-9.

Gonzalez, M., Poncet, A., Combescure, C., Robert, J., Ris, H. B., & Gervaz, P. (2013). Risk factors for survival after lung metastasectomy in colorectal cancer patients: a systematic review and meta-analysis. *Annals of Surgical Oncology*, 20(2), 572–579. https://doi.org/10.1245/s10434-012-2726-3.

Graff, R. E., Möller, S., Passarelli, M. N., Witte, J. S., Skytthe, A., Christensen, K., et al. (2017). Familial Risk and Heritability of Colorectal Cancer in the Nordic Twin Study of Cancer. *Clinical Gastroenterology and Hepatology*, 15(8), 1256–1264. https://doi.org/10.1016/j.cgh.2016.12.041.

Guinney, J., Dienstmann, R., Wang, X., De Reyniès, A., Schlicker, A., Soneson, C., et al. (2015). The consensus molecular subtypes of colorectal cancer. *Nature Medicine*, 21(11), 1350–1356. https://doi.org/10.1038/nm.3967.

Harriss, D. J., Atkinson, G., George, K., Tim Cable, N., Reilly, T., Haboubi, N., et al. (2009). Lifestyle factors and colorectal cancer risk (1): systematic review and meta-analysis of associations with body mass index. *Colorectal Disease*, 11(6), 547–563. https://doi.org/10.1111/j.1463-1318.2009.01766.x.

Holch, J. W., Ricard, I., Stintzing, S., Modest, D. P., & Heinemann, V. (2017). The relevance of primary tumour location in patients with metastatic colorectal cancer: a meta-analysis of first-line clinical trials. *European Journal of Cancer*, 70, 87–98. https://doi.org/10.1016/j.ejca.2016.10.007.

Hoorn, B., Sommeijer, D., & Vermeulen, L. (2021). Clinical Value of Consensus Molecular Subtypes in Colorectal Cancer: a Systematic Review and Meta-Analysis. *JNCI: Journal of the National Cancer Institute*.

Jasperson, K. W., Tuohy, T. M., Neklason, D. W., & Burt, R. W. (2010). Hereditary and Familial Colon Cancer. *Gastroenterology*, 138(6), 2044–2058. https://doi.org/10.1053/j.gastro.2010.01.054.

Keum, N. N., & Giovannucci, E. (2019). Global burden of colorectal cancer: emerging trends, risk factors and prevention strategies. *Nature Reviews Gastroenterology and Hepatology*, 16(12), 713–732. https://doi.org/10.1038/s41575-019-0189-8.

Koppe, M. J., Boerman, O. C., Oyen, W. J. G., & Bleichrodt, R. P. (2006). Peritoneal carcinomatosis of colorectal origin: incidence and current treatment strategies. *Annals of Surgery*, 243(2), 212–222. https://doi.org/10.1097/01.sla.0000197702.46394.16.

Kranenburg, O., Speeten, K. v. d., & Hingh, I. d. (2021). Peritoneal Metastases From Colorectal Cancer: defining and Addressing the Challenges. *Frontiers in oncology*, 11. https://doi.org/10.3389/fonc.2021.650098.

László, L., Kurilla, A., Takács, T., Kudlik, G., Koprivanacz, K., Buday, L., et al. (2021). Recent updates on the significance of kras mutations in colorectal cancer biology. *Cells*, 10(3), 1–19. https://doi.org/10.3390/cells10030667.

Lee, M. S., Menter, D. G., & Kopetz, S. (2017). Right versus left colon cancer biology: integrating the consensus molecular subtypes. *JNCCN Journal of the National Comprehensive Cancer Network*, 15(3), 411–419. https://doi.org/10.6004/jnccn.2017.0038.

Li, J., Yuan, Y., Yang, F., Wang, Y., Zhu, X., Wang, Z., et al. (2019). Expert consensus on multidisciplinary therapy of colorectal cancer with lung metastases (2019 edition). *Journal of Hematology and Oncology*, 12(1). https://doi.org/10.1186/s13045-019-0702-0.

Liang, P. S., Chen, T. Y., & Giovannucci, E. (2009). Cigarette smoking and colorectal cancer incidence and mortality: systematic review and meta-analysis. *International Journal of Cancer*, 124(10), 2406–2415. https://doi.org/10.1002/ijc.24191.

Liu, P. H., Wu, K., Ng, K., Zauber, A. G., Nguyen, L. H., Song, M., et al. (2019). Association of Obesity with Risk of Early-Onset Colorectal Cancer among Women. *JAMA oncology*, 5(1), 37–44. https://doi.org/10.1001/jamaoncol.2018.4280.

Loupakis, F., Yang, D., Yau, L., Feng, S., Cremolini, C., Zhang, W., et al. (2015). Primary tumor location as a prognostic factor in metastatic colorectal cancer. *JNCI: Journal of the National Cancer Institute*, 107(3), 6. https://doi.org/10.1093/jnci/dju427.

Ma, P., Yao, Y., Sun, W., Dai, S., & Zhou, C. (2017). Daily sedentary time and its association with risk for colorectal cancer in adults. *Medicine*, 96(22), e7049. https://doi.org/10.1097/MD.0000000000007049.

Malki, A., Elruz, R. A., Gupta, I., Allouch, A., Vranic, S., Moustafa, A., et al. (2021). Molecular mechanisms of colon cancer progression and metastasis: recent insights and advancements. *International Journal of Molecular Sciences*, 22(1), 1–24. https://doi.org/10.3390/ijms22010130.

Manfredi, S., Lepage, C., Hatem, C., Coatmeur, O., Faivre, J., & Bouvier, A. M. (2006). Epidemiology and management of liver metastases from colorectal cancer. *Annals of Surgery*, 244(2), 254–259. https://doi.org/10.1097/01.sla.0000217629.94941.cf.

Milosevic, M., Edwards, J., Tsang, D., Dunning, J., Shackcloth, M., Batchelor, T., et al. (2020). Pulmonary Metastasectomy in Colorectal Cancer: updated analysis of 93 randomized patients – control survival is much better than previously assumed. *Colorectal Disease*, 22(10), 1314–1324. https://doi.org/10.1111/codi.15113.

Modest, D. P., Ricard, I., Heinemann, V., Hegewisch-Becker, S., Schmiegel, W., Porschen, R., et al. (2016). Outcome according to KRAS-, NRAS- and BRAF-mutation as well as KRAS mutation variants: pooled analysis of five randomized trials in metastatic colorectal cancer by the AIO colorectal cancer study group. *Annals of Oncology*, 27(9), 1746–1753. https://doi.org/10.1093/annonc/mdw261.

Mooi, J. K., Wirapati, P., Asher, R., Lee, C. K., Savas, P., Price, T. J., et al. (2018). The prognostic impact of consensus molecular subtypes (CMS) and its predictive effects for bevacizumab benefit in metastatic colorectal cancer: molecular analysis of the AGITG MAX clinical trial. *Annals of Oncology*, 29(11), 2240–2246. https://doi.org/10.1093/annonc/mdy410.

Mousavi, S. M., Fallah, M., Sundquist, K., & Hemminki, K. (2012). Age- and time-dependent changes in cancer incidence among immigrants to Sweden: colorectal, lung, breast and prostate cancers. *International Journal of Cancer*, 131(2), E122–E128. https://doi.org/10.1002/ijc.27334.

Nguyen, L. H., Liu, P.-H., Zheng, X., Keum, N., Zong, X., Li, X., et al. (2018). Sedentary Behaviors, TV Viewing Time, and Risk of Young-Onset Colorectal Cancer. JNCI Cancer Spectrum, 2(4), 73. Epub 2019 Jan 25. PMID: 30740587; PMCID: PMC6361621. doi:https://doi.org/10.1093/jncics/pky073

Okita, A., Takahashi, S., Ouchi, K., Inoue, M., Watanabe, M., Endo, M., et al. (2018). Consensus molecular subtypes classification of colorectal cancer as a predictive factor for chemotherapeutic efficacy against metastatic colorectal cancer. *Oncotarget*, 9(27), 18698–18711. https://doi.org/10.18632/oncotarget.24617.

Pearlman, R., Frankel, W. L., Swanson, B., Zhao, W., Yilmaz, A., Miller, K., et al. (2017). Prevalence and spectrum of germline cancer susceptibility gene mutations among patients with early-onset colorectal cancer. *JAMA oncology*, 3(4), 464–471. https://doi.org/10.1001/jamaoncol.2016.5194.

Pereira, A. A. L., Rego, J. F. M., Morris, V., Overman, M. J., Eng, C., Garrett, C. R., et al. (2015). Association between KRAS mutation and lung metastasis in advanced colorectal cancer. *British Journal of Cancer,* 112(3), 424–428. https://doi.org/10.1038/bjc.2014.619.

Pikoulis, E., Margonis, G. A., Andreatos, N., Sasaki, K., Angelou, A., Polychronidis, G., et al. (2016). Prognostic role of braf mutations in colorectal cancer liver metastases. *Anticancer Research,* 36(9), 4805–4811. https://doi.org/10.21873/anticanres.11040.

Prasanna, T., Karapetis, C. S., Roder, D., Tie, J., Padbury, R., Price, T., et al. (2018). The survival outcome of patientswith metastatic colorectal cancer based on the site of metastases and the impact of molecularmarkers and site of primary cancer on metastatic pattern. Acta Oncologica, 57(11), 1438–1444. Epub 2018 Jul 23. PMID: 30035653. doi:https://doi.org/10.1093/jncics/pky073

Prasanna, T., Craft, P. S., Chua, Y. J., Karapetis, C. S., Gibbs, P., Wong, R., et al. (2017). The outcome of patients (pts) with metastatic colorectal cancer (mCRC) based on site of metastases (mets) and the impact of molecular markers and site of primary cancer on metastatic pattern. *Journal of Clinical Oncology,* 3560. https://doi.org/10.1200/jco.2017.35.15_suppl.3560.

Provenzale, D., Ness, R. M., Llor, X., Weiss, J. M., Abbadessa, B., Cooper, G., et al. (2020). NCCN Guidelines Insights: colorectal Cancer Screening, Version 2.2020. *Journal of the National Comprehensive Cancer Network,* 18(10), 1312–1320. https://doi.org/10.6004/jnccn.2020.0048.

Reinhart, K., Bannert, C., Dunkler, D., Salzl, P., Trauner, M., Renner, F., et al. (2013). Prevalence of flat lesions in a large screening population and their role in colonoscopy quality improvement. *Endoscopy,* 45(5), 350–356. https://doi.org/10.1055/s-0032-1326348.

Rex, D. K., Boland, C. R., Dominitz, J. A., Giardiello, F. M., Johnson, D. A., Kaltenbach, T., et al. (2017). Colorectal Cancer Screening: recommendations for Physicians and Patients from the U.S. Multi-Society Task Force on Colorectal Cancer. *American Journal of Gastroenterology,* 112(7), 1016–1030. https://doi.org/10.1038/ajg.2017.174.

Scott, R. B., Rangel, L. E., Osler, T. M., & Hyman, N. H. (2016). Rectal cancer in patients under the age of 50 years: the delayed diagnosis. *American Journal of Surgery,* 211(6), 1014–1018. https://doi.org/10.1016/j.amjsurg.2015.08.031.

Siegel, R. L., Miller, K. D., Sauer, G., A. , F., S. , A., Butterly, L. F., et al. (2020). Colorectal cancer statistics, 2020. *CA Cancer Journal for Clinicians,* 70(3), 145–164. https://doi.org/10.3322/caac.21601.

Stintzing, S., Wirapati, P., Lenz, H. J., Neureiter, D., Fischer von Weikersthal, L., Decker, T., et al. (2019). Consensus molecular subgroups (CMS) of colorectal cancer (CRC) and first-line efficacy of FOLFIRI plus cetuximab or bevacizumab in the FIRE3 (AIO KRK-0306) trial. *Annals of Oncology,* 30(11), 1796–1803. https://doi.org/10.1093/annonc/mdz387.

Talseth-Palmer, B. A. (2017). The genetic basis of colonic adenomatous polyposis syndromes. *Hereditary Cancer in Clinical Practice,* 15(1). https://doi.org/10.1186/s13053-017-0065-x.

Testa, U., Pelosi, E., & Castelli, G. (2018). Colorectal Cancer: genetic Abnormalities, Tumor Progression, Tumor Heterogeneity, Clonal Evolution and Tumor-Initiating Cells. *Medical Sciences,* 31. https://pubmed.ncbi.nlm.nih.gov/29652830/#:~:text=Testa%20U%2C%20Pelosi%20E%2C%20Castelli%20G.%20Colorectal%20cancer%3A%20genetic%20abnormalities%2C%20tumor%20progression%2C%20tumor%20heterogeneity%2C%20clonal%20evolution%20and%20tumor%2Dinitiating%20cells.%20Med%20Sci%20(Basel).%202018%20Apr%2013%3B6(2)%3A31.%20doi%3A%2010.3390/medsci6020031.%20PMID%3A%2029652830%3B%20PMCID%3A%20PMC6024750.

Thanki, K., Nicholls, e., & Gajjar, a. (2017). Consensus Molecular Subtypes of Colorectal Cancer and their Clinical Implications. *Int Biol Biomed J,* 3, 105–111.

Tran, B., Kopetz, S., Tie, J., Gibbs, P., Jiang, Z. Q., Lieu, C. H., et al. (2011). Impact of BRAF mutation and microsatellite instability on the pattern of metastatic spread and prognosis in metastatic colorectal cancer. *Cancer,* 117(20), 4623–4632. https://doi.org/10.1002/cncr.26086.

Ubink, I., van Eden, W. J., Snaebjornsson, P., Kok, N. F. M., van Kuik, J., van Grevenstein, W. M. U., et al. (2018). Histopathological and molecular classification of colorectal cancer and corresponding peritoneal metastases. *British Journal of Surgery,* 105(2), e204–e211. https://doi.org/10.1002/bjs.10788.

Umar, A., Boland, C. R., Terdiman, J. P., Syngal, S., de la Chapelle, A., Rüschoff, J., et al. (2004). Revised Bethesda Guidelines for hereditary nonpolyposis colorectal cancer (Lynch syndrome) and microsatellite instability. *JNCI: Journal of the National Cancer Institute,* 96(4), 261–268. https://doi.org/10.1093/jnci/djh034.

van der Geest, L. G. M., Lam-Boer, J., Koopman, M., Verhoef, C., Elferink, M. A. G., & de Wilt, J. H. W. (2015). Nationwide trends in incidence, treatment and survival of colorectal cancer patients with synchronous metastases. *Clinical and Experimental Metastasis*, 32(5), 457–465. https://doi.org/10.1007/s10585-015-9719-0.

Vieira, A. R., Abar, L., Chan, D. S. M., Vingeliene, S., Polemiti, E., Stevens, C., et al. (2017). Foods and beverages and colorectal cancer risk: a systematic review and meta-analysis of cohort studies, an update of the evidence of the WCRF-AICR Continuous Update Project. *Annals of Oncology*, 28(8), 1788–1802. https://doi.org/10.1093/annonc/mdx171.

Win, A. K., Young, J. P., Lindor, N. M., Tucker, K. M., Ahnen, D. J., Young, G. P., et al. (2012). Colorectal and other cancer risks for carriers and noncarriers from families with a DNA mismatch repair gene mutation: a prospective cohort study. *Journal of Clinical Oncology*, 30(9), 958–964. https://doi.org/10.1200/JCO.2011.39.5590.

Wolf, A. M. D., Fontham, E. T. H., Church, T. R., Flowers, C. R., Guerra, C. E., LaMonte, S. J., et al. (2018). Colorectal cancer screening for average-risk adults: 2018 guideline update from the American Cancer Society. *CA Cancer Journal for Clinicians*, 68(4), 250–281. https://doi.org/10.3322/caac.21457.

Yaeger, R., Cowell, E., Chou, J. F., Gewirtz, A. N., Borsu, L., Vakiani, E., et al. (2015). RAS mutations affect pattern of metastatic spread and increase propensity for brain metastasis in colorectal cancer. *Cancer*, 121(8), 1195–1203. https://doi.org/10.1002/cncr.29196.

You, Y. N., Lee, L. D., Deschner, B. W., & Shibata, D. (2020). Colorectal cancer in the adolescent and young adult population. *Journal of Oncology Practice*, 16(1), 19–27. https://doi.org/10.1200/JOP.19.00153.

CHAPTER

2

The tumor microenvironment of colorectal cancer liver metastases: Molecular mediators and future therapeutic targets

Peter M. Siegel[a,b], *Hanna Nyström*[c,d] and *Pnina Brodt*[b,e,f,g]

[a]Goodman Cancer Institute, McGill University, Montreal, Québec, QC, H3A 1A3, Canada [b]Department of Medicine, Faculty of Medicine, McGill University, Montreal, Québec, QC, H3A 1A1, Canada [c]Department of Surgical and Perioperative Sciences, Surgery, Umeå University, Sweden [d]Wallenberg Centre for Molecular Medicine, Umeå University, Sweden [e]Department of Surgery, Montreal, QC, H4A 3J1 [f]Medicine and Oncology, Montreal, QC, H4A 3J1 [g]McGill University and the Cancer Program of the Research Institute of the McGill University Health Center, Montreal, QC, H4A 3J1

Introduction

The liver is the most frequent site of metastases in colorectal cancer (CRC) patients. Importantly, the development of liver metastases (LM) is associated with poor prognosis and is the most common cause of cancer-related death (Helling and Martin, 2014). Several factors contribute to the relatively high frequency of LM in CRC patients. Among them are the rich blood supply that supports the liver, entering via the portal circulation that drains the GI tract (Lautt, Granger, and Granger, 2010) and the unique immune-tolerant and pro-metastatic liver microenvironment (LME). Five major phases have been identified in the progression of liver metastasis: (i) establishment of a pre-metastatic niche; (ii) the microvascular phase, whereby cancer cells arrest in the sinusoidal vessels leading to cancer cell death or extravasation; (iii) the extravascular, pre-angiogenic phase that entails recruitment and activation of hepatic stromal

Contemporary Management of Metastatic Colorectal Cancer: A Precision Medicine Approach
DOI: https://doi.org/10.1016/B978-0-323-91706-3.00011-4

cells and myeloid cells that infiltrate avascular metastases. At this stage cancer cells may assume a dormant phenotype or progress to form overt metastases. The latter is associated with (iv) an angiogenic phase that involves endothelial cell recruitment/tumor neovascularization or cooption of an existing vascular network and (v) the growth phase whereby metastases expand and become clinically detectable (Van den Eynden et al., 2013; Vidal-Vanaclocha, 2008).

Upon entry into the liver, and at each phase of the metastatic cascade, CRC cells encounter a unique microenvironment consisting of resident hepatic cells programed to carry out the metabolic/synthetic functions of the liver and protect the liver from immune hyper-reactivity. They include the liver sinusoidal endothelial cells (LSEC), Kupffer cells (KC), dendritic cells (DC), hepatic stellate cells (HSC) and hepatocytes (Table 2.1). Each of these specialized cell populations can play a role in antigen presentation and the response to pathogens. They can also respond to and control the fate of invading cancer cells.

Recent progress in the development of effective immunotherapies, including antibodies directed against immune checkpoint proteins such as programmed death 1 (PD-1) and cytotoxic T-lymphocyte-associated protein four (CTLA-4), has had significant impact on the management and outcome of several malignancies. PD-1 and CTLA-4 negatively regulate T cell dependent immune responses to prevent immune system over-activation and auto-reactivity. In the context of malignant disease, T cell exhaustion triggered by immune checkpoint engagement dampens anti-tumor immunity and limits the ability of cytotoxic T cells (CTL) to eradicate malignant cells. Immune checkpoint inhibitors (ICIs) can block the interaction of checkpoint molecules with their ligands and thereby enable CTL activation and cancer cell elimination. ICIs have markedly improved clinical outcomes for some malignancies such as melanoma, lung cancer and renal cell carcinoma (Hu et al., 2019; Queirolo, Boutros, Tanda, Spagnolo, and Quaglino, 2019; Wilky, 2019; Xu, Atkins, and McDermott, 2020). Other solid cancers have also demonstrated durable ICI responses, including a specific subset of CRC with microsatellite-instability high (MSI-H) or mismatch-repair (MMR) deficient disease (Le et al., 2015; Overman et al., 2018). However, many patients with metastatic CRC (mCRC) do not respond to checkpoint inhibition and, moreover, LM is one of several factors predicting a poor response to immunotherapy, even in responsive malignancies such as melanoma and lung cancer (Yu et al., 2021).

The liver has evolved to maintain tissue homeostasis and a state of immune – unresponsiveness in the face of constant exposure to food-derived and commensal microbial products entering through the portal circulation. This is achieved by the unique properties of cells residing in the liver that function to dampen adaptive immune responses. Here we will survey the unique features of the liver microenvironment that contribute to this general state of immune-tolerance and render the liver particularly "hospitable" to incoming metastatic cancer cells. The diverse cell types and unique liver ECM, which collectively control the progression of metastasis and can act to curtail or promote the process, will be described and recent insight into their respective roles highlighted.

The unique immune microenvironment of the liver

Role of liver sinusoidal endothelial cells

Upon entry into the liver, cancer cells first encounter the highly specialized liver sinusoidal endothelial cells (LSEC) that line the network of sinusoidal vessels draining the hepatic

TABLE 2.1 Dendritic cells of the liver

Cell type	Main Cell surface markers	Subtypes and additional markers	Functions	References
Conventional myeloid DCs (mDC)	$CD45^+CD11c^+MHCII^+$	$CD141^+$ (thrombomodulin, BDCA-3) subtype $CD1c^+$ (BDCA-1) subtype	Can present antigen but produce IL-10 and induce IL-10 and IL-4 production in T cells i.e.-**poor T cell activators**	(Friedman, S. L., 2008a; Friedman, S. L., 2008b)
Plasmacytoid DCs (pDC) (human)	$CD11c^-$	Clec4C ILT7 (LILRA4) CD4 CD68 ILT3 (LILRB4) CD123	Type-I interferon (IFN) responses **produce IL-27 and IDO to induce Treg**	(Fiegle et al., 2019)
Plasmacytoid DCs (mice)	CD11c- intermediate levels	B220 Ly6C BST2 (tetherin14) Siglec-H)	Express a low Delta4/Jagged1 Notch ligand ratio, **skewing response towards Th2 differentiation and apoptosis of $CD4^+$ T cells. Express PD-L1** to bind exhausted $PD\text{-}1^+$ T cells	(Dou et al., 2018; Fiegle et al., 2019; Geissmann et al., 2005; Germann et al., 2020)
Lymphoid-related DC (in mice)	Express lymphoid cell markers	Subtype 1 - $CD11c^+CD8^+$	Induce a Th1-type response that results in IL-12 and TNFα production	(Erstad et al., 2020; Fiegle et al., 2019; Freire Valls et al., 2019)
		Subtype 2 - $CD11c^+NK1.1^+$	Produce IFNγ, can activate T cells, retain cytolytic activity	(Chen et al., 2007; Coffelt et al., 2016)

and portal circulations. The LSEC barrier contains fenestrations of approximately 100 nm in diameter organized into structures known as sieve plates. Through these fenestrations, hepatocytes and cells residing in the space of Disse are exposed to the content of the blood. Under normal physiological conditions, LSECs together with Kupffer cells (KC) - the resident liver macrophages located in the sinusoids (see below) screen the portal blood and remove pathogens and foreign molecules. They can also produce inflammatory cytokines that recruit additional innate immune cells. Cancer cells entering the sinusoidal vessels can be rapidly eliminated by KC-mediated phagocytosis or the tumoricidal action of mediators such as TNF, nitric oxide (NO) and oxygen radicals that are released by KCs and LSECs. This local inflammatory response is, however, a double-edged sword because it can result in the induction of vascular adhesion receptors such as E-selectin, P-selectin and VCAM-1 on the surface of LSECs. The increase in these receptors enables cancer cell adhesion to the vessel wall through counter-receptors, such as $sLew^X$ and VLA4, or indirectly via attachment to circulating platelets or neutrophils. This can enable rapid exit of the cancer cells into the space of Disse (extravasation), where they are protected from the phagocytic activity of KCs (Reviewed in (Brodt, 2016; Chen et al., 2007; Pillarisetty, Katz, Bleier, Shah, and Dematteo, 2005; Van den Eynden et al., 2013; Vidal-Vanaclocha, 2008) and can progress to form overt metastases. A recent study also identified the interaction between ICAM-1 expressed on LSECs and LFA-1 present on CRC cells as a driver of liver metastasis. It was shown that inflammatory factors released by both LSECs and bound CRC cells contribute to hepatic stellate cell (HSC) activation. Activated HSCs subsequently increased the production of VEGF and metalloproteinases (MMPs), thereby enhancing the pro-metastatic microenvironment in the liver (Benedicto et al., 2019).

LSECs can also contribute to an immune tolerant state within the liver that can be exploited by cancer cells. While LSECs can present antigen to T cells, they also express PD-L1 and induce immune cell exhaustion and anergy of PD-1 expressing T cells. Additionally, Klugewitz et al. have reported that LSECs selectively suppress the expansion of IFN-producing T cells, while promoting the outgrowth of IL-4-expressing Th2 cells, thereby dampening T cell mediated immunoreactivity (Klugewitz et al., 2002).

The natural killer cells of the liver

The liver contains the largest population of natural killer (NK) cells in the body, potentially up to half of all liver lymphocytes (Crispe, 2009; Doherty and O'Farrelly, 2000). In the mouse, two major NK cell populations derived from distinct lineages were identified namely, the circulating NKs (cNK) and the liver resident NKs (lrNK) (Male, 2017). The cNKs depend on the transcription factor Eomes and can circulate freely, while lrNKs are Tbet dependent, found in the liver sinusoids and cannot leave the liver (Male, 2017). These innate lymphocytes, rarely found in other tissues, play a key role in resistance to infection and clearance of cancer cells by screening cells for the absence of 'self' markers. This unique property enables them to recognize cancer cells that have downregulated antigen-presenting molecules, such as MHC-I, thereby avoiding immune surveillance by the adaptive immune system (Crispe, 2009). A unique NK population, the invariant NK T cells (iNKT) are also found in the liver. Derived from thymic $CD4^-CD8^-$ double-negative precursors, they develop into $CD4^+CD8^+$ double-positive cells, and circulate to several organs such as the liver, spleen and lungs (Benlagha, Kyin, Beavis, Teyton, and Bendelac, 2002; Dashtsoodol et al., 2017). In the liver, they highly express the chemokine receptors CCR5 and CXCR3. These receptors mediate iNKT cell recruitment to sites of inflammation. Under normal conditions, iNKT cells continually crawl along the sinusoid walls, independently of the blood flow, scanning for ligands. When activated, they firmly adhere to LSEC, presumably by binding to CD1d molecules on endothelial cells and macrophages (Geissmann et al., 2005; Gumperz, Miyake, Yamamura, and Brenner, 2002). Once activated, iNKT can acquire effector functions (Gumperz et al., 2002) and elicit strong anti-tumor cytotoxicity (Dashtsoodol et al., 2017) (reviewed extensively in (Kubes and Jenne, 2018).

The dendritic cells of the liver contribute to immune-tolerance

The heterogeneous liver dendritic cell population

Dendritic cells are the classical antigen-presenting cells (APC) of the lymphatic system (Table 2.1). Hepatic dendritic cells also initiate and orchestrate immune responses, but they are programmed to contribute to liver tolerance rather than activate an immunogenic T cell response (Dou, Ono, Chen, Thomson, and Chen, 2018). Hepatic DCs reside in the subcapsular region of the liver, interstitially between hepatocytes, in periportal areas and within the vasculature (Dou et al., 2018). Both in humans and in mice, they constitute a heterogenous population, identifiable by specific cell surface markers and transcription factors. In humans, the two main subtypes are the conventional myeloid DCs (mDC) that are $CD45^+CD11c^+MHCII^+$ and the plasmacytoid DCs (pDC), which express no (in human) or intermediate levels of CD11c. Two distinct subsets of mDCs, the $CD141^+$ (thrombomodulin or BDCA-3) and $CD1c^+$ (BDCA-1) DCs have been identified in the liver, as well as pDCs. pDCs constitute a unique DC subset specializing in type-I interferon (IFNs) responses. They selectively express the C type lectin BDCA2 (also known as Clec4C), the immunoglobulin-like transcript 7 (ILT7; also known as LILRA4), CD4, CD68, ILT3 (also known as LILRB4) and the IL3 receptor α-subunit (also known as CD123). However, these cells undergo phenotypic changes at different developmental stages and/or activation states (Swiecki and Colonna, 2015). In mice, pDCs are identified based on expression of CD11c, B220, LY6C, bone marrow stromal antigen 2 (BST2; also known as tetherin14) and sialic acid-binding immunoglobulinlike lectin H (SiglecH)(26). In addition to mDC and pDC, two lymphoid-related DC, the $CD11c^+CD8^+$ DCs and $CD11c^+NK1.1^+$ DC have also been identified in mice, although their roles are not fully understood (Crispe, 2011; Doherty, 2016; Tiegs and Lohse, 2010) (For summary, please see Table 2.1).

Liver dendritic cell functions

pDCs and mDCs express MHC class II and co-stimulatory molecules, which allow them to present antigens to $CD4^+$ T cells. However, depending on the context, DCs can lead to either $CD4^+$ T cell activation or tolerance. Hepatic mDCs and pDCs are poor T cell activators, due to production of IL-10 (as opposed to IL-12 produced by immunogenic, skin mDCs) and their ability to induce IL-10 and IL-4 production in T cells, rather than T cell proliferation (Bamboat et al., 2009; Goddard, Youster, Morgan, and Adams, 2004). The differentiation of bone marrow-derived progenitors into liver DCs that produce high IL-10 and low IL-12 levels is regulated, at least in part, by liver stroma-derived macrophage colony-stimulating factor (M-CSF) (Xia et al., 2008). Hepatic pDCs also produce IL-27 and indoleamine 2,3-dioxygenase 1 (IDO1). These factors can, in turn, suppress T cell responsiveness by inducing immunosuppressive

Tregs and metabolizing tryptophan, respectively (Doherty, 2016). In addition, liver pDCs express a low Delta4/Jagged1 Notch ligand ratio and this skews the response towards Th2 cell differentiation/cytokine production and $CD4^+$ T cell apoptosis (Tokita et al., 2008). Liver pDCs also express PDL-1 and can induce T cell exhaustion by engaging the checkpoint molecule PD-1 on T cells (reviewed in (Doherty, 2016; Heymann and Tacke, 2016; Swiecki and Colonna, 2015)). It has also been suggested that the lipid content of human DCs may help determine their activity, as a low lipid content predisposes these cells to tolerogenic functions (Ibrahim et al., 2012). Unlike mDCs and pDCs, $CD11c^+CD8^+$ DCs generate a Th1-type response that results in IL-12 and TNFα production (Doherty, 2016; Heymann and Tacke, 2016). $CD11c^+NK1.1^+$ cells can produce cytokines, such as IFNγ, to activate immune T cells, while also retaining cytolytic activity that could generate cellular antigens for T cell activation (Chen et al., 2007; Pillarisetty et al., 2005). Thus, T cell activation and CTL generation in the liver may ultimately be determined by the balance between the immunogenic and tolerogenic functions of this heterogeneous liver DC population.

Myeloid cells can play diverse and opposing roles in colorectal cancer liver metastasis

The tumor-resident and bone-marrow derived macrophages

Macrophage populations play an important role in modulating the formation and growth of colorectal liver metastases (CRLMs) and can be sub-divided into liver-resident macrophages (Kupffer Cells: KC) and infiltrating bone marrow-derived macrophages (BoMs) (Keirsse et al., 2018). KCs originate from the extraembryonic yolk sac and subsequently from fetal liver monocytes; whereas, BoMs are derived from circulating monocytes once hematopoiesis has shifted to the bone marrow (Keirsse et al., 2018).

Role of kupffer cells

KCs play opposing roles in controlling the formation of CRLMs. During early metastatic phases, KCs can impair seeding/colonization of metastatic cancer cells; however, KCs can also help promote the growth of established CRLMs (Matsumura et al., 2014; Wen, Ager, and Christophi, 2013). KCs can directly kill cancer cells via their enhanced phagocytic activity or indirectly through the release of soluble factors that augment the anti-tumor effects of infiltrating immune cells (reviewed in (Brodt, 2016; Tsilimigras et al., 2021)). For example, it was recently shown that expression of both Dectin-2 and Dectin-3 in KCs was required for efficient KC-mediated cancer cell engulfment, which resulted in liver metastasis suppression, a requirement not shared by BoMs (Kimura et al., 2016).

Metastatic CRC cells that survive initial interactions with KCs can ultimately benefit from KC-mediated functions, including enhancing CRC cell extravasation through the release of inflammatory cytokines that activate adhesion molecules on LSECs and the establishment of an immunosuppressive microenvironment, to promote the formation of LM (Khatib et al., 2005, 1999). Recently, it was shown that KCs contribute to increased vascular leakiness through the release of MMP-9, thereby enhancing CRC cell extravasation and liver metastasis. Interestingly, the uptake of angiopoietin like protein −1 (ANGPTL1)-containing extracellular vesicles by KCs resulted in a reduction in MMP-9 secretion, an increase in vascular integrity and impaired liver metastasis (Jiang et al., 2021). KCs have also been implicated in modulating the composition and organization of extracellular matrix components to foster enhanced liver metastasis. It was recently reported that mice lacking the angiotensin II subtype receptor 1a (AT1a) exhibited decreased formation of CRLMs relative to wild-type littermates (Shimizu et al., 2017). The decrease in metastatic burden was associated with reduced numbers of $CD31^+$ endothelial cells and $F4/80^+$ macrophages in the livers of AT1a knockout mice relative to wild-type controls. Interestingly, the transfer of wild-type bone marrow cells into irradiated AT1a knockout mice failed to rescue efficient CRC liver metastasis, suggesting that the $F4/80^+$ cells within metastases-bearing livers were resident KCs and not BoMs (Shimizu et al., 2017). Mechanistically, $F4/80^+$ KCs were shown to produce TGFb, which in turn, stimulated collagen I production by hepatic stellate cells and the ablation of $F4/80^+$ KCs resulted in a reduction in CRLM.

KCs can also present antigen. Located within the liver sinusoids, they are optimally located to interact with T cells recruited to the liver. However, this interaction does not generally lead to T cell activation. This may be due to lower expression of MHCII and costimulatory molecules B7-1 and B7-2 than in other APCs, such as DCs (You, Cheng, Kedl, and Ju, 2008). In addition, antigen-presentation by KCs can lead to PD-L1 upregulation and the release of immunosuppressive molecules such as IL-10, TGFβ, prostaglandin E2 (PGE2), IDO1 and/or arginase that cumulatively result in T cell suppression and the induction of immunosuppressive regulatory T cells (iTregs) (extensively reviewed in (Doherty, 2016). However, in the presence of inflammatory cytokines, Poly I:C or pathogen-associated molecules such as TLR3 and TLR9 ligands, KCs can transform into T cell-activating APCs due, in part, to increased MHCII expression (Abo, Kawamura, and Watanabe, 2000; You et al., 2008). Moreover, KCs can potently activate iNKTs and consequently contribute to reactivity against non-MHC expressing cells. In this context, it should be noted that KCs likely consist of distinct subpopulations that differ in their development, life span and antigen presenting ability. Using an unbiased cytometry by "time of flight" (CyTOF) approach, David et al. observed two distinct KC populations, one positive and one negative for CD11c, and this was confirmed by imaging. These cells may therefore represent distinct subpopulations with divergent potential to present antigen (David et al., 2016).

Bone marrow-derived macrophages

Macrophages that infiltrate LMs, often referred to as tumor-associated macrophages (TAMs), can exhibit a great degree of plasticity depending on the local microenvironment (Guc and Pollard, 2021). The functional states of TAMs encompass a spectrum ranging from M1 polarized macrophages (inflammatory, anti-tumor phenotypes) to M2 polarized macrophages (alternatively activated, pro-tumor phenotypes).

Metastasis-suppressing macrophages

The importance of macrophage polarization was recently demonstrated by examining liver metastases in mice lacking N-myc downstream-regulated gene 2 (NDRG2). NDRG2-deficient mice developed fewer LM, when injected with different cancer cell types, including CRC cells (Li et al., 2018). Analysis of the immune cell composition revealed that Ndrg2-/- mice possessed a higher proportion of $Ly6C^{lo}MHCII^{hi}$ (M1-like) macrophages and a lower proportion of $Ly6C^{lo}MHCII^{lo}$ (M2-like) macrophages. Bone marrow transplant studies confirmed that Ndrg2-/- bone marrow-derived macrophages were important suppressors of CRLM (Li et al., 2018). These observations are consistent with a previous study demonstrating that CRC cells engineered to overexpress CXCL16 failed to efficiently form LMs compared with controls (Kee et al., 2014). In this study, CRC-derived CXCL16 recruited M1 macrophages that expressed TNF-a, which induced cancer cell apoptosis and causing a reduction in liver metastases (Kee et al., 2014).

Pro-metastatic macrophages

Growing evidence points to an important role of macrophages in promoting the establishment and expansion of CRLMs. Indeed, polarization of macrophages to an M2-like phenotype is associated with enhanced liver metastasis in CRC models. For example, injection of CRC cells into ICAM-1 deficient mice resulted in a significantly increased liver-metastatic burden when compared to ICAM-1 proficient mice, and this was attributed to an increase in M2 macrophage infiltration into the liver (Yang, Liu, Piao, Shao, and Du, 2015). Complement factor 5a has been shown to promote an M2 phenotype in macrophages infiltrating CRLMs and loss of C5aR, which is expressed in M2-like macrophages, impaired liver metastasis (Piao et al., 2018). CRC cell-derived miRNAs, packaged in exosomes, were recently shown to induce an M2 phenotype in infiltrating macrophages. These M2 polarized macrophages increased CRC liver metastasis by promoting an epithelial-to-mesenchymal transition (EMT) in cancer cells and releasing VEGF into the metastatic ME (Wang et al., 2020). These observations align with previous reports showing that infiltrating macrophages can induce an EMT in CRC cells, thereby enhancing the malignant phenotype (Wei et al., 2019). Moreover, the presence of infiltrating VEGFR1$^+$ macrophages within CRLMs correlated with poor patient outcomes (Freire Valls et al., 2019).

Collectively, these data highlight how polarization of infiltrating macrophages can have a dramatic effect on the formation of LMs. Indeed, a recent study used macrophage morphology as a proxy for polarization status and examined their prognostic value in patients with CRLM. They discovered that larger TAMs (L-TAMs) were present with increased frequency in CRLM - bearing patients with poor outcomes when compared to smaller TAMs (S-TAMs). RNA-seq data obtained from these two macrophage populations revealed that S-TAMs expressed pro-inflammatory genes whereas L-TAMs expressed genes of the complement family, scavenger receptors and cholesterol related genes, suggesting that different functional macrophage states were associated with distinct morphologies (Donadon et al., 2020). Of particular relevance is a recent study that investigated the mechanisms underlying the relative failure of IT to provide therapeutic benefit in patients with LM. Using multiple mouse models, the study has shown that LMs siphon activated CD8$^+$ T cells from the circulation. Antigen-specific Fas$^+$CD8$^+$ T cells then interact with FasL$^+$CD11b$^+$F4/80$^+$ monocyte-derived macrophages in the liver and undergo apoptosis, depleting the organ and the circulation of antigen-specific CTLs. This could be rectified by liver-directed radiotherapy that eliminated immunosuppressive macrophages and increased hepatic T cell survival. In patients harboring liver metastatic disease, a similar reduction in the number of peripheral T cells and a diminished T cell function were observed (Yu et al., 2021). Thus, recruited monocytes not only exert direct metastasis–promoting effects, they can also subvert a CTL response and thereby contribute indirectly to metastatic expansion and dampen the effect of IT.

Neutrophils opposing roles in liver metastasis progression

Neutrophils have emerged as an extremely important innate immune cell type that regulates metastatic progression in numerous cancer types. Several studies have revealed that a high neutrophil-to-lymphocyte ratio (NLR) in the peripheral blood of patients with CRLM, prior to resection or administration of therapy is associated with poor clinical outcomes (Erstad et al., 2020; Giakoustidis, Neofytou, Khan, and Mudan, 2015; Mao et al., 2019; McCluney et al., 2018; Verter et al., 2021).

It has become clear that neutrophils do not represent a uniform population of innate immune cells but rather exhibit a great degree of heterogeneity. In an analogous fashion to macrophages, neutrophils can exhibit either metastases-suppressing or metastases-promoting functions (Coffelt, Wellenstein, and de Visser, 2016; Hsu, Shen, and Siegel, 2020). The importance of neutrophil polarization within the context of CRC liver metastasis was revealed in mice engineered to undergo short or long-term type 1 insulin like growth factor (IGF-1) depletion. While neutrophils could still accumulate in metastasis bearing livers with long term IGF-1 depletion, they failed to polarize to a pro-metastatic phenotype, which was associated with reduced liver-metastatic burden (Rayes et al., 2018).

The ability of neutrophils to enhance metastatic progression can be attributed to several distinct neutrophil effector functions including induction of an immunosuppressive ME, enhancing angiogenesis and production of neutrophil extracellular traps (NETs) through a process termed NETosis.

Neutrophil-mediated immunosuppression

Infiltrating neutrophils can induce an immunosuppressive microenvironment in numerous solid cancers via suppression of both cytotoxic T cells and NK cells (Coffelt et al., 2016; Hsu et al., 2020). In a CRC transgenic model, it was recently shown that infiltrating neutrophils were abundant in primary CRC adenomas and that neutrophils isolated from these lesions could suppress T cell proliferation in vitro. Notably, neutrophil depletion in vivo resulted in reduced CRC tumor burden and increased T cell infiltration (Germann et al., 2020). Mechanistically, infiltrating neutrophils expressed MMP-9, which could activate latent TGF-b to suppress T cell activation (Germann et al., 2020). Similarly, NOTCH1 activation in CRC cells was shown to mediate the TGFβ2-dependent recruitment of immunosuppressive neutrophils within the liver, which promoted the formation of LM.

Neutrophil-mediated angiogenesis

A major pro-metastatic function of neutrophils is the induction of an angiogenic response. Indeed, it has been shown that neutrophils recruited into the liver-metastatic ME produce FGF2, which drives angiogenesis and growth of nascent CRC-derived hepatic metastases (Gordon-Weeks et al., 2017). Neutrophils can also release other pro-angiogenic factors, such as Bv8. Using a syngeneic CRC model, it has recently been shown that LM infiltrating $Bv8^+$ neutrophils caused resistance to VEGF neutralizing antibodies (Itatani et al., 2020).

NETosis

Neutrophils release chromatin decorated with granule constituents forming extracellular structures termed NETs (Papayannopoulos, 2018). It has been shown that ischemia/reperfusion (I/R) triggered by liver resection caused increased NETosis and reduced survival in patients with mCRC (Tohme et al., 2016). Similarly, a hepatic I/R model in mice bearing CRLM revealed an increase in NET formation relative to sham controls, and this enhanced the growth of metastatic lesions. Importantly, degrading NETs with DNase abrogated the growth of LM following I/R (Tohme et al., 2016). Mechanistically, NETs were shown to induce Toll-like receptor 9 (TLR9) activation in CRC cells, leading to engagement of p38, STAT3, JNK and the p65 subunit of NF-kB, which contributed to the growth of CRLM (Tohme et al., 2016). Likewise, LPS-induced NETs were shown to enhance the formation of CRLM and this could be inhibited by the administration of DNase 1 (Yang et al., 2020). In the latter study, the NETs were shown to induce the expression of IL-8 in CRC cells and IL-8, in turn, engaged tumor cell intrinsic NF-kB signaling (Yang et al., 2020).

Recently, it was shown that in mice bearing sub-cutaneous lung carcinoma cells, NET formation is enhanced and this increases cancer cell adhesion to the liver sinusoids and promotes the formation of lung and CRC-derived LM following intrasplenic/portal injection (Rayes et al., 2019). These effects were diminished if NETs were degraded by DNase I or NETosis was blocked by neutrophil elastase inhibitors. These data suggest that primary tumors can induce the formation of NETs in the absence of sepsis or surgically induced systemic inflammation (Rayes et al., 2019). Specific NET components may play distinct roles in the metastasis-promoting effects of NETosis. For example, CECAM1 has been shown to be a constituent of NETs produced by both mouse and human neutrophils and CEACAM1-containing NETs enhanced the adhesion of CRC cells to the sinusoidal endothelium in the liver (Rayes et al., 2020). The critical role that neutrophils and NETosis play in augmenting CRC liver metastasis have raised interest in targeting NETosis as a therapeutic strategy (Khan et al., 2021). Several studies described above have shown that the administration of DNase 1 can block NETosis-enhanced CRLM in pre-clinical models. Recently, the therapeutic feasibility of this approach was explored by using an adeno-associated virus (AAV) gene therapy vector to deliver DNase 1 to the liver (Xia et al., 2020). Consistent with their postulated role, elimination of NETs via DNase 1 delivery to the liver reduced CRLM. AAV-DNase 1 treated mice possessed fewer neutrophils and this was associated with an influx of $CD8^+$ CTLs around the metastatic lesions (Xia et al., 2020).

Myeloid-derived suppressor cells (MDSCs) promote liver metasasis by diverse mechanisms

MDSCs are bone-marrow derived innate immune cells that induce an immunosuppressive ME in the context of cancer (Table 2.2). MDSCs include precursors of the monocyte and granulocyte lineages and can therefore be subdivided into monocytic (M-MDSCs) and granulocytic (G-MDSCs) MDSCs (Dou and Fang, 2021). A considerable body of evidence implicates MDSCs in the establishment and growth of CRLM. In mice bearing primary CRC tumors that had not yet formed hepatic metastases, MDSCs were found in the liver at higher numbers than in non-tumor bearing mice (Zeng et al., 2021). Transcriptomic analysis of pre-metastatic liver tissue indicated that markers associated with T cell suppression were more highly expressed in these livers than in the controls (Zeng et al., 2021). G-MDSCs were implicated in establishing a pre-metastatic niche in the liver (Wang, Sun, Wei, Cen, and DuBois, 2017). Indeed, VEGF-A expressing CRC cells could induce CXCL1 expression in macrophages, in turn, increasing the infiltration of $CXCR2^+$ G-MDSCs into the pre-metastatic liver and around established LM. Pharmacological inhibition of CXCR2 resulted in decreased recruitment of G-MDSCs and a reduction in liver metastatic burden (Wang et al., 2017).

TABLE 2.2 Myeloid Cells in the Liver Microenvironment.

Cell Type	Main Cell Surface Markers	Subtypes/Additional Markers	Functions	Refs.
Resident Macrophage Populations: Kupffer Cells (KCs)				
KCs: Anti-tumor	Human: CD68+, Mouse: F4/80+	Dectin 1,2 IL-1b, IL-6, IL-12, IL-18, TNFa	- Phagocytose/direct tumor cell killing - Enhance CTL/NK mediated tumor cell killing via the release of inflammatory cytokines/chemokines - Function as antigen-presenting cells	(Brodt, 2016; Jiang et al., 2021; Keirsse et al., 2018; Kimura et al., 2016; Shimizu et al., 2017; Tsilimigras et al., 2021)
KCs: Pro-tumor	Human: CD68+, Mouse: F4/80+	MMP9 TGFb	- Enhance cancer cell extravasation via activation of LSECs - Activate hepatic stellate cells - Contribute to CTL suppression/induction of Tregs	(Brodt, 2016; Doherty, 2016; Keirsse et al., 2018; Khatib et al., 2005, 1999; Tsilimigras et al., 2021)
Bone Marrow-Derived Macrophage Populations				
M1-like macrophages: Anti-tumor	Human: CD68+, CD11b+ Mouse: F4/80+, CD11b+	Human: CD40+, CD86+, iNOS, HLADR+ Mouse: Ly6Clow, MHCII+, CD86+, iNOS	- Direct tumor cell killing/phagocytosis - Anti-angiogenic - Antigen presentation	(Abo et al., 2000; Guc and Pollard, 2021)
M2-Like macrophages: Pro-tumor	Human: CD68+, CD11b+ Mouse: F4.80+, CD11b+	Human: CD163+, CD206+ Mouse: CD206+	- Pro-angiogenic - Matrix remodeling activity - Contribute to immunosuppression	(Abo et al., 2000; Piao et al., 2018; Yang et al., 2015)

(*continued on next page*)

Neutrophil Populations				
N1 (Mature): Anti-tumor	Human: CD14-, CD15+, CD11b+ Mouse: CD11b+, Ly6C-, Ly6G+	High Density, segmented nuclei	- Direct tumor killing (ROS) - Antigen presentation	(Abo et al., 2000; Mao et al., 2019; McCluney et al., 2018)
N2 (Immature): Pro-tumor	Human: CD14-, CD15+, CD11b+ Mouse: CD11b+, Ly6C-, Ly6G+	Low Density, unsegmented nuclei	- Pro-angiogenic - Matrix remodeling activity - Undergo NETosis - Contribute to immunosuppression	(Abo et al., 2000; Coffelt et al., 2016; Germann et al., 2020; Gordon-Weeks et al., 2017; Hsu et al., 2020; Itatani et al., 2020; Mao et al., 2019; McCluney et al., 2018; Papayannopoulos, 2018; Rayes et al., 2018; Tohme et al., 2016; Yang et al., 2020)
Myeloid Derived Suppressor Cells (MDSCs)				
Monocytic-MDSCs	Human:CD14+, CD15-, CD11b+ Mouse: CD11b+, Ly6C^{high}, Ly6G-	Human: CD133^{high}, HLADR-	- Immunosuppression - Pro-angiogenic	(Abo et al., 2000; Ham et al., 2015; Khan et al., 2021; Kiyasu et al., 2020; Wang et al., 2017; Zeng et al., 2021)
Granulocytic-MDSCs	Human: CD14-, CD15+, CD11b+ Mouse: CD11b+, Ly6C-, Ly6G+	Human: CD133^{mid}, HLADR-	- immunosuppression	(Abo et al., 2000; Dou and Fang, 2021; Khan et al., 2021)

Numerous studies have shown that infiltrating MDSCs modulate the local immune ME to favor immunosuppression and growth of LM. CCR1$^+$MDSCs were shown to accumulate in primary CRC tumors and LM and Ccr1-deficient mice exhibited decreased primary tumor growth and liver metastasis (Kiyasu et al., 2020). Irradiated mice receiving wild-type bone marrow transplants exhibited robust growth of primary CRC tumors and LM, but this was impaired in recipients of the Ccr1 $^{-/-}$ bone marrow transplants. Analysis of primary tumors and LM revealed an increase in CD8$^+$ CTL and a reduction in FoxP3$^+$ regulatory T cells in mice receiving Ccr1 $^{-/-}$ bone marrow transplants versus WT bone marrow recipients (Kiyasu et al., 2020). Similarly, loss of TNFR2 in MDSCs was associated with diminished MDSC recruitment and reduced CRLM, which coincided with a reduction in FoxP3$^+$ regulatory T cells (Ham et al., 2015). Notably, a sexual dimorphism was identified in the regulatory role that TNFR2 plays in MDSC recruitment to LM and estrogen was identified as a regulator of MDSC recruitment and an immunosuppressive ME in the livers of female mice, suggesting that anti-estrogens may have potential utility in the management of liver metastatic disease (Milette et al., 2019).

MDSCs can also promote the growth of liver metastases through alterations in the vasculature that supports CRLM. Using a CD11b-diptheria toxin receptor (DTR) "suicide gene", investigators were able to deplete MDSCs through administration of diptheria toxin, leading to a reduction in the formation of CRLM (Lim et al., 2015). Interestingly, loss of CD11b$^+$ myeloid cells was associated with a decrease in vascular density within, and around CRLMs. Elimination of MDSCs resulted in increased Angiopoietin Like 7 (ANGPTL7) expression in the cancer cells and overexpression of ANGPTL7 in lung or colon carcisnoma cells resulted in a reduction in LM burden, coincident with reduced vascularity (Lim et al., 2015) (For a summary of myeloid cell populations infiltrating CRLM and their functions see Table 2.2 and also Fig. 2.1).

Role of hepatic stellate cells

The Hepatic stellate cells (HepSC) are major drivers of the fibrotic response within the liver. Normally quiescent within the space of Disse, they are activated in response to tissue damage and inflammatory factors, acquire a myofibroblast- like phenotype including expression of α-smooth muscle actin (αSMA) and deposit extracellular proteins such as collagen I and IV and fibronectin to promote tissue repair (Friedman, 2008; Olaso, Santisteban, Bidaurrazaga, Gressner, and Rosenbaum, 1997; Vidal-Vanaclocha, 2011). Chemokines and cytokines released by HepSCs, such as CCL2, CCL5 and CCL21, recruit inflammatory and immune cells into the liver microenvironment while TGFβ and proangiogenic factors, such as VEGF and angiopoietin-1, promote a pro-metastatic microenvironment (Friedman, 2008; Nielsen et al., 2016; Zhao et al., 2014). In addition, the ECM proteins deposited by HepSCs and ECM degrading proteinases produced by these cells, including MMP2, MMP9 and MMP13, stimulate angiogenesis by providing a scaffold for migrating endothelial cells (Copple, Bai, Burgoon, and Moon, 2011; Smedsrod et al., 2009; Taura et al., 2008) and also facilitate cancer cell invasion (Brodt, 2016; Kang, Shah, and Urrutia, 2015; Milette, Sicklick, Lowy, and Brodt, 2017; Olaso et al., 2003; Vidal-Vanaclocha, 2011). HepSCs can present antigens to T cells and induce an immune response against cancer cells because they express MHC class I and II proteins (Friedman, 2008; Vinas et al., 2003) and are exposed to blood-borne antigens through LSEC fenestrations. Like other APCs in the liver, however, HepSCs express PD-L1 and this can lead to T cell

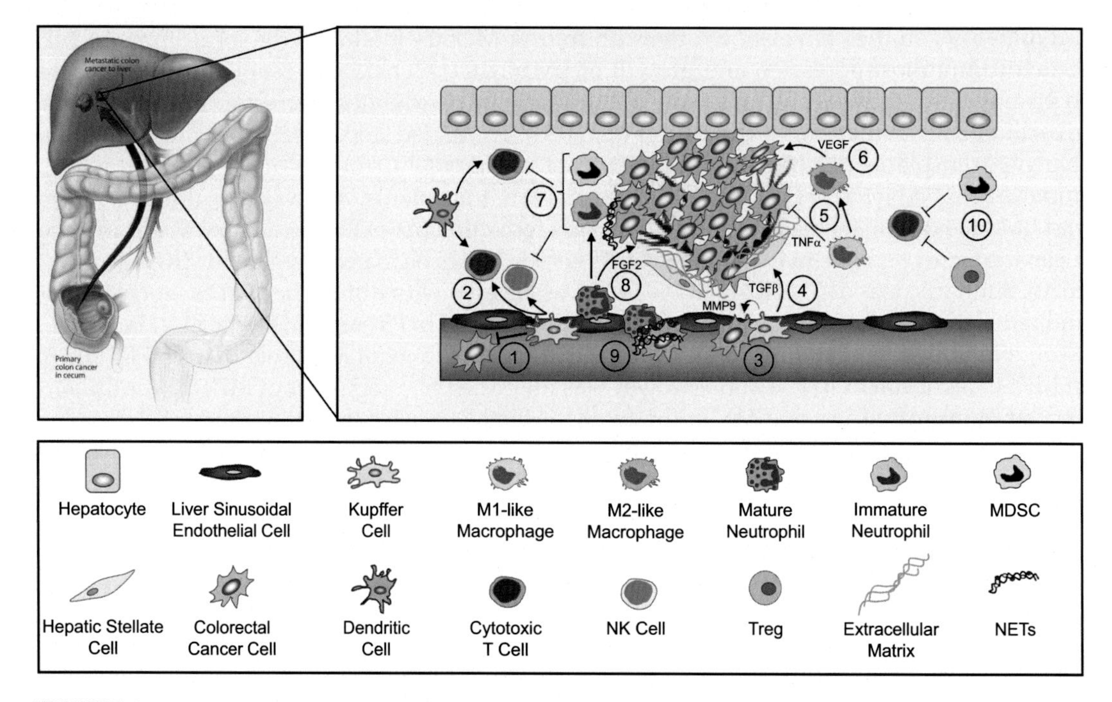

FIGURE 2.1 Complex interactions between cancer cells and host cells in the liver metastasis microenvironment can impair or promote the formation of CRC liver metastases. Liver resident KCs can 1) eliminate CRC cells as they seed the liver sinusoids or 2) enhance the infiltration of cytotoxic T cells or NK cells that can remove CRC cells. Conversely, KCs can 3) enhance CRC extravasation or 4) activate hepatic stellate cells to promote the seeding and successful establishment of CRC liver metastases. Infiltrating 5) M1-like macrophages can directly eliminate cancer cells within the liver or 6) polarization towards M2-like macrophages can induce an epithelial-to-mesenchymal transition in CRC cells that enhances the formation of hepatic metastases. 7) The recruitment of immature neutrophils or PMN-MDSCs into the liver microenvironment can suppress CTL or NK-mediated CRC cell killing. Neutrophils can also 8) promote neo-angiogenesis within CRC liver metastases via the release for angiogenic factors or 9) enhance the entrapment of CRC cells within the liver sinusoids to facilitate their extravasation. 10) The microenvironment that forms around CRC liver metastases is immunosuppressive due to the infiltration of MDSCs and Tregs that impair CTL-mediated CRC cell killing.

exhaustion via PD-1 engagement. In addition, HepSCs produce IL-6, IL-10 and TGFβ (Charles et al., 2013), can induce the expansion of $CD4^+$ $CD25^+$ $FoxP3^+$ regulatory T cells in an IL-2-dependent manner (Jiang et al., 2008) and promote transition of monocytes to MDSCs in a CD44-dependent manner (Hochst et al., 2013), thereby enhancing the immunosuppressive TME.

Multiple factors combine to inhibit a cytolytic T cell response to metastatic cancer cells

The presence of metastatic cancer cells in the liver can potentially activate specific T-cell mediated immune responses that may curtail metastatic expansion through different cytolytic mechanisms (for review see (Hadrup, Donia, and Thor Straten, 2013). However, as already summarized above, antigen presentation by local APC can result in immune tolerance and a diminished cytotoxic T cell response. Metastatic cells can also express the PD-1 ligands, PD-L1 and PD-L2 and thereby directly evade $CD4^{+}$ T helper cell and $CD8^{+}$ CTL-mediated kill. In addition, the recruitment of immunosuppressive lymphoid and myeloid cell subsets such as Tregs and MDSC, respectively, can augment the state of immune unresponsiveness in the liver. T cells recruited to the liver may also polarize into Tregs (inducible Treg, iTreg) due to the presence of TGFβ and IL-2 in the liver (Petronilho, Roesler, and Schwartsmann, 2007) and this coincides with the upregulation of the CTLA-4 co-inhibitory receptor. In this TGFβ-rich TME, neutrophils and monocytes can also acquire immunosuppressive (i.e. M2 and N2) phenotypes (reviewed in (Chanmee, Ontong, Konno, and Itano, 2014; Kim and Bae, 2016)). As indicated above, this state of T cell immune dysfunction clearly has systemic consequences and likely contributes to the poor response to immunotherapy in patients harboring hepatic metastases (See Fig. 2.2).

The extracellular matrix regulates cancer cell survival and growth in the liver

The unique extracellular matric (ECM) of the liver and liver metastases

The extracellular matrix (ECM), previously thought to provide a mere scaffold for maintaining tissue integrity, is presently recognized as a critical component of the TME. The ECM compartment regulates multiple cellular functions including cell adhesion, proliferation, differentiation and migration (Bonnans, Chou, and Werb, 2014). It also serves as a reservoir of molecular mediators such as cytokines, growth factors and nanovesicle-associated mediators (Huleihel et al., 2016; Hynes, 2009). The compositions of the normal liver ECM and LM-associated ECM have recently been reviewed in detail (Nystrom, 2021).

The ECM lining the LSEC and separating it from the Space of Disse is unique as it does not form a continuous typical basement membrane (BM) barrier (Martinez-Hernandez and Amenta, 1993). Rather, it consists of BM proteins including fibronectin, some collagen type I, and minor quantities of types III, IV, V, and VI collagen that provide cells with adhesion and BM-related functions, without forming a tightly sealed compartment. This enables passage of plasma molecules from the sinusoids through LSEC fenestrations into the space of Disse and the parenchyma. It has, in fact, been shown that the numbers and morphology of LSEC fenestrations are regulated by the ECM (McGuire, Bissell, Boyles, and Roll, 1992).

A recent study showed that ECM composition and content differ between primary CRC and CRLMs and suggested that peptidylarginine deiminase (PAD)4-dependent citrullination of ECM proteins, such as type I collagen may be involved in the progression of CRLM (Yuzhalin et al., 2018). Another study identified an ECM-specific mRNA signature in CRLM tissue of patients that underwent surgery prior to chemotherapy. Up to 50% of the genes identified were involved in ECM remodeling, including mediators of cell adhesion, ECM organization and angiogenesis (Del Rio et al., 2013). A recent study using whole exome RNA sequencing of CRLM tissue revealed that transcripts encoding molecules involved in ECM-receptor interactions and focal adhesion formation were uniquely up-regulated within the CRLMs, but not in the matched primary tumors (Oga et al., 2019). Ishaque et al., using

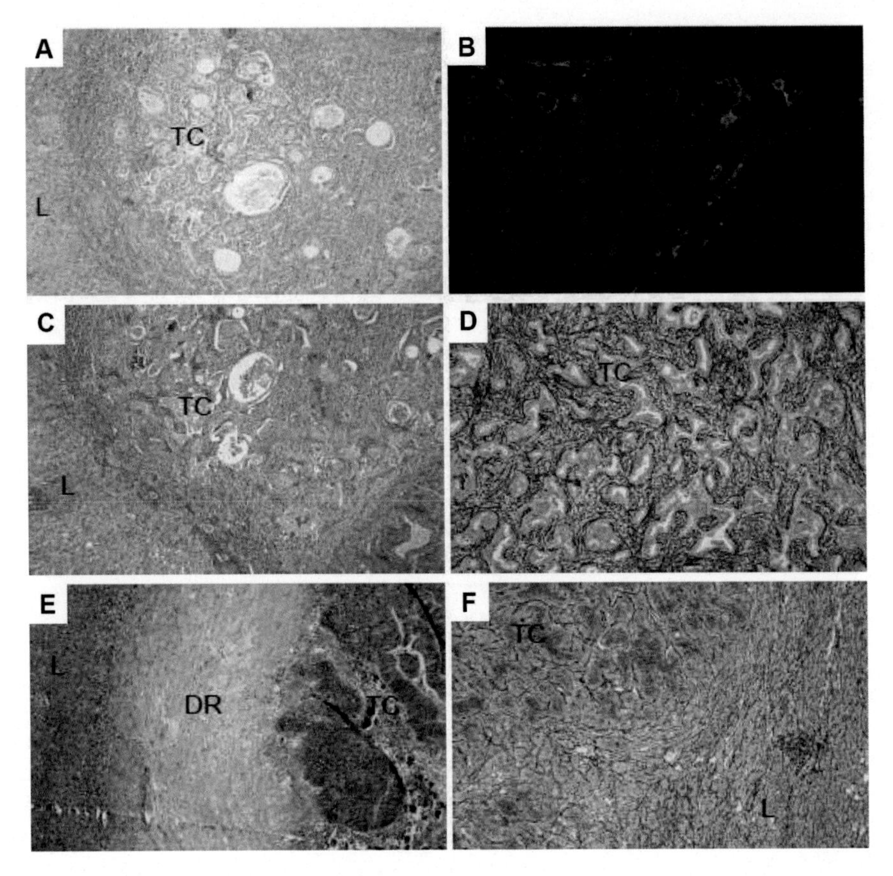

FIGURE 2.2 The ECM of colorectal cancer liver metastases. Shown in (A) are IHC images of CRCLM. Type I collagen is shown in brown, cells are counterstained in blue. Type I collagen is expressed strongly in the stroma of the tumor (mag. X10). Shown in (B) are immunofluorescence images of CRCLM. Type IV collagen in shown red, CD31 in green and nuclei in blue. Intense production of type IV collagen is evident within the ECM of the CRCLM (mag x20). Shown in (C and D) are chemical stain images. Surgical specimens were stained with Picrosirius Red (C) showing type I and III collagen fibers in red or with a Reticulin Stain (D) showing reticular fibers in Black. Cell nuclei (C) are in blue and CRC cells (D) are in pink (mag. X10) Shown in (E) are H&E stained Desmoplastic type CRCLM, showing how a desmoplastic reaction (DR) separates tumor cells from normal liver. Shown in (F) are reticulin stained Replacement type CRCLM showing how tumor cells invade the existing liver architecture without desmoplasia (mag x10). TC- Tumor cells, L- Liver.

whole genome sequencing, found that canonical pathways enriched in CRLM were related to actin cytoskeleton polymerization and hepatic fibrosis/stellate cell activation, indicating that metastatic cells evoke a host response conducive to liver-specific metastatic colonization (Ishaque et al., 2018).

Type IV collagen (COL IV), the major BM protein was shown to be up-regulated in CRLM (Burnier et al., 2011; Gulubova, 2004; Nystrom et al., 2012) and in CRC that metastasize to the liver (Nystrom et al., 2012). The collagen trimer 112 is found in both normal liver and in CRLMs (Nystrom, Naredi, Hafstrom, and Sund, 2011) and circulating COL IV was identified as a potential biomarker for CRLM (Nystrom et al., 2011; Nyström, Tavelin, Björklund, Naredi, and Sund, 2015; Rolff et al., 2016) (For images, see Table 2.2). In a recent study, using human colon carcinoma cell lines KM12SM and KM12C that have high and low liver metastasizing potential, respectively, it was shown that the chemokines CCL-5 and CCL-7 were regulated by COL IV via integrin signaling and that this was associated with increased liver-metastatic potential (Vaniotis et al., 2018). In the same study, high expression of CCL-5, CCL-7 that correlated with COL IV levels, was documented in resected human CRLMs (Vaniotis et al., 2018). Type I and III collagens were also shown to be highly expressed in CRLMs (Nystrom et al., 2012). The glycoprotein Tenascin was found to be highly expressed in CRLM, and increased tenascin levels in the primary tumor correlated with LM incidence, postoperative survival and LM-free survival (Murakami et al., 2017). The expression of Laminin 511, a component of the BM, was associated with reduced survival in several independent CRC cohorts. Furthermore, angiogenesis signatures and vessel density significantly correlated with Laminin-511 expression levels (Gordon-Weeks et al., 2019). In a CRC animal model, Laminin 511 was shown to promote branching angiogenesis and modulate Notch signaling and was required for growth of LMs (Gordon-Weeks et al., 2019).

Importantly, in a recent study using decellularized human matrix scaffolds, D´Angelo and colleagues found that the ECM matrix alone can regulate the cancer cell phenotype. In this study, human CRC HT-29 cells were grown in 3D matrices consisting of decellularized scaffolds derived from normal colon, normal liver, CRC and CRLM. The HT-29 cells had enhanced proliferation and migration when grown in 3D ECM derived from tumor samples. HT-29 cells cultured in CRLM matrix also expressed EMT markers, highlighting the importance of the tumor-ECM interaction to tumor cell behavior (D'Angelo et al., 2020).

The ECM and cell adhesion molecules

Integrins represent the major ECM adhesion receptors. Upon binding to ECM proteins, integrins activate signaling pathways that control cell shape, maintain cell polarity, protect cells from anoikis (cell detachment induced apoptosis) and regulate cell migration and invasion.

A study using the colon cancer cell line HCT-116 showed that hepatocytes and the ECM modulated $\alpha5\beta1$ integrin activity in HCT-116 cells, leading to FAK phosphorylation in response to cell adhesion to fibronectin. Furthermore, integrin $\alpha5\beta1$ modulated the expression/activity of integrin $\alpha2\beta1$, the major collagen receptor (Pelillo, Bergamo, Mollica, Bestagno, and Sava, 2015). Integrins have been investigated as possible targets for treatment of cancer and metastatic disease. However, despite initial promising results in animal models, no benefit was seen in clinical trials (extensively reviewed in (Alday-Parejo, Stupp, and Ruegg, 2019). An important factor is likely the complexity of integrin function and biology. There is presently a paucity of clinical data on the role of specific integrins in CRLM, and their role in the human disease remains to be fully understood.

The effect of ECM stiffness

Tissue stiffness is determined by a combination of factors including the cell cytoskeleton and the ECM. Fibrillar collagens are the most abundant ECM proteins. ECM remodeling involving type I collagen (COL I) has been identified as a major factor in tissue stiffening during cancer progression (Pickup, Mouw, and Weaver, 2014).

Cancer-associated fibroblasts (CAFs) are likely a major source of tumor-associated ECM proteins and can further modify the TME by expression of lysyl oxidase (LOX), which mediates collagen crosslinking. LOX-induced collagen crosslinking has been described as one potential mechanism for increased ECM stiffness in CRC and CRLMs. Increased matrix stiffness was shown to activate FAK/Src-signaling, resulting in increased FAK/Src phosphorylation and the induction of highly proliferative and invasive phenotypes (Baker, Bird, Lang, Cox, and Erler, 2013). CAFs can also increase contractility by expressing α-SMA, causing further shrinkage and stiffening of the ECM (Follonier Castella, Gabbiani, McCulloch, and Hinz, 2010).

Tissue stiffness was found to be higher in CRLMs when compared to primary CRC tumors. In patients with CRLM receiving anti-VEGF therapy in combination with Renin-Angiotensin System inhibitors prior to liver resection, CRLM tissue had reduced stiffness and the treatment was associated with longer survival (Shen et al., 2020). It has been shown that metastases-associated fibroblasts (MAFs) are the main modulators of ECM stiffness in CRLM and they express high levels of all Renin-Angiotensin System components. The Renin-Angiotensin Systeminhibitors affected matrix remodeling by reducing LOX expression, collagen production and Rho GTPase-mediated cell contractility in the MAFs (Shen et al., 2020). This identifies tumor stiffness, the altered ECM compartment, as well as the stromal cell compartment of CRLM as potential targets for therapy in mCRC (see more below). The origin of MAFs within CRLM and whether they are derived from activated HepSC, portal fibroblasts or both remains to be resolved.

Potential strategies for targeting the microenvironment of CRLM and increasing immunotherapy efficacy in patients with liver metastatic disease

As described in the previous sections, infiltrating innate immune cells including macrophages, neutrophils and MDSCs can collectively have diverse effects on the establishment and growth of liver metastases (Table 2.1 and Table 2.2). Principle among these is direct immunosuppression of the adaptive arm of the immune system, most notably T cell suppression or elimination. It has recently been shown that the immune microenvironments of primary CRC tumors and LM can be highly heterogeneous with respect to immune cell infiltration, both in immune cell composition and in their distribution within the lesions (Van den Eynde et al., 2018). Importantly, the immune phenotype of the least-infiltrated metastases had a stronger association with patient outcome than other metastases and was associated with poor overall and disease-free survival (Van den Eynde et al., 2018).

The major challenge associated with the effective introduction of immunotherapy in patients with CRC that has spread to the liver is abolishing or reprogramming this immunosuppressive microenvironment. One possible approach focuses on the central role that signaling via STAT3 plays in promoting immunosuppression in both cancer cells and myeloid cells (Zou et al., 2020). Recently, it was shown that STAT3 inhibitors could impair the formation of CRLM and reduce the accumulation of MDSCs in the liver ME due to enhanced MDSC apoptosis (Guha et al., 2019). MDSCs isolated from LM of mice treated with STAT3 inhibitors exhibited impaired ability to suppress T cell proliferation/activation when compared to vehicle treated controls. Interestingly, STAT3 inhibitors were shown to increase the anti-tumor efficacy of CAR-T immunotherapy in this model (Guha et al., 2019). TGFb is a known inducer of an immunosuppressive ME and another potential target in mCRC. Using a transgenic mouse model of mCRC, TGFb blockade was shown to increase the anti-tumor efficacy of immunotherapies targeting PD-1/PD-L1 (Tauriello et al., 2018). In female patients, the potential of anti-estrogen therapy to decrease MDSC recruitment and increase IT therapy warrants further investigation (Milette et al., 2019). Finally, as recently shown in an orthotopic CRC model, combinatorial immunotherapy targeting multiple immune checkpoints, such as CTLA-4 and PD-L1, may increase the efficacy of this therapy in the treatment of LM (Fiegle et al., 2019).

Of note, an added layer of complexity in targeting the immune ME of CRLM is the diversity in histopathological growth patterns (HGP) of LM. Desmoplastic (DHGP) metastases are characterized by a desmoplastic rim that separates the CRLMs from the liver parenchyma while replacement (RHGP) liver metastases arise through the replacement of hepatocytes by cancer cells as the lesions expand (van Dam et al., 2017) (See images in Table 2.2). Moreover, the immune microenvironments associated with DHGP and RHGP CRLM have distinct features. Thus, DHGP CRLM are characterized by a higher infiltration of $CD8^{+}$ cytotoxic T cells when compared to RHGP lesions (Hoppener et al., 2020; Liang et al., 2020), and this was shown to correlate with the better clinical outcomes associated with untreated patients presenting with DHGP CRLM (Galjart et al., 2019; Nielsen, Rolff, and Eefsen, 2014; Van den Eynden et al., 2013, 2014, 2012). In addition, neutrophils expressing lysyl oxidase like-4 (LOXL4) were found to be enriched in CRLM that displayed the replacement type growth pattern (Palmieri et al., 2020), suggesting that distinct neutrophil subpopulations may be implicated in the formation of angiogenic or vessel-co-opting CRLM.

Clearly, the HGP of LM can have a profound effect on how patients respond to specific therapeutic strategies and this could potentially represent a basis for patient stratification, especially in this era of immunotherapy and immune modulating therapies (van Dam et al., 2018). It is also likely that unique therapeutic targets will be present in DHGP or RHGP-type CRLMs. Indeed, it was recently shown that claudin-8 expression was increased in DHGP lesions; whereas, claudin-2 is preferentially expressed in RHGP CRLMs (Tabaries et al., 2021). In order for the HGP to be useful for patient stratification, a reliable method for their classification prior to treatment will be required and this technology is not yet available for clinical management of CRLM.

As discussed above, the evidence also suggests that ECM stiffness may be potentially useful as a target in CRLM treatment. The addition of anti-VEGF therapy in patients with CRLM only improves survival by months, likely due to acquired resistance. An analysis performed in 2016 showed that patients treated with the addition of anti-VEGF therapy had increased hyaluronic acid (HA) deposition within the tumors and this was also seen in syngeneic mouse models (Rahbari et al., 2016). The changes in the ECM resulted in increased tumor stiffness, likely resulting from treatment-induced tumor hypoxia. In animal models, this acquired resistance to anti-VEGF therapy could be reversed by enzymatic depletion of HA, suggesting that targeting ECM components may improve the effect of systemic oncological treatment such as anti-VEGF therapy (Rahbari et al., 2016). Similar results were obtained by Schiffman et al., who showed that in human CRLM tissue, COL IV and ECM deposition were increased following anti-VEGF therapy (Schiffmann et al., 2017). Studies in animal models by the same group showed that a combination of low-dose anti-VEGF therapy and a tyrosine kinase inhibitor had similar growth inhibition effects on the metastases but did not alter ECM deposition. The treatment combination resulted in better-preserved vascular normalization and improved oxygenation, thus enabling perfusion and better drug access for therapy (Schiffmann et al., 2017). Collectively, these studies suggest that combining standard of care therapy with drugs that target ECM production or stiffness may improve treatment outcomes.

Conclusion

CRC remains one of the most common cancers globally. Despite significant progress in the management of CRC, mortality for patients who develop CRLM remains high. Surgery in combination with standard-of-care drug therapy still represents the best treatment option for these patients. For patients who are not candidates for liver surgery, drug treatment can slow disease progression and prolong survival, but is ultimately non-curative. Targeted therapy directed towards the microenvironment of CRLM may improve patient outcomes, but will require a thorough understanding of the complex and multifactorial microenvironment of CRLM. The liver is naturally programmed toward muted immune responses and this state of unresponsiveness is further enhanced by myeloid and lymphoid cells that acquire immunosuppressive and pro-metastatic properties in the TME. This decreased activity of immune cells enables metastatic expansion, while alsocausing systemic consequences and reduced patient responses to IT. To counter this permissive immune microenvironment, a multi-pronged approach that combines standard-of-care therapy and/or immunotherapy with targeted strategies for reprograming the pro-metastatic ME of CRLM will be critical. As our understanding of the factors underlying the recruitment, accumulation and survival of immunosuppressive cells within the TME of the liver improves, optimization of such strategies could become a clinical reality.

Acknowledgements

The authors gratefully acknowledge grants from the following funding agencies in support of their work on cellular and molecular aspects of liver metastasis: The Canadian Institute of Health Research (to PMS and PB), the Terry Fox Research Institute (to PMS), the Québec Ministère de l'Économie, de l'Innovation et des Exportations (to PB), the Swedish Cancer Society, Knut and Alice Wallenberg Foundation, Västerbotten County Council and the Swedish Research Council (To HN).

References

Abo, T., Kawamura, T., & Watanabe, H. (2000). Physiological responses of extrathymic T cells in the liver. *Immunological Reviews, 174*, 135–149.

Alday-Parejo, B., Stupp, R., & Ruegg, C. (2019). Are Integrins Still Practicable Targets for Anti-Cancer Therapy? *Cancers (Basel), 11*(7), 978–1007.

Baker, A. M., Bird, D., Lang, G., Cox, T. R., & Erler, J. T. (2013). Lysyl oxidase enzymatic function increases stiffness to drive colorectal cancer progression through FAK. *Oncogene, 32*(14), 1863–1868.

Bamboat, Z. M., Stableford, J. A., Plitas, G., Burt, B. M., Nguyen, H. M., Welles, A. P., …, & DeMatteo, R. P. (2009). Human liver dendritic cells promote T cell hyporesponsiveness. *Journal of Immunology, 182*(4), 1901–1911.

Benedicto, A., Herrero, A., Romayor, I., Marquez, J., Smedsrod, B., Olaso, E., & Arteta, B. (2019). Liver sinusoidal endothelial cell ICAM-1 mediated tumor/endothelial crosstalk drives the development of liver metastasis by initiating inflammatory and angiogenic responses. *Scientific Reports, 9*(1), 13111–13122.

Benlagha, K., Kyin, T., Beavis, A., Teyton, L., & Bendelac, A. (2002). A thymic precursor to the NK T cell lineage. *Science, 296*(5567), 553–555.

Bonnans, C., Chou, J., & Werb, Z. (2014). Remodelling the extracellular matrix in development and disease. *Nature Reviews Molecular Cell Biology, 15*(12), 786–801.

Brodt, P. (2016). Role of the Microenvironment in Liver Metastasis: from Pre- to Prometastatic Niches. *Clinical Cancer Research, 22*(24), 5971–5982.

Burnier, J. V., Wang, N., Michel, R. P., Hassanain, M., Li, S., Lu, Y., …, & Brodt, P. (2011). Type IV collagen-initiated signals provide survival and growth cues required for liver metastasis. *Oncogene, 30*(35), 3766–3783.

Castella, L. F., Gabbiani, G., McCulloch, C. A., & Hinz, B. (2010). Regulation of myofibroblast activities: calcium pulls some strings behind the scene. *Experimental Cell Research, 316*(15), 2390–2401.

Chanmee, T., Ontong, P., Konno, K., & Itano, N. (2014). Tumor-associated macrophages as major players in the tumor microenvironment. *Cancers (Basel), 6*(3), 1670–1690.

Charles, R., Chou, H. S., Wang, L., Fung, J. J., Lu, L., & Qian, S. (2013). Human hepatic stellate cells inhibit T-cell response through B7-H1 pathway. *Transplantation, 96*(1), 17–24.

Chen, L., Calomeni, E., Wen, J., Ozato, K., Shen, R., & Gao, J. X. (2007). Natural killer dendritic cells are an intermediate of developing dendritic cells. *Journal of leukocyte biology, 81*(6), 1422–1433.

Coffelt, S. B., Wellenstein, M. D., & de Visser, K. E. (2016). Neutrophils in cancer: neutral no more. *Nature Reviews Cancer, 16*(7), 431–446.

Copple, B. L., Bai, S., Burgoon, L. D., & Moon, J-O. K. (2011). Hypoxia-inducible Factor-1α Regulates Expression of Genes in Hypoxic Hepatic Stellate Cells Important for Collagen Deposition and Angiogenesis. *Liver international: Official journal of the International Association for the Study of the Liver, 31*(2), 230–244.

Crispe, I. N. (2009). The liver as a lymphoid organ. *Annual Review of Immunology, 27*, 147–163.

Crispe, I. N. (2011). Liver antigen-presenting cells. *Journal of Hepatology, 54*(2), 357–365.

D'Angelo, E., Natarajan, D., Sensi, F., Ajayi, O., Fassan, M., Mammano, E., …, & Agostini, M. (2020). Patient-Derived Scaffolds of Colorectal Cancer Metastases as an Organotypic 3D Model of the Liver Metastatic Microenvironment. *Cancers (Basel)*, 12(2), 1–20, 364.

Dashtsoodol, N., Shigeura, T., Aihara, M., Ozawa, R., Kojo, S., Harada, M., …, & Taniguchi, M. (2017). Alternative pathway for the development of Valpha14(+) NKT cells directly from CD4(-)CD8(-) thymocytes that bypasses the CD4(+)CD8(+) stage. *Nature Immunology, 18*(3), 274–282.

David, B. A., Rezende, R. M., Antunes, M. M., Santos, M. M., Freitas Lopes, M. A., Diniz, A. B., …, & Menezes, G. B. (2016). Combination of Mass Cytometry and Imaging Analysis Reveals Origin, Location, and Functional Repopulation of Liver Myeloid Cells in Mice. *Gastroenterology, 151*(6), 1176–1191.

Del Rio, M., Mollevi, C., Vezzio-Vie, N., Bibeau, F., Ychou, M., & Martineau, P. (2013). Specific extracellular matrix remodeling signature of colon hepatic metastases. *Plos One, 8*(9), 1–13, e74599.

Doherty, D. G. (2016). Immunity, tolerance and autoimmunity in the liver: a comprehensive review. *Journal of Autoimmunity, 66*, 60–75.

Doherty, D. G., & O'Farrelly, C (2000). Innate and adaptive lymphoid cells in the human liver. *Immunological Reviews, 174*, 5–20.

Donadon, M., Torzilli, G., Cortese, N., Soldani, C., Di Tommaso, L., Franceschini, B., …, & Marchesi, F. (2020). Macrophage morphology correlates with single-cell diversity and prognosis in colorectal liver metastasis. *Journal of Experimental Medicine, 217*(11), 1–15, e20191847.

Dou, A., & Fang, J. (2021). Heterogeneous Myeloid Cells in Tumors. *Cancers (Basel), 13*(15), 1–25, 3772.

Dou, L., Ono, Y., Chen, Y. F., Thomson, A. W., & Chen, X. P. (2018). Hepatic Dendritic Cells, the Tolerogenic Liver Environment, and Liver Disease. *Seminars in Liver Disease, 38*(2), 170–180.

Erstad, D. J., Taylor, M. S., Qadan, M., Axtell, A. L., Fuchs, B. C., Berger, D. L., …, & Ferrone, C. R. (2020). Platelet and neutrophil to lymphocyte ratios predict survival in patients with resectable colorectal liver metastases. *American Journal of Surgery, 220*(6), 1579–1585.

Fiegle, E., Doleschel, D., Koletnik, S., Rix, A., Weiskirchen, R., Borkham-Kamphorst, E., …, & Lederle, W. (2019). Dual CTLA-4 and PD-L1 Blockade Inhibits Tumor Growth and Liver Metastasis in a Highly Aggressive Orthotopic Mouse Model of Colon Cancer. *Neoplasia, 21*(9), 932–944.

Freire Valls, A., Knipper, K., Giannakouri, E., Sarachaga, V., Hinterkopf, S., Wuehrl, M., …, & Schmidt, T. (2019). VEGFR1(+) Metastasis-Associated Macrophages Contribute to Metastatic Angiogenesis and Influence Colorectal Cancer Patient Outcome. *Clinical Cancer Research, 25*(18), 5674–5685.

Friedman, S. L. (2008a). Mechanisms of hepatic fibrogenesis. *Gastroenterology, 134*(6), 1655–1669.

Friedman, S. L. (2008b). Hepatic stellate cells: protean, multifunctional, and enigmatic cells of the liver. *Physiological Reviews, 88*(1), 125–172.

Galjart, B., Nierop, P. M. H., van der Stok, E. P., van den Braak, R., Höppener, D. J., Daelemans, S., …, & Grünhagen, D. J. (2019). Angiogenic desmoplastic histopathological growth pattern as a prognostic marker of good outcome in patients with colorectal liver metastases. *Angiogenesis, 22*(2), 355–368.

Geissmann, F., Cameron, T. O., Sidobre, S., Manlongat, N., Kronenberg, M., Briskin, M. J., …, & Littman, D. R. (2005). Intravascular immune surveillance by CXCR6+ NKT cells patrolling liver sinusoids. *Plos Biology, 3*(4), 650–661, e113.

Germann, M., Zangger, N., Sauvain, M. O., Sempoux, C., Bowler, A. D., Wirapati, P., …, & Radtke, F. (2020). Neutrophils suppress tumor-infiltrating T cells in colon cancer via matrix metalloproteinase-mediated activation of TGFbeta. *EMBO Molecular Medicine, 12*(1), 1–16, e10681.

Giakoustidis, A., Neofytou, K., Khan, A. Z., & Mudan, S. (2015). Neutrophil to lymphocyte ratio predicts pattern of recurrence in patients undergoing liver resection for colorectal liver metastasis and thus the overall survival. *Journal of Surgical Oncology, 111*(4), 445–450.

Goddard, S., Youster, J., Morgan, E., & Adams, D. H. (2004). Interleukin-10 Secretion Differentiates Dendritic Cells from Human Liver and Skin. *The American Journal of Pathology, 164*(2), 511–519.

Gordon-Weeks, A., Lim, S. Y., Yuzhalin, A., Lucotti, S., Vermeer, J. A. F., Jones, K., …, & Muschel, R. J. (2019). Tumour-Derived Laminin alpha5 (LAMA5) Promotes Colorectal Liver Metastasis Growth, Branching Angiogenesis and Notch Pathway Inhibition. *Cancers (Basel), 11*(5), 630–648.

Gordon-Weeks, A. N., Lim, S. Y., Yuzhalin, A. E., Jones, K., Markelc, B., Kim, K. J., …, & Muschel, R. (2017). Neutrophils promote hepatic metastasis growth through fibroblast growth factor 2-dependent angiogenesis in mice. *Hepatology, 65*(6), 1920–1935.

Guc, E., & Pollard, J. W. (2021). Redefining macrophage and neutrophil biology in the metastatic cascade. *Immunity, 54*(5), 885–902.

Guha, P., Gardell, J., Darpolor, J., Cunetta, M., Lima, M., Miller, G., …, & Katz, S. C. (2019). STAT3 inhibition induces Bax-dependent apoptosis in liver tumor myeloid-derived suppressor cells. *Oncogene, 38*(4), 533–548.

Gulubova, M. V. (2004). Collagen type IV, laminin, alpha-smooth muscle actin (alphaSMA), alpha1 and alpha6 integrins expression in the liver with metastases from malignant gastrointestinal tumours. *Clinical & Experimental Metastasis, 21*(6), 485–494.

Gumperz, J. E., Miyake, S., Yamamura, T., & Brenner, M. B. (2002). Functionally distinct subsets of CD1d-restricted natural killer T cells revealed by CD1d tetramer staining. *Journal of Experimental Medicine, 195*(5), 625–636.

Hadrup, S., Donia, M., & Thor Straten, P. (2013). Effector CD4 and CD8 T cells and their role in the tumor microenvironment. *Cancer Microenvironment: official journal of the International Cancer Microenvironment Society, 6*(2), 123–133.

Ham, B., Wang, N., D'Costa, Z., Fernandez, M. C., Bourdeau, F., Auguste, P., …, & Brodt (2015). TNF Receptor-2 Facilitates an Immunosuppressive Microenvironment in the Liver to Promote the Colonization and Growth of Hepatic Metastases. *Cancer Research, 75*(24), 5235–5247.

Helling, T. S., & Martin, M. (2014). Cause of death from liver metastases in colorectal cancer. *Annals of Surgical Oncology, 21*(2), 501–506.

Heymann, F., & Tacke, F. (2016). Immunology in the liver–from homeostasis to disease. *Nature reviews Gastroenterology & hepatology, 13*(2), 88–110.

Höchst, B., Schildberg, F. A., Sauerborn, P., Gäbel, Y. A., Gevensleben, H., Goltz, D., …, & Diehl, L. (2013). Activated human hepatic stellate cells induce myeloid derived suppressor cells from peripheral blood monocytes in a CD44-dependent fashion. *Journal of Hepatology, 59*(3), 528–535.

Höppener, D. J., Nierop, P. M. H., Hof, J., Sideras, K., Zhou, G., Visser, L., …, & Verhoef, C. (2020). Enrichment of the tumour immune microenvironment in patients with desmoplastic colorectal liver metastasis. *British Journal of Cancer, 123*(2), 196–206.

Hsu, B. E., Shen, Y., & Siegel, P. M. (2020). Neutrophils: orchestrators of the Malignant Phenotype. *Frontiers in immunology, 11*, 1–10, 1778.

Hu, Z., Li, M., Chen, Z., Zhan, C., Lin, Z., & Wang, Q. (2019). Advances in clinical trials of targeted therapy and immunotherapy of lung cancer in 2018. *Translational lung cancer research, 8*(6), 1091–1106.

Huleihel, L., Hussey, G. S., Naranjo, J. D., Zhang, L., Dziki, J. L., Turner, N. J., ..., & Badylak, S. F. (2016). Matrix-bound nanovesicles within ECM bioscaffolds. *Science Advances, 2*(6), 1–11, e1600502.

Hynes, R. O. (2009). The extracellular matrix: not just pretty fibrils. *Science, 326*(5957), 1216–1219.

Ibrahim, J., Nguyen, A. H., Rehman, A., Ochi, A., Jamal, M., Graffeo, C. S., ..., & Miller, G. (2012). Dendritic Cell Populations With Different Concentrations of Lipid Regulate Tolerance and Immunity in Mouse and Human Liver. *Gastroenterology, 143*(4), 1061–1072.

Ishaque, N., Abba, M. L., Hauser, C., Patil, N., Paramasivam, N., Huebschmann, D., ..., & Allgayer, H. (2018). Whole genome sequencing puts forward hypotheses on metastasis evolution and therapy in colorectal cancer. *Nature communications, 9*(1), 1–14, 4782.

Itatani, Y., Yamamoto, T., Zhong, C., Molinolo, A. A., Ruppel, J., Hegde, P., ..., & Ferrara, N. (2020). Suppressing neutrophil-dependent angiogenesis abrogates resistance to anti-VEGF antibody in a genetic model of colorectal cancer. *Proc Natl Acad Sci U S A.,, 117*(35), 21598–21608.

Jiang, G., Yang, H.-R., Wang, L., Wildey, G. M., Fung, J., Qian, S., & Lu, L. (2008). Hepatic stellate cells preferentially expand allogeneic CD4+ CD25+ FoxP3+ regulatory T cells in an IL-2-dependent manner. *Transplantation, 86*(11), 1492–1502.

Jiang, K., Chen, H., Fang, Y., Chen, L., Zhong, C., Bu, T., ..., & Ding, K. (2021). Exosomal ANGPTL1 attenuates colorectal cancer liver metastasis by regulating Kupffer cell secretion pattern and impeding MMP9 induced vascular leakiness. *Journal of Experimental & Clinical Cancer Research, 40*(1), 1–13, 21.

Kang, N., Shah, V. H., & Urrutia, R. (2015). Membrane-to-Nucleus Signals and Epigenetic Mechanisms for Myofibroblastic Activation and Desmoplastic Stroma: potential Therapeutic Targets for Liver Metastasis? *Molecular Cancer Research, 13*(4), 604–612.

Kee, J. Y., Ito, A., Hojo, S., Hashimoto, I., Igarashi, Y., Tsuneyama, K., ..., & Koizumi, K. (2014). CXCL16 suppresses liver metastasis of colorectal cancer by promoting TNF-alpha-induced apoptosis by tumor-associated macrophages. *Bmc Cancer [Electronic Resource], 14*(949), 1–11.

Keirsse, J., Van Damme, H., Geeraerts, X., Beschin, A., Raes, G., & Van Ginderachter, J. A. (2018). The role of hepatic macrophages in liver metastasis. *Cellular Immunology, 330*, 202–215.

Khan, U., Chowdhury, S., Billah, M. M., Islam, K. M. D., Thorlacius, H., & Rahman, M. (2021). Neutrophil Extracellular Traps in Colorectal Cancer Progression and Metastasis. *International Journal of Molecular Sciences, 22*(14), 1–18.

Khatib, A. M., Auguste, P., Fallavollita, L., Wang, N., Samani, A., Kontogiannea, M., ..., & Brodt, P. (2005). Characterization of the host proinflammatory response to tumor cells during the initial stages of liver metastasis. *American Journal of Pathology, 167*(3), 749–759.

Khatib, A. M., Kontogiannea, M., Fallavollita, L., Jamison, B., Meterissian, S., & Brodt, P. (1999). Rapid induction of cytokine and E-selectin expression in the liver in response to metastatic tumor cells. *Cancer Research, 59*(6), 1356–1361.

Kim, J., & Bae, J. S. (2016). Tumor-Associated Macrophages and Neutrophils in Tumor Microenvironment. *Mediators of Inflammation, 2016*, 1–11, 6058147.

Kimura, Y., Inoue, A., Hangai, S., Saijo, S., Negishi, H., Nishio, J., ..., & Taniguchi, T. (2016). The innate immune receptor Dectin-2 mediates the phagocytosis of cancer cells by Kupffer cells for the suppression of liver metastasis. *Proc Natl Acad Sci U S A.,, 113*(49), 14097–14102.

Kiyasu, Y., Kawada, K., Hirai, H., Ogawa, R., Hanada, K., Masui, H., ..., & Sakai, Y. (2020). Disruption of CCR1-mediated myeloid cell accumulation suppresses colorectal cancer progression in mice. *Cancer Letters, 487*, 53–62.

Klugewitz, K., Blumenthal-Barby, F., Schrage, A., Knolle, P. A., Hamann, A., & Crispe, I. N. (2002). Immunomodulatory effects of the liver: deletion of activated CD4+ effector cells and suppression of IFN-gamma-producing cells after intravenous protein immunization. *Journal of Immunology, 169*(5), 2407–2413.

Kubes, P., & Jenne, C. (2018). Immune Responses in the Liver. *Annual Review of Immunology, 36*, 247–277.

Lautt, W. W., Granger, D. N., & Granger, J. (2010). Resistance in the Venous System. *Hepatic Circulation: Physiology and Pathophysiology* (pp. 53–61). San Rafael, CA: Morgan & Claypool Life Sciences.

Le, D. T., Uram, J. N., Wang, H., Bartlett, B. R., Kemberling, H., Eyring, A. D., ..., & Diaz, L. A., Jr. (2015). PD-1 Blockade in Tumors with Mismatch-Repair Deficiency. *New England Journal of Medicine, 372*(26), 2509–2520.

Li, M., Lai, X., Zhao, Y., Zhang, Y., Li, M., Li, D., ..., & Zhang, J. (2018). Loss of NDRG2 in liver microenvironment inhibits cancer liver metastasis by regulating tumor associate macrophages polarization. *Cell death & disease, 9*(2), 1–14, 248.

Liang, J. Y., Xi, S. Y., Shao, Q., Yuan, Y. F., Li, B. K., Zheng, Y., …, & Li, Y. H. (2020). Histopathological growth patterns correlate with the immunoscore in colorectal cancer liver metastasis patients after hepatectomy. *Cancer Immunology, Immunotherapy, 69*(12), 2623–2634.

Lim, S. Y., Gordon-Weeks, A., Allen, D., Kersemans, V., Beech, J., Smart, S., & Muschel, R. (2015). Cd11b(+) myeloid cells support hepatic metastasis through down-regulation of angiopoietin-like 7 in cancer cells. *Hepatology, 62*(2), 521–533.

Male, V. (2017). Liver-Resident NK Cells: the Human Factor. *Trends in Immunology, 38*(5), 307–309.

Mao, R., Zhao, J. J., Bi, X. Y., Zhang, Y. F., Li, Z. Y., Huang, Z., …, & Cai, J. Q. (2019). A Low Neutrophil to Lymphocyte Ratio Before Preoperative Chemotherapy Predicts Good Outcomes After the Resection of Colorectal Liver Metastases. *Journal of Gastrointestinal Surgery, 23*(3), 563–570.

Martinez-Hernandez, A., & Amenta, P. S. (1993). The hepatic extracellular matrix. I. Components and distribution in normal liver. *Virchows Archiv. A, Pathological Anatomy and Histopathology, 423*(1), 1–11.

Matsumura, H., Kondo, T., Ogawa, K., Tamura, T., Fukunaga, K., Murata, S., & Ohkohchi, N. (2014). Kupffer cells decrease metastasis of colon cancer cells to the liver in the early stage. *International Journal of Oncology, 45*(6), 2303–2310.

McCluney, S. J., Giakoustidis, A., Segler, A., Bissel, J., Valente, R., Hutchins, R. R., …, & Kocher, H. M. (2018). Neutrophil: lymphocyte ratio as a method of predicting complications following hepatic resection for colorectal liver metastasis. *Journal of Surgical Oncology, 117*(5), 1058–1065.

McGuire, R. F., Bissell, D. M., Boyles, J., & Roll, F. J. (1992). Role of extracellular matrix in regulating fenestrations of sinusoidal endothelial cells isolated from normal rat liver. *Hepatology, 15*(6), 989–997.

Milette, S., Hashimoto, M., Perrino, S., Qi, S., Chen, M., Ham, B., …, & Brodt, P. (2019). Sexual dimorphism and the role of estrogen in the immune microenvironment of liver metastases. *Nature communications, 10*(1), 1–16, 5745.

Milette, S., Sicklick, J. K., Lowy, A. M., & Brodt, P. (2017). Molecular Pathways: targeting the Microenvironment of Liver Metastases. *Clinical Cancer Research, 23*(21), 6390–6399.

Murakami, T., Kikuchi, H., Ishimatsu, H., Iino, I., Hirotsu, A., Matsumoto, T., …, & Konno, H. (2017). Tenascin C in colorectal cancer stroma is a predictive marker for liver metastasis and is a potent target of miR-198 as identified by microRNA analysis. *British Journal of Cancer, 117*(9), 1360–1370.

Nielsen, K., Rolff, H. C., & Eefsen, R. L. (2014). Vainer B. The morphological growth patterns of colorectal liver metastases are prognostic for overall survival. *Modern Pathology, 27*(12), 1641–1648.

Nielsen, S. R., Quaranta, V., Linford, A., Emeagi, P., Rainer, C., Santos, A., …, & Schmid, M. C. (2016). Macrophage-secreted granulin supports pancreatic cancer metastasis by inducing liver fibrosis. *Nature Cell Biology, 18*(5), 549–560.

Nystrom, H. (2021). Extracellular matrix proteins in metastases to the liver - Composition, function and potential applications. *Seminars in Cancer Biology, 71*, 134–142.

Nystrom, H., Naredi, P., Berglund, A., Palmqvist, R., Tavelin, B., & Sund, M. (2012). Liver-metastatic potential of colorectal cancer is related to the stromal composition of the tumour. *Anticancer Research, 32*(12), 5183–5191.

Nystrom, H., Naredi, P., Hafstrom, L., & Sund, M. (2011). Type IV collagen as a tumour marker for colorectal liver metastases. *European Journal of Surgical Oncology, 37*(7), 611–617.

Nyström, H., Tavelin, B., Björklund, M., Naredi, P., & Sund, M. (2015). Improved tumour marker sensitivity in detecting colorectal liver metastases by combined type IV collagen and CEA measurement. *Tumour Biology, 36*(12), 9839–9847.

Oga, T., Yamashita, Y., Soda, M., Kojima, S., Ueno, T., Kawazu, M., …, & Mano, H. (2019). Genomic profiles of colorectal carcinoma with liver metastases and newly identified fusion genes. *Cancer Science, 110*(9), 2973–2981.

Olaso, E., Salado, C., Egilegor, E., Gutierrez, V., Santisteban, A., Sancho-Bru, P., …, & Vidal-Vanaclocha, F. (2003). Proangiogenic role of tumor-activated hepatic stellate cells in experimental melanoma metastasis. *Hepatology, 37*(3), 674–685.

Olaso, E., Santisteban, A., Bidaurrazaga, J., Gressner, A. M., Rosenbaum, J., & Vidal-Vanaclocha, F. (1997). Tumor-dependent activation of rodent hepatic stellate cells during experimental melanoma metastasis. *Hepatology, 26*(3), 634–642.

Overman, M. J., Lonardi, S., Wong, K. Y. M., Lenz, H. J., Gelsomino, F., Aglietta, M., …, & André, T. (2018). Durable Clinical Benefit With Nivolumab Plus Ipilimumab in DNA Mismatch Repair-Deficient/Microsatellite Instability-High Metastatic Colorectal Cancer. *Journal of Clinical Oncology, 36*(8), 773–779.

Palmieri, V., Lazaris, A., Mayer, T. Z., Petrillo, S. K., Alamri, H., Rada, M., …, & Metrakos, M. (2020). Neutrophils expressing lysyl oxidase-like 4 protein are present in colorectal cancer liver metastases resistant to anti-angiogenic therapy. *Journal of Pathology, 251*(2), 213–223.

Papayannopoulos, V. (2018). Neutrophil extracellular traps in immunity and disease. *Nature Reviews Immunology, 18*(2), 134–147.

Pelillo, C., Bergamo, A., Mollica, H., Bestagno, M., & Sava, G. (2015). Colorectal Cancer Metastases Settle in the Hepatic Microenvironment Through alpha5beta1 Integrin. *Journal of Cellular Biochemistry, 116*(10), 2385–2396.

Petronilho, F., Roesler, R., Schwartsmann, G., & Dal Pizzol, F. (2007). Gastrin-releasing peptide receptor as a molecular target for inflammatory diseases. *Inflamm Allergy Drug Targets, 6*(4), 197–200.

Piao, C., Zhang, W. M., Li, T. T., Zhang, C. C., Qiu, S., Liu, Y., …, & Du, J. (2018). Complement 5a stimulates macrophage polarization and contributes to tumor metastases of colon cancer. *Experimental Cell Research, 366*(2), 127–138.

Pickup, M. W., Mouw, J. K., & Weaver, V. M. (2014). The extracellular matrix modulates the hallmarks of cancer. *Embo Reports, 15*(12), 1243–1253.

Pillarisetty, V. G., Katz, S. C., Bleier, J. I., Shah, A. B., & Dematteo, R. P. (2005). Natural killer dendritic cells have both antigen presenting and lytic function and in response to CpG produce IFN-gamma via autocrine IL-12. *Journal of Immunology, 174*(5), 2612–2618.

Queirolo, P., Boutros, A., Tanda, E., Spagnolo, F., & Quaglino, P. (2019). Immune-checkpoint inhibitors for the treatment of metastatic melanoma: a model of cancer immunotherapy. *Seminars in Cancer Biology, 59*, 290–297.

Rahbari, N. N., Kedrin, D., Incio, J., Liu, H., Ho, W. W., Nia, H. T., …, & Fukumura, D. (2016). Anti-VEGF therapy induces ECM remodeling and mechanical barriers to therapy in colorectal cancer liver metastases. *Science Translational Medicine, 8*(360), 1–25, 360ra135.

Rayes, R. F., Milette, S., Fernandez, M. C., Ham, B., Wang, N., Bourdeau, F., …, & Brodt, P. (2018). Loss of neutrophil polarization in colon carcinoma liver metastases of mice with an inducible, liver-specific IGF-I deficiency. *Oncotarget, 9*(21), 15691–15704.

Rayes, R. F., Mouhanna, J. G., Nicolau, I., Bourdeau, F., Giannias, B., Rousseau, S., …, & Spicer, J. D. (2019). Primary tumors induce neutrophil extracellular traps with targetable metastasis promoting effects. *JCI Insight, 4*(16), 1–14, e128008.

Rayes, R. F., Vourtzoumis, P., Bou Rjeily, M., Seth, R., Bourdeau, F., Giannias, B., …, & Ferri, L. E. (2020). Neutrophil Extracellular Trap-Associated CEACAM1 as a Putative Therapeutic Target to Prevent Metastatic Progression of Colon Carcinoma. *Journal of Immunology, 204*(8), 2285–2294.

Rolff, H. C., Christensen, I. J., Vainer, B., Svendsen, L. B., Eefsen, R. L., Wilhelmsen, M., …, & Illemann, M. (2016). The Prognostic and Predictive Value of Soluble Type IV Collagen in Colorectal Cancer: a Retrospective Multicenter Study. *Clinical Cancer Research, 22*(10), 2427–2434.

Schiffmann, L. M., Brunold, M., Liwschitz, M., Goede, V., Loges, S., Wroblewski, M., …, & Coutelle, O. (2017). A combination of low-dose bevacizumab and imatinib enhances vascular normalisation without inducing extracellular matrix deposition. *British Journal of Cancer, 116*(5), 600–608.

Shen, Y., Wang, X., Lu, J., Salfenmoser, M., Wirsik, N. M., Schleussner, N., …, & Schmidt, T. (2020). Reduction of Liver Metastasis Stiffness Improves Response to Bevacizumab in Metastatic Colorectal Cancer. *Cancer Cell, 37*(6), 800–817, e7.

Shimizu, Y., Amano, H., Ito, Y., Betto, T., Yamane, S., Inoue, T., …, & Majima, M. (2017). Angiotensin II subtype 1a receptor signaling in resident hepatic macrophages induces liver metastasis formation. *Cancer Science, 108*(9), 1757–1768.

Smedsrod, B., Le Couteur, D., Ikejima, K., Jaeschke, H., Kawada, N., Naito, M., …, & Yamaguchi, N. (2009). Hepatic sinusoidal cells in health and disease: update from the 14th International Symposium. *Liver International, 29*(4), 490–501.

Swiecki, M., & Colonna, M. (2015). The multifaceted biology of plasmacytoid dendritic cells. *Nature Reviews Immunology, 15*(8), 471–485.

Tabariès, S., Annis, M. G., Lazaris, A., Petrillo, S. K., Huxham, J., Abdellatif, A., …, & Peter, M. (2021). Claudin-2 promotes colorectal cancer liver metastasis and is a biomarker of the replacement type growth pattern. *Commun Biol, 4*(1), 657–670. doi:10.1038/s42003-021-02189-9.34079064.

Taura, K., De Minicis, S., Seki, E., Hatano, E., Iwaisako, K., Osterreicher, C. H., …, & Brenner, D. A. (2008). Hepatic Stellate Cells Secrete Angiopoietin 1 That Induces Angiogenesis in Liver Fibrosis. *Gastroenterology, 135*(5), 1729–1738.

Tauriello, D. V. F., Palomo-Ponce, S., Stork, D., Berenguer-Llergo, A., Badia-Ramentol, J., Iglesias, M., …, & Batlle, E. (2018). TGFbeta drives immune evasion in genetically reconstituted colon cancer metastasis. *Nature, 554*(7693), 538–543.

Tiegs, G., & Lohse, A. W. (2010). Immune tolerance: what is unique about the liver. *Journal of Autoimmunity, 34*(1), 1–6.

Tohme, S., Yazdani, H. O., Al-Khafaji, A. B., Chidi, A. P., Loughran, P., Mowen, K., …, & Tsung, A. (2016). Neutrophil Extracellular Traps Promote the Development and Progression of Liver Metastases after Surgical Stress. *Cancer Research, 76*(6), 1367–1380.

Tokita, D., Sumpter, T. L., Raimondi, G., Zahorchak, A. F., Wang, Z., Nakao, A., …, & Thomson, A. W. (2008). Poor allostimulatory function of liver plasmacytoid DC is associated with pro-apoptotic activity, dependent on regulatory T cells. *Journal of Hepatology, 49*(6), 1008–1018.

Tsilimigras, D. I., Brodt, P., Clavien, P. A., Muschel, R. J., D'Angelica, M. I., Endo, I., …, & Pawlik, T. M. (2021). Liver metastases. *Nature reviews Disease primers, 7*(1), 27–49.

van Dam, P. J., Daelemans, S., Ross, E., Waumans, Y., Van Laere, S., Latacz, E., …, & Vermeulen, P. B. (2018). Histopathological growth patterns as a candidate biomarker for immunomodulatory therapy. *Seminars in Cancer Biology, 52*(Pt 2), 86–93.

van Dam, P. J., van der Stok, E. P., Teuwen, L. A., Van den Eynden, G. G., Illemann, M., Frentzas, S., …, & Vermeulen, P. B. (2017). International consensus guidelines for scoring the histopathological growth patterns of liver metastasis. *British Journal of Cancer, 117*(10), 1427–1441.

Van den Eynde, M., Mlecnik, B., Bindea, G., Fredriksen, T., Church, S. E., Lafontaine, L., …, & Galon, J. (2018). The Link between the Multiverse of Immune Microenvironments in Metastases and the Survival of Colorectal Cancer Patients. *Cancer Cell, 34*(6), 1012–1026, e3.

Van den Eynden, G. G., Bird, N. C., Dirix, L. Y., Eefsen, R. L., Gao, Z. H., Hoyer-Hansen, G., …, & Brodt, P. (2014). Tumor stromal phenotypes define VEGF sensitivity–letter. *Clinical Cancer Research, 20*(19), 5140.

Van den Eynden, G. G., Bird, N. C., Majeed, A. W., Van Laere, S., Dirix, L. Y., & Vermeulen, P. B. (2012). The histological growth pattern of colorectal cancer liver metastases has prognostic value. *Clinical & Experimental Metastasis, 29*(6), 541–549.

Van den Eynden, G. G., Majeed, A. W., Illemann, M., Vermeulen, P. B., Bird, N. C., Hoyer-Hansen, G., …, & Brodt, P. (2013). The multifaceted role of the microenvironment in liver metastasis: biology and clinical implications. *Cancer Research, 73*(7), 2031–2043.

Vaniotis, G., Rayes, R. F., Qi, S., Milette, S., Wang, N., Perrino, S., …, & Brodt, P. (2018). Collagen IV-conveyed signals can regulate chemokine production and promote liver metastasis. *Oncogene, 37*(28), 3790–3805.

Verter, E., Berger, Y., Perl, G., Peretz, I., Tovar, A., Morgenstern, S., …, & Sadot, E. (2021). Neutrophil-to-Lymphocyte Ratio Predicts Recurrence Pattern in Patients with Resectable Colorectal Liver Metastases. *Annals of Surgical Oncology, 28*(8), 4320–4329.

Vidal-Vanaclocha, F. (2008). The Prometastatic Microenvironment of the Liver. *Cancer Microenvironment, 1*(1), 113–129.

Vidal-Vanaclocha, F. (2011). The Tumor Microenvironment at Different Stages of Hepatic Metastasis. In P. Brodt (Ed.), *Liver Metastasis: Biology and Clinical Management* (pp. 43–87). Dordrecht: Springer Science+Business Media B.V. online resource.

Vinas, O., Bataller, R., Sancho-Bru, P., Gines, P., Berenguer, C., Enrich, C., …, & Rodés, J. (2003). Human hepatic stellate cells show features of antigen-presenting cells and stimulate lymphocyte proliferation. *Hepatology, 38*(4), 919–929.

Wang, D., Sun, H., Wei, J., Cen, B., & DuBois, R. N. (2017). CXCL1 Is Critical for Premetastatic Niche Formation and Metastasis in Colorectal Cancer. *Cancer Research, 77*(13), 3655–3665.

Wang, D., Wang, X., Si, M., Yang, J., Sun, S., Wu, H., …, & Yu, X. (2020). Exosome-encapsulated miRNAs contribute to CXCL12/CXCR4-induced liver metastasis of colorectal cancer by enhancing M2 polarization of macrophages. *Cancer Letters, 474*, 36–52.

Wei, C., Yang, C., Wang, S., Shi, D., Zhang, C., Lin, X., …, & Xiong, B. (2019). Crosstalk between cancer cells and tumor associated macrophages is required for mesenchymal circulating tumor cell-mediated colorectal cancer metastasis. *Molecular Cancer [Electronic Resource], 18*(1), 1–23 64.

Wen, S. W., Ager, E. I., & Christophi, C. (2013). Bimodal role of Kupffer cells during colorectal cancer liver metastasis. *Cancer Biology & Therapy, 14*(7), 606–613.

Wilky, B. A. (2019). Immune checkpoint inhibitors: the linchpins of modern immunotherapy. *Immunological Reviews, 290*(1), 6–23.

Xia, S., Guo, Z., Xu, X., Yi, H., Wang, Q., & Cao, X. (2008). Hepatic microenvironment programs hematopoietic progenitor differentiation into regulatory dendritic cells, maintaining liver tolerance. *Blood, 112*(8), 3175–3185.

Xia, Y., He, J., Zhang, H., Wang, H., Tetz, G., Maguire, C. A., …, & Tsung, A. (2020). AAV-mediated gene transfer of DNase I in the liver of mice with colorectal cancer reduces liver metastasis and restores local innate and adaptive immune response. *Mol Oncol, 14*(11), 2920–2935.

Xu, W., Atkins, M. B., & McDermott, D. F. (2020). Checkpoint inhibitor immunotherapy in kidney cancer. *Nat Rev Urol, 17*(3), 137–150.

Yang, L., Liu, L., Zhang, R., Hong, J., Wang, Y., Wang, J., …, & Hao, H. (2020). IL-8 mediates a positive loop connecting increased neutrophil extracellular traps (NETs) and colorectal cancer liver metastasis. *Journal of Cancer, 11*(15), 4384–4396.

Yang, M., Liu, J., Piao, C., Shao, J., & Du, J. (2015). ICAM-1 suppresses tumor metastasis by inhibiting macrophage M2 polarization through blockade of efferocytosis. *Cell Death & Disease, 6*, 1–12 e1780.

You, Q., Cheng, L., Kedl, R. M., & Ju, C. (2008). Mechanism of T cell tolerance induction by murine hepatic Kupffer cells. *Hepatology, 48*(3), 978–990.

Yu, J., Green, M. D., Li, S., Sun, Y., Journey, S. N., Choi, J. E., …, & Zou, W. (2021). Liver metastasis restrains immunotherapy efficacy via macrophage-mediated T cell elimination. *Nature Medicine, 27*(1), 152–164.

Yuzhalin, A. E., Gordon-Weeks, A. N., Tognoli, M. L., Jones, K., Markelc, B., Konietzny, R., …, & Muschel, R. J. (2018). Colorectal cancer liver metastatic growth depends on PAD4-driven citrullination of the extracellular matrix. *Nature communications, 9*(1), 1–15, 4783.

Zeng, D., Wang, M., Wu, J., Lin, S., Ye, Z., Zhou, R., …, & Liao, W. (2021). Immunosuppressive Microenvironment Revealed by Immune Cell Landscape in Pre-metastatic Liver of Colorectal Cancer. *Frontiers in oncology, 11*, 1–15, 620688.

Zhao, W., Zhang, L., Xu, Y., Zhang, Z., Ren, G., Tang, K., …, & Wang, X. (2014). Hepatic stellate cells promote tumor progression by enhancement of immunosuppressive cells in an orthotopic liver tumor mouse model. *Laboratory Investigation; A Journal of Technical Methods and Pathology, 94*(2), 182–191.

Zou, S., Tong, Q., Liu, B., Huang, W., Tian, Y., & Fu, X. (2020). Targeting STAT3 in Cancer Immunotherapy. *Molecular Cancer [Electronic Resource], 19*(1), 1–19, 145.

CHAPTER

3

Pre-operative imaging, response evaluation, and surgical planning – CT, PET, radiomics, and FLR measurement

Elizabeth Y. Liu, BA[a], *Azarakhsh Baghdadi, MD, MAS*[a], *Timothy M. Pawlik, MD, MPH, MTS, PhD*[b] *and Ihab R. Kamel, MD, PhD*[a]

[a]Department of Radiology and Radiological Science, Johns Hopkins Hospital, Baltimore, MD, USA [b]Department of Surgery, The Ohio State University Wexner Medical Center, The James Comprehensive Cancer Center, Columbus, OH, USA

Introduction

Colorectal cancer (CRC) is one of the most common malignancies and a leading cause of cancer morbidity and mortality worldwide. Many factors can impact survival including the development of metastases. The most common site of colorectal cancer metastases is the liver, as almost 20 percent of patients with CRC have liver metastasis at presentation. Among patients without liver metastases at presentation, about 25 percent will develop metachronous liver metastasis at some point in their disease course.

Different treatment options are available for patients with CRC and colorectal liver metastases (CRLM) including locoregional and systemic therapies. Surgical resection remains, however, the best chance at long-term survival and cure. In general, CRLMs are considered to be resectable if:

1. Macroscopic and microscopic resection of disease is feasible (via resection alone or combined with radiofrequency ablation or chemotherapy)
2. At least two adjacent liver segments can be spared along with sufficient vascular and biliary flow
3. There is an adequate liver remnant volume

Contemporary Management of Metastatic Colorectal Cancer: A Precision Medicine Approach
DOI: https://doi.org/10.1016/B978-0-323-91706-3.00003-5

Contrary to prior belief, the number of liver metastases is not a contraindication to surgery. Patients with colorectal cancer and CRLM can fall into four categories of resectability:

1. Initially resectable by standard approach
2. Initially resectable by extended approach (i.e. staged resections, preoperative portal vein embolization, two-stage hepatectomy, resection plus ablation)
3. Initially unresectable, but likely convertible
4. Initially unresectable and unlikely convertible

In this chapter, we aim to describe the different imaging modalities used to evaluate and stage patients with CRLM. We describe the role that each imaging modality plays and discuss the elements of hepatic imaging related to evaluation of response to preoperative therapy, as well as surgical planning.

Role of imaging in CRLM

With advances in radiological imaging and surgical techniques, the pool of patients with potentially resectable CRLM has grown over time. Identifying and assessing patients for potential surgical resection with the appropriate radiologic imaging techniques is critical. Among the various available imaging modalities, ultrasonography (US), computed tomography (CT), magnetic resonance imaging (MRI), and ^{18}F fluoro-2-deoxy-D-glucose (FDG) positron emission tomography (PET) can be used to assess patients with CRLM. CT and MRI are generally the two most commonly used techniques to stage patients and assess patients in the preoperative setting; transabdominal US is most often used to guide lesion biopsies. Additionally, US plays an important role in identifying and confirming lesions intraoperatively.

The goals of imaging are generally:

- To determine initial staging and quantify burden of disease
- To evaluate the size, number, and distribution of CRLMs
- To determine the patient's eligibility for surgical resection
- To predict and assess pre-operative treatment response
- To assist with pre-surgical planning and future liver remnant measurement
- To identify lesions intraoperatively
- To follow-up with treatment surveillance

Pre-operative imaging of CRLMs

Initial staging

Assessment of colorectal cancer disease stage is important to define the optimal treatment plan. Tumor staging offers the greatest insight into overall prognosis, with the presence of distant metastasis and extrahepatic disease being among the most important determinants of survival. The different imaging modalities available to stage CRC as well as assess for and evaluate CRLMs include CT, MRI, and FDG-PET.

Ultrasonography (US)

US is the most accessible imaging modality worldwide and one of the major imaging tests used to evaluate CRLM in many countries. US is not ideal for staging CRC when CT and MRI are available, but it can still play a role in pre-operative imaging. Specifically, it can play a complementary role to evaluate CT or MRI lesions that are deemed indeterminant. In addition, US guidance is preferred over CT guidance when performing percutaneous biopsies of suspicious lesions.

3.5–5 MHz curved-array transducers can be used for transabdominal evaluation of CRLMs. For contrast-enhanced US (CE-US), second generation microbubble contrast agents are injected. There are distinct enhancement phases: arterial phase images can be collected up to 25 s post-injection, PVP images are measured from 25 to 45 s post-injection, and late phase images can be visualized up to 2 min post-injection.

On US, CRLM typically appear as round, well-circumscribed hypoechoic lesions. There is typically a hypoechoic halo surrounding the lesion, giving it a target-shaped appearance due to compression of the normal liver parenchyma (Fig. 3.1A). On CE-US, the lesions demonstrate rapid enhancement during the arterial phase as most lesions are supplied by the hepatic artery. During PVP and delayed phase, almost all metastases will show washout.

With contrast enhancement, US has an 87–91 percent accuracy to characterize and detect liver lesions. However, conventional US without contrast enhancement has a significantly lower sensitivity (54–77 percent) compared with CT or MRI. In addition, US results are highly dependent on operator expertise.

US is also critical for intraoperative imaging. During the procedure, the surgical team should routinely perform an intraoperative ultrasonography (IOUS) exam or contrast-enhanced IOUS of the liver to attempt to detect CRLMs that were unable to be visualized during preoperative imaging or undetectable by palpation during surgery. These intraoperative imaging techniques have been found to have a higher detection rate of unrecognized synchronous liver metastases during primary colorectal cancer resection or during resection of previously known hepatic masses versus preoperative US, CT, CE-CT, and MRI, especially for lesions less than 10 mm in diameter. IOUS is also used by the surgeon to plan the parenchymal dissection.

Computed tomagraphy (CT)

CT is the most commonly used imaging method for detecting CRLM. Multidetector row CT (MDCT) scanners allow for a complete liver scan in a single breath-hold resulting in decreased motion artifact and, often, more precise imaging. MDCT also has the ability to image other potential sites of disease or metastasis during a single examination (i.e., lungs). Use of contrast is necessary, with contrast-enhanced CT (CE-CT) typically the mainstay modality for CRC staging.

The efficacy of CT is dependent on the technique and parameters used, such as slice thickness, kilovolt (peak) (kV[*p*]), milliamperes (mA), and contrast delivery. In practice, an axial slice thickness of 2–4 mm is sufficient to evaluate metastatic lesions to the liver. A slice thickness of 2–4mm results in better multiplanar reconstructed images and therefore provides better detection and characterization of liver lesions. Slices thinner than 2–4 mm are not

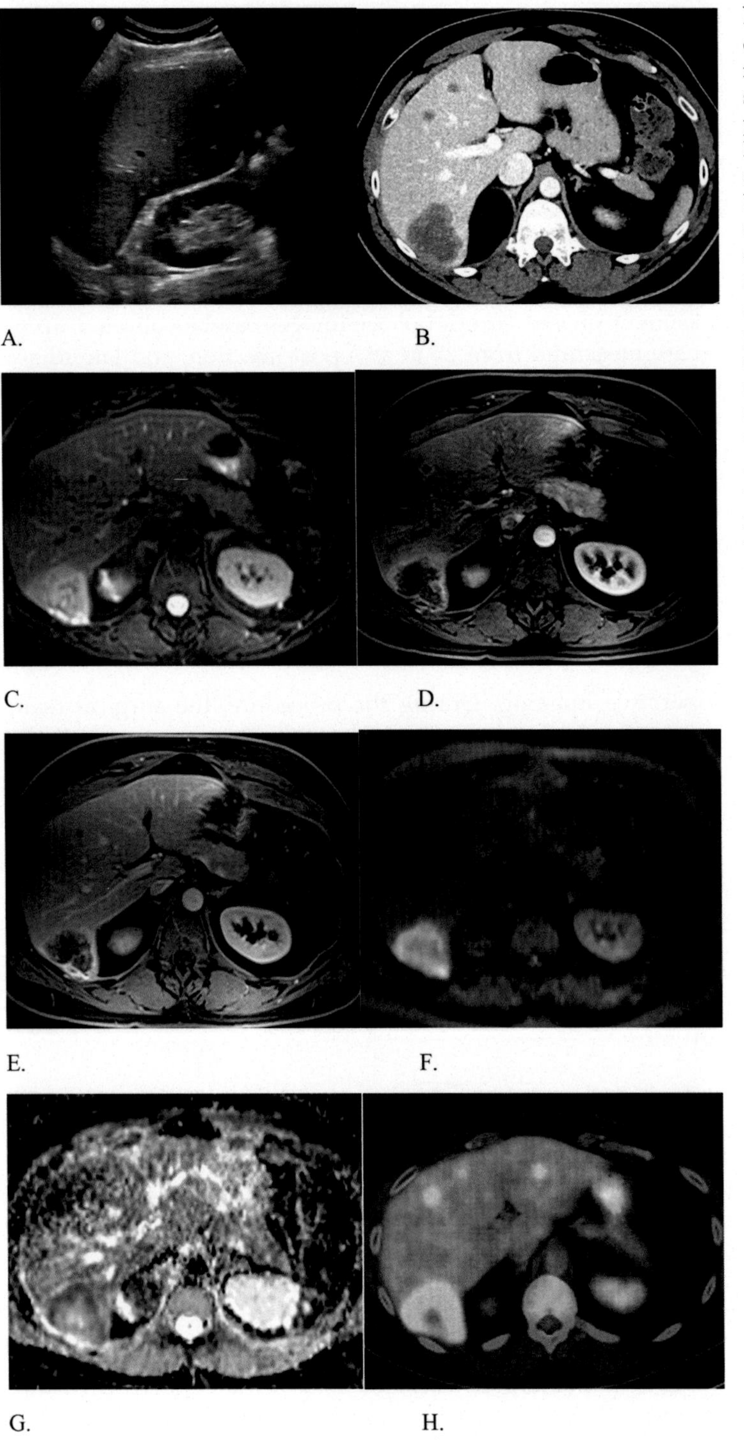

FIGURE 3.1 47-year-old with colorectal adenocarcinoma with metastasis to the liver. Ultrasound shows a well circumscribed hypoechoic lesion surrounded by a hypoechoic halo which gives it a target appearance (A). CT at baseline shows a hypodense lesion (B) with slight hyperintensity on T2 weighted MRI (C). Hepatic arterial phase images show a hypointense lesion with a hyperintense rim (D), which is seen as a hypointense lesion on portal venous phase images (E). DWI shows a hyperintense lesion (F) with restricted diffusion on the ADC map compatible with metastasis (G). FDG-PET images show multiple hypermetabolic lesions with a target appearance seen in the largest lesion (H).

recommended, as it does not increase lesion detection and also increases noise. The optimal kV and mA ratios are 120 to 150 kV(p)/80 to 300 mA. Contrast enhancement can be achieved using 2mL/kg of non-ionic contrast media injected via IV using a power injector at a rate of 3- to 5-mL/second. Scans should be performed 20–25 s post-injection to obtain arterial phase images and 60–65 s for portal venous phase (PVP) images. To best evaluate CRLMs, images should be captured in the PVP. Oral contrast is not recommended as it may degrade image reconstruction of the arterial phase and PVP images. Instead, 750–1,000mL of water may be used as a negative contrast agent.

On CT, CRLM lesions classically appear as hypodense or isodense lesions in pre-contrast images and as rim-enhancing lesions with hypodense foci in arterial phase images. The lesions are most conspicuous on PVP images, as the hyperenhancing liver parenchyma offers a clear delineation of the hypoenhancing CRLM lesions. This pattern of hypoenhancement is due to the hallmark hypovascularity of CRLMs (Fig. 3.1B). CT has a sensitivity of 85–91.5 percent when detecting CRLM on the PVP. A small subset of CRLM lesions include calcifications, which are best seen on pre-contrast images.

The strengths of using MDCT with contrast enhancement include faster acquisition of images – a single breath-hold is sufficient to scan the entire liver once. However, CT has limited success in identifying lesions under 10 mm, and decreasing axial slice thickness to 1 mm does not significantly improve the detection of smaller liver lesions yet can result in an increased false-negative rate.

Magnetic resonance imaging (MRI)

MRI provides radiologists with multiple sequences – T1-weighted, T2-weighted, diffusion-weighted, and contrast-enhanced imaging, which provide a very thorough evaluation of liver lesions. Diffusion-weighted imaging (DWI) is a relatively newer MRI sequence that uses the diffusion of water molecules to generate contrast on MR images by measuring the Brownian motion of water molecules. The sequence also includes an apparent diffusion coefficient (ADC) parameter, which is a map that displays information regarding physiologic restriction and pathologic restriction of water. This technique reflects the degree of diffusion and allows for a more informed decision regarding true pathology. In fact, DWI is significantly more sensitive than T2-weighted MRI to detect CRLMs, with a sensitivity of 82 percent and a specificity of 90 percent. DWI can detect lesions smaller than 10 mm and can also be safely used in patients with contrast allergies or poor renal function.

Images are ideally acquisitioned with a magnet strength of 1.5 Tesla or greater using a phased-array torso coil. A slice thickness of 5 mm or less is preferred for all sequences, but a slice thickness of 3 mm or less is ideal for T1 pre-contrast and post-contrast sequences. Extracellular MRI contrast media such as gadobutrol allows for delineation of metastatic disease particularly in the venous or delayed phases.

CRLMs have several distinct features when assessed with MRI. CRLM lesions generally present as hypointense on T1, hyperintense with intermediate to high signal intensity on T2 (Figs. 3.1C, 3.2C, and 3.3A), and restricted diffusion on DWI (Fig. 3.1F and 3.3B), which can be confirmed by ADC map (Fig. 3.1G). On extracellular gadolinium-based contrast-enhanced MRI, larger CRLM lesions demonstrate rim enhancement with hypointense foci on the arterial phase images (Fig. 3.1D, 3.2A) and hypointensity in the PVP (Fig. 3.1E, 3.2B, 3.3C) and delayed

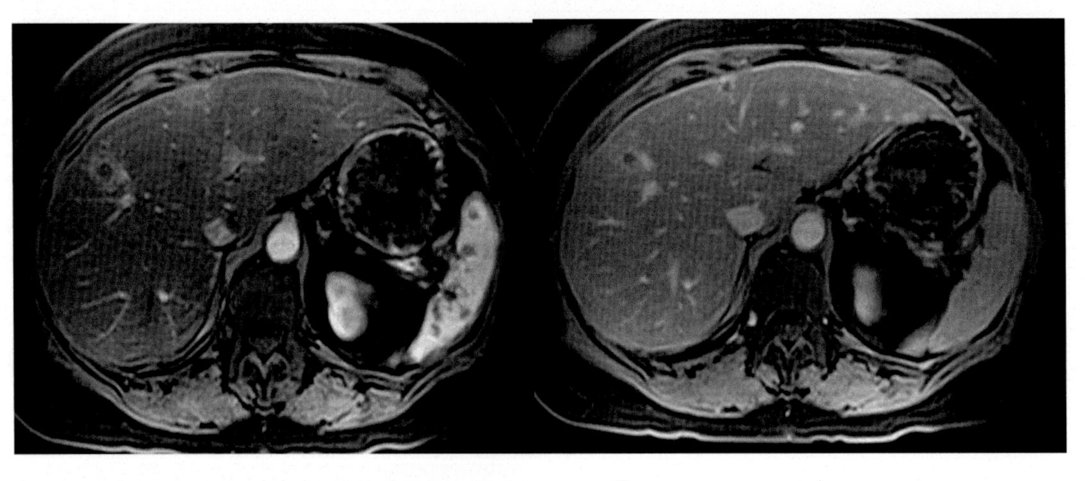

A. B.

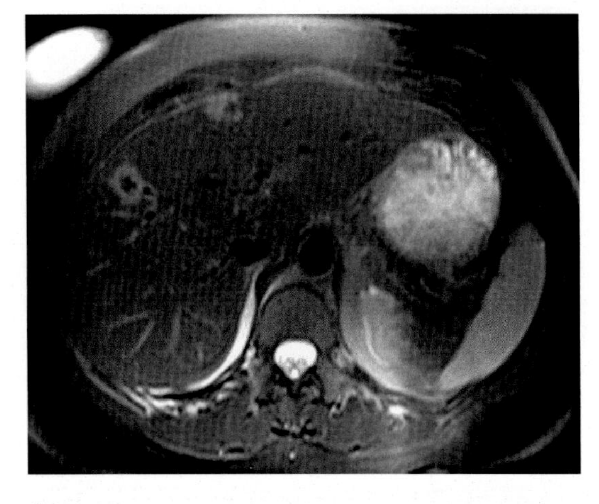

C.

FIGURE 3.2 61-year-old woman with liver metastasis from CRC who initially presented with abdominal pain and partial bowel obstruction. T1-weighted images show hypointense lesions with rim enhancement in the hepatic arterial phase (A) that persist on portal venous phase images (B). T2-weighted images (C) reveal multiple lesions with slightly hyperintense rim.

phase images. Some CRLMs may not have these features and are at risk of being missed by MRI. These metastases are more likely to be detected on DWI. In addition to traditional extracellular MRI contrast media, hepatocelluar MR contrast agents such as gadoxetic acid and gadobenate dimeglumine can improve lesion characterization as these agents have significant uptake by functioning hepatocytes and excretion via the biliary system. In particular, these hepatocellular contrast agents have selective biphasic uptake by normally functioning hepatocytes first immediately after contrast administration and then in the hepatobiliary phase, about 20 min post contrast administration, whereas metastases do not uptake gadolinium-based contrast (Fig. 3.3D).

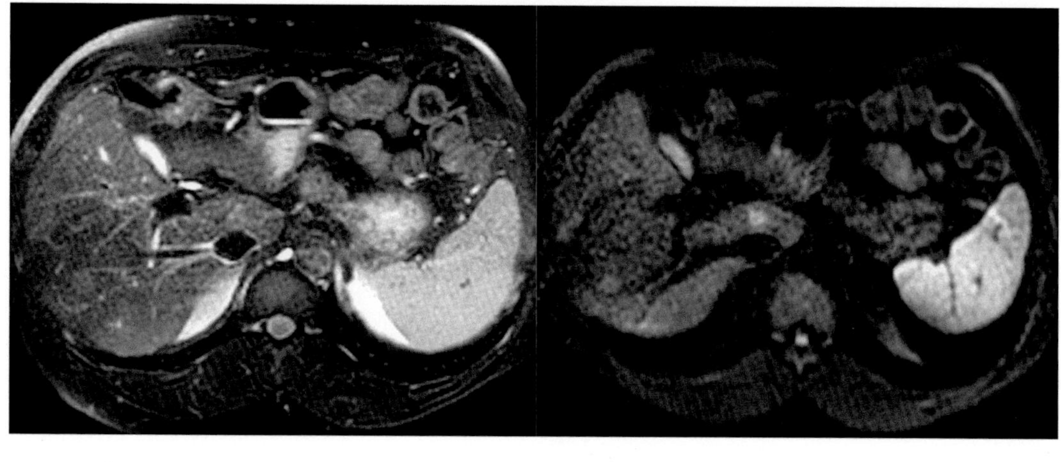

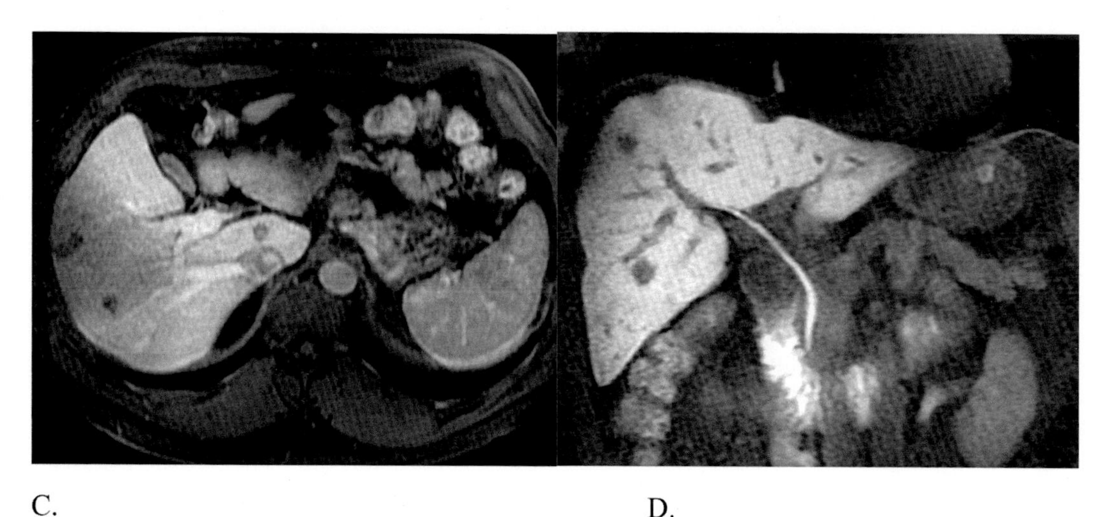

FIGURE 3.3 50-year-old man with rectal adenocarcinoma and liver metastasis who initially presented with hematochezia. (A) Subtle hyperintense lesions are seen on T2-weighted images, better visualized on DWI (B). The lesions are hypovascular on portal venous phase images (C) with no uptake on hepatobiliary phase coronal images after EOVIST injection (D)

With multiple imaging sequences, MRI provides greater information of hepatic lesions and allows for more in-depth evaluation. In addition, MRI is more accurate than CT when detecting liver metastases in the setting of hepatic steatosis and post-neoadjuvant therapy. There is an added benefit to MRI of reduced radiation exposure as well. However, MRI cannot be used to evaluate for certain extrahepatic metastatic lesions such as lung lesions, which severely limits its role in CRC staging. MRI also may not be available to all patients, especially those who live in resource-limited areas and those with contraindications such as metal devices and implants.

In spite of significant improvements in MRI gradients allowing faster acquisition, MRI has a slower acquisition speed than CT. MRI images can also be subject to significant breathing and motion artifact.

Historically, gadolinium-based contrast agents were not be used in those with renal insufficiency due to side effects such as nephrogenic systemic fibrosis (NSF). More recently, Group II contrast agents including Gadobutrol (Gadavist) and Gadoterate acid (Dotarem) have been approved for patients with impaired renal function since they have been associated with few if any unconfounded cases of NSF. Harboring MRI-unsafe implants (eg. Pacemakers) is another contraindication for MRI.

Fluorodeoxyglucose-positron emission tomography (FDG-PET)

CT and MRI have been accepted as the preferred modalities for staging CRC, however multimodality imaging can improve detection of disease versus a single modality. Specifically, FDG-PET/CT and FDG-PET/MRI provide anatomical and functional information in an image and allows for improved characterization and identification of suspicious hepatic lesions. The ^{18}F-FDG typically used in PET is a glucose analog that is taken up by metabolically active cells. The standardized uptake value (SUV) – which takes into account tissue radioactivity concentration, administered FGD dose, and the patient's body weight – is the most common parameter used to evaluate the uptake of the radioactive tracer.

Patient preparation is key when undergoing a PET study. Patients must fast for at least four hours prior to acquisition and finger stick blood glucose measurement prior to ^{18}F-FDG injection must be <200 mg/dL. On imaging, cells with high uptake of ^{18}F-FDG will have increased SUV values (Fig. 3.1H). While the normal liver parenchyma itself has a typical SUV of 2–5, tumor lesions are expected to be even more FDG-avid with higher SUV. The PET modality can also detect abnormal glucose metabolism that may precede anatomical changes.

The strengths of PET in conjunction with CT or MRI lie with its ability to determine anatomical characteristics as well functional status resulting in improved lesion characterization. Some CRLM lesions are not detectable by PET, however. For instance, mucinous tumors (which account for 17 percent of colorectal cancers) do not uptake FDG and therefore cannot be visualized by PET. In addition, PET/CT has limited value to detect lesions less than 10 mm, although PET/MRI can overcome this limitation.

Assessment of prognosis and surgical candidacy

Possible prognostic factors for CRLM lesions include the number of metastases, size and location of the lesions, response to pre-surgical treatments such as chemotherapy, hypoechogenicity of the lesions on ultrasound, disease on initial presentation, vascular invasion, and composition of the underlying liver. While the number of tumor lesions is not an absolute contraindication to hepatic tumor resection, imaging is important to plan an R0 (i.e. microscopically negative) resection, as well as assess response to preoperative chemotherapy prior to surgical resection.

Tumor Size: Tumor size measurements are important for prognosis and operative planning. The techniques must be highly consistent, objective, and reproducible in order to successfully assess for treatment response or disease progression. With advances in diagnostic imaging, radiologists can construct three-dimensional images and measure total tumor volume (TTV); some data have suggested that TTV was associated with recurrence-free survival, overall survival, and unresectable recurrence. The size of the tumor can also affect the size of the liver remnant, surgical approach, and the surgeon's ability to obtain negative margins.

Tumor Distribution and Location: Bilateral distribution of CRLM does not affect overall survival and should not be considered a contraindication so long as an R0 resection with sufficient residual liver volume is achievable. Additionally, pre-operative interventions such as neoadjuvant chemotherapy, as well as two-stage hepatectomy can improve the odds of resection with tumor-free surgical margins in these clinical situations. These interventions are discussed further in this chapter.

Vascular Involvement: Determination of vascular involvement is important for surgical planning. Tumors that infiltrate vascular structures are frequently resectable, yet patients with CRLM and vascular invasion have worse prognosis versus patients without CRLM vascular invasion. CE-CT and CE-MRI can be used to demonstrate vascular anatomy, aberrations and to create a vascular map on pre-surgical evaluation. CE-CT can better illustrate vascular anatomy and small segmental vessels of the liver and is the preferred modality for vascular evaluation before surgery.

Hepatic Function and Volumetrics: Prior to surgery, select patients should undergo assessment of hepatic functional reserve. In particular, patients who have compromised underlying liver function (i.e., fatty liver, cirrhosis, fibrosis) or individuals in whom an extended resection is being planned. Hepatic functional reserve can be evaluated by determining the volume of the future remnant liver, as well as assessing liver function on laboratory testing. Depending on the functional status of the liver, a future liver remnant of 20–30 percent of the liver's original volume or a ratio of remnant liver to body weight of greater than 0.5 percent is typically sufficient. Patients who have bilateral metastases, large tumor burden, or abnormal liver function are particularly at risk for developing postoperative liver failure and may need a 30–40 percent liver remnant volume. Modern imaging techniques and programs can be used to create three dimensional (3D) reconstructions, with 3D CT being the preferred technique. This allows for evaluation of CRLM volume, as well as the volume of the remaining non-tumorous liver parenchyma, in addition to assessment of the relationship between the vessels and the tumors to optimize surgical strategy.

Extrahepatic Involvement: The presence of extrahepatic metastases can change the overall therapeutic plan and thus can impact surgical decision-making. The preferred means to evaluate for extrahepatic lesions include CT chest and abdomen only or PET/CT. In particular, FDG-PET has been suggested as the most accurate modality for detection of extrahepatic disease and occult metastasis.

Use of imaging for surgical planning

Surgical planning and approach are dependent on the presence of arterial variants, the anatomy of the arteries feeding the tumor, and the arterial supply of the normal hepatic parenchyma in order to ensure tumor-free margins and to prevent liver and biliary ischemia. The Michels classification of hepatic artery variants can assist in preoperative planning, further detailed in Table 3.2.

Hepatic venous variants are present in the population as well, and must also be evaluated on imaging, on a case-by-case basis when planning for surgical resection to prevent ischemia and venous congestion. The right hepatic vein is one dominant vein in the majority of the population. For a typical right lobe resection, the middle and left hepatic veins should be preserved. For a typical left lateral segment resection, the right and middle hepatic veins should be preserved and the left hepatic vein should be resected at or above the confluence of the middle hepatic vein. Hepatic venous variants can be seen in 16–33 percent of individuals, with accessory hepatic veins draining directly into the inferior vena cava (IVC) being the most common variant. An accessory right inferior hepatic vein draining segment 5 and/or 6 directly into the IVC is the most common accessory hepatic vein. The presence of accessory veins has implications when planning surgical resection as they must be ligated when removing their corresponding hepatic segments.

The portal vein supplies roughly 75 percent of the blood flow to the liver. Thus, any variations to portal venous anatomy must be taken into account prior to hepatectomy. The overall prevalence of portal vein anatomic variation is estimated to be 20–30 percent. The most common variant is portal vein trifurcation, where the main portal vein divides into three branches: the right anterior portal vein, the right posterior portal vein, and the left portal vein. This can be found in about 6.8 percent of cases. For these patients, ligation of the left portal vein proximal to the right anterior portal vein can lead to ischemia and atrophy of hepatic segments 4, 5, and 8. The second most common variant is a right posterior vein originating as the first branch of the main portal vein. This can be seen in about 5.0 percent of cases. This is especially important to consider for patients undergoing extended right hepatectomy as ligating only the right anterior branch or only the right posterior branch would lead to active bleeding from the other.

Biliary complications have been found to occur in up to 8.1 percent of hepatic tumor resections and are highly associated with liver failure and surgical mortality. There is a higher prevalence of biliary complications after left-sided hepatectomy, likely associated with anatomy factors. In addition, bile leakage is a serious biliary complication that is associated with resections involving segments 1 and 6. One of the most common bile duct variants is the right posterior hepatic duct draining into the left hepatic duct. This has been found in 15.6 percent of cases in one case series and are best demonstrated by magnetic resonance cholangiopancreatography. For these patients, care should be exercised when performing left lobe resection. In cases where the left hepatic duct drains directly into the right hepatic duct, approaches to right liver lobe resection may need to be altered. For patients with biliary duct trifurcation, both right lobe and left lobe resection approaches will need to be altered.

Pre-operative treatment and response evaluation of CRLM

Advances in preoperative chemotherapy can facilitate resection of extensive CRLM. In many instances, long term survival of patients with high-burden disease treated with neoadjuvant chemotherapy followed by surgical resection can be similar to outcomes among individuals with initially resectable disease. As such, goals of preoperative interventions for patients with high-burden CRLM should include decreasing tumor volume and, in some instances, increasing normal liver parenchyma volume.

Downsizing of initially unresectable lesions

Systemic chemotherapy aims to decrease the size of the metastatic lesions. Specifically, up to 20–40 percent of patients with initially unresectable CRLMs can be converted to resectable disease following chemotherapy. For initially unresectable patients with multiple CRLMs, preoperative chemotherapy can down-size disease in a portion of patients to facilitate resection and improved overall survival. Tumors that respond to treatment will first undergo functional metabolic changes, making FGD-PET a useful tool to assess early metabolic response to chemotherapy. CT or MRI can be used to assess anatomic and morphologic response, though these changes tend to be apparent after functional changes occur. Early evaluation of response can inform the appropriate length of chemotherapy to maximize response prior to surgery. Pattern of response detected on imaging can also determine prognosis and likelihood of relapse post-surgery.

For some patients, chemotherapy can result in complete radiological resolution of disease, where CRLMs seen on initial staging imaging are undetectable on imaging after treatment with preoperative chemotherapy. Although a radiologic complete response may seem encouraging, it may not correlate to a durable resolution of disease. In addition, there may be difficulties identifying and resecting CRLMs that have "disappeared" (i.e., disappearing liver metastases, DLMs). FDG-PET has limited value for evaluation of DLMs, as it has poor sensitivity for detection of lesions smaller than 10 mm, and there is aberrant glucose metabolism following chemotherapy. Therefore, radiologists should exercise caution when reporting a complete response.

While neoadjuvant chemotherapy can improve oncological outcomes for patients with initially unresectable CRLMs, treatment can also cause chemotherapy-associated liver injury. This may impact the volume of liver parenchyma necessary to achieve an adequate functional remanent liver. Common agents used for chemotherapy including oxaliplatin, irinotecan, and 5-fluorouracil have been observed to cause liver toxicity. In particular, oxaliplatin has been associated with sinusoidal dilation in up to 19 percent of patients and irinotecan has been associated with steatohepatitis in up to 20 percent of patients. In addition to steatosis and sinusoidal dilation, chemotherapeutic agents may also cause hemorrhagic central lobar necrosis. A portion of patients who develop liver toxicity also develop secondary splenic hypertrophy, causing symptoms similar to portal hypertension, with associated thrombocytopenia and varices.

Chemotherapy-induced changes to the liver parenchyma and to tumors themselves can pose challenges to monitoring known CRLMs by imaging and diagnosing new CRLMs. Steatosis and steatohepatitis cause the liver parenchyma to appear hyperechoic, compromising the performance of US. CT is also less sensitivity for detecting CRLMs among patients who have received preoperative chemotherapy. In these instances, MRI is the best imaging modality to monitor and diagnose CRLMs in patients who have undergone systemic chemotherapy.

TABLE 3.1 Definitions of lesions and response categories from the RECIST 1.1 criteria.

Criterion	RECIST 1.1
Measurable lesions	Minimum size = 10mm on CT
Measurement method	Longest diameter
Number of lesions measured	5 lesions (≤2 in any one organ)
Response category	
Complete Response	Disappearance of all target lesions or lymph nodes <10mm on short axis
Partial Response	>30 percent decrease in SLD of target lesions
Progressive Disease	>20 percent increase in SLD of target lesions with an absolute increase of ≥5mm; new lesions; detailed description of unequivocal progression
Stable Disease	None of the above

SLD = sum of longest diameters.

It is also important to keep in mind that progression of disease, whether metastases to new sites or growth of previously identified metastases, can occur during the administration of preoperative chemotherapy. Therefore, subsequent imaging should evaluate response of known lesions as well as identification of new lesions.

Preoperative treatment response is best assessed according to Response Evaluation Criteria In Solid Tumors (RECIST) criteria, version 1.1. Details are listed in Table 3.1.

Increasing future remnant liver volume and volumetric assessment

In order to be eligible for surgical resection, patients must have enough remaining functional liver parenchyma after the hepatectomy to prevent postoperative liver failure. For patients with normal liver parenchyma, surgical resection is generally contraindicated if the future liver remnant is estimated to be less than 20–30 percent of the total liver volume. Patients who have decreased liver function, such as those who have undergone multiple rounds of chemotherapy, should aim to have a future liver remnant that is at least 40 percent of their liver volume.

Volumetric assessment

Accurate measurements of liver volume may be obtained with CT, which is the standard method for evaluating the future liver remnant (FLR), with a less than 5 percent error rate. IV contrast is necessary to demonstrate segmental vascular landmarks. To measure gross liver volume, total and segmental liver contours are outlined on each slice and the surface area is multiplied by slice thickness.

Traditionally, measurements included total liver volume and the volume of the areas to be respected. Total liver volume (TLV) can be calculated by subtracting the volume (V) of all tumors from the measured volume of liver. The FLR may then be calculated as the percentage of non-tumor bearing liver by dividing liver remnant volume (LRV) by TLV

TABLE 3.2 Common anatomic variants in hepatic arterial blood flow with prevalence and possible surgical implications.

Type	Prevalence	Description	Surgical implications
I	55.0–61.0 percent	Hepatic trunk arises from the CHA	Surgical modification due to hepatic artery anatomy is likely unnecessary.
II	3.0–10.0 percent	Replaced LHA	Surgical modification is necessary if tumors are present in the left lobe. LHA should be ligated where it arises from the LGA
III	8.0–11.0 percent	Replaced RHA	Surgical modification is necessary if tumors are present in the right lobe. RHA should be ligated where it arises from the SMA
IV	~1.0 percent	Replaced LHA and replaced RHA	Surgical modification is necessary regardless of tumor location.
V	8.0–11.0 percent	Accessory LHA arising from the LGA	Surgical modification is necessary if tumors are present in the left lobe. The accessory LHA should be ligated where it arises from the LGA
VI	1.5–7.0 percent	Accessory RHA arising from the SMA	Surgical modification is necessary if tumors are present in the right lobe. The accessory RHA should be ligated where it arises from the SMA
VII	~1.0 percent	Accessory LHA and accessory the RHA	Surgical modification is necessary regardless of tumor location.
VIII	~2.5 percent	Accessory LHA or RHA with replaced RHA or LHA	Surgical modification is dependent on which replaced artery is present and will require ligation of the accessory artery.
IX	2.0–4.5 percent	Replaced CHA arising from the SMA	Surgical modification is necessary regardless of tumor location.
X	~0.5 percent	Replaced CHA arising from the LGA	Surgical modification is necessary regardless of tumor location.

CHA = common hepatic artery, LHA = left hepatic artery, RHA = right hepatic artery, LGA = left gastric artery, SMA = superior mesenteric artery.

$$TLV_{measured} = V_{Total\ Liver} - V_{Measured\ Total\ Liver\ Tumor}$$

$$FLR_{Measured} = LRV/TLV_{Measured} \times 100\ \text{percent}$$

For patients with multiple CRLMs, each individual tumor must be individually measured, which may lead to cumulative mathematical errors and a less accurate FLR estimation. This technique does not consider functional liver volume in patients with biliary dilation or those with compromised liver parenchyma (eg. vascular obstruction, prolonged cholangitis). Moreover, measurement of total liver volume is affected by liver atrophy following PVE. Additionally, this method may yield inaccurate results in patients with large tumors or patients with cirrhosis.

Total liver volume has been shown to be linearly associated with body surface area ($TLV_{Standard} = (1267.28 \times BSA) - 794.41$, $FLR_{Standard} = LRV/TLV_{Standard} \times 100$ percent). Therefore, an alternate method measures total estimated liver volume taking into account each patient's characteristics, in addition to the TLV measured on imaging. To obtain $FLR_{standard}$, LRV is measured on imaging, however, total liver volume is estimated based on $TLV_{standard}$. This method allows for FLR comparison among patients based on height and weight and is the preferred technique for estimating FLR.

Increasing future remnant liver volume

Interventions such as portal vein embolization (PVE) and two-stage hepatectomy aim to increase the FLR volume to increase the chances that a patient would be eligible for hepatectomy.

PVE is a procedure that embolizes one size of the portal venous system in order to induce hypertrophy of the other liver lobe, known as the FLR. This procedure is ideal for patients with metastases that are limited to a single hemi-liver, with the contralateral lobe free of disease. There are two different methods: the percutaneous transhepatic approach and the transileocolic approach via laparotomy. Ultrasound or fluoroscopic guidance is used during the percutaneous approach to visualize the portal vein. After the procedure, CT is used to monitor hepatic volume as well as to re-evaluate for disease recurrence. In 4–6 weeks, total liver volume may increase by 14 percent.

A two-stage hepatectomy is performed by conducting two separate hepatectomies, one after the other. This procedure is typically performed when bilateral CRLMs are still too large after neoadjuvant chemotherapy and the future liver remnant is too small. During the first hepatectomy, the CRLMs are resected from the hemi-liver with a lesser amount of tumor burden. During the second hepatectomy, the remaining CRLMs are resected from the contralateral lobe. In the time between the two resections, the liver is allowed to regenerate, creating a larger FRL. In order to prevent tumor growth between the two hepatectomies and to optimize liver regeneration, chemotherapy is typically administered 3 weeks after the first hepatectomy. The timing of the second hepatectomy is determined by speed of liver regeneration, chemotherapeutic control of the remnant liver tumors, and the likelihood that the second resection would be curative.

If the estimated FRL is not sufficient (e.g., less than 20–30 percent of the liver parenchyma for patients with normal functioning livers or less than 40 percent of the liver parenchyma for patients with decreased liver function from heavy chemotherapy, steatosis, etc.), PVE or portal vein ligation (in a procedure known as Associating Liver Partition and Portal Vein Ligation for Staged Hepatectomy (ALPPS)) may be performed during the first hepatectomy (Figs. 3.4A–3.4G).

Alternative therapies for CRLM

For patients who are not initial candidates for surgical resection and who are still not considered candidates after initial treatment, radiofrequency ablation (RFA), microwave ablation, hepatic artery infusion (HAI), and selective internal radiation therapy (SIRT) can be used as alternative treatments.

Ablation

Ablation involves heating tumor cells via an image-guided needle that emits electrical currents or microwaves. Successful ablation occurs when the entire tumor as well as a portion

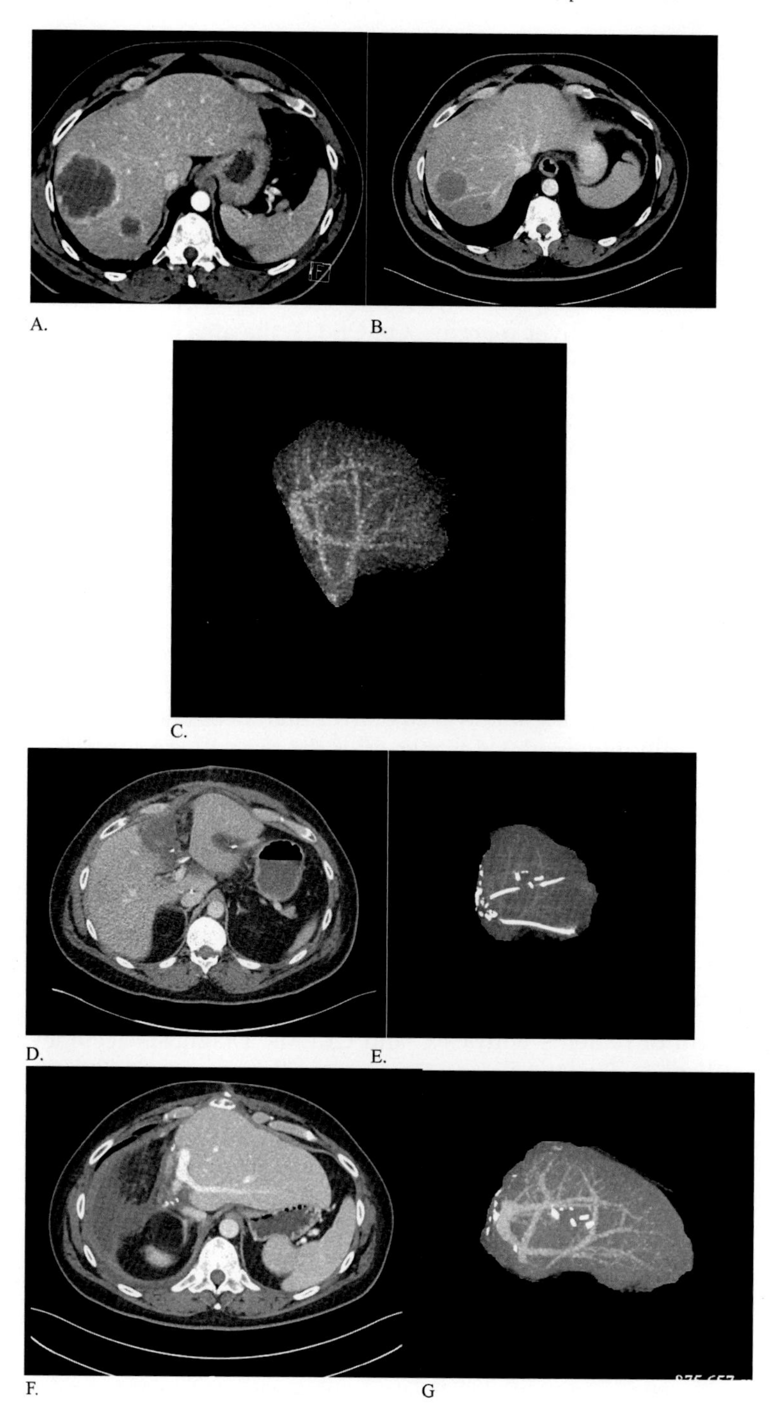

FIGURE 3.4 47-year-old male with CRC and metastasis to the liver. CT shows hypodense lesions with rim enhancement before therapy (A). The lesions decreased in size after chemotherapy and immunotherapy (B). Volume of remnant liver was 392cc (C), which was inadequate to maintain liver function. Patient underwent the first portion of the ALPPS procedure. One week after the first stage, the remnant volume was 550cc on CT (D, E). Patient underwent the second part of the ALPPS procedure, and at six weeks post-operation, the remaining liver volume was 875cc on CT (F, G).

of the surrounding normal liver parenchyma are destroyed within the target region. However, if any tumors are missed or not completely ablated, residual tumor tissue can cause disease recurrence. Disease recurrence can occur in up to 40–60 percent of patients after the procedure. Therefore, patients must obtain imaging ideally within 1 week after the procedure to assess for successful ablation, as well as every 3 to 4 months post-procedure to evaluate for disease progression or new tumors. Post-ablation results are best evaluated by CE-CT or CE-MRI during the PVP. A CRLM tumor is considered to have been successfully ablated when there is a 5 mm or greater margin of normal hepatic parenchyma surrounding the ablation site during the PVP in short-term follow-up imaging, as CRLMs may have adjacent microscopic tumor cell extension without clear lesion-to-liver margins. On CE-CT, the area of ablation is a non-enhancing area of low attenuation that will gradually involute over time. If imaging is performed shortly after ablation, there may be rim-enhancement due to hyperemia from thermal injury. Rim-enhancement due to hyperemia can have an irregular contour with variations in thickness. It is circumferential and will subside over time. Discrete, nodular enhancement that does not completely surround the ablation area is suspicious for residual tumor or recurrent disease.

Hepatic artery infusion (HAI) and selective internal radiation therapy (SIRT)

HAI and SIRT are locoregional treatments that target tumor tissue locally, and response to these treatments can be evaluated with CT or MRI. HAI involves infusion of anti-cancer drugs directly into the arterial vessels supplying the liver to deliver high dose chemotherapy locally. Follow up imaging is generally obtained 3–4 weeks after the procedure with CT or dynamic MRI. Similarly, SIRT involves arterial catheter based therapy involving the delivery of radioactive microspheres to the liver. Typically, patients obtain a follow up CT or MRI 3 to 6 months post-procedure.

Conclusion

Multidisciplinary efforts and precision medicine will continue to be of utmost importance to the evaluation and management of patients with CRC and CRLMs. Diagnosis accuracy, pre-surgical planning, and prediction of post-surgical outcomes will improve as imaging techniques continue to evolve. Pre-operative evaluation of patients with CRLMs include contrast-enhanced US, high quality CT or MRI, and FDG-PET if available. Calculation of liver volumetrics is also important for tailoring disease management. Determination of alternative treatment eligibility and treatment response evaluation rely on CT or MRI, with FDG-PET playing a limited role.

Bibliography

Adam, R, Laurent, A, Azoulay, D, Castaing, D, & Bismuth, H. (2000). Two-Stage Hepatectomy: A Planned Strategy to Treat Irresectable Liver Tumors. *Annals of Surgery, 232*(6), 777. doi:10.1097/00000658-200012000-00006.

Baghdadi, A, Ghadimi, M, Mirpour, S, et al. (2021). Imaging neuroendocrine tumors: Characterizing the spectrum of radiographic findings. *Surgical Oncology, 37*, 101529. doi:10.1016/j.suronc.2021.101529.

Baghdadi, A, Mirpour, S, Ghadimi, M, et al. (2021). Imaging of Colorectal Liver Metastasis. *Journal of Gastrointestinal Surgery, 18* Published online October. doi:10.1007/s11605-021-05164-1.

Bennett P, Mintz A, Perry B, Trout AT, Vergara-Wentland P, eds. Approach to Interpretation. In: Specialty Imaging: PET (pp. 813). (2018). Elsevier. doi:10.1016/B978-0-323-52484-1.50010-8.

Bismuth, H, Adam, R, Lévi, F, et al. (1996). Resection of nonresectable liver metastases from colorectal cancer after neoadjuvant chemotherapy. *Annals of surgery, 224*(4), 509–522. doi:10.1097/00000658-199610000-00009.

Caraiani, C, Petresc, B, Dong, Y, & Dietrich, CF. (2019). Contraindications and adverse effects in abdominal imaging. *Medical Ultrasonography, 21*(4), 456–463. doi:10.11152/mu-2145.

Catalano, O, Nunziata, A, Lobianco, R, & Siani, A. (2005). Real-Time Harmonic Contrast Material–specific US of Focal Liver Lesions. *Radiographics, 25*(2), 333–349. doi:10.1148/RG.252045066.

Catalano, OA, Singh, AH, Uppot, RN, Hahn, PF, Ferrone, CR, & Sahani, DV (2008). Vascular and Biliary Variants in the Liver: Implications for Liver Surgery1. *Radiographics, 28*(2), 359–378. doi:10.1148/RG.282075099.

Covey, AM, Brody, LA, Maluccio, MA, Getrajdman, GI, & Brown, KT. (2002). Variant Hepatic Arterial Anatomy Revisited: Digital Subtraction Angiography Performed in 600 Patients. *Radiology, 224*(2), 542–547. doi:10.1148/RADIOL.2242011283.

Dixon, M, Cruz, J, Sarwani, N, & Gusani, N. (2021). The Future Liver Remnant: Definition, Evaluation, and Management. *American Surgeon, 87*(2), 276–286. doi:10.1177/0003134820951451.

Ellebæk, SB, Fristrup, CW, & Mortensen, MB. (2017). Intraoperative Ultrasound as a Screening Modality for the Detection of Liver Metastases during Resection of Primary Colorectal Cancer – A Systematic Review. *Ultrasound International Open, 3*(2), E60. doi:10.1055/S-0043-100503.

Folprecht, G. (2016). Liver Metastases in Colorectal Cancer. *American Society of Clinical Oncology Educational Book, 3*(5), 278–279. doi:10.1200/EDBK_159185.

Fong, Y, Fortner, J, Sun, RL, Brennan, MF, & Blumgart, LH. (1999). Clinical Score for Predicting Recurrence After Hepatic Resection for Metastatic Colorectal Cancer: Analysis of 1001 Consecutive Cases. *Annals of Surgery, 230*(3), 309. doi:10.1097/00000658-199909000-00004.

Frydrychowicz, A, Lubner, MG, Brown, JJ, et al. (2012). Hepatobiliary MR imaging with gadolinium-based contrast agents. *Journal of Magnetic Resonance Imaging, 35*(3), 492–511. doi:10.1002/jmri.22833.

Ghadimi, M, Pandey, P, Rezvani Habibabadi, R, et al. (2021). Role of volumetric multiparametric MRI in distinguishing between intraductal papillary mucinous neoplasms and serous cystadenoma. *Abdominal Radiology, 46*(4), 1629–1639. doi:10.1007/s00261-020-02792-0.

Hale, HL, Husband, JE, Gossios, K, Norman, AR, & Cunningham, D. (1998). CT of calcified liver metastases in colorectal carcinoma. *Clinical Radiology, 53*(10), 735–741. doi:10.1016/S0009-9260(98)80315-2.

Hazhirkarzar, B, Tang, H, Ghadimi, M, et al. (2021). Predicting early necrosis of colorectal liver metastases using volumetric enhancement on baseline MRI and oil deposition on post-cTACE unenhanced CT. *Abdominal Radiology, 46*(10), 4610–4618. doi:10.1007/s00261-021-03133-5.

Hernandez-Alejandro, R, Ruffolo, LI, Alikhanov, R, Björnsson, B, Torres, OJM, & Serrablo, A. (2020). Associating Liver Partition and Portal Vein Ligation for Staged Hepatectomy (ALPPS) procedure for colorectal liver metastasis. *International Journal of Surgery, 82*, 103–108. doi:10.1016/J.IJSU.2020.04.009.

Ito, K, Govindarajan, A, Ito, H, & Fong, Y. (2010). Surgical treatment of hepatic colorectal metastasis: Evolving role in the setting of improving systemic therapies and ablative treatments in the 21st century. *Cancer Journal, 16*(2), 103–110. doi:10.1097/PPO.0B013E3181D7E8E5.

Jaeck, D, Oussoultzoglou, E, Rosso, E, Greget, M, Weber, JC, & Bachellier, P. (2004). A Two-Stage Hepatectomy Procedure Combined With Portal Vein Embolization to Achieve Curative Resection for Initially Unresectable Multiple and Bilobar Colorectal Liver Metastases. *Annals of Surgery, 240*(6), 1037. doi:10.1097/01.SLA.0000145965.86383.89.

Jaeck, D, & Pessaux, P. (2008). Bilobar Colorectal Liver Metastases: Treatment Options. *Surgical Oncology Clinics of North America, 17*, 553–568. doi:10.1016/j.soc.2008.02.006.

Kaur, H, Hindman, NM, Al-Refaie, WB, et al. (2017). ACR Appropriateness Criteria® Suspected Liver Metastases. *Journal of the American College of Radiology, 14*(5), S314–S325. doi:10.1016/J.JACR.2017.01.037.

Khaliq, AA, Nsiah, E, Bilal, NH, & Hughes, DR (2014). Duszak R. The Scope and Distribution of Imaging Services at Critical Access Hospitals. *Journal of the American College of Radiology, 11*(9), 857–862. doi:10.1016/J.JACR.2014.02.013.

Kinkel, K, Lu, Y, Both, M, Warren, RS, & Thoeni, RF. (2002). Detection of Hepatic Metastases from Cancers of the Gastrointestinal Tract by Using Noninvasive Imaging Methods (US, CT, MR Imaging, PET): A Meta-Analysis. *Radiology, 224*(3), 748–756. doi:10.1148/RADIOL.2243011362.

Kodzwa R. ACR Manual on Contrast Media: 2018 Updates. Vol 91; 2019.

Kornprat, P, Jarnagin, WR, Gonen, M, et al. (2006). Outcome After Hepatectomy for Multiple (Four or More) Colorectal Metastases in the Era of Effective Chemotherapy. *Annals of Surgical Oncology, 14*(3), 1151–1160. doi:10.1245/S10434-006-9068-Y.

Lang, H, Baumgart, J, & Mittler, J. (2020). Associated Liver Partition and Portal Vein Ligation for Staged Hepatectomy (ALPPS) Registry: What Have We Learned? *Gut and Liver, 14*(6), 699. doi:10.5009/GNL19233.

Liapi, E, & Kamel, IR (2008). The Role of Imaging in the Management of Patients with Potentially Resectable Colorectal Metastases. In JL Marshall, & MA Choti (Eds.), *Managing Colorectal Cancer: The Resectable and Potentially Resectable Patient - A Multidisciplinary Approach* (pp. 17–41). CMPMedica.

Limanond, P, Zimmerman, P, Raman, SS, Kadell, BM, & Lu, DSK. (2012). Interpretation of CT and MRI After Radiofrequency Ablation of Hepatic Malignancies. *American Journal of Roentgenology, 181*(6), 1635–1640. doi:10.2214/AJR.181.6.1811635.

Llimpe, FLR, Di Fabio, F, Ercolani, G, et al. (2014). Imaging in resectable colorectal liver metastasis patients with or without preoperative chemotherapy: results of the PROMETEO-01 study. *British Journal of Cancer, 111*(4), 667. doi:10.1038/BJC.2014.351.

Mainenti, PP. (2015). Non-invasive diagnostic imaging of colorectal liver metastases. *World Journal of Radiology, 7*(7), 157. doi:10.4329/wjr.v7.i7.157.

Manfredi, S, Lepage, C, Hatem, C, Coatmeur, O, Faivre, J, & Bouvier, AM. (2006). Epidemiology and management of liver metastases from colorectal cancer. *Annals of Surgery, 244*(2), 254–259. doi:10.1097/01.SLA.0000217629.94941.CF.

Mathew, RP, & Venkatesh, SK. (2018). Liver vascular anatomy: a refresher. *Abdominal Radiology, 43*(8), 1886–1895. doi:10.1007/S00261-018-1623-Z.

May, BJ, & Madoff, DC. (2012). Portal vein embolization: Rationale, technique, and current application. *Seminars in Interventional Radiology, 29*(2), 81–89. doi:10.1055/s-0032-1312568.

Park, MH, Hyunchul, R, Kim, YS, Dongil, C, & Hyo, KL (2008). Won JL. Spectrum of CT findings after radio-frequency ablation of hepatic tumors. *Radiographics, 28*(2), 379–390. doi:10.1148/RG.282075038/ASSET/IMAGES/LARGE/G08MR01G15C.JPEG.

Pawlik, TM, Schulick, RD, & Choti, MA. (2008). Expanding Criteria for Resectability of Colorectal Liver Metastases. *The Oncologist, 13*(1), 51–64. doi:10.1634/THEONCOLOGIST.2007-0142.

Scatarige, JC, Fishman, EK, Saksouk, FA, & Siegelman, SS. (1983). Computed Tomography of Calcified Liver Masses. *Journal of Computer Assisted Tomography, 7*(1), 83–89.

Schmidt, S, Demartines, N, Soler, L, Schnyder, P, & Denys, A (2008). Portal Vein Normal Anatomy and Variants: Implication for Liver Surgery and Portal Vein Embolization. *Seminars in Interventional Radiology, 25*(2), 86. doi:10.1055/S-2008-1076688.

Shaghaghi, M, AliyariG hasabeh, M, Ameli, S, et al. (2020). Role of tumor margin and ADC change in defining the need for additional treatments after the first TACE in patients with unresectable HCC. *European Journal of Radiology, 133*, 109389. doi:10.1016/j.ejrad.2020.109389.

Spelt, L, Andersson, B, Nilsson, J, & Andersson, R. (2012). Prognostic models for outcome following liver resection for colorectal cancer metastases: A systematic review. *European journal of surgical oncology : the journal of the European Society of Surgical Oncology and the British Association of Surgical Oncology, 38*(1), 16–24. doi:10.1016/J.EJSO.2011.10.013.

Sung, H, Ferlay, J, Siegel, RL, et al. (2021). Global Cancer Statistics 2020: GLOBOCAN Estimates of Incidence and Mortality Worldwide for 36 Cancers in 185 Countries. *CA: A Cancer Journal for Clinicians, 71*(3), 209–249. doi:10.3322/CAAC.21660.

Sureka, B, Patidar, Y, Bansal, K, Rajesh, S, Agrawal, N, & Arora, A. (2015). Portal vein variations in 1000 patients: surgical and radiological importance. *The British Journal of Radiology, 88*, 1055. doi:10.1259/BJR.20150326.

Tai, K, Komatsu, S, Sofue, K, et al. (2020). Total tumour volume as a prognostic factor in patients with resectable colorectal cancer liver metastases. *BJS Open, 4*(3), 456–466. doi:10.1002/BJS5.50280.

van Kessel, CS, Buckens, CFM, van den Bosch, MAAJ, van Leeuwen, MS, van Hillegersberg, R, & Verkooijen, HM (2012). Preoperative Imaging of Colorectal Liver Metastases After Neoadjuvant Chemotherapy: A Meta-Analysis. *Annals of Surgical Oncology, 19*(9), 2805. doi:10.1245/S10434-012-2300-Z.

van Vledder, MG, Torbenson, MS, Pawlik, TM, et al. (2010). The Effect of Steatosis on Echogenicity of Colorectal Liver Metastases on Intraoperative Ultrasonography. *Archives of Surgery, 145*(7), 661–667. doi:10.1001/ARCHSURG.2010.124.

Vauthey, JN, Pawlik, TM, Ribero, D, et al. (2016). Chemotherapy Regimen Predicts Steatohepatitis and an Increase in 90-Day Mortality After Surgery for Hepatic Colorectal Metastases. *Journal of Clinical Oncology, 24*(13), 2065–2072. doi:10.1200/JCO.2005.05.3074.

Vilgrain, V, Esvan, M, Ronot, M, Caumont-Prim, A, Aubé, C, & Chatellier, G. (2016). A meta-analysis of diffusion-weighted and gadoxetic acid-enhanced MR imaging for the detection of liver metastases. *European Radiology, 26*(12), 4595–4615. doi:10.1007/S00330-016-4250-5.

Wong, S, Mangu, P, Choti, M, et al. (2010). American Society of Clinical Oncology 2009 clinical evidence review on radiofrequency ablation of hepatic metastases from colorectal cancer. *Journal of clinical oncology : official journal of the American Society of Clinical Oncology, 28*(3), 493–508. doi:10.1200/JCO.2009.23.4450.

CHAPTER

4

Use of molecular markers and other personalized factors in treatment decisions for metastatic colorectal cancer

Alex B. Blair, MD[a], *Laura L. Tenner, MD, MPH*[b] *and Bradley N. Reames, MD, MS, FACS*[c]

[a]Department of Surgery, Johns Hopkins Hospital, Baltimore, MD, USA [b]Division of Medical Oncology, Department of Internal Medicine, University of Nebraska Medical Center, Omaha, NE, USA [c]Division of Surgical Oncology, Department of Surgery, University of Nebraska Medical Center, Omaha, NE, USA

Introduction

Colorectal cancer (CRC) is a leading cause of cancer death. While overall survival of non-metastatic disease exceeds 60 percent, a significant portion of patients will develop metastasis and succumb to disease. Furthermore, nearly a quarter of patients present with metastasis at the time of diagnosis, a majority of which are not initially amenable to curative resection. Even among those patients who are eligible for curative intent surgical exploration, 10-year survival is less than 25 percent and over half will experience disease recurrence by 5 years (Bredt and Rachid, 2014; Fong, Fortner, Sun, Brennan, and Blumgart, 1999). As a result, a better understanding of cancer biology (how cancer cells grow, invade, establish metastatic potential, metastasize, adapt to foreign environments, and persist despite treatment) is imperative to continued improvements in therapeutic effectiveness and oncologic outcomes. With the evolution of combination chemotherapy, targeted therapeutics and aggressive multidisciplinary approaches, patient survival for metastatic colorectal cancer (mCRC) has greatly improved in recent decades and is now over 36 months for patients with unresectable disease (Fakih, 2015; Hamers et al., 2019).

Contemporary Management of Metastatic Colorectal Cancer: A Precision Medicine Approach
DOI: https://doi.org/10.1016/B978-0-323-91706-3.00002-3

Nevertheless, CRC remains a biologically heterogenous disease with diverse genetic origins, molecular and clinical presentations, treatment responses and outcomes. Historical one-size-fits-all approaches to systemic therapy have slowly evolved to more personalized approaches, guided by emerging evidence that the effectiveness of systemic therapy may be improved if tailored to the genetic, molecular, and disease characteristics of each unique patient. As a result, the identification of unique patient or disease characteristics that influence tumor biology or therapeutic response are essential for multidisciplinary management of mCRC.

Prognostic versus predictive

Modern approaches to personalized therapy for mCRC require a thorough understanding of the differences between a "prognostic" and a "predictive" biomarker. In this context, "biomarker" is defined as any measurement variable that is associated with a disease outcome (Ballman, 2015). A biomarker may take many different forms, from a single measurement (carcinoembryonic antigen [CEA] level) to a collection of measurements (signature), such as a colorectal mutation panel. As detailed below, relevant biomarkers to the personalized management of mCRC include various disease characteristics, histology, pharmacogenetic genotype, germline and tumor genotype, primary tumor sidedness, and other emerging measurements.

Biomarkers used to inform management of mCRC may be prognostic, predictive, or both. A prognostic biomarker provides information regarding a likely cancer outcome (e.g. recurrence or death) independent of the therapy received (Ballman, 2015). Examples of prognostic biomarkers relevant to mCRC management include certain histologies (mucinous adenocarcinoma or signet-ring cell adenocarcinoma) and mutations in Kristin-ras (KRAS) or Serine/threonine-protein kinase B-Raf (BRAF). A prognostic biomarker is distinguished from a predictive biomarker, which predicts a differential treatment effect between patients that are biomarker-positive and biomarker-negative (Ballman, 2015). Examples in mCRC include certain enzyme deficiencies (described below) that predict increased toxicity from specific chemotherapeutic agents, and the absence of KRAS mutation (wild-type status), which predicts benefit from the use of an EGFR inhibitor. This chapter will summarize both prognostic and predictive biomarkers currently utilized to inform a personalized approach to multidisciplinary management of mCRC (Table 4.1).

Disease characteristics

Prior to advances in molecular genotyping and targeted therapy, individualized recommendations for multidiscplinary management of mCRC relied heavily on clinical and disease characteristics identified through history, laboratory and imaging evaluations. Multidiscplinary management recommendations regarding the perceived benefit of metastasectomy were informed by the accumulation of disease characteristics associated with worse survival or increased recurrence. Such characteristics included synchronous (vs. metachronous) disease, primary tumor nodal status, margin status following primary tumor resection, disease free

TABLE 4.1 Prognostic and predictive biomarkers in the personalized management of metastatic colorectal cancer.

Biomarker	*Prognostic value*	*Predictive value*
Clinical disease characteristics: **(1)** Synchronous disease **(2)** Nodal metastasis in primary **(3)** Positive margin after resection **(4)** Short disease-free interval **(5)** Increased size **(6)** Increased number **(7)** Presence of extrahepatic disease	Worse prognosis and shorter overall survival	–
Mucinous histology	Worse prognosis and shorter overall survival	Worse response to first line chemotherapeutics, may have better response to irinotecan-based regimens as compared to oxaliplatin
Signet-ring cell histology	Worse prognosis and shorter overall survival. Nearly double the rate of recurrence as conventional adenocarcinoma	–
Deficiency in DPYD	–	Severe toxicity with Fluoropyrimidine-based therapy due to variability in drug clearance
Deficiency in UGT1A1	–	Severe toxicity with Irinotecan-based therapy requiring dose reductions and modifications in deficient patients
KRAS mutation	Worse prognosis, increased risk of aggressive biology, metastatic spread, shorter overall and recurrence free survival Worse survival following hepatic resection in the setting of KRAS codon 12 mutation	EGFR inhibitor therapies such as cetuximab and panitumumab are not effective in KRAS mutated tumors as compared to wild type counterparts Unresectable wild type KRAS tumors see clear benefit with combination EGFR inhibitor plus doublet chemotherapy
BRAF mutation	Worse prognosis and shorter overall survival	Opportunity for therapeutic response with BRAF inhibition with vemurafenib in combination with EGFR inhibitors
HER2 mutation	–	Opportunity for therapeutic response with HER2 inhibition with trastuzumab and/or pertuzumab

(*continued on next page*)

TABLE 4.1 Prognostic and predictive biomarkers in the personalized management of metastatic colorectal cancer—cont'd

Biomarker	***Prognostic value***	***Predictive value***
DNA microsatellite instability	Superior prognosis independent of treatment as compared to microsatellite stable disease Worse prognosis however if MSI in combination with BRAF mutation	Opportunity for therapeutic response with targeted anti-PD1 checkpoint therapy
Right sided colonic disease	Worse overall survival as compared to left sided disease Identifies patients with greater likelihood of KRAS and BRAF mutations	–
Circulating tumor cells (CTCs) and cell free DNA	Worse survival and increased rates of progression when compared to patients without detectable CTCs	Future potential to identify molecular characteristics of metastatic cells feasibly identifying therapeutic targets

interval, number of prior cycles of chemotherapy, CEA levels, presence of extrahepatic disease, and the number, size and location of liver metastases, among others (Fong et al., 1999; Passot et al., 2017). Several clinical scoring systems utilizing combinations of the above characteristics were created to assist individualized management decisions, with the most widely used developed in 1999 by Fong et al. (Fong et al., 1999) to predict outcomes following hepatic resection for mCRC and inform recommendations for surgery. However, while these disease characteristics may assist the differentiation of patients into prognostic subgroups, they do not predict personalized responses to therapy. As the science of personalized therapy has evolved, the influence of disease characteristics on multidisciplinary management of mCRC has lessened.

Histology

Certain histologic subtypes of colorectal adenocarcinoma provide prognostic information for treatment planning. While a majority of CRC are conventional adenocarcinomas, 5–15 percent are mucinous adenocarcinomas, and 1 percent are signet-ring cell adenocarcinomas. Mucinous adenocarcinomas are characterized by an abundance of extracellular mucin that comprises >50 percent of the total tumor mass, while signet-ring cell adenocarcinomas contain cells of peripherally placed nuclei displaced by intracytoplasmic mucin in >50 percent of the total tumor mass (Fadel et al., 2021).

Mucinous adenocarcinomas have a slight female predominance, more commonly occur in the right colon (compared to the left colon or rectum), and present with larger tumors at advanced stages (Fadel et al., 2021). Compared to conventional adenocarcinomas, mucinous adenocarcinomas are more likely to be metastatic (33.6 percent, vs. 27.6 percent respectively), have multiple sites of metastasis (58.6 percent vs. 49.9 percent), and develop carcinomatosis (Hugen, van de Velde, de Wilt, and Nagtegaal, 2014). Following first-line therapy with oxaliplatin and/or irinotectan, mucinous mCRC had significantly lower overall response rates

(18.4 percent) and median overall survivals (14.0 months), when compared to non-mucinous histologies (49 percent and 23.4 months, respectively) (Catalano et al., 2009). Subsequent subgroup analyses suggest improved survival outcomes for patients with mucinous adeno-caricnoma when treated with irinotecan-based regimens, as compared to oxaliplatin-based regimens (Catalano et al., 2018).

Similar to mucinous adenocarcinomas, signet-ring cell adenocarcinomas more frequently occur in the right colon, and present with larger tumors and more advanced stages. Compared to conventional adenocarcinoma, signet-ring adenocarcinomas are also more likely to exhibit metastatic disease (61.2 percent vs. 27.6 percent), have multiple sites of metastasis (70.7 percent vs. 49.9 percent), and develop carcinomatosis (Fadel et al., 2021; Hugen et al., 2014). Five year survival ranges from 0–12 percent, and rates of recurrence are nearly double (77 percent) rates for conventional adenocarcinoma (38 percent) (Tajiri et al., 2017). Molecular studies of signet-ring cell colorectal adenocarcinomas suggest increased rates of BRAF mutations and microsatellite instability (Tajiri et al., 2017). Consequently, microsatellite analysis should be performed routinely, and immunotherapy should be considered for any patients with MSI-high tumors.

Pharmacogenetics for conventional cytotoxic chemotherapy

Pharmacogenetics is the analysis of how genetic variation can lead to a differential response to a pharmacologic agent. Despite significant progress in the development of immunotherapy and molecular targeted agents, cytotoxic chemotherapy regimens remain the primary treatment in mCRC. Though there are no specific biomarkers used in practice to help guide cytotoxic chemotherapy treatments, some pharmacogenetic tools are available to guide individualized evaluation if patients experience significant toxicities from a given chemotherapy. Deficiencies in dihydropyrimidine dehydrogenase (DPYD) and uridine diphosphate glucuronosyltransferase (UGT)1A1, though rare, are two examples of pharmacogenetic biomarkers currently utilized to guide personalized therapy in mCRC.

Fluoropyrimidines, such as 5-FU and capecitabine, are cornerstones of systemic therapy for mCRC. 5-FU is a fluorine-substituted analogue of uracil whose active metabolites cause cytotoxicity and apoptosis through disruption of DNA synthesis. DPYD is responsible for the initial and rate-limiting step of 5-FU catabolism, and converts 80 percent of 5-FU in the liver to inactive dihydrofluorouracil. Patients with genetic variants leading to a deficiency of DPYD may experience variable systemic clearance of fluoropyrimidies, leading to increased rates of drug toxicity (Varughese et al., 2020). While the role of empiric testing remains unclear, patients experiencing severe toxicity with fluoropyrimidines should receive DPYD testing. Patients with partial deficiency may tolerate a reduced dose, but therapy with fluoropyrimidines is contraindicated in those with a complete deficiency. As a result, DPYD deficiency can limit available therapeutics, and negatively impact prognosis.

Irinotecan is another commonly used chemotherapeutic for mCRC. Similar to fluoropyrimidines, irinotectan is a prodrug that undergoes conversion to active metabolites, which exert cytotoxic effects through inhibition of topoisomerase I leading to irreparable DNA damage and cell cycle arrest. UGT1A1 is a critical enzyme in the metabolism of active metabolites of irinotecan, which results in elimination through bile (70 percent) or urine (30 percent).

Similar to DPYD deficiency, polymorphisms in the UGT1A1 gene may result in varying levels of enzyme activity, impaired elimination of active metabolites of irinotecan, and severe dose-limiting toxicities (particularly neutropenia) in up to 25 percent of patients. Patients exhibiting severe toxicity while receiving irinotectan should be tested, and guidelines exist to guide dose reductions and subsequent dose modifications in patients found to be deficient (Varughese et al., 2020).

KRAS

Kristin-ras (KRAS) is a proto-oncogene that encodes a GTPase protein and plays a key role in the intracellular signal transduction downstream of membrane-bound receptors such as epidermal growth factor receptor (EGFR). Mutation in KRAS leads to constitutive activation in the mitogen activated protein kinase (MAPK) pathway irrespective of independent activation of the upstream EGFR receptor, resulting in unregulated cell growth, proliferation, survival, migration, and invasion (Fig. 4.1) (Tan and Du, 2012). Activating KRAS mutations are described in multiple malignancies and are identified in nearly 30–50 percent of CRC cases (Karapetis et al., 2008).

KRAS in an important prognostic and predictive biomarker in the treatment of metastatic colorectal cancer. Prognostically, KRAS mutated tumors in mCRC are associated with worse outcomes, including an increased risk of aggressive biology, metastatic spread, recurrence, and death (Margonis et al., 2015; Vauthey et al., 2013; Yaeger et al., 2015). Data from patients undergoing hepatic resection for mCRC show KRAS mutation was independently associated with worse PFS and OS (Margonis et al., 2015; Vauthey et al., 2013). Within variants of KRAS mutations, KRAS codon 12 (a glycine to valine, G12V, or glycine to serine, G12S) has been associated with worse recurrence free survival across all stages of mCRC (Andreyev et al., 2001; Margonis et al., 2015). Because of the prognostic implications of KRAS mutations, data suggest curative resection may not be beneficial in the metastatic setting in KRAS mutant patients who also have other poor clinical prognostic features, such as node positive disease or large metastases (Passot et al., 2017).

The presence of a KRAS mutation also serves as a predictive biomarker for the therapeutic effectiveness of certain treatments, such as EGFR inhibitor therapy. Cetuximab is a recombinant human-mouse chimeric monoclonal antibody that binds to the extracellular domain of EGFR, blocking phosphorylation and thus the activation of downstream kinases. Cetuximab and panitumumab, an alternative EGFR inhibitor, are both approved by the FDA for use in advanced mCRC (Vale et al., 2012). Multiple clinical trials have demonstrated the benefit of anti-EGFR therapy in KRAS wild-type (KRASWT) tumors. Mechanistically, anti-EGFR therapy is not beneficial in KRAS mutated patients because of the independent constitutive activation of KRAS downstream of EGFR, which continually promotes cell growth and division.

The OPUS trial investigated the use of combination chemotherapy with and without cetuximab for unresectable mCRC. Results indicated a superior overall response and PFS in KRAS WT tumors treated with cetuximab, while patients with KRAS mutated tumors derived no benefit (Bokemeyer et al., 2009). The CRYSTAL trial similarly investigated FOLFIRI with and without cetuximab as first line therapy for mCRC. The trial found that the addition of

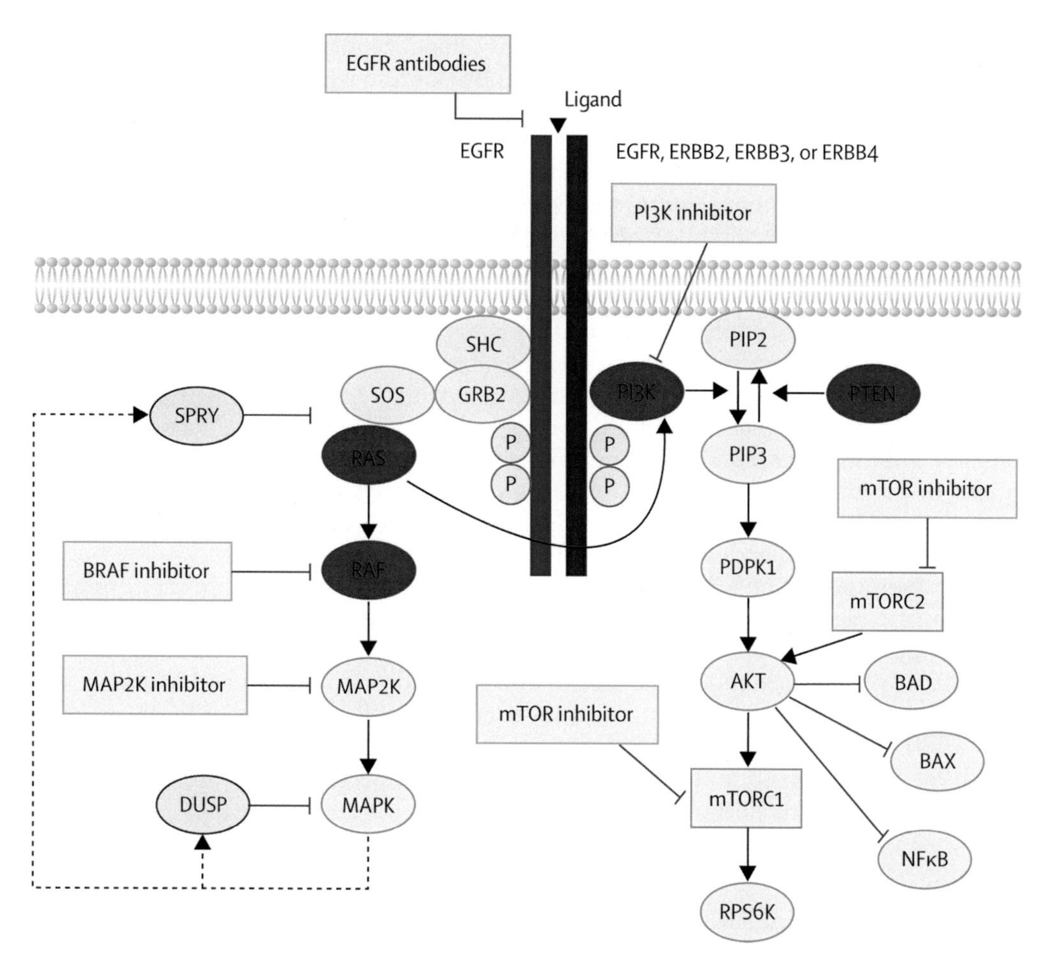

FIGURE 4.1 EGFR-mediated signalling pathways and possible targeted therapy options (Adopted from: De Roock W at al. KRAS, BRAF, PIK3CA, and PTEN mutations: implications for targeted therapies in metastatic colorectal cancer; Lancet Oncol. 2011;12:594–603).

cetuximab to FOLFIRI resulted in significantly longer PFS (9.9 months vs. 8.4 months) and OS (23.5 months vs. 20.0 months) in a subgroup of patients with KRAS WT versus KRAS mutated tumors (Van Cutsem et al., 2011, 2009). Similar studies evaluating panitumumab in combination with best supportive care for KRAS WT patients progressing on standard chemotherapy demonstrated improved PFS with the addition of an EGFR-inhibitor compared to FOLFOX alone (Douillard et al., 2014; Van Cutsem et al., 2007).

Trials evaluating use of cetuximab in the perioperative setting for patients with initially unresectable mCRC corroborate results seen in the palliative setting for patients with unresectable disease. Numerous trials evaluating cetuximab in combination with FOLFOX or FOLFIRI have published rates of R0 resection in initially unresectable KRAS WT patients that are significantly improved compared to rates following chemotherapy alone (Poston et al., 2017). In the BELIEF study, for example, R0 resection rates with cetuximab were

26.7 percent, vs. 6.3 percent with chemotherapy alone. Similarly promising results were reported in the prospective nonrandomized trial by Somashekhar at al. Among 46 patients with initially unresectable KRAS WT mCRC that received cetuximab and chemotherapy, all patients that experienced objective response (28, 60.9 percent) went on to receive R0 resections (Somashekhar, Ashwin, Zaveri, Rauthan, and Patil, 2016). Thus, in the setting of initially unresectable metastatic liver lesions, data support the preferential use of the combination of an EGFR inhibitor plus doublet chemotherapy for the conversion of unresectable lesions to potentially treat with curative intent resection in KRAS wt mCRC patients.

However, despite clear evidence of benefit for patients with unresectable KRAS WT mCRC, a multicenter, phase III trial for patients with resectable disease suggested a survival detriment with the addition of cetuximab to perioperative treatment. The New EPOC trial randomized KRAS WT patients with resectable mCRC to receive chemotherapy with or without cetuximab before and after liver resection. Although no statistical difference was seen in the primary endpoint of progression-free survival, median overal survival was 26 months shorter for patients that received cetuximab (81.0 vs. 55.4 months) (Bridgewater et al., 2020). As a result, cetuximab is not recommended for mCRC patients with resectable disease.

Though the majority of KRAS WT tumor respond to EGFR inhibition, there remains a proportion of patients who fail to respond, likely indicating mechanisms of resistance requiring further investigation. Mutations in other RAS family oncogenes such as NRAS and HRAS similarly identify tumor resistance to anti-EGFR therapy (Shaib and Mahajan, 2013). Other genes in the phosphorylation pathway functioning downstream of EGFR, including PI3K, PTEN, MAPK, MEK, have not proven to be reliable predictive biomarkers of EGFR response for mCRC (Shaib and Mahajan, 2013), and investigations into the origins of anti-EGFR resistance in this cohort of patients is ongoing.

BRAF

Serine/threonine-protein kinase B-Raf (BRAF) is a protein kinase that plays a critical role in the MAPK cell signaling pathway downstream of KRAS. BRAF mutations are identified in fewer than 10 percent of all CRC cases. BRAF signaling exists in the same MAPK pathway as KRAS, and functional mutations in each of these genes result in a similar phenotype with similar therapeutic implications (Fig. 4.1). BRAF mutation is a prognostic biomarker associated with higher rates of peritoneal and distant lymph node involvement for mCRC, worse outcomes, and poorer survival (Tie and Desai, 2015; Tran et al., 2011). Among patients with mCRC undergoing curative intent hepatectomy, BRAF mutation was associated with decreased survival compared to both BRAF WT and KRAS mutated tumors (Karagkounis et al., 2013; Schirripa et al., 2015).

In addition, BRAF also acts as a predictive marker. Early efforts in targeted drug therapy in melanoma discovered a direct BRAF inhibitor, vemurafenib. Studies were conducted to see if there was similar benefit for BRAF inhibition in colorectal cancer. OS benefit was obtained when BRAF inhibition was combined with EGFR inhibitors (Le et al., 2015; Lochhead et al., 2013). Newer generation BRAF inhibition therapy, encorafenib in combination with EGFR inhibition, is an effective treatment option in BRAF mutated mCRC patients.

HER2

Human epidermal growth factor 2 (HER2) plays a critical role in intracellular signal transduction and is an additional attractive target for mCRC. The role of HER2 in the pathogenesis of breast cancer as well as the targeted use of trastuzumab and other HER2 inhibition agents is well established. Even though a small portion of the mCRC population (less than 10 percent) overexpresses HER2, numerous studies have focused on HER2 mutations in this population because of the multiple targeted options available (Meric-Bernstam et al., 2019; Sartore-Bianchi et al., 2016; Siena et al., 2021). The landmark study was a phase II trial investigating the use of HER2 inhibition in treatment-refractory HER2 mutated mCRC and identified a 32 percent objective response rate, with 2 percent having a complete response (Meric-Bernstam et al., 2019). HER2 inhibition options have expanded to include combinations of trastuzumab with pertuzumab, trastuzumab with lapatinib, or Fam-trastuzumab deruxtecan-nxki. While only representing a small proportion of all mCRC patients, HER2 amplified disease serves as a predictive biomarker for HER2 targeted therapy with the opportunity for therapeutic response (Hainsworth et al., 2018; Meric-Bernstam et al., 2019; Wang et al., 2020).

DNA microsatellite instability and immunotherapy

Microsatellites are repetitive units within DNA maintained by the mismatch repair (MMR) system. Deficiencies in specific genes in the MMR system (MLH1, MSH2, MSH6, PMS2 or TACSTD1) result in high levels of microsatellite instability (MSI-H) which predisposes genomic instability and subsequent tumor proliferation. These MMR deficiencies can arise sporadically as hypermethylation or as germline mutations (Goldstein et al., 2014). Microsatellite instability (MSI) is both an effective prognostic and predictive biomarker. Compared to patients with mCRC and microsatellite stable (MSS) disease, MSI-H CRC confers a superior prognosis independent of treatment (Goldstein et al., 2014; Koopman et al., 2009). If a BRAF mutation is also present, it identifies hypermethylation as the origin of MSI-H, and thus a sporadic (not germline) mutation. The finding of concomitant BRAF mutation decreases the likelihood of Lynch syndrome and is associated with a significantly worse OS when compared to MSI-H BRAF WT counterparts (Goldstein et al., 2014; Lochhead et al., 2013).

Immunotherapy has emerged as a revolutionary therapy for certain immunogenic metastatic cancers. Monoclonal antibodies against different immune checkpoints, such as cytotoxic T-lymphocyte antigen 4 (CTLA-4), or programmed cell death protein 1 (PD1), promote increased cancer antigen recognition by the native immune system, and in some cases have led to dramatic therapeutic responses in metastatic patients. Anti-PD1 IgG4 monoclonal antibodies, such as nivolumab and pembrolizumab, have been developed to target PD-1 resulting in increased T cell activation, activity, and subsequent tumor regression. Anti-PD-1 therapies have shown dramatic responses in a small cohort of mCRC patients. A seminal paper by Le et al. leveraged the unique immunogenic phenotype of MSI-H mCRC and investigated the use of targeted anti-PD1 therapy in 28 patients with MMR deficient/MSI-H and 25 patients with proficient MMR/MSS mCRC, respectively (Le et al., 2015). Median PFS and OS was

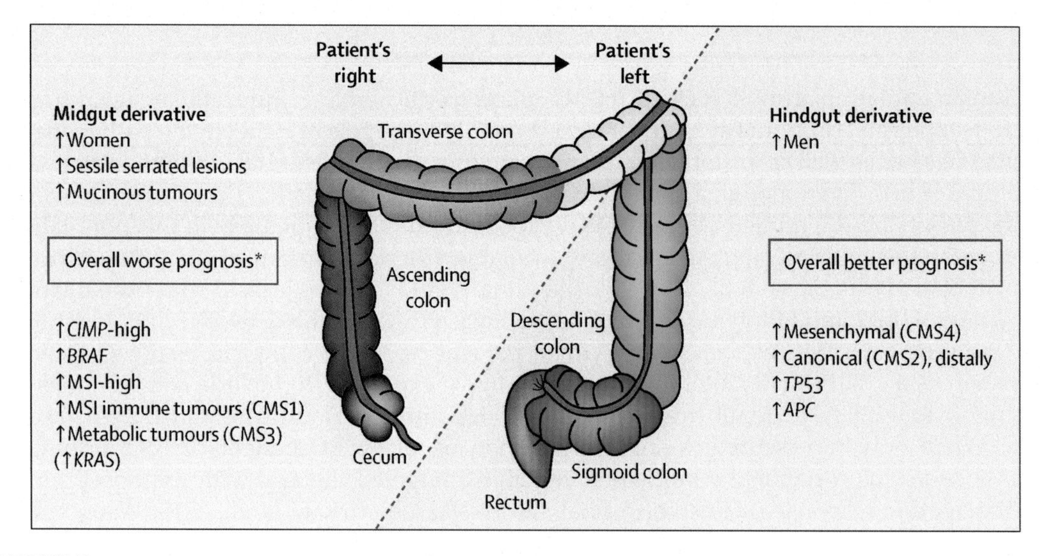

FIGURE 4.2 Clinical, histologic, and molecular differences between right-sided and left-sided colorectal cancer. (Adopted from: Dekker E et al. Colorectal Cancer. Lancet 2019 Oct 19;394 (10,207):1467–80).

not reached for MSI-H patients, compared to 2.4 and 6 months respectively for the MSS cohort, strongly supporting that MMR status predicted a clinical benefit of immune checkpoint blockade (Le et al., 2015). Patients with sporadic MSI-H mutations had a 100 percent objective response to immunotherapy compared to only 27 percent in those with Lynch syndrome (Le et al., 2015). This led to FDA approval for anti-PD1 checkpoint therapy for MSI-H mCRC. These findings are further supported by multiple subsequent trials reporting a durable benefit of anti-PD1 checkpoint therapy in patients with MSI-H mCRC and now represent a standard of care option for first line treatment (Casak et al., 2021; Overman et al., 2017). However, as only a small subset of patients have mCRC with MSI-H and will potentially benefit from immunotherapy, further research is needed to investigate the effectiveness of immunotherapy in mCRC outside of this niche population.

Tumor sidedness

Studies show cancers arising from the right and the left regions of large intestine are clinically and molecular distinct (Fig. 4.2) (de Boer et al., 2020; Malakorn et al., 2021). This is hypothesized to result from the distinct embryologic origins of these two regions. As a result, the location of the primary tumor itself can serve as a prognostic indicator for individuals with mCRC. The right side of the colon (cecum, ascending colon and proximal two-thirds of the transverse colon) arises from the embryologic midgut and is supplied by the superior mesenteric artery, while the left side (distal one third of transverse colon, descending colon, sigmoid and rectum) arises from the embryologic hindgut and is supplied by the inferior mesenteric artery. Molecular characterizations of right-sided CRC are more commonly hypermutated with increasing prevalence of MSI, RAS and BRAF mutations, while left-sided

CRC more frequently exhibit loss of heterozygosity and chromosomal instability (Fig. 4.2) (Benedix et al., 2010). After adjusting for clinical factors, tumor sidedness has been shown to be a prognostic biomarker, with significantly better OS seen in patients with left-sided colon cancer compared to right-sided counterparts. (Shida et al., 2020).

In addition, sidedness of the primary tumor can help inform therapeutic decisions, such as anti-VEGF and anti-EGFR targeted therapeutics (Petrelli et al., 2017). A recent meta-analysis indicated that left sided mCRC patients with KRAS WT and BRAF WT tumors experienced improved responses and longer OS when treated with anti-VEGF therapies compared to patients with right-sided tumors (Loupakis et al., 2018). Furthermore, numerous trials investigating the use of anti-EGFR targeted therapy for mCRC show benefit in patients with left-sided tumors, with improvements in survival compared to chemotherapy alone or chemotherapy with anti-VEGF therapies (Holch, Ricard, Stintzing, Modest, and Heinemann, 2017; Petrelli et al., 2017; Tejpar et al., 2017). When analyzing right-sided KRAS WT cohorts, numerous studies reported poorer responses to anti-EGFR therapies (Holch et al., 2017; Petrelli et al., 2017; Tejpar et al., 2017).

Circulating tumor cells and cell free DNA

Circulating tumor cells (CTCs) can be measured in the peripheral blood of patients with mCRC and are an intriguing prognostic biomarker associated with disease progression and poor survival, when compared to patients without detectable CTCs (Groot Koerkamp, Rahbari, Buchler, Koch, and Weitz, 2013). Recent studies suggest identification of CTCs in the perioperative setting is associated with early recurrence and may inform prognosis following hepatic resection of mCRC (Koch et al., 2005). CTCs may also serve to assess therapeutic response in mCRC, as conversion from high to low CTCs during or after therapy suggests improved prognosis, while persistently high CTCs, even despite radiographic response, is associated with shorter survivals (Barbazan et al., 2014).

Circulating tumor DNA (ctDNA) are fragments of nucleic acid not associated with tumor cells found in the peripheral blood. Similar to CTCs, the detection of ctDNA and their corresponding levels are associated with response to therapy and subsequent radiographic response (Tie et al., 2015). Analysis of ctDNA "liquid biopsies" may serve as a platform to generate molecular profiles to capture the heterogeneity of an individual patient's mCRC. The genomic phenotype of ctDNA or CTCs in theory may more accurately represent the molecular characteristics of metastatic cells compared to the primary tumor. Though the literature on routine use of CTC and ctDNA in mCRC is evolving, the ease of collection and longitudinal assessment identify them as attractive biomarkers to inform tumor biology, assess treatment efficacy, detect emergence of tumor resistance, guide therapeutic changes, and identify patients at highest risk of recurrence. Further efforts to improve the isolation, characterization, detection and interpretation of CTCs and ctDNA are ongoing.

Gut microbiome

The gut microbiome is another exciting area of research in the personalized management of mCRC. Emerging literature suggests CRC causes compositional and ecological changes in

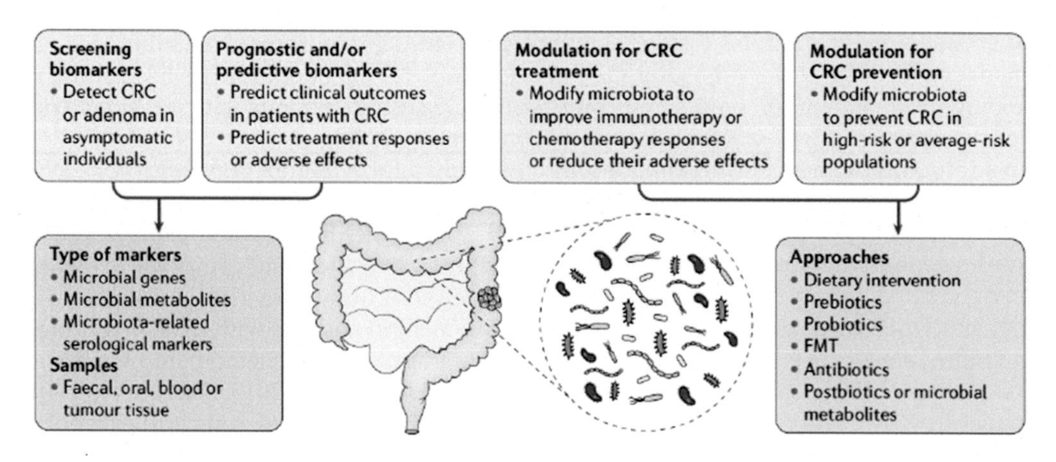

FIGURE 4.3 Possible clinical applications related to gut microbiota in metastatic colorectal cancer (Adopted from: Wong SH et al. Gut microbiota in colorectal cancer: mechanisms of action and clinical applications. Nat Rev Gast Hep. 2019;16:690–704).

the gut microbiome, while studies in animals have indicated various bacteria have important roles in carcinogenesis (Fig. 4.3). Other evidence suggests gut microbiota is involved in CRC progression and response to therapy. As our understanding of the relationship between gut microbiota and CRC continues to evolve, changes in microbiota or detection of specific bacteria may serve as a future biomarker for screening, prognosis, or assessment of treatment response. In addition, modulation of the gut microbiota may one day serve as a strategy to enhance the effectiveness of treatment and reduce adverse events in patient with CRC (Wong and Yu, 2019).

Conclusions

The treatment approach for metastat metastatic colorectal cancer continues to evolve away from the historical approach of broadly-applied recommendations for cytotoxic chemotherapeutic regimens. Instead, systemic therapy choices are increasingly guided by pathologic and molecular biomarkers of the individual patient and their tumor, which inform the provider's understanding of overall prognosis, and potential increased effectiveness of certain therapies. These biomarkers include tumor histology, sidedness and consequent biologic behavior, pharmacogenetics and associated changes in gene expression, specific tumor mutations with corresponding therapeutic targets, and microsatellite instability, which provides opportunities for immunotherapeutics. There is hope that survival for metastatic colorectal cancer will continue to improve with ongoing research and investment in identification of reliable prognostic and predictive biomarkers to optimize thearapeutic decision making for individual patients.

References

Andreyev, H. J., Norman, A. R., Cunningham, D., Oates, J., Dix, B. R., Iacopetta, B. J., …, & Urosevic, N. (2001). Kirsten ras mutations in patients with colorectal cancer: the 'RASCAL II' study. *British Journal of Cancer*, 85(5), 692–696.

Ballman, K. V. (2015). Biomarker: predictive or Prognostic? *Journal of Clinical Oncology*, 33(33), 3968–3971.

Barbazan, J., Muinelo-Romay, L., Vieito, M., Candamio, S., Diaz-Lopez, A., Cano, A., …, & Lopez-Lopez, R. (2014). A multimarker panel for circulating tumor cells detection predicts patient outcome and therapy response in metastatic colorectal cancer. *International Journal of Cancer*, 135(11), 2633–2643.

Benedix, F., Kube, R., Meyer, F., Schmidt, U., Gastinger, I., & Lippert, H. (2010). Comparison of 17,641 patients with right- and left-sided colon cancer: differences in epidemiology, perioperative course, histology, and survival. *Diseases of the Colon and Rectum*, 53(1), 57–64.

Bokemeyer, C., Bondarenko, I., Makhson, A., Hartmann, J. T., Aparicio, J., de Braud, F., …, & Koralewski, P. (2009). Fluorouracil, leucovorin, and oxaliplatin with and without cetuximab in the first-line treatment of metastatic colorectal cancer. *Journal of Clinical Oncology*, 27(5), 663–671.

Bredt, L. C., & Rachid, A. F. (2014). Predictors of recurrence after a first hepatectomy for colorectal cancer liver metastases: a retrospective analysis. *World J Surg Oncol*, 12, 391.

Bridgewater, J. A., Pugh, S. A., Maishman, T., Eminton, Z., Mellor, J., Whitehead, A., …, & Primrose, J. N. (2020). Systemic chemotherapy with or without cetuximab in patients with resectable colorectal liver metastasis (New EPOC): long-term results of a multicentre, randomised, controlled, phase 3 trial. *The Lancet Oncology*, 21(3), 398–411.

Casak, S. J., Marcus, L., Fashoyin-Aje, L., Mushti, S. L., Cheng, J., Shen, Y. L., …, & Lemery, S. J. (2021). FDA Approval Summary: pembrolizumab for the First-line Treatment of Patients with MSI-H/dMMR Advanced Unresectable or Metastatic Colorectal Carcinoma. *Clinical Cancer Research*, 27(17), 4680–4684.

Catalano, V., Bergamo, F., Cremolini, C., Vincenzi, B., Negri, F., Giordani, P., …, & Graziano, F. (2018). Optimizing the use of first-line chemotherapy in metastatic colorectal cancer patients with mucinous histology: a multicenter, retrospective combined analysis on 897 patients. *Annals of Oncology*, 29, v97.

Catalano, V., Loupakis, F., Graziano, F., Torresi, U., Bisonni, R., Mari, D., …, & Fedeli, S. L. (2009). Mucinous histology predicts for poor response rate and overall survival of patients with colorectal cancer and treated with first-line oxaliplatin- and/or irinotecan-based chemotherapy. *British Journal of Cancer*, 100(6), 881–887.

de Boer, N. L., Rovers, K., Burger, J. W. A., Madsen, E. V. E., Brandt-Kerkhof, A. R. M., Kok, N. F. M., …, & Verhoef, C. (2020). A population-based study on the prognostic impact of primary tumor sidedness in patients with peritoneal metastases from colon cancer. *Cancer medicine*, 9(16), 5851–5859.

Douillard, J. Y., Siena, S., Cassidy, J., Tabernero, J., Burkes, R., Barugel, M., …, & Sidhu, R. (2014). Final results from PRIME: randomized phase III study of panitumumab with FOLFOX4 for first-line treatment of metastatic colorectal cancer. *Annals of Oncology*, 25(7), 1346–1355.

Fadel, M., Malietzis, G., Constantinides, V., Pellino, G., Tekkis, P., & Kontovounisios, C. (2021). Clinicopathological factors and survival outcomes of signet-ring cell and mucinous carcinoma versus adenocarcinoma of the colon and rectum: a systematic review and meta-analysis. *Discover Oncology*, 12(1), 1–12.

Fakih, M. G. (2015). Metastatic colorectal cancer: current state and future directions. *Journal of Clinical Oncology*, 33(16), 1809–1824.

Fong, Y., Fortner, J., Sun, R. L., Brennan, M. F., & Blumgart, L. H. (1999). Clinical score for predicting recurrence after hepatic resection for metastatic colorectal cancer: analysis of 1001 consecutive cases. *Annals of Surgery*, 230(3), 309–318 discussion 18-21.

Goldstein, J., Tran, B., Ensor, J., Gibbs, P., Wong, H. L., Wong, S. F., …, & Overman, M. J. (2014). Multicenter retrospective analysis of metastatic colorectal cancer (CRC) with high-level microsatellite instability (MSI-H). *Annals of Oncology*, 25(5), 1032–1038.

Groot Koerkamp, B., Rahbari, N. N., Buchler, M. W., Koch, M., & Weitz, J. (2013). Circulating tumor cells and prognosis of patients with resectable colorectal liver metastases or widespread metastatic colorectal cancer: a meta-analysis. *Annals of Surgical Oncology*, 20(7), 2156–2165.

Hainsworth, J. D., Meric-Bernstam, F., Swanton, C., Hurwitz, H., Spigel, D. R., Sweeney, C., …, & Kurzrock, R. (2018). Targeted Therapy for Advanced Solid Tumors on the Basis of Molecular Profiles: results From MyPathway, an Open-Label, Phase IIa Multiple Basket Study. *Journal of Clinical Oncology*, 36(6), 536–542.

Hamers, P., Bos, A. C. R. K., May, A. M., Punt, C. J., Koopman, M., & Vink, G. R. (2019). Recent changes in overall survival of real-life stage IV colorectal cancer patients. *Journal of Clinical Oncology*, 37(15), 3522.

Holch, J. W., Ricard, I., Stintzing, S., Modest, D. P., & Heinemann, V. (2017). The relevance of primary tumour location in patients with metastatic colorectal cancer: a meta-analysis of first-line clinical trials. *European Journal of Cancer*, 70, 87–98.

Hugen, N., van de Velde, C. J. H., de Wilt, J. H. W., & Nagtegaal, I. D. (2014). Metastatic pattern in colorectal cancer is strongly influenced by histological subtype. *Annals of Oncology*, 25(3), 651–657.

Karagkounis, G., Torbenson, M. S., Daniel, H. D., Azad, N. S., Diaz, L. A., Jr., Donehower, R. C., …, & Choti, M. A. (2013). Incidence and prognostic impact of KRAS and BRAF mutation in patients undergoing liver surgery for colorectal metastases. *Cancer*, 119(23), 4137–4144.

Karapetis, C. S., Khambata-Ford, S., Jonker, D. J., O'Callaghan, C. J., Tu, D., Tebbutt, N. C., …, & Zalcberg, J. R. (2008). K-ras mutations and benefit from cetuximab in advanced colorectal cancer. *New England Journal of Medicine*, 359(17), 1757–1765.

Koch, M., Kienle, P., Hinz, U., Antolovic, D., Schmidt, J., Herfarth, C., …, & Wetiz, J. (2005). Detection of hematogenous tumor cell dissemination predicts tumor relapse in patients undergoing surgical resection of colorectal liver metastases. *Annals of Surgery*, 241(2), 199–205.

Koopman, M., Kortman, G. A., Mekenkamp, L., Ligtenberg, M. J., Hoogerbrugge, N., Antonini, N. F., …, & van Kreiken, J. H. J. M. (2009). Deficient mismatch repair system in patients with sporadic advanced colorectal cancer. *British Journal of Cancer*, 100(2), 266–273.

Le, D. T., Uram, J. N., Wang, H., Bartlett, B. R., Kemberling, H., Eyring, A. D., …, & Diaz, L. A. (2015). PD-1 Blockade in Tumors with Mismatch-Repair Deficiency. *New England Journal of Medicine*, 372(26), 2509–2520.

Lochhead, P., Kuchiba, A., Imamura, Y., Liao, X., Yamauchi, M., Nishihara, R., …, & Ogino, S. (2013). Microsatellite instability and BRAF mutation testing in colorectal cancer prognostication. *JNCI: Journal of the National Cancer Institute*, 105(15), 1151–1156.

Loupakis, F., Hurwitz, H. I., Saltz, L., Arnold, D., Grothey, A., Nguyen, Q. L., …, & Lenz, H. (2018). Impact of primary tumour location on efficacy of bevacizumab plus chemotherapy in metastatic colorectal cancer. *British Journal of Cancer*, 119(12), 1451–1455.

Malakorn, S., Ouchi, A., Hu, C. Y., Sandhu, L., Dasari, A., You, Y. N., …, & Chang, G. J. (2021). Tumor Sidedness, Recurrence, and Survival After Curative Resection of Localized Colon Cancer. *Clinical Colorectal Cancer*, 20(1), e53–e60.

Margonis, G. A., Spolverato, G., Kim, Y., Karagkounis, G., Choti, M. A., & Pawlik, T. M. (2015). Effect of KRAS Mutation on Long-Term Outcomes of Patients Undergoing Hepatic Resection for Colorectal Liver Metastases. *Annals of Surgical Oncology*, 22(13), 4158–4165.

Meric-Bernstam, F., Hurwitz, H., Raghav, K. P. S., McWilliams, R. R., Fakih, M., VanderWalde, A., …, & Hainsworth, J. (2019). Pertuzumab plus trastuzumab for HER2-amplified metastatic colorectal cancer (MyPathway): an updated report from a multicentre, open-label, phase 2a, multiple basket study. *The Lancet Oncology*, 20(4), 518–530.

Overman, M. J., McDermott, R., Leach, J. L., Lonardi, S., Lenz, H. J., Morse, M. A., …, & Andre, T. (2017). Nivolumab in patients with metastatic DNA mismatch repair-deficient or microsatellite instability-high colorectal cancer (CheckMate 142): an open-label, multicentre, phase 2 study. *The Lancet Oncology*, 18(9), 1182–1191.

Passot, G., Denbo, J. W., Yamashita, S., Kopetz, S. E., Chun, Y. S., Maru, D., …, & Vauthey, J. N. (2017). Is hepatectomy justified for patients with RAS mutant colorectal liver metastases? An analysis of 524 patients undergoing curative liver resection. *Surgery*, 161(2), 332–340.

Petrelli, F., Tomasello, G., Borgonovo, K., Ghidini, M., Turati, L., Dallera, P., …, & Barni, S. (2017). Prognostic Survival Associated With Left-Sided vs Right-Sided Colon Cancer: a Systematic Review and Meta-analysis. *JAMA oncology*, 3(2), 211–219.

Poston, G., Adam, R., Xu, J., Byrne, B., Esser, R., Malik, H., …, & Xu, J. (2017). The role of cetuximab in converting initially unresectable colorectal cancer liver metastases for resection. *European Journal of Surgical Oncology*, 43(11), 2001–2011.

Sartore-Bianchi, A., Trusolino, L., Martino, C., Bencardino, K., Lonardi, S., Bergamo, F., …, & Siena, S. (2016). Dual-targeted therapy with trastuzumab and lapatinib in treatment-refractory, KRAS codon 12/13 wild-type, HER2-positive metastatic colorectal cancer (HERACLES): a proof-of-concept, multicentre, open-label, phase 2 trial. *The Lancet Oncology*, 17(6), 738–746.

Schirripa, M., Bergamo, F., Cremolini, C., Casagrande, M., Lonardi, S., Aprile, G., …, & Falcone, A. (2015). BRAF and RAS mutations as prognostic factors in metastatic colorectal cancer patients undergoing liver resection. *British Journal of Cancer*, 112(12), 1921–1928.

Shaib, W., & Mahajan, R. (2013). El-Rayes B. Markers of resistance to anti-EGFR therapy in colorectal cancer. *J Gastrointest Oncol*, 4(3), 308–318.

Shida, D., Inoue, M., Tanabe, T., Moritani, K., Tsukamoto, S., Yamauchi, S., …, & Kanemitsu, Y. (2020). Prognostic impact of primary tumor location in Stage III colorectal cancer-right-sided colon versus left-sided colon versus rectum: a nationwide multicenter retrospective study. *Journal of Gastroenterology, 55*(10), 958–968.

Siena, S., Di Bartolomeo, M., Raghav, K., Masuishi, T., Loupakis, F., Kawakami, H., …, & Yoshino, T. (2021). Trastuzumab deruxtecan (DS-8201) in patients with HER2-expressing metastatic colorectal cancer (DESTINY-CRC01): a multicentre, open-label, phase 2 trial. *The Lancet Oncology, 22*(6), 779–789.

Somashekhar, S. P., Ashwin, K. R., Zaveri, S. S., Rauthan, A., & Patil, P. (2016). Assessment of Tumor Response and Resection Rates in Unresectable Colorectal Liver Metastases Following Neoadjuvant Chemotherapy with Cetuximab. *Indian J Surg Oncol, 7*(1), 11–17.

Tajiri, K., Sudou, T., Fujita, F., Hisaka, T., Kinugasa, T., & Akagi, Y. (2017). Clinicopathological and Corresponding Genetic Features of Colorectal Signet Ring Cell Carcinoma. *Anticancer Research, 37*(7), 3817–3823.

Tan, C., & Du, X. (2012). KRAS mutation testing in metastatic colorectal cancer. *World Journal of Gastroenterology: Wjg, 18*(37), 5171–5180.

Tejpar, S., Stintzing, S., Ciardiello, F., Tabernero, J., Van Cutsem, E., Beier, F., …, & Heinemann, V. (2017). Prognostic and Predictive Relevance of Primary Tumor Location in Patients With RAS Wild-Type Metastatic Colorectal Cancer: retrospective Analyses of the CRYSTAL and FIRE-3 Trials. *JAMA oncology, 3*(2), 194–201.

Tie, J., & Desai, J. (2015). Targeting BRAF mutant metastatic colorectal cancer: clinical implications and emerging therapeutic strategies. *Target Oncol, 10*(2), 179–188.

Tie, J., Kinde, I., Wang, Y., Wong, H. L., Roebert, J., Christie, M., …, & Gibbs, P. (2015). Circulating tumor DNA as an early marker of therapeutic response in patients with metastatic colorectal cancer. *Annals of Oncology, 26*(8), 1715–1722.

Tran, B., Kopetz, S., Tie, J., Gibbs, P., Jiang, Z. Q., Lieu, C. H., …, & Desai, J. (2011). Impact of BRAF mutation and microsatellite instability on the pattern of metastatic spread and prognosis in metastatic colorectal cancer. *Cancer, 117*(20), 4623–4632.

Vale, C. L., Tierney, J. F., Fisher, D., Adams, R. A., Kaplan, R., Maughan, T. S., …, & Meade, A. M. (2012). Does anti-EGFR therapy improve outcome in advanced colorectal cancer? A systematic review and meta-analysis. *Cancer Treatment Reviews, 38*(6), 618–625.

Van Cutsem, E., Kohne, C. H., Hitre, E., Zaluski, J., Chang Chien, C. R., Makhson, A., …, & Rougier, P. (2009). Cetuximab and chemotherapy as initial treatment for metastatic colorectal cancer. *New England Journal of Medicine, 360*(14), 1408–1417.

Van Cutsem, E., Kohne, C. H., Lang, I., Folprecht, G., Nowacki, M. P., Cascinu, S., …, & Ciardiello, F. (2011). Cetuximab plus irinotecan, fluorouracil, and leucovorin as first-line treatment for metastatic colorectal cancer: updated analysis of overall survival according to tumor KRAS and BRAF mutation status. *Journal of Clinical Oncology, 29*(15), 2011–2019.

Van Cutsem, E., Peeters, M., Siena, S., Humblet, Y., Hendlisz, A., Neyns, B., …, & Amado, R. G. (2007). Open-label phase III trial of panitumumab plus best supportive care compared with best supportive care alone in patients with chemotherapy-refractory metastatic colorectal cancer. *Journal of Clinical Oncology, 25*(13), 1658–1664.

Varughese, L. A., Lau-Min, K. S., Cambareri, C., Damjanov, N., Massa, R., Reddy, N., …, & Tuteja, S. (2020). DPYD and UGT1A1 Pharmacogenetic Testing in Patients with Gastrointestinal Malignancies: an Overview of the Evidence and Considerations for Clinical Implementation. *Pharmacotherapy, 40*(11), 1108–1129.

Vauthey, J. N., Zimmitti, G., Kopetz, S. E., Shindoh, J., Chen, S. S., Andreou, A., …, & Maru, D. M. (2013). RAS mutation status predicts survival and patterns of recurrence in patients undergoing hepatectomy for colorectal liver metastases. *Annals of Surgery, 258*(4), 619–626 discussion 26-7.

Wang, G., He, Y., Sun, Y., Wang, W., Qian, X., Yu, X., …, & Pan, Y. (2020). Prevalence, prognosis and predictive status of HER2 amplification in anti-EGFR-resistant metastatic colorectal cancer. *Clinical & translational oncology: official publication of the Federation of Spanish Oncology Societies and of the National Cancer Institute of Mexico, 22*(6), 813–822.

Wong, S. H., & Yu, J. (2019). Gut microbiota in colorectal cancer: mechanisms of action and clinical applications. *Nature reviews Gastroenterology & hepatology, 16*(11), 690–704.

Yaeger, R., Cowell, E., Chou, J. F., Gewirtz, A. N., Borsu, L., Vakiani, E., …, & Kemeny, Y. (2015). RAS mutations affect pattern of metastatic spread and increase propensity for brain metastasis in colorectal cancer. *Cancer, 121*(8), 1195–1203.

CHAPTER

5

Role of Neoadjuvant therapy in the treatment of patients with colorectal liver metastases

Jeremy Sharib, MD[a], Bryan Clary, MD[b] and Michael E Lidsky, MD[a]

[a] Duke University Medical Center, Department of Surgery, Division of Surgical Oncology, USA [b] University of California San Diego, Department of Surgery, USA

Introduction

Approximately 50 percent of patients with colorectal cancer will develop liver metastases during the course of their lifetime (Moghadamyeghaneh, Alizadeh, and Phelan, 2016). Untreated colorectal liver metastases (CRLM) are associated with poor survival of less than 6 months following presentation (Rougier, Milan, and Lazorthes, 1995), whereas, complete surgical resection is associated with a probability of survival of 30–60 percent at 5-years and 20–25 percent at 10-years (Choti, Sitzmann, and Tiburi, 2002; Rees, Tekkis, Welsh, O'Rourke, and John, 2008; Scheele, Stang, Altendorf-Hofmann, and Paul, 1995). Despite these considerations, hepatectomy remains an underutilized therapeutic modality to this day, perhaps due to perceptions regarding the high probability of recurrence on the part of referring physicians including medical oncologists as well as general and colorectal surgeons (Raoof, Jutric, and Haye, 2020; Vega, Salehi, and Nicolaescu, 2021). In an effort to improve upon the high rates of recurrence following hepatectomy, investigators have explored the use of adjuvant systemic therapy. While a more thorough review of adjuvant therapy following resection of CRLM is provided in Chapter 16, retrospective and limited randomized data utilizing adjuvant 5-flourouracil (5-FU) alone are inconsistent, with some studies suggesting an improvement in progression free (PFS), but no difference in overall survival (OS) (Kanemitsu, Shimizu, and Mizusawa, 2021; Mitry, Fields, and Bleiberg, 2008; Parks, Gonen, and Kemeny, 2007; Portier, Elias, and Bouche, 2006). Most would agree that if there is a benefit, it is quite modest. In the past two decades, highly potent combination systemic therapies have improved tumor

Contemporary Management of Metastatic Colorectal Cancer: A Precision Medicine Approach

DOI: https://doi.org/10.1016/B978-0-323-91706-3.00013-8

response rates and OS in advanced colorectal cancer, including patients with unresectable CRLM (Biller and Schrag, 2021; de Gramont, Figer, and Seymour, 2000; Giacchetti, Itzhaki, and Gruia, 1999; Goldberg, Sargent, and Morton, 2004; Hochster, Hart, and Ramanathan, 2008; Loupakis, Cremolini, and Masi, 2014). The increased effectiveness of these regimens has led many groups to explore and incorporate their use prior to hepatectomy in potentially resectable patients.

Preoperative systemic therapy for CRLM can be given either as a true neoadjuvant therapy in the context of resectable disease, or as a method to convert unresectable disease to resectable disease, also described as "conversion". Both approaches are supported widely by surgical and medical oncologists, as well as consensus guidelines (Adam, de Gramont, and Figueras, 2015; National Comprehensive Cancer Network, 2021). The definition of resectable disease, which is discussed in detail in chapters 7 and 8, depends on technical and oncologic considerations, including proximity to vascular inflow and outflow, number of tumors, disease burden, bilaterality, and the size of the future liver remnant, and remains controversial even among surgeons (Adam and Kitano, 2019; Rocha and Helton, 2012; Tzeng and Aloia, 2013). Unfortunately, determination of resectability is often made without the involvement of liver surgeon (Aubin, Bressan, and Grondin, 2018; Raoof et al., 2020; Shah and Clary, 2013; Vega et al., 2021). As a result, the term neoadjuvant chemotherapy, which implies systemic therapy that is given to patients with resectable disease prior to curative intent resection, is inconsistent in the literature. Additionally, there are no prospective data evaluating neoadjuvant therapy as a singular modality, and therefore all inferences are made in the context of perioperative and adjuvant chemotherapy, and the purported benefits and limitations of each. Despite these shortcomings in the literature, this chapter will review the rationale and reported experience for preoperative systemic therapy in patients with unresectable and resectable CRLM.

Rationale for perioperative chemotherapy for colorectal liver metastases

Preoperative therapy has been shown to offer a survival benefit in several primary gastrointestinal malignancies (Cunningham, Allum, and Stenning, 2006; Sauer, Liersch, and Merkel, 2012; Sohal, Duong, and Ahmad, 2021). The unifying rationale for neoadjuvant therapy in each of these malignancies is to provide early treatment of micrometastatic disease; decrease tumor size to enable a less morbid, more complete (R0) operation; and guarantee that all patients who undergo resection receive combined multimodality therapy. In addition, a window of upfront therapy is used to identify patients with poor biology who should not undergo surgery. The theoretical benefits for preoperative therapy for colorectal liver disease are similarly to a) treat micrometastatic disease- the existence and the ability of which has already proven capable of presiding within distant tissue; b) select patients who will benefit most from hepatectomy and prevent those with aggressive disease from an unnecessary and morbid hepatic resection; c) dictate choice of post hepatectomy chemotherapy; and more uniquely, d) convert a major hepatectomy to a minor or parenchymal sparing hepatectomy. In patients with initially unresectable disease, all of the above apply with the further intent to facilitate complete (R0) resection. There are also a number of potential disadvantages that include increased perioperative complications related to general and liver-specific side-effects as well as the possibility that response to therapy will impair the ability to detect clinically relevant

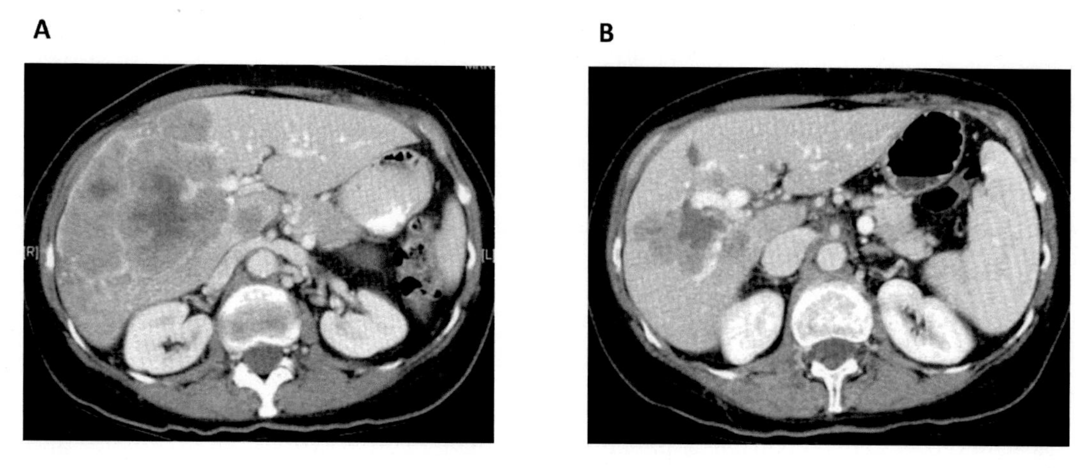

FIGURE 5.1 Neoadjuvant chemotherapy as a means to "convert" technically unresectable colorectal liver metastases to resectable liver metastases. A. Extensive right sided disease, including potential vascular invasion into right posterior portal pedicle and tumor extension to the anterior portal pedicle and middle hepatic vein, which would require extended right hepatectomy and small future liver remnant. B. Following 6 cycles FOLFOX, there has been significant response and retraction from the middle hepatic vein and right anterior portal pedicle. The patient's liver disease was cleared with a standard right hepatectomy.

disease at the time of surgery. The paragraphs that follow will discuss in greater detail these and other considerations for patients with initially unresectable disease followed by those with resectable situations.

Preoperative chemotherapy for patients with unresectable liver metastases

Up to 80–90 percent of patients presenting with colorectal liver metastases will present with unresectable disease (Altendorf-Hofmann and Scheele, 2003; Jatzko et al., 1991; Mitry et al., 2008). Systemic therapy represents the initial standard-of-care option for these patients, and thus there is little controversy with its use as a primary therapy in this setting. Historically, long term cure with 5-FU or 5-FU/leucovorin (LV) regimens alone was achieved in less than 5 percent of patients (Dy, Hobday, and Nelson, 2009). Although response rates were modest by today's standards, the potential for cure through conversion to a resectable state was identified and explored by a number of groups (Fig. 5.1). Bismuth, Adam, and Levi (1996) Conversion occurred in up to 10–15 percent of patients treated with 5-FU regimens and was not associated with an increase in operative morbidity following partial hepatectomy. Moreover, in patients who converted and underwent resection, recurrence and survival rates approximate that of initially resectable patients (Adam, Delvart, and Pascal, 2004).

With the introduction of potent multiagent regimens in the early 2000's that combine oxaliplatin and irinotecan with 5-FU/LV, upfront chemotherapy as a method to downstage initially unresectable tumors became a widely accepted strategy (Kalofonos, Aravantinos, and Kosmidis, 2005; Saltz, Cox, and Blanke, 2000). The likelihood of conversion utilizing oxaliplatin, irinotecan, or both when added to 5-FU has been reported to occur in as few as 5–10 percent to up to 50–60 percent of patients (Adam, Wicherts, and de Haas, 2009; Alberts et al., 2003; Jones et al., 2014; Masi, Loupakis, and Pollina, 2009; Ychou, Viret, and Kramar, 2008). The variability in these studies reflects a number of factors including whether patients with extrahepatic disease were included and also whether defined criteria for resection and review by experts in hepatic surgery were incorporated into the assessments. In patients with unresectable disease confined only to the liver, the preponderance of the literature suggests that resection can be achieved in approximately 33–45 percent of patients (Alberts et al., 2003; Giacchetti et al., 1999; Pozzo, Basso, and Cassano, 2004). In prospective data (Table 5.1), the most potent systemic chemotherapy regimen to convert unresectable metastases appears to the triplet regimen including 5-FU, oxaliplatin, and irinotecan (FOLFOXIRI). In METHEP, a randomized phase 2 study comparing standard multiagent chemotherapy (FOLFOX/FOLFIRI) to intensified regimens (including FOLFOXIRI), curative intent resection was performed in 40 percent versus 67 percent of patients, respectively, however R0 resection was achieved in only 30 percent of patients who received FOLFOXIRI. (Ychou, Rivoire, and Thezenas, 2013) Additionally, in a similar phase 3 randomized controlled trial comparing FOLFIRI to FOLFOXIRI as first line therapy for metastatic colorectal cancer, 36 percent of patients with liver only disease randomized to FOLFOXIRI underwent hepatectomy, compared to 12 percent in the FOLFIRI group ($p = 0.017$) (Falcone, Ricci, and Brunetti, 2007). Across both studies, median OS following initial treatment of unresectable disease with FOLFOXIRI was 23–48 months, and five-year OS reached as high as 30–35 percent in patients who underwent resection, compared to five-year survival rates around 10 percent with multidrug chemotherapy regimens alone.

More recently, targeted agents, including vascular endothelial growth factor (VEGF) or epidermal growth factor receptor (EGFR) inhibitors, have been added to the multiagent chemotherapy regimens in metastatic colorectal cancer. Bevacizumab, a monoclonal antibody against VEGF, improves PFS, OS, and response duration when added to irinotecan based chemotherapy and improves PFS when added to oxaliplatin based or triplet chemotherapy for metastatic colon cancer (Hurwitz, Fehrenbacher, and Novotny, 2004; Loupakis et al., 2014; Saltz, Clarke, and Diaz-Rubio, 2008). Its use was also shown to promote early response, within 8 weeks of therapy, in greater than 60 percent of patients, which could allow for downstaging and possible resection prior to the onset of significant hepatic toxicity (Cremolini, Loupakis, and Antoniotti, 2015; Wong, Cunningham, and Barbachano, 2011). In the OLIVIA trial, a randomized phase II study comparing bevacizumab plus modified FOLFOX or FOLFOXIRI in treatment-naïve patients with initially unresectable liver only metastases, 49 percent versus 61 percent underwent resection with R0 rates (including planned two-staged hepatectomy) of 31 percent versus 54 percent, respectively (Gruenberger, Bridgewater, and Chau, 2015). Treatment response associated with conversion to resectability occurred after median 3.1 months in both groups. Overall PFS in the intent-to-treat population was also improved in the FOLFOXIRI plus bevacizumab arm (18.6 vs 11.5 mo, HR 0.43 [95 percent CI 0.26–0.72]). In patients who underwent resection, median PFS was 31.8 months. Median OS was not reached at the time of publication, but in meta-analyses of prospective data which included FOLFOXIRI plus bevacizumab in liver only metastatic colorectal cancer, median OS was 30.1 months across all patients. Survival was higher in RAS/BRAF-wild type patients (37.1 mo) compared to RAS-mutated patients (25.6 months) or BRAF-mutated patients (13.4 months) (Cremolini, Loupakis, and Antoniotti, 2015; Tomasello et al., 2017). These regimens

TABLE 5.1 Prospective trials investigating neoadjuvant chemotherapy in patients with initially unresectable colorectal liver metastases

Study	Regimens	*n*	Response (95% CI), %	R0 resections (95% CI), %	Surgical mortality, %	Median PFS (95% CI), mo	Median OS (95% CI), mo
Chemotherapy alone							
METHEP[38,a]	FOLFOX4/FOLFIRI	30	60 (41–77)	23 (NR)	0	9.2 (6.8–13.4)	17.7 (13.7–43.0)
	FOLFIRI–HD	32	62 (44–79)	25 (–)	0	12.1 (10.3–16.6)	29.4 (26.1–42.4)
	FOLFOX7	30	57 (37–75)	23 (–)	0	8.5 (6.4–10.9)	26.9 (18.7–45.0)
	FOLFOXIRI	30	73 (54–88)	30 (–)	5	14.1 (11.2–21.7)	48.8 (21.9–NR)
Falcone[39]	FOLFIRI	122	41 (32–50)	12[b] (–)	–	6.9 (–)	16.7 (–)
	FOLFOXIRI	122	66 (56–74)	36[b] (2)	–	9.8 (–)	22.6 (–)
Cetuximab-based regimens[c]							
CELIM[51-2]	Cetuximab + FOLFOX6	56	68 (54–80)	38 (25–52)	9	11.2 (7.2–15.3)	35.8 (28.1–43.6)
	Cetuximab + FOLFIRI	55	57 (42–70)	30 (18–44)	0	10.5 (8.9–12.2)	29.0 (16.0–41.9)
Ye[51]	mFOLFOX6/FOLFIRI	68	29 (–)	7 (–)	0	5.8 (3.9–6.1)	21.0 (16.7–23.4)
	Cetuximab + mFOL-FOX6/FOLFIRI	70	57 (–)	26 (–)	0	10.2 (8.6–11.4)	30.9 (16.5–41.5)
Bevacizumab-based regimens							
BOXER[43]	Bevacizumab + CAPOX	46	78 (63–89)	20 (–)	–	12.0 (–)	NR
OLIVIA[44]	Bevacizumab + mFOLFOX6	39	62 (45–77)	31 (17–48)[d]	11	11.5 (9.6–13.6)	32.2 (0.7–59.6)
	Bevacizumab + FOLFOXIRI	41	81 (65–91)	54 (37–69)[d]	0	18.6 (12.9–22.3)	NR (0–56.0)
TRIBE[45]	Bevacizumab + FOLFIRI	256	53.1 (46.8–59.3)	12 (–)	–	9.7 (9.3–10.9)	25.8 (22.7–30.8)
	Bevacizumab + FOLFOXIRI	252	65.1 (58.8–70.9)	15 (7)	–	12.1 (10.9–13.2)	31.0 (26.9–35.1)

[a] 1–3 resectable lung metastases (<2cm) permitted.
[b] In patients with liver only disease.
[c] CELIM included patients with KRAS wild-type (70%) and KRAS mutated (30%) tumours. Ye et al. included only patients with KRAS wildtype tumours.
[d] Includes RO obtained during second surgeryAbbreviations: CAPOX=capecitabine plus oxaliplatin; Cl=confidence interval; FOLFIRI=infused 5-fluorouracil, folinic acid plus irinotecan; FOLFIRI-HD=infused 5-fluorouracil, folinic acid plus high-dose irinotecan; (m)FOLFOX=(modified) infused 5-fluorouracil, folinic acid plus oxaliplatin; FOLFOXIRI=infused 5-fluorouracil, folinic acid, oxaliplatin plus irinotecan; NR=not reached; ORR=overall response rate; OS=overall survival.Adapted from Gruenberger T, et. al. Ann Oncol. 2015 Apr;26(4):702-708.

are not without toxicity, however. In OLIVIA, 84 percent treated with FOLFOX and 95 percent treated with FOLFOXIRI experienced grade 3 or higher adverse events during chemotherapy and 20 percent and 35 percent, respectively, discontinued bevacizumab prematurely. Surgical morbidity related to bevacizumab occurred in 32 percent, with 4.5 percent mortality (deaths occurred in two heavily pretreated patients).

Cetuximab and panitumimab are monoclonal antibodies against endothelial growth factor receptor (EGFR) that similarly improve response rate when added to FOLFOX or FOLFIRI in the first-line setting for KRAS-wild type metastatic colorectal cancer (Bokemeyer, Bondarenko, and Makhson, 2009; Douillard, Siena, and Cassidy, 2014; Maughan, Adams, and Smith, 2011; Van Cutsem, Kohne, and Hitre, 2009; Ye, Liu, and Ren, 2013). While the impact of anti-EGFR therapy on PFS and OS is unclear, improved tumor response could theoretically benefit survival outcomes in unresectable patients who are able to undergo resection after neoadjuvant therapy. In the CELIM trial, a randomized phase 2 study evaluating cetuximab added to FOLFOX or FOLFIRI in patients with liver only unresectable metastases, response rates were equivalent (68 percent versus 57 percent, Odds ratio (OR) 1.62, [0.74–3.59]; $p = 0.23$) after a median 5.1 months of treatment (Folprecht, Gruenberger, and Bechstein, 2010). Resection and/or ablation was completed in 46 percent of patients overall, but R0 resection rates were a modest (35 percent), despite inclusion of many potentially resectable patients on retrospective review. Postoperative liver failure occurred in only 1 patient (2.2 percent) greater than 60 days after surgery and mortality was 4.4 percent. While the trial design did not initially stratify by RAS mutation status, patients whose tumors were KRAS-wild type and underwent resection, however, achieved 54 month median OS, with 46 percent of patients alive at 5 years (Folprecht, Gruenberger, and Bechstein, 2014). Due to the improved response rates for bevacizumab and anti-EGFR therapies in unresectable liver only metastatic colorectal cancer patients, the impact of molecular subtypes on regimens containing targeted agents is a topic for ongoing study (Huiskens, van Gulik, and van Lienden, 2015). However, it's important to weigh risks and benefits of these multiagent regimens in the context of existing goals of therapy.

In summary, "neoadjuvant" chemotherapy is highly effective in its ability to facilitate curative intent resection in patients with initially unresectable colorectal metastases and in doing so is an important tool to significantly prolong survival for patients with advanced disease (Adam and Kitano, 2019). Current regimens are associated with a reduction in tumor burden in more than 65–70 percent and partial responses by RECIST criteria in approximately 50 percent, in chemo-naïve patients. Contemporary studies that incorporate rigorous criteria for resection and expert review are associated with conversion rates of approximately 30–50 percent. Resection remains a critical element of treatment as PFS remains under 1 year in the absence of resection, in part reflecting the fact that complete pathologic response to chemotherapy occurs in only 4–9 percent of patients (Adam et al., 2009; Adam, Wicherts, and de Haas, 2008; Blazer, Kishi, and Maru, 2008). Long-term survival in patients who convert to resection is regularly seen with most studies demonstrating 5-year survival estimates exceeding 30 percent (Adam et al., 2004). Early involvement of a liver surgeon in the care of patients with unresectable liver only or limited extrahepatic disease is critical to identify patients in which conversion may be possible and in whom aggressive treatment is thus warranted (Raoof et al., 2020; Reddy, Barbas, and Clary, 2009; Shah and Clary, 2013). In addition to appropriate patient selection, the goals of systemic therapy must be narrowed to optimize chances of successful resection. This includes limiting the amount of chemotherapy to convert to resectable disease rather than to maximal benefit in order to minimize preoperative liver toxicity. Given the lack of alternatives to ongoing systemic treatment, one can accept longer preoperative treatment if inadequate response is not seen, but a maximum preoperative duration should be determined on a case-by-case basis. Finally, while beyond the scope of this chapter, additional liver-directed strategies to convert patients with unresectable liver disease, including hepatic artery infusion, radiofrequency ablation, and radioembolization may also be utilized in the appropriate clinical setting under the same parameters as described above.

Neoadjuvant chemotherapy for resectable liver metastases

Randomized trials exploring the role of adjuvant chemotherapy following hepatectomy for resectable colorectal liver metastases suggest a modest benefit in PFS (Hasegawa, Saiura, and Takayama, 2016; Kanemitsu et al., 2021; Portier et al., 2006). While not designed to answer the question of overall survival benefit, treatment and control OS curves in these studies are generally overlapping. In addition, it is not clear from the literature at this point time whether contemporary multiagent regimens improves PFS or OS compared to 5-FU alone (Ychou, Hohenberger, and Thezenas, 2009). In response to data in the adjuvant setting and in the context of the advances seen in unresected patients with more contemporary regimens, neoadjuvant sequencing of systemic therapy in patients with resectable disease is theoretically attractive as a means of improving outcomes following resection and perhaps in better selecting patients for potentially morbid procedures.

Early experiences with neoadjuvant chemotherapy for resectable CRLM have demonstrated that treatment response is an important predictive factor. Response to neoadjuvant chemotherapy for synchronous liver metastases before or after resection of the primary tumor is associated with improved median OS following resection in several series (Adam, Pascal, and Castaing, 2004; Allen et al., 2003; Gruenberger et al., 2008). Specifically, radiographic (RECIST), biologic (CEA <200ng/dL), or pathologic (tumor regression grade score) response have all demonstrated usefulness as prognostic tools for OS (Berardi, De Man, and Laurent, 2018; Gallagher, Zheng, and Capanu, 2009). Progression during neoadjuvant chemotherapy occurs in <10 percent of patients, and in most series is associated with poor outcomes. Progression on therapy has been proposed by many to be a strong relative contraindication to hepatectomy even when patients remain within standard anatomic criteria for resectability. This recommendation remains controversial particularly in patients with tumors <5cm and limited disease (<3 lesions). Retrospective experiences in patients meeting these criteria have documented the possibility of long-term survival (Allen et al., 2003; Gallagher et al., 2009; Neumann, Thelen, and Rocken, 2009; Vigano, Capussotti, and Barroso, 2012). In addition to informing prognosis, response to neoadjuvant chemotherapy provides guidance regarding choice of postoperative chemotherapy for patients in whom additional therapy is recommended.

At present there are no completed trials that have evaluated pure neoadjuvant therapy followed by hepatectomy in the management of resectable patients. The European Organization for the Research and Treatment of Cancer (EORTC) conducted a trial (40983) to assess

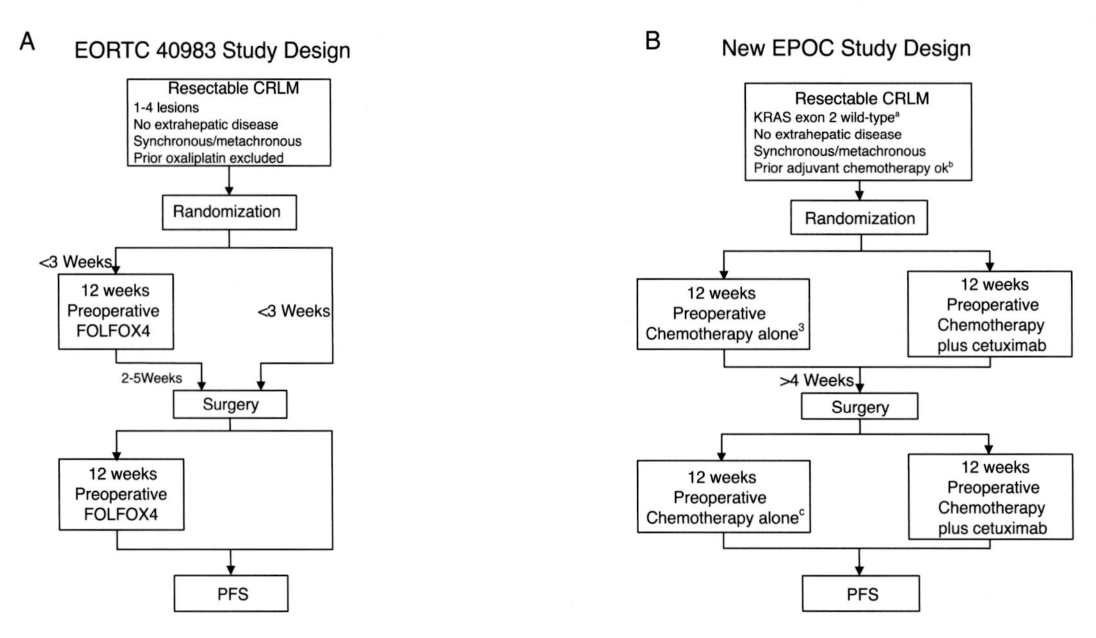

FIGURE 5.2 Study designs for two randomized controlled trials evaluating neoadjuvant chemotherapy regimens for colorectal liver metastases A. Study design for EORTC 40983 (Nordlinger et al., 2008). B. Study design for the New EPOC trial.[82] [a]Amended to include only KRAS exon 2 WT patients after 22 patients enrolled (14 randomized) [b]If completed 6 months or more before trial entry. Previous radiation therapy for rectal tumors also allowed. Prior chemotherapy for metastatic disease excluded. [c]FOLFIRI included for patients who received prior oxaliplatin.

the combination of perioperative chemotherapy and surgery compared to surgery alone for patients with small volume, initially resectable colorectal liver metastases (Nordlinger, Sorbye, and Glimelius, 2008). EORTC 40983 was a randomized, controlled, parallel-group, phase 3 study from 78 hospitals across Europe which randomized 364 patients (182 in each group) who had histologically proven colorectal cancer and up to 4 potentially resectable CRLM to either perioperative FOLFOX4 or surgery alone (Fig. 5.2A). Perioperative chemotherapy included 6 cycles prior to resection, followed by surgery 2–5 weeks after the last administration of preoperative chemotherapy, and finally completion of an additional 6 cycles of chemotherapy after resection. Patients with both synchronous metastases, whose primary tumor was also considered resectable, and metachronous metastases, whose primary tumor was previously removed by an R0 resection, were included. The study was powered to detect a 40 percent increase in the primary outcome of 3-year PFS, from an anticipated 21.0 percent to 32.8 percent. At a median follow-up of 3.9 years, 3-year PFS was 28.1 percent versus 35.4 percent (HR 0.79 [95 percent confidence interval (CI) 0.62–1.02]; $p = 0.58$), which failed to meet the primary outcome in the intent to treat analysis (Fig. 5.3A). However, when considering eligible patients only, 3-year PFS did reach significance, 28.1 percent% versus 36.2 percent (HR 0.77 [95 percent CI 0.60–1.00]; $p = 0.041$; Fig. 5.3B). Though not powered for OS, these curves were nearly overlapping in the two arms and not statistically different (5-year OS 51.2 percent vs 47.8 percent; HR 0.88 [95 percent CI 0.68–1.14]; $p = 0.34$; Fig. 5.3C-D) (Nordlinger, Sorbye, and Glimelius, 2013).

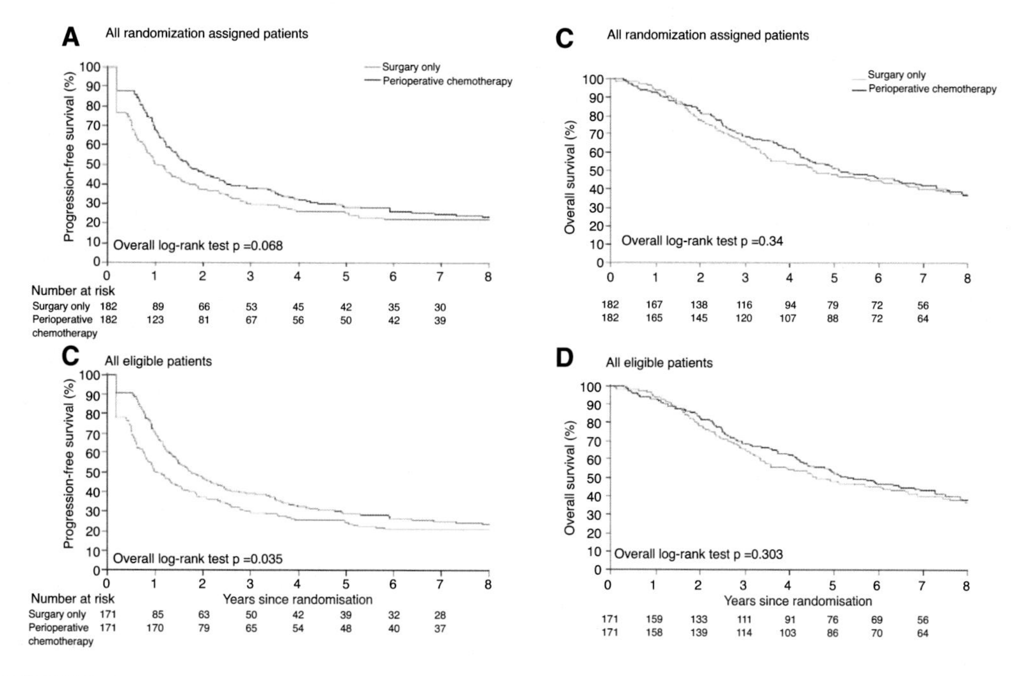

FIGURE 5.3 Survival outcomes for perioperative chemotherapy for resectable colorectal liver metastases. A-B. Long term progression free survival for all randomized (A) and eligible (B) patients from EORTC 40983. C-D. Long term overall survival for all randomized (A) and eligible (B) patients. Used with permission from Lancet Oncol. 2013;14(12):1208–15.

While EORTC 40983 failed to reach its primary outcome, deft trial execution and analysis of secondary outcomes allow for several conclusions to be made. First, investigators successfully reached pre-specified accrual goals, and <10 percent in each group failed to initiate therapy due to ineligibility. Follow-up was also strong, as 92 percent of patients were followed for median 8.5 years. Second, preoperative therapy was well tolerated, but it was associated with increased operative morbidity. Eighty-three percent in the perioperative chemotherapy arm received all 6 preoperative cycles of chemotherapy and underwent resection, compared to 84 percent of patients in the control arm. Planned postoperative chemotherapy was initiated in 63 percent of resected patients in the treatment arm (44 percent completed). Non-hematologic grade 3–4 complications during preoperative chemotherapy occurred in only 38 percent or patients. Importantly, perioperative chemotherapy was associated with increased reversible postoperative complications in 25 percent versus 16 percent patients ($p = 0.04$). The excess morbidity was principally related to biliary fistula (8 percent versus 4 percent), prolonged hepatic failure (6 percent versus 3 percent), and intra-abdominal infection (7 percent versus 2 percent). Additionally, a single patient could not undergo resection due to liver damage related to chemotherapy. Mortality was <1 percent in both groups. Third, preoperative chemotherapy was associated with high response rates, but did not improve resection rates. Only 7 percent of patients progressed during the relatively short course of preoperative chemotherapy, and again, the number of patients resected in each arm was identical. These data suggest that short courses of FOLFOX in patients with low volume oligometastases is an inadequate strategy on its own to identify patients least likely to benefit from exploration or resection, yet does predispose 95 percent of patients to an increased risk of perioperative morbidity due to hepatic chemotoxicity. Reinforcing this concept, patients in the perioperative chemotherapy group had similar non-therapeutic laparotomies (5 percent vs 11 percent, $p = 0.069$). Additionally, as noted, the resection rates did not differ between groups, however, the potential to prevent early progression appears to influence PFS as the separation between the curves occurred early, but remained parallel through the follow-up period. Unfortunately, there are no randomized trials to date which include all chemotherapy given prior to surgery, which could further take advantage of the pretreatment response, likely due to the concern for increased toxicity as described above. Fourth, the ability for preoperative chemotherapy to impact the magnitude of hepatectomy is unclear from these data. The majority of patients included (51 percent vs 52 percent) had only 1 lesion, and there was no difference in distribution of wedge/minor hepatectomy compared to major hepatectomy in the two groups. In patients with multiple lesions, or greater than four lesions (which were excluded) neoadjuvant chemotherapy may facilitate more limited resection. Fifth, colorectal liver metastases are a surgical disease, both as primary and salvage therapy. The study design is notable that patients in the surgery arm do not undergo chemotherapy prior to disease progression. This is inconsistent with current guidelines and likely would not be ethically possible to replicate in current era. However despite this, nearly 30 percent of patients following surgery alone are without relapse at long term follow-up and OS is equivalent. In addition 40 percent of patients in the surgery group and 46 percent of patients in the perioperative chemotherapy group underwent secondary salvage operations to treat recurrence, again with equal OS. To summarize, conclusions made from this study do not definitively demonstrate the utility of neoadjuvant chemotherapy for resectable colorectal liver metastases, nor do they strongly dissuade its use, particularly in patients with extensive or high risk disease. It should be noted that there is significant controversy regarding the interpretation of EORTC 40983 with many considering it a positive trial. At best, perioperative FOLFOX in patients with low volume, resectable disease has a modest benefit in delaying recurrence without clear benefit in overall survival. The findings should give some comfort in settings where patients are adamantly opposed to, or have contraindications to systemic therapy. Ongoing trials are currently working to address neoadjuvant chemotherapy in patients with greater burdens of disease (Ayez, van der Stok, and de Wilt, 2015).

Following EORTC 40983, contemporary trials attempted to determine whether the addition of targeted agents may improve outcomes when given in the neoadjuvant setting. For many, bevacizumab is an intriguing option for neoadjuvant therapy in part because it appears to ameliorate FOLFOX-associated hepatotoxicity. While it has not proven active in the adjuvant setting (Snoeren, van Hillegersberg, and Schouten, 2017), improved response rates and PFS in advanced disease and its use in enhancing conversion of unresectable patients provide a theoretical advantage for the neoadjuvant setting in resectable patients (Garcia-Alfonso, Ferrer, and Gil, 2015; Kawaguchi and Vauthey, 2020; Loupakis et al., 2014). Retrospective data from patients with resectable liver metastases has indeed shown consistently improved radiographic and pathologic response rates following neoadjuvant regimens which included bevacizumab (38–40 percent) compared to those that did not (10–27 percent), as well as potential protection from sinusoidal injury (Chun, Vauthey, and Boonsirikamchai, 2009; Klinger, Tamandl, and Eipeldauer, 2010; Ribero, Wang, and Donadon, 2007; Vera, Gomez Dorronsoro, and Lopez-Ben, 2014). A nonrandomized prospective phase II study of perioperative capecitabine with oxaliplatin (XELOX) plus bevacizumab showed high rates of pathologic response (73 percent) and R0 resection (93 percent). Despite these response rates, only patients who went on to complete adjuvant chemotherapy had benefit in PFS (26.2 months versus 7.4 months, $p < 0.05$) and OS (47.9 months versus 27.7 months, $p < 0.05$) (Gruenberger, Arnold, and Rubbia-Brandt, 2012, 2008). While some may consider addition of bevacizumab to multiagent chemotherapy to elicit a greater response in patients with unresectable CRLM to facilitate conversion to resection, there is currently no randomized data for neoadjuvant chemotherapy plus bevacizumab for patients with resectable colorectal liver metastases.

As described previously, anti-EGFR agents have also been shown to improve response rates in the advanced metastatic colorectal cancer setting in patients with KRAS-wild type tumors. The New EPOC trial was a randomized, multicenter, phase 3 study which sought to determine whether cetuximab added to perioperative chemotherapy (FOLFOX, XELOX, or FOLFIRI in patients who had previously received oxaliplatin) for patients with resectable, KRAS-wild type colorectal liver metastases could improve the primary outcome of PFS (Fig. 5.2B) (Primrose, Falk, and Finch-Jones, 2014). After median follow-up of 20.7 months, there was no difference in response rates between groups (72 percent versus 61 percent, $p = 0.383$), and PFS was significantly lower in the chemotherapy plus cetuximab cohort (14.1 versus 20.5 months, HR 1.48 [95 percent CI 1.04–2.12]; $p = 0.03$). The trial was closed early after reaching a predefined futility criteria for the primary outcome. On long term follow-up (median 66.7 months) PFS was shown to be equivalent between the two groups (15.5 versus 22.2 months, HR 1.45 [95 percent CI 0.87–1.56]; $p = 0.304$), but overall survival was shorter in the cetuximab group (55.4 versus 81.0 months, HR 1.45 [95 percent CI 1.02–2.05, $p = 0.036$) (Bridgewater, Pugh, and Maishman, 2020). The authors concluded that cetuximab in combination with chemotherapy cannot be recommended for patients with resectable colorectal liver metastases. This conclusion is met with some controversy as concerns regarding the trial's rigor abound, but the use of cetuximab in the neoadjuvant setting have largely fell out of favor (Nordlinger, Poston, and Goldberg, 2015).

Safety of neoadjuvant chemotherapy for colorectal liver metastases

Many chemotherapeutic agents cause direct hepatic toxicity, and the success of hepatic surgery relies, in large part on the health of the remnant liver. As a result, neoadjuvant chemotherapy prior to hepatic resection for liver metastases requires unique considerations regarding the choice of regimen and length of therapy to prevent unintended hepatic toxicity that can increase postoperative morbidity, or at the extreme, render a patient unresectable despite anatomically favorable disease. Oxaliplatin-based regimens are significantly associated with sinusoidal dilation (19 percent versus 2 percent, $p < 0.001$) in retrospective data (Kandutsch et al., 2008; Vauthey, Pawlik, and Ribero, 2006). Another commonly used agent, irinotecan, is associated with high rates of steatohepatitis (20 percent versus 4 percent, $p < 0.001$), which when present is associated with post-hepatectomy liver insufficiency (5.8 percent versus 0.8 percent, $p = 0.01$) and 90-day mortality (14.7 percent versus 1.6 percent, $p = 0.001$) (Kandutsch et al., 2008; Vauthey et al., 2006). Independent of the regimen, postoperative morbidity is also associated with the number of chemotherapy cycles administered, and hepatic toxicity of any type is associated with increased post-hepatectomy mortality (6.5 percent versus 1.6 percent, $p = 0.01$) (Karoui, Penna, and Amin-Hashem, 2006;

Vauthey et al., 2006). Increased morbidity was demonstrated prospectively in EORTC 40983 as shown above, with all cause surgical morbidity significantly greater in the chemotherapy arm, including double the rates of biliary fistula and hepatic insufficiency (Nordlinger et al., 2008).

Bevacizumab is theorized to have a protective effect against oxaliplatin induced sinusoidal obstruction syndrome, indirectly by decreasing the number of cycles of cytotoxic chemotherapy required for response, and directly, due to its effect on intratumoral fluid dynamics secondary to vascular stabilization (Hochster et al., 2008; Willett, Boucher, and di Tomaso, 2004). Indeed, pathologic assessments of resected liver tumors show decreased sinusoidal dilation in patients treated with bevacizumab compared to those treated with FOLFOX alone (any grade- 27.4 percent versus 53.5 percent, moderate to severe- 8.1 percent versus 27.9 percent, both $p < 0.01$) (Ribero et al., 2007). In two prospective, non-randomized trials which included a bevacizumab arm, sinusoidal dilation was reduced in the bevacizumab group (42.3 percent versus 52.2 percent, $p < 0.05$), and severe, grade 3 sinusoidal dilation was reduced several fold (1.9 percent versus 23.9 percent, $p < 0.001$) (Klinger, Eipeldauer, and Hacker, 2009; Ribero et al., 2007). In the same study, perisinusoidal fibrosis (17.3 percent versus 37 percent, $p < 0.05$) and hepatocyte ballooning (28.2 percent versus 68.1 percent, $p < 0.05$), but not hepatic fibrosis were also reduced in patients who received bevacizumab.

In practice, when neoadjuvant chemotherapy is used, toxicity can be mitigated by limiting duration to less than 6 cycles, with special consideration of the ongoing risks and benefits for more cycles given on a patient-by-patient basis. In general, FOLFOX is the most commonly used regimen for these patients, unless patient-specific factors dictate using FOLFIRI, or when additional response is needed to downstage to parenchymal preserving resection. In the latter case, FOLFOXIRI may be considered with or without bevacizumab. The enhanced response and mitigation of hepatotoxicity associated with the addition of bevacizumab must be weighed against the potential for wound healing and bleeding complications.

Conclusions

While definitive evidence to support improvements in long-term survival endpoints is currently lacking, there are a number of practical benefits to the application of neoadjuvant therapy in patients with colorectal liver metastases. For patients with unresectable hepatic tumor burdens, conversion to resection is the best opportunity for long term survival. Surgically fit patients should thus undergo evaluation by a hepatic surgeon, and all patients with potential to convert to resection should receive aggressive chemotherapy with that intent. Response can be evaluated early and if conversion is achieved, the patient should be brought to surgery rather than continue neoadjuvant therapy and risk preoperative liver injury.

For initially resectable patients, the perceived benefits of neoadjuvant chemotherapy are less certain and must be weighed against the possibility of increased perioperative complications. Retrospective and randomized trials show only modest improvement to PFS in this patient population, and consistently fail to show improvement in OS, some data even suggesting detriment in certain populations (Bridgewater et al., 2020). Other rationale for neoadjuvant therapy, including its use a biologic 'test' to improve patient selection, has neither been consistently demonstrated nor included as a defined endpoint in clinical trials to date

(Gruenberger et al., 2008; Neumann et al., 2009; Vigano et al., 2012). Though not evident from available data, the risk of neoadjuvant approaches may, however, be justified when the goal is to convert a major hepatectomy to a minor or parenchyma-preserving hepatectomy. Studies with targeted or more active regimens in well selected patients are ongoing and may change the narrative, but currently available neoadjuvant chemotherapy regimens for resectable colorectal liver metastases should be used strategically given the risk of increased perioperative morbidity.

Future clinical trials should address specific rationale for neoadjuvant chemotherapy beyond survival considerations, and examine novel technologies which may define optimal populations for neoadjuvant therapy, such as circulating tumor DNA (ctDNA), radiomics, or molecular profiling. Additionally, while it is unlikely that future trials for colorectal liver metastases will compare interventions to resection alone, well powered trials comparing survival outcomes for neoadjuvant and perioperative therapy are needed. Decisions regarding resectability, utilization and the proper sequencing of treatment modalities are therefore nuanced and should be made in a multidisciplinary fashion, including input from hepatic surgeons.

References

Adam, R., de Gramont, A., Figueras, J., Kokudo, N., Kunstlinger, F., Loyer, E., & ...of the, E. g. (2015). Managing synchronous liver metastases from colorectal cancer: a multidisciplinary international consensus. *Cancer Treatment Reviews, 41*(9), 729–741. doi:10.1016/j.ctrv.2015.06.006.

Adam, R., Delvart, V., Pascal, G., Valeanu, A., Castaing, D., Azoulay, D., ..., & Bismuth, H. (2004). Rescue surgery for unresectable colorectal liver metastases downstaged by chemotherapy: a model to predict long-term survival. *Annals of Surgery, 240*(4), 644–657 discussion 657-648. doi:10.1097/01.sla.0000141198.92114.f6.

Adam, R., & Kitano, Y. (2019). Multidisciplinary approach of liver metastases from colorectal cancer. *Ann Gastroenterol Surg, 3*(1), 50–56. doi:10.1002/ags3.12227.

Adam, R., Pascal, G., Castaing, D., Azoulay, D., Delvart, V., Paule, B., ..., & Bismuth, H. (2004). Tumor progression while on chemotherapy: a contraindication to liver resection for multiple colorectal metastases? *Annals of Surgery, 240*(6), 1052–1061 discussion 1061-1054. doi:10.1097/01.sla.0000145964.08365.01.

Adam, R., Wicherts, D. A., de Haas, R. J., Aloia, T., Levi, F., Paule, B., ..., & Castaing, D. (2008). Complete pathologic response after preoperative chemotherapy for colorectal liver metastases: myth or reality? *Journal of Clinical Oncology, 26*(10), 1635–1641. doi:10.1200/JCO.2007.13.7471.

Adam, R., Wicherts, D. A., de Haas, R. J., Ciacio, O., Levi, F., Paule, B., ..., & Castaing, D. (2009). Patients with initially unresectable colorectal liver metastases: is there a possibility of cure? *Journal of Clinical Oncology, 27*(11), 1829–1835. doi:10.1200/JCO.2008.19.9273.

Alberts, S. R., Horvath, W. L., Sternfeld, W. C., Goldberg, R. M., Mahoney, M. R., Dakhil, S. R., ..., & Donohue, J. H. (2005). Oxaliplatin, fluorouracil, and leucovorin for patients with unresectable liver-only metastases from colorectal cancer: a North Central Cancer Treatment Group phase II study. *Journal of Clinical Oncology, 23*, 9243. doi:10.1200/JCO.2005.07.740.

Allen, P. J., Kemeny, N., Jarnagin, W., DeMatteo, R., Blumgart, L., & Fong, Y. (2003). Importance of response to neoadjuvant chemotherapy in patients undergoing resection of synchronous colorectal liver metastases. *Journal of Gastrointestinal Surgery, 7*(1), 109–117. doi:10.1016/S1091-255X(02)00121-X.

Altendorf-Hofmann, A., & Scheele, J. (2003). A critical review of the major indicators of prognosis after resection of hepatic metastases from colorectal carcinoma. *Surgical Oncology Clinics of North America, 12*(1), 165–192 xi. doi:10.1016/s1055-3207(02)00091-1.

Aubin, J. M., Bressan, A. K., Grondin, S. C., Dixon, E., MacLean, A. R., Gregg, S., ..., & Ball, C. G. (2018). Assessing resectability of colorectal liver metastases: How do different subspecialties interpret the same data? *Canadian Journal of Surgery, 61*(4), 251–256.

Ayez, N., van der Stok, E. P., de Wilt, H., Radema, S. A., van Hillegersberg, R., Roumen, R. M., …, & Grünhagen, D. J. (2015 Mar 26). Neo-adjuvant chemotherapy followed by surgery versus surgery alone in high-risk patients with resectable colorectal liver metastases: the CHARISMA randomized multicenter clinical trial. *BMC cancer, 15*, 180 PMID: 25884448; PMCID: PMC4377036. doi:10.1186/s12885-015-1199-8.

Berardi, G., De Man, M., Laurent, S., Smeets, P., Tomassini, F., Ariotti, R., …, & Troisi, R. I. (2018). Radiologic and pathologic response to neoadjuvant chemotherapy predicts survival in patients undergoing the liver-first approach for synchronous colorectal liver metastases. *European Journal of Surgical Oncology, 44*(7), 1069–1077. doi:10.1016/j.ejso.2018.03.008.

Biller, L. H., & Schrag, D. (2021). Diagnosis and Treatment of Metastatic Colorectal Cancer: A Review. *Jama, 325*(7), 669–685. doi:10.1001/jama.2021.0106.

Bismuth, H., Adam, R., Levi, F., Farabos, C., Waechter, F., Castaing, D., …, & Engerran, L. (1996). Resection of nonresectable liver metastases from colorectal cancer after neoadjuvant chemotherapy. *Annals of Surgery, 224*(4), 509–520 discussion 520-502. doi:10.1097/00000658-199610000-00009.

3rd Blazer, D. G., Kishi, Y., Maru, D. M., Kopetz, S., Chun, Y. S., Overman, M. J., …, & Vauthey, J. N. (2008). Pathologic response to preoperative chemotherapy: a new outcome end point after resection of hepatic colorectal metastases. *Journal of Clinical Oncology, 26*(33), 5344–5351. doi:10.1200/JCO.2008.17.5299.

Bokemeyer, C., Bondarenko, I., Makhson, A., Hartmann, J. T., Aparicio, J., de Braud, F., …, & Koralewski, P. (2009). Fluorouracil, leucovorin, and oxaliplatin with and without cetuximab in the first-line treatment of metastatic colorectal cancer. *Journal of Clinical Oncology, 27*(5), 663–671. doi:10.1200/JCO.2008.20.8397.

Bridgewater, J. A., Pugh, S. A., Maishman, T., Eminton, Z., Mellor, J., Whitehead, A., …, & New, E. i. (2020). Systemic chemotherapy with or without cetuximab in patients with resectable colorectal liver metastasis (New EPOC): long-term results of a multicentre, randomised, controlled, phase 3 trial. *The Lancet Oncology, 21*(3), 398–411. doi:10.1016/S1470-2045(19)30798-3.

Choti, M. A., Sitzmann, J. V., Tiburi, M. F., Sumetchotimetha, W., Rangsin, R., Schulick, R. D., …, & Cameron, J. L. (2002). Trends in long-term survival following liver resection for hepatic colorectal metastases. *Annals of Surgery, 235*(6), 759–766. doi:10.1097/00000658-200206000-00002.

Chun, Y. S., Vauthey, J. N., Boonsirikamchai, P., Maru, D. M., Kopetz, S., Palavecino, M., …, & Loyer, E. M. (2009). Association of computed tomography morphologic criteria with pathologic response and survival in patients treated with bevacizumab for colorectal liver metastases. *Jama, 302*(21), 2338–2344. doi:10.1001/jama.2009.1755.

Cremolini, C., Loupakis, F., Antoniotti, C., Lonardi, S., Masi, G., Salvatore, L., …, & Falcone, A. (2015). Early tumor shrinkage and depth of response predict long-term outcome in metastatic colorectal cancer patients treated with first-line chemotherapy plus bevacizumab: results from phase III TRIBE trial by the Gruppo Oncologico del Nord Ovest. *Annals of Oncology, 26*(6), 1188–1194. doi:10.1093/annonc/mdv112.

Cremolini, C., Loupakis, F., Antoniotti, C., Lupi, C., Sensi, E., Lonardi, S., …, & Falcone, A. (2015). FOLFOXIRI plus bevacizumab versus FOLFIRI plus bevacizumab as first-line treatment of patients with metastatic colorectal cancer: updated overall survival and molecular subgroup analyses of the open-label, phase 3 TRIBE study. *The Lancet Oncology, 16*(13), 1306–1315. doi:10.1016/S1470-2045(15)00122-9.

Cunningham, D., Allum, W. H., Stenning, S. P., Thompson, J. N., Van de Velde, C. J., Nicolson, M., …, & Participants, M. T. (2006). Perioperative chemotherapy versus surgery alone for resectable gastroesophageal cancer. *New England Journal of Medicine, 355*(1), 11–20. doi:10.1056/NEJMoa055531.

de Gramont, A., Figer, A., Seymour, M., Homerin, M., Hmissi, A., Cassidy, J., …, & Bonetti, A. (2000). Leucovorin and fluorouracil with or without oxaliplatin as first-line treatment in advanced colorectal cancer. *Journal of Clinical Oncology, 18*(16), 2938–2947. doi:10.1200/JCO.2000.18.16.2938.

Douillard, J. Y., Siena, S., Cassidy, J., Tabernero, J., Burkes, R., Barugel, M., …, & Sidhu, R. (2014). Final results from PRIME: randomized phase III study of panitumumab with FOLFOX4 for first-line treatment of metastatic colorectal cancer. *Annals of Oncology, 25*(7), 1346–1355. doi:10.1093/annonc/mdu141.

Dy, G. K., Hobday, T. J., Nelson, G., Windschitl, H. E., O'Connell, M. J., Alberts, S. R., …, & Sargent, D. J. (2009). Long-term survivors of metastatic colorectal cancer treated with systemic chemotherapy alone: a North Central Cancer Treatment Group review of 3811 patients, N0144. *Clinical Colorectal Cancer, 8*(2), 88–93.

Falcone, A., Ricci, S., Brunetti, I., Pfanner, E., Allegrini, G., Barbara, C., …, & Gruppo Oncologico Nord, O. (2007). Phase III trial of infusional fluorouracil, leucovorin, oxaliplatin, and irinotecan (FOLFOXIRI) compared with infusional fluorouracil, leucovorin, and irinotecan (FOLFIRI) as first-line treatment for metastatic colorectal cancer: the Gruppo Oncologico Nord Ovest. *Journal of Clinical Oncology, 25*(13), 1670–1676. doi:10.1200/JCO.2006.09.0928.

Folprecht, G., Gruenberger, T., Bechstein, W., Raab, H. R., Weitz, J., Lordick, F., …, & Kohne, C. H. (2014). Survival of patients with initially unresectable colorectal liver metastases treated with FOLFOX/cetuximab or FOLFIRI/cetuximab in a multidisciplinary concept (CELIM study). *Annals of Oncology, 25*(5), 1018–1025. doi:10.1093/annonc/mdu088.

Folprecht, G., Gruenberger, T., Bechstein, W. O., Raab, H. R., Lordick, F., Hartmann, J. T., …, & Kohne, C. H. (2010). Tumour response and secondary resectability of colorectal liver metastases following neoadjuvant chemotherapy with cetuximab: the CELIM randomised phase 2 trial. *The Lancet Oncology, 11*(1), 38–47. doi:10.1016/S1470-2045(09)70330-4.

Gallagher, D. J., Zheng, J., Capanu, M., Haviland, D., Paty, P., Dematteo, R. P., …, & Kemeny, N. (2009). Response to neoadjuvant chemotherapy does not predict overall survival for patients with synchronous colorectal hepatic metastases. *Annals of Surgical Oncology, 16*(7), 1844–1851. doi:10.1245/s10434-009-0348-1.

Garcia-Alfonso, P., Ferrer, A., Gil, S., Duenas, R., Perez, M. T., Molina, R., …, & Lara, R. (2015). Neoadjuvant and conversion treatment of patients with colorectal liver metastasis: the potential role of bevacizumab and other antiangiogenic agents. *Target Oncol, 10*(4), 453–465. doi:10.1007/s11523-015-0362-0.

Giacchetti, S., Itzhaki, M., Gruia, G., Adam, R., Zidani, R., Kunstlinger, F., …, & Levi, F. (1999). Long-term survival of patients with unresectable colorectal cancer liver metastases following infusional chemotherapy with 5-fluorouracil, leucovorin, oxaliplatin and surgery. *Annals of Oncology, 10*(6), 663–669. doi:10.1023/a:1008347829017.

Goldberg, R. M., Sargent, D. J., Morton, R. F., Fuchs, C. S., Ramanathan, R. K., Williamson, S. K., …, & Alberts, S. R. (2004). A randomized controlled trial of fluorouracil plus leucovorin, irinotecan, and oxaliplatin combinations in patients with previously untreated metastatic colorectal cancer. *Journal of clinical oncology: official journal of the American Society of Clinical Oncology, 22*(1), 23–30. doi:10.1200/JCO.2004.09.046.

Gruenberger, B., Scheithauer, W., Punzengruber, R., Zielinski, C., Tamandl, D., & Gruenberger, T. (2008). Importance of response to neoadjuvant chemotherapy in potentially curable colorectal cancer liver metastases. *BMC cancer, 8*, 120 Apr 25PMID: 18439246; PMCID: PMC2386791. doi:10.1186/1471-2407-8-120.

Gruenberger, B., Tamandl, D., Schueller, J., Scheithauer, W., Zielinski, C., Herbst, F., & Gruenberger, T. (2008). Bevacizumab, capecitabine, and oxaliplatin as neoadjuvant therapy for patients with potentially curable metastatic colorectal cancer. *Journal of Clinical Oncology, 26*(11), 1830–1835. doi:10.1200/JCO.2007.13.7679.

Gruenberger, T., Arnold, D., & Rubbia-Brandt, L. (2012). Pathologic response to bevacizumab-containing chemotherapy in patients with colorectal liver metastases and its correlation with survival. *Surgical Oncology, 21*(4), 309–315. doi:10.1016/j.suronc.2012.07.003.

Gruenberger, T., Bridgewater, J., Chau, I., Garcia Alfonso, P., Rivoire, M., Mudan, S., …, & Adam, R. (2015). Bevacizumab plus mFOLFOX-6 or FOLFOXIRI in patients with initially unresectable liver metastases from colorectal cancer: the OLIVIA multinational randomised phase II trial. *Annals of Oncology, 26*(4), 702–708. doi:10.1093/annonc/mdu580.

Hasegawa, K., Saiura, A., Takayama, T., Miyagawa, S., Yamamoto, J., Ijichi, M., …, & Kokudo, N. (2016). Adjuvant Oral Uracil-Tegafur with Leucovorin for Colorectal Cancer Liver Metastases: A Randomized Controlled Trial. *Plos One, 11*(9), e0162400. doi:10.1371/journal.pone.0162400.

Hochster, H. S., Hart, L. L., Ramanathan, R. K., Childs, B. H., Hainsworth, J. D., Cohn, A. L., …, & Hedrick, E. (2008). Safety and efficacy of oxaliplatin and fluoropyrimidine regimens with or without bevacizumab as first-line treatment of metastatic colorectal cancer: results of the TREE Study. *Journal of Clinical Oncology, 26*(21), 3523–3529. doi:10.1200/JCO.2007.15.4138.

Huiskens, J., van Gulik, T. M., van Lienden, K. P., Engelbrecht, M. R., Meijer, G. A., van Grieken, N. C., …, & Punt, C. J. (2015). Treatment strategies in colorectal cancer patients with initially unresectable liver-only metastases, a study protocol of the randomised phase 3 CAIRO5 study of the Dutch Colorectal Cancer Group (DCCG). *BMC cancer, 15*, 365. doi:10.1186/s12885-015-1323-9.

Hurwitz, H., Fehrenbacher, L., Novotny, W., Cartwright, T., Hainsworth, J., Heim, W., …, & Kabbinavar, F. (2004). Bevacizumab plus irinotecan, fluorouracil, and leucovorin for metastatic colorectal cancer. *New England Journal of Medicine, 350*(23), 2335–2342. doi:10.1056/NEJMoa032691.

Jatzko, G., Wette, V., Muller, M., Lisborg, P., Klimpfinger, M., & Denk, H. (1991). Simultaneous resection of colorectal carcinoma and synchronous liver metastases in a district hospital. *International Journal of Colorectal Disease, 6*(2), 111–114. doi:10.1007/BF00300206.

Jones, R. P., Hamann, S., Malik, H. Z., Fenwick, S. W., Poston, G. J., & Folprecht, G. (2014). Defined criteria for resectability improves rates of secondary resection after systemic therapy for liver limited metastatic colorectal cancer. *European Journal of Cancer, 50*(9), 1590–1601. doi:10.1016/j.ejca.2014.02.024.

Kalofonos, H. P., Aravantinos, G., Kosmidis, P., Papakostas, P., Economopoulos, T., Dimopoulos, M., …, & Fountzilas, G. (2005). Irinotecan or oxaliplatin combined with leucovorin and 5-fluorouracil as first-line treatment in advanced colorectal cancer: a multicenter, randomized, phase II study. *Annals of Oncology, 16*(6), 869–877. doi:10.1093/annonc/mdi193.

Kandutsch, S., Klinger, M., Hacker, S., Wrba, F., Gruenberger, B., & Gruenberger, T. (2008). Patterns of hepatotoxicity after chemotherapy for colorectal cancer liver metastases. *European Journal of Surgical Oncology, 34*(11), 1231–1236. doi:10.1016/j.ejso.2008.01.001.

Kanemitsu, Y., Shimizu, Y., Mizusawa, J., Inaba, Y., Hamaguchi, T., Shida, D., …, & Fukuda, H.JCOG Colorectal Cancer Study Group. (2021). Hepatectomy Followed by mFOLFOX6 Versus Hepatectomy Alone for Liver-Only Metastatic Colorectal Cancer (JCOG0603): A Phase II or III Randomized Controlled Trial. *Journal of Clinical Oncology, 39*(34), 3789–3799 Dec 1Epub 2021 Sep 14. PMID: 34520230. doi:10.1200/JCO.21.01032.

Karoui, M., Penna, C., Amin-Hashem, M., Mitry, E., Benoist, S., Franc, B., …, & Nordlinger, B. (2006). Influence of preoperative chemotherapy on the risk of major hepatectomy for colorectal liver metastases. *Annals of Surgery, 243*(1), 1–7. doi:10.1097/01.sla.0000193603.26265.c3.

Kawaguchi, Y., & Vauthey, J. N. (2020). The Landmark Series: Randomized Control Trials Examining Perioperative Chemotherapy and Postoperative Adjuvant Chemotherapy for Resectable Colorectal Liver Metastasis. *Annals of Surgical Oncology, 27*(11), 4263–4270. doi:10.1245/s10434-020-08777-z.

Klinger, M., Eipeldauer, S., Hacker, S., Herberger, B., Tamandl, D., Dorfmeister, M., …, & Gruenberger, T. (2009). Bevacizumab protects against sinusoidal obstruction syndrome and does not increase response rate in neoadjuvant XELOX/FOLFOX therapy of colorectal cancer liver metastases. *European Journal of Surgical Oncology, 35*(5), 515–520. doi:10.1016/j.ejso.2008.12.013.

Klinger, M., Tamandl, D., Eipeldauer, S., Hacker, S., Herberger, B., Kaczirek, K., …, & Gruenberger, T. (2010). Bevacizumab improves pathological response of colorectal cancer liver metastases treated with XELOX/FOLFOX. *Annals of Surgical Oncology, 17*(8), 2059–2065. doi:10.1245/s10434-010-0972-9.

Loupakis, F., Cremolini, C., Masi, G., Lonardi, S., Zagonel, V., Salvatore, L., …, & Falcone, A. (2014). Initial therapy with FOLFOXIRI and bevacizumab for metastatic colorectal cancer. *New England Journal of Medicine, 371*(17), 1609–1618. doi:10.1056/NEJMoa1403108.

Masi, G., Loupakis, F., Pollina, L., Vasile, E., Cupini, S., Ricci, S., …, & Falcone, A. (2009). Long-term outcome of initially unresectable metastatic colorectal cancer patients treated with 5-fluorouracil/leucovorin, oxaliplatin, and irinotecan (FOLFOXIRI) followed by radical surgery of metastases. *Annals of Surgery, 249*(3), 420–425. doi:10.1097/SLA.0b013e31819a0486.

Maughan, T. S., Adams, R. A., Smith, C. G., Meade, A. M., Seymour, M. T., Wilson, R. H., …, & Investigators, M. C. T. (2011). Addition of cetuximab to oxaliplatin-based first-line combination chemotherapy for treatment of advanced colorectal cancer: results of the randomised phase 3 MRC COIN trial. *Lancet, 377*(9783), 2103–2114. doi:10.1016/S0140-6736(11)60613-2.

Mitry, E., Fields, A. L., Bleiberg, H., Labianca, R., Portier, G., Tu, D., …, & Rougier, P. (2008). Adjuvant chemotherapy after potentially curative resection of metastases from colorectal cancer: a pooled analysis of two randomized trials. *Journal of clinical oncology : official journal of the American Society of Clinical Oncology, 26*(30), 4906–4911. doi:10.1200/JCO.2008.17.3781.

Moghadamyeghaneh, Z., Alizadeh, R. F., Phelan, M., Carmichael, J. C., Mills, S., Pigazzi, A., …, & Stamos, M. J. (2016). Trends in colorectal cancer admissions and stage at presentation: impact of screening. *Surgical Endoscopy, 30*(8), 3604–3610. doi:10.1007/s00464-015-4662-3.

National Comprehensive Cancer Network. (2021). Colon Cancer (Version 3.2021). Retrieved from https://www.nccn.org/professionals/physician_gls/pdf/colon.pdf

Neumann, U. P., Thelen, A., Rocken, C., Seehofer, D., Bahra, M., Riess, H., …, & Neuhaus, P. (2009). Nonresponse to pre-operative chemotherapy does not preclude long-term survival after liver resection in patients with colorectal liver metastases. *Surgery, 146*(1), 52–59. doi:10.1016/j.surg.2009.02.004.

Nordlinger, B., Poston, G. J., & Goldberg, R. M. (2015). Should the results of the new EPOC trial change practice in the management of patients with resectable metastatic colorectal cancer confined to the liver? *Journal of Clinical Oncology, 33*(3), 241–243. doi:10.1200/JCO.2014.58.3989.

Nordlinger, B., Sorbye, H., Glimelius, B., Poston, G. J., Schlag, P. M., Rougier, P., & …Federation Francophone de Cancerologie, D. (2008). Perioperative chemotherapy with FOLFOX4 and surgery versus surgery alone for resectable liver metastases from colorectal cancer (EORTC Intergroup trial 40983): a randomised controlled trial. *Lancet, 371*(9617), 1007–1016. doi:10.1016/S0140-6736(08)60455-9.

Nordlinger, B., Sorbye, H., Glimelius, B., Poston, G. J., Schlag, P. M., Rougier, P., & ...Federation Francophone de Cancerologie, D. (2013). Perioperative FOLFOX4 chemotherapy and surgery versus surgery alone for resectable liver metastases from colorectal cancer (EORTC 40983): long-term results of a randomised, controlled, phase 3 trial. *The Lancet Oncology, 14*(12), 1208–1215. doi:10.1016/S1470-2045(13)70447-9.

Parks, R., Gonen, M., Kemeny, N., Jarnagin, W., D'Angelica, M., DeMatteo, R., ..., & Fong, Y. (2007). Adjuvant chemotherapy improves survival after resection of hepatic colorectal metastases: analysis of data from two continents. *Journal of the American College of Surgeons, 204*(5), 753–761 discussion 761-753. doi:10.1016/j.jamcollsurg.2006.12.036.

Portier, G., Elias, D., Bouche, O., Rougier, P., Bosset, J. F., Saric, J., ..., & Bedenne, L. (2006). Multicenter randomized trial of adjuvant fluorouracil and folinic acid compared with surgery alone after resection of colorectal liver metastases: FFCD ACHBTH AURC 9002 trial. *Journal of Clinical Oncology, 24*(31), 4976–4982. doi:10.1200/JCO.2006.06.8353.

Pozzo, C., Basso, M., Cassano, A., Quirino, M., Schinzari, G., Trigila, N., ..., & Barone, C. (2004). Neoadjuvant treatment of unresectable liver disease with irinotecan and 5-fluorouracil plus folinic acid in colorectal cancer patients. *Annals of Oncology, 15*(6), 933–939. doi:10.1093/annonc/mdh217.

Primrose, J., Falk, S., Finch-Jones, M., Valle, J., O'Reilly, D., Siriwardena, A., ..., & Bridgewater, J. (2014). Systemic chemotherapy with or without cetuximab in patients with resectable colorectal liver metastasis: the New EPOC randomised controlled trial. *The Lancet Oncology, 15*(6), 601–611. doi:10.1016/S1470-2045(14)70105-6.

Raoof, M., Jutric, Z., Haye, S., Ituarte, P. H. G., Zhao, B., Singh, G., ..., & Fong, Y. (2020). Systematic failure to operate on colorectal cancer liver metastases in California. *Cancer medicine, 9*(17), 6256–6267. doi:10.1002/cam4.3316.

Reddy, S. K., Barbas, A. S., & Clary, B. M. (2009). Synchronous colorectal liver metastases: is it time to reconsider traditional paradigms of management? *Annals of Surgical Oncology, 16*(9), 2395–2410. doi:10.1245/s10434-009-0372-1.

Rees, M., Tekkis, P. P., Welsh, F. K., O'Rourke, T., & John, T. G. (2008). Evaluation of long-term survival after hepatic resection for metastatic colorectal cancer: a multifactorial model of 929 patients. *Annals of Surgery, 247*(1), 125–135. doi:10.1097/SLA.0b013e31815aa2c2.

Ribero, D., Wang, H., Donadon, M., Zorzi, D., Thomas, M. B., Eng, C., ..., & Vauthey, J. N. (2007). Bevacizumab improves pathologic response and protects against hepatic injury in patients treated with oxaliplatin-based chemotherapy for colorectal liver metastases. *Cancer, 110*(12), 2761–2767. doi:10.1002/cncr.23099.

Rocha, F. G., & Helton, W. S. (2012). Resectability of colorectal liver metastases: an evolving definition. *HPB (Oxford), 14*(5), 283–284. doi:10.1111/j.1477-2574.2012.00451.x.

Rougier, P., Milan, C., Lazorthes, F., Fourtanier, G., Partensky, C., Baumel, H., & Faivre, J. (1995). Prospective study of prognostic factors in patients with unresected hepatic metastases from colorectal cancer. Fondation Francaise de Cancerologie Digestive. *British Journal of Surgery, 82*(10), 1397–1400. doi:10.1002/bjs.1800821034.

Saltz, L. B., Clarke, S., Diaz-Rubio, E., Scheithauer, W., Figer, A., Wong, R., ..., & Cassidy, J. (2008). Bevacizumab in combination with oxaliplatin-based chemotherapy as first-line therapy in metastatic colorectal cancer: a randomized phase III study. *Journal of Clinical Oncology, 26*(12), 2013–2019. doi:10.1200/JCO.2007.14.9930.

Saltz, L. B., Cox, J. V., Blanke, C., Rosen, L. S., Fehrenbacher, L., Moore, M. J., ..., & Miller, L. L. (2000). Irinotecan plus fluorouracil and leucovorin for metastatic colorectal cancer. Irinotecan Study Group. *New England Journal of Medicine, 343*(13), 905–914. doi:10.1056/NEJM200009283431302.

Sauer, R., Liersch, T., Merkel, S., Fietkau, R., Hohenberger, W., Hess, C., ..., & Rodel, C. (2012). Preoperative versus postoperative chemoradiotherapy for locally advanced rectal cancer: results of the German CAO/ARO/AIO-94 randomized phase III trial after a median follow-up of 11 years. *Journal of Clinical Oncology, 30*(16), 1926–1933. doi:10.1200/JCO.2011.40.1836.

Scheele, J., Stang, R., Altendorf-Hofmann, A., & Paul, M. (1995). Resection of colorectal liver metastases. *World Journal of Surgery, 19*(1), 59–71. doi:10.1007/BF00316981.

Shah, K., & Clary, B. (2013). Synchronous colorectal liver metastases: the "surgeon as oncologist" perspective. *Minerva Chirurgica, 68*(1), 49–76.

Snoeren, N., van Hillegersberg, R., Schouten, S. B., Bergman, A. M., van Werkhoven, E., Dalesio, O., & ...Hepatica study, g. (2017). Randomized Phase III Study to Assess Efficacy and Safety of Adjuvant CAPOX with or without Bevacizumab in Patients after Resection of Colorectal Liver Metastases: HEPATICA study. *Neoplasia, 19*(2), 93–99. doi:10.1016/j.neo.2016.08.010.

Sohal, D. P. S., Duong, M., Ahmad, S. A., Gandhi, N. S., Beg, M. S., Wang-Gillam, A., ..., & Hochster, H. S. (2021). Efficacy of Perioperative Chemotherapy for Resectable Pancreatic Adenocarcinoma: A Phase 2 Randomized Clinical Trial. *JAMA oncology, 7*(3), 421–427. doi:10.1001/jamaoncol.2020.7328.

Tomasello, G., Petrelli, F., Ghidini, M., Russo, A., Passalacqua, R., & Barni, S. (2017). FOLFOXIRI Plus Bevacizumab as Conversion Therapy for Patients With Initially Unresectable Metastatic Colorectal Cancer: A Systematic Review and Pooled Analysis. *JAMA oncology, 3*(7), e170278. doi:10.1001/jamaoncol.2017.0278.

Tzeng, C. W., & Aloia, T. A. (2013). Colorectal liver metastases. *Journal of Gastrointestinal Surgery, 17*(1), 195–201 quiz p 201-192. doi:10.1007/s11605-012-2022-3.

Van Cutsem, E., Kohne, C. H., Hitre, E., Zaluski, J., Chang Chien, C. R., Makhson, A., …, & Rougier, P. (2009). Cetuximab and chemotherapy as initial treatment for metastatic colorectal cancer. *New England Journal of Medicine, 360*(14), 1408–1417. doi:10.1056/NEJMoa0805019.

Vauthey, J. N., Pawlik, T. M., Ribero, D., Wu, T. T., Zorzi, D., Hoff, P. M., …, & Abdalla, E. K. (2006). Chemotherapy regimen predicts steatohepatitis and an increase in 90-day mortality after surgery for hepatic colorectal metastases. *Journal of Clinical Oncology, 24*(13), 2065–2072. doi:10.1200/JCO.2005.05.3074.

Vega, E. A., Salehi, O., Nicolaescu, D., Dussom, E. M., Alarcon, S. V., Kozyreva, O., Simonds, J., Schnipper, D., & Conrad, C. (2021 Nov). Failure to Cure Patients with Colorectal Liver Metastases: The Impact of the Liver Surgeon. *Annals of Surgical Oncology, 28*(12), 7698–7706 Epub 2021 Apr 30. Erratum in: Ann Surg Oncol. 2021 May 18;: PMID: 33939045. doi:10.1245/s10434-021-10030-0.

Vera, R., Gomez Dorronsoro, M., Lopez-Ben, S., Viudez, A., Queralt, B., Hernandez, I., …, & Figueras, J. (2014). Retrospective analysis of pathological response in colorectal cancer liver metastases following treatment with bevacizumab. *Clinical & translational oncology, 16*(8), 739–745. doi:10.1007/s12094-013-1142-x.

Vigano, L., Capussotti, L., Barroso, E., Nuzzo, G., Laurent, C., Ijzermans, J. N., …, & Adam, R. (2012). Progression while receiving preoperative chemotherapy should not be an absolute contraindication to liver resection for colorectal metastases. *Annals of Surgical Oncology, 19*(9), 2786–2796. doi:10.1245/s10434-012-2382-7.

Willett, C. G., Boucher, Y., di Tomaso, E., Duda, D. G., Munn, L. L., Tong, R. T., …, & Jain, R. K. (2004). Direct evidence that the VEGF-specific antibody bevacizumab has antivascular effects in human rectal cancer. *Nature Medicine, 10*(2), 145–147. doi:10.1038/nm988.

Wong, R., Cunningham, D., Barbachano, Y., Saffery, C., Valle, J., Hickish, T., …, & Chau, I. (2011). A multicentre study of capecitabine, oxaliplatin plus bevacizumab as perioperative treatment of patients with poor-risk colorectal liver-only metastases not selected for upfront resection. *Annals of Oncology, 22*(9), 2042–2048. doi:10.1093/annonc/mdq714.

Ychou, M., Hohenberger, W., Thezenas, S., Navarro, M., Maurel, J., Bokemeyer, C., …, & Santoro, A. (2009). A randomized phase III study comparing adjuvant 5-fluorouracil/folinic acid with FOLFIRI in patients following complete resection of liver metastases from colorectal cancer. *Annals of Oncology, 20*(12), 1964–1970. doi:10.1093/annonc/mdp236.

Ychou, M., Rivoire, M., Thezenas, S., Quenet, F., Delpero, J. R., Rebischung, C., …, & Assenat, E. (2013). A randomized phase II trial of three intensified chemotherapy regimens in first-line treatment of colorectal cancer patients with initially unresectable or not optimally resectable liver metastases. The METHEP trial. *Annals of Surgical Oncology, 20*(13), 4289–4297. doi:10.1245/s10434-013-3217-x.

Ychou, M., Viret, F., Kramar, A., Desseigne, F., Mitry, E., Guimbaud, R., …, & Nordlinger, B. (2008). Tritherapy with fluorouracil/leucovorin, irinotecan and oxaliplatin (FOLFIRINOX): a phase II study in colorectal cancer patients with non-resectable liver metastases. *Cancer Chemotheraphy and Pharmacology, 62*(2), 195–201. doi:10.1007/s00280-007-0588-3.

Ye, L. C., Liu, T. S., Ren, L., Wei, Y., Zhu, D. X., Zai, S. Y., …, & Xu, J. (2013). Randomized controlled trial of cetuximab plus chemotherapy for patients with KRAS wild-type unresectable colorectal liver-limited metastases. *Journal of Clinical Oncology, 31*(16), 1931–1938. doi:10.1200/JCO.2012.44.8308.

CHAPTER

6

Management of the disappeared colorectal liver metastasis

Sidra Bonner and Hari Nathan

Department of Surgery, University of Michigan, Ann Arbor, MI

Introduction

Among individuals diagnosed with colorectal cancer, about 25–30 percent will develop liver metastases (Engstrand, Nilsson, Strömberg, Jonas, and Freedman, 2018; Hackl et al., 2014; Manfredi et al., 2006). Historically, less than 25 percent of these patients present with resectable disease due to the presence of extra-hepatic metastatic disease, involvement of critical vascular or biliary structures, or insufficient functional liver remnant [(Adam et al., 2004; Hackl et al., 2014). The surgical management of colorectal liver metastases (CLM) has significantly changed in the last several decades due to increased surgical safety and greater availability of liver-directed and parenchyma-sparing therapies. Additionally, increased effectiveness of systemic therapy for CLM has allowed some patients to convert to resectability (Adam et al., 2004). Even for patients with initially resectable disease, administration of pre-operative chemotherapy remains common, despite lack of conclusive evidence of benefit.

There has been a modest increase in response rates of CLM with modern systemic therapy regimens (Adam et al., 2004). Standard combination chemotherapy regimens including 5-fluorouracil (5-FU) with folinic acid (FA) plus oxaliplatin (FOLFOX), 5-FU/FA with irinotecan(FOLFIRI), capecitabine plus oxaliplatin (Capeox) and capecitabine plus irinotecan (CAPIRI) yield response rates of 39 percent−62 percent (Goldberg et al., 2004; Nordlinger et al., 2013; Saltz et al., 2000). Targeted monoclonal antibody therapy in addition to combination therapy regimens have also been found to increase response rates. (Ikoma, Raghav, and Chang, 2017; Xie, Chen, and Fang, 2020). While radiographic response is typically associated with improved outcomes, a complete radiographic response or disappearance of CLM following systemic therapy presents a diagnostic and therapeutic challenge. The complete disappearance of CLM after chemotherapy occurs in approximately 5–25 percent of patients (Auer et al., 2010; Lucidi, Hendlisz, Van Laethem, and Donckier, 2016). The prognostic role of disappearing liver metastases (DLM) is unclear given that radiologic complete response does not fully correlate with pathologic complete response. The wide range of management pathways of

DOI: https://doi.org/10.1016/B978-0-323-91706-3.00018-7

DLM including observation, additional systemic therapy, and/or resection of original site of disease currently lack significant evidence regarding oncologic outcomes to guide high level recommendations (Araujo et al., 2020; Kuhlmann, van Hilst, Fisher, and Poston, 2016). Thus, interdisciplinary teams should be central to the current management of DLM for patients with colorectal cancer. In this chapter, the current challenges of diagnostic modalities and management of DLM are discussed.

Defining disappearing colorectal liver metastasis (DLM)

Disappearing liver metastasis (DLM) is defined as a colorectal liver metastasis that becomes undetectable on cross sectional imaging, typically following the receipt of systemic therapy. The modality of cross-sectional imaging used for patients with CLM is central to the identification of DLMs. The sensitivity and specificity of each type of imaging technique is key to determining if a prior liver metastasis has disappeared. The most common imaging techniques used include computed tomography (CT), fluorodeoxyglucose positron emission tomography (FDG-PET), and magnetic resonance imaging (MRI). CT imaging is the most used study for the monitoring of liver metastases during administration of systemic therapy. Dual phase, contrast-enhanced CT has a sensitivity of 60–85 percent with specificity near 90 percent (Kamel et al., 2003; Van Kessel et al., 2012). Hepatic steatosis, which is present in 10–45 percent of the general population and increases in prevalence among patients who have received chemotherapy, impairs the diagnostic performance of CT (Browning et al., 2004; Lazo et al., 2013). The lower density of steatotic liver parenchyma on CT leads to less contrast enhancement and less liver-to-lesion contrast, which limits the detection of metastases (Van Kessel et al., 2012).

FDG-PET imaging, with or without concurrent CT, has been used as a complementary study for the detection of CLM and overall tumor burden. FDG-PET imaging alone does not provide anatomical detail but has high sensitivity for the detection of intrahepatic and extrahepatic disease (Van Kessel et al., 2012). Studies to date have also demonstrated that FDG-PET alone is not superior to CT imaging. However, combined FDG-PET/CT allows for increased sensitivity and detection of clear anatomic location compared to FDG-PET alone (Van Kessel et al., 2012; Tsilimigras et al., 2019). The CT included in FDG-PET/CT is for registration only and is typically a non-contrast, low-resolution scan that should not be used for operative planning. Treatment with chemotherapy has significant impact on the sensitivity of both FDG-PET and FDG-PET/CT. A prior meta-analysis demonstrated that in the setting of systemic chemotherapy, the sensitivity for detecting CLM significantly decreased for FDG-PET and FDG-PET/CT compared to the setting of chemo-naivety. This is due to induced necrosis and reduced metabolic activity of cancer cells which leads to decreased visualization of lesions (Lucidi et al., 2016). The role of FDG-PET/CT in the detection of DLM has been limited to few studies and its role remains unclear in the management of DLM (Kamel et al., 2003).

MRI is the most sensitive and specific diagnostic modality for CLM. MRI imaging has a sensitivity of 80–85 percent and specificity of 90–95 percent for the detection of CLM (Van Kessel et al., 2012). Prior research comparing CT to contrast enhanced MRI imaging has demonstrated that liver MRI consistently has higher sensitivity and specificity (Bhattacharjya et al., 2004; Choi et al., 2018; Park et al., 2017; Rappeport et al., 2007). Unlike PET/CT and CT

TABLE 6.1 The relationship between DLM on imaging and pathologic response.

	Pathologic DLM	Radiologic DLM	NPV	95 percent CI
CT				
Auer et al., 2010	75	118	0.64	(0.55–0.72)
Benoist et al. (2006)	14	66	0.21	(0.13–0.33)
Tanaka et al. (2009)	44	86	0.51	(0.41–0.62)
MRI				
Auer et al. (2010)	33	44	0.75	(0.60–0.86)
Ntourakis et al. (2016)	30	77	0.39	(0.29–0.50)
Park et al. (2017)	43	55	0.78	(0.65–0.87)

imaging, MRI imaging maintains a high sensitivity in the setting of hepatic steatosis. A prior meta-analysis demonstrated a pooled sensitivity of 85.7 percent among patients receiving systemic therapy (Van Kessel et al., 2012). A recent study found that MRI imaging had a significantly higher positive predictive value for the detection of DLM compared to contrast-enhanced CT (Park et al., 2017). These findings support that the standard of practice should be to use MRI imaging as the primary initial imaging modality for detection of CLM (Muaddi et al., 2021).

To improve the diagnostic sensitivity and specificity, liver MRI are often performed with the gadolinium-based contrast agent gadoxetate disodium (Eovist). Eovist is a hepatobiliary contrast agent that is uptaken and excreted by hepatocytes. Eovist MRI has increased sensitivity in the detection of smaller CLM and in the setting of hepatic steatosis compared to other MRI contrast agents (Owen et al., 2016). A systematic review of the diagnostic accuracy of Eovist -MRI for liver metastases compared to contrast CT demonstrated that it was significantly more sensitive (RR=1.29, 95 percent CI=1.18–1.7, $p < 0.001$) (Vreugdenburg et al., 2016). Studies have found that Eovist-MRI has higher sensitivity for smaller lesions (<1cm) with greater diagnostic confidence and interobserver concordance (Kim et al., 2017; Vreugdenburg et al., 2016).

New techniques to better delineate anatomy and detect subtle lesions are being studied with a primary focus on the utility of augmented reality. This modality uses a three-dimensional model of a patient's anatomy built from the superimposition of images from CT imaging onto real-time images of a patient to improve identification and visualization of anatomic structures (Nicolau, Soler, Mutter, and Marescaux, 2011). Other investigations have demonstrated potential benefit of augmented reality to help detect DLM intra-operatively (Ntourakis et al., 2016). However, larger-scale studies will be necessary to understand the utility of this technique (Table 6.1).

The complex association between DLM on imaging and pathologic response is central to the management challenge of DLM. The correlation of radiologic disappearance of liver metastases to pathologic response has varied in multiple studies. The variability in findings is due to differences in neoadjuvant therapies and radiologic modalities studied. For instance, a retrospective study using CT imaging demonstrated that 66 percent of CT defined DLM represented a "true complete response," defined as no tumor detected in the resection specimen or no repeat appearance on follow up imaging at 1 year. This study also included analysis which determined that hepatic arterial infusion (HAI) chemotherapy, inability to observe the DLM on additional MRI imaging, and normalization of serum carcinoembryonic antigen levels were independently associated with a true complete response (Auer et al., 2010). A contrasting study on DLM defined by CT imaging observed residual disease in 83 percent of DLMs determined by persistent macroscopic disease at time of laparotomy, microscopic disease, or early recurrence within 1 year (Benoist et al., 2006). Taken in combination, these two studies highlight the limitations of CT imaging as the imaging modality of choice for frequent imaging during neoadjuvant therapy.

Comparatively, studies using MRI have demonstrated a stronger association between DLM on imaging and pathologic response. For instance, a retrospective review of 200 CLM identified that 77 of the 200 metastases (38.5 percent) disappeared on Eovist-MRI. Of those lesions, approximately 55 percent demonstrated viable tumor on pathologic review or recurred within 1 year on follow up imaging (Owen et al., 2016). An additional study demonstrated that patients with DLM, who underwent both EOVIST MRI and diffusion weighted imaging had recurrence rates of 10.9 percent and 15.7 percent at 1 and 2 years respectively (Kim et al., 2017). A prior study of MRI with gadolinium-based contrast compared to contrast enhanced CT demonstrated had a significantly higher positive predictive value for pathologic response (78 percent; 95 percent CI: 63.68 percent–87.74 percent vs. 35.2 percent; 95 percent CI:25.11 percent–46.79 percent; $P<.001$) (Park et al., 2017). These findings suggest that disappearance on MRI imaging alone, despite high sensitivity, doesn't completely predict a complete pathologic response. However, the association between imaging and pathologic findings is stronger for MRI than CT imaging. Therefore, MRI imaging, preferably with gadoxetate disodium, is the preferable imaging study for patients with CLM.

Predictors of DLM pathologic response

Given that systemic treatment regimens are routinely used for individuals with unresectable disease and increasingly being used for individuals with initially resectable metastatic disease, several studies have sought to identify factors might contribute to higher rates of true pathologic complete response. Patient factors, characteristics of metastases on imaging studies and specific systemic therapy regimens are associated with higher complete pathologic responses. Patients factors including age under 60 years old, BMI < 30 kg/m2, and lower baseline CEA or normalization of CEA levels are associated with complete pathologic response (Adam et al., 2004; Auer et al., 2010; Spolverato et al., 2015). Characteristics of CLM associated with the development of DLM included smaller size (< 3 cm) and multiple metastases (>3 lesions) (Adam et al., 2004; Benoist et al., 2006; van Vledder et al., 2010). Additionally, assessment of MRI imaging characteristics demonstrated that non-reticular hypodensity of liver parenchyma was associated with no early recurrence of DLM. Lastly, increased number of cycles of systemic therapy prior to surgery and platin-based chemotherapy have been found to be associated with higher rates of development of DLM (van Vledder et al., 2010). However, despite these factors correlating with a true pathologic response of a DLM, this can only be confirmed by surgical resection or recurrent imaging over a sustained period (Table 6.2).

The management challenges posed by the discordance between imaging findings and pathologic response highlights the consequences of when systemic treatment for CLM is continued for maximal response as opposed to resectability. The National Comprehensive Cancer

TABLE 6.2 Addressing the end-point of neo-adjuvant chemotherapy

Authors (Year)	No. of Patients with DLM	No. of DLM evaluated	Percent true complete response
Auer et al. (2010)	39	118	66 percent
Benoist et al. (2006)	38	66	17 percent
van Vledder et al. (2010)	40	127	47 percent
Ferrero et al. (2012)	33	67	38 percent
Tanaka et al. (2009)	23	86	69 percent

Network (NCCN) in the United States currently recommends synchronous or staged colorectal resection with liver resection as the preferred treatment for resectable disease (Benson et al., 2021). The NCCN guidelines also note that at institutions with experience in surgical and medical oncologic expertise, hepatic artery infusion with systemic neoadjuvant therapy for 2–3 months followed by synchronous or staged primary colorectal and liver resection can be done (Benson et al., 2021). The use of systemic therapy for lesions that are initially resectable remains controversial. Yet, there are cases when a short pre-defined course of systemic therapy may aid surgical resection, such as in the case of parenchymal sparing hepatectomy (Chua, Saxena, Liauw, Kokandi, and Morris, 2010; Matsumura et al., 2016; Moris et al., 2017; Nordlinger et al., 2013). If a patient receives chemotherapy for resectable disease, high quality imaging should be performed with MRI prior to therapy and as needed to supplement CT during the administration of therapy. The primary goal of systemic therapy administration for patients with resectable disease should be safe resection as opposed to maximal response of the metastasis. For patients with initially unresectable metastases, for which systemic therapy is standard of care, the NCCN recommends that patients be re-evaluated for conversion to resectability every 2 months with liver MR or CT imaging.

Intra-Operative evaluation of DLM

The use of intraoperative ultrasonography (IOUS) is a standard method used for the detection of DLM at the time of resection. IOUS in conjunction with intraoperative palpation and visualization can improve the detection of DLM. A prior study of IOUS detection found that during open laparotomy of patients with a total 67 DLM, only 6 lesions were identified with direct visualization and palpation with an additional 39 lesions identified with IOUS (Leen et al., 2006)]. These findings along with additional reports have found that 10–60 percent of DLM can be identified when IOUS is used (Auer et al., 2010; Benoist et al., 2006; Ferrero et al., 2012). Contrast-enhanced IOUS (CE-IOUS) using sulfurhexafluoride and perflubutane, as contrast agents, is a novel technique with prior research indicating that it may be superior in identifying more liver metastases than conventional IOUS imaging resulting in a change in surgical planning in 15 percent—30 percent of cases (Leen et al., 2006; Takahashi et al., 2012). Research of CE-IOUS is limited in the setting of DLM, however in one study of 32 DLMs, 4 lesions were identified with using IOUS and CE-IOUS allowed the detection of an additional 12 lesions. Within this study, of the pathologically confirmed metastases, CE-IOUS identified 79 percent compared to 21 percent with IOUS (p=.004) (Arita et al., 2014).

A surgeon's ability to detect DLM even with standard intraoperative methods of direct visualization, palpation and IOUS with or without contrast enhancement are affected by other anatomic factors. The depth and anatomic location of DLM in addition to the degree of hepatic steatosis have significant effect on the detection of DLM intra-operatively. For example, subcapsular lesions that have disappeared on imaging may still be visible intra-operatively as a capsular scar. Due to these challenges, the use of fiducials as an additional modality for identification of DLM has been assessed. The utility of identifying high risk lesions and performing image guided percutaneous placement of intrahepatic fiducial markers has been investigated as a method to improve localization of DLM. Published reports of appropriate technique have stated that the fiducial should be placed at the posterior edge to aid with intraoperative detection of resection depth to achieve a negative posterior margin (Passot et al., 2016; Zalinski, Abdalla, Mahvash, and Vauthey, 2009). However, there are no specific current studies detailing the effectiveness of fiducial placement prior to systemic therapy and the intra-operative detection of DLM. Given that the fiducial placement is a procedure with specific procedural risks and associated costs, it is important to evaluate fully the added clinical benefit for patients.

Surgical resection versus surveillance of DLM

The primary management strategies of DLMs include additional systemic therapy, surgical resection, ablation or surveillance with definitive surgical or ablative therapy for recurrent disease. To date, there have been very few studies comparing these various treatment pathways and associated recurrence-free survival and overall survival. In a prior study comparing surgery to surveillance alone, patients receiving surveillance alone demonstrated intrahepatic recurrence free survival of 40.2 percent at 1 year and 16.1 percent at 3 years compared to 68.8 percent and 35.1 percent in patients undergoing surgical resection (van Vledder et al., 2010). Additional studies have found that DLM left in situ with ongoing surveillance have recurrence free survival at 5 years of 23 percent to 41 percent (Gaujoux et al., 2011; Tanaka et al., 2009). For DLM left in situ, most recurrent lesions occur within 24 months and almost half of patients that develop local recurrence at the site of the untreated DLM will develop recurrence at another site (Elias et al., 2007; Tanaka et al., 2009; van Vledder et al., 2010). Given the high rates of residual disease at individual DLM and the risk of recurrence, many advocate that liver resection or ablation at the original sites of disease should be performed if possible (Bischof, Clary, Maithel, and Pawlik, 2013; Kuhlmann et al., 2016). When the original site of disease is unresectable, patients will require regular follow-up imaging with MRI to guide management of any recurrent disease.

Surgeon management of DLM remains variable given the absence of evidence identifying a superior management strategy in survival for patients. A study of hepatobiliary surgeons found 99 percent had managed patients with DLM and 63 percent waited a few-months to assess for sustained response prior to proceeding with surgical or ablative therapy. For superficial DLM, 49 percent of surgeons elect for observation and 31 percent resect the lesion. Additionally, only one-quarter of surgeons reported using fiducial markers for lesions <1 cm (Melstrom et al., 2021). The variation in practice management highlights the importance interdisciplinary management with tailored approaches based on patient and tumor characteristics. Our approach to management of DLM is provided in Fig. 6.1.

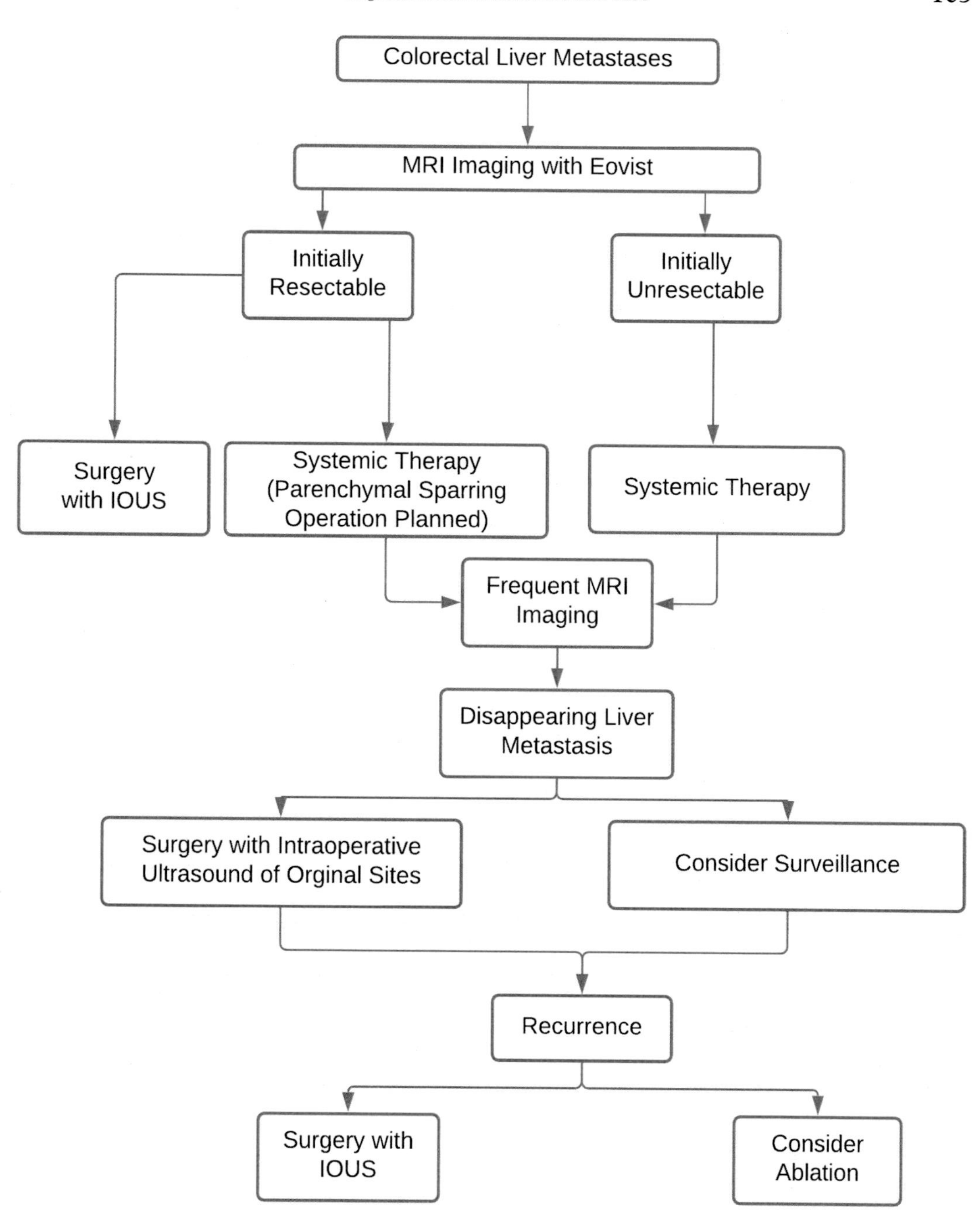

FIGURE 6.1 Algorithm for clinical approach to Disappearing Liver Metastases. Management of Disappearing Liver Metastases.

Summary

Disappearing liver metastases following systemic therapy presents a unique challenge. Whether a lesion has truly disappeared is related to the quality of the imaging modality chosen. It is critical that all patients receive MRI imaging prior to initiation of systemic therapy in order to provide an accurate baseline assessment of disease. The complete response of CLM imaging should not be mistaken for a full pathologic response given the high levels of residual disease detected on final pathology. Rather than treating lesions to maximal response, surgical resection should usually be performed once a lesion is resectable, or has reached a pre-defined tumor burden goal to facilitate parenchymal sparing operations.

References

Adam, R., Delvart, V., Pascal, G., Valeanu, A., Castaing, D., Azoulay, D., et al. (2004). Rescue surgery for unresectable colorectal liver metastases downstaged by chemotherapy: a model to predict long-term survival. *Annals of Surgery*, 240(4), 644–658. https://doi.org/10.1097/01.sla.0000141198.92114.f6.

Araujo, R. L. C., Milani, J. M., Armentano, D. P., Moreira, R. B., Pinto, G. S. F., de Castro, L. A., et al. (2020). Disappearing colorectal liver metastases: strategies for the management of patients achieving a radiographic complete response after systemic chemotherapy. *Journal of Surgical Oncology*, 121(5), 848–856. https://doi.org/10.1002/jso.25784.

Arita, J., Ono, Y., Takahashi, M., Inoue, Y., Takahashi, Y., & Saiura, A. (2014). Usefulness of contrast-enhanced intraoperative ultrasound in identifying disappearing liver metastases from colorectal carcinoma after chemotherapy. *Annals of Surgical Oncology*, 21(3), S390–S397. https://doi.org/10.1245/s10434-014-3576-y.

Auer, R. C., White, R. R., Kemeny, N. E., Schwartz, L. H., Shia, J., Blumgart, L. H., et al. (2010). Predictors of a true complete response among disappearing liver metastases from colorectal cancer after chemotherapy. *Cancer*, 116(6), 1502–1509. https://doi.org/10.1002/cncr.24912.

Benoist, S., Brouquet, A., Penna, C., Julié, C., El Hajjam, M., Chagnon, S., et al. (2006). Complete response of colorectal liver metastases after chemotherapy: does it mean cure? *Journal of Clinical Oncology*, 24(24), 3939–3945. https://doi.org/10.1200/JCO.2006.05.8727.

Benson, A. B., Al-Hawary, M. M., Azad, C., Y.-J. , C., K. , K., Cohen, S., et al. (2021). *NCCN Guidelines Version 3.2021 Colon Cancer Continue NCCN Guidelines Panel Disclosures*.

Bhattacharjya, S., Bhattacharjya, T., Baber, S., Tibballs, J. M., Watkinson, A. F., & Davidson, B. R. (2004). Prospective study of contrast-enhanced computed tomography, computed tomography during arterioportography, and magnetic resonance imaging for staging colorectal liver metastases for liver resection. *British Journal of Surgery*, 91(10), 1361–1369. https://doi.org/10.1002/bjs.4699.

Bischof, D. A., Clary, B. M., Maithel, S. K., & Pawlik, T. M. (2013). Surgical management of disappearing colorectal liver metastases. *British Journal of Surgery*, 100(11), 1414–1420. https://doi.org/10.1002/bjs.9213.

Browning, J. D., Szczepaniak, L. S., Dobbins, R., Nuremberg, P., Horton, J. D., Cohen, J. C., et al. (2004). Prevalence of hepatic steatosis in an urban population in the United States: impact of ethnicity. *Hepatology*, 40(6), 1387–1395. https://doi.org/10.1002/hep.20466.

Choi, S. H., Kim, S. Y., Park, S. H., Kim, K. W., Lee, J. Y., Lee, S. S., et al. (2018). Diagnostic performance of CT, gadoxetate disodium-enhanced MRI, and PET/CT for the diagnosis of colorectal liver metastasis: systematic review and meta-analysis. *Journal of Magnetic Resonance Imaging*, 47(5), 1237–1250. https://doi.org/10.1002/jmri.25852.

Chua, T. C., Saxena, A., Liauw, W., Kokandi, A., & Morris, D. L. (2010). Systematic review of randomized and nonrandomized trials of the clinical response and outcomes of neoadjuvant systemic chemotherapy for resectable colorectal liver metastases. *Annals of Surgical Oncology*, 17(2), 492–501. https://doi.org/10.1245/s10434-009-0781-1.

Elias, D., Goere, D., Boige, V., Kohneh-Sharhi, N., Malka, D., Tomasic, G., et al. (2007). Outcome of posthepatectomy-missing colorectal liver metastases after complete response to chemotherapy: impact of adjuvant intra-arterial hepatic oxaliplatin. *Annals of Surgical Oncology*, 14(11), 3188–3194. https://doi.org/10.1245/s10434-007-9482-9.

Engstrand, J., Nilsson, H., Strömberg, C., Jonas, E., & Freedman, J. (2018). Colorectal cancer liver metastases - a population-based study on incidence, management and survival. *BMC Cancer*, 18(1), 78, Published 2018 Jan 15. https://doi.org/10.1186/s12885-017-3925-x.

Ferrero, A., Langella, S., Russolillo, N., Vigano', L., Tesoriere, R. L., & Capussotti, L. (2012). Intraoperative Detection of Disappearing Colorectal Liver Metastases as a Predictor of Residual Disease. *Journal of Gastrointestinal Surgery, 16*(4), 806–814. https://doi.org/10.1007/s11605-011-1810-5.

Gaujoux, S., Goéré, D., Dumont, F., Souadka, A., Dromain, C., Ducreux, M., et al. (2011). Complete radiological response of colorectal liver metastases after chemotherapy: what can we expect? *Digestive Surgery, 28*(2), 114–120. https://doi.org/10.1159/000323820.

Goldberg, R. M., Sargent, D. J., Morton, R. F., Fuchs, C. S., Ramanathan, R. K., Williamson, S. K., et al. (2004). A randomized controlled trial of fluorouracil plus leucovorin, irinotecan, and oxaliplatin combinations in patients with previously untreated metastatic colorectal cancer. *Journal of Clinical Oncology, 22*(1), 23–30. https://doi.org/10.1200/JCO.2004.09.046.

Hackl, C., Neumann, P., Gerken, M., Loss, M., Klinkhammer-Schalke, M., & Schlitt, H. J. (2014). Treatment of colorectal liver metastases in Germany: a ten-year population-based analysis of 5772 cases of primary colorectal adenocarcinoma. *BMC Cancer, 14*, 810. https://doi.org/10.1186/1471-2407-14-810.

Ikoma, N., Raghav, K., & Chang, G. (2017). An Update on Randomized Clinical Trials in Metastatic Colorectal Carcinoma. *Surgical Oncology Clinics of North America, 26*(4), 667–687. https://doi.org/10.1016/j.soc.2017.05.007.

Kamel, I. R., Choti, M. A., Horton, K. M., Braga, H. J. V., Birnbaum, B. A., Fishman, E. K., et al. (2003). Surgically staged focal liver lesions: accuracy and reproducibility of dual-phase helical CT for detection and characterization. *Radiology, 227*(3), 752–757. https://doi.org/10.1148/radiol.2273011768.

Kim, S. S., Song, K. D., Kim, Y. K., Kim, H. C., Huh, J. W., Park, Y. S., et al. (2017). Disappearing or residual tiny ($\leq$5 mm) colorectal liver metastases after chemotherapy on gadoxetic acid-enhanced liver MRI and diffusion-weighted imaging: is local treatment required? *European Radiology, 27*(7), 3088–3096. https://doi.org/10.1007/s00330-016-4644-4.

Kuhlmann, K., van Hilst, J., Fisher, S., & Poston, G. (2016). Management of disappearing colorectal liver metastases. *European Journal of Surgical Oncology, 42*(12), 1798–1805. https://doi.org/10.1016/j.ejso.2016.05.005.

Lazo, M., Hernaez, R., Eberhardt, M. S., Bonekamp, S., Kamel, I., Guallar, E., et al. (2013). Prevalence of nonalcoholic fatty liver disease in the United States: the third national health and nutrition examination survey, 1988-1994. *American Journal of Epidemiology, 178*(1), 38–45. https://doi.org/10.1093/aje/kws448.

Leen, E., Ceccotti, P., Moug, S. J., Glen, P., MacQuarrie, J., Angerson, W. J., et al. (2006). Potential value of contrast-enhanced intraoperative ultrasonography during partial hepatectomy for metastases: an essential investigation before resection? *Annals of Surgery, 243*(2), 236–240. https://doi.org/10.1097/01.sla.0000197708.77063.07.

Lucidi, V., Hendlisz, A., Van Laethem, J. L., & Donckier, V. (2016). Missing metastases as a model to challenge current therapeutic algorithms in colorectal liver metastases. *World Journal of Gastroenterology, 22*(15), 3937–3944. https://doi.org/10.3748/wjg.v22.i15.3937.

Manfredi, S., Lepage, C., Hatem, C., Coatmeur, O., Faivre, J., & Bouvier, A. M. (2006). Epidemiology and management of liver metastases from colorectal cancer. *Annals of Surgery, 244*(2), 254–259. https://doi.org/10.1097/01.sla.0000217629.94941.cf.

Matsumura, M., Mise, Y., Saiura, A., Inoue, Y., Ishizawa, T., Ichida, H., et al. (2016). Parenchymal-Sparing Hepatectomy Does Not Increase Intrahepatic Recurrence in Patients with Advanced Colorectal Liver Metastases. *Annals of Surgical Oncology, 23*(11), 3718–3726. https://doi.org/10.1245/s10434-016-5278-0.

Melstrom, L. G., Warner, S. G., Wong, P., Sun, V., Raoof, M., Singh, G., et al. (2021). Management of disappearing colorectal liver metastases: an international survey. *HPB, 23*(4), 506–511. https://doi.org/10.1016/j.hpb.2020.10.005.

Moris, D., Ronnekleiv-Kelly, S., Rahnemai-Azar, A. A., Felekouras, E., Dillhoff, M., Schmidt, C., et al. (2017). Parenchymal-Sparing Versus Anatomic Liver Resection for Colorectal Liver Metastases: a Systematic Review. *Journal of Gastrointestinal Surgery, 21*(6), 1076–1085. https://doi.org/10.1007/s11605-017-3397-y.

Muaddi, H., Silva, S., Choi, W. J., Coburn, N., Hallet, J., Law, C., et al. (2021). When is a Ghost Really Gone? A Systematic Review and Meta-analysis of the Accuracy of Imaging Modalities to Predict Complete Pathological Response of Colorectal Cancer Liver Metastases After Chemotherapy. *Annals of Surgical Oncology, 28*(11), 6805–6813. https://doi.org/10.1245/s10434-021-09824-z.

Nicolau, S., Soler, L., Mutter, D., & Marescaux, J. (2011). Augmented reality in laparoscopic surgical oncology. *Surgical Oncology, 20*(3), 189–201. https://doi.org/10.1016/j.suronc.2011.07.002.

Nordlinger, B., Sorbye, H., Glimelius, B., Poston, G. J., Schlag, P. M., Rougier, P., et al. (2013). Perioperative FOLFOX4 chemotherapy and surgery versus surgery alone for resectable liver metastases from colorectal cancer (EORTC

40983): long-term results of a randomised, controlled, phase 3 trial. *The Lancet Oncology*, 14(12), 1208–1215. https://doi.org/10.1016/S1470-2045(13)70447-9.

Ntourakis, D., Memeo, R., Soler, L., Marescaux, J., Mutter, D., & Pessaux, P. (2016). Augmented Reality Guidance for the Resection of Missing Colorectal Liver Metastases: an Initial Experience. *World Journal of Surgery*, 40(2), 419–426. https://doi.org/10.1007/s00268-015-3229-8.

Owen, J. W., Fowler, K. J., Doyle, M. B., Saad, N. E., Linehan, D. C., & Chapman, W. C. (2016). Colorectal liver metastases: disappearing lesions in the era of Eovist hepatobiliary magnetic resonance imaging. *HPB*, 18(3), 296–303. https://doi.org/10.1016/j.hpb.2015.10.009.

Park, M. J., Hong, N., Han, K., Kim, M. J., Lee, Y. J., Park, Y. S., et al. (2017). Use of imaging to predict complete response of colorectal liver metastases after chemotherapy: MR imaging versus CT imaging. *Radiology*, 284(2), 423–431. https://doi.org/10.1148/radiol.2017161619.

Passot, G., Odisio, B. C., Zorzi, D., Mahvash, A., Gupta, S., Wallace, M. J., et al. (2016). Eradication of Missing Liver Metastases After Fiducial Placement. *Journal of Gastrointestinal Surgery*, 20(6), 1173–1178. https://doi.org/10.1007/s11605-016-3079-1.

Rappeport, E. D., Loft, A., Berthelsen, A. K., Von Der Recke, P., Larsen, P. N., Mogensen, A. M., et al. (2007). Contrast-enhanced FDG-PET/CT vs. SPIO-enhanced MRI vs. FDG-PET vs. CT in patients with liver metastases from colorectal cancer: a prospective study with intraoperative confirmation. *Acta Radiologica*, 48(4), 369–378. https://doi.org/10.1080/02841850701294560.

Saltz, L. B., Cox, J. V., Blanke, C., Rosen, L. S., Fehrenbacher, L., Moore, M. J., et al. (2000). Irinotecan plus fluorouracil and leucovorin for metastatic colorectal cancer. *New England Journal of Medicine*, 343(13), 905–914. https://doi.org/10.1056/NEJM200009283431302.

Spolverato, G., Vitale, A., Ejaz, A., Cosgrove, D., Cowzer, D., Cillo, U., et al. (2015). Hepatic Resection for Disappearing Liver Metastasis: a Cost-Utility Analysis. *Journal of Gastrointestinal Surgery*, 19(9), 1668–1675. https://doi.org/10.1007/s11605-015-2873-5.

Takahashi, M., Hasegawa, K., Arita, J., Hata, S., Aoki, T., Sakamoto, Y., et al. (2012). Contrast-enhanced intraoperative ultrasonography using perfluorobutane microbubbles for the enumeration of colorectal liver metastases. *British Journal of Surgery*, 99(9), 1271–1277. https://doi.org/10.1002/bjs.8844.

Tanaka, K., Takakura, H., Takeda, K., Matsuo, K., Nagano, Y., & Endo, I. (2009). Importance of complete pathologic response to prehepatectomy chemotherapy in treating colorectal cancer metastases. *Annals of Surgery*, 250(6), 935–942. https://doi.org/10.1097/SLA.0b013e3181b0c6e4.

Tsilimigras, D. I., Ntanasis-Stathopoulos, I., Paredes, A. Z., Moris, D., Gavriatopoulou, M., Cloyd, J. M., et al. (2019). Disappearing liver metastases: a systematic review of the current evidence. *Surgical Oncology*, 29, 7–13. https://doi.org/10.1016/j.suronc.2019.02.005.

Van Kessel, C. S., Buckens, C. F. M., Van Den Bosch, M. A. A. J., Van Leeuwen, M. S., Van Hillegersberg, R., & Verkooijen, H. M. (2012). Preoperative imaging of colorectal liver metastases after neoadjuvant chemotherapy: a meta-analysis. *Annals of Surgical Oncology*, 19(9), 2805–2813. https://doi.org/10.1245/s10434-012-2300-z.

van Vledder, M. G., de Jong, M. C., Pawlik, T. M., Schulick, R. D., Diaz, L. A., & Choti, M. A. (2010). Disappearing Colorectal Liver Metastases after Chemotherapy: should we be Concerned? *Journal of Gastrointestinal Surgery*, 14(11), 1691–1700. https://doi.org/10.1007/s11605-010-1348-y.

Vreugdenburg, T. D., Ma, N., Duncan, J. K., Riitano, D., Cameron, A. L., & Maddern, G. J. (2016). Comparative diagnostic accuracy of hepatocyte-specific gadoxetic acid (Gd-EOB-DTPA) enhanced MR imaging and contrast enhanced CT for the detection of liver metastases: a systematic review and meta-analysis. *International Journal of Colorectal Disease*, 31(11), 1739–1749. https://doi.org/10.1007/s00384-016-2664-9.

Xie, Y. H., Chen, Y. X., & Fang, J. Y. (2020). Comprehensive review of targeted therapy for colorectal cancer. *Signal Transduction and Targeted Therapy*, 5(1), 22. https://doi.org/10.1038/s41392-020-0116-z.

Zalinski, S., Abdalla, E. K., Mahvash, A., & Vauthey, J. N. (2009). A marking technique for intraoperative localization of small liver metastases before systemic chemotherapy. *Annals of Surgical Oncology*, 16(5), 1208–1211. https://doi.org/10.1245/s10434-009-0328-5.

CHAPTER

7

Approach to small liver remnant – strategies to increase resectability

Flavio Rocha (G), MD, FACS, FSSO and Kimberly Washington, MD, FACS

Division of Surgical Oncology, Knight Cancer Institute, Oregon Health and Science University, Portland, OR, United States

Introduction

Management of liver metastasis from colon and rectal cancer has shifted in recent years from palliative systemic chemotherapy to multi-disciplinary management including resection with curative intent. With clearance of metastatic disease from the liver comes the concern for leaving an adequate liver volume to prevent post-hepatectomy liver failure (PHLF). Although the potential for PHLF in the small liver remnant is greatest amongst those undergoing extended hepatectomies, it is relevant for those undergoing formal right or left hepatectomy, particularly after prolonged use of chemotherapy or intrinsic liver disease. Therefore, measuring FLR volume is essential for pre-operative planning and prevention of PHLF from a small liver remnant.

In the event that the expected liver remnant is small and the patient would be at risk of PHLF, there are options to increase volume of the liver remnant pre-operatively. Historically, intraoperative portal vein ligation (PVL) was performed as a first stage procedure. Currently, portal vein embolization (PVE) is the most commonly used technique, often used for increasing volume of the left liver in preparation for a right or extended right hepatectomy (formerly known as trisectionectomy). Further, hepatic vein embolization in addition to PVE has been found to increase hypertrophy beyond that which is seen with PVE alone. Additional surgical options include Associating Liver Partition and Portal Vein Ligation (ALPPS) - a surgical technique that results in faster hypertrophy, but requires two operative procedures. This chapter will detail techniques to prevent the small liver remnant including current practices, ongoing and future trials.

Contemporary Management of Metastatic Colorectal Cancer: A Precision Medicine Approach
DOI: https://doi.org/10.1016/B978-0-323-91706-3.00012-6

Future liver remnant (FLR)

The ability to preserve an adequate future liver remnant (FLR) volume is the cornerstone of surgical planning in hepatectomy for large or multifocal tumors. As the indications for hepatectomy for primary liver tumors and metastatic disease have expanded, determining accurate liver volume is essential. This begins with high-quality, multi-phase cross-sectional computed tomography (CT) imaging of the liver with three-dimensional reconstruction. In addition, for liver metastasis and particularly after systemic chemotherapy, magnetic resonance imaging (MRI) with gadoxetate sodium offers more enhanced detection of liver metastasis that may not be as clearly visible on CT imaging due to steatosis or other liver parenchymal changes.

Calculating FLR

FLR volume should be calculated as the absolute volume of the fully functioning portion of liver after resection (Jarnigan, Allen, and Chapman, 2016). Several formulas have been proposed to accurately calculate liver volume. A total of 16 unique formulas have been published; however, only two are commonly used. The first technique calculates FLR as a function of non-tumor-bearing liver, using the following formula:

$$TLV_{Measured} = V_{TotalLiver} - V_{Tumor}$$

$$FLR_{Measured} = LRV/TLV_{Measured} \times 100\%$$

Total liver volume ($V_{Total\ Volume}$) is calculated by determining volume of the entire liver through three-dimensional cross-sectional imaging. Next, the volume of each individual tumor is measured and totaled as V_{Tumor}, which is used to calculate $TLV_{Measured}$. Measured future liver remnant ($FLR_{Measured}$) is determined as a percentage of the intended liver remaining after resection and the calculated $TLV_{Measured}$. The greatest advantage of this technique is that it theoretically provides the most accurate measurement of FLR. However, it is tedious to measure each individual tumor volume which introduces the inherent risk of error.

The standardized future liver remnant ($FLR_{Standard}$) is the most commonly used calculating method. It estimates total liver volume based on body surface area (BSA), as studies have shown the linear relationship between these two values. The first use of BSA to estimate TLV was done by Urata, et al. in 96 Japanese children and adults to determine adequate size for donor liver transplantation to prevent small for size syndrome (Urata et al., 1995). Vauthey, et al. modified the calculation after finding the Japanese formula underestimated TLV in Western patients. Their cohort was larger ($n = 292$) with median weight of 71kg and BSA of 1.82m^2, which more closely reflected the Western adult population (Vauthey et al., 2002).

The $FLR_{standard}$ is calculated as follows:

$$TLV_{Standard} = (1267.28 \times BSA) - 794.41$$

$$FLR_{Measured} = LRV/TLV_{Standard} \times 100\%$$

High quality cross-sectional imaging is required to measure the volume of liver the surgeon intends to leave behind. $FLR_{standard}$ is determined as a percentage of the liver remnant volume and $TLV_{standard}$ as calculated by BSA. The advantage of this technique is the relative ease of use. The major disadvantage is that Vauthey's patient cohort did not include patients with cirrhosis, fibrosis, steatosis, biliary disease, or other liver disease. However, subsequent studies have consistently upheld this calculation.

Optimal future liver volume

Once FLR is calculated, one must determine the minimum percentage necessary to decrease risk of post-hepatectomy liver failure (PHLF). Kishi, et al. analyzed patients who underwent extended right hepatectomy and were stratified based on size of FLR: <20 percent, 2–30 percent, or >30 percent. This study found amongst patients with FLR of >30 percent, the incidence of PHLF was 15 percent and death from liver failure was 2 percent. On the other hand, in those with FLR <20 percent, the incidence of PHLF was 34 percent ($p = 0.010$) and death from liver failure was 11 percent ($p = 0.021$). It is important to note the vast majority of these patients had no evidence of significant liver dysfunction prior to hepatectomy (Kishi et al., 2009).

For those with underlying liver disease, optimal FLR must be adjusted. In colorectal liver metastases, a significant portion of patients receive pre-operative chemotherapy that can have adverse effects on the background liver. The most commonly used chemotherapy regimen for colorectal cancer is 5-fluorouracil with leucovorin, and oxaliplatin (FOLFOX). Oxaliplatin is known to cause sinusoidal obstruction syndrome, also called blue liver, a condition marked by congestion of the small vessels of the liver which over time lead to portal hypertension. Irinotecan, a chemotherapeutic agent in FOLFIRI (folinic acid, flurouracil, and irinotecan) also has a known adverse effect of steatohepatitis, or yellow liver. In steatohepatitis, inflammation of the liver parenchyma is associated with fatty replacement of hepatocytes. Unfortunately, many patients with CRLM receive prolonged pre-hepatectomy chemotherapy, especially those with metachronous disease. Therefore adjustments must be made in the FLR minimums to prevent PHLF.

Shindoh, et al. reported a 194 patient cohort who underwent extended right hepatectomy, all with FLR >20 percent, stratified into three groups: no pre-operative chemotherapy, short-course chemotherapy (<12 weeks) and long-course chemotherapy (>12 weeks). They found no patients experiencing PHLF amongst those with FLR of at least 30 percent who had no pre-operative chemotherapy. On the other hand, for those with FLR <30 percent, 5.1 percent of patients who received short-course chemotherapy developed PHLF and 16.3 percent of those who received long-course chemotherapy ($p = 0.006$). Therefore, it is suggested that patients who received long-course chemotherapy should have an FLR >30 percent to reduce risk of PHLF (Shindoh et al., 2013).

In patients with underlying fibrosis or cirrhosis, hepatocyte functional assessment is as valuable as anatomic volumetric assessment. Combining volume and functional data can be used to stratify those who need portal vein embolization (PVE) in the preoperative setting. The Makuuchi criteria uses plasma retention rate of indocyanine green at 15 min (ICG R15) as an element in determining safety of hepatic resection (Miyagawa, Makuuchi, Kawasaki, and Kakazu, 1995). Fig. 7.1 ICG is taken up by hepatocytes and cleared in the bile. Its rate of clearance is used to assess liver function. This test is not currently available in the United States, but has been used for over two decades in Asia to assess hepatic function. Technetium 99m galactosyl human serum albumin scintigraphy (99m Tc-GSA) is thought to be a more reliable

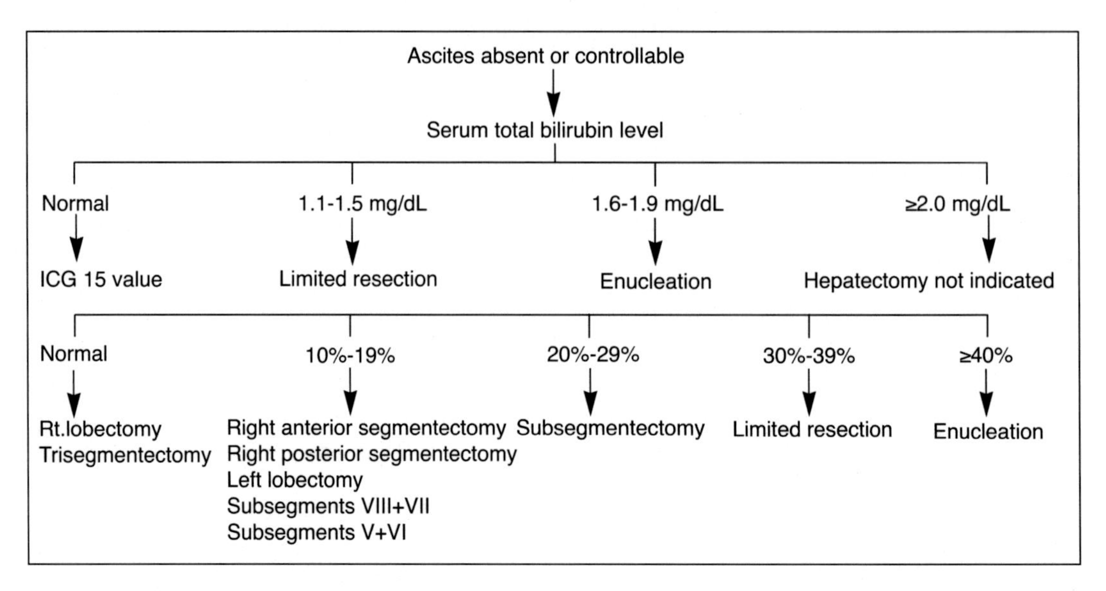

FIGURE 7.1 Criteria for Hepatectomy in Chronic Liver Disease From Miyagawa, S., Makuuchi, M., Kawasaki, S. & Kakazu, T. (1995). Criteria for safe hepatic resection. American Journal of Surgery, 169(6), 589–594. Criteria for hepatectomy in patients with chronic liver disease used by surgeons at the First Department of Surgery, Shinshu University Hospital, Japan, between 1990 and December 1992. The extent of hepatic resection was based on serum total bilirubin level and the plasma retention rate of indocyanine green at 15 min (ICG 15 value).

test for assessing hepatic functional reserve. The value of 99mTc-GSA is in its ability to be applied to jaundiced patients since its uptake is not directly inhibited by hyperbilirubinemia (Ohkura et al., 2014). Currently, there is no standardized method available in the United States to assess hepatic function prior to hepatectomy.

Portal vein embolization (PVE)

The most common preoperative procedure performed to increase FLR volume is portal vein embolization (PVE). Its purpose is two-fold: a) redirect portal flow to the intended liver remnant, thereby increasing volume and b) shift hepatic functional reserve resulting in atrophy of the embolized liver. PVE is most effective when portal blood flow is completely cut off to the liver that will be removed thereby allowing the non-tumor bearing liver to hypertrophy. PVE increases functional capacity of the liver remnant and can increase contralateral lobe volume by up to 20 percent, with the peak in growth occurring within 2–4 weeks (Eshkenazy et al., 2014).

Indications and contraindications for PVE

PVE should be considered in the pre-operative setting for any patient with marginal estimated FLR. There are two absolute contraindications to PVE: known portal hypertension and ipsilateral portal vein tumor thrombosis. PVE causes increased portal pressures in the contralateral portal vein, which could worsen other complications of portal hypertension such as splenomegaly, esophageal varices and bleeding and should, therefore, be avoided in this setting.

Portal vein ligation, a historical perspective

The first published evidence of portal vein ligation was by Dr Ichio Honjo in 1975, where the right or left branch of the portal vein supplying the affected hepatic lobe was surgically ligated. Dr Honjo based his technique on prior experimental animal studies by Rous et al. where selective ligation of the portal vein branch resulted in atrophy of the hepatic lobe and hypertrophy of the contralateral lobe (Rous and Larimore, 1920). Similarly, Kraus et al. identified regression of experimentally produced carcinoma of the liver with selective portal vein ligation in rats (KRAUS and BELTRAN, 1959). Honjo, et al. described 12 patients with primary carcinoma of the liver and 8 patients with metastatic disease. In most patients, the portal vein was ligated ipsilateral to the large, unresectable tumor. Two patients underwent left lateral sectionectomy to clear the remnant liver while simultaneously undergoing right portal vein ligation. There were no serious postoperative complications reported and an overall survival of 12.6 months (2.5 to 39.5 months) was reported. Interestingly, each patient underwent a preoperative hepatic angiogram to determine if the lesion(s) were hypervascular or ischemic. The mean survival in those with ischemic tumors (12.3 mo) was significantly different compared with those with hypervascular tumors (7.4 mo). The correlation between prolonged survival after PVL in patients with ischemic tumors and slowed progression of disease was first reported in this study (Honjo, Suzuki, Ozawa, Takasan, and Kitamura, 1975).

Technical aspects of PVE

Portal vein embolization was first described by Dr Masatoshi Makuuchi in 1990 to increase the safety of major hepatectomy for hilar cholangio carcinoma. The technique involved mesenteric venous access with a 7F polyethylene catheter inserted into the portal vein at laparotomy through the ileocolic vein. The portal vein was identified and embolized under fluoroscopic guidance. The portal pressure was measured pre- and post-embolization. The embolizing material was a mixture of Gelfoam cubes or powder, diatrizoate sodium meglumine, and gentamicin. At a mean interval between PVE and hepatectomy of 17 days (6–41 days) only one out of 14 patients developed PHLF resulting in death (Makuuchi et al., 1990). The invasiveness of this approach warranted an alternative option for portal vein cannulation.

The most common technique for accessing the portal vein for embolization is percutaneous transhepatic approach. A meta-analysis of 1088 patients demonstrated safety and effectiveness of PVE as a means to induce liver hypertrophy and decrease risk of post-hepatectomy liver failure (Abulkhir et al., 2008).

There are two methods for percutaneous transhepatic PVE: ipsilateral (access portal vein through tumor bearing liver) or contralateral (access portal vein through the remnant liver). The advantage of the ipsilateral approach is that no catheters are placed within the FLR. Therefore this approach minimizes the risk of injury to the FLR during PVE and provides a more direct access to segment IV portal veins (Madoff et al., 2005; M Nagino, Nimura, Kamiya, Kondo, and Kanai, 1996). The right PV has sharp angles often necessitating usage of reverse-curve catheters or balloon occlusion catheters to access. The preferred puncture location is the anterior segment of the right PV, as this is associated with the lowest complication rate (Kodama, Shimizu, Endo, Miyamoto, and Miyasaka, 2002). When embolization is being performed in preparation for extended right hepatectomy, embolization of segment IV should be performed first so as to avoid catheter change through the embolized right PV risking dislodgement of embolic material.

Choice of embolizing agents

The first widely used embolic agent for percutaneous PVE was polyvinyl alcohol particles (Contour SE Microspheres: Boston Scientific, Natick, MA). Most studies on choice of embolic agent are small retrospective cohort studies. There are no large randomized trials that compare embolic agents, therefore no evidence of superiority of any one embolic agent over another exists.

A mixture of N–butyl–cryanoacrylate (NBCA) and ethiodized oil is currently the most common embolic agent used in the United States. It induces substantial FLR hypertrophy with low morbidity rates. Gautier, et al. showed use of ethylene-vinyl alcohol copolymer (EVOH – Onyx R, LES, Covidien, Plymouth, MN) in addition to NBCA is useful for occluding portal vein branches as NBCA carries a risk of non-target embolization (Gautier et al., 2021). Optimization of embolizing agent for PVE is still a matter of debate, but animal and human studies have strongly suggested that permanent embolizing agents and especially cryanoacrylate (glue) are safe and induced greater liver hypertrophy than other agents (van den Esschert et al., 2012). Non-permanent embolizing materials are associated with an increased incidence of recanalization of the embolized portal vein.

Post-PVE hypertrophy/kinetic growth rate

After PVE, it is important to assess the rate and degree of hypertrophy of the planned FLR. This is most commonly assessed via high-quality, multi-phase cross-sectional imaging with implementation of volumetry. Often the first post-procedure scan is performed two weeks after PVE and the difference in remnant liver volume is calculated, indicating the degree of hypertrophy (DH). From this growth change, the kinetic growth rate (KGR) scan be calculated from the following formula:

$$KGR = DH\ (\%\ percent)\ /\ time\ elapsed\ since\ PVE\ (weeks)$$

Shindoh, et al. demonstrated that KGR >2 percent per week is the strongest predictor of resection without hepatic insufficiency (Shindoh et al., 2013). As the leading cause of post-operative mortality in major liver resections, identifying patients with minimal hypertrophy response to PVE has undoubtedly contributed to the lower perioperative deaths in recent decades. Very few studies have assessed the impact of neoadjuvant chemotherapy on the ability of the liver to hypertrophy after PVE. Fischer, et al. describes 64 patients, in whom 25 were administered chemotherapy between PVE and resection. Progression of disease occurred in 18.9 percent of tumors in patients who underwent chemotherapy compared with 34.2 percent of tumors in patients who had no chemotherapy. In their patient cohort,

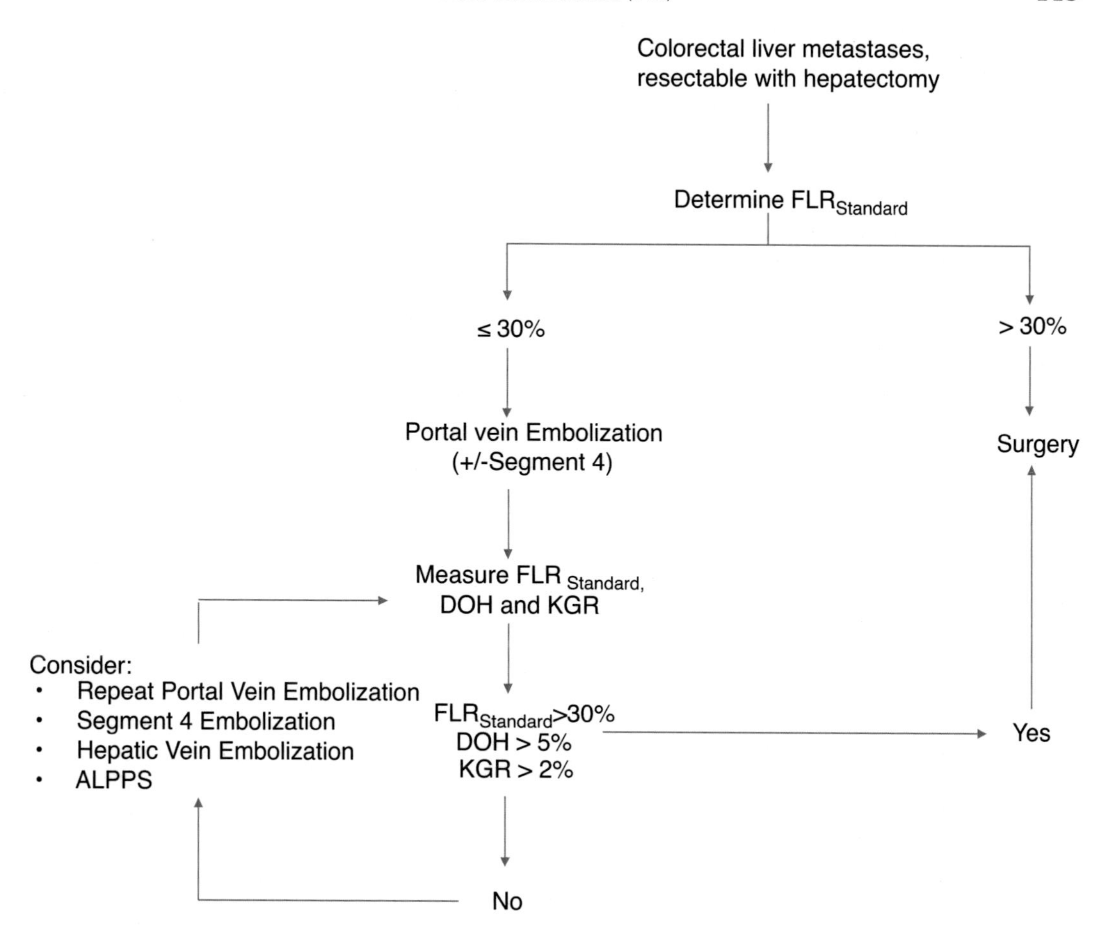

FIGURE 7.2 Evaluation and Management of the Future Liver Remnant *From Dixon, M., Cruz, J., Sarwani, N. & Gusani, N. (2021). The Future Liver Remnant: Definition, Evaluation, and Management. The American Surgeon, 87(2), 276–286.* https://doi.org/10.1177/0003134820951451. Summary for evaluation and management of the future liver remnant in patients with colorectal liver metastases that are resectable with a major hepatectomy. ALPPS indicates associating liver partition and portal vein occlusion for staged hepatectomy; DOH, degree of hypertrophy; FLRStandard, standardized future liver remnant; KGR, kinetic growth rate.

those who underwent preoperative chemotherapy were found to have 20 percent contralateral liver hypertrophy compared with 19 percent in those who received no chemotherapy (Fischer et al., 2013). Conversely, Beal, et al. demonstrated impaired hypertrophy in those receiving post-PVE chemotherapy (mostly oxaliplatin-based regimen) compared with those who did not receive post-PVE chemotherapy (89 mL verses 135 mL, respectively, $p = 0.016$) (Beal et al., 2006). The role of PVE on liver hypertrophy in patients receiving preoperative chemotherapy is one of active investigation (Fig. 7.2) (Dixon, Cruz, Sarwani, and Gusani, 2021).

Combined portal vein & hepatic vein embolization

In some circumstances, portal vein embolization (PVE) alone does not produce the appropriate degree of contralateral parenchymal hypertrophy to avoid post-hepatectomy liver failure. PVE combined with hepatic vein embolization (HVE) was first described by Nagino, et al. to induce hypertrophy which allowed for extended hepatectomy in a patient with initial volumetrics suggesting a 25 percent remnant liver. After simultaneous PVE and HVE, the patient underwent left trisegmentectomy and caudate lobectomy. Liver regeneration was reported to be adequate at three months following hepatectomy (Masato Nagino et al., 2003).

In the largest study to date, 37 patients with estimated FLR/TLV ratio of less than 25 percent underwent simultaneous PVE and HVE with 61 percent increased liver volume at four weeks compared to 29 percent volume increase in patients who underwent PVE alone ($p < 0.0001$). Laurent, et al. described this technique as a "radiological simultaneous portohepatic vein embolization" (RASPE) likening it to a radiographical associating liver partition and portal vein ligation (ALLPS) without the need for two operative procedures. With similar morbidity in the PVE and RASPE groups, the only drawback of simultaneous embolization over ALLPS is the longer interval between embolization and resection compared to the interval between first and second stage ALPPS (Laurent et al., 2020).

Ongoing research is necessary to determine the appropriate patient population that would benefit the most from combined PVE and HVE prior to hepatectomy. The HYPER-LIV01 trial (NCT03841305) is a multicenter phase II randomized trial comparing percentage of change in FLR volume at three weeks after combined PVE/HVE (also termed liver venous deprivation) compared with PVE alone for colorectal liver metastases. Similarly, the DRAGON-2 trial (NCT04272931) continues to accrue comparing the same approaches in a similar population of patients (Deshayes et al., 2020).

Associating liver partition and portal vein ligation

In 2007, Dr Hans Schlitt planned an extended right hepatectomy for perihilar cholangiocarcinoma but realized intraoperatively that the liver remnant would be too small to prevent post-hepatectomy liver failure. Therefore, he performed a left hepaticojejunostomy which necessitated dividing the liver parenchyma along the falciform ligament, thereby devascularizing segment IV. Additionally, he ligated the right portal vein with the intent to cause hypertrophy of segment II and III. Approximately one week after this procedure, the patient underwent computed tomography (CT) scan revealing significant growth of the left liver much to Dr Schlitt's surprise. With an adequate liver remnant now, the patient returned to the operating room for extended right hepatectomy without significant immediate postoperative complications.

This technique was repeated by other German surgeons and subsequently published by Schnitzbauer, et al. detailing 25 cases performed in 5 German centers. This group reported an impressive rate of hypertrophy – 74 percent volume increase of the remnant liver within a mean of 9 days after ALPPS (Schnitzbauer et al., 2012). Prior to this technique, the only options for liver hypertrophy were endovascular portal vein embolization (PVE) or surgical portal vein ligation (PVL). Notably, PVE using various methods of embolization only leads to increase FLR of 10–46 percent after 2–8 weeks (Liu and Zhu, 2009). Similarly, PVL has been shown to result in parenchymal hypertrophy of 38 percent at 8 weeks (Belghiti and Benhaïm, 2009).

The traditional ALPPS procedure describes complete transection of the liver parenchyma at segment IV in the initial operation with wrapping of the liver in plastic bag to prevent adhesion formation and contain any possible bile leaks with a planned return to operating room for completion hepatectomy between 9 and 14 days after imaging of confirmed adequate hypertrophy (Fig. 7.3) (Abbasi et al., 2018). It has been proposed that the reason for significant parenchymal hypertrophy in an abbreviated period is due to complete (arterial and venous) devascularization of segment IV. This prevents formation of vascular collaterals between the left and right lobes of the liver, the proposed cause of lower hypertrophy rates in patients who undergo PVE alone.

The LIGRO trial was the first prospective, multicenter randomized trial comparing ALPPS ($n = 48$) to two-stage hepatectomy ($n = 49$) for colorectal liver metastasis (CRLM). Participants were deemed unresectable as a one stage procedure due to future liver remnant (FLR)/standardized total liver volume (sTLV) <30 percent. All patients were treated with preoperative chemotherapy and enrolled after multidisciplinary review. The resection rate was 92 percent in the ALPPS arm compared with 57 percent in the two-stage hepatectomy arm. Of the patients in the two-stage hepatectomy arm that failed to reach FLR of 30 percent, 12 were successfully treated with subsequent ALPPS making this an important salvage technique (Sandström et al., 2018).

Various modifications of ALPPS have been reported to improve upon the technical aspects of the originally described procedure. Associating liver tourniquet and portal vein ligation (ALTPS) entails placement of a tourniquet along Cantle's line between the right and middle hepatic veins. The tourniquet is knotted tightly enough to occlude all vessels. Patients underwent second stage hepatectomy within median time of 11 days (8–28 days) after the initial procedure (Robles et al., 2014). An anterior approach is described with the intent to decrease perihepatic inflammation by avoiding liver mobilization. This approach was borne out a desire to eliminate the need for the plastic wrap in the initial operation. It describes a complete parenchymal split down to the inferior vena cava (IVC) with Cavitron Ultrasonic Surgical Aspirator (CUSA) without mobilization of the right liver (Chan, Pang, and Poon, 2014).

As we continue to push the limits of hepatectomy, monosegmental ALPPS has been described in which only one liver segment constitutes the FLR (Steinbrück, D'Oliveira, Cano, and Enne, n.d.). Scadde, et al. describes 12 patient in 6 centers who underwent monosegmental ALPPS with median time to second stage hepatectomy of 13 days and median hypertrophy of liver remnant of 160 percent (Schadde et al., 2015).

ALPPS is a highly specialized procedure that is best performed by those who have experience with the technique as well as proper patient selection. This is especially true when using ALPPS in a rescue fashion for those who had inadequate hypertrophy after PVE (Björnsson, Gasslander, and Sandström, 2013; Tschuor et al., 2013; Vyas et al., 2014). Not to be overlooked are the significant complications associated with ALPPS including PHLF, biliary leak, and sepsis. Ratti, et al. reports a higher complication rate in their ALPPS group compared to the two stage hepatectomy group (83.3 percent vs 38.2 percent, respectively; $p = 0.011$)

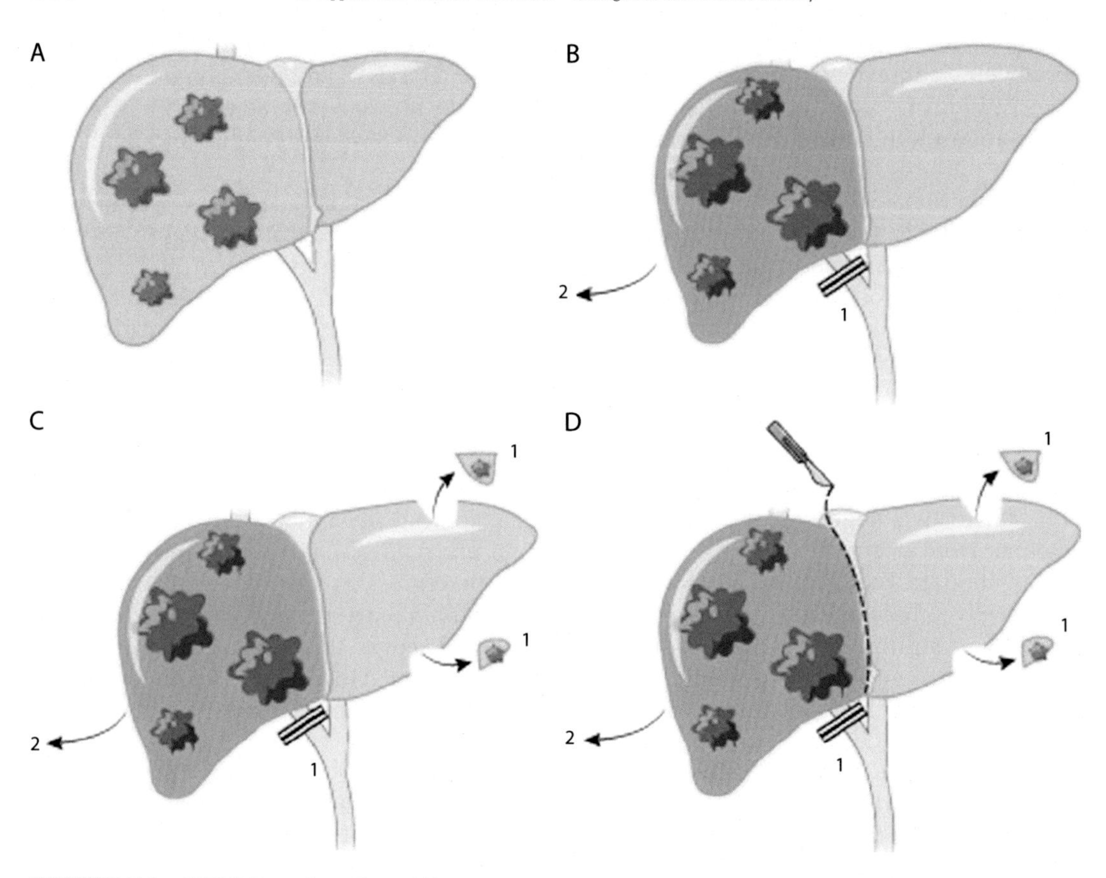

FIGURE 7.3 ALPPS Procedure *From Abbasi, A., Rahnemai-Azar, AA, Merath, K., Weber, SM, Abbott, DE, Dillhoff, M., Cloyd, J. & Pawlik, T. M. (2018). Role of associating liver partition and portal vein ligation in staged hepatectomy (ALPPS)-strategy for colorectal liver metastases. Translational Gastroenterology and Hepatology, 3, 66.* https://doi.org/10.21037/tgh.2018.09.03. Visualization of pre- or peri–operative interventions and their effect on liver remnant volume. (A) Malignant liver disease; (B) embolization/ligation of the right portal branch, [1] resulting in atrophy of the right hemi-liver and compensatory growth of the left hemi-liver, which can be removed when appropriate hypertrophy has been achieved [2]; (C) removal of tumours from the left hemi-liver and occlusion of the right portal branch [1]. After 4–6 weeks, the volume of the left hemi-liver is increased and the right hemi-liver can be removed [2]; (D) removal of tumours from the left hemi-liver, in situ splitting of the hemi-livers, and simultaneous ligation of the right portal vein branch [1]. After 1-week, augmented hypertrophy of the left hemi-liver permits removal of the right hemi-liver [2].

(Ratti et al., 2015). However, this difference in complication rate was not seen in a later study by Adams, et al. that showed no difference in major complications between the two groups (Adam et al., 2016). It remains unclear if there is a benefit to swift (less than 14 days) hypertrophy followed by resection compared to PVE with resection approximately four weeks post-procedure. Olthof et al. compared patients with extensive liver disease who underwent ALPPS to those with unresectable CRLM receiving palliative chemotherapy and found no difference in OS (24 vs 17.6 months, $p = 0.088$) (Olthof et al., 2017). These concerns have resulted in lower adoption of ALPPS as a standard technique to decrease risk of PHLF due to a small liver remnant.

Conclusion

Management of colorectal liver metastasis continues to evolve as precision oncology advances with chemotherapy and immunotherapy providing a more durable tumor response. These advances open the possibilities for aggressive surgical curative-intent resection in patients with liver only metastatic disease. For optimal post-operative results, avoiding PHLF from a small liver remnant is essential. Post-hepatectomy liver failure can be minimized with attention to calculating the future liver remnant volume prior to operative resection. For those with normal background liver, >20 percent total liver volume after resection is associated with lower PHLF. For those who have undergone long-course (>12 weeks) of pre-resection chemotherapy, >30 percent total liver volume is necessary. For those with cirrhosis or severe fibrosis, >40 percent total liver volume is necessary. In an effort to achieve these volumes, portal vein embolization is commonly performed, often through the tumor bearing liver in an effort to prevent injury to the future liver remnant. With appropriate training and adequate patient selection, ALPPS is also an option, but requires two operative procedures to successfully complete. In the event that PVE does not procedure appropriate hypertrophy, performing hepatic vein embolization can produce greater hypertrophy or rescue ALPPS can be utilized. Ultimately, the intent is to remove all disease. If this can be completed successfully with parenchymal sparing approaches, it will greatly benefit the patient in the event of recurrence.

References

Abbasi, A., Rahnemai-Azar, A. A., Merath, K., Weber, S. M., Abbott, D. E., Dillhoff, M., et al. (2018). Role of associating liver partition and portal vein ligation in staged hepatectomy (ALPPS)-strategy for colorectal liver metastases. *Translational Gastroenterology and Hepatology*, 3, 1–8. https://doi.org/10.21037/tgh.2018.09.03.

Abulkhir, A., Limongelli, P., Healey, A. J., Damrah, O., Tait, P., Jackson, J., et al. (2008). Preoperative portal vein embolization for major liver resection: a meta-analysis. *Annals of Surgery*, 247(1), 49–57.

Adam, R., Imai, K., Castro Benitez, C., Allard, M.-A., Vibert, E., Sa Cunha, A., et al. (2016). Outcome after associating liver partition and portal vein ligation for staged hepatectomy and conventional two-stage hepatectomy for colorectal liver metastases. *British Journal of Surgery*, 103(11), 1521–1529. https://doi.org/10.1002/bjs.10256.

Beal, I. K., Anthony, S., Papadopoulou, A., Hutchins, R., Fusai, G., Begent, R., et al. (2006). Portal vein embolisation prior to hepatic resection for colorectal liver metastases and the effects of periprocedure chemotherapy. *Bjr*, 79(942), 473–478.

Belghiti, J., & Benhaïm, L. (2009). Portal vein occlusion prior to extensive resection in colorectal liver metastasis: a necessity rather than an option!. *Annals of Surgical Oncology*, 16(5), 1098–1099. https://doi.org/10.1245/s10434-009-0379-7.

Björnsson, B., Gasslander, T., & Sandström, P. (2013). In situ split of the liver when portal venous embolization fails to induce hypertrophy: a report of two cases. *Case Rep Surg*, 2013, 1–4, 238675. https://doi.org/10.1155/2013/238675.

Chan, A. C. Y., Pang, R., & Poon, R. T. P. (2014). Simplifying the ALPPS procedure by the anterior approach. *Annals of Surgery*, 260(2), 1–7. https://doi.org/10.1097/SLA.0000000000000736.

Deshayes, E., Piron, L., Bouvier, A., Lapuyade, B., Lermite, E., Vervueren, L., et al. (2020). Study protocol of the HYPER-LIV01 trial: a multicenter phase II, prospective and randomized study comparing simultaneous portal and hepatic vein embolization to portal vein embolization for hypertrophy of the future liver remnant before major hepatectomy for colo-rectal liver metastases. *BMC cancer*, 20(1), 574. https://doi.org/10.1186/s12885-020-07065-z.

Dixon, M., Cruz, J., Sarwani, N., & Gusani, N. (2021). The Future Liver Remnant : definition, Evaluation, and Management. *American Surgeon*, 87(2), 276–286. https://doi.org/10.1177/0003134820951451.

Eshkenazy, R., Dreznik, Y., Lahat, E., Zakai, B. B., Zendel, A., & Ariche, A. (2014). Small for size liver remnant following resection: prevention and management. *Hepatobiliary Surg Nutr*, 3(5), 303–312. https://doi.org/10.3978/j.issn.2304-3881.2014.09.08.

Fischer, C., Melstrom, L. G., Arnaoutakis, D., Jarnagin, W., Brown, K., D'Angelica, M., et al. (2013). Chemotherapy after portal vein embolization to protect against tumor growth during liver hypertrophy before hepatectomy. *JAMA Surg*, 148(12), 1103–1108. https://doi.org/10.1001/jamasurg.2013.2126.

Gautier, S., Chevallier, O., Mastier, C., d'Athis, P., Falvo, N., Pilleul, F., et al. (2021). Portal vein embolization with ethylene-vinyl alcohol copolymer for contralateral lobe hypertrophy before liver resection: safety, feasibility and initial experience. *Quant Imaging Med Surg*, 11(2), 797–809. https://doi.org/10.21037/qims-20-808.

Honjo, I., Suzuki, T., Ozawa, K., Takasan, H., & Kitamura, O. (1975). Ligation of a branch of the portal vein for carcinoma of the liver. *American Journal of Surgery*, 130(3), 296–302.

Jarnigan, W., Allen, P., & Chapman, W. (2016). Blumgart's Surgery of the Liver, Biliary Tract, and Pancreas. In W. Jarnigan. (Ed.), *Hepatic resection for benign disease and for liver and biliary tumors* (6th ed.) (2, pp. 1522–1577). Philadelphia, PA: Elsevier.

Kishi, Y., Abdalla, E. K., Chun, Y. S., Zorzi, D., Madoff, D. C., Wallace, M. J., et al. (2009). Three hundred and one consecutive extended right hepatectomies: evaluation of outcome based on systematic liver volumetry. *Annals of Surgery*, 250(4), 540–548. https://doi.org/10.1097/SLA.0b013e3181b674df.

Kodama, Y., Shimizu, T., Endo, H., Miyamoto, N., & Miyasaka, K. (2002). Complications of percutaneous transhepatic portal vein embolization. *Journal of Vascular and Interventional Radiology : JVIR,*, 13(12), 1233–1237.

KRAUS, G. E., & BELTRAN, A. (1959). Effect of induced infarction on rat liver implanted with Walker carcinoma 256. *Archives of Surgery*, 79, 769–774 (Chicago, Ill. : 1960).

Laurent, C., Fernandez, B., Marichez, A., Adam, J.-P., Papadopoulos, P., Lapuyade, B., et al. (2020). Radiological Simultaneous Portohepatic Vein Embolization (RASPE) Before Major Hepatectomy: a Better Way to Optimize Liver Hypertrophy Compared to Portal Vein Embolization. *Annals of Surgery*, 272(2), 199–205. https://doi.org/10.1097/SLA.0000000000003905.

Liu, H., & Zhu, S. (2009). Present status and future perspectives of preoperative portal vein embolization. *American Journal of Surgery*, 197(5), 686–690. https://doi.org/10.1016/j.amjsurg.2008.04.022.

Madoff, D. C., Abdalla, E. K., Gupta, S., Wu, T.-T., Morris, J. S., Denys, A., et al. (2005). Transhepatic ipsilateral right portal vein embolization extended to segment IV: improving hypertrophy and resection outcomes with spherical particles and coils. *Journal of Vascular and Interventional Radiology : JVIR,*, 16(2 Pt 1), 215–225.

Makuuchi, M., Thai, B. L., Takayasu, K., Takayama, T., Kosuge, T., Gunvén, P., et al. (1990). Preoperative portal embolization to increase safety of major hepatectomy for hilar bile duct carcinoma: a preliminary report. *Surgery*, 107(5), 521–527.

Miyagawa, S., Makuuchi, M., Kawasaki, S., & Kakazu, T. (1995). Criteria for safe hepatic resection. *American Journal of Surgery*, 169(6), 589–594.

Nagino, M., Nimura, Y., Kamiya, J., Kondo, S., & Kanai, M. (1996). Selective percutaneous transhepatic embolization of the portal vein in preparation for extensive liver resection: the ipsilateral approach. *Radiology*, 200(2), 559–563.

Nagino, M., Yamada, T., Kamiya, J., Uesaka, K., Arai, T., & Nimura, Y. (2003). Left hepatic trisegmentectomy with right hepatic vein resection after right hepatic vein embolization. *Surgery*, 133(5), 580–582.

Ohkura, Y., Mizuno, S., Kishiwada, M., Hamada, T., Usui, M., Sakurai, H., et al. (2014). Benefit of technetium-99m galactosyl human serum albumin scintigraphy instead of indocyanine green test in patients scheduled for hepatectomy. *Hepatology Research : The Official Journal of the Japan Society of Hepatology,*, 44(10), E118–E128. https://doi.org/10.1111/hepr.12248.

Olthof, P. B., Huiskens, J., Wicherts, D. A., Huespe, P. E., Ardiles, V., Robles-Campos, R., et al. (2017). Survival after associating liver partition and portal vein ligation for staged hepatectomy (ALPPS) for advanced colorectal liver metastases: a case-matched comparison with palliative systemic therapy. *Surgery*, 161(4), 909–919. https://doi.org/10.1016/j.surg.2016.10.032.

Ratti, F., Schadde, E., Masetti, M., Massani, M., Zanello, M., Serenari, M., et al. (2015). Strategies to Increase the Resectability of Patients with Colorectal Liver Metastases: a Multi-center Case-Match Analysis of ALPPS and Conventional Two-Stage Hepatectomy. *Annals of Surgical Oncology*, 22(6), 1933–1942. https://doi.org/10.1245/s10434-014-4291-4.

Robles, R., Parrilla, P., López-Conesa, A., Brusadin, R., de la Peña, J., Fuster, M., et al. (2014). Tourniquet modification of the associating liver partition and portal ligation for staged hepatectomy procedure. *British Journal of Surgery, 101*(9), 1129–1134. discussion 1134 https://doi.org/10.1002/bjs.9547 .

Rous, P., & Larimore, L. D. (1920). RELATION OF THE PORTAL BLOOD TO LIVER MAINTENANCE : a DEMONSTRATION OF LIVER ATROPHY CONDITIONAL ON COMPENSATION. *Journal of Experimental Medicine, 31*(5), 609–632.

Sandström, P., Røsok, B. I., Sparrelid, E., Larsen, P. N., Larsson, A. L., Lindell, G., et al. (2018). ALPPS Improves Resectability Compared With Conventional Two-stage Hepatectomy in Patients With Advanced Colorectal Liver Metastasis: results From a Scandinavian Multicenter Randomized Controlled Trial (LIGRO Trial). *Annals of Surgery, 267*(5), 833–840. https://doi.org/10.1097/SLA.0000000000002511.

Schadde, E., Malagó, M., Hernandez-Alejandro, R., Li, J., Abdalla, E., Ardiles, V., et al. (2015). Monosegment ALPPS hepatectomy: extending resectability by rapid hypertrophy. *Surgery, 157*(4), 676–689. https://doi.org/10.1016/j.surg.2014.11.015.

Schnitzbauer, A. A., Lang, S. A., Goessmann, H., Nadalin, S., Baumgart, J., Farkas, S. A., et al. (2012). Right portal vein ligation combined with in situ splitting induces rapid left lateral liver lobe hypertrophy enabling 2-staged extended right hepatic resection in small-for-size settings. *Annals of Surgery, 255*(3), 405–414. https://doi.org/10.1097/SLA.0b013e31824856f5.

Shindoh, J., Truty, M. J., Aloia, T. A., Curley, S. A., Zimmitti, G., Huang, S. Y., et al. (2013). Kinetic growth rate after portal vein embolization predicts posthepatectomy outcomes: toward zero liver-related mortality in patients with colorectal liver metastases and small future liver remnant. *Journal of the American College of Surgeons, 216*(2), 201–209. https://doi.org/10.1016/j.jamcollsurg.2012.10.018.

Shindoh, J., Tzeng, C.-W. D., Aloia, T. A., Curley, S. A., Zimmitti, G., Wei, S. H., et al. (2013). Optimal future liver remnant in patients treated with extensive preoperative chemotherapy for colorectal liver metastases. *Annals of Surgical Oncology, 20*(8), 2493–2500. https://doi.org/10.1245/s10434-012-2864-7.

Steinbrück, K., D'Oliveira, M., Cano, R., & Enne, M. (n.d.). Monosegmental ALPPS after Bilateral Hepatectomy. Annals of Hepatology, *16*(5), 814–817. https://doi.org/10.5604/01.3001.0010.2825

Tschuor, C., Croome, K. P., Sergeant, G., Cano, V., Schadde, E., Ardiles, V., et al. (2013). Salvage parenchymal liver transection for patients with insufficient volume increase after portal vein occlusion – an extension of the ALPPS approach. *European Journal of Surgical Oncology : The Journal of the European Society of Surgical Oncology and the British Association of Surgical Oncology,, 39*(11), 1230–1235. https://doi.org/10.1016/j.ejso.2013.08.009.

Urata, K., Kawasaki, S., Matsunami, H., Hashikura, Y., Ikegami, T., Ishizone, S., et al. (1995). Calculation of child and adult standard liver volume for liver transplantation. *Hepatology, 21*(5), 1317–1321.

van den Esschert, J. W., van Lienden, K. P., Alles, L. K., van Wijk, A. C., Heger, M., Roelofs, J. J., et al. (2012). Liver regeneration after portal vein embolization using absorbable and permanent embolization materials in a rabbit model. *Annals of Surgery, 255*(2), 311–318. https://doi.org/10.1097/SLA.0b013e31823e7587.

Vauthey, J.-N., Abdalla, E. K., Doherty, D. A., Gertsch, P., Fenstermacher, M. J., Loyer, E. M., et al. (2002). Body surface area and body weight predict total liver volume in Western adults. *Liver Transplantation : Official Publication of the American Association for the Study of Liver Diseases and the International Liver Transplantation Society, 8*(3), 233–240.

Vyas, S. J., Davies, N., Grant, L., Imber, C. J., Sharma, D., Davidson, B. R., et al. (2014). Failure of portal venous embolization. ALPPS as salvage enabling successful resection of bilobar liver metastases. *J Gastrointest Cancer, 45*(Suppl (1)), 233–236. https://doi.org/10.1007/s12029-014-9643-6.

CHAPTER

8

Two-stage versus ALPPS for large intrahepatic burden of colorectal liver metastasis

Victoria Ardiles, MD,PhD[a], *Martin de Santibañes, MD,PhD*[b] *and Eduardo de Santibañes, MD, PhD*[c]

[a]Coordinator Surgical Department, Liver Transplant Unit. Hospital Italiano de Buenos Aires. Buenos Aires, Argentina [b]General Surgery Service and Liver Transplant Unit. Hospital Italiano de Buenos Aires. Buenos Aires, Argentina [c]Honorary Chaiman General Surgery Service. Hospital Italiano de Buenos Aires. Buenos Aires, Argentina

Surgical resection is currently the only potentially curative treatment in patients with multiple and bilobar colorectal cancer liver metastases (CRLM) with 5-year survival up to 60 percent (House et al., 2010). However, resectability criteria have changed over the years due to the reduction in morbidity and mortality associated with liver resection, better patient selection, better understanding of the disease and the routine use of modern chemotherapy regimens. Currently, a tumor is considered resectable when the potential resection margin is negative and the future liver remnant (FLR) volume is sufficient to maintain liver function, preserving at least two contiguous segments with adequate afferent and efferent bile and vascular flow (Charnsangavej et al., 2006).

This paradigm shift based on the remaining liver and not on the quantity, size, and distribution of the lesions, is founded on the relationship between the FLR volume and postoperative liver function, with the risk of post hepatectomy liver failure (PHLF) inversely proportional to the FLR volume (Ribero et al., 2007). In this way, leaving a sufficient FLR volume decreases the incidence of PHLF, which is the main cause of death after this type of surgery (Rahbari et al., 2011).

Contemporary Management of Metastatic Colorectal Cancer: A Precision Medicine Approach
DOI: https://doi.org/10.1016/B978-0-323-91706-3.00019-9

The recovery of liver function after major liver resection is not only directly related to the volume, but also the quality of the remaining liver after surgery (Mullen et al., 2007). In healthy livers, a FLR volume of 25–30 percent of the total liver volume would be enough to maintain good liver function, reducing postoperative morbidity and mortality. There are certain situations in which the capacity for liver regeneration may be impaired, such as in elderly or diabetics patients, in fibrotic, steatotic, or cholestatic livers, or patients who have received prior chemotherapy. In these cases, a minimal FLR volume of 35–40 percent would be necessary; > 40 percent FLR is likely needed in patients with liver cirrhosis (Mullen et al., 2007; Vauthey et al., 2004).

Oncological liver surgery represents a dilemma for the surgeon, who, on the one hand, has to completely resect the tumor (sometimes requiring extensive hepatectomies) and, on the other, must preserve enough remaining functional parenchyma to avoid PHLF. In recent years, to achieve this goal, various techniques have been developed that make it possible to surgically rescue these patients.

The need to have an adequate FLR volume motivated the scientific community to develop techniques to induce its hypertrophy. In 1982, Masatoshi Makuuchi introduced the concept of portal embolization (PVE) to induce FLR hypertrophy, achieving growth rates between 10 percent and 40 percent in 4 to 8 weeks (Makuuchi et al., 1990). A few years later, the group of Belghitti, and simultaneously Cappusotti, suggested that the effect on the FLR hypertrophy could be achieved with similar efficiency by portal vein ligation (PVL) (Capussotti et al., 2008; Farges et al., 2003). However, at present, it is preferred to perform PVE since simultaneous occlusion of segment 4 portal branches can be accomplished and the lack of portal flow in the embolized parenchyma can be verified. In addition, better results have been reported in terms of FLR hypertrophy (Shindoh et al., 2013).

The concept of two-stage hepatectomies (TSH) was first introduced in 1992 and published in 2000 by Paul Brouse's group, to treat patients with multiple unresectable bilateral liver metastases (Adam et al., 2000a). In the original series by R Adam et al., 6 out of 13 patients underwent concomitant PVE to obtain greater FLR hypertrophy. Subsequently, the Strasbourg group, led by D. Jaeck, proposed the routine use of PVE associated with TSH after the first period followed by a second operation to "clean-up" lesions in the remaining parenchyma (Jaeck et al., 2004a). Since then, several specialized centers have adopted, developed, and modified this strategy (Imai et al., 2015; Lam et al., 2013a; Wicherts et al., 2008a).

The TSH is limited to multiple and bilateral tumors that cannot be resected in a single stage, either in combination with PVE or PVL or with local ablation therapies (Aussilhou et al., 2008; Farges et al., 2003). Portal occlusion (by PVE or PVL) is usually performed during the first stage together with a minor or non-anatomical hepatectomy to clean up the FLR, as well as with local ablation procedures in the case of more deeply localized lesions. At the second stage, after having achieved sufficient hypertrophy, the hepatectomy is completed. Five-year survival of TSH for CRLM varies between 32 percent and 64 percent with a mean survival of 24 to 44 months (Capussotti et al., 2008; Giuliante et al., 2014; Tsai et al., 2010a; Wicherts et al., 2008a).

In an update of the two-stage hepatectomy series at the Paul Brouse Hospital, between 1992 and 2012, 139 out of 1116 consecutive patients with a CRLM diagnosis with an indication for liver resection, were scheduled for TSH. Of these patients, 33 percent experienced disease progression after the first stage and were unable to complete the second stage. In the

TABLE 8.1 Failure to complete second stage in two-stage hepatectomy.

Author	year	n	second stage not completed
Adam	2000	16	3 (19 percent)
Jaeck	2004	33	8 (24 percent)
Tsai	2010	35	10 (29 percent)
Wicherts	2008	59	19 (31 percent)
Brouquet	2011	65	18 (33 percent)

intention-to-treat survival analysis, patients who were scheduled for TSH had a lower survival compared with patients who had a conventional one-stage hepatectomy (5-year survival of 31.8 vs. 47.1 percent, mean survival: 38.4 vs. 55.2 months, $p = 0.0004$). However, when considering only patients in which the TSH could be completed, both approaches had a similar overall survival (5-year survival: 41.3 vs. 48.0 percent, mean survival 44.3 vs. 56.6 months, $p = 0.40$) (Imai and Adam, 2017). These findings suggest that if both stages can be completed, overall survival is comparable to that of a single stage hepatectomy.

Despite the benefits already mentioned, the potential simultaneous and more accelerated growth of the oncological disease, both in the remaining liver and in other organs during the waiting period before complete resection, is a potential disadvantage of this method (Adam et al., 2000a; Brouquet et al., 2011a; De Graaf, Van Den Esschert, Van Lienden, and Van Gulik, 2009; Elias et al., 1999) Table 8.1 (Adam et al., 2000b; Jaeck et al., 2004b; Tsai et al., 2010b; Wicherts et al., 2008b).

The effectiveness of portal occlusion and TSH to complete the hepatectomy is only 60–80 percent and the main cause of failure is tumor progression during the waiting time between both steps (Giuliante et al., 2014; Muratore et al., 2012; Tsai et al., 2010a; Wicherts et al., 2008a). In 2012, Schnitzbauer et al. described the in-situ liver partition technique obtaining FLR hypertrophy of 40 to 160 percent in just 6 days, being able to complete the hepatectomy in one weeks (Schnitzbauer et al., 2012). This new strategy of two-stage hepatectomy with a short interval between both procedures, took the name of ALPPS for Associating Liver Partition and Portal vein occlusion for Stage hepatectomy (De Santibañes and Clavien, 2012). Despite the enormous diffusion of ALPPS worldwide, the high morbidity and mortality reported in various series produced a great debate about its safety (J. Li et al., 2013; Torres et al., 2013). In large published multicenter experiences, such as the Brazilian one with 39 patients and the German one with 25 patients, morbidity of 59 to 68 percent and mortality of 12 percent were reported (Schnitzbauer et al., 2012; Torres et al., 2013). In the same way, a cooperative series on the initial experience of ALPPS in Italy reported morbidity greater than 54 percent and mortality of 20 percent (Serenari et al., 2016).

After the first International ALPPS Consensus, held in Hamburg in February 2015, the analysis resulting from the International ALPPS Registry database showed that the highest mortality occurred after the second step and that, most of the time it, could be related to inappropriate patients' selection and the wrong decision of when to perform the second stage (Schadde et al., 2015). Subsequently, less invasive technical variants began to be developed and patient selection was improved, thus improving perioperative results

(Alvarez, Ardiles, De Santibañes, Pekolj, and De Santibañes, 2015a; de Santibañes, Alvarez, Ardiles, Pekolj, and de Santibañes, 2016; Gall et al., 2015; Jun Li et al., 2016; Robles et al., 2014). Also, now there is enough follow-up of ALPPS patients to draw conclusions of oncological results (Hasselgren et al., 2021a; Petrowsky et al., 2020a).

In both TSH and ALLPS, the objectives to be achieved are: 1) to obtain a sufficient FLR to be able to complete the resection avoiding PHLF, 2) with low associated morbidity and mortality and 3) with adequate oncological results.

FLR hypertrophy and feasibility to complete both stages

ALPPS is distinguished by the fact that it offers rapid and considerable FLR hypertrophy that is superior to traditional portal occlusion and TSH strategies (Adam et al., 2000a; Alvarez, Ardiles, Sanchez Claria, Pekolj, and de Santibañes, 2013; Lam et al., 2013a; Schadde et al., 2014a; Schnitzbauer et al., 2012). This accelerated hypertrophy in ALPPS reduces drop-out in patients with marginally resectable disease and translates into greater resectability Table 8.2 (Adam et al., 2016; Baumgart et al., 2019; Bednarsch et al., 2020; Croome et al., 2015; Knoefel et al., 2013; Ratti et al., 2015; Sandström et al., 2018a; Schadde et al., 2014b; Tanaka et al., 2015).

The first comparative study of ALPPS versus PVE and TSH was published by Shindoh et al. (Shindoh et al., 2013). In this paper, the authors compared their historical series of PVE and TSH with the initial ALPPS series reported by Schnitbauer et al. (Schnitzbauer et al., 2012). Among 144 PVE and TSH patients, only two-thirds of patients underwent curative resection. Thus, the feasibility of completing R0 resection was 77 percent with mean hypertrophy of 62 percent in 34 days. At that time, the first analysis of the international ALPPS registry reported mean hypertrophy of 80 percent in 7 days, allowing both procedures to be completed in 98 percent of cases (Schadde et al., 2014a). Later, in a multicenter experience published by Schadde et al., ALPPS was associated with a higher chance of resectability versus hepatectomy combined with PVE or PVL (83 percent vs 66 percent, p. 0.027) (Schadde et al., 2014). Other authors have reported similar results when comparing ALPPS versus TSH (Table 8.2).

Some recently published systematic reviews and meta-analysis noted no differences in the percentage of hypertrophy between these two strategies. However, in ALPPS patients, the hypertrophy was faster and therefore the kinetic growth rate (KGR:%percent hypertrophy/week) was also significantly higher. Complete resection was achieved in 90 percent of ALPPS patients (range 83.3–100 percent) versus 74,6 percent of THS patients (range 63.4–100 percent) (Liu, Yang, Gu, and Tang, 2019; Moris et al., 2018; Shen et al., 2018; Zhou et al., 2017). There is only one RCT comparing TSH and ALPPS in CRLM patients (LIGRO Trial) whose primary endpoint was the resection rate, which was significantly higher in ALPPS patients (92 percent versus 52 percent) (Sandström et al., 2018b).

An important advantage of ALPPS is that it can be used as a rescue strategy after portal occlusion or TSH with insufficient FLR hypertrophy. Rescue ALPPS was initially reported by Tschuor et al. in 3 patients with insufficient FLR hypertrophy after portal occlusion. All patients finally reached a sufficient FLR volume and could be resected (Tschuor et al., 2013). Other authors reported similar experiences becoming a useful strategy before ruling out the possibility of completing the resection due to insufficient FLR In the LIGRO trial, in 13 patients

TABLE 8.2 Resectability in studies comparing two-stage hepatectomy and ALPPS.

Author	year	design	n	%percent resectability
Knoefel	2013	RCS	ALPPS =7	100
			PVE=15	80
Schadde	2014	RCS	ALPPS = 48	83
			PVE/PVL= 83	66
Croome	2015	RCS	ALPPS = 15	100
			PVE = 53	79
Ratti	2015	RCS (case match)	ALPPS = 12	100
			TSH = 36	94
Tanaka	2015	RCS	ALPPS = 11	100
			TSH = 54	80
Adam	2016	RCS	ALPSS= 17	100
			TSH = 41	61
Baumgart	2019	RCS	ALPPS= 8	72
			TSH=50	100
Sandström	2018	RCT	ALPPS = 48	92
			TSH = 49	57
Bednarsch	20	RCS	ALPPS = 21	100
			TSH/PVE= 37	88

RCS: retrospective cohort study; RCT: randomized control trial. r:range; THS: two-stage hepatectomy; PVE: portal vein embolizarion; PVL: portal vein ligation.

of the TSH group FLR hypertrophy was insufficient. In 12 patients, a rescue ALPPS was performed allowing a complete resection in 8 to 16 days (Sandström et al., 2018b).

Another important advantage of this technique is that due to this accelerated hypertrophy, and since the liver to be resected can act as an "auxiliary liver" between both surgical steps, there is the possibility of carrying out large FLR cleaning (usually through atypical resections) and even leaving an FLR composed by only one liver segment (Erik Schadde et al., 2015). Until the development of ALPPS, remaining livers composed of a single segment had only been obtained by two surgical procedures with an interval of several months between them, which represents more a repeated liver resection than a TSH. In this scenario, the ALPPS approach presents a change to the classic paradigm of resectability since it has been shown that even a single segment can be sufficient in extreme situations when aggressive cleaning of the FLR is performed (Charnsangavej et al., 2006).

Although there are several reports in the literature that have confirmed the accelerated increase in FLR volume with ALPPS, there are still not many reports on the biological substrate that leads to this change. At the beginning of the ALPPS experience, some detractors of this technique suggested that the increase in liver volume was mainly due to edema and not to the proliferation of hepatocytes. However, even though there are studies that demonstrate proliferative and architectural changes at the histological level accompanying the macroscopic hypertrophy observed in ALPPS, there is still a lack of information on whether there is an equivalent increase in liver function (de Santibañes et al., 2016; Eshmuminov et al., 2017). When analyzing the FLR parenchyma post ALPPS, Matsuo et al. noted immaturity of the hepatocytes and the bile canaliculi, which reflects that, despite the increase in volume observed in the FLR, it could not be accompanied by a parallel increase in function (Matsuo et al., 2016).

With the development of ALPPS, it became clear that achieving sufficient FLR volume (which until now guided the decision to proceed to the second stage) did not necessarily imply having achieved sufficient function. Several reports have shown the discrepancy between FLR function and volume in this setting (Rassam et al., 2020; Serenari et al., 2018; Truant et al., 2017). Measuring liver function to select when to proceed to the second stage is of crucial importance to reduce the incidence of PHLF, breaking with the usual paradigm of only FLR volume measurement.

Morbidity and Mortality

Proponents of TSH argue that ALPPS has excessively high morbidity and mortality rates. However, recently published results by the Beaujon Hospital in France on 87 initially unresectable CRLM patients who underwent major TSH after preoperative chemotherapy, do not seem to fully support such a claim. (54) Overall morbidity and mortality in this series was 84 percent and 10 percent respectively, being higher (19 percent) in patients who had received several cycles of preoperative chemotherapy

Furthermore, a publication that compares a highly selected series of PVE and TSH (78 percent as 1-time hepatectomy) with the initial multicenter German experience of ALPPS, failed to demonstrate a significant difference in overall morbidity and mortality between the two methods (Shindoh et al., 2013). In a recent publication of the MD Anderson Cancer Center including 65 patients undergoing TSH, morbidity rates of 49 percent and mortality of 6.4 percent were reported despite considering only the second surgery (Brouquet et al., 2011b). Regarding the experience in TSH published by the Paul Brousse Hospital´s group on 59 patients, morbidity of 59 percent and mortality of 7 percent were reported after the second surgery (Wicherts et al., 2008a). Additionally, in a cooperative experience published by Tsai et al. that included 45 patients from 2 large HPB centers, an overall mortality rate of 8.8 percent was reported (4 percent after the first surgery and 5 percent after the second) (Tsai et al., 2010a). Based on these results from the most important series of TSH, it is observed that the reported morbidity and mortality rates are similar to those obtained with ALPPS in experienced centers. Also, it should be noted that the mortality of ALPPS in CRLM was lower and even nil in some series Table 8.3 (Alvarez, Ardiles, De Santibañes, Pekolj, and De Santibañes, 2015b; Brouquet et al., 2011a; Cauchy et al., 2012; Lam et al., 2013b; Petrowsky et al., 2020b; Sandström et al., 2018a; Tsai et al., 2010b; Wanis et al., 2018; Wicherts et al., 2008b).

Of note, the ALPPS series that showed the highest mortality were the initial ones, in which there was very little experience in the technique, patient selection and management, timing of

TABLE 8.3 Morbidity and mortality of two-stage hepatectomy and ALPPS series.

Author	year	Surgery	n	Morbidity	Mortality
Lam	2013	TSH	459	40	3
Cauchy	2012	TSH	87	30	10
Brouquet	2011	TSH	65	29	6.4
Tsai	2010	TSH	45	28	8.8
Wicherts	2008	TSH	59	59	7
Alvarez	2015	ALPPS	30	53	6.6
Wanis	2018	ALPPS	58	21	0
Sandström	2018	ALPPS	48	43	9.1
		TSH	49	43	10.1
Petrowsky	2021	ALPPS	510	21	2.5

THS: two-stage hepatectomy.

the second stage, etc. It should not be forgotten that the mortality from TSH proposed by the Paul Brousse Hospital group fell from 15 percent in the inaugural series in 2000 to 7 percent in 2008 (Adam et al., 2000a; Wicherts et al., 2008a). Similar to other procedures, i the number of ALPPS cases performed seems to be related to mortality. In fact, the mortality reported in the International ALPPS Registry for CRLM patients in centers with ⟨8 procedures was 13 percent versus 4 percent in centers with⟩ 8 ALPPS ($p < 0.001$) (Huiskens et al., 2019). These data highlight the importance of the learning curve in the new surgical procedures.

A recent publication on the International ALPPS Registry analyzed the evolution of morbidity and mortality and the selection criteria of patients in centers that have performed more than 10 ALPPS per year during the last 3 years (Linecker et al., 2017). A total of 437 patients from 16 centers were included, observing that the CRLM as an indication increased from 55 percent of the total ALPPS performed to 77 percent, with a decrease in the application of this strategy in biliary tumors (from 24 percent to 9 percent). In parallel with this adjustment in patient selection, a decrease in mortality was observed at 90 days, from 17 percent at the beginning of the series to 4 percent 5 years more recently (p 0.002). In addition, complications greater than grade IIIb decreased from 10 percent to 3 percent (p 0.011). Furthermore, a survey carried out in the participating centers showed that 100 percent adjusted in some way the selection of patients during their experience, and 75 percent modified some aspect of the surgical technique to reduce morbidity and mortality.

The systematic reviews and meta-analysis discussed above demonstrate greater morbidity and mortality from ALPPS. However, the series included are the initial series in the experience of each center in which the learning curve had not been overcome. The only RCT comparing ALPPS with TSH shows no difference in morbidity and mortality between the two groups (Sandström et al., 2018b). The decrease in morbidity and mortality, as a result of the increased experience in the application of ALPPS, can be explained both by a refinement in the selection of patients as well as by the technical variations that were carried out. Since the creation of the International ALPPS Registry, one of its main objectives has been to determine the criteria for adjusting the selection of patients who would benefit the most from ALPPS. In this sense, in 2014 the first analysis of 220 patients from 41 centers was published. In this study, factors associated with severe postoperative complications (> IIIb according to the Clavien-Dindo classification) were identified: age older than 60, the indication for tumors other than CRLM, the need for transfusion, and the duration of the procedure longer than 6 h (Schadde et al., 2014a). Based on these findings, it can be stated that the increase in complications is related both to the inadequate patient selection and to the technical challenges imposed by performing ALPPS. At that time, an analysis of the factors associated with mortality was not carried out since there were not enough events to perform a robust analysis. A year later, during the First International Consensus of ALPPS, an analysis of associated factors for mortality was presented (Schadde et al., 2015). This analysis shows that the risk factors previously reported for morbidity (age, tumor type, duration of the first surgical time, and intraoperative transfusions) are also risk factors for mortality. These data reinforce the concept that ALPPS should be used with great caution in patients older than 60 years and with tumors other than CRLM.

Additionally, this study of the International ALPPS Registry advanced a step that was fundamental for adjusting patient selection, more precisely, the moment in which the second stage should be performed. In this study, it was observed that 93 percent of postoperative deaths occur after the second stage of ALPPS and that PHLF was the main cause in 75 percent of them. In fact, the alteration in liver function reflected by a MELD score greater than 10 before the second step of ALPPS was an independent predictor of 90 days mortality (Schadde et al., 2015). Performing a second surgery in a patient who is recovering from a major surgical procedure, and who is experiencing PHLF, carries a higher risk of mortality after the second stage. The first stage of ALPPS can be considered as a stress test of liver function and, therefore, patients who develop PHLF after this first procedure would not be good candidates to proceed to the second stage. This highlights the need to select for each individual patient the correct moment to perform the second stage and not to do it routinely in a week as it was originally stated (Alvarez et al., 2013). Although the analysis of the International Registry attempts to provide evidence to prevent mortality after the second stage by evaluating liver function and choosing the best time to complete the ALPPS, it is important to emphasize that the initial selection of patients must remain restrictive, since once the first step has been carried out, the quality of life and survival of the patient can be significantly compromised.

The other variables identified as risk factors for increased morbidity and mortality (duration of the procedure and intraoperative transfusions) are clear markers of the severity and complexity of this surgery. Different groups have proposed technical modifications of the ALPPS (Mini ALPPS, Hybrid ALPPS, ALTPS, RALPP, laparoscopic ALPPS), all of them using less invasive techniques to reduce the complexity of the procedure (de Santibañes et al., 2016; Gall et al., 2015; Jun Li et al., 2016; Robles et al., 2014). These variations, in combination with better patient selection, have helped to reduce morbidity and mortality to the currently observed rates which are similar to those of TSH (Wanis et al., 2021).

Oncological results

From the beginning of ALPPS, skeptics raised speculative concerns regarding the oncological results of this approach as a consequence of tumor manipulation and considered it a

TABLE 8.4 Overall Survival and disease-free survival of two-stage hepatectomy and ALPPS series.

			Overall survial		Disease-free survival	
Autor	Surgery	n	3 years	5 years	3 years	5 years
Lam	TSH	459	59%percent(r28-84)	42 percent(r32-64)	20 percent (r 6–27)	r 13–20 percent
Brouquet	TSH	65	67 percent	51 percent	20 percent	20 percent
Wicherts	THS	59	—	31 percent	26 percent	13 percent
Petrowsky	ALPPS	510	59 percent	33 percent	19 percent	12 percent
Hasselgren	ALPPS	48	Median OS 48 months			
	TSH	49	Median OS 26 months			

r: range; THS: two-stage hepatectomy.

technique with a high risk of early tumor recurrence (Aloia and Vauthey, 2012). However, for the population of patients with CRLM in our series, overall survival at 1 and 3 years from the time of diagnosis of metastases was 96 percent and 53 percent, respectively, while survival at 1 and 3 years from the ALPSP was 83 percent and 49 percent.

These results are encouraging when compared with the existing series of TSH, even more considering that some of these studies only analyzed the survival of those patients who could undergo the second surgery Table 8.4 (Brouquet et al., 2011a; Hasselgren et al., 2021b; Lam et al., 2013b; Petrowsky et al., 2020b; Wicherts et al., 2008b).

It should be considered, when analyzing survival, that patients treated with ALPPS are in general initially judged unresectable by a multidisciplinary committee and have an aggressive behavior of their disease, which may be seen reflected in the high percentage of patients with synchronous metastases, bilobar disease, positive nodes in the primary tumor, and several cycles of preoperative chemotherapy (Petrowsky et al., 2020a). Therefore, this population has a high chance of recurrence and worse survival, when ALPPS was performed as the only chance of potentially curative treatment.

Activating K/N-RAS mutations are present in 35 percent to 45 percent of patients with CRLM and have been associated with poor survival, poor radiologic and/or pathologic responses to chemotherapy, and high rates of margin-positive resections (Brudvik et al., 2016). K/N-RAS mutation was also identified as an independent predictor of poor survival after ALPPS Both median cancer-related survival and disease-free survival were worse in K/N-RAS mutated tumors (Petrowsky et al., 2020a; Serenari et al., 2018a). The impact of K/N-RAS mutation on survival after ALPPS was observed for both right- and left-sided primary tumors but was more pronounced in patients with right-sided tumors. Lower survival was also related to tumor characteristics (primary T4, right colon), and poor response to chemotherapy (Petrowsky et al., 2020a). These findings will help to optimize patient selection, both avoiding futile surgical indications and maximizing the benefit for patients with extensive disease who are otherwise exposed to high-risk aggressive surgery.

Post-resection recurrence of CRLM occurs in up to 73 percent of patients, and most of these recurrences appear within 2 years after surgery (Hallet et al., 2016). ALPPS series report early recurrence in the follow-up, but these poor results could be more consequence of aggressive tumor biology than just the result of stimulation of tumor growth by systemic factors released during the surgery itself, as was stated by some authors. ALPPS candidates themselves represent a high-risk subgroup, with aggressive biological behavior, and in whom poor disease-free survival should not be surprising. However, disease-free survival is no longer a reliable predictor of overall survival in patients with CRLM, since repeat resections for recurrence and other multimodal therapies will substantially improve overall survival outcomes. Repeated resections after ALPPS for CRLM in selected patients are safe and feasible with low morbidity and no mortality. Survival seems to be comparable with repeated resections after conventional hepatectomy.

The mean disease-free survival of 11 months recently reported in ALPPS is higher than the 7.5 months and 7.1 months reported in the experiences of classic TSH in two referral centers (Abbott, Sohn, Hanseman, and Curley, 2014; Adam et al., 2016; Faitot et al., 2014; Petrowsky et al., 2020b). A recently published study aimed to compare the intention-to-treat survival of ALPPS ($n = 17$) versus classic 2-stage hepatectomy ($n = 41$) in CRLM (Adam et al., 2016). Surprisingly, even though disease-free survival was not significantly different between both strategies, it was found that the estimated overall survival at 2 years was lower after ALPPS than after classic TSH (42 percent vs 77 percent, $p = 0.006$) and more importantly, that the overall survival of the patients who did not complete the second period in the classical strategy was comparable to that of the ALPPS. However, the results of this study must be carefully interpreted. First, the positive margin rate in ALPPS was 64 percent versus 29 percent in the classic TSH group. Second, salvage surgery for liver recurrence was performed less frequently after ALPPS than after classic TSH, which could reflect a more aggressive recurrence pattern but also a different policy in patient management treated during the learning curve of an innovative surgical approach. Finally, the French group did not report the incidence of K/N RAS mutations between the ALPPS group and the classic TSH, which has been identified as a significant risk factor associated with worse results (Petrowsky et al., 2020b; Serenari et al., 2018b).

Olthof et al. performed an analysis of the oncological outcomes of CRLM patients with CRLM in the International ALPPS Registry. From a total of 211 patients with complete data in the registry, they were divided into two groups according to the presence or absence of at least two factors chosen as markers of unresectability and where ALPPS would be the only surgical option with curative intent. Thus, the 70 patients with two or more criteria (≥ 6 metastases, ≥ 2 metastases in the FLR and ≥ 6 compromised segments) were compared with the 141 patients with less than 2 criteria. Two-year survival was significantly lower in the group with ≥ 2 criteria (49 percent versus 72 percent, $p < 0.001$) as was the mean overall survival (20 months versus 35 months). In the same way, the mean disease-free survival was significantly lower in the first group (6 versus 12 months respectively) and 37 percent of patients with ≥ 2 criteria had recurrence before 6 months compared to 24 percent in patients with less than 2 criteria. In a subgroup analysis, patients with ≥ 2 criteria were compared with a cohort of patients with ≥ 6 metastases who had been included in two palliative treatment protocols with systemic chemotherapy (CAIRO and CAIRO2) (matched by age, sex, and synchronicity). Surprisingly, the overall survival of the subgroup of patients with ALPPS with poorer prognosis criteria was comparable to that of those patients undergoing palliative chemotherapy treatments (Olthof et al., 2017). Although this study has many limitations, mainly due to its retrospective nature and the analysis of the available variables leaving aside some other important ones from the oncological point of view, it shows that the fact that a patient is technically resectable using ALPPS does not necessarily mean that we are offering a benefit in oncological terms. Patients in whom ALPPS is indicated belong to a subgroup with very advanced disease and with several poor prognostic factors (synchronous, multiple metastases, several compromised segments, high incidence of positive lymph nodes in the primary tumor, extensive preoperative chemotherapy treatments, etc.). Therefore, it is essential to select those patients who will benefit the most from an invasive procedure that carries morbidity and mortality.

In the updated follow-up of the RCT comparing ALPPS versus TSH, patients randomized to ALPPS had significantly longer survival than those randomized to TSH (46 vs 26 months, respectively). This finding may be explained by the higher resection rate in the ALPPS group because the difference was no longer significant when the comparison was made for resected patients (Hasselgren et al., 2021b).

Regarding the quality of life of these patients, we recently carried out together with another pioneering center with great experience in this surgery an analysis of the long-term quality of life of patients with CRLM who had undergone ALPPS (Wanis et al., 2018). The results showed that, despite having an advanced disease that required aggressive liver resection, patients report few functional limitations and symptoms. The quality of life reported in this series is similar to the reference values of the general population (Langenhoff, Krabbe, Peerenboom, Wobbes, and Ruers, 2006).

Conclusion

Considering that the main disadvantage of ALPPS is the greater morbidity and mortality, and the main disadvantage of classic two-stage hepatectomy is the possibility of progression during the waiting time between stages, various groups have proposed variations of both procedures to solve these drawbacks, such as the classic ALPPS modifications (Hybrid ALPPS, ALTPS, RALPP, laparoscopic ALPPS, MiniALPPS, etc.), all of them using less invasive techniques, and the fast track TSH with the aim to reduce the time between procedures and therefore the probability of tumor progression.

Currently, ALPPS and TSH show excellent technical feasibility, good security patterns, and comparable long-term oncologic outcomes in CRLM patients. Both are two-stage hepatectomies that differ at the time of performing the second stage. The key to improve results is to have an adequate patient´s selection and properly define the timing to complete the procedure based not only on the FLR volume increase but fundamentally on the clinical status of the patient and the FLR function, waiting the necessary time for the patient to be in optimal conditions to perform the second stage.

References

Abbott, D. E., Sohn, V. Y., Hanseman, D., & Curley, S. A. (2014). Cost-effectiveness of simultaneous resection and RFA versus 2-stage hepatectomy for bilobar colorectal liver metastases. *Journal of Surgical Oncology*, 109(6), 516–520. https://doi.org/10.1002/jso.23539.

Adam, R., Imai, K., Castro Benitez, C., Allard, M. A., Vibert, E., Sa Cunha, A., et al. (2016). Outcome after associating liver partition and portal vein ligation for staged hepatectomy and conventional two-stage hepatectomy for colorectal liver metastases. *British Journal of Surgery*, 103(11), 1521–1529. https://doi.org/10.1002/bjs.10256.

Adam, R., Laurent, A., Azoulay, D., Castaing, D., Bismuth, H., Buchler, M., et al. (2000a). Two-stage hepatectomy: a planned strategy to treat irresectable liver tumors. *Annals of Surgery,* 232(6), 777–785. https://doi.org/10.1097/00000658-200012000-00006.

Adam, R., Laurent, A., Azoulay, D., Castaing, D., Bismuth, H., Buchler, M., et al. (2000b). Two-stage hepatectomy: a planned strategy to treat irresectable liver tumors. *Annals of Surgery,* 232(6), 777–785. https://doi.org/10.1097/00000658-200012000-00006.

Aloia, T. A., & Vauthey, J. N. (2012). Associating liver partition and portal vein ligation for staged hepatectomy (ALPPS): what is gained and what is lost? *Annals of Surgery,* 256(3), e9. https://doi.org/10.1097/SLA.0b013e318265fd3e.

Alvarez, F. A., Ardiles, V., De Santibañes, M., Pekolj, J., & De Santibañes, E. (2015a). Associating liver partition and portal vein ligation for staged hepatectomy offers high oncological feasibility with adequate patient safety: a prospective study at a single center. *Annals of Surgery,* 261(4), 723–732. https://doi.org/10.1097/SLA.0000000000001046.

Alvarez, F. A., Ardiles, V., De Santibañes, M., Pekolj, J., & De Santibañes, E. (2015b). Associating liver partition and portal vein ligation for staged hepatectomy offers high oncological feasibility with adequate patient safety: a prospective study at a single center. *Annals of Surgery,* 261(4), 723–732. https://doi.org/10.1097/SLA.0000000000001046.

Alvarez, F. A., Ardiles, V., Sanchez Claria, R., Pekolj, J., & de Santibañes, E. (2013). Associating Liver Partition and Portal Vein Ligation for Staged Hepatectomy (ALPPS): tips and Tricks. *Journal of Gastrointestinal Surgery,* 17(4), 814–821. https://doi.org/10.1007/s11605-012-2092-2.

Aussilhou, B., Lesurtel, M., Sauvanet, A., Farges, O., Dokmak, S., Goasguen, N., et al. (2008). Right portal vein ligation is as efficient as portal vein embolization to induce hypertrophy of the left liver remnant. *Journal of Gastrointestinal Surgery,* 12(2), 297–303. https://doi.org/10.1007/s11605-007-0410-x.

Baumgart, J., Jungmann, F., Bartsch, F., Kloth, M., Mittler, J., Heinrich, S., et al. (2019). Two-Stage Hepatectomy and ALPPS for Advanced Bilateral Liver Metastases: a Tailored Approach Balancing Risk and Outcome. *Journal of Gastrointestinal Surgery,* 23(12), 2391–2400. https://doi.org/10.1007/s11605-019-04145-9.

Bednarsch, J., Czigany, Z., Sharmeen, S., Van Der Kroft, G., Strnad, P., Ulmer, T. F., et al. (2020). ALPPS versus two-stage hepatectomy for colorectal liver metastases - -a comparative retrospective cohort study. *World J Surg Oncol, 18*(1), 140. PMID: 32580729; PMCID: PMC7315489. doi:10.1186/s12957-020-01919-3.

Brouquet, A., Abdalla, E. K., Kopetz, S., Garrett, C. R., Overman, M. J., Eng, C., et al. (2011a). High survival rate after two-stage resection of advanced colorectal liver metastases: response-based selection and complete resection define outcome. *Journal of Clinical Oncology,* 29(8), 1083–1090. https://doi.org/10.1200/JCO.2010.32.6132.

Brouquet, A., Abdalla, E. K., Kopetz, S., Garrett, C. R., Overman, M. J., Eng, C., et al. (2011b). High survival rate after two-stage resection of advanced colorectal liver metastases: response-based selection and complete resection define outcome. *Journal of Clinical Oncology,* 29(8), 1083–1090. https://doi.org/10.1200/JCO.2010.32.6132.

Brudvik, K. W., Mise, Y., Chung, M. H., Chun, Y. S., Kopetz, S. E., Passot, G., et al. (2016). RAS Mutation Predicts Positive Resection Margins and Narrower Resection Margins in Patients Undergoing Resection of Colorectal Liver Metastases. *Annals of Surgical Oncology,* 23(8), 2635–2643. https://doi.org/10.1245/s10434-016-5187-2.

Capussotti, L., Muratore, A., Baracchi, F., Lelong, B., Ferrero, A., Regge, D., et al. (2008). Portal vein ligation as an efficient method of increasing the future liver remnant volume in the surgical treatment of colorectal metastases. *Archives of Surgery,* 143(10), 978–982. https://doi.org/10.1001/archsurg.143.10.978.

Cauchy, F., Aussilhou, B., Dokmak, S., Fuks, D., Gaujoux, S., Farges, O., et al. (2012). Reappraisal of the risks and benefits of major liver resection in patients with initially unresectable colorectal liver metastases. *Annals of Surgery,* 256(5), 746–754. https://doi.org/10.1097/sla.0b013e3182738204.

Charnsangavej, C., Clary, B., Fong, Y., Grothey, A., Pawlik, T. M., & Choti, M. A. (2006). Selection of patients for resection of hepatic colorectal metastases: expert consensus statement. *Annals of Surgical Oncology,* 13(10), 1261–1268. https://doi.org/10.1245/s10434-006-9023-y.

Croome, K. P., Hernandez-Alejandro, R., Parker, M., Heimbach, J., Rosen, C., & Nagorney, D. M. (2015). Is the liver kinetic growth rate in ALPPS unprecedented when compared with PVE and living donor liver transplant? A multicentre analysis. *HPB,* 17(6), 477–484. https://doi.org/10.1111/hpb.12386.

De Graaf, W., Van Den Esschert, J. W., Van Lienden, K. P., & Van Gulik, T. M. (2009). Induction of tumor growth after preoperative portal vein embolization: is it a real problem? *Annals of Surgical Oncology,* 16(2), 423–430. https://doi.org/10.1245/s10434-008-0222-6.

de Santibañes, E., Alvarez, F.A., Ardiles, V., Pekolj, J., & de Santibañes, M. (2016). Inverting the ALPPS paradigm by minimizing first stage impact: the Mini-ALPPS technique. Langenbeck's Archives of Surgery, *401*(4), 557–563. https://doi.org/10.1007/s00423-016-1424-1

De Santibañes, E., & Clavien, P. A. (2012). Playing play-doh to prevent postoperative liver failure: the \aLPPS\ approach. *Annals of Surgery*, 255(3), 415–417. https://doi.org/10.1097/SLA.0b013e318248577d.

de Santibañes, M., Dietrich, A., Alvarez, F. A., Ardiles, V., Loresi, M., D'adamo, M., et al. (2016). Biological Substrate of the Rapid Volumetric Changes Observed in the Human Liver During the Associating Liver Partition and Portal Vein Ligation for Staged Hepatectomy Approach. *Journal of Gastrointestinal Surgery*, 20(3), 546–553. https://doi.org/10.1007/s11605-015-2982-1.

Elias, D., De Baere, T., Roche, A., Ducreux, M., Leclere, J., & Lasser, P. (1999). During liver regeneration following right portal embolization the growth rate of liver metastases is more rapid than that of the liver parenchyma. *British Journal of Surgery*, 86(6), 784–788. https://doi.org/10.1046/j.1365-2168.1999.01154.x.

Eshmuminov, D., Tschuor, C., Raptis, D. A., Boss, A., Wurnig, M. C., Sergeant, G., et al. (2017). Rapid liver volume increase induced by associating liver partition with portal vein ligation for staged hepatectomy (ALPPS): is it edema, steatosis, or true proliferation? *Surgery (United States)*, 161(6), 1549–1552. https://doi.org/10.1016/j.surg.2017.01.005.

Faitot, F., Faron, M., Adam, R., Elias, D., Cimino, M., Cherqui, D., et al. (2014). Two-Stage hepatectomy versus 1-Stage Resection combined with radiofrequency for bilobar colorectal metastases a case-matched analysis of surgical and oncological outcomes. *Annals of Surgery*, 260(5), 822–828. Lippincott Williams and Wilkins https://doi.org/10.1097/SLA.0000000000000976.

Farges, O., Belghiti, J., Kianmanesh, R., Regimbeau, J. M., Santoro, R., Vilgrain, V., et al. (2003). Portal Vein Embolization before Right Hepatectomy: prospective Clinical Trial. *Annals of Surgery*, 237(2), 208–217. https://doi.org/10.1097/00000658-200302000-00010.

Gall, T. M. H., Sodergren, M. H., Frampton, A. E., Fan, R., Spalding, D. R., Habib, N. A., et al. (2015). Radio-frequency-assisted liver partition with portal vein ligation (RALPP) for liver regeneration. *Annals of Surgery*, 261(2), e45–e46. https://doi.org/10.1097/SLA.0000000000000607.

Giuliante, F., Ardito, F., Ferrero, A., Aldrighetti, L., Ercolani, G., Grande, G., et al. (2014). Tumor progression during preoperative chemotherapy predicts failure to complete 2-stage hepatectomy for colorectal liver metastases: results of an Italian multicenter analysis of 130 patients. *Journal of the American College of Surgeons*, 219(2), 285–294. https://doi.org/10.1016/j.jamcollsurg.2014.01.063.

Hallet, J., Sa Cunha, A., Adam, R., Goéré, D., Bachellier, P., Azoulay, D., et al. (2016). Factors influencing recurrence following initial hepatectomy for colorectal liver metastases. *British Journal of Surgery*, 103(10), 1366–1376. https://doi.org/10.1002/bjs.10191.

Hasselgren, K., Røsok, B. I., Larsen, P. N., Sparrelid, E., Lindell, G., Schultz, N. A., et al. (2021a). ALPPS Improves Survival Compared With TSH in Patients Affected of CRLM: survival Analysis From the Randomized Controlled Trial LIGRO. *Annals of Surgery*, 273(3), 442–448. https://doi.org/10.1097/SLA.0000000000003701.

Hasselgren, K., Røsok, B. I., Larsen, P. N., Sparrelid, E., Lindell, G., Schultz, N. A., et al. (2021b). ALPPS Improves Survival Compared With TSH in Patients Affected of CRLM: survival Analysis From the Randomized Controlled Trial LIGRO. *Annals of Surgery*, 273(3), 442–448. https://doi.org/10.1097/SLA.0000000000003701.

House, M. G., Ito, H., Gönen, M., Fong, Y., Allen, P. J., DeMatteo, R. P., et al. (2010). Survival after Hepatic Resection for Metastatic Colorectal Cancer: trends in Outcomes for 1,600 Patients during Two Decades at a Single Institution. *Journal of the American College of Surgeons*, 210(5), 744–752. https://doi.org/10.1016/j.jamcollsurg.2009.12.040.

Huiskens, J., Schadde, E., Lang, H., Malago, M., Petrowsky, H., de Santibañes, E., et al. (2019). Avoiding postoperative mortality after ALPPS–development of a tumor-specific risk score for colorectal liver metastases. *HPB*, 21(7), 898–905. https://doi.org/10.1016/j.hpb.2018.11.010.

Imai, K., & Adam, R. (2017). Two-stage liver surgery. *Extreme Hepatic Surgery and Other Strategies: Increasing Resectability in Colorectal Liver Metastases* (pp. 203–215). Cham, Switzerland, Springer International Publishing.

Imai, K., Benitez, C. C., Allard, M. A., Vibert, E., Cunha, A. S., Cherqui, D., et al. (2015). Failure to achieve a 2-stage hepatectomy for colorectal liver metastases. *Annals of Surgery*, 262(5), 772–779. https://doi.org/10.1097/SLA.0000000000001449.

Jaeck, D., Oussoultzoglou, E., Rosso, E., Greget, M., Weber, J.-C., & Bachellier, P. (2004a). A Two-Stage Hepatectomy Procedure Combined With Portal Vein Embolization to Achieve Curative Resection for Initially Unresectable Multiple and Bilobar Colorectal Liver Metastases. *Annals of Surgery*, 240(6), 1037–1051. https://doi.org/10.1097/01.sla.0000145965.86383.89.

Jaeck, D., Oussoultzoglou, E., Rosso, E., Greget, M., Weber, J.-C., & Bachellier, P. (2004b). A Two-Stage Hepatectomy Procedure Combined With Portal Vein Embolization to Achieve Curative Resection for Initially Unresectable

Multiple and Bilobar Colorectal Liver Metastases. *Annals of Surgery*, 240(6), 1037–1051. https://doi.org/10.1097/01.sla.0000145965.86383.89.

Knoefel, W. T., Gabor, I., Rehders, A., Alexander, A., Krausch, M., Schulte Am Esch, J., et al. (2013). In situ liver transection with portal vein ligation for rapid growth of the future liver remnant in two-stage liver resection. *British Journal of Surgery*, 100(3), 388–394. https://doi.org/10.1002/bjs.8955.

Lam, V. W. T., Laurence, J. M., Johnston, E., Hollands, M. J., Pleass, H. C. C., & Richardson, A. J. (2013a). A systematic review of two-stage hepatectomy in patients with initially unresectable colorectal liver metastases. *HPB*, 15(7), 483–491. https://doi.org/10.1111/j.1477-2574.2012.00607.x.

Lam, V. W. T., Laurence, J. M., Johnston, E., Hollands, M. J., Pleass, H. C. C., & Richardson, A. J. (2013b). A systematic review of two-stage hepatectomy in patients with initially unresectable colorectal liver metastases. *HPB*, 15(7), 483–491. https://doi.org/10.1111/j.1477-2574.2012.00607.x.

Langenhoff, B. S., Krabbe, P. F. M., Peerenboom, L., Wobbes, T., & Ruers, T. J. M. (2006). Quality of life after surgical treatment of colorectal liver metastases. *British Journal of Surgery*, 93(8), 1007–1014. https://doi.org/10.1002/bjs.5387.

Li, J., Girotti, P., Königsrainer, I., Ladurner, R., Königsrainer, A., & Nadalin, S. (2013). ALPPS in Right Trisectionectomy: a Safe Procedure to Avoid Postoperative Liver Failure? *Journal of Gastrointestinal Surgery*, 17(5), 956–961. https://doi.org/10.1007/s11605-012-2132-y.

Li, J., Kantas, A., Ittrich, H., Koops, A., Achilles, E. G., Fischer, L., et al. (2016). Avoid "All-Touch" by Hybrid ALPPS to Achieve Oncological Efficacy. *Annals of Surgery*, *1*, e6–e7. https://doi.org/10.1097/SLA.0000000000000845.

Linecker, M., Björnsson, B., Stavrou, G. A., Oldhafer, K. J., Lurje, G., Neumann, U., et al. (2017). Risk Adjustment in ALPPS Is Associated with a Dramatic Decrease in Early Mortality and Morbidity. *Annals of Surgery*, 266(5), 779–786. https://doi.org/10.1097/SLA.0000000000002446.

Liu, Y., Yang, Y., Gu, S., & Tang, K. (2019). A systematic review and meta-analysis of associating liver partition and portal vein ligation for staged hepatectomy (ALPPS) versus traditional staged hepatectomy. *Medicine*, 98(15), e15229. https://doi.org/10.1097/md.0000000000015229.

Makuuchi, M., Thai, B. L., Takayasu, K., Takayama, T., Kosuge, T., Gunven, P., et al. (1990). Preoperative portal embolization to increase safety of major hepatectomy for hilar bile duct carcinoma: a preliminary report. *Surgery*, 107(5), 521–527.

Matsuo, K., Murakami, T., Kawaguchi, D., Hiroshima, Y., Koda, K., Yamazaki, K., et al. (2016). Histologic features after surgery associating liver partition and portal vein ligation for staged hepatectomy versus those after hepatectomy with portal vein embolization. *Surgery (United States)*, 159(5), 1289–1298. https://doi.org/10.1016/j.surg.2015.12.004.

Moris, D., Ronnekleiv-Kelly, S., Kostakis, I. D., Tsilimigras, D. I., Beal, E. W., Papalampros, A., et al. (2018). Operative Results and Oncologic Outcomes of Associating Liver Partition and Portal Vein Ligation for Staged Hepatectomy (ALPPS) Versus Two-Stage Hepatectomy (TSH) in Patients with Unresectable Colorectal Liver Metastases: a Systematic Review and Meta-Analysis. *World Journal of Surgery*, 42(3), 806–815. https://doi.org/10.1007/s00268-017-4181-6.

Mullen, J. T., Ribero, D., Reddy, S. K., Donadon, M., Zorzi, D., Gautam, S., et al. (2007). Hepatic Insufficiency and Mortality in 1,059 Noncirrhotic Patients Undergoing Major Hepatectomy. *Journal of the American College of Surgeons*, 204(5), 854–862. https://doi.org/10.1016/j.jamcollsurg.2006.12.032.

Muratore, A., Zimmitti, G., Ribero, D., Mellano, A., Viganò, L., & Capussotti, L. (2012). Chemotherapy between the first and second stages of a two-stage hepatectomy for colorectal liver metastases: should we routinely recommend it? *Annals of Surgical Oncology*, 19(4), 1310–1315. https://doi.org/10.1245/s10434-011-2069-5.

Olthof, P. B., Huiskens, J., Wicherts, D. A., Huespe, P. E., Ardiles, V., Robles-Campos, R., et al. (2017). Survival after associating liver partition and portal vein ligation for staged hepatectomy (ALPPS) for advanced colorectal liver metastases: a case-matched comparison with palliative systemic therapy. *Surgery (United States)*, 161(4), 909–919. https://doi.org/10.1016/j.surg.2016.10.032.

Petrowsky, H., Linecker, M., Raptis, D. A., Kuemmerli, C., Fritsch, R., Kirimker, O. E., et al. (2020a). First Long-term Oncologic Results of the ALPPS Procedure in a Large Cohort of Patients With Colorectal Liver Metastases. *Annals of Surgery*, 272(5), 793–800. https://doi.org/10.1097/SLA.0000000000004330.

Petrowsky, H., Linecker, M., Raptis, D. A., Kuemmerli, C., Fritsch, R., Kirimker, O. E., et al. (2020b). First Long-term Oncologic Results of the ALPPS Procedure in a Large Cohort of Patients With Colorectal Liver Metastases. *Annals of Surgery*, 272(5), 793–800. https://doi.org/10.1097/SLA.0000000000004330.

Rahbari, N. N., Garden, O. J., Padbury, R., Brooke-Smith, M., Crawford, M., Adam, R., et al. (2011). Posthepatectomy liver failure: a definition and grading by the International Study Group of Liver Surgery (ISGLS). *Surgery,*, 149(5), 713–724. https://doi.org/10.1016/j.surg.2010.10.001.

Rassam, F., Olthof, P. B., van Lienden, K. P., Bennink, R. J., Erdmann, J. I., Swijnenburg, R.-J., et al. (2020). Comparison of functional and volumetric increase of the future remnant liver and postoperative outcomes after portal vein embolization and complete or partial associating liver partition and portal vein ligation for staged hepatectomy (ALPPS). *Annals of translational medicine, 8*(7), 436. https://doi.org/10.21037/atm.2020.03.191.

Ratti, F., Schadde, E., Masetti, M., Massani, M., Zanello, M., Serenari, M., et al. (2015). Strategies to Increase the Resectability of Patients with Colorectal Liver Metastases: a Multi-center Case-Match Analysis of ALPPS and Conventional Two-Stage Hepatectomy. *Annals of Surgical Oncology,* 22(6), 1933–1942. https://doi.org/10.1245/s10434-014-4291-4.

Ribero, D., Abdalla, E. K., Madoff, D. C., Donadon, M., Loyer, E. M., & Vauthey, J. N. (2007). Portal vein embolization before major hepatectomy and its effects on regeneration, resectability and outcome. *British Journal of Surgery,* 94(11), 1386–1394. https://doi.org/10.1002/bjs.5836.

Robles, R., Parrilla, P., Lõpez-Conesa, A., Brusadin, R., De La Peña, J., Fuster, M., et al. (2014). Tourniquet modification of the associating liver partition and portal ligation for staged hepatectomy procedure. *British Journal of Surgery,* 101(9), 1129–1134. https://doi.org/10.1002/bjs.9547.

Sandström, P., Røsok, B. I., Sparrelid, E., Larsen, P. N., Larsson, A. L., Lindell, G., et al. (2018a). ALPPS Improves Resectability Compared with Conventional Two-stage Hepatectomy in Patients with Advanced Colorectal Liver Metastasis: results from a Scandinavian Multicenter Randomized Controlled Trial (LIGRO Trial). *Annals of Surgery,*, 267(5), 833–840. https://doi.org/10.1097/SLA.0000000000002511.

Sandström, P., Røsok, B. I., Sparrelid, E., Larsen, P. N., Larsson, A. L., Lindell, G., et al. (2018b). ALPPS Improves Resectability Compared with Conventional Two-stage Hepatectomy in Patients with Advanced Colorectal Liver Metastasis: results from a Scandinavian Multicenter Randomized Controlled Trial (LIGRO Trial). *Annals of Surgery,*, 267(5), 833–840. https://doi.org/10.1097/SLA.0000000000002511.

Schadde, E., Ardiles, V., Robles-Campos, R., Malago, M., Machado, M., Hernandez-Alejandro, R., et al. (2014a). Early survival and safety of ALPPS first report of the international ALPPS registry. *Annals of Surgery,* 260(5), 829–838. https://doi.org/10.1097/SLA.0000000000000947.

Schadde, E., Ardiles, V., Robles-Campos, R., Malago, M., Machado, M., Hernandez-Alejandro, R., et al. (2014b). Early survival and safety of ALPPS first report of the international ALPPS registry. *Annals of Surgery,* 260(5), 829–838. https://doi.org/10.1097/SLA.0000000000000947.

Schadde, E., Ardiles, V., Slankamenac, K., Tschuor, C., Sergeant, G., Amacker, N., et al. (2014). ALPPS offers a better chance of complete resection in patients with primarily unresectable liver tumors compared with conventional-staged hepatectomies: results of a multicenter analysis. *World Journal of Surgery,* 38(6), 1510–1519. https://doi.org/10.1007/s00268-014-2513-3.

Schadde, E., Raptis, D. A., Schnitzbauer, A. A., Ardiles, V., Tschuor, C., Lesurtel, M., et al. (2015). Prediction of mortality after ALPPS Stage-1. *Annals of Surgery,*, 262(5), 780–786. https://doi.org/10.1097/SLA.0000000000001450.

Schadde, E., Malagó, M., Hernandez-Alejandro, R., Li, J., Abdalla, E., Ardiles, V., et al. (2015). Monosegment ALPPS hepatectomy: extending resectability by rapid hypertrophy. *Surgery,* 157(4), 676–689. https://doi.org/10.1016/j.surg.2014.11.015.

Schnitzbauer, A. A., Lang, S. A., Goessmann, H., Nadalin, S., Baumgart, J., Farkas, S. A., et al. (2012). Right portal vein ligation combined with in situ splitting induces rapid left lateral liver lobe hypertrophy enabling 2-staged extended right hepatic resection in small-for-size settings. *Annals of Surgery,* 255(3), 405–414. https://doi.org/10.1097/SLA.0b013e31824856f5.

Serenari, M., Alvarez, F. A., Ardiles, V., De Santibañes, M., Pekolj, J., & De Santibañes, E. (2018a). The ALPPS Approach for Colorectal Liver Metastases: impact of KRAS Mutation Status in Survival. *Digestive Surgery,* 35(4), 303–310. https://doi.org/10.1159/000471930.

Serenari, M., Alvarez, F. A., Ardiles, V., De Santibañes, M., Pekolj, J., & De Santibañes, E. (2018b). The ALPPS Approach for Colorectal Liver Metastases: impact of KRAS Mutation Status in Survival. *Digestive Surgery,* 35(4), 303–310. https://doi.org/10.1159/000471930.

Serenari, M., Collaud, C., Alvarez, F. A., De Santibañes, M., Giunta, D., Pekolj, J., et al. (2018). Interstage Assessment of Remnant Liver Function in ALPPS Using Hepatobiliary Scintigraphy: prediction of Posthepatectomy Liver Failure and Introduction of the HIBA Index. *Annals of Surgery,* 267(6), 1141–1147. https://doi.org/10.1097/SLA.0000000000002150.

Serenari, M., Zanello, M., Schadde, E., Toschi, E., Ratti, F., Gringeri, E., et al. (2016). Importance of primary indication and liver function between stages: results of a multicenter Italian audit of ALPPS 2012-2014. *HPB*, 18(5), 419–427. https://doi.org/10.1016/j.hpb.2016.02.003.

Shen, Y. N., Guo, C. X., Wang, L. Y., Pan, Y., Chen, Y. W., Bai, X. L., et al. (2018). Associating liver partition and portal vein ligation versus 2-stage hepatectomy A meta-analysis. *Medicine (United States), 97*(35), e12082. https://doi.org/10.1097/MD.0000000000012082.

Shindoh, J., Truty, M. J., Aloia, T. A., Curley, S. A., Zimmitti, G., Huang, S. Y., et al. (2013). Kinetic growth rate after portal vein embolization predicts posthepatectomy outcomes: toward zero liver-related mortality in patients with colorectal liver metastases and small future liver remnant. *Journal of the American College of Surgeons*, 216(2), 201–209. https://doi.org/10.1016/j.jamcollsurg.2012.10.018.

Shindoh, J., Vauthey, J. N., Zimmitti, G., Curley, S. A., Huang, S. Y., Mahvash, A., et al. (2013). Analysis of the efficacy of portal vein embolization for patients with extensive liver malignancy and very low future liver remnant volume, including a comparison with the associating liver partition with portal vein ligation for staged hepatectomy approach. *In Journal of the American College of Surgeons*, 217(1), 126–133. https://doi.org/10.1016/j.jamcollsurg.2013.03.004.

Tanaka, K., Matsuo, K., Murakami, T., Kawaguchi, D., Hiroshima, Y., Koda, K., et al. (2015). Associating liver partition and portal vein ligation for staged hepatectomy (ALPPS): short-term outcome, functional changes in the future liver remnant, and tumor growth activity. *European Journal of Surgical Oncology*, 41(4), 506–512. https://doi.org/10.1016/j.ejso.2015.01.031.

Torres, O. J. o. M., Fernandes, E. d. S. M. a., Oliveira, C. V. i. C., Lima, C. X. a., Waechter, F. L. u., Moraes-Junior, J. M. a. A., et al. (2013). Associating liver partition and portal vein ligation for staged hepatectomy (ALPPS): the Brazilian experience. *Arquivos Brasileiros de Cirurgia Digestiva : ABCD = Brazilian Archives of Digestive Surgery*, 26(1), 40–43.

Truant, S., Baillet, C., Deshorgue, A. C., El Amrani, M., Huglo, D., & Pruvot, F. R. (2017). Contribution of hepatobiliary scintigraphy in assessing ALPPS most suited timing. *Updates Surg*, 69(3), 411–419. https://doi.org/10.1007/s13304-017-0481-5.

Tsai, S., Marques, H. P., De Jong, M. C., Mira, P., Ribeiro, V., Choti, M. A., et al. (2010a). Two-stage strategy for patients with extensive bilateral colorectal liver metastases. *HPB*, 12(4), 262–269. https://doi.org/10.1111/j.1477-2574.2010.00161.x.

Tsai, S., Marques, H. P., De Jong, M. C., Mira, P., Ribeiro, V., Choti, M. A., et al. (2010b). Two-stage strategy for patients with extensive bilateral colorectal liver metastases. *HPB*, 12(4), 262–269. https://doi.org/10.1111/j.1477-2574.2010.00161.x.

Tschuor, C., Croome, K. P., Sergeant, G., Cano, V., Schadde, E., Ardiles, V., et al. (2013). Salvage parenchymal liver transection for patients with insufficient volume increase after portal vein occlusion - An extension of the ALPPS approach. *European Journal of Surgical Oncology*, 39(11), 1230–1235. https://doi.org/10.1016/j.ejso.2013.08.009.

Vauthey, J. N., Pawlik, T. M., Abdalla, E. K., Arens, J. F., Nemr, R. A., Wei, S. H., et al. (2004). Is Extended Hepatectomy for Hepatobiliary Malignancy Justified? *Annals of Surgery*, 239(5), 722–732. https://doi.org/10.1097/01.sla.0000124385.83887.d5.

Wanis, K. N., Ardiles, V., Alvarez, F. A., Tun-Abraham, M. E., Linehan, D., de Santibañes, E., et al. (2018). Intermediate-term survival and quality of life outcomes in patients with advanced colorectal liver metastases undergoing associating liver partition and portal vein ligation for staged hepatectomy. *Surgery (United States)*, 163(4), 691–697. https://doi.org/10.1016/j.surg.2017.09.044.

Wanis, K. N., Linecker, M., Madenci, A. L., Müller, P. C., Nüssler, N., Brusadin, R., et al. (2021). Variation in complications and mortality following ALPPS at early-adopting centers. *HPB*, 23(1), 46–55. https://doi.org/10.1016/j.hpb.2020.04.009.

Wicherts, D. A., Miller, R., De Haas, R. J., Bitsakou, G., Vibert, E., Veilhan, L. A., et al. (2008a). Long-term results of two-stage hepatectomy for irresectable colorectal cancer liver metastases. *Annals of Surgery*, 248(6), 994–1003. https://doi.org/10.1097/SLA.0b013e3181907fd9.

Wicherts, D. A., Miller, R., De Haas, R. J., Bitsakou, G., Vibert, E., Veilhan, L. A., et al. (2008b). Long-term results of two-stage hepatectomy for irresectable colorectal cancer liver metastases. *Annals of Surgery*, 248(6), 994–1003. https://doi.org/10.1097/SLA.0b013e3181907fd9.

Zhou, Z., Xu, M., Lin, N., Pan, C., Zhou, B., Zhong, Y., et al. (2017). Associating liver partition and portal vein ligation for staged hepatectomy versus conventional two-stage hepatectomy: a systematic review and meta-analysis. *World J Surg Oncol, 15*(1), 227. https://doi.org/10.1186/s12957-017-1295-0.

CHAPTER

9

Synchronous colorectal liver metastasis – simultaneous vs. staged approach

Colin M. Court and Alice C. Wei

Department of Surgery, Memorial Sloan Kettering Cancer Center, New York, New York, United States of America

Introduction

Up to 15–25 percent of patients with colorectal cancer have synchronous colorectal liver metastases (sCRLM) identified at the time of initial diagnosis (R. Martin et al., 2003; R. C. G. Lykoudis et al., 2014; Martin et al., 2009; Martin, Augenstein, Reuter, Scoggins, and McMasters, 2009; Lykoudis, O'Reilly, Nastos, and Fusai, 2014; Martin et al., 2003). The multimodal management of sCRLM includes local, regional, and systemic approaches, reflecting the unique biology of this disease. While liver metastases constitute stage IV disease, both retrospective and prospective studies suggest that long-term cure is possible with surgical extirpation of liver-only metastases. Thus, for patients with synchronous liver metastases as the only extra-colonic site of disease, some form of liver-directed therapy should be considered as part of the initial treatment plan. The exact timing of these interventions has become more complex as more effective systemic therapies and locoregional options become available. At the same time, advances in surgical quality and perioperative care have allowed more aggressive surgical approaches while decreasing surgical morbidity and mortality.

Sequencing of care for sCRLM

For potentially resectable sCRLM, successful resection is the most important prognostic indicator. Clearance of all macroscopic and microscopic liver disease (i.e., R0 resection) conveys a 5-year overall survival (OS) as high as 60 percent (Giuliante, Vigano, Rose, and M, 2021; Mayo et al., 2013; Pawlik et al., 2005). Importantly, surgery is the only potentially

Contemporary Management of Metastatic Colorectal Cancer: A Precision Medicine Approach
DOI: https://doi.org/10.1016/B978-0-323-91706-3.00015-1

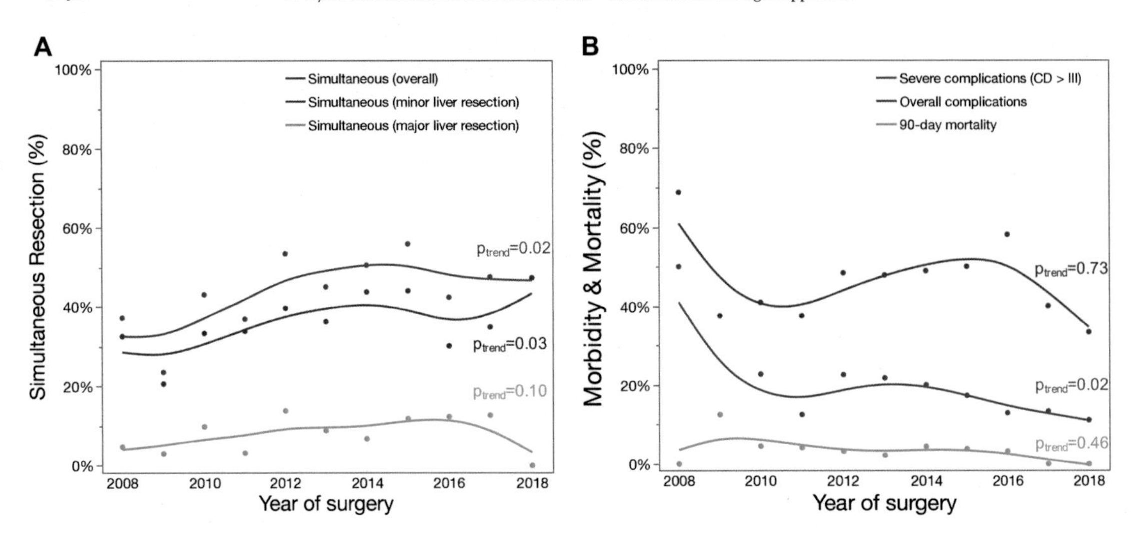

FIGURE 9.1 Illustration of the different surgical approaches to sCRLM. A simultaneous approach includes resection of both the primary tumor and the sCRLM in the same operation. Staged approaches include both primary-first and liver-first options.

curative therapy; of patients who undergo liver metastasectomy, 20–25 percent have disease-free intervals >10 years (Tomlinson et al., 2007). There is still considerable debate regarding the timing of liver metastasectomy within a given patient's overall treatment plan. Both a simultaneous approach (hepatectomy at the time of primary resection) and staged approaches have been advocated (Fig. 9.1). For staged approaches, the traditional (primary-first) approach involves liver resection after resection of the primary colorectal cancer tumor, while a liver-first approach involves hepatectomy followed by resection of the primary tumor at a separate, later procedure. All of these approaches are routinely used but their use has varied with time (Fig. 9.2) (Tsilimigras et al., 2021).

The timing of colorectal primary resection and liver metastasectomy must also be considered within the context of available adjunctive perioperative therapies. For sCRLM, this includes systemic therapies like chemotherapy and/or targeted therapy, as well as regional therapy, such as radiation for the primary tumor, and liver-directed therapy for sCRLM (e.g., thermal ablation of liver metastases, and hepatic artery infusion [HAI] chemotherapy). While the indications and timing of these interventions are discussed elsewhere in this book, their timing and order may differ for sCRLM depending on symptoms and technical considerations of surgery. For example, in the case of a very bulky rectal cancer tumor, it may be more clinically beneficial to proceed with chemotherapy as the initial treatment even if the liver resection is likely to be a straightforward procedure.

Factors that are important to consider when determining treatment sequence include patient symptoms (e.g., colonic obstruction, pain, liver function abnormalities, etc.), technical issues related to resectablilty of both the primary and the liver metastases, the need for pelvic radiation, as well as liver resection considerations, such as a marginal future liver remnant size

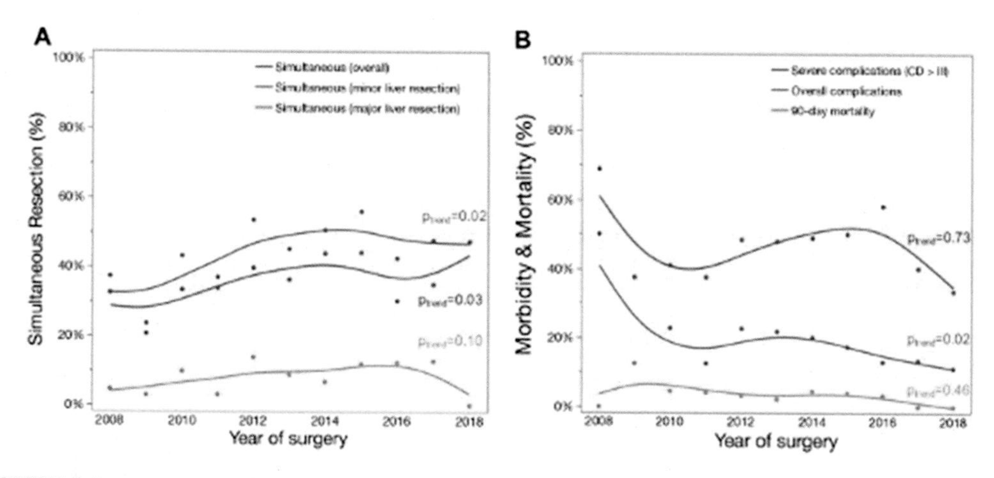

FIGURE 9.2 (A) Trends in the use of simultaneous liver resection for synchronous CRLM between 2008 and 2018 per extent of liver resection. (B) Trends in morbidity and mortality among patients who underwent simultaneous resection for synchronous CRLM between 2008 and 2018. CD, Clavien-Dindo; CRLM, colorectal liver metastases. *From Tsilimigras, DI, Sahara, K., Hyer, JM, Diaz, A., Moris, D., Bagante, F., Guglielmi, A., Ruzzenente, A., Alexandrescu, S., Poultsides, G., Sasaki, K., Aucejo, F., Ejaz, A., Cloyd, J. M. & Pawlik, T. M. (2021). Trends and outcomes of simultaneous versus staged resection of synchronous colorectal cancer and colorectal liver metastases. Surgery, 170(1), 160–166.* https://doi.org/10.1016/j.surg.2021.01.041.

or threatened margins. Furthermore, there may be logistical considerations, as there may not be the right combination of experienced colorectal and hepatopancreatobiliary (HPB) surgeons to perform a simultaneous procedure at the same institution required, even when clinically appropriate. In the US, this may be especially difficult if either the colorectal primary or the liver metastases are borderline resectable and patients are not receiving care at high volume centers.

Given the number of clinical components that must be integrated to decide on a treatment plan for an individual patient, homogenous guidelines are not available. At a minimum, these complex cases should be reviewed by a multidisciplinary team that includes specialists in colorectal surgery, HPB surgery, medical and radiation oncology, radiology, gastroenterology, and other allied specialties. An individualized plan can then be developed for each patient that integrates and prioritizes the most urgent clinical problem for sequential management.

Perioperative chemotherapy

Survival for patients with sCRLM is driven by treatment of the metastases, both by local interventions, as well as regional therapies and systemic chemotherapy. For upfront unresectable liver metastases, systemic chemotherapy remains the mainstay of treatment. Modern chemotherapy regimens have proven efficacious at downsizing patients to surgical resection using a conversion strategy (discussed further below) (Bismuth et al., 1996). However, results have been mixed for adjuvant and neoadjuvant trials in patients with resectable sCRLM. Proponents of a chemotherapy-first approach believe that it allows an effective test of the biology and aggressiveness of the tumor, while offering few downsides in terms of progression or symptoms of the primary tumor. For example, in the FOxTROT trial, the rate of obstruction was only 3 percent when using modern neoadjuvant therapy for locally advanced colon cancers, and in the NSABPC-10 trial, the major morbidity rate from an intact primary tumor in patients with metastatic colon cancer was 14 percent (Khatri, 2009; McCSeligmann et al., 2020; McCahill et al., 2012). In a study from Memorial Sloan Kettering Cancer Center (MSK), 93 percent of 233 patients with stage IV disease and CRLM did not require any surgical intervention for their primary tumor during treatment of their metastatic disease (Poultsides et al., 2009).

As mentioned above, chemotherapy may downsize originally unresectable sCRLM and convert them to resectable lesions. One of the first reports of downsizing was by Bismuth et al., who analyzed 53 patients with CRLM initially deemed unresectable and treated with 5-FU based chemotherapy (Bismuth et al., 1996). The authors reported a 16 percent conversion rate to resectable, with a 40 percent 5-year OS, comparable to initially resectable CRLM patients. Since, many large cohort studies and clinical trials have confirmed these results, with studies showing that up to 30 percent of unresectable CRLM may become resectable after chemotherapy (Abdalla et al., 2006; Quan et al., 2012; Reddy, Barbas, and Clary, 2009).

Recurrence after surgery alone in sCRLM occurs in about two-thirds of patients, with half of those recurrences in the liver alone, while the other half are extrahepatic (Buisman et al., 2020; De Jong et al., 2009). Given this high recurrence rate, numerous studies have looked at the utility of either pre- or post-op systemic chemotherapy for patients with sCRLM. A recent study analyzed 2020 patients with CRLM, of whom 1442 (71 percent) received perioperative systemic chemotherapy (Buisman et al., 2020). The authors used the clinical risk score (CRS) to stratify patients as high or low risk of recurrence. They found that systemic chemotherapy decreased the risk of extrahepatic recurrence in high-risk patients but not low-risk patients and did not affect the risk of intrahepatic recurrence in either subgroup. They further found that perioperative systemic therapy improved OS in high-risk patients but made no difference for low-risk patients.

Several prospective trials have attempted to address the utility of perioperative chemotherapy in sCRLM. The EORTC 40,983 trial was a randomized, phase 3, parallel-group study involving 78 hospitals for patients with up to 4 CRLMs. Patients were randomized to either surgery alone or perioperative FOLFOX4 (six 14-day cycles both before and after hepatectomy). While the initial report demonstrated improved progression-free survival (Nordlinger et al., 2008), a subsequent report with longer follow-up showed no difference in 5-year OS (Nordlinger et al., 2013). The Japanese JCOG0603 trial was recently published demonstrating similar results (Kanemitsu, Shimizu, and Mizusawa, 2021). In a phase II/III trial, 149 patients underwent hepatectomy alone versus 151 patients who received adjuvant mFOLFOX6. The trial was terminated early because DFS was significantly longer in patients treated with hepatectomy followed by chemotherapy. Yet, overall 5-year OS was comparable between the two groups. The EPOC trial evaluted cetuximab in patients with KRAS exon 2 wild-type CRLMs. Patients were randomized 1:1 to receive chemotherapy with or without cetuximab before and after hepatectomy. A total of 257 patients underwent randomization and the median OS was 20.7 months. Surprisingly, the addition of cetuximab resulted in shorter progression-free survival. A pooled analysis of two randomized trials looking at adjuvant therapy following hepatectomy for CRLM found a small but significant benefit (Mitry et al., 2008).

The duration of chemotherapy must also be considered in liver surgery, as numerous chemotherapeutic agents have hepatic toxicity. Bevacizumab has demonstrated tumor regression when included in an oxaliplatin or irinotecan regimen, but requires a 4-week delay after the last dose before hepatectomy (Castellanos and Merchant, 2014; Walter and Thomas, 2013). Oxaliplatin-based regimens are associated with liver sinusoid abnormalities in many patients (Rubbia-Brandt et al., 2004). Similarly, irinotecan has been associated with the development of hepatic steatosis in up to two-thirds of patients (Kooby et al., 2003).

While all of these factors must be considered for individual patients, current guidelines tend to favor the use of systemic chemotherapy. The National Comprehensive Cancer Network (NCCN) guidelines for patients with resectable sCRLM are to proceed with a simultaneous resection followed by adjuvant therapy (FOLFOX or CapeOx), or neoadjuvant therapy for 3 months prior to any surgery (Benson et al., 2021). For KRAS exon 2 wild-type tumors, the addition of anti-EGFR therapy using panitumumab or cetuximab may be considered but is controversial. Additional testing for MSI status and possible immunotherapy is also recommended. The number of additional biomarkers and systemic agents is likely to increase in the coming years.

Simultaneous approach

The benefits of a simultaneous approach are obvious for both the clinician and the patients: only a single operation. In a recent population-based cohort study from Ontario, Canada, the average cost of a staged resection was higher at $54,321 CAD vs. $41,286 for a simultaneous resection (Wang et al., 2020). This was primarily due to the longer hospitalization with a staged vs. a simultaneous approach (11 vs. 8 days, respectively). Unfortunately, early experience from the 1990s with a simultaneous approach reported higher operative morbidity and mortality than with the traditional primary-first approach (Bismuth, Castaing, and Traynor, 1988; Bolton and Fuhrman, 2000; Lillemoe and Vauthey, 2020; Nordlinger et al., 1996). Bolton et al. performed a retrospective review of 165 patients and concluded that hepatectomy should be delayed if a major hepatectomy is required due to higher postoperative mortality (Bolton and Fuhrman, 2000). Nordlinger et al. similarly concluded that the increased risk of major hepatectomy precluded a simultaneous approach and developed a scoring system to improve case selection based on outcomes from 1568 patients with sCRLM (Nordlinger et al., 1996). However, as the science of liver surgery has advanced, the combined approach has become increasingly common. Newer series have found acceptable rates of complications even with major simultaneous cases (Fig. 9.3) (Tsilimigras et al., 2021). In a study from MSK, the outcomes of 106 patients who underwent a traditional primary-first surgical approach were compared to 134 patients who had a combined approach for sCRLM. The combined approach group had a shorter median hospital length of stay (10 vs. 18 days, $p < 0.001$), as well as fewer overall complications (49 percent vs. 67 percent, $p < 0.003$) and similar mortality as the primary-first cohort. In a large ($n = 610$ patients) retrospective multicenter study comparing simultaneous versus staged approaches, the authors concluded that outcomes were largely based on the type of hepatectomy (minor vs. major) (Reddy et al., 2007). Patients undergoing minor hepatectomy did the same or better with a simultaneous approach; however, the

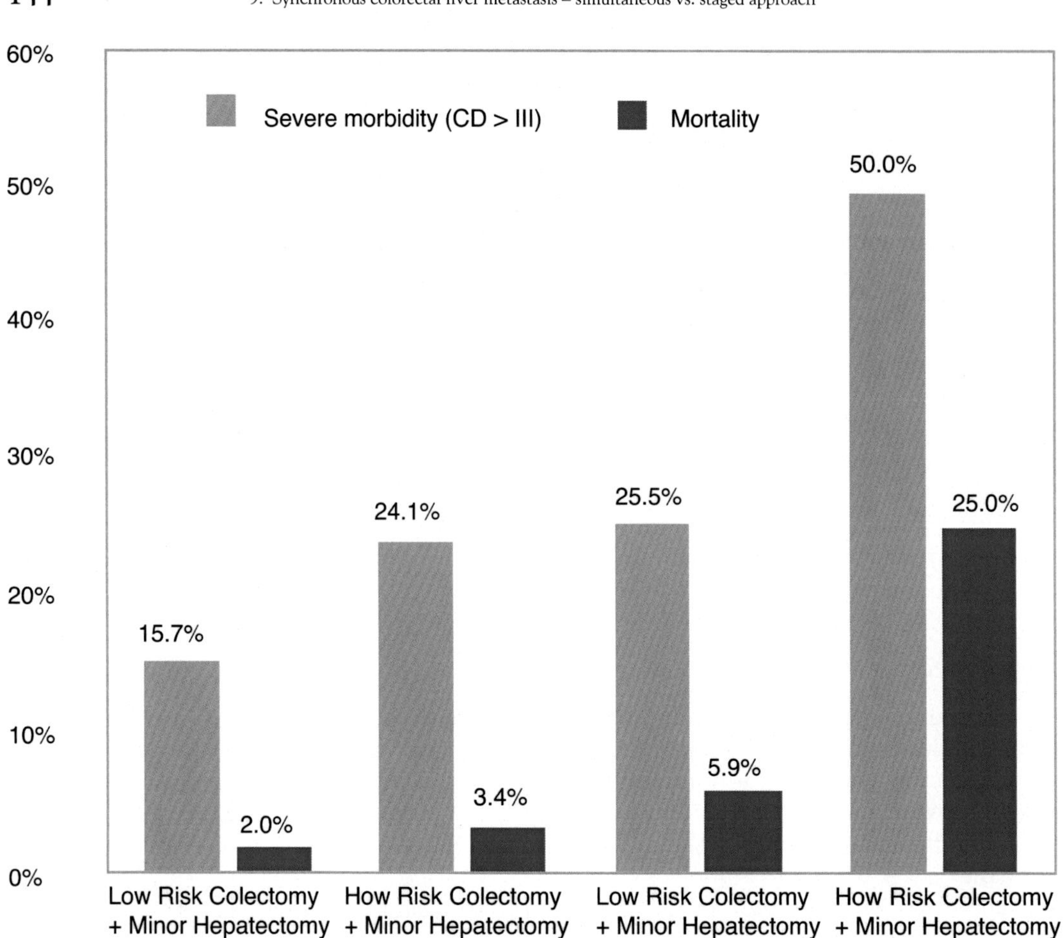

FIGURE 9.3 Observed incidence of severemorbidity and 90-day mortality among patients undergoing simultaneous low/high-risk colectomy and minor/major liver resection.ww CD, Clavien-Dindo. *From Tsilimigras, DI, Sahara, K., Hyer, JM, Diaz, A., Moris, D., Bagante, F., Guglielmi, A., Ruzzenente, A., Alexandrescu, S., Poultsides, G., Sasaki, K., Aucejo, F., Ejaz, A., Cloyd, J. M. & Pawlik, T. M. (2021). Trends and outcomes of simultaneous versus staged resection of synchronous colorectal cancer and colorectal liver metastases. Surgery, 170(1), 160–166.* https://doi.org/10.1016/j.surg.2021.01.041.

34 patients who underwent a simultaneous surgery that included a major hepatectomy had higher rates of severe morbidity (36 percent vs. 15 percent, $p < 0.05$) and mortality (8 percent vs. 1 percent, $p < 0.05$) than those who had a minor hepatectomy. The authors concluded that while a simultaneous approach may be advantageous for limited liver disease, surgeons should question using a simultaneous approach when a major hepatectomy is required. In the current era when parenchymal preserving strategies are preferred, non-anatomic, minor liver resections are now the norm which allows safer simultaneous procedures. This likely contributes to the observed secular trends which shows an increased number of simultaneous procedures being performed (see Fig. 9.2A).

Several studies have attempted to compare the three methods – simultaneous, primary-first, and liver-first – to determine the optimal timing of and approach to surgery for sCRLM. Unfortunately, almost each of these studies are retrospective; little prospective data exist to answer this question. In a large study of 1004 patients with sCRLM treated between 1982 and 2011($n = 329$ simultaneous approach, $n = 647$ traditional primary-first approach, $n = 34$ liver-first approach), (Mayo et al., 2013) the authors found no difference in either mortality ($\sim$3 percent in all groups) or major postoperative morbidity. Overall survival was the same between simultaneous and staged approaches. A liver-first approach was more often used with bilateral disease, and a staged approach was more commonly used when >3 hepatic segments were resected.

Two large meta-analyses have attempted to answer the question of optimal timing. In a cohort of 2880 patients, Yin et al. found that patients undergoing a simultaneous approach had a lower incidence of postoperative complications (Yin et al., 2013). Based on their findings, the authors concluded that a simultaneous approach was appropriate if the following criteria were met: liver resection involves <4 segments, and the patient is <70 years old, without severe comorbid conditions. A similar study by Slesser et al. looked at a total of 3159 patients undergoing either simultaneous ($n = 1381$) or staged ($n = 1778$) resection (Slesser et al., 2013). They found no difference in OS, disease-free survival, complications, operative mortality, or blood loss; however, the authors noted that there was a bias towards a staged approach in patients having significantly larger, and more frequently bilobar, liver metastases. Ongoing studies (Serrano et al., 2018) will hopefully help clarify the indications for a simultaneous approach to sCRLM.

Staged approaches: primary-first

The traditional, or primary-first, approach to sCRLM involves resection of the primary tumor followed by a resection of the liver metastases at a later date. Proponents of this approach feel that early removal of the primary tumor prevents further metastases from developing, as well as complications, such as obstruction, perforation, or bleeding. Initially, this approach was advocated as it was felt that the higher morbidity of liver resections would make a combined approach prohibitively risky, and ensuing complications could prevent patients from receiving adjuvant systemic chemotherapy. In addition, a primary-first approach gives time for aggressive tumor biology to become apparent prior to subjecting the patient to a potentially morbid a liver resection (Bolton and Fuhrman, 2000; Shimizu et al., 2007; Lambert, Colacchio, and Barth, 2000).

Some of the arguments for primary-first surgery (i.e., high primary-related complication rate and prohibitively high risk of combined surgery) were true in the 80s and 90s, but advancements in both chemotherapy and surgical safety have dramatically changed the factors being weighed. While historical trials found bowel obstruction rates to be as high as 30 percent in patients with stage IV colorectal cancer (Winner et al., 2013), modern chemotherapy regimens are far more efficacious, and rates of intestinal complications during chemotherapy are much lower at 5–15 percent (Benoist et al., 2005; Tebbutt et al., 2003).

Arguments against the primary-first approach are based on the fact that survival is driven by the liver metastases, not the primary tumor. Upfront colorectal resection delays both chemotherapy and liver resection by weeks to and possibly months. Moreover, complications occur in up to 30 percent of patients undergoing colorectal resection, further delaying therapy for metastatic disease (Alves et al., 2005; Longo et al., 2000). For patients with complications after colorectal surgery, chemotherapy or liver resection may never be an option, eliminating the two most efficacious treatments from those patients' treatment plans.

Staged approaches: liver-first

Survival in patients with sCRLM is primarily driven by management of the metastatic disease, and proponents of a liver-first approach focus on aggressive management of the liver metastases followed by management of the primary tumor (De Jong et al., 2011). This approach was first described in a cohort of 20 patients in 2006, and demonstrated excellent outcomes (Lillemoe and Vauthey, 2020; Mentha et al., 2006). It was noted to be particularly suitable for rectal cancer patients, given the need for pelvic chemoradiotherapy prior to primary resection. Subsequent studies have confirmed the safety and outcomes of this approach. In a study of the prospective multi-institutional global registry, LiverMetSurvey, Andres et al. found patients who underwent a liver-first approach ($n = 58$) had similar OS and disease-free survival to a group of 729 patients who had a primary-first approach (Andres et al., 2012). In a recent follow-up to this study, the authors compared a liver-first approach to both simultaneous and the traditional primary-first approach and found a survival benefit with the liver-first approach in patients with multiple bilobar lesions (Giuliante et al., 2021).

Systematic reviews have reached similar conclusions. Jegatheeswaran et al. performed a systematic review of 417 articles and identified 4 studies with 121 patients undergoing a liver-first approach. Of these 121 patients, 90 (74 percent) were able to complete the full course of treatment, and 19 percent had disease progression during the protocol period (Jegatheeswaran, Mason, Hancock, and Siriwardena, 2013). Similarly, another study of 82 patients with sCRLM demonstrated a relapse rate of 25 percent with a liver-first approach and reported a 3-year OS of 30 percent with low morbidity and mortality from hepatectomy (De Rosa et al., 2013). In this study, 17 percent of patients did not have their primary tumor resected either due to complete response to chemoradiotherapy or progression of disease. In a systematic review of 4 trials, median overall survival in this study was 40 months and the recurrence rate after complete resection was 52 percent. Overall, the data supports the liver-first approach as a viable alternative to simultaneous and primary-first approaches.

Surgical approach summary

The available data demonstrate that all three approaches – primary-first, simultaneous, and liver-first – are reasonable options. Without large prospective studies, it is unlikely that the question of which sequence of treatment is the best approach will ever be definitively answered. However, the available data suggest that the best approach is one that is tailored to patients' needs. In a North American practice survey of 234 surgeons, there was good overall agreement with regards to the operative approach to take (Griffiths et al., 2020). When presented with clinical vignettes involving low complexity colorectal surgery and minor hepatectomy, 83 percent of general surgeons and 98 percent of hepatobiliary surgeons supported a simultaneous approach. As the clinical scenarios became increasingly complex, surgeons moved to a staged approach. For complex colorectal procedures and major hepatectomies, 0 percent of general surgeons and 3 percent of hepatobiliary surgeons would perform simultaneous resection. These findings suggest there is general agreement among surgeons on the surgical approach offered which appears to be based on the surgical complexity of each case.

MSK approach

At MSK, we tailor our approach to each patient, beginning with a multidisciplinary discussion with the colorectal surgery, HPB surgery, and medical oncology teams. For most patients with sCLRM, we favor induction chemotherapy for asymptomatic primary tumors. In general, we favor a simultaneous approach when possible, given the benefits for the patient in terms of convenience, timing, and cost. Even for major liver resections combined with colon resections, we have found the complication rate to be acceptable (Martin et al., 2003; Silberhumer et al., 2016). Staged resections are usually performed when there is a rate-limiting factor for one of the two resections, such as borderline resectable liver disease. Furthermore, we often combine surgery and systemic therapy with HAI chemotherapy to maximize locoregional liver control (Groot Koerkamp et al., 2017). When HAI is used, a subcutaneous pump placement is performed at the time of surgery floxuridine is administered into the pump every 4 weeks in addition to systemic therapy, for downstaging/ disease control or adjuvant strategy, depending on the extent of residual liver metastases present (D'Angelica et al., 2015; Groot Koerkamp et al., 2017). A discussion of the use of HAI chemotherapy is beyond the scope of this chapter but is discussed elsewhere in this book.

Case-based learning

A 47-year-old male without significant past medical history presented to his primary care provider with decreased stool caliber, diarrhea and intermittent blood and mucus in his stools. He had recently travelled outside the country and thought this might be traveler's diarrhea. A CT scan was ordered which demonstrated nonspecific sigmoid wall thickening. Due to COVID-19 his colonoscopy was delayed for a year. When eventually performed it demonstrated a fungating mass in the sigmoid colon at 20 cm that was traversed, and his colonoscopy was complete to the terminal ileum. Biopsy revealed a moderately differentiated microsatellite-stable invasive adenocarcinoma. Staging CT scans demonstrated a 7.1 cm mass in the sigmoid colon with regional adenopathy as well as two prominent masses within the left lobe of the liver. There was no evidence of extrahepatic metastatic disease. He had a single family member with breast cancer diagnosed in her 60s. He was physically active without other operative risk factors.

He was seen by members of the colorectal and hepato-pancreato-biliary surgery teams. An MRI of the liver was performed which demonstrated a dominant 5.6 cm segment 2–4A mass with an adjacent segment 4A satellite lesion measuring 1.7 cm (Fig. 9.4). The lesions involved the left hepatic vein and were close to but free of the middle vein. His-CEA was 4.1 and clinical risk score was 3.

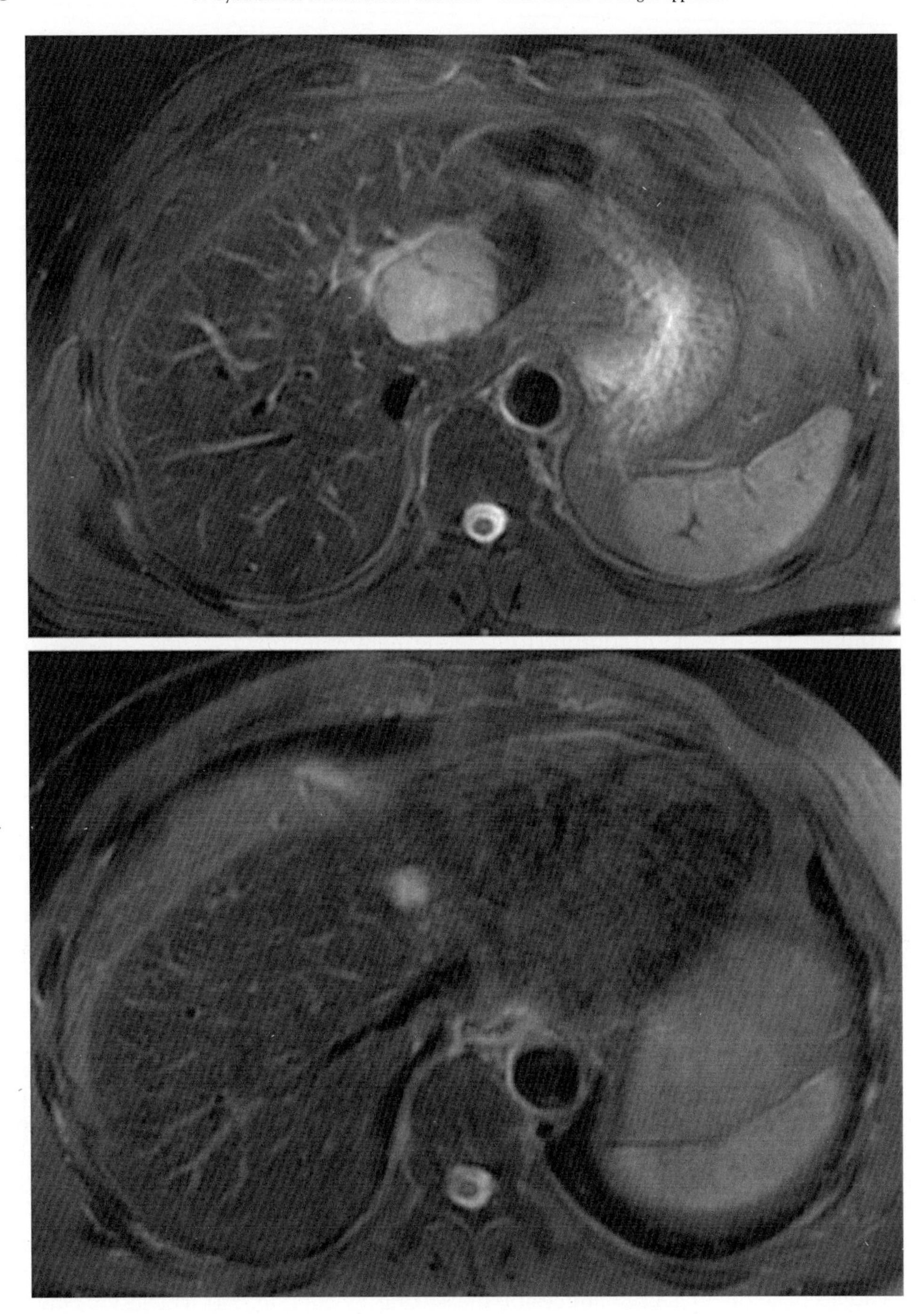

FIGURE 9.4 Relevant preoperative T1 MRI images of sCRLM for the case discussion showing a dominant 5.6 cm segment 2–4A mass with an adjacent segment 4A satellite lesion measuring 1.7 cm.

Multimodal therapy was discussed with him including surgery for his primary cancer, surgery for his liver metastases and systemic treatment. The patient declined adjuvant HAI chemotherapy. He underwent 6 cycles of preoperative FOLFOX with stable disease and underwent a simultaneous open sigmoid colectomy and left hemi-hepatectomy (segments 2/3/4A/4B) using an intra-glissonean approach. The parenchymal transection was accomplished with hydro jet dissection and the Aquamantys (saline enhanced monopolar coagulator) with vascular staplers used for the left hepatic vein and pedicle.

Postoperatively he had an uneventful recovery and was discharged on post-operative day 6. He was started on post-operative FOLFOX about a month after surgery to complete the remainder of his 12 planned perioperative cycles.

References

Abdalla, E. K., Adam, R., Bilchik, A. J., Jaeck, D., Vauthey, J. N., & Mahvi, D. (2006). Improving resectability of hepatic colorectal metastases: expert consensus statement. *Annals of Surgical Oncology*, 13(10), 1271–1280. https://doi.org/10.1245/s10434-006-9045-5.

Alves, A., Panis, Y., Mathieu, P., Mantion, G., Kwiatkowski, F., & Slim, K. (2005). Postoperative mortality and morbidity in French patients undergoing colorectal surgery: results of a prospective multicenter study. *Archives of Surgery*, 140(3), 278–283. https://doi.org/10.1001/archsurg.140.3.278.

Andres, A., Toso, C., Adam, R., Barroso, E., Hubert, C., Capussotti, L., et al. (2012). A survival analysis of the liver-first reversed management of advanced simultaneous colorectal liver metastases: a LiverMetSurvey-based study. *Annals of Surgery*, 256(5), 772–779.

Benoist, S., Pautrat, K., Mitry, E., Rougier, P., Penna, C., & Nordlinger, B. (2005). Treatment strategy for patients with colorectal cancer and synchronous irresectable liver metastases. *British Journal of Surgery*, 92(9), 1155–1160. https://doi.org/10.1002/bjs.5060.

Benson, A. B., Venook, A. P., Al-Hawary, M. M., Arain, M. A., Chen, Y.-J., Ciombor, K. K., et al. (2021). Colon Cancer, Version 2.2021, NCCN Clinical Practice Guidelines in Oncology. *Journal of the National Comprehensive Cancer Network*, 19(3), 329–359. https://doi.org/10.6004/jnccn.2021.0012.

Bismuth, H., Adam, R., Lévi, F., Farabos, C., Waechter, F., Castaing, D., et al. (1996). Resection of nonresectable liver metastases from colorectal cancer after neoadjuvant chemotherapy. *Annals of Surgery*, 224(4), 509–522. https://doi.org/10.1097/00000658-199610000-00009.

Bismuth, H., Castaing, D., & Traynor, O. (1988). Surgery for synchronous hepatic metastases of colorectal cancer. *Scandinavian Journal of Gastroenterology*, 23(149), 144–149. https://doi.org/10.3109/00365528809096972.

Bolton, J. S., & Fuhrman, G. M. (2000). Survival after resection of multiple bilobar hepatic metastases from colorectal carcinoma. *Annals of Surgery*, 231(5), 743–751. https://doi.org/10.1097/00000658-200005000-00015.

Buisman, F. E., Galjart, B., van der Stok, E. P., Balachandran, V. P., Boerner, T., Drebin, J. A., et al. (2020). Recurrence Patterns After Resection of Colorectal Liver Metastasis are Modified by Perioperative Systemic Chemotherapy. *World Journal of Surgery*, 44(3), 876–886. https://doi.org/10.1007/s00268-019-05121-9.

Castellanos, J. A., & Merchant, N. B. (2014). Strategies for Management of Synchronous Colorectal Metastases. *Curr Surg Rep*, 44(3), 876–886. https://doi.org/10.1007/s40137-014-0062-1.

D'Angelica, M. I., Correa-Gallego, C., Paty, P. B., Cercek, A., Gewirtz, A. N., Chou, J. F., et al. (2015). Phase ii trial of hepatic artery infusional and systemic chemotherapy for patients with unresectable hepatic metastases from colorectal cancer conversion to resection and long-term outcomes. *Annals of Surgery*, 261(2), 353–360. https://doi.org/10.1097/SLA.0000000000000614.

De Jong, M. C., Pulitano, C., Ribero, D., Strub, J., Mentha, G., Schulick, R. D., et al. (2009). Rates and patterns of recurrence following curative intent surgery for colorectal liver metastasis: an international multi-institutional analysis of 1669 patients. *Annals of Surgery*, 250(3), 440–447. https://doi.org/10.1097/SLA.0b013e3181b4539b.

De Jong, M. C., Van Dam, R. M., Maas, M., Bemelmans, M. H. A., Olde Damink, S. W. M., Beets, G. L., et al. (2011). The liver-first approach for synchronous colorectal liver metastasis: a 5-year single-centre experience. *HPB*, 13(10), 745–752. https://doi.org/10.1111/j.1477-2574.2011.00372.x.

De Rosa, A., Gomez, D., Hossaini, S., Duke, K., Fenwick, S. W., Brooks, A., et al. (2013). Stage IV colorectal cancer: outcomes following the liver-first approach. *Journal of Surgical Oncology*, 108(7), 444–449. https://doi.org/10.1002/jso.23429.

Giuliante, F., Vigano, L., Rose, D., M, A., et al. (2021). Liver-First Approach for Synchronous Colorectal Metastases: analysis of 7360 Patients from the LiverMetSurvey Registry. *Annals of Surgical Oncology*, 108(7), 444–449.

Griffiths, C., Bogach, J., Simunovic, M., Parpia, S., Ruo, L., Hallet, J., et al. (2020). Simultaneous resection of colorectal cancer with synchronous liver metastases; a practice survey. *HPB*, 22(5), 728–734. https://doi.org/10.1016/j.hpb.2019.09.012.

Groot Koerkamp, B., Sadot, E., Kemeny, N. E., Gonen, M., Leal, J. N., Allen, P. J., . . . D'Angelica, M. I. (2017). Perioperative hepatic arterial infusion pump chemotherapy is associated with longer survival after resection of colorectal liver metastases: a propensity score analysis. *Journal of Clinical Oncology*, 35(17), 1938–1944. doi:10.1200/JCO.2016.71.8346.

Jegatheeswaran, S., Mason, J. M., Hancock, H. C., & Siriwardena, A. K. (2013). The liver-first approach to the management of colorectal cancer with synchronous hepatic metastases: a systematic review. *JAMA Surg*, 148(4), 385–391. doi:10.1001/jamasurg.2013.1216.

Kanemitsu, Y., Shimizu, Y., & Mizusawa (2021). Hepatectomy Followed by mFOLFOX6 Versus Hepatectomy Alone for Liver-Only Metastatic Colorectal Cancer (JCOG0603): a Phase II or III Randomized Controlled Trial. *Journal of Clinical Oncology*.

Khatri, V. P. (2009). Synchronous colorectal liver metastases: triumph of prospective randomized trials over observational bias leads to paradigm shift. *Annals of Surgical Oncology*, 16(7), 1762–1764. https://doi.org/10.1245/s10434-009-0369-9.

Kooby, D. A., Fong, Y., Suriawinata, A., Gonen, M., Allen, P. J., Klimstra, D. S., et al. (2003). Impact of steatosis on perioperative outcome following hepatic resection. *Journal of Gastrointestinal Surgery*, 7(8), 1034–1044. Elsevier Inc. https://doi.org/10.1016/j.gassur.2003.09.012 .

Lambert, L. A., Colacchio, T. A., & Barth, R. J. (2000). Interval hepatic resection of colorectal metastases improves patient selection. *Archives of Surgery*, 135(4), 473–480. American Medical Association https://doi.org/10.1001/archsurg.135.4.473 .

Lillemoe, H.A., & Vauthey, J.-N. (2020). Surgical approach to synchronous colorectal liver metastases: staged, combined, or reverse strategy. *Hepatobiliary Surgery and Nutrition*, 25–34. https://doi.org/10.21037/hbsn.2019.05.14.

Longo, W. E., Virgo, K. S., Johnson, F. E., Oprian, C. A., Vernava, A. M., Wade, T. P., et al. (2000). Risk factors for morbidity and mortality after colectomy for colon cancer. *Diseases of the Colon and Rectum*, 43(1), 83–91. https://doi.org/10.1007/BF02237249.

Lykoudis, P. M., O'Reilly, D., Nastos, K., & Fusai, G. (2014). Systematic review of surgical management of synchronous colorectal liver metastases. *British Journal of Surgery*, 101(6), 605–612. https://doi.org/10.1002/bjs.9449.

Martin, R. C. G., Augenstein, V., Reuter, N. P., Scoggins, C. R., & McMasters, K. M. (2009). Simultaneous Versus Staged Resection for Synchronous Colorectal Cancer Liver Metastases. *Journal of the American College of Surgeons*, 208(5), 842–850. https://doi.org/10.1016/j.jamcollsurg.2009.01.031.

Martin, R., Paty, P. B., Fong, Y., Grace, A., Cohen, A., DeMatteo, R., et al. (2003). Simultaneous liver and colorectal resections are safe for synchronous colorectal liver metastasis. *Journal of the American College of Surgeons*, 197(2), 233–241. https://doi.org/10.1016/S1072-7515(03)00390-9.

Mayo, S. C., Pulitano, C., Marques, H., Lamelas, J., Wolfgang, C. L., De Saussure, W., et al. (2013). Surgical management of patients with synchronous colorectal liver metastasis: a multicenter international analysis. *Journal of the American College of Surgeons*, 216(4), 707–716. https://doi.org/10.1016/j.jamcollsurg.2012.12.029.

McCahill, L. E., Yothers, G., Sharif, S., Petrelli, N. J., Lai, L. L., Bechar, N., et al. (2012). Primary mFOLFOX6 plus bevacizumab without resection of the primary tumor for patients presenting with surgically unresectable metastatic colon cancer and an intact asymptomatic colon cancer: definitive analysis of NSABP Trial C-10. *Journal of Clinical Oncology*, 30(26), 3223–3228. https://doi.org/10.1200/JCO.2012.42.4044.

Mentha, G., Majno, P. E., Andres, A., Rubbia-Brandt, L., Morel, P., & Roth, A. D. (2006). Neoadjuvant chemotherapy and resection of advanced synchronous liver metastases before treatment of the colorectal primary. *British Journal of Surgery*, 93(7), 872–878. https://doi.org/10.1002/bjs.5346.

Mitry, E., Fields, A. L. A., Bleiberg, H., Labianca, R., Portier, G., Tu, D., et al. (2008). Adjuvant chemotherapy after potentially curative resection of metastases from colorectal cancer: a pooled analysis of two randomized trials. *Journal of Clinical Oncology*, 26(30), 4906–4911. https://doi.org/10.1200/JCO.2008.17.3781.

Nordlinger, B., Guiguet, M., Vaillant, J. C., Balladur, P., Boudjema, K., Bachellier, P., et al. (1996). Surgical resection of colorectal carcinoma metastases to the liver: a prognostic scoring system to improve case selection, based on 1568 patients. *Cancer, 77*(7), 1254–1262. https://doi.org/10.1002/(SICI)1097-0142(19960401)77. 7<1254::AID-CNCR5>3.0.CO;2-I.

Nordlinger, B., Sorbye, H., Glimelius, B., Poston, G. J., Schlag, P. M., Rougier, P., et al. (2008). Perioperative chemotherapy with FOLFOX4 and surgery versus surgery alone for resectable liver metastases from colorectal cancer (EORTC Intergroup trial 40983): a randomised controlled trial. *The Lancet,* 371(9617), 1007–1016. https://doi.org/10.1016/S0140-6736(08)60455-9.

Nordlinger, B., Sorbye, H., Glimelius, B., Poston, G. J., Schlag, P. M., Rougier, P., et al. (2013). Perioperative FOLFOX4 chemotherapy and surgery versus surgery alone for resectable liver metastases from colorectal cancer (EORTC 40983): long-term results of a randomised, controlled, phase 3 trial. *The Lancet Oncology,* 14(12), 1208–1215. https://doi.org/10.1016/S1470-2045(13)70447-9.

Pawlik, T.M., Scoggins, C.R., Zorzi, D., Abdalla, E.K., Andres, A., Eng, C., et al. (2005). Effect of surgical margin status on survival and site of recurrence after hepatic resection for colorectal metastases. In *Annals of Surgery* (Vol. *241*, Issue (5), pp. 715–724). https://doi.org/10.1097/01.sla.0000160703.75808.7d.

Poultsides, G. A., Servais, E. L., Saltz, L. B., Patil, S., Kemeny, N. E., Guillem, J. G., et al. (2009). Outcome of primary tumor in patients with synchronous stage IV colorectal cancer receiving combination chemotherapy without surgery as initial treatment. *Journal of Clinical Oncology,* 27(20), 3379–3384. https://doi.org/10.1200/JCO.2008.20.9817.

Quan, D., Gallinger, S., Nhan, C., Auer, R. A., Biagi, J. J., Fletcher, G. G., et al. (2012). The role of liver resection for colorectal cancer metastases in an era of multimodality treatment: a systematic review. *Surgery,* 151(6), 860–870. https://doi.org/10.1016/j.surg.2011.12.018.

Reddy, S. K., Barbas, A. S., & Clary, B. M. (2009). Synchronous colorectal liver metastases: is it time to reconsider traditional paradigms of management? *Annals of Surgical Oncology,* 16(9), 2395–2410. https://doi.org/10.1245/s10434-009-0372-1.

Reddy, S. K., Pawlik, T. M., Zorzi, D., Gleisner, A. L., Ribero, D., Assumpcao, L., et al. (2007). Simultaneous resections of colorectal cancer and synchronous liver metastases: a multi-institutional analysis. *Annals of Surgical Oncology,* 14(12), 3481–3491. https://doi.org/10.1245/s10434-007-9522-5.

Rubbia-Brandt, L., Audard, V., Sartoretti, P., Roth, A. D., Brezault, C., Le Charpentier, M., et al. (2004). Severe hepatic sinusoidal obstruction associated with oxaliplatin-based chemotherapy in patients with metastatic colorectal cancer. *Annals of Oncology,* 15(3), 460–466. https://doi.org/10.1093/annonc/mdh095.

Seligmann, J. F., & the FOxTROT Collaborative Group (2020). FOxTROT: neoadjuvant FOLFOX chemotherapy with or without panitumumab (Pan) for patients (pts) with locally advanced colon cancer (CC). *Journal of Clinical Oncology,* 38(15_suppl), 4013-4013. doi:10.1200/JCO.2020.38.15_suppl.4013.

Serrano, P. E., Gafni, A., Parpia, S., Ruo, L., Simunovic, M., Meyers, B. M., et al. (2018). Simultaneous resection of colorectal cancer with synchronous liver metastases (RESECT), a pilot study. *International Journal of Surgery Protocols,* 8, 1–6. https://doi.org/10.1016/j.isjp.2018.01.001.

Shimizu, Y., Yasui, K., Sano, T., Hirai, T., Kanemitsu, Y., Komori, K., et al. (2007). Treatment strategy for synchronous metastases of colorectal cancer: is hepatic resection after an observation interval appropriate? *Langenbeck's Archives of Surgery, 392*(5), 535–538. https://doi.org/10.1007/s00423-007-0153-x.

Silberhumer, G. R., Paty, P. B., Denton, B., Guillem, J., Gonen, M., Araujo, R. L. C., et al. (2016). Long-term oncologic outcomes for simultaneous resection of synchronous metastatic liver and primary colorectal cancer. *Surgery (United States),* 160(1), 67–73. https://doi.org/10.1016/j.surg.2016.02.029.

Slesser, A. A. P., Simillis, C., Goldin, R., Brown, G., Mudan, S., & Tekkis, P. P. (2013). A meta-analysis comparing simultaneous versus delayed resections in patients with synchronous colorectal liver metastases. *Surgical Oncology,* 22(1), 36–47. https://doi.org/10.1016/j.suronc.2012.11.002.

Tebbutt, N. C., Norman, A. R., Cunningham, D., Hill, M. E., Tait, D., Oates, J., et al. (2003). Intestinal complications after chemotherapy for patients with unresected primary colorectal cancer and synchronous metastases. *Gut,* 52(4), 568–573. https://doi.org/10.1136/gut.52.4.568.

Tomlinson, J. S., Jarnagin, W. R., DeMatteo, R. P., Fong, Y., Kornprat, P., Gonen, M., et al. (2007). Actual 10-year survival after resection of colorectal liver metastases defines cure. *Journal of Clinical Oncology,* 25(29), 4575–4580. https://doi.org/10.1200/JCO.2007.11.0833.

Tsilimigras, D. I., Sahara, K., Hyer, J. M., Diaz, A., Moris, D., Bagante, F., et al. (2021). Trends and outcomes of simultaneous versus staged resection of synchronous colorectal cancer and colorectal liver metastases. *Surgery,* 170(1), 160–166. https://doi.org/10.1016/j.surg.2021.01.041.

Walter, H., & Thomas, A. L. (2013). Liver resection following FOLFOXIRI plus bevacizumab: a detailed pathological review. *British Journal of Cancer,* 108(12), 2417–2418. https://doi.org/10.1038/bjc.2013.244.

Wang, J., Griffiths, C., Simunovic, M., Parpia, S., Gu, C. S., Gafni, A., et al. (2020). Simultaneous versus staged resection for synchronous colorectal liver metastases: a population-based cost analysis in Ontario, Canada - Health economic evaluation. *International Journal of Surgery,* 78, 75–82. https://doi.org/10.1016/j.ijsu.2020.04.044.

Winner, M., Mooney, S. J., Hershman, D. L., Feingold, D. L., Allendorf, J. D., Wright, J. D., et al. (2013). Incidence and predictors of bowel obstruction in elderly patients with stage IV colon cancer: a population-based cohort study. *JAMA Surgery,* 148(8), 715–722. https://doi.org/10.1001/jamasurg.2013.1.

Yin, Z., Liu, C., Chen, Y., Bai, Y., Shang, C., Yin, R., et al. (2013). Timing of hepatectomy in resectable synchronous colorectal liver metastases (SCRLM): simultaneous or delayed? *Hepatology,* 57(6), 2346–2357. https://doi.org/10.1002/hep.26283.

CHAPTER

10

Minimally invasive approaches to colorectal liver metastases

Ahmad Hamad, MD, Timothy M. Pawlik, MD, MPH, MTS, PhD and Aslam Ejaz, MD, MPH[1]

Department of Surgery, The Ohio State University Wexner Medical Center, The James Comprehensive Cancer Center, Columbus, OH, USA

Introduction

Colorectal cancer (CRC) is the third most common cause of cancer death in both men and women in the United States (US) with an estimated 53,200 related-deaths in 2020 (Siegel et al., 2020). There is an increase in the incidence of late stage metastatic colorectal cancer with the most common site of metastasis being the liver (Benson et al., 2018). Nearly 20 percent of patients present with synchronous liver metastasis on initial evaluation and about a third of patients will develop liver metastases at some point during their treatment course (Jegatheeswaran et al., 2013; Kow, 2019). In eligible patients, surgical resection of liver metastases provides the best hope for long-term survival with an improvement in 5-year survival rates of 40–60 percent for those who undergo curative-intent resection (Abdalla et al., 2006; De Jong, Pulitano, and Ribero, 2009).

Minimally invasive techniques have been increasingly used in liver surgery over the last few decades since their introduction in their 1990s (Buell, Thomas, and Doty, 2004; Cherqui, Husson, and Hammoud, 2000). Initially, laparoscopic liver resections (LLR) were limited to wedge resections but have since evolved to include major hepatectomies (Nguyen, Gamblin, and Geller, 2009). With improved multidisciplinary planning, imaging techniques, and technological advances, LLR and even robotic liver resections (RLR) are feasible. The robotic platform overcomes some of the limitations of laparoscopy as it has added the benefit of three-dimensional visualization, stabilization of tremor, reduced operative fatigue, and improved ergonomics from the console-surgeon interface. Minimally invasive liver resection (MILR) not only has similar oncologic outcomes to open liver resection (OLR) but also has some short-term advantages such as reduced postoperative length of stay (LOS) (Lin, Ye, and Zhu, 2015).

[1] Division of Surgical Oncology, The Ohio State University, Wexner Medical Center, Columbus, OH, USA. aslam.ejaz@osumc.edu

Contemporary Management of Metastatic Colorectal Cancer: A Precision Medicine Approach

DOI: https://doi.org/10.1016/B978-0-323-91706-3.00001-1

The hope from MILR is to minimize tissue damage, surgical trauma, and immunosuppression in order to improve both short- and long-term postoperative outcomes. In this chapter, we will discuss minimally invasive techniques in the management of colorectal liver metastases (CRLM).

Laparoscopic liver resection

Background

The first LLR for benign disease was performed in 1992 by Gagner et al. and was followed by Azagra et al. reporting the first laparoscopic anatomical liver resection in 1993. However, the first LLR for CRLM was performed by Wayand and Woisetchläger (Azagra, Goergen, Gilbart, and Jacobs, 1996; Gagner, Rheault, and Dubuc, 1992; Wayand and Woisetschläger, 1993). Since then, the laparoscopic approach has been adopted by many surgeons and has been reported for various indications ranging from benign to malignant (Nguyen et al., 2009). In 2008, experts convened in Louisville, KY and concluded that laparoscopic liver surgery is a safe and effective approach to the management of liver disease if performed by trained and experienced surgeons. Moreover, LLR was accepted as a gold standard with OLR for CRLM (Buell, Cherqui, and Geller, 2009). The second international conference held in Morioka, Japan concluded that minor LLR had become the standard of care while major LLR were still innovative procedures in the explorative phase (Wakabayashi, Cherqui, and Geller, 2015). Minor LLR was defined as the resection of two or less Couinaud segments not including the posterior-superior segments (Wakabayashi et al., 2015). The indications for LLR include a wide range of benign diagnoses such as hemangiomas, focal nodular hyperplasia, symptomatic giant hepatic cysts, and benign adenoma and malignant lesions such as CRLM and hepatocellular carcinoma (HCC) (Nguyen et al., 2009). More than 50 percent of LLR reported in large series are now for malignant diagnoses, primarily HCC and CRLM. (Geller and Tsung, 2015) LLR offers benefits such as smaller incisions, less intraoperative blood loss, shorter hospital LOS, and comparative morbidity and mortality when compared to OLR (Ciria, Cherqui, Geller, Briceno, and Wakabayashi, 2016; Nguyen et al., 2009, 2011).

Outcomes

Since the Morioka conference, one randomized controlled trial (RCT) comparing OLR vs. LLR has been published (Fretland, Dagenborg, and Bjørnelv, 2018) in addition to the numerous case series, case control studies, and meta-analyses that exist in the literature (Wakabayashi et al., 2015). The OSLO–COMET trial was the first RCT comparing OLR and LLR in the treatment of CRLM (Fretland et al., 2018). The authors showed that LLR was associated with a lower postoperative complication rate (LLR: 19 percent vs. OLR: 31 percent; $P = 0.021$) and shorter hospital LOS (LLR: 53 h vs. OLR 96 h; $P < 0.001$) without compromising oncologic outcomes such as resection margin status or postoperative morbidity. Moreover, there were no differences in blood loss and operation time with equal overall cost. Most importantly, patients undergoing LLR gained a 0.011 quality-adjusted life years when compared to patients undergoing OLR (Fretland et al., 2018). A recent systematic review and meta-analysis compared oncologic outcomes between both approaches (Xie, Xiong, and Liu, 2017). The authors

TABLE 10.1 Published literature comparing laparoscopic liver resections to open liver resections.

Year	Author	Publication Type	Diagnosis	Number of Patients
2009	Nguyen et al	Retrospective	CRLM	LLR: 109
2010	Abu Hilal et al.	Retrospective	CRLM	LLR: 135
2013	Feroci et al.	Retrospective	CRLM	188 (LLR: 68 vs. OLR: 120)
2013	Guerron et al.	Retrospective	CRLM	80 (LLR: 40 vs. OLR: 40)
2013	Zhou et al.	Meta-analysis	CRLM	695 (LLR: 268 vs. OLR: 427)
2014	Luo et al.	Meta-analysis	CRLM	624 (LLR: 241 vs. OLR: 383)
2014	Wei et al.	Meta-analysis	CRLM	975 (LLR: 376 vs. OLR: 599)
2015	Schiffman et al.	Meta-analysis	CRLM	610 (LLR: 242 vs. OLR: 368)
2016	Hallet et al.	Meta-analysis	CRLM	2017 (LLR: 580 vs. OLR: 1437)
2016	Fretland et al.	Randomized controlled trial	CRLM	280 (LLR: 133 vs. OLR: 147)
2017	Xie et al.	Systematic Review and Meta-analysis	CRLM	4697 (LLR: 1809 vs. OLR: 2888)
2018	Ratti et al.	Retrospective	CRLM	885 (LLR: 187 vs. OLR: 698)

included 4697 patients from 32 non-randomized studies and demonstrated that patients in the LLR group had higher rates of R0 resection margins (OR: 1.64, 95 percent CI 1.32–2.05, $P < 0.00001$) without any significant differences in 3- or 5-year overall survival (OS), disease-free survival (DFS), or disease recurrence. Additionally, LLR was associated with less intraoperative blood loss, fewer blood transfusions, shorter hospital LOS, less overall morbidity, but longer operative time (Xie et al., 2017). Other meta-analyses showed similar results thus demonstrating the feasibility and safety of LLR in patients with CRLM (Hallet et al., 2016; Luo, Yu, and Bai, 2014; Schiffman, Kim, Tsung, Marsh, and Geller, 2015; Wei et al., 2014; Zhou, Xiao, Wu, Li, and Li, 2013). In addition, several retrospective single and multi-center studies have been published demonstrating superior outcomes in terms of intraoperative blood loss, postoperative complications, and LOS associated with LLR for CRLM when compared to OLR, without compromising oncologic outcomes, disease recurrence, and mortality rates (Abu Hilal, Underwood, Zuccaro, Primrose, and Pearce, 2010; Feroci, Baraghini, and Lenzi, 2013; Guerron, Aliyev, and Agcaoglu, 2013; Nguyen, Laurent, and Dagher, 2009; Pilgrim, To, Usatoff, and Evans, 2009; Ratti et al., 2018). Overall, LLR was shown to be superior to OLR by decreasing hospital LOS, postoperative morbidity, intraoperative transfusions, while showing comparable short- and long-term oncologic outcomes (Table 10.1).

Robotic liver resection

Background

The robotic platform overcomes many shortcomings associated with the laparoscopic approach including limited range of instrument motion, inferior surgeon ergonomics, and two-dimensional visualization. The first RLR was performed and published by Giulianotti et al. in 2001 (Giulianotti, Coratti, and Angelini, 2003). Since then, there has been an uptake in the utilization of the robotic platform for hepatobiliary operations in recent years (Ejaz, Sachs, and He, 2014). The robot allows for better and more accurate tissue manipulation to be able to perform more anatomically challenging resections when compared to the rigid laparoscopic instruments. It would allow surgeons to perform resections on lesions in posterior-superior segments which require curved transections that are difficult to perform laparoscopically (Boggi et al., 2015; Nota, Woo, and Raoof, 2019; Wu, Chen, Lee, Liang, and Wu, 2019). Despite these advantages, RLR is currently still considered a novel technique that's under investigation.

Outcomes

Like LLR, there is one published RCT that is currently running and enrolling patients with CRLM with the aim to evaluate the safety and feasibility of the robotic platform. The authors of that RCT were able to publish short-term outcomes in 2017 after 4 years of accrual (Xu, Wei, and Chang, 2017). Patients randomized to RLR had less intraoperative blood loss, shorter LOS, shorter time to pass flatus, quicker time to advance diet, decreased major complication rates (Clavien-Dindo grade III/IV: RLR: 6.7 percent vs OLR: 20.0 percent; $P = 0.032$), despite having longer operating times. The authors recommended the robotic platform for CRLM patients with less than 3 liver metastases and maximum lesion size of 5 cm (Xu et al., 2017).

Several meta-analyses and systematic reviews have been published in the literature comparing RLR to LLR and RLR to OLR. Almost a decade ago, a meta-analysis by Abood et al. demonstrated that RLR was safe and feasible for both minor and major liver resections as it showed comparable rates of intraoperative blood loss, LOS, and postoperative complications (Abood and Tsung, 2013). Machairas et al. demonstrated that patients undergoing RLR for various indications including CRLM had lower overall morbidity rates and shorter LOS, however had longer operative times. Moreover, there were no differences in intraoperative blood loss, blood transfusion requirements, R0 resection rates, and mortality rates (Machairas, Papaconstantinou, and Tsilimigras, 2019). A similar systematic review by Diamantis et al. showed similar oncologic outcomes between RLR and OLR and LLR in patients with malignant diagnoses including HCC, CRLM and others (Tsilimigras, Moris, Vagios, Merath, and Pawlik, 2018). On the other hand, a meta-analysis comparing RLR to LLR showed that the robotic approach was associated with higher intraoperative blood loss and operative times while the conversion rate, R1 resection rate, LOS, mortality, and postoperative morbidity were similar in both cohorts (Montalti, Berardi, Patriti, Vivarelli, and Troisi, 2015). Another similar meta-analysis comparing RLR and LLR demonstrated higher operative times in the RLR cohort while there were no differences in intraoperative blood loss, conversion rates, R0 resection rates, morbidity, and mortality (Qiu, Chen, and Chengyou, 2016). Another more recent meta-analysis further cemented the safety and feasibility of the robotic platform after comparing patients undergoing RLR vs. LLR. Compared to LLR, RLR was associated with higher intraoperative blood loss, longer operative times and longer time to first nutritional intake, however, there was no significant differences in LOS, conversion rates, R0 resection rates, postoperative morbidity, and mortality (Hu et al., 2018).

Giulianotti et al. first published the largest series on RLR in 2011 which included 70 patients with malignant diagnoses with 16 patients with CRLM (Giulianotti, Coratti, and Sbrana, 2011). Moreover, Tsung et al. performed a 1:2 matched analysis comparing RLR and LLR in patients with malignant diagnoses including CRLM. In this series, matched patients displayed no differences in operative and postoperative outcomes including intraoperative blood loss, transfusion rates, R0 resection rates, LOS, and 90-day mortality (Tsung, Geller, and Sukato, 2014). A more recent retrospective single-institution study looking at RLR for CRLM again showed the feasibility of the robotic platform and even showed a potential positive role for patients with multiple metastases and previous or synchronous surgery (Guadagni, Furbetta, and Di Franco, 2019).

In conclusion, this data shows the safety and feasibility of the robotic platform in tackling liver resections of benign and malignant diagnosis including CRLM. More importantly, by improving postoperative outcomes such as decreasing postoperative morbidity and shortening LOS, patients who underwent MILR for CRLM are more likely to receive adjuvant therapy sooner than patients undergoing OLR, which translates into improved OS (Tohme, Goswami, and Han, 2015). RLR has been shown to have comparable short- and long-term outcomes to OLR and RLR. We do still need more data on long-term outcomes such as disease recurrence and overall survival.

Laparoscopic radiofrequency ablation

Surgical resection provides the best hope for cure for patients with CRLM. However, hepatic resection for this patient population is limited to patients with good liver function. Moreover, hepatic resections are associated with significant morbidity and mortality. Only 10 percent to 25 percent of patients with CRLM are candidates for surgical resection due to tumor number, location or concern for inadequate functional hepatic reserve postoperatively (Nordlinger, Van Cutsem, and Rougier, 2007; Wong, Mangu, and Choti, 2010). Thus, alternative ablative techniques have been used to complement or replace surgical resection when indicated. These techniques include radiofrequency ablation (RFA) and microwave coagulation (MWC).

Background

RFA is a treatment modality that uses a form of alternating electrical current for interstitial tissue destruction. The radiofrequency energy is supplied by a generator that is attached to a needle electrode or applicator and dispersive electrodes or adhesive grounding pads. The generator applies a high-frequency alternating electrical current, causing ionic agitation that heats the tissue in the area of the applicator tip which results in cell death due to the irreversible coagulation of proteins, including enzymes, intranuclear proteins, DNA proteins, and DNA, and that finally leads to the targeted tumor and adjacent liver tissue being thermally destroyed (Wong et al., 2010). The first RFA of liver lesions was described in 1990 by McGahan et al. (McGahan, Browning, Brock, and Tesluk, 1990).

Outcomes

The first and one of the largest series of laparoscopic RFA (LRFA) for unresectable CRLM was described by Siperstein et al. (Siperstein, Berber, Ballem, and Parikh, 2007). In this series, 234 patients with unresectable CRLM due to tumor location, or number or non-responsive to chemotherapy, or the presence of extrahepatic disease, underwent 292 LRFA with a median survival of 32 months. Patients with 3 or more lesions or CEA higher than 200ng/ml had worse OS (Siperstein et al., 2007). The EORTC trial compared patients undergoing RFA (including open, laparoscopic, and percutaneous) with systemic therapy vs. patients receiving systemic therapy alone. This was the first RCT on the efficacy of RFA and it concluded that RFA combined with systemic therapy resulted in significantly longer progression-free survival (PFS) (Ruers, Punt, and Van Coevorden, 2012). Another large retrospective series analyzing LRFA was published by Kennedy et al. in 2012 (Kennedy et al., 2013). 130 patients underwent LRFA with a median survival of 40.4 months, a 5-year survival of 28.8 percent, and a local recurrence rate of 9.2 percent. Larger tumor size and bilobar disease were both associated with worse survival on multivariate analysis (Kennedy et al., 2013). A retrospective study comparing LRFA to surgical resection in resectable CRLM demonstrated comparable long-term survival between both cohorts in carefully selected patients (Hammill et al., 2011). Berber et al. demonstrated that selectivity of patients undergoing LRFA as patients with comorbidities, extrahepatic disease, or difficult tumor locations were referred to LRFA instead of resection and still achieved long-term survival while having unresectable tumors (Berber, Tsinberg, Tellioglu, and Simpfendorfer, 2008). Aliyev et al. compared LRFA to resection in patients with solitary CRLM ≤3 cm. LRFA demonstrated hopeful results in high-risk patients with solitary tumors (5-year survival rate 47 percent and median DFS of 25 months), however, the local recurrence rates were high (18 percent vs. 4 percent after resection) (Aliyev, Agcaoglu, and Aksoy, 2013). When comparing overall costs between patients undergoing LRFA or surgical resection, Takahashi et al. demonstrated that the mean operating room and hospital costs were 51 percent and 55 percent higher in patients undergoing surgical resection while not compromising OS and DFS in carefully selected patients (Takahashi, Akyuz, and Kahramangil, 2018).

In conclusion, LRFA has been shown to be beneficial for high-risk patients, with extrahepatic disease, with difficult technical requirements and mostly for patients with inoperable disease. Nevertheless, surgical resection remains the gold standard and is the best hope for cure for patients with CRLM. LRFA has shown promising results in a highly selected patient cohort but the local recurrence rates remain high, necessitating frequent or close follow-up.

Laparoscopic microwave coagulation

Background

Microwave coagulation (MWC) is a form of high frequency (900 MHz to 2.45 GHz) electromagnetic radiation that creates heat through excitation of water molecules with the resulting thermal damage leading to coagulation necrosis and ablation of tumor (Padma, Martinie, and Iannitti, 2009; Rocha and D'Angelica, 2010). MCW produces active heating of tissue and is not affected by tissue dessication thus allowing for a greater zone of intratumoral thermal injury over a shorter period of time (Rocha and D'Angelica, 2010). Tabuse et al. reported the first MWC in 1979 where it was used as a hemostatic technique to minimize bleeding during hepatic resections (Tabuse, 1979). The technique of laparoscopic MWC (LMWC) was first described in 2005 by Simon et al. (Simon, Dupuy, and Mayo-Smith, 2005).

Outcomes

A phase II trial first described a series of 87 patients with primary and secondary liver tumors including CRLM undergoing MWC including 7 undergoing LMWC in 2007. The authors showed the safety and feasibility of MWC for hepatic tumor ablation (Iannitti, Martin, and Simon, 2007). The was followed by another series describing patients with CRLM undergoing only LMWC. The authors performed LMWC on 57 patients with HCC and other metastases such as CRLM and again showed the feasibility of this technique when compared to an open approach with an OS of 22.6 months (Jagad, Koshariya, and Kawamoto, 2008). A recent retrospective series at a single institution in China described a cohort of patients undergoing LMWC and LRFA. LMWC cohort had a significantly less local tumor progression rate (1.4 percent vs. 10.2 percent; $P = 0.046$) but OS, DFS, and complication rates were similar on both cohorts (Yang and Li, 2017). Overall, LMWC has shown promising results with improved local control compared to LRFA but we still need large cohort studies and RCTs to prove its effectivity.

Conclusion

Minimally invasive liver surgery has been increasingly used over the last few decades for CRLM (Buell et al., 2004; Cherqui et al., 2000). With improved multidisciplinary planning, imaging techniques, and technological advances, LLR and even robotic liver resections (RLR) are feasible. LLR has become the standard of care for minor liver resections. The robotic platform overcomes some of the limitations of laparoscopy but remains a novel technique. Minimally invasive liver resection (MILR) not only has similar oncologic outcomes to open liver resection (OLR) but also has some short-term advantages (Lin et al., 2015). Adjunct techniques such as LRFA and LMWC have provided hope for patients with inoperable disease with the goal to achieve local control. Nevertheless, surgical resection remains the standard of care and presents the best chance of cure for patients with CRLM.

References

Abdalla, E. K., Adam, R., Bilchik, A. J., Jaeck, D., Vauthey, J. N., & Mahvi, D. (2006). Improving resectability of hepatic colorectal metastases: expert consensus statement. *Annals of Surgical Oncology*, 13(10), 1271–1280. Epub 2006 Sep 6. PMID: 16955381. doi:10.1245/s10434-006-9045-5.

Abood, G. J., & Tsung, A. (2013). Robot-assisted surgery: improved tool for major liver resections? *J Hepatobiliary Pancreat Sci*, 20(2), 151–156. doi:10.1007/s00534-012-0560-4.

Abu Hilal, M., Underwood, T., Zuccaro, M., Primrose, J., & Pearce, N. (2010). Short- and medium-term results of totally laparoscopic resection for colorectal liver metastases. *British Journal of Surgery*, 97(6), 927–933. doi:10.1002/bjs.7034.

Aliyev, S., Agcaoglu, O., Aksoy, E., Taskin HE, E., Vogt, D., Fung, J., Siperstein, A., & Berber, E. (2013). Efficacy of laparoscopic radiofrequency ablation for the treatment of patients with small solitary colorectal liver metastasis. *Surgery*, 154(3), 556–562. Epub 2013 Jul 13. PMID: 23859307. doi:10.1016/j.surg.2013.03.009.

Azagra, J. S., Goergen, M., Gilbart, E., & Jacobs, D. (1996). Laparoscopic anatomical (hepatic) left lateral segmentectomy-technical aspects. *Surgical Endoscopy*, 10(7), 758–761. doi:10.1007/BF00193052.

Benson, A. B., Venook, A. P., Al-Hawary, M. M., Cederquist, L., Chen, Y. J., Ciombor, K. K., & Freedman-Cass, D. A. (2018). Rectal cancer, version 2.2018 clinical practice guidelines in Oncology. *JNCCN J Natl Compr Cancer Netw,* 16(7), 874–901 2018 Jul; PMID: 30006429. doi:10.6004/jnccn.2018.0061.

Berber, E., Tsinberg, M., Tellioglu, G., & Simpfendorfer, C. H. (2008). Siperstein AE. Resection versus laparoscopic radiofrequency thermal ablation of solitary colorectal liver metastasis. *J Gastrointest Surg Off J Soc Surg Aliment Tract,* 12(11), 1967–1972. doi:10.1007/s11605-008-0622-8.

Boggi, U., Caniglia, F., Vistoli, F., Costa, F., Pieroni, E., & Perrone, V. G. (2015). Laparoscopic robot-assisted resection of tumors located in posterosuperior liver segments. *Updates Surg,* 67(2), 177–183. doi:10.1007/s13304-015-0304-5.

Buell, J. F., Cherqui, D., Geller, D. A., O'Rourke, N., Iannitti, D., Dagher, I., & Chari, R. S. (2009). The international position on laparoscopic liver surgery: the Louisville Statement, 2008. *Annals of Surgery,* 250(5), 825–830. PMID: 19916210. doi:10.1097/sla.0b013e3181b3b2d8.

Buell, J. F., Thomas, M. J., Doty, T. C., Gersin, K. S., Merchen, T. D., Gupta, M., & Woodle, E. S. (2004). An initial experience and evolution of laparoscopic hepatic resectional surgery. *Surgery,* 136(4), 804–811. PMID: 15467665. doi:10.1016/j.surg.2004.07.002.

Cherqui, D., Husson, E., Hammoud, R., Malassagne, B., Hammoud, R., Stéphan, F., Bensaid, S., & Fagniez, P. L. (2000). Laparoscopic liver resections: a feasibility study in 30 patients. *Annals of Surgery,* 232(6), 753–762. PMID: 11088070; PMCID: PMC1421268. doi:10.1097/00000658-200012000-00004.

Ciria, R., Cherqui, D., Geller, D. A., Briceno, J., & Wakabayashi, G. (2016). Comparative Short-term Benefits of Laparoscopic Liver Resection: 9000 Cases and Climbing. *Annals of Surgery,* 263(4), 761–777. doi:10.1097/SLA.0000000000001413.

De Jong, M. C., Pulitano, C., Ribero, D., Strub, J., Mentha, G., Schulick, R. D., Choti, M. A., & Pawlik, T. M. (2009). Rates and patterns of recurrence following curative intent surgery for colorectal liver metastasis: an international multi-institutional analysis of 1669 patients. *Annals of Surgery,* 250(3), 440–448. PMID: 19730175. doi:10.1097/SLA.0b013e3181b4539b.

Ejaz, A., Sachs, T., He, J., et al. (2014). A comparison of open and minimally invasive surgery for hepatic and pancreatic resections using the nationwide inpatient sample. *Surg (United States).* doi:10.1016/j.surg.2014.03.046.

Feroci, F., Baraghini, M., Lenzi, E., Garzi, A., Vannucchi, A., Cantafio, S., & Scatizzi, M. (2013). Laparoscopic surgery improves postoperative outcomes in high-risk patients with colorectal cancer. *Surgical Endoscopy,* 27(4), 1130–1137 Epub 2012 Oct 6. PMID: 23052534. doi:10.1007/s00464-012-2559-y.

Fretland, Å. A., Dagenborg, V. J., Bjørnelv, G. M. W., Kazaryan, A. W., Kristiansen, R., Fagerland, M. W., & Edwin, B. (2018). Laparoscopic Versus Open Resection for Colorectal Liver Metastases: the OSLO-COMET Randomized Controlled Trial. *Annals of Surgery,* 267(2), 199–207. PMID: 28657937. doi:10.1097/SLA.0000000000002353.

Gagner, M., Rheault, M., & Dubuc, J. (1992). Laparoscopic partial hepatectomy for liver tumor (abstract). *Surgical Endoscopy,* 6, 97–98.

Geller, D. A., & Tsung, A. (2015). Long-term outcomes and safety of laparoscopic liver resection surgery for hepatocellular carcinoma and metastatic colorectal cancer. *J Hepatobiliary Pancreat Sci,* 22(10), 728–730. doi:10.1002/jhbp.278.

Giulianotti, P. C., Coratti, A., Angelini, M., Angelini, M., Sbrana, F., Cecconi, S., Balestracci, T., & Caravaglios, G. (2003). Robotics in general surgery: personal experience in a large community hospital. *Archives of Surgery,* 138(7), 777–784. PMID: 12860761. doi:10.1001/archsurg.138.7.777.

Giulianotti, P. C., Coratti, A., Sbrana, F., Addeo, P., Bianco, F. M., Buchs, N. C., & Benedetti, E. (2011). Robotic liver surgery: results for 70 resections. *Surgery,* 149(1), 29–39 . Epub 2010 Jun 8. PMID: 20570305. doi:10.1016/j.surg.2010.04.002.

Guadagni, S., Furbetta, N., Di Franco, G., Palmeri , M., Gianardi, D., Bianchini, M., & Morelli, L. (2019). Robotic-assisted surgery for colorectal liver metastasis: a single-centre experience. *J Minim Access Surg,* 16(2), 160–165. Epub ahead of print. PMID: 30777992; PMCID: PMC7176011. doi:10.4103/jmas.JMAS_265_18.

Guerron, A. D., Aliyev, S., Agcaoglu, O., Aksoy, E., Taskin, H. E., Aucejo, F., & Berber, E. (2013). Laparoscopic versus open resection of colorectal liver metastasis. *Surgical Endoscopy,* 27(4), 1138–1143. Epub 2012 Oct 10. PMID: 23052537. doi:10.1007/s00464-012-2563-2.

Hallet, J., Beyfuss, K., Memeo, R., Karanicolas, P. J., Marescaux, J., & Pessaux, P. (2016). Short and long-term outcomes of laparoscopic compared to open liver resection for colorectal liver metastases. *Hepatobiliary Surg Nutr,* 5(4), 300–310. doi:10.21037/hbsn.2016.02.01.

Hammill, C. W., Billingsley, K. G., Cassera, M. A., Wolf, R. F., Ujiki, M. B., & Hansen, P. D. (2011). Outcome after laparoscopic radiofrequency ablation of technically resectable colorectal liver metastases. *Annals of Surgical Oncology,* 18(7), 1947–1954. doi:10.1245/s10434-010-1535-9.

Hu, L., Yao, L., Li, X., Jin, P., Yang, K., & Guo, T. (2018). Effectiveness and safety of robotic-assisted versus laparoscopic hepatectomy for liver neoplasms: a meta-analysis of retrospective studies. *Asian Journal of Surgery*, 41(5), 401–416. doi:10.1016/j.asjsur.2017.07.001.

Iannitti, D. A., Martin, R. C. G., Simon, C. J., Hope, W. W., Newcomb, W. L., McMasters, K. M., & Dupuy, D. (2007). Hepatic tumor ablation with clustered microwave antennae: the US Phase II trial. *HPB (Oxford)*, 9(2), 120–124. PMID: 18333126; PMCID: PMC2020783. doi:10.1080/13651820701222677.

Jagad, R. B., Koshariya, M., Kawamoto, J., Papastratis, P., Kefalourous, H., Patris, V., & Lygidakis, N. J. (2008). Laparoscopic microwave ablation of liver tumors: our experience. *Hepato-Gastroenterology*, 55(81), 27–32. PMID: 18507073.

Jegatheeswaran, S., Mason, J. M., Hancock, H. C., & Siriwardena, A. K. (2013). The liver-first approach to the management of colorectal cancer with synchronous hepatic metastases: a systematic review. *JAMA Surg*, 148(4), 385–391. PMID: 23715907. doi:10.1001/jamasurg.2013.1216.

Kennedy, T. J., Cassera, M. A., Khajanchee, Y. S., Diwan, T. S., Hammill, C. W., & Hansen, P. D. (2013). Laparoscopic radiofrequency ablation for the management of colorectal liver metastases: 10-year experience. *Journal of Surgical Oncology*, 107(4), 324–328. doi:10.1002/jso.23268.

Kow, A. W. C. (2019). Hepatic metastasis from colorectal cancer. *J Gastrointest Oncol*, 10(6), 1274–1298. PMID: 31949948; PMCID: PMC6955002. doi:10.21037/jgo.2019.08.06.

Lin, Q., Ye, Q., Zhu, D., Wei, Y., Ren, L., Zheng, P., & Xu, J. (2015). Comparison of minimally invasive and open colorectal resections for patients undergoing simultaneous R0 resection for liver metastases: a propensity score analysis. *International Journal of Colorectal Disease*, 30(3), 385–395. Epub 2014 Dec 12. PMID: 25503803. doi:10.1007/s00384-014-2089-2.

Luo, l., Yu, Z.-Y., & Bai, Y.-N. (2014). Laparoscopic hepatectomy for liver metastases from colorectal cancer: a meta-analysis. *Journal of Laparoendoscopic & Advanced Surgical Techniques. Part A*, 24(4), 213–222. doi:10.1089/lap.2013.0399.

Machairas, N., Papaconstantinou, D., Tsilimigras, D. I., Moris, D., Prodromidou, A., Paspala, A., & Kostakis, I. D. (2019). Comparison between robotic and open liver resection: a systematic review and meta-analysis of short-term outcomes. *Updates Surg*, 71(1), 39–48. Epub 2019 Feb 4. PMID: 30719624. doi:10.1007/s13304-019-00629-0.

McGahan, J. P., Browning, P. D., Brock, J. M., & Tesluk, H. (1990). Hepatic ablation using radiofrequency electrocautery. *Investigative Radiology*, 25(3), 267–270. doi:10.1097/00004424-199003000-00011.

Montalti, R., Berardi, G., Patriti, A., Vivarelli, M., & Troisi, R. I. (2015). Outcomes of robotic vs laparoscopic hepatectomy: a systematic review and meta-analysis. *World Journal of Gastroenterology: Wjg*, 21(27), 8441–8451. doi:10.3748/wjg.v21.i27.8441.

Nguyen, K. T., Gamblin, T. C., & Geller, D. A. (2009). World review of laparoscopic liver resection-2,804 patients. *Annals of Surgery*, 250(5), 831–841. doi:10.1097/SLA.0b013e3181b0c4df.

Nguyen, K. T., Laurent, A., Dagher, I., Geller, D. A., Steel, J., Thomas, M. T., & Gamblin, T. C. (2009). Minimally invasive liver resection for metastatic colorectal cancer: a multi-institutional, international report of safety, feasibility, and early outcomes. *Annals of Surgery*, 250(5), 842–848. PMID: 19806058. doi:10.1097/SLA.0b013e3181bc789c.

Nguyen, K. T., Marsh, J. W., Tsung, A., Steel, J. J. L., Gamblin, T. C., & Geller, D. A. (2011). Comparative benefits of laparoscopic vs open hepatic resection: a critical appraisal. *Archives of Surgery*, 146(3), 348–356. doi:10.1001/archsurg.2010.248.

Nordlinger, B., Van Cutsem, E., Rougier, P., Köhne, C. H., Ychou, M., Sobrero, A., & Poston, G. (2007). Does chemotherapy prior to liver resection increase the potential for cure in patients with metastatic colorectal cancer? A report from the European Colorectal Metastases Treatment Group. *European Journal of Cancer*, 43(14), 2037–2045. Epub 2007 Sep 4. PMID: 17766104. doi:10.1016/j.ejca.2007.07.017.

Nota, C. L., Woo, Y., Raoof, M., Boerner, T., Molenaar, I. Q., Choi, G. H., & Fong, Y. (2019). Robotic Versus Open Minor Liver Resections of the Posterosuperior Segments: a Multinational, Propensity Score-Matched Study. *Annals of Surgical Oncology*, 26(2), 583–590. Epub 2018 Oct 17. PMID: 30334196; PMCID: PMC7883340. doi:10.1245/s10434-018-6928-1.

Padma, S., Martinie, J. B., & Iannitti, D. A. (2009). Liver tumor ablation: percutaneous and open approaches. *Journal of Surgical Oncology*, 100(8), 619–634. doi:10.1002/jso.21364.

Pilgrim, C. H. C., To, H., Usatoff, V., & Evans, P. M. (2009). Laparoscopic hepatectomy is a safe procedure for cancer patients. *HPB*, 11(3), 247–251. doi:10.1111/j.1477-2574.2009.00045.x.

Qiu, J., Chen, S., & Chengyou, D. (2016). A systematic review of robotic-assisted liver resection and meta-analysis of robotic versus laparoscopic hepatectomy for hepatic neoplasms. *Surgical Endoscopy,* 30(3), 862–875. doi:10.1007/s00464-015-4306-7.

Ratti, F., Fiorentini, G., Cipriani, F., Catena, M., Paganelli, M., & Aldrighetti, L. (2018). Laparoscopic vs Open Surgery for Colorectal Liver Metastases. *JAMA Surg,* 153(11), 1028–1035. doi:10.1001/jamasurg.2018.2107.

Rocha, F. G., & D'Angelica, M. (2010). Treatment of liver colorectal metastases: role of laparoscopy, radiofrequency ablation, and microwave coagulation. *Journal of Surgical Oncology,* 102(8), 968–974. doi:10.1002/jso.21720.

Ruers, T., Punt, C., Van Coevorden, F., Pierie, J. P. E. N., Borel-Rinkes, I., Ledermann, J. A., & Nordlinger, B. (2012). Radiofrequency ablation combined with systemic treatment versus systemic treatment alone in patients with non-resectable colorectal liver metastases: a randomized EORTC Intergroup phase II study (EORTC 40004). *Ann Oncol Off J Eur Soc Med Oncol,* 23(10), 2619–2626. Epub 2012 Mar 19. PMID: 22431703; PMCID: PMC3457746. doi:10.1093/annonc/mds053.

Schiffman, S. C., Kim, K. H., Tsung, A., Marsh, J. W., & Geller, D. A. (2015). Laparoscopic versus open liver resection for metastatic colorectal cancer: a metaanalysis of 610 patients. *Surgery,* 157(2), 211–222. doi:10.1016/j.surg.2014.08.036.

Siegel, R. L., Miller, K. D., Goding Sauer, A., Fedewa, S. A., Butterly, L. F., Anderson, J. A., & Jemal, A. (2020). Colorectal cancer statistics, 2020. *CA: A Cancer Journal for Clinicians,* 70(3), 145–164. Epub 2020 Mar 5. PMID: 32133645. doi:10.3322/caac.21601.

Simon, C. J., Dupuy, D. E., & Mayo-Smith, W. W. (2005). Microwave ablation: principles and applications. *Radiogr a Rev Publ Radiol Soc North Am Inc,* 25(Suppl (1)), S69–S83. doi:10.1148/rg.25si055501.

Siperstein, A. E., Berber, E., Ballem, N., & Parikh, R. T. (2007). Survival after radiofrequency ablation of colorectal liver metastases: 10-year experience. *Annals of Surgery,* 246(4), 557–559. doi:10.1097/SLA.0b013e318155a7b6.

Tabuse, K. (1979). A new operative procedure of hepatic surgery using a microwave tissue coagulator. *Nihon Geka Hokan,* 48(2), 160–172.

Takahashi, H., Akyuz, M., Kahramangil, B., Kose, E., Aucejo, F., Fung, J., & Berber, E. (2018). A Comparison of the Initial Cost Associated With Resection Versus Laparoscopic Radiofrequency Ablation of Small Solitary Colorectal Liver Metastasis. *Surgical Laparoscopy, Endoscopy & Percutaneous Techniques,* 28(6), 371–374. PMID: 30222692. doi:10.1097/SLE.0000000000000577.

Tohme, S., Goswami, J., Han, K., Chidi, A. P., Geller, D. A., Reddy, S., & Tsung, A. (2015). Minimally Invasive Resection of Colorectal Cancer Liver Metastases Leads to an Earlier Initiation of Chemotherapy Compared to Open Surgery. *Journal of Gastrointestinal Surgery,* 19(12), 2199–2206. Epub 2015 Oct 5. PMID: 26438480; PMCID: PMC4892107. doi:10.1007/s11605-015-2962-5.

Tsilimigras, D. I., Moris, D., Vagios, S., Merath, K., & Pawlik, T. M. (2018). Safety and oncologic outcomes of robotic liver resections: a systematic review. *Journal of Surgical Oncology,* 117(7), 1517–1530. doi:10.1002/jso.25018.

Tsung, A., Geller, D. A., Sukato, D. C., Sabbaghian, S., Tohme, S., Steel, J., & Bartlett, D. L. (2014). Robotic versus laparoscopic hepatectomy: a matched comparison. *Annals of Surgery,* 259(3), 549–555. PMID: 24045442. doi:10.1097/SLA.0000000000000250.

Wakabayashi, G., Cherqui, D., Geller, D. A., Buell, J. F., Kaneko, H., Han, H. S., & Strasberg, S. M. (2015). Recommendations for laparoscopic liver resection: a report from the second international consensus conference held in Morioka. *Annals of Surgery,* 261(4), 619–629. PMID: 25742461. doi:10.1097/SLA.0000000000001184.

Wayand, W., & Woisetschläger, R. (1993). [*Laparoscopic resection of liver metastasis*]. *Chirurg,* 64(3), 195–197.

Wei, M., He, Y., Wang, J., Chen, N., Zhou, Z., & Wang, Z. (2014). Laparoscopic versus open hepatectomy with or without synchronous colectomy for colorectal liver metastasis: a meta-analysis. *Plos One,* 9(1), e87461. PMID: 24489916; PMCID: PMC3906170. doi:10.1371/journal.pone.0087461.

Wong, S. L., Mangu, P. B., Choti, M. A., Crocenzi, T. S., Dodd 3rd, G. D., Dorfman, G. S., & Benson 3rd, A. B. (2010). American Society of Clinical Oncology 2009 clinical evidence review on radiofrequency ablation of hepatic metastases from colorectal cancer. *J Clin Oncol Off J Am Soc Clin Oncol,* 28(3), 493–508. Epub 2009 Oct 19. PMID: 19841322. doi:10.1200/JCO.2009.23.4450.

Wu, C.-Y., Chen, P.-D., Lee, C.-Y., Liang, J.-T., & Wu, Y.-M. (2019). Robotic-assisted right posterior segmentectomies for liver lesions: single-center experience of an evolutional method in left semi-lateral position. *J Robot Surg,* 13(2), 231–237. doi:10.1007/s11701-018-0842-1.

Xie, S.-M., Xiong, J.-J., Liu, X.-T., Chen, H. Y., Iglesia-García, D., Altaf, K., & Liu, X. B. (2017). Laparoscopic Versus Open Liver Resection for Colorectal Liver Metastases: a Comprehensive Systematic Review and Meta-analysis. *Science Reports,* 7(1), 1012. PMID: 28432295; PMCID: PMC5430829. doi:10.1038/s41598-017-00978-z.

Xu, J., Wei, Y., Chang, W., Jian, M., Ye, Q., Wang, X., & Fan, J. (2017). Robot-assisted procedure versus open surgery for simultaneous resection of colorectal cancer with liver metastases: short-term outcomes of a randomized controlled study. *Annals of Oncology*, 35(15 Suppl), 3575. doi:10.1093/annonc/mdx659.001.

Yang, B., & Li, Y. (2017). A comparative study of laparoscopic microwave ablation with laparoscopic radiofrequency ablation for colorectal liver metastasis. *J BUON*, 22(3), 667–672.

Zhou, Y., Xiao, Y., Wu, L., Li, B., & Li, H. (2013). Laparoscopic liver resection as a safe and efficacious alternative to open resection for colorectal liver metastasis: a meta-analysis. *Bmc Surgery [Electronic Resource]*, 13, 44. PMID: 24083369; PMCID: PMC3849970. doi:10.1186/1471-2482-13-44.

CHAPTER

11

Hepatic resection of colorectal liver metastasis in the presence of extrahepatic disease

Rachel V. Guest and Rowan Parks

Department of Clinical Surgery, University of Edinburgh, Edinburgh, United Kingdom

Incidence of extrahepatic disease

Population studies estimate that 25 – 30% of patients with colorectal cancer develop liver metastases during the course of their disease and 24.5% of patients will have EHD at the time of diagnosis (Engstrand et al., 2018). This is most commonly in the lung (16.9%), followed by the peritoneum (7.1%) and distant lymph nodes (4.8%). Patients with metachronously detected liver metastases are diagnosed significantly more frequently with lung metastases (56.6% vs. 44.10%, p=0.042), which are also seen more commonly in left-sided and rectal cancers (19.7% vs. 13.2%, p=0.010). Peritoneal metastases are more commonly diagnosed in right-sided cancers (10.6% vs 5.5% p=0.003). Although most studies have analyzed survival in patients with EHD according to individual site, some epidemiological studies have evaluated overall outcomes in patients with EHD. In the Swedish national registry study, patients without any metastatic disease had a 5-year overall survival (OS) of 75.1% compared to 25.2% for patients with liver-only metastases, 45.7% for patients with lung-only metastases and 12.7% in those with liver and lung metastases combined (Engstrand et al., 2018) (Fig. 11.1).

Alternative data suggests that the number of metastases rather than their location has a greater influence on overall survival (Elias et al., 2005). In a retrospective analysis of 308 patients undergoing resection for CRLM, the total number of metastases (inside or outside the liver), rather than the presence or absence of EHD appeared to be a more powerful prognostic factor; with 5-year survival rates of 38% (SD 4%) in patients with 1-3 metastases, 29% (SD 5%) in those with 4-5 metastases and 18% (SD 5%) in those with >6 metastases (p=0.002).

Contemporary Management of Metastatic Colorectal Cancer: A Precision Medicine Approach
DOI: https://doi.org/10.1016/B978-0-323-91706-3.00008-4

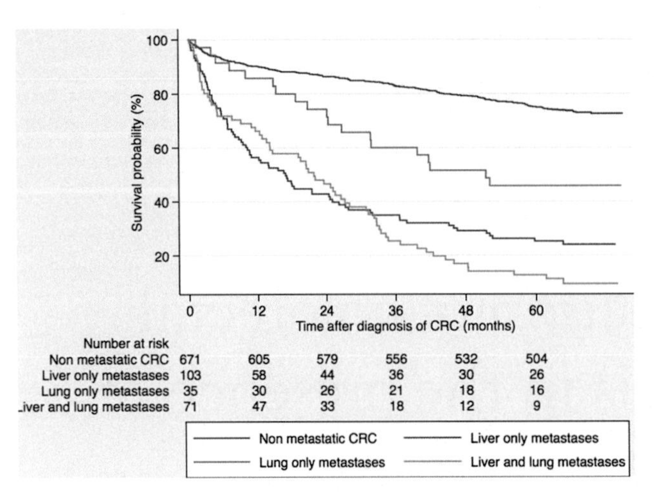

FIGURE 11.1 Kaplan-Meier analyses of overall survival in patients with varying patterns of colorectal metastases. Liver and lung metastases versus liver only metastases, median survival 1.8 and 1.4 years respectively, p=0.204 (log rank). Liver only metastases versus lung only metastases, median survival 1.4 versus 4.3 years respectively, p=0.006 (log rank). Lung only metastases versus non-metastatic colorectal cancer p=0.001 (log rank). (Reproduced with permission from Engstrand et al. 2018). From Engstrand, J., Nilsson, H., Strömberg, C., Jonas, E. & Freedman, J. (2018). Colorectal cancer liver metastases - a population-based study on incidence, management and survival. BMC Cancer, 18(1). https://doi.org/10.1186/s12885-017-3925-x.

Diagnosis of extrahepatic disease

The detection of EHD can be a critical factor in determining the curative versus palliative intent of management of patients with CRLM. Computed Tomography (CT), Magnetic Resonance Imaging (MRI) with liver-specific contrast agents and Flurodeoxyglucose-Positron Emission Tomography (FDG-PET) are considered standard of care in the diagnosis of intrahepatic CRLM. The use of FDG-PET is estimated to detect EHD in 10 – 32% of patients with otherwise resectable liver metastases and is reported to alter clinical management in 25% of patients (17% due to detection of EHD) (Yang et al., 2007). Diagnostic laparoscopy with laparoscopic ultrasound has also been proposed as a means to avoid unnecessary laparotomy in patients with apparently resectable CRLM, although the proportion of patients in whom unsuspected intra- or extrahepatic disease is identified is relatively small and a selective approach is generally advocated, for example in patients with high clinical risk scores (Grobmyer et al., 2004).

Role of surgery in patients with extrahepatic disease

The survival benefits conferred by surgical resection for patients with liver-only colorectal metastases are well established. The benefits of surgery for patients with EHD are less well defined, however in the era of modern chemotherapy, the presence of EHD is no longer considered a contraindication to surgery and acceptable long-term survival in selected patients is reported by an increasing number of centers. This has been exemplified by a number of studies, the largest of which is a retrospective review of patients undergoing resection of synchronous CRLM and EHD over a 20-year period (1992-2012) at Memorial Sloan Kettering Cancer Center (MSKCC) (Leung et al., 2017). Of 2,693 patients who underwent surgery, 219 patients with EHD were eligible for inclusion. Systemic chemotherapy was used in almost all patients (56.2% neoadjuvant; 82.2% adjuvant). These were principally modern regimes (FOLFOX/ FOLFIRI +/- cetuximab or bevacizumab), but in this series, 23.3% of patients received either neoadjuvant or adjuvant hepatic arterial infusion of floxuridine. The median 3-, 5- and 10-year overall survival rates were 34.4 months, 49%, 28% and 10% respectively. The site of EHD affected survival, with portal nodes, retroperitoneal nodes and multisite EHD associated with the worst prognosis.

Similar data were reported in a consecutive series of 840 patients undergoing liver resection at Hôpital Paul-Brousse, Paris in which 186 (22%) patients had concomitant resectable EHD (Adam et al., 2011). Patients with EHD had a lower 5-year survival than those without (28% vs 55%, p=<0.001). Five poor prognostic factors were identified at multivariate analysis: EHD location other than lung, EHD concomitant to recurrence of colorectal liver metastasis, CEA >10ng/ml, at least 6 colorectal liver metastases and right-sided colon cancer.

A systematic review of 50 studies including 3,481 patients with CRLM and EHD also found similar survival figs. with a median survival of 30.5 months (range 9 – 98), 3- and 5-year overall survival of 42.4% (20.6 – 77%) and 28% (0 – 61%) respectively. Operative morbidity and mortality rates were similar to those seen in patients without EHD (10.7 – 58% and 0 – 4.2% respectively) and 78% of patients achieved an R0 resection (Hwang et al., 2014).

A prospective phase II non-randomised study has sought to examine the role of surgery specifically in patients with synchronous hepatic and extrahepatic colorectal metastases (Wei et al., 2016). Patients with any number of intrahepatic metastases and up to 3 foci of EHD deemed to be resectable with R0 margins were eligible. The primary outcomes were perioperative morbidity and mortality and follow-up was for 2 years. Modest numbers of patients were recruited to the study and 77% completed the protocol procedures, which included 46% undergoing planned sequential resections (26). The median recurrence free survival (RFS) was 5 months (range 0 – 17 months), however overall survival was 50 months (range 7 – 133) for all patients (ITT analysis) and 54 months (range 7 – 133) for patients who completed protocol procedures. An initial deterioration in quality of life scores (EORTC and FACT-Hep instruments) were observed at 4 and 8 months following surgery, however this appeared to be transient and had returned to baseline by 12 months.

Recurrence

The majority of patients who undergo resection of CRLM and EHD will exhibit disease recurrence. In their retrospective review of 219 patients with EHD over 20 years (1992 – 2012), Leung and colleagues identified recurrence in 185 patients (90.2%) at a median of 8 months (Leung et al., 2017). In this cohort, intrahepatic recurrence occurred in 84% patients at a median of 8 months and 51.7% of patients suffered recurrence both within and outside the liver. Recurrence at the initial site of EHD resection occurred in 76.9% of patients. Forty one of 185 patients (22.3%) with recurrence were able to undergo salvage surgery or ablation with an associated median survival of 57 months (3- and 5-year survival of 66% and 48% respectively from the time of salvage). The No Evidence of Disease (NED) rate was 6.6% with 8 actual 10-year survivors (5 of whom had NED). Of these, 5 patients had NED at 10 years, all of whom had a solitary liver metastasis, had complete resection of EHD and had stable or responsive disease on chemotherapy.

Several clinical risk scores have been developed to identify factors associated with survival in patients with CRLM and predict those at high risk of early recurrence who may be better served by a non-operative approach. The details and utility of these scores are covered elsewhere in the book, however the presence of EHD, the site of EHD (portal/retroperitoneal nodes or multiple sites vs. all other sites) and incomplete resection of EHD have been identified on multivariate analysis as independent negative prognostic factors affecting overall and recurrence free survival (Fong et al., 1999; Leung et al., 2017).

Lung metastases

The lung is the second most common site of colorectal metastases after the liver and resection has become an increasing part of multimodal treatment pathways. Liver and lung metastases are more commonly diagnosed in left-sided colon cancers (28.4% vs 22.1%, p = 0.029 and 19.7% vs 13.2%, p = 0.010, respectively), despite the extent of metastases and associated mortality reported as greater for right-sided cancers (Engstrand et al., 2018). Data from the national Swedish patient registry suggests that patients with extrahepatic metastases confined to the lung have superior survival outcomes following surgery (50 months, 95% CI 39 – 60) compared to those with lymph node metastases (32 months, 95% CI 7 – 58, p=0.022) or peritoneal disease (28 months, 95% CI 14-41, p=0.012) (Hasselgren et al., 2020).

The current evidence to support a survival benefit from pulmonary metastectomy over a policy of active surveillance is based on retrospective and prospective series and non-comparative data but indicates that selected patients with limited lung and liver metastases can achieve comparable outcomes to those with liver-only disease (Miller et al., 2007; Mineo et al., 2003; Shah et al., 2006). A meta-analysis of 25 such studies between 2000 and 2011 identified prognostic factors predictive of survival in patients undergoing pulmonary metastectomy (Gonzalez et al., 2013). Of 2925 patients, four variables were associated with poor survival: (1) a short disease-free interval (DFI) between primary tumour resection and development of lung metastases (Hazard Ratio (HR) 1.59, 95% CI 1.27 – 1.98); (2) multiple lung metastases (HR 2.04, 95% CI 1.72–2.41); (3) positive hilar and/or mediastinal lymph nodes (HR 1.65, 95% CI 1.35 – 2.02) and (4) elevated prethoracotomy CEA (HR 1.91, 95% CI 1.57 – 2.32). This meta-analysis reported an overall 5-year survival rate of 27 – 68% in patients who underwent complete resection, however it should be noted that 75% of patients included presented with isolated lung metastases and had not previously undergone hepatic resection. Indeed, such heterogeneity in presentation patterns has been a major confounder for the interpretation of survival data in this field. The temporal pattern between liver and lung metastases, the number and extent of lesions, use of peri-operative chemotherapy and the number of previous procedures for recurrence are biases which have frequently hampered interpretation of data and led to a wide range of reported survival rates.

The Pulmonary Metastectomy versus Continued Active Monitoring in Colorectal Cancer (PulMiCC) trial was a two-stage, phase III, parallel-arm, non-inferiority trial which aimed to compare outcomes of patients randomized to either pulmonary metastectomy or active monitoring (Treasure et al., 2019). The study was terminated early due to poor recruitment (65 patients over 6 years across 24 centres). Sixty-five patients were randomized; however, 155 further patients were lost to randomization principally due to clinicians' decision making, although interestingly there was only one crossover from the control to treatment group. The 5-year survival of patients who underwent metastectomy was 38% (23 – 62%), a rate

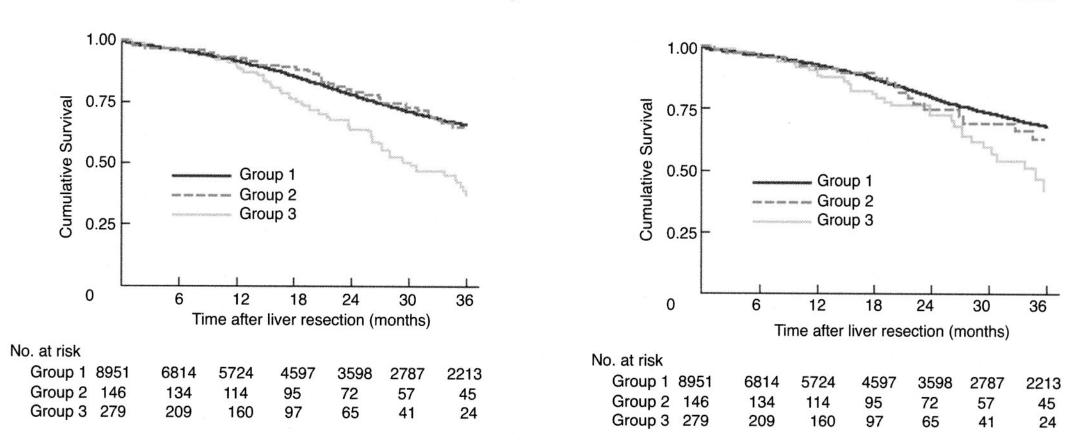

FIGURE 11.2 Overall Survival (OS) is superior in patients following liver resection (Group 1) or liver and lung resection (Group 2) compared with patients undergoing liver resection alone in the presence of unresected lung metastases (Group 3) both before (left-hand panel) and after adjustment for co-variables (right-hand panel). Reproduced with permission from Andres et al. 2015. Reproduced from Andres A, Mentha G, Adam R, Gerstel E, Skipenko OG, Barroso E, et al. Surgical management of patients with colorectal cancer and simultaneous liver and lung metastases. Br J Surg. 2015;102(6):691-9.

comparable to that cited by observational studies. However, the observed survival in the control arm of 29% (16 – 52%) was better than figures widely cited in the literature for untreated colorectal lung metastases. The trial authors and other commentators have speculated that this difference may prove narrower than many in this field have previously assumed, and that although metastectomy may offer long-term survival in those patients in whom lung metastases are the only residue of their colorectal cancer, they challenge the assertion that that there is a very low likelihood of 5-year survival without surgical intervention in comparable patients. In the continued absence of non-operative or surveillance control arms in studies addressing this question, the putative survival benefit from pulmonary metastectomy remains hotly debated.

The management of simultaneously diagnosed liver and lung metastases (SLLM) (diagnosis ≤3 months apart) continues to be controversial. A prospective registry study based on the international LiverMetSurvey involving 253 centers in 66 countries analyzed outcomes in patients with colorectal cancer and liver and/or lung metastases surgically treated between 2000 and 2012 (Andres et al., 2015). Of the 9,619 included patients, 9,185 underwent surgical resection for isolated liver metastases (group 1), 149 underwent resection for lung and liver metastases (group 2) and 285 patients underwent surgical resection of liver metastases with unresected lung metastases (group 3). Crude overall 5-year survival was similar in group 1 and group 2 patients (50.0% vs 40.7% respectively), but superior in both these groups to patients undergoing liver resection with unresected lung metastases (group 3) (9.4%, p=<0.001). Groups were found to differ significantly in age, tumor and nodal stage, number and extent of liver metastases, timing of surgery (synchronous vs. metachronous), CEA, use of embolization, extent of surgery, initial resectability, use of chemotherapy and site of lung metastases (unilateral vs. bilateral). After adjustment for such co-variables, 5-year survival was again similar between groups 1 and 2 (51.5% vs. 44.5%, p = 0.675), but significantly inferior in group 3 (14.3%, p = 0.001) (Fig. 11.2).

Current guidelines dictate that patients must meet the following criteria for surgery: R0 resection is technically feasible with maintenance of adequate function postoperatively, patient must be able to tolerate pulmonary resection, there is control of the primary tumour and no evidence of an extrathoracic lesion (Engstrom et al., 2003). Of the prognostic factors identified by Gonzalez et al., mediastinal lymph node involvement should be investigated pre-operatively with CT-PET and when suspected, mediastinoscopy should be performed before proceeding with pulmonary metastectomy. Elevated CEA is not considered a contraindication to surgery if tumour clearance is deemed feasible and would be expected to return to normal levels following pulmonary metastectomy. The surgical approach must be individualized to each patient; however, a synchronous procedure can be considered depending on the complexity of the procedure, comorbid disease, surgical exposure and surgeon expertise. Minimally invasive and transdiaphragmatic approaches have been developed to minimise the impact of the thoracic incision for patients with tumours suitable for synchronous resection (Mise et al., 2014).

In addition, or as an alternative to surgical resection, Local Ablative Therapies (LAT) and Stereotactic Body Radiotherapy (SBRT) have been used to treat oligometastatic colorectal lung metastases (Hasegawa et al., 2005). As has been seen with pulmonary metastectomy, selection bias and the retrospective, non-randomised nature of existing data have made interpretation of outcomes challenging. A comparative cohort study has analysed survival outcomes in patients undergoing either surgery (n=142) or SRBT (n=28) as first-line local therapy for lung metastases between 2005 and 2012 (Filippi et al., 2016). Overall survival at 1 and 2 years was comparable between these size discrepant groups 89% and 77% respectively for SRBT; 96% and 82% respectively for surgical resection, p = 0.134). Although an inferior PFS was observed in the SBRT arm, the two groups had differing post-procedural surveillance protocols and the authors have cautioned against over-interpretation of these data. Given the difficulties in recruiting patients with oligometastatic disease to the PulMICC trial, the feasibility of a large-scale randomized trial of SBRT or ablation against active monitoring seems a far-off ideal, however this question as well as a comparison of surgical and non-surgical treatments in patients with metastatic colorectal cancer in the lung have been set as research recommendations by the UK National Institute for Health and Care Excellence.

Lymph node metastases

Involvement of the portal lymph nodes is considered locoregional spread from colorectal liver metastases and as such is termed 're-metastases'. This is seen in 3 - 33% of patients with CRLM and confers an especially poor prognosis, with a 5-year survival of 0 – 5% in patients undergoing perihepatic lymphadenectomy (Rodgers & McCall, 2000). These poor survival data are recapitulated by a more recent study by Okuno and colleagues, who analysed 174 patients undergoing hepatectomy and lymphadenectomy for CRLM, 54 (31%) of whom had lymph node involvement. Recurrence free survival (RFS) and overall survival (OS) were significantly inferior in patients with perihepatic lymph node involvement (RFS: 5·3 vs 13·8 months, $P < 0 \cdot 001$; OS: 20·5 vs 71·3 months; $P < 0 \cdot 001$) (Okuno et al., 2018) (Fig. 11.3).

It is likely that improvements in reported survival over time are a consequence of improved systemic chemotherapy regimens, inclusion of patients with microscopic/occult disease rather

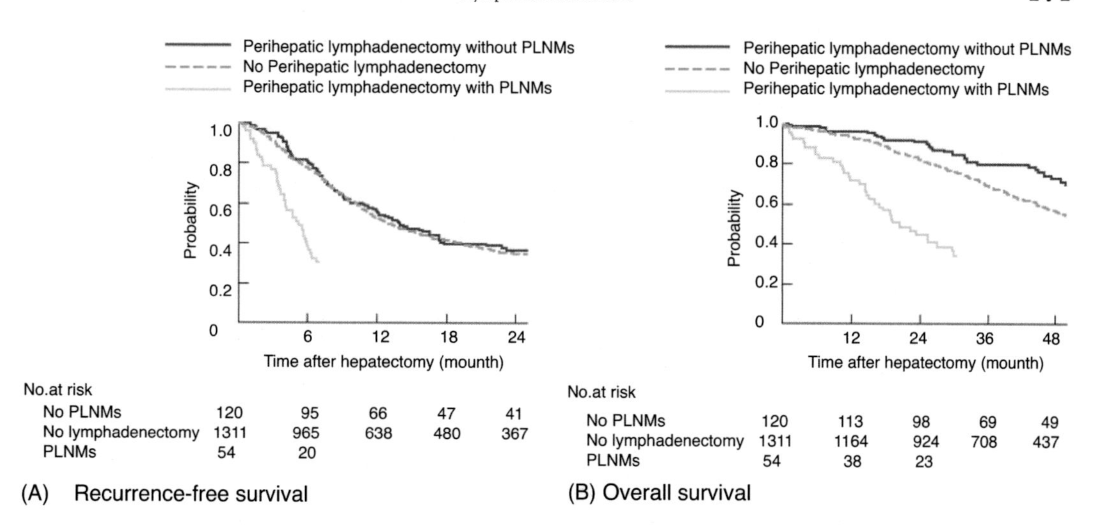

FIGURE 11.3 Recurrence Free Survival (RFS) (*A*) and Overall Survival (OS) (*B*) are significantly reduced in patients with portal lymph node metastases. Reproduced with permission from Okuno et al. 2018. Reproduced From Okuno, M., Goumard, C., Mizuno, T., Kopetz, S., Omichi, K., Tzeng, C. W. D., Chun, Y. S., Lee, J. E., Vauthey, J. N. & Conrad, C. (2018). Prognostic impact of perihepatic lymph node metastases in patients with resectable colorectal liver metastases. British Journal of Surgery, 105(9), 1200–1209. https://doi.org/10.1002/bjs.10822.

than macroscopic/palpable nodal involvement and refinements in staging and imaging. Moreover, routine assessment of lymph nodes using immunohistochemistry for cytokeratins has been proposed to further enhance the sensitivity of detection, to identify patients at higher risk of recurrence who would benefit from post-operative adjuvant chemotherapy (Bennett et al., 2008). Nevertheless, portal nodal involvement appears to be an unfavorable site of EHD compared with pulmonary or peritoneal involvement (Leung et al., 2017); a phenomenon that has been highlighted as contradictory to the classical surgical oncological paradigm whereby local nodal disease is generally a superior prognostic factor compared with distant metastatic spread.

Although no randomized data are yet available to assess any survival effect of portal lymphadenectomy (Gurusamy et al., 2008), prospective cohort studies have been undertaken in which patients with palpable or macroscopically involved nodes are excluded in order to draw comparison between the survival of patients without nodal disease and those with occult metastases (Elias et al., 2004; Laurent et al., 2004; Jaeck et al., 2002; Grobmyer et al., 2006; Ercolani et al., 2004). These series cite the rate of microscopic node involvement as 11-15%, with some authors suggesting this to be sufficiently high to recommend that routine lymphadenectomy should be performed in all patients undergoing CRLM resection to provide prognostic information that can guide postoperative management, for example administration of systemic therapy (Elias et al., 2004; Laurent et al., 2004; Ercolani et al., 2004). This argument has been contested by others who have examined the sensitivity of staging imaging modalities and argue that the majority of patients with involved perihepatic nodes can be identified using a combination of CT, PET and operative assessment (Yang et al., 2007; Grobmyer et al., 2006). A retrospective, single institution, cohort study has analyzed outcomes from 81 patients who underwent either routine or selective lymphadenectomy during hepatectomy for CRLM depending on the primary operator (Pindak et al., 2017). Patients were matched for age, ASA score and Fong's prognostic criteria. They observed no difference in long-term survival between the selective and routine groups (median overall survival (mOS) 61.62 vs. 60.12 months; HR 0.90 95%; confidence interval (CI) 0.52-1.58, p=0.7). A significant difference in survival was observed between patients with positive and those with negative nodes (mOS 29.6 vs. 66.97 months, HR 6.33; 95% CI 2.16-18.57, p=0.0001).

Prospective studies have shown the location of involved lymph nodes to be a prognostic factor for survival. The lymphatic drainage of the liver is described by Ito et al. to take three principal routes through the hepatoduodenal ligament to reach the para-aortic nodal basin: the main pathway is the cholecystoretropancreatic (right) route, which runs spirally and posteriorly from the anterior surface of the common bile duct to the right, as well as posteriorly straight down the posterior surface of the bile duct. Two further routes, the cholecystoceliac pathway and the cholecystomesenteric pathway (left route), converge with the abdominoaortic lymph nodes near the left renal vein (Moszkowicz et al., 2012) (Fig. 11.4).

In a study of 160 patients undergoing hepatectomy for CRLM, Jaeck and colleagues identified 17 patients with nodal involvement (40 metastases among 127 dissected lymph nodes) and found survival significantly inferior in patients with involvement of ≥1 nodal basin (9 patients) compared to those with involved nodes confined to the hepatic hilum (8 patients) (Jaeck et al., 2002). A study from MD Anderson identified 54 patients with lymph node involvement, 34 of whom had metastases along the hepatoduodenal ligament, 8 along the common hepatic and celiac arteries and 12 in the para-aortic basin (Okuno et al., 2018). Median OS was superior in patients with para-aortic nodal involvement, compared to those with hepatoduodenal ligament nodes (58.2 months vs 15.5 months, p=0.012). In concordance with Jaeck et al., they found patients with just 1 or 2 involved nodes had significantly better median OS than patients with 3 or more (25.4 vs 16.3 months, p=0.039).

These data, suggesting superior survival in patients with nodes outside of the hepatoduodenal ligament, are in contrast to the findings of other investigators. This includes a study of 47 patients undergoing simultaneous hepatectomy and lymphadenectomy for CRLM in which the location of metastatic nodes strongly influenced survival, with an observed 5-year OS of 25% in patients with involved pedicle nodes, but 0% in those with celiac or para-aortic involvement (Jaeck et al., 2002; Adam et al., 2008). Results from this study indicate that in selected patients with CRLM, simultaneous hepatectomy with lymphadenectomy can offer a 5-year survival rate of 18%, with no post-operative mortality, in patients who have had a pre-operative response to chemotherapy (25% 5-year survival in patients with isolated hepatoduodenal node involvement) (Adam et al., 2008). The decision as to whether to proceed with resection when nodal involvement is discovered intra-operatively remains highly controversial, with no widely held consensus, although decision making is commonly guided by factors including tumour burden, clinical risk score and therapeutic response.

Peritoneal metastases

Due to its association with poor survival, the presence of peritoneal metastases was historically considered as systemic tumour dissemination representative of advanced metastatic

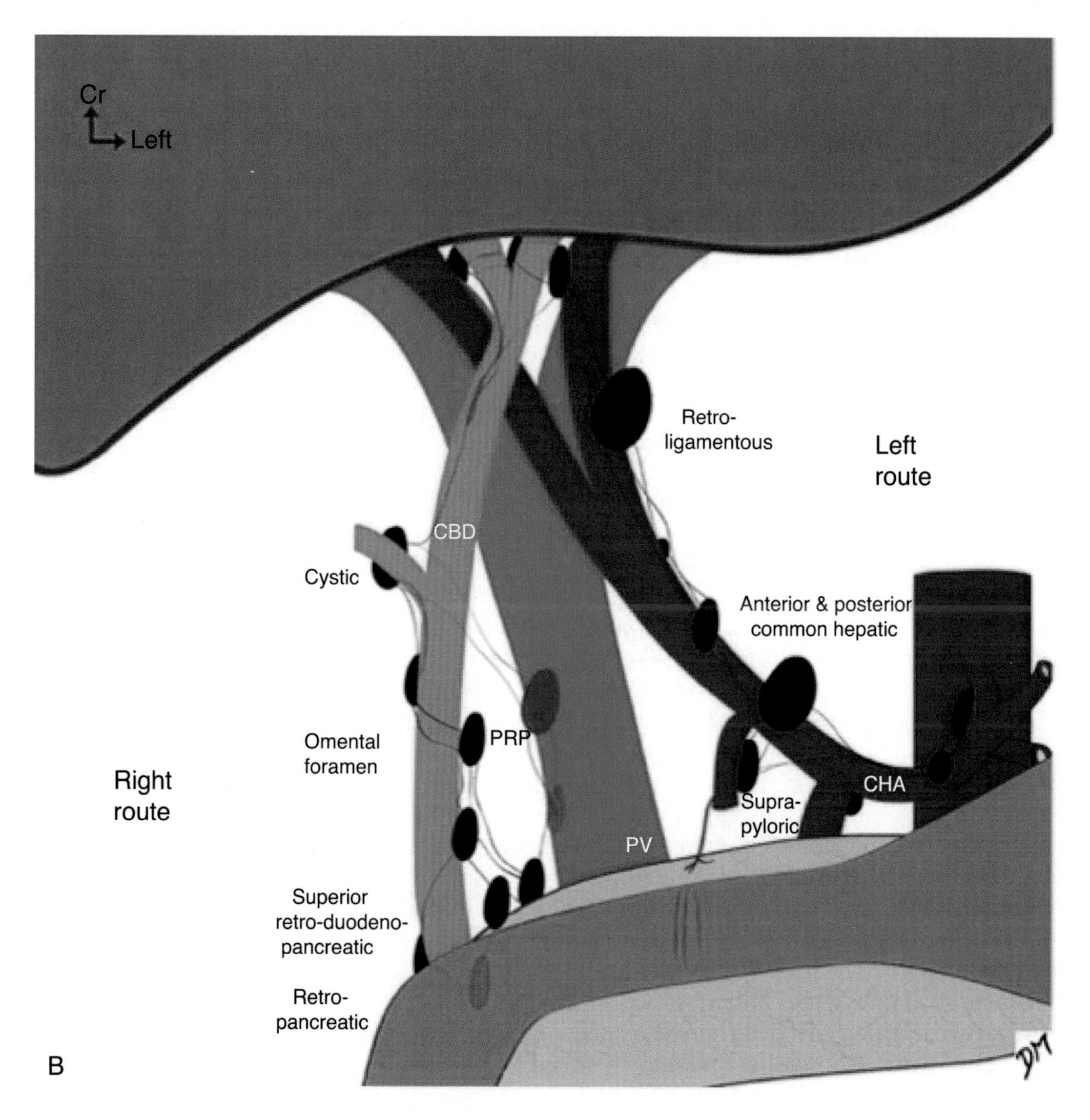

FIGURE 11.4 Schematic of lymphatic drainage routes of the liver as described by Ito et al. Reproduced with permission from Moskowicz et al., 2012. Reproduced from Moszkowicz, D., Cauchy, F., Dokmak, S. & Belghiti, J. (2012). Routine pedicular lymphadenectomy for colorectal liver metastases. Journal of the American College of Surgeons, 214(6), e39–e45. https://doi.org/10.1016/j.jamcollsurg.2012.02.015.

disease and a contraindication to surgery. Peritoneal disease is estimated to occur in 13% of patients with colorectal cancer (61% synchronously; 39% metachronously) and is associated with a median survival of 7 months (Jayne et al., 2002). The identification of a group of patients with metastatic CRC involving the peritoneum as the solitary site of recurrence, without other organ involvement, led Paul Sugarbaker and others to hypothesize that in some patients with localized peritoneal disease as a result of regional transcelomic spread, there might be a role for cytoreductive surgery and/or hyperthermic intraperitoneal chemotherapy (HIPEC) (Sugarbaker, 1999).

Two randomised controlled trials have sought to address this issue. The first was a single centre study that randomised 105 patients to either systemic chemotherapy or cytoreductive surgery followed by HIPEC (Verwaal et al., 2003). Procedure related mortality was high in the surgery arm (8%) and median duration of surgery (485 minutes, range 315 – 765); blood loss (3.9 litres, range 0.5 – 30.0) and hospital stay (23 days) reflected the challenges of this type of surgery. However, median overall survival in the control arm was 12.6 months compared with 22.4 months in the HIPEC group (p=0.032, median 21.6 months follow up), with the best prognosis seen in patients in whom a complete resection was achieved. The long-term follow up (median 8 years, range 72 – 115 months) of these patients was reported in a subsequent publication, in which the median progression-free survival was 7.7 months in the control group and 12.6 months in the HIPEC group (p=0.020) (Verwaal et al., 2008). Median disease-specific survival was 12.6 months in the control arm and 22.2 months in the HIPEC arm (p=0.028). Five-year survival was 45% when R1 resection was achieved. The second trial (PRODIGE-7) was a multicentre French study that randomised 265 patients undergoing cytoreductive surgery to receive HIPEC using Oxaliplatin or surgery alone (Quénet et al., 2021). No difference in overall 5-year survival was observed, however survival rates for all patients were higher than anticipated (median survival 42 months), suggesting a benefit for high-quality surgery. No difference was seen in 30-day mortality, but high-dose Oxaliplatin HIPEC was associated with greater morbidity (24.1% vs 13.6%, p=0.030).

The Peritoneal Carcinomatosis Index (PCI) has been validated as a predictor of survival in patients with peritoneal metastases, with a recommendation that patients with a PCI <12 can proceed to cytoreductive surgery and HIPEC (Faron et al., 2016)(39). This includes patients with limited hepatic metastases, although studies specifically looking at patients undergoing simultaneous resection of liver and peritoneal metastases are few and retrospective (Kianmanesh et al., 2007). In one series of 43 patients with colorectal cancer undergoing cytoreductive surgery and HIPEC for peritoneal carcinomatosis, 16 patients (37%) had concomitant liver metastases. Of these, three had previous liver resection, 10 had simultaneous resection and three had deferred hepatic resection (Kianmanesh et al., 2007). Actuarial 2- and 4-year survival rates were 72% and 44% respectively and multivariate analysis showed median survival was principally determined by the completeness of surgery and was no different between patients who had cytoreductive surgery and HPIEC alone versus those who had associated liver resection (median survival 35.3 vs 36 months, p=0.73).

Conclusions

The challenges of selection bias, high rates of cross-over between different groups, difficulties in randomization (e.g., once histological diagnosis of nodal involvement is confirmed) and attrition in intention to treat analyses, have resulted in an evidence base in this field of study that is almost exclusively based on observational retrospective data. Furthermore, comprehensive long-term follow-up has rarely been available. Despite such issues, the studies discussed in this chapter have shown that in the presence of EHD, 5-year survival rates of

30% or even higher can be achieved, especially in patients with single sites of EHD (most favorably the lung) who have shown a good response to systemic therapy and in whom an R0 resection can be achieved. Although it is important that patient expectations are managed appropriately, it seems fair to conclude that the presence of EHD can no longer in itself be considered a contraindication to surgery and each patient's situation should be assessed on an individual basis in the context of contemporary multimodal treatment pathways.

References

Adam, R., De Haas, R. J., Wicherts, D. A., Vibert, E., Salloum, C., Azoulay, D., et al. (2011). Concomitant extrahepatic disease in patients with colorectal liver metastases: when is there a place for surgery? *Annals of Surgery, 253*(2), 349–359. https://doi.org/10.1097/SLA.0b013e318207bf2c.

Adam, R., Wicherts, D. A., De Haas, R. J., Aloia, T., Lévi, F., Paule, B., et al. (2008). Complete pathologic response after preoperative chemotherapy for colorectal liver metastases: myth or reality? *Journal of Clinical Oncology, 26*(10), 1635–1641. https://doi.org/10.1200/JCO.2007.13.7471.

Andres, A., Mentha, G., Adam, R., Gerstel, E., Skipenko, O. G., Barroso, E., et al. (2015). Surgical management of patients with colorectal cancer and simultaneous liver and lung metastases. *British Journal of Surgery, 102*(6), 691–699. https://doi.org/10.1002/bjs.9783.

Bennett, J. J., Schmidt, C. R., Klimstra, D. S., Grobmyer, S. R., Ishill, N. M., D'Angelica, M., et al. (2008). Perihepatic lymph node micrometastases impact outcome after partial hepatectomy for colorectal metastases. *In Annals of Surgical Oncology, 15*(4), 1130–1136. https://doi.org/10.1245/s10434-007-9802-0.

Elias, D., Liberale, G., Vernerey, D., Pocard, M., Ducreux, M., Boige, V., et al. (2005). Hepatic and extrahepatic colorectal metastases: when resectable, their localization does not matter, but their total number has a prognostic effect. *Annals of Surgical Oncology, 12*(11), 900–909. https://doi.org/10.1245/ASO.2005.01.010.

Elias, D., Sideris, L., Pocard, M., Ouellet, J. F., Boige, V., Lasser, P., et al. (2004). Results of R0 resection for colorectal liver metastases associated with extrahepatic disease. *Annals of Surgical Oncology, 11*(3), 274–280. https://doi.org/10.1245/ASO.2004.03.085.

Engstrand, J., Nilsson, H., Strömberg, C., Jonas, E., & Freedman, J. (2018). Colorectal cancer liver metastases - a population-based study on incidence, management and survival. *BMC cancer, 18*(1). https://doi.org/10.1186/s12885-017-3925-x.

Engstrom, P. F., Benson, A. B., Saltz, L., & Network, N. C. C. (2003). Colon cancer. Clinical practice guidelines in oncology. *Journal of the National Comprehensive Cancer Network : JNCCN,, 1*(1), 40–53. https://doi.org/10.6004/jnccn.2003.0006.

Ercolani, G., Grazi, G. L., Ravaioli, M., Grigioni, W. F., Cescon, M., Gardini, A., et al. (2004). The Role of Lymphadenectomy for Liver Tumors: further Considerations on the Appropriateness of Treatment Strategy. *Annals of Surgery, 239*(2), 202–209. https://doi.org/10.1097/01.sla.0000109154.00020.e0.

Faron, M., Macovei, R., Goéré, D., Honoré, C., Benhaim, L., & Elias, D. (2016). Linear Relationship of Peritoneal Cancer Index and Survival in Patients with Peritoneal Metastases from Colorectal Cancer. *Annals of Surgical Oncology, 23*(1), 114–119. https://doi.org/10.1245/s10434-015-4627-8.

Filippi, A. R., Guerrera, F., Badellino, S., Ceccarelli, M., Castiglione, A., Guarneri, A., et al. (2016). Exploratory Analysis on Overall Survival after Either Surgery or Stereotactic Radiotherapy for Lung Oligometastases from Colorectal Cancer. *Clinical Oncology, 28*(8), 505–512. https://doi.org/10.1016/j.clon.2016.02.001.

Fong, Y., Fortner, J., Sun, R. L., Brennan, M. F., & Blumgart, L. H. (1999). Clinical Score for Predicting Recurrence After Hepatic Resection for Metastatic Colorectal Cancer. *Annals of Surgery, 230*(3), 309. https://doi.org/10.1097/00000658-199909000-00004.

Gonzalez, M., Poncet, A., Combescure, C., Robert, J., Ris, H. B., & Gervaz, P. (2013). Risk factors for survival after lung metastasectomy in colorectal cancer patients: a systematic review and meta-analysis. *Annals of Surgical Oncology, 20*(2), 572–579. https://doi.org/10.1245/s10434-012-2726-3.

Grobmyer, S. R., Fong, Y., D'Angelica, M., DeMatteo, R. P., Blumgart, L. H., & Jarnagin, W. R. (2004). Diagnostic laparoscopy prior to planned hepatic resection for colorectal metastases. *Archives of Surgery, 139*(12), 1326–1330. https://doi.org/10.1001/archsurg.139.12.1326.

Grobmyer, S. R., Wang, L., Gonen, M., Fong, Y., Klimstra, D., D'Angelica, M., et al. (2006). Perihepatic lymph node assessment in patients undergoing partial hepatectomy for malignancy. *Annals of Surgery, 244*(2), 260–264. https://doi.org/10.1097/01.sla.0000217606.59625.9d.

Gurusamy, K. S., Imber, C., & Davidson, B. R. (2008). Management of the hepatic lymph nodes during resection of liver metastases from colorectal cancer: a systematic review. *Hpb Surgery*. https://doi.org/10.1155/2008/684150.

Hasegawa, K., Kokudo, N., Imamura, H., Matsuyama, Y., Aoki, T., Minagawa, M., et al. (2005). Prognostic impact of anatomic resection for hepatocellular carcinoma. *Annals of Surgery, 242*(2), 252–259. https://doi.org/10.1097/01.sla.0000171307.37401.db.

Hasselgren, K., Isaksson, B., Ardnor, B., Lindell, G., Rizell, M., Strömberg, C., et al. (2020). Liver resection is beneficial for patients with colorectal liver metastases and extrahepatic disease. *Annals of translational medicine*, 109. https://doi.org/10.21037/atm.2019.12.125.

Hwang, M., Jayakrishnan, T. T., Green, D. E., George, B., Thomas, J. P., Groeschl, R. T., et al. (2014). Systematic review of outcomes of patients undergoing resection for colorectal liver metastases in the setting of extra hepatic disease. *European Journal of Cancer, 50*(10), 1747–1757. https://doi.org/10.1016/j.ejca.2014.03.277.

Jaeck, D., Nakano, H., Bachellier, P., Inoue, K., Weber, J. C., Oussoultzoglou, E., et al. (2002). Significance of hepatic pedicle lymph node involvement in patients with colorectal liver metastases: a prospective study. *Annals of Surgical Oncology, 9*(5), 430–438. https://doi.org/10.1245/aso.2002.9.5.430.

Jayne, D. G., Fook, S., Loi, C., & Seow-Choen, F. (2002). Peritoneal carcinomatosis from colorectal cancer. *British Journal of Surgery, 89*(12), 1545–1550. https://doi.org/10.1046/j.1365-2168.2002.02274.x.

Kianmanesh, R., Scaringi, S., Sabate, J. M., Castel, B., Pons-Kerjean, N., Coffin, B., et al. (2007). Iterative cytoreductive surgery associated with hyperthermic intraperitoneal chemotherapy for treatment of peritoneal carcinomatosis of colorectal origin with or without liver metastases. *Annals of Surgery, 245*(4), 597–603. https://doi.org/10.1097/01.sla.0000255561.87771.11.

Laurent, C., Sa Cunha, A., Rullier, E., Smith, D., Rullier, A., & Saric, J. (2004). Impact of microscopic hepatic lymph node involvement on survival after resection of colorectal liver metastasis. *Journal of the American College of Surgeons, 198*(6), 884–891. https://doi.org/10.1016/j.jamcollsurg.2004.01.017.

Leung, U., Gönen, M., Allen, P. J., Kingham, T. P., DeMatteo, R. P., Jarnagin, W. R., et al. (2017). Colorectal cancer liver metastases and concurrent extrahepatic disease treated with resection. *Annals of Surgery, 265*(1), 158–165. https://doi.org/10.1097/SLA.0000000000001624.

Miller, G., Biernacki, P., Kemeny, N. E., Gonen, M., Downey, R., Jarnagin, W. R., et al. (2007). Outcomes after Resection of Synchronous or Metachronous Hepatic and Pulmonary Colorectal Metastases. *Journal of the American College of Surgeons, 205*(2), 231–238. https://doi.org/10.1016/j.jamcollsurg.2007.04.039.

Mineo, T. C., Ambrogi, V., Tonini, G., Bollero, P., Roselli, M., Mineo, D., et al. (2003). Longterm results after resection of simultaneous and sequential lung and liver metastases from colorectal carcinoma. *Journal of the American College of Surgeons, 197*(3), 386–391. https://doi.org/10.1016/S1072-7515(03)00387-9.

Mise, Y., Mehran, R. J., Aloia, T. A., & Vauthey, J. N. (2014). Simultaneous lung resection via a transdiaphragmatic approach in patients undergoing liver resection for synchronous liver and lung metastases. *Surgery (United States), 156*(5), 1197–1203. https://doi.org/10.1016/j.surg.2014.04.050.

Moszkowicz, D., Cauchy, F., Dokmak, S., & Belghiti, J. (2012). Routine pedicular lymphadenectomy for colorectal liver metastases. *Journal of the American College of Surgeons, 214*(6), e39–e45. https://doi.org/10.1016/j.jamcollsurg.2012.02.015.

Okuno, M., Goumard, C., Mizuno, T., Kopetz, S., Omichi, K., Tzeng, C. W. D., et al. (2018). Prognostic impact of perihepatic lymph node metastases in patients with resectable colorectal liver metastases. *British Journal of Surgery, 105*(9), 1200–1209. https://doi.org/10.1002/bjs.10822.

Pindak, D., Pavlendova, J., Tomas, M., Dolnik, J., Duchon, R., & Pechan, J. (2017). Selective versus routine lymphadenectomy in the treatment of liver metastasis from colorectal cancer: a retrospective cohort study. *Bmc Surgery [Electronic Resource], 17*(1). https://doi.org/10.1186/s12893-017-0233-y.

Quénet, F., Elias, D., Roca, L., Goéré, D., Ghouti, L., Pocard, M., et al. (2021). Cytoreductive surgery plus hyperthermic intraperitoneal chemotherapy versus cytoreductive surgery alone for colorectal peritoneal metastases (PRODIGE 7): a multicentre, randomised, open-label, phase 3 trial. *The Lancet Oncology, 22*(2), 256–266. https://doi.org/10.1016/S1470-2045(20)30599-4.

Rodgers, M. S., & McCall, J. L. (2000). Surgery for colorectal liver metastases with hepatic lymph node involvement: a systematic review. *British Journal of Surgery, 87*(9), 1142–1155. https://doi.org/10.1046/j.1365-2168.2000.01580.x.

Shah, S. A., Haddad, R., Al-Sukhni, W., Kim, R. D., Greig, P. D., Grant, D. R., et al. (2006). Surgical resection of hepatic and pulmonary metastases from colorectal carcinoma. *Journal of the American College of Surgeons, 202*(3), 468–475. https://doi.org/10.1016/j.jamcollsurg.2005.11.008.

Sugarbaker, P.H. (1999). Management of peritoneal-surface malignancy: the surgeon's role. Langenbeck's Archives of Surgery, 384(6), 576–587. https://doi.org/10.1007/s004230050246

Treasure, T., Farewell, V., Macbeth, F., Monson, K., Williams, N. R., Brew-Graves, C., et al. (2019). Pulmonary Metastasectomy versus Continued Active Monitoring in Colorectal Cancer (PulMiCC): a multicentre randomised clinical trial. *Trials, 20*(1). https://doi.org/10.1186/s13063-019-3837-y.

Verwaal, V. J., Bruin, S., Boot, H., Van Slooten, G., & Van Tinteren, H. (2008). 8-Year follow-up of randomized trial: cytoreduction and hyperthermic intraperitoneal chemotherapy versus systemic chemotherapy in patients with peritoneal carcinomatosis of colorectal cancer. *Annals of Surgical Oncology, 15*(9), 2426–2432. https://doi.org/10.1245/s10434-008-9966-2.

Verwaal, V. J., van Ruth, S., de Bree, E., van Slooten, G. W., van Tinteren, H., Boot, H., et al. (2003). Randomized trial of cytoreduction and hyperthermic intraperitoneal chemotherapy versus systemic chemotherapy and palliative surgery in patients with peritoneal carcinomatosis of colorectal cancer. *Journal of Clinical Oncology, 21*(20), 3737–3743. https://doi.org/10.1200/JCO.2003.04.187.

Wei, A. C., Coburn, N. G., Devitt, K. S., Serrano, P. E., Moulton, C. A., Cleary, S. P., et al. (2016). Survival Following Resection of Intra- and Extra-Hepatic Metastases from Colorectal Cancer: a Phase II Trial. *Annals of Surgical Oncology, 23*(8), 2644–2651. https://doi.org/10.1245/s10434-016-5189-0.

Yang, Y. Y. L., Fleshman, J. W., & Strasberg, S. M. (2007). Detection and management of extrahepatic colorectal cancer in patients with resectable liver metastases. *Journal of Gastrointestinal Surgery, 11*(7), 929–944. https://doi.org/10.1007/s11605-006-0067-x.

CHAPTER

12

Locoregional approaches to colorectal liver metastasis – ablation

Jian Zheng and David A. Geller

Department of Surgery, University of Pittsburgh Medical Center, Pittsburgh, PA

Introduction

Colorectal cancer is the second leading cause of cancer-related death in the United States (Siegel et al., 2020). About half of patients diagnosed with colorectal cancer will have synchronous (20 percent) or develop metachronous (additional 30 percent) colorectal liver metastasis (CRLM) in their lifetime (Takahashi and Berber, 2020; Puijk et al., 2018; Gurusamy et al., 2018). Curative-intent liver resection of CRLM can lead to 5-year survival rates of 40–60 percent, but only 10–20 percent of patients with CRLM are candidates for resection (Ruers et al., 2017; Fong et al., 1999). Only a minority of patients are eligible for resection because of an inadequate future liver remnant, unfavorable anatomical location of tumors, or due to physiologic contraindications and an inability to tolerate hepatectomy (Puijk et al., 2018; Meijerink et al., 2018). Even though CRLM represents metastatic disease, curative hepatectomy can prolong long-term survival. On the other hand, the median overall survival of patients with untreated CRLM is only 4.5–12 months. Systemic therapy can prolong survival to 15 to 35 months, but the 5-year survival without liver resection is low at < 15 percent (Puijk et al., 2018; Meijerink et al., 2018).

Although liver resection is the standard of care for patients with resectable CRLM, thermal ablation is an excellent alternative for many patients who cannot undergo hepatectomy. Previous retrospective series have reported comparable overall survival for patients with CRLM who undergo ablation versus hepatectomy, but liver resection remains the gold standard and the best hope for long-term survival (Eltawil et al., 2014; Faitot et al., 2014; Hof et al., 2016; Karanicolas et al., 2013). Both the COLLISON and LAVA trials are prospective, randomized trials currently enrolling patients with CRLM to compare long-term outcomes of ablation versus resection (Puijk et al., 2018; Gurusamy et al., 2018). For patients with unresectable CRLM, the EORTC–CLOCC trial published in 2017 demonstrated that aggressive local control

Contemporary Management of Metastatic Colorectal Cancer: A Precision Medicine Approach
DOI: https://doi.org/10.1016/B978-0-323-91706-3.00006-0

TABLE 12.1 Indications and contraindications to thermal ablations (Takahashi and Berber, 2020; Ruers et al., 2017).

Indications	Contraindications
• Unresectable liver metastases, <8 in number with involvement of <20% of liver volume, and the largest lesion <4 cm • In combination with hepatectomy to expand the pool of resectable patients, such as treating bilobar disease with concomitant resection and ablation • In patients who are unfit to undergo resection due to their medical comorbidities or performance status • A small (<3 cm) solitary metastasis that would otherwise require a major hepatectomy • Patient prefer ablation over resection	• Larger CRLM due to higher rate of incomplete ablation and subsequent local recurrence. Common maximum lesion size is 3–4 cm • Contraindications for general anesthesia for open or laparoscopic surgery • Uncorrectable coagulopathy • Jaundice or biliary dilatation • Decompensated ascites • Tumor location abutting either the liver hilum or the right/left hepatic ducts • Untreatable extrahepatic disease or diffuse metastatic liver disease • Metallic devices such as pacemaker are contraindicated for RFA, but are acceptable with MWA

of unresectable CRLM treated by ablation with or without resection can significantly improve their overall survival compared to systemic chemotherapy alone (Ruers et al., 2017). Thus, ablation should be considered for patients with CRLM with contraindications to resection.

Indications and contraindications

The indications and contraindication to thermal ablations are summarized in Table 12.1. Ablation should be considered for patients with unresectable liver metastases or with resectable disease but in patients with poor performance status who are unable to tolerate hepatectomy (Takahashi and Berber, 2020). Retrospective studies have demonstrated that for patients with small (<3 cm) solitary CRLM, thermal ablation leads to similar oncologic long-term outcomes as surgical resection, but results from ongoing prospective randomized trials are needed before ablation can be recommended in patients with small resectable CRLM (Takahashi and Berber, 2020). Another indication for thermal ablation is for a small solitary lesion that is centrally located and would otherwise require a major hepatectomy (Takahashi and Berber, 2020). Since ablation allows parenchymal preservation, it is also helpful in patients with bilobar metastases. Ablation and liver resection can be performed concomittantly to treat bilobar disease with parenchymal preservation, and spare the need for two-stage hepatectomy and its associated operative morbidities (Takahashi and Berber, 2020). Given the different options available, patients should be evaluated in a multidisciplinary tumor board to make recommendations after considering their specific indications and contraindications for resection, ablation, and other alternatives.

Radiofrequency vs microwave ablations

Thermal ablation includes radiofrequency ablation (RFA) and microwave ablation (MWA). RFA was first recognized in the early 1990s and became widely accepted in 2000s for liver tumors given its effectiveness with relatively low morbidity (Takahashi and Berber, 2020). MWA became popular after FDA approved the newer microwave thermosphere ablation (MTA) device in 2014 (Takahashi and Berber, 2020). Cryoablation of CRLM was also used in the 1990s, but it largely has been replaced by RFA or MWA due to smaller needle probes and the incidence of fewer complications (Wells et al., 2015; Petre and Sofocleous, 2017).

Both RFA and MWA modalities use thermal energy to destroy cancer cells with its adjacent liver parenchyma. RFA uses alternating electrical current at a high frequency of 400 MHz to generate thermal energy to heat an ablation zone that is about 5 cm area from the probe tip (Takahashi and Berber, 2020; Wells et al., 2015). The dose delivered for RFA varies in different patients depending on target ablation zone diameter (Gurusamy et al., 2018). The goal temperature in the tumor is 60 °C to achieve coagulative necrosis while keeping the electrode tip temperature < 100 °C to avoid charring and vaporization of tissue (Gurusamy et al., 2018). In contrast, MWA uses electromagnetic wave at microwave frequency greater than 900 MHz to agitate water molecules to generate thermal energy to destroy cancer cells (Wells et al., 2015; Martin et al., 2007). It works well in the liver and other tissues with high percentage of water molecules.

Both RFA and MWA have their own advantages and disadvantages. For example, the RFA electrodes have multiple tines, and it can be difficult to account for the exact needle tip location of each tine which could result in thermal damage to a vital structure. RFA may take up to 20–30 min for larger tumors in the 3–4 cm range. And is susceptible to the heat-sink effect, making it difficult to treat lesions close to large vessels (>3 mm diameter) due to loss of thermal energy with adjacent blood flow (Pillai et al., 2015). RFA can also cause thermal injury to adjacent organs, large vessels and major bile ducts (Puijk et al., 2018). Moreover, aside from the initial innovation of a powerful generator (200 W) that can produce maximum ablation zones of 4–5 cm, overlapping needle deployments are often needed and RFA technology has not been significantly improved upon over the recent years (Takahashi and Berber, 2020). Oncologically, RFA has been reported to have a high rate of local recurrence, up to 20–40 percent in some series, especially when the tumor size is 3 cm or greater (Wong et al., 2010; Takahashi et al., 2017).

MWA has multiple advantages over RFA in that MWA requires less time to achieve tumoricidal temperature in the tissue, is less susceptible to the heat-sink effect, allows wider penetration and margin, creates more homogenous tissue heating, and does not require a grounding pad or cooling system (Pillai et al., 2015). MWA can thus lead to a larger and more homogenous zone of active heating, both within the targeted zone and next to blood vessels (Puijk et al., 2018). Compared to RFA, MWA also has significantly reduced ablation time (37±3 vs. 19±3 min, $P < 0.001$) and thus shorter operative time (202±13 vs. 154±3 min, $P = 0.009$) (Takahashi et al., 2018). Given the numerous advantages of MWA over RFA, many institutions including our liver cancer center have transitioned from RFA to MWA in the past 5 years. Currently, we use RFA for small tumors < 1 cm, and MWA for tumors 1–4 cm in size. The details of radiofrequency and microwave ablations are compared on Table 12.2.

Ablation approaches

Ablation can be performed via open, laparoscopic, and percutaneous approaches. An open approach carries the morbidity of a laparotomy, whereas laparoscopic and percutaneous approaches have the advantage of being minimally-invasive and are associated with less

TABLE 12.2 Comparison of radiofrequency and microwave ablations (Takahashi and Berber, 2020; Gurusamy et al., 2018).

RFA	MWA
• Alternating electrical current	• Electromagnetic wave
• Longer time to achieve goal temperature	• Shorter time to achieve tumoricidal temperature
• Heat-sink effect	• Less susceptible to heat-sink effect
• Tissue charring and boiling cause increased impedance which reduces conductivity	• Rapid and homogenous heating
• Unpredictable ablation zone	• Predictable ablation zone
	• Challenging for precise sub-cm ablation zone
• Treats single lesion	• Simultaneous treatment of multiple lesions
• Smaller ablation volume	• Larger ablation volume
• Treats lesions up to 3–4 cm	• Treats lesions up to 5–6 cm
• Surgical clips or pacemakers are contraindicated	• Clips or pacemakers are not contraindicated
• Need grounding pads	• No grounding pads needed

post-procedural pain and a shorter hospital length of stay (Takahashi and Berber, 2020). Open and laparoscopic approaches need general anesthesia, but they have the advantage of a more thorough evaluation for complete peritoneal staging to rule out any occult metastasis (Takahashi and Berber, 2020). Open and laparoscopic approaches are supplemented by intraoperative ultrasound for precise targeting of the target CRLM and for thorough evaluation of the remnant liver for any additional occult liver metastasis that were not identified on preoperative imaging (Takahashi and Berber, 2020). This is important as up to 50 percent of additional lesions can be identified with intraoperative ultrasound that were not detected preoperatively (Sietses et al., 2010). An operating view of performing an ultrasound-guided laparoscopic RFA of a CRLM was captured on Fig. 12.1.

Percutaneous approach is the least invasive approach and it can be performed with local anesthesia or sedation. It does require different image techniques such as ultrasound, computational tomography (CT), or magnetic resonance imaging (MRI) to guide the placement of the ablation probe (Takahashi and Berber, 2020). The percutaneous approach is limited by inability to survey for occult liver or peritoneal metastases (Takahashi and Berber, 2020). In addition, since the liver cannot be mobilized during the percutaneous ablation, superficial lesions close to other organs cannot be safely ablated (Takahashi and Berber, 2020). These open, laparoscopic, and percutaneous approaches are compared in Table 12.3.

Post-ablation complications

Thermal ablation is generally considered a relatively safe procedure with low morbidity rates of 4–9 percent and 90-day mortality rates $<$ 1 percent (Wong et al., 2010; Gillams et al., 2015; Correa-Gallego et al., 2014). Post-ablation complications can be categorized into three general groups (Correa-Gallego et al., 2014; Birsen et al., 2014; Mulier et al., 2002; Rhim et al., 2008):

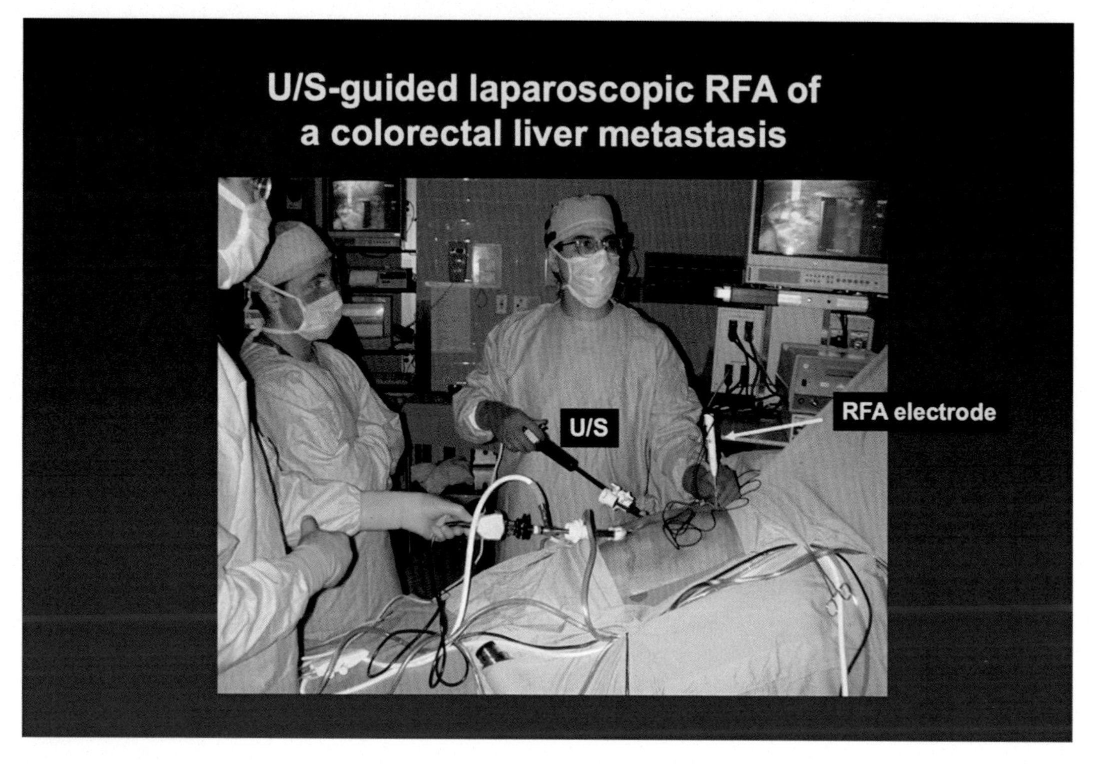

FIGURE 12.1 An ultrasound-guided laparoscopic RFA of a CRLM.

TABLE 12.3 Comparison of open, laparoscopic, and percutaneous approaches (Takahashi and Berber, 2020).

Open	Laparoscopic	Percutaneous
• General anesthesia • Invasive • Evaluate occult disease • Can mobilize liver to treat lesions close to other organs	• General anesthesia • Less invasive • Evaluate occult disease • Can mobilize liver to treat lesions close to other organs	• Local, sedation, or general anesthesia • Least invasive • Limited evaluation of occult disease • Cannot mobilize liver and thus cannot treat surface lesions close to other organs

1. Complications related to probe placement such as bleeding, infection (liver abscess or superficial wound infection), tumor seeding, or incorrect insertion position causing pneumothorax
2. Complications related to transfer of energy such as direct thermal damage to surrounding structures including bowel, gallbladder, or bile ducts causing biloma or biliary stricture, or grounding pad burns, post-ablation syndrome, hepatic vascular damage, liver failure

3. Complications associated with any invasive procedure, such as thromboembolism, referred pain, fever, nausea or emesis, or acute kidney injury

Complication rates between RFA and MWA are comparable (Correa-Gallego et al., 2014). In one retrospective study that matched 254 tumors to MWA or RFA, the morbidity rates were similar between the two groups (27 percent vs. 24 percent for MWA and RFA, respectively, $p = 0.80$) (Correa-Gallego et al., 2014). In this study, the majority of patients had ablation performed in combination with resection. The most common complications were wound infections (16 percent), followed by intra-abdominal fluid collections (8 percent), and pleural effusions (4 percent) (Correa-Gallego et al., 2014).

However, in a meta-analysis of multiple retrospective studies, it was concluded that complication rates for RFA for unresectable CRLMs were lower compared to resection, but MWA complication rates were similar to resection (Meijerink et al., 2018). It is important to note that the quality of evidence inputted for this meta-analysis were low quality as they were retrospective studies on heterogenous populations (Meijerink et al., 2018). Furthermore, there were significant inherent selection biases when comparing complications of patients who underwent thermal ablation versus resection. Because many patients referred to ablation had underlying comorbidities and poor performance status, and thus they may have been at higher risk for cardiopulmonary and other complications compared to healthier patients selected for resection (Meijerink et al., 2018).

Surveillance

After an ablative therapy, surveillance scan (triphasic liver CT or MRI) is typically obtained in 1–3 months after the procedure to evaluate the completeness of the ablation zone and to assess for any missed lesions (Takahashi and Berber, 2020). When a concerning lesion is identified on the surveillance scan, repeat ablation is a feasible option (Takahashi and Berber, 2020). For ongoing cancer surveillance, cross-sectional imaging should be repeated every 3 months along with serial carcinoembryonic antigen (CEA) levels and clinical examination for the first 2 years, and then can be spaced out to every 6 months for up to 5 to 10 years if patients remain without evidence of disease (Puijk et al., 2018; Hof et al., 2016).

Local recurrence rates

After RFA, local recurrence rates have been quoted between 2 and 40 percent, with 5-year survival rates estimated around 14–50 percent (Takahashi and Berber, 2020; Takahashi et al., 2017; Kennedy et al., 2013). Risk factors for local recurrence included tumor size $\geq$ 3m, ablation margin $<$ 0.5 cm, and tumors close to large vasculature due to the heat-sink effect (Petre and Sofocleous, 2017; Takahashi et al., 2017; Shady et al., 2016). Thus, RFA should preferentially be utilized only for CRLM $<$ 3 cm that are distant from large vessels with a goal of a 1 cm ablation margin in order to decrease the risk of local recurrence (Puijk et al., 2018).

Studies evaluating MWA have found lower local recurrence rates compared to RFA and are quoted between 6 and 10 percent (Takahashi et al., 2018; Martin et al., 2010; Groeschl et al., 2014; Leung et al., 2015). While predictors for local recurrence following MWA are similar to RFA, including tumors $>$ 3 cm and ablation margin $<$ 0.5 cm, proximity to large vasculature

TABLE 12.4 Summary of the recent literatures on outcomes in CRLM following RFA or MWA +/− resection

Authors	Year	Patients	Modality	Median follow-up (months)	Median disease-free survival (months)	Median overall survival (months)
(Tinguely et al., 2020)	2020	82	MWA	25.2	–	43.4
(Shady et al., 2016)	2016	162	Percutaneous RFA	55	26	36
(Hof et al., 2016)	2016	261 26 75 69	Resection Open RFA Perc RFA Resection + RFA	38.6	45.5	55.6
(Philips et al., 2016)	2016	100 101	MWA Resection + MWA	–	9.3 10.1	42.2 38.4

was not found to be a significant risk factor because MWA is less susceptible to heat-sink effect (Takahashi et al., 2018; Correa-Gallego et al., 2014; Takahashi et al., 2018).

Long-term outcomes

For patients with unresectable CRLM, the EORTC–CLOCC trial was the first multicenter randomized, prospective trial which found that local treatment with thermal ablation +/− resection along with systemic therapy improved both progression-free and overall survival compared to palliative chemotherapy alone (Ruers et al., 2017; Ruers et al., 2012). This phase II trial included 119 patients with unresectable CRLM ($n < 10$ tumors and without extrahepatic metastasis) from 22 centers from Europe between 2002 and 2007 (Ruers et al., 2017; Ruers et al., 2012). The median progression-free survival in the combined treatment cohort was 16.8 months (95 percent CI = 12.0 to 21.9 months) as compared to 9.9 months (95 percent CI = 9.1 to 12.9 months) in the systemic only arm (Ruers et al., 2012). After a median follow up of 9.7 years, the combined treatment group also had significant improved overall survival (HR= 0.58, CI= 0.38–0.88, $p = 0.01$) compared to those receiving systemic therapy alone (Ruers et al., 2017). The combined treatment cohort had a median overall survival of 45.6 months (95 percent CI = 30.3 to 67.8 months), as compared to 40.5 months (95 percent CI = 27.5 to 47.7 months) in the systemic only cohort (Ruers et al., 2017). The combined treatment cohort had 3-, 5-, and 8- year overall survival rates of 56.9 percent (95 percent CI = 43.3 percent to 68.5 percent), 43.1 percent (95 percent CI = 30.3 percent to 55.3 percent), 35.9 percent (95 percent CI = 23.8 percent to 48.2 percent), respectively, whereas the systemic treatment alone cohort had lower rates of long-term survival at 55.2 percent (95 percent CI = 41.6 percent to 66.9 percent), 30.3 percent (95 percent CI = 19.0 percent to 42.4 percent), and 8.9 percent (95 percent CI = 3.3 percent to 18.1 percent), respectively (Ruers et al., 2017).

A summary of the recent literatures on long-term outcomes in patients with CRLM treated by RFA or MWA with or without concomitant resection is listed in Table 12.4.

Long-term outcomes of the multi-modality treatments

Based on a recent systematic review and meta-analysis, Meijerink et al. concluded that RFA plus systemic chemotherapy was superior to chemotherapy alone and that resection was superior to RFA alone. However, RFA and systemic chemotherapy were not found to be superior to RFA plus resection or to MWA (Meijerink et al., 2018). In separate studies, the oncologic outcomes for patients with CRLM were found to be comparable between ablation and resection (Hof et al., 2016; Karanicolas et al., 2013; Aliyev et al., 2013; Tinguely et al., 2020). However, results from further ongoing prospective studies are needed to demonstrate true superiority of ablation over hepatectomy. With the current low-quality evidence available, hepatectomy remains the standard of care in patients with resectable CRLM

It is important to note that selection criteria tend to be very different for patients considering ablation versus resection. Surgeons may opt for ablation if the intention is to preserve liver parenchyma, to downstage multinodular tumors as part of two-stage operation, or to treat patients who could not tolerate major hepatectomy due to underlying comorbidities or poor performance status (Takahashi and Berber, 2020). Thus, because of these selection biases, studies evaluating the long-term outcomes of ablation versus resection should be interpreted with caution. COLLISON and LAVA trials should be able to provide a better comparison in the future.

The COLLISON and LAVA trials are prospective, randomized trials currently enrolling patients with CRLM to undergo ablation versus resection (Puijk et al., 2018; Gurusamy et al., 2018). The COLLISON trial is a two-arm, single-blind phase-III clinical trial in the Netherlands with an enrollment goal of 318 patients with at least 1 CRLM $\leq$3 cm without extrahepatic disease eligible for both ablation and resection as well as additional lesions that are ablatable or resectable (Puijk et al., 2018). This study is expected to take 13 years, including a 10-year follow-up period (Puijk et al., 2018). The LAVA trial plans to accrue 330 patients in the United Kingdom and Netherlands to demonstrate the non-inferiority of ablation compared to resection (Gurusamy et al., 2018).

Summary points

Ablation should be recommended for patients with small unresectable CRLM. In the EORTC–CLOCC trial, local treatment with thermal ablation +/− resection along with systemic therapy had shown to significantly improve progression-free and overall survival compared to palliative chemotherapy alone in patients with unresectable CRLM

For patients with resectable CRLM, resection remains the standard of care. Although the oncologic outcomes may be comparable between thermal ablation and resection in small solitary CRLM, ongoing trials such as COLLISON and LAVA trials will better clarify their roles.

Ablations are often performed concomitantly with resection to treat multinodular or bilobar disease in order to spare patient the morbidity of two-stage hepatectomy.

More institutions have shifted practice from RFA to MWA in the recent years because MWA has multiple advantages such that MWA requires less time to achieve tumoricidal temperature in the tissue, is less susceptible to the heat-sink effect, allows wider penetration and margin, creates more homogenous tissue heating, does not require grounding pad or cooling system, and are associated with lower local recurrence.

Disclosure statement

The authors have nothing to disclose.

References

Aliyev, S., Agcaoglu, O., Aksoy, E., et al. (Sep 2013). Efficacy of laparoscopic radiofrequency ablation for the treatment of patients with small solitary colorectal liver metastasis. *Surgery, 154*(3), 556–562. http://doi.org/10.1016/j.surg.2013.03.009.

Birsen, O., Aliyev, S., Aksoy, E., et al. (Jun 2014). A critical analysis of postoperative morbidity and mortality after laparoscopic radiofrequency ablation of liver tumors. *Annals of Surgical Oncology, 21*(6), 1834–1840. http://doi.org/10.1245/s10434-014-3526-8.

Correa-Gallego, C., Fong, Y., Gonen, M., et al. (2014). A retrospective comparison of microwave ablation vs. radiofrequency ablation for colorectal cancer hepatic metastases. *Annals of Surgical Oncology, 21*(13), 4278–4283. Dec http://doi.org/10.1245/s10434-014-3817-0.

Eltawil, K. M., Boame, N., Mimeault, R., et al. (2014). Patterns of recurrence following selective intraoperative radiofrequency ablation as an adjunct to hepatic resection for colorectal liver metastases. *Journal of Surgical Oncology, 110*(6), 734–738. Nov http://doi.org/10.1002/jso.23689.

Faitot, F., Faron, M., Adam, R., et al. (2014). Two-stage hepatectomy versus 1-stage resection combined with radiofrequency for bilobar colorectal metastases: a case-matched analysis of surgical and oncological outcomes. *Annals of Surgery, 260*(5), 822–827. Nov. discussion 827-8. http://doi.org/10.1097/SLA.0000000000000976.

Fong, Y., Fortner, J., Sun, R. L., Brennan, M. F., & Blumgart, L. H. (1999). Clinical score for predicting recurrence after hepatic resection for metastatic colorectal cancer: analysis of 1001 consecutive cases. *Annals of Surgery, 230*(3), 309–318. Sepdiscussion 318-21 http://doi.org/10.1097/00000658-199909000-00004.

Gillams, A., Goldberg, N., Ahmed, M., et al. (2015). Thermal ablation of colorectal liver metastases: a position paper by an international panel of ablation experts, The Interventional Oncology Sans Frontieres meeting 2013. *European Radiology, 25*(12), 3438–3454. Dec http://doi.org/10.1007/s00330-015-3779-z.

Groeschl, R. T., Pilgrim, C. H., Hanna, E. M., et al. (2014). Microwave ablation for hepatic malignancies: a multiinstitutional analysis. *Annals of Surgery, 259*(6), 1195–1200. Jun http://doi.org/10.1097/SLA.0000000000000234.

Gurusamy, K., Corrigan, N., Croft, J., et al. (2018). Liver resection surgery versus thermal ablation for colorectal LiVer MetAstases (LAVA): study protocol for a randomised controlled trial. *Trials, 19*(1), 105. Feb 13 http://doi.org/10.1186/s13063-018-2499-5.

Hof, J., Wertenbroek, M. W., Peeters, P. M., Widder, J., Sieders, E., & de Jong, K. P. (2016). Outcomes after resection and/or radiofrequency ablation for recurrence after treatment of colorectal liver metastases. *British Journal of Surgery, 103*(8), 1055–1062. Jul http://doi.org/10.1002/bjs.10162.

Karanicolas, P. J., Jarnagin, W. R., Gonen, M., et al. (2013). Long-term outcomes following tumor ablation for treatment of bilateral colorectal liver metastases. *JAMA Surgery, 148*(7), 597–601. Jul http://doi.org/10.1001/jamasurg.2013.1431.

Kennedy, T. J., Cassera, M. A., Khajanchee, Y. S., Diwan, T. S., Hammill, C. W., & Hansen, P. D. (2013). Laparoscopic radiofrequency ablation for the management of colorectal liver metastases: 10-year experience. *Journal of Surgical Oncology, 107*(4), 324–328. Mar http://doi.org/10.1002/jso.23268.

Leung, U., Kuk, D., D'Angelica, M. I., et al. (2015). Long-term outcomes following microwave ablation for liver malignancies. *British Journal of Surgery, 102*(1), 85–91. Jan http://doi.org/10.1002/bjs.9649.

Martin, R. C., Scoggins, C. R., & McMasters, K. M. (2007). Microwave hepatic ablation: initial experience of safety and efficacy. *Journal of Surgical Oncology, 96*(6), 481–486. Nov 1 http://doi.org/10.1002/jso.20750.

Martin, R. C., Scoggins, C. R., & McMasters, K. M. (2010). Safety and efficacy of microwave ablation of hepatic tumors: a prospective review of a 5-year experience. *Annals of Surgical Oncology, 17*(1), 171–178. Jan http://doi.org/10.1245/s10434-009-0686-z.

Meijerink, M. R., Puijk, R. S., van Tilborg, A., et al. (2018). Radiofrequency and Microwave Ablation Compared to Systemic Chemotherapy and to Partial Hepatectomy in the Treatment of Colorectal Liver Metastases: a Systematic Review and Meta-Analysis. *Cardiovascular and Interventional Radiology, 41*(8), 1189–1204. Aug http://doi.org/10.1007/s00270-018-1959-3.

Mulier, S., Mulier, P., Ni, Y., et al. (2002). Complications of radiofrequency coagulation of liver tumours. *British Journal of Surgery, 89*(10), 1206–1222. Oct http://doi.org/10.1046/j.1365-2168.2002.02168.x.

Petre, E. N., & Sofocleous, C. (2017). Thermal Ablation in the Management of Colorectal Cancer Patients with Oligometastatic Liver Disease. *Visc Med, 33*(1), 62–68. Mar http://doi.org/10.1159/000454697.

Philips, P., Groeschl, R. T., Hanna, E. M., et al. (2016). Single-stage resection and microwave ablation for bilobar colorectal liver metastases. *British Journal of Surgery, 103*(8), 1048–1054. Jul http://doi.org/10.1002/bjs.10159.

Pillai, K., Akhter, J., Chua, T. C., et al. (2015). Heat sink effect on tumor ablation characteristics as observed in monopolar radiofrequency, bipolar radiofrequency, and microwave, using ex vivo calf liver model. *Medicine, 94*(9), e580. Mar http://doi.org/10.1097/MD.0000000000000580.

Puijk, R. S., Ruarus, A. H., Vroomen, L., et al. (2018). Colorectal liver metastases: surgery versus thermal ablation (COLLISION) - a phase III single-blind prospective randomized controlled trial. *BMC cancer, 18*(1), 821. Aug 15 http://doi.org/10.1186/s12885-018-4716-8.

Rhim, H., Lim, H. K., Kim, Y. S., Choi, D., & Lee, W. J. (2008). Radiofrequency ablation of hepatic tumors: lessons learned from 3000 procedures. *Journal of Gastroenterology and Hepatology, 23*(10), 1492–1500. Oct http://doi.org/10.1111/j.1440-1746.2008.05550.x.

Ruers, T., Punt, C., Van Coevorden, F., et al. (2012). Radiofrequency ablation combined with systemic treatment versus systemic treatment alone in patients with non-resectable colorectal liver metastases: a randomized EORTC Intergroup phase II study (EORTC 40004). *Annals of oncology: official journal of the European Society for Medical Oncology /ESMO, 23*(10), 2619–2626. Oct http://doi.org/10.1093/annonc/mds053.

Ruers, T., Van Coevorden, F., Punt, C. J., et al. (2017). Local Treatment of Unresectable Colorectal Liver Metastases: results of a Randomized Phase II Trial. *JNCI: Journal of the National Cancer Institute, 109*(9). Sep 1 http://doi.org/10.1093/jnci/djx015.

Shady, W., Petre, E. N., Gonen, M., et al. (2016). Percutaneous Radiofrequency Ablation of Colorectal Cancer Liver Metastases: factors Affecting Outcomes–A 10-year Experience at a Single Center. *Radiology, 278*(2), 601–612. Feb http://doi.org/10.1148/radiol.2015142489.

Siegel, R. L., Miller, K. D., Goding, S. A., et al. (2020). Colorectal cancer statistics, 2020. *CA: A Cancer Journal for Clinicians, 70*(3), 145–164. May http://doi.org/10.3322/caac.21601.

Sietses, C., Meijerink, M. R., Meijer, S., & van den Tol, M. P. (2010). The impact of intraoperative ultrasonography on the surgical treatment of patients with colorectal liver metastases. *Surgical Endoscopy, 24*(8), 1917–1922. Aug http://doi.org/10.1007/s00464-009-0874-8.

Takahashi, H., Akyuz, M., Aksoy, E., Karabulut, K., & Berber, E. (2017). Local recurrence after laparoscopic radiofrequency ablation of malignant liver tumors: results of a contemporary series. *Journal of Surgical Oncology, 115*(7), 830–834. Jun http://doi.org/10.1002/jso.24599.

Takahashi, H., Akyuz, M., Kahramangil, B., et al. (2018). A Comparison of the Initial Cost Associated With Resection Versus Laparoscopic Radiofrequency Ablation of Small Solitary Colorectal Liver Metastasis. *Surgical Laparoscopy, Endoscopy & Percutaneous Techniques, 28*(6), 371–374. Dec http://doi.org/10.1097/SLE.0000000000000577.

Takahashi, H., & Berber, E. (2020). Role of thermal ablation in the management of colorectal liver metastasis. *Hepatobiliary Surg Nutr, 9*(1), 49–58. Feb http://doi.org/10.21037/hbsn.2019.06.08.

Takahashi, H., Kahramangil, B., & Berber, E. (2018). Local recurrence after microwave thermosphere ablation of malignant liver tumors: results of a surgical series. *Surgery, 163*(4), 709–713. Apr http://doi.org/10.1016/j.surg.2017.10.026.

Takahashi, H., Kahramangil, B., Kose, E., & Berber, E. (2018). A comparison of microwave thermosphere versus radiofrequency thermal ablation in the treatment of colorectal liver metastases. *HPB: the official journal of the International Hepato Pancreato Biliary Association, 20*(12), 1157–1162. Dec http://doi.org/10.1016/j.hpb.2018.05.012.

Tinguely, P., Dal, G., Bottai, M., Nilsson, H., Freedman, J., & Engstrand, J. (2020). Microwave ablation versus resection for colorectal cancer liver metastases - A propensity score analysis from a population-based nationwide registry. *European journal of surgical oncology: the journal of the European Society of Surgical Oncology and the British Association of Surgical Oncology, 46*(3), 476–485. Mar http://doi.org/10.1016/j.ejso.2019.12.002.

Wells, S. A., Hinshaw, J. L., Lubner, M. G., Ziemlewicz, T. J., Brace, C. L., & Lee, F. T., Jr. (2015). Liver Ablation: best Practice. *Radiologic Clinics of North America, 53*(5), 933–971. Sep http://doi.org/10.1016/j.rcl.2015.05.012.

Wong, S. L., Mangu, P. B., Choti, M. A., et al. (2010). American Society of Clinical Oncology 2009 clinical evidence review on radiofrequency ablation of hepatic metastases from colorectal cancer. *Journal of clinical oncology: official journal of the American Society of Clinical Oncology, 28*(3), 493–508. Jan 20 http://doi.org/10.1200/JCO.2009.23.4450.

CHAPTER

13

Locoregional approaches to colorectal liver metastasis – intra-arterial

David G. Brauer and Michael I D'Angelica

Memorial Sloan Kettering Cancer Center, New York, NY, United States

Introduction

Colorectal liver metastases (CRLM) represent advanced disease, although significant improvements in survival have been possible through developments in both systemic and locoregional therapies. The liver-directed therapy that is the treatment of choice, when possible, is complete resection, the details and benefits of which are covered elsewhere in this text. Progressive or recurrent hepatic disease is the cause of death in most patients with CRLM and, unfortunately, more than 75 percent of patients with CRLM present with unresectable hepatic disease at the time of diagnosis (Creasy et al., 2018; Engstrand, Nilsson, Stromberg, Jonas, & Freedman, 2018). Common reasons for unresectable hepatic disease include involvement of vital structures, inadequate future liver remnant, or an extensive burden of bilobar disease. Other reasons such as the patient's functional status or inability to tolerate a hepatic resection are equally important. Patients able to undergo complete resection of their disease have significantly greater overall survival and are potentially cured, emphasizing the importance of identifying treatment modalities that can make surgery possible or otherwise treat or palliate hepatic disease (Creasy et al., 2018). Several locoregional liver-directed therapies have been developed and serve as adjuncts to hepatic resection or alternatives when hepatic resection is not possible.

Certain liver-directed therapies utilize intraarterial strategies to treat regionally confined disease. These approaches take advantage of the rich and duplicate blood supply of the liver and include transarterial embolization (TAE), transarterial chemoembolization (TACE), transarterial radioembolization (TARE), and hepatic artery infusion chemotherapy (HAIC). The hepatic parenchyma has a dual blood supply from the hepatic artery and the portal vein, although the majority of the blood supply comes from the portal venous circulation.

Contemporary Management of Metastatic Colorectal Cancer: A Precision Medicine Approach
DOI: https://doi.org/10.1016/B978-0-323-91706-3.00009-6

CRLM derive their blood supply predominantly from the arterial circulation, as do most malignant liver tumors, making intra-arterial therapies applicable to a broad range of liver malignancies. Segall in 1923 identified this arterial predominance in two autopsy specimens of liver metastases (Segall, 1923). Despite this historic observation, the exact mechanism of this arterial predominance is unclear. For CRLM, the presumed route of spread from the primary tumor to the liver is by hematogenous spread through the portal venous circulation. Whether lymphatic spread is a necessary intermediate in the development of colorectal liver metastases is debated and beyond the scope of this text. Once the tumor has established itself in the liver, the tumor develops an arterial predominance by locally invading and eventually obliterating the veins, an observation made in the 1950s that is still commonly accepted (Breedis and Young, 1954). Angiogenesis – or, more specifically, arteriogenesis – also plays a significant role in increasing the degree of arterial inflow to a tumor (Carmeliet, 2000; Hanahan and Folkman, 1996). This arterial predominance set the stage for the targeted delivery of therapies through the hepatic arterial system directly to the tumor(s), with relative sparing of the normal hepatic parenchyma.

Particularly relevant to the delivery of intraarterial therapies is a thorough understanding of hepatic arterial anatomy, as variant anatomy is quite common. Conventional hepatic arterial anatomy, in which the left and right hepatic arteries arise from the proper hepatic artery off the common hepatic artery and celiac axis, occurs in up to 80 percent of patients. The most common variants, with incidences of 10 percent or more each, include a replaced right hepatic artery arising from the superior mesenteric artery or a replaced left hepatic artery arising from the left gastric artery. These variants can occur simultaneously, as can a number of other variants with myriad different branching patterns (Noussios et al., 2017). Extrahepatic collateral arteries to either the normal hepatic circulation or from neovascularization by a tumor (e.g., phrenic arteries) must also be considered, although these are more common in hepatocellular carcinoma than with CRLM (Kim et al., 2005; Moustafa et al., 2017).

Here we will review the indications for and data supporting four intra-arterial liver-directed therapies: TAE, TACE, TARE and HAIC. TACE and TAE will be grouped together as embolic therapies.

Embolic therapies

TAE and TACE rely on the principle of vascular occlusion to induce tumor necrosis. Vascular occlusion by surgical arterial ligation was initially proposed by Markowitz after his findings of arterial-predominant flow in tumors and a now-infamous case report of accidental hepatic artery ligation that resulted in marked necrosis of a metastatic liver tumor relative to the surrounding parenchyma (Mori et al., 1966). Operative hepatic artery ligation was subsequently introduced as a therapeutic option but was only performed in cases of extensive tumor burden where no other surgical or systemic options were possible. Over time, TAE was ultimately able to be performed using percutaneous access and embolization, and a transition was made from embolizing proximally at the proper hepatic artery to embolizing more selectively in distal hepatic artery branches closer to the tumor (Chuang and Wallace, 1981). Common vascular occlusive agents include Gelfoam® (Pfizer, New York, NY), coils, alcohol, and microspheres. Recanalization or neovascularization occurs over time with any of these agents, so multiple interventions may be needed over time.

TACE is an extension of TAE that involves the catheter-based delivery of a single dose of chemotherapy to selective arteries supplying a tumor followed by embolization. The embolization serves to (1) induce cell death as with TAE and (2) reduce or eliminate blood flow to reduce the washout of the delivered chemotherapy, theoretically prolonging the exposure of the tumor to the delivered chemotherapy. An additional advancement in prolonging the effect of arterially-delivered chemotherapy has been the introduction of different carrier particles such as drug eluting beads (DEB). These were proposed to increase the half-life of local chemotherapy by over 1,000 times (Lewis et al., 2006). However, a recent review suggested that the half-life of the chemotherapy component of TACE is limited to a few hours or less (Richardson et al., 2013).

Contraindications to embolic therapies include pre-procedural vascular abnormalities such as hepatic artery thrombosis, portal vein thrombosis, extensive hepatic replacement with tumor, extrahepatic collateral arterial supply that cannot safely be accessed, and biliary strictures.

Complications of TAE or TACE include non-target embolization of adjacent organs and post-embolization syndrome. Non-target embolization can be iatrogenic (from mistakes in catheter placement or medication delivery) or from pre-existing or tumor-induced intrahepatic vascular shunts. The gallbladder, duodenum, stomach, and lungs can be easily affected by inadvertent embolization or after distribution of embolization material. This can lead to off-target ischemic complications such as cholecystitis, pancreatitis, gastrointestinal bleeding, gastrointestinal perforations, or pulmonary complications. Pre-treatment arteriograms – either before the procedure or at the beginning of the procedure prior to drug delivery – are necessary to confirm that the proposed treatment area excludes off-target organs. Postembolization syndrome is a common outcome following TAE or TACE. It occurs in up to 90 percent of patients and is characterized by fever, abdominal pain, nausea, vomiting, and leukocytosis. When severe, this is an indication for inpatient observation following embolization, although embolization can be done as an outpatient procedure if symptoms are minimal. Increased incidence of postembolization syndrome has been seen with higher doses of administered chemotherapy (Leung et al., 2001). More significant but less common adverse events following TAE or TACE include liver failure (incidence between 3 and 5 percent, with a lower incidence in patients with CRLM than in patients with primary hepatic malignancies likely related to lower rates of underlying liver disease), hepatic abscess (1–2 percent, more common with a prior bilio-enteric anastomosis), contrast-induced kidney injury (3–10 percent), and mortality (0–4 percent) (Gaba et al., 2017).

Indications and outcomes

Early reports and trials

Although TAE or TACE are technically feasible in most clinical scenarios, particularly in cases of unresectable disease not amenable to other therapies, the indications must be considered in the context of the data supporting the effectiveness of these interventions. The role of TAE and TACE in the treatment of CRLM is largely historic, owing to limited efficacy relative to modern systemic chemotherapy. One of the earliest case series of TAE was reported by the MD Anderson Cancer Center in the 1970s. Of 47 patients treated with TAE for liver tumors, 19 had CRLM. Response rates were as high as 90 percent in this cohort and subsequent reports from this group, and median overall survival (OS) from the time of TAE in this cohort was 11.5 months. However, the response rates reported predate the use of cross-sectional imaging to more accurately measure tumor volume and assess response, and there was heterogeneity within the group between proximal and distal embolization. In 1990, a group of 22 patients undergoing proximal hepatic artery embolization was reported within the context of a clinical trial. Response rates were not reported, but median OS in the TAE group was 7 months, similar to the 7.9 month median OS in a control arm consisting of 20 untreated patients (Hunt et al., 1990). A 1994 trial compared TAE and TACE by randomizing 24 patients to either TAE with polyvinyl alcohol or TACE with 5-FU and alpha- 2a-interferon (Martinelli et al., 1994). Results were pooled between the two interventions, but more patients progressed ($n = 7$) than responded ($n = 6$) in the combined analysis. Median OS was 9 months.

TACE versus systemic chemotherapy

A 2012 phase III trial from multiple institutions in Italy randomized 74 patients with unresectable CRLM to either systemic chemotherapy (fluorouracil, leucovorin, and irinotecan - FOLFIRI) or DEB-TACE with irinotecan (DEBIRI) (Fiorentini et al., 2012). All patients had their primary tumor resected and received adjuvant systemic chemotherapy after primary resection prior to enrollment. Hepatic response was observed in 69 percent of patients in the DEBIRI group and only 20 percent in the FOLFIRI group. Median PFS was longer in the DEBIRI group (7 months vs 4 months; $p = 0.006$) and median OS was longer in the DEBIRI group (22 months vs 15 months; $p = 0.031$). All patients experienced extrahepatic progression by the end of the study (median follow-up 50 months). Toxicities in the DEBIRI group included LFT elevations and fever and were much lower than toxicities in the systemic treatment group. No patients in the DEBIRI group experienced dose reductions or delays in treatments, and patients in the DEBIRI group had a longer time before quality of life decline (8 months vs 3 months; $p < 0.001$).

Systemic chemotherapy with or without TACE

A 2015 multi-institutional trial from the Americas randomized 69 patients to either systemic chemotherapy with FOLFOX and bevacizumab or FOLFOX, bevacizumab, and DEBIRI (FOLFOX-DEBIRI) in the first-line setting in patients with CRLM (Martin et al., 2015). Significant adverse events were more than three times higher in the FOLFOX-DEBIRI group largely due to complications of TACE including symptoms of postembolization syndrome requiring hospitalization. Response rates were significantly higher in the FOLFOX-DEBIRI group at 2 months (98 percent vs 82 percent), but these responses were not durable. Hepatic PFS was greater in the FOLFOX-DEBIRI group, 17 months vs 12 months ($p = 0.05$), with no differences in extrahepatic progression-free survival.

A recent trial of TACE randomized 168 patients with CRLM progressive on first-line systemic therapy at a single center in China to either systemic therapy alone (FOLFOX or FOLFIRI, with or without cetuximab or bevacizumab) or systemic therapy with TACE using an emulsion of raltitrexed (a thymidylate synthase inhibitor), oxaliplatin, and irinotecan (Liu et al., 2021). Median follow-up was short at 12 months. There was no difference in response rate between the groups. Patients in the TACE arm had longer PFS (6.7 months vs 3.8 months; $p = 0.009$) but similar OS (18.4 months vs 14.8 months; $p = 0.7$). A similar percentage of patients were able to undergo surgery in each arm (17 percent in the entire cohort), however, all of these resected patients ultimately developed hepatic and pulmonary recurrences in follow-up (median disease-free postoperative survival 7 months). Rates and sites of recurrences were not different between the groups. Adverse events were not compared between groups, although overall rates of Common Terminology Criteria for Adverse Events (CTCAE) grade 3 or higher toxicities were <10 percent overall.

Summary of embolic therapies

Currently there is little role for embolic arterially-directed therapies in the management of CRLM. Modern data does not support the routine use of TAE or TACE in this disease. Randomized trials evaluating these therapies have been underpowered with substantial heterogeneity, particularly for adjuvant chemotherapy reigmens, as well as methodologic flaws that complicate their interpretation. Further, they have failed to show convincing evidence for durable clinical benefit outside of select reports. As such, TAE and TACE are not recommended treatment modalities for CRLM in evidence-based guidelines such as those from the National Comprehensive Cancer Network.

Transarterial radioembolization (TARE)

A distinct arterially-directed therapy is TARE. This involves the delivery of a radioactive isotope – most commonly yttrium-90 ("Y-90") – for localized radiation treatment to a tumor. Similar to TACE, TARE is used in cases of unresectable liver tumors in patients with adequate hepatic function. Additional details and data for this approach are covered in-depth in a separate chapter in this text on radiation approaches (Chapter 14), but will be reviewed here briefly. A combined analysis of three multi-institutional randomized trials comparing systemic chemotherapy to systemic chemotherapy with TARE in the first-line setting for colorectal cancer with synchronous CRLM was published in 2017 (Wasan et al., 2017). After a median follow-up of 43 months, there was no significant difference in overall survival between the groups: median survival 23 months in the TARE arm and 22 months in the no TARE arm ($p = 0.61$). Serious adverse events of any grade were higher in the TARE arm, 54 percent vs 43 percent. Similar findings were seen using TARE as second-line therapy in the EPOCH trial (Mulcahy et al., 2021). Four hundred twenty-eight patients with CRLM who progressed on systemic oxaliplatin or irinotecan-based chemotherapy were randomized to second-line chemotherapy of choice with or without TARE. PFS and hepatic PFS (hPFS) were both reported as significantly longer in the TARE arm, but the absolute differences were modest: 8 months vs 7.2 months for PFS ($p = 0.001$) and 9.1 months vs 7.2 months for hPFS ($p < 0.001$). Response rates in the TARE arm were 34 percent versus 21 percent in the chemotherapy-alone arm. Median overall survival was no different between the groups, 14.4 months vs 14 months ($p = 0.7$). Grade 3 adverse events were higher in the TARE arm, 68 percent vs 49 percent. In summary, the randomized data shows no survival benefit along with increased harm using

TARE over systemic chemotherapy in either the first-line or second-line, suggesting that TARE is not an effective treatment strategy for CRLM

TARE was compared to TACE and DEB-TACE in a meta-analysis of 23 prospective studies of arterial therapies for CRLM (Levy et al., 2018). Similar response rates were observed for all approaches (23 – 36 percent). TARE was associated with significantly lower one-year overall survival (41 percent compared to 70 percent for TACE and 80 percent for DEB-TACE), although heterogeneity across studies precluded definitive conclusions on superiority or inferiority of any one approach.

Hepatic artery infusion chemotherapy (HAIC)

Intra-arterial infusion of chemotherapy to a tumor was first reported in 1950, again inspired from clinical observations stemming from an accident, this time the inadvertent infusion of the nitrogen mustard HN-2 into the brachial artery of a patient with Hodgkin's lymphoma (Klopp et al., 1950). Over the following decades, a number of case reports described high response rates using various cytotoxic drugs for a wide range of pathologies including CRLM. A comprehensive review of competing arterially-delivered drugs for CRLM published in the 1980s determined that, among the many agents being used at the time, only 5-fluorouracil (5-FU) had the desirable properties of (1) rapid hepatic clearance so that systemic toxicity is not reached, which allows for more concentrated drug dosing than could be tolerated systemically, and (2) response rates exceeding those for systemic therapy alone for hepatic tumors at the time. Subsequent work by Ensminger and colleagues determined that the fluoropyrimidine 5-Fluoro-2'-deoxyuridine (FUDR) had even more favorable pharmacokinetics than 5-FU, and FUDR has remained the mainstay of hepatic artery infusion (Chen and Gross, 1980; Ensminger et al., 1978; Ensminger and Gyves, 1983).

HAIC requires the insertion of infusion catheters into the hepatic artery, either surgically or percutaneously. If performed surgically, a catheter is placed directly into a branch of the hepatic artery (most commonly the gastroduodenal artery) and is connected to a subcutaneous infusion pump, allowing for continuous infusion of chemotherapy. If administered percutaneously, a catheter is advanced from an access point to the target vessel and can be used for a single infusion or is similarly connected to a subcutaneous infusion port (not pump) that allows for intermittent administration of bolus chemotherapy. As compared to TACE, HAIC allows for more frequent or continuous administration of chemotherapy to the target lesions. Early descriptions of HAIC utilized chemotherapy infusion through percutaneous arterial catheters, first described in 1970 by a team from the Lahey Clinic (Watkins et al., 1970). At the time, infusion catheters were fraught with complications including extra-vascular leaking, clotting, and infectious complications, leading to the implementation of the subcutaneous hepatic artery infusion pump (HAIP). The HAIP was first intended for continuous infusion of heparin for patients requiring systemic anticoagulation and was incorporated into the treatment of liver tumors by a group from the University of Minnesota (Buchwald et al., 1980). This first case series included 5 patients: one pump was nonfunctional and was removed within 24 h, but the other patients received an average of four months of FUDR without any pump-related complications.

HAIP: function and insertion

This section will focus largely on HAIC via HAIP, although catheter-based HAIC will also be discussed. At present, the Intera 3000 (Intera Oncology, Boston, MA) HAIP is the only FDA-approved device for the infusion of FUDR into the hepatic artery. This pump had previously been called the Codman® 3000 pump (Johnson and Johnson, New Brunswick, NJ). Other infusion pumps repurposed for HAIC include the SynchroMed™ II intrathecal pump from Medtronic (Minneapolis, MN). The Intera pump is made of titanium and uses an internal chamber of a body-heat-activated propellant to exert force on a second internal chamber containing the instilled chemotherapy. The chemotherapy passes through a filter and flow-restrictor before exiting through the catheter. This system ensures a constant pressure and flow rate and is not reliant on batteries or motors, allowing for life-long use. The flow rate is preset and can be affected by body temperature and altitude, and dosing adjustments may be necessary depending on how these variables affect the intended dose as calculated from the flow rate and concentration of chemotherapy administered. The reservoir holds 30ml and must be refilled every two weeks to maintain catheter patency. If a patient is off treatment, glycerin can be instilled and can extend the necessary refill time to 8 weeks while maintaining catheter patency.

HAIPs have traditionally been placed surgically via laparotomy, although minimally invasive approaches are now commonly used (Qadan et al., 2017). A CT angiogram is obtained preoperatively to delineate hepatic arterial anatomy. In the case of normal hepatic arterial anatomy, the gastroduodenal artery (GDA) is dissected, ligated distally, and an arteriotomy is made through which the catheter is advanced and secured in the proximal GDA at the takeoff from the hepatic artery. Arterial branches from the GDA and hepatic artery within 2 cm of the GDA origin are ligated to eliminate potential chemotherapy infusion to nearby organs such as the stomach, duodenum, and pancreas. After the catheter is inserted, methylene blue is injected to evaluate for extrahepatic perfusion. If extrahepatic blue dye is identified, contributing branches are ligated. For variant arterial anatomy, the best strategy remains to place the catheter in the GDA and ligate accessory/replaced hepatic arteries; strategies for other arterial variants are beyond the scope of this review. The pump is positioned subcutaneously, frequently in the left lateral abdominal wall between the ribs and the anterior superior iliac spine, and is secured at the level of the fascia. A postoperative Technecium-99m labeled albumin HAIP perfusion study is performed to assess for extrahepatic perfusion, and additional extrahepatic perfusion can be addressed through embolization using percutaneous interventional techniques. For further detail regarding technique, including pre-procedure planning and postoperative management, we recommend additional reading (Thiels and D'Angelica, 2020) as well as studying protocols from the trials and series cited in this chapter.

Pump insertion is an invasive procedure and can be the source of treatment-related complications. The Memorial Sloan Kettering Cancer Center (MSKCC) experience of 544 consecutive HAIP placements was published in 2005 (Allen et al., 2005). The overall rate of pump complications was 22 percent. Complication rates were higher when the pump was placed in an artery other than the gastroduodenal artery. Complications decreased over time and with higher surgeon volume. The majority of complications were arterial, including thrombosis or extrahepatic perfusion. Sixteen percent of all complications were related to the pump pocket (surgical site infection, pump migration, etc.) and 26 percent were catheter-related (occlusion, dislodgement, or erosion). Of note, this series reported cases through 2001 and less than 20 percent of this cohort used the current pump technology. A more recent series reported a 10 percent complication rate associated with HAIP placement and function, and most pump complications were able to be remedied with an intervention and same-day discharge (Buisman et al., 2019).

Indications, contraindications, and other complications

Indications for HAIC have expanded since the earliest reports in the 1980s and 1990s, when it was initially used as a salvage therapy for patients with unresectable CRLM with unresponsive or progressive disease on systemic chemotherapy. HAIC now plays a role alongside resection, ablation, and systemic chemotherapy for patients with CRLM. Specific indications described in detail in this chapter include unresectable CRLM, converting unresectable patients to resectable disease, and as adjuvant therapy.

There are various contraindications to HAIC, some absolute and others relative. High tumor burden (>70 percent of hepatic parenchyma replaced by tumor), inadequate baseline liver function, or vascular abnormalities (portal hypertension, portal vein thrombus, or hepatic artery occlusion) are generally considered absolute contraindications. The lack of an identifiable target vessel to insert the catheter into is also a contraindication, although vascular grafts can address this barrier. Patients must be able to tolerate general anesthesia if the HAIC is to be placed surgically.

A frequent long-term adverse event of HAIP chemotherapy is biliary sclerosis. The incidence of biliary sclerosis is 5.5 percent after HAIP insertion combined with hepatectomy and 2 percent in cases of unresectable disease with HAIP insertion alone, and is associated with abnormal postoperative flow scans, postoperative infections, and higher doses of HAIC (Ito et al., 2012). Surveillance of liver function tests and adjustments to HAIC dosing is performed by medical oncologists while a patient is on HAIC to monitor for biliary sclerosis and hepatic toxicity.

Unresectable disease

Initial case series and, eventually, randomized trials of HAIC versus systemic chemotherapy for CRLM were published from several institutions from the 1980s to the early 2000s. A meta-analysis of 10 randomized trials through 2006 included over 1,200 patients and reported significant improvements in response rate with HAIC versus systemic chemotherapy (43 percent vs 18 percent, $p < 0.001$) and a non-significant difference in median OS (16 months vs 12 months, $p = 0.24$) (Table 13.1) (Mocellin et al., 2007). Due to this modest and non-significant survival difference, this meta-analysis suggested this was "the end of an era" for HAIC as a sole therapy for CRLM. Although meta-analyses attempt to control for heterogeneity across studies, the HAIC studies to date had heterogeneity that could not be easily accounted for using statistical methods, including variations in HAIC and systemic chemotherapy regimens, crossover, and the inclusion of both pump-based and catheter-based HAIC. One of the included trials, the multi-institutional CALGB 9481 trial from 2006, is often cited as the standard for comparing HAIC with systemic therapy. One hundred and thirty-five patients were randomized to either HAIC with FUDR or systemic 5-FU and leucovorin,

TABLE 13.1 Summary of multiple cohort and randomized trials of hepatic artery infusion chemotherapy published thorugh 2006.

			Hepatic artery infusion		Systemic	
Reference	n	Crossover allowed	Drug	Response rate (percent)	Drug	Response rate (percent)
Chang et al. (1987)	64	No	FUDR	62	FUDR	17
Kemeny et al. (1987)	99	Yes	FUDR	53	FUDR	21
Hohn et al. (1989)	143	Yes	FUDR	42	FUDR	9
Martin et al. (1990)	74	No	FUDR	48	FU	21
Wagman et al. (1990)	41	Yes	FUDR	55	FU	20
Rougier et al. (1992)	163	No	FUDR	41	FU	9
Allen-Mersh et al. (1994)	100	No	FUDR	NR	FU or best supportive care	NR
Lorenz and Müller (2000)	168	Yes	FUDR or FU/ leucovorin	44	FU/leucovorin	27
Kerr et al. (2003)	290	No	FU/leucovorin	22	FU/leucovorin	19
Kemeny et al. (2006)	135	No	FUDR	47	FU/leucovorin	24

with no crossover allowed (N. E. Kemeny et al., 2006). The HAIC group had significantly greater response rates (47 percent vs 24 percent, $p = 0.012$), longer time to hepatic progression (9.8 months vs 7.3 months, $p = 0.034$) and longer overall survival (median 24.4 months vs 20 months, $p = 0.003$). Patients in the HAIC arm had lower rates of neutropenia, diarrhea, and stomatitis, although they did experience bilirubin elevations and some required biliary drainage for biliary sclerosis as a result of HAIC. Criticisms of this trial include a modest survival difference and no difference in the time to disease progression (hepatic or extrahepatic), along with a substantial rate of early extrahepatic recurrence in the HAIC group. Additionally, the systemic regimen used is no longer the standard of care. These limitations were addressed in studies already underway at the time of publication in which HAIC was combined with systemic chemotherapy.

A phase I study published by Dr Nancy Kemeny and colleagues from MSKCC showed safety when combining HAIC with either systemic 5-FU or irinotecan (Nancy Kemeny et al., 1993). Despite enrolled patients having already received systemic fluorouracil, response rates with HAIC fluoropyrimidine therapy were as high as 77 percent, prompting further studies of this combined approach. A number of further early phase prospective trials have been reported demonstrating response rates of up to 90 percent in the first line and 50 to 75 percent in the second line setting (N Kemeny et al., 2001; Pak et al., 2018). No subsequent randomized trials with comparisons to modern systemic chemotherapy have been reported.

The excellent response rate with HAIC despite prior systemic chemotherapy represents a significant treatment option for patients with disease that is progressing despite failure of multiple lines of systemic chemotherapy. A case series from MSKCC published in 2016 highlighted 110 patients with progression on at least three systemic agents: fluorouracil, oxaliplatin, and irinotecan. Patients with liver-only disease had a response rate of 33 percent and median overall survival of 20 months, an impressive outcome for patients with chemo-refractory disease (Cercek et al., 2016).

Converting patients to resectable disease

Noting the above response rates, HAIC has been implemented as a treatment modality to convert patients with CRLM from unresectable to resectable liver disease. This approach has the therapeutic goal of achieving complete responses or reducing the size of tumors allowing for resection based on adequate future liver remnant or by improving the relationship of tumors to vital structures to allow for an adequate margin of resection and/or ablation. A phase I study from MSKCC published in 2009 reported on 49 patients with unresectable CRLM treated with HAIC with FUDR combined with systemic chemotherapy (N. E. Kemeny et al., 2009). Response rate were 92 percent, and 47 percent were able to undergo complete resection. Higher rates of conversion to resection were seen in females and chemotherapy-naïve patients; other clinical variables such as tumor number, size, and distribution were not associated with conversion. Median disease-free survival in the subset of patients who underwent resection was 8 months. A subsequent phase 2 trial of 64 patients with unresectable CRLM treated with HAIP at MSKCC showed a 73 percent response rate and a 52 percent conversion rate to surgery, with conversion being the only identifiable variable associated with improved PFS and OS (Pak et al., 2018). Of patients alive at one year after enrollment, median overall survival was not reached for patients undergoing resection compared to median overall survival of 18 months for patients who did not convert within a year. Median overall survival was significantly longer for patients who were chemotherapy-naïve on enrollment compared to previously-treated patients, 78 months vs 30 months ($p = 0.02$). Nine patients (8 resected) appeared to be cured of their disease being free of any recurrence for approximately 5 years since their last intervention, highlighting the curative potential of resection using this approach.

Although HAIC through a HAIP is the most frequent route of administration reported, protocols including hepatic artery infusion catheters and non-FUDR-based infusion chemotherapies have been reported. A small retrospective cohort study from France utilized an arterial infusion of oxaliplatin, leucovorin, and fluorouracil every two weeks through a percutaneous catheter (Allard et al., 2015). Eighteen patients were converted to resection, with 33 percent exhibiting pathologic complete response compared to 10 percent in a matched cohort of patients receiving only systemic chemotherapy ($p = 0.03$). The OPTILIV trial, also from France, treated 64 patients with catheter infusion of irinotecan, oxaliplatin, and 5-FU, along with systemic cetuximab (Lévi et al., 2016). Response rate was 41 percent, with 30 percent of patients converting to resection. Resected patients had significantly longer disease-free survival, 16 months vs 9 months. Overall, response rates and conversion rates in these catheter and port-based HAI protocols are lower than responses in the HAIP-based cohorts reviewed above.

Adjuvant

The use of HAIC in the adjuvant setting after resection for CRLM has evolved over time. The concept initially arose from the observation that, despite curative-intent resection, disease-specific survival was less than 50 percent at five years (Creasy et al., 2018). An early randomized trial of adjuvant HAIC in the 1980s showed no difference in five-year disease-specific survival or OS, although patients in the HAIC arm had a lower rate of hepatic disease at the time of first recurrence (Rudroff et al., 1999). A randomized trial of 156 patients from MSKCC published in 1999 showed significant improvements in all outcomes (OS, PFS and hepatic PFS) for HAIC in combination with systemic 5-FU compared to systemic therapy with 5-FU alone after resection(N Kemeny et al., 1999). The exact mechanism for this improvement is unclear: HAIC may treat micrometastatic disease present at the time of surgery but not visible on cross-sectional imaging or at the time or surgery, or it may prevent new metastatic deposits.

A common criticism of these adjuvant HAIC data is that they predate modern systemic chemotherapy. In order to address this issue, a large retrospective analysis from MSKCC reported on the outcomes between patients receiving adjuvant HAIP and no HAIP after complete resection of CRLM (Koerkamp et al., 2017). Of 1,442 patients receiving perioperative oxaliplatin or irinotecan-based chemotherapies, 47 percent received adjuvant combination HAIP. Median overall survival with HAIP in the modern treatment era was 72 months compared to 51 months without HAIP, and adjuvant HAIP was independently associated with prolonged survival (Fig. 13.1).

Another common criticism of HAIC data is that most reports come from a single instutition, MSKCC. However, many other institutions are incorporating HAIC adjuvant protocols and a consortium of HAIC centers now has over 50 participating member institutions. Certain institutions are targeting HAIC to patients at highest risk for recurrence using risk factors known at the time of presentation of CRLM, usually some variation of the five variables within the Clinical Risk Score published by Fong et al. in 1999 (Table 13.2) (Fong et al., 1999; House et al., 2010). A single-institution retrospective analysis from France published in 2013 showed that three-year disease-free survival was significantly longer in patients at high risk of recurrence who received systemic therapy with catheter-based oxaliplatin HAIC compared to those who received systemic therapy alone (33 percent vs 5 percent, $p < 0.001$) (Goéré et al., 2013). An ongoing randomized trial in France will evaluate adjuvant HAIC for patients at high-risk of recurrence (NCT02494973).

Although it seems reasonable that patients at highest-risk would benefit from more aggressive interventions, retrospective data suggests that patients at lower-risk of recurrence may benefit more from adjuvant HAIP. In the MSKCC retrospective cohort study, variables associated with longer overall survival after HAIP include lower Clinical Risk Score, lower CEA, fewer tumors resected, and node-negative primary (Table 13.3). This has prompted an ongoing randomized trial in the Netherlands that will evaluate adjuvant HAIC for patients at low-risk of recurrence (Netherlands Trial Register 7493).

Extrahepatic disease

Applying HAIC to patients with extrahepatic disease is a subject of debate. HAIC is regularly used in combination with systemic disease, so the presence of small-volume extrahepatic disease that is responding to or at least controlled on systemic chemotherapy

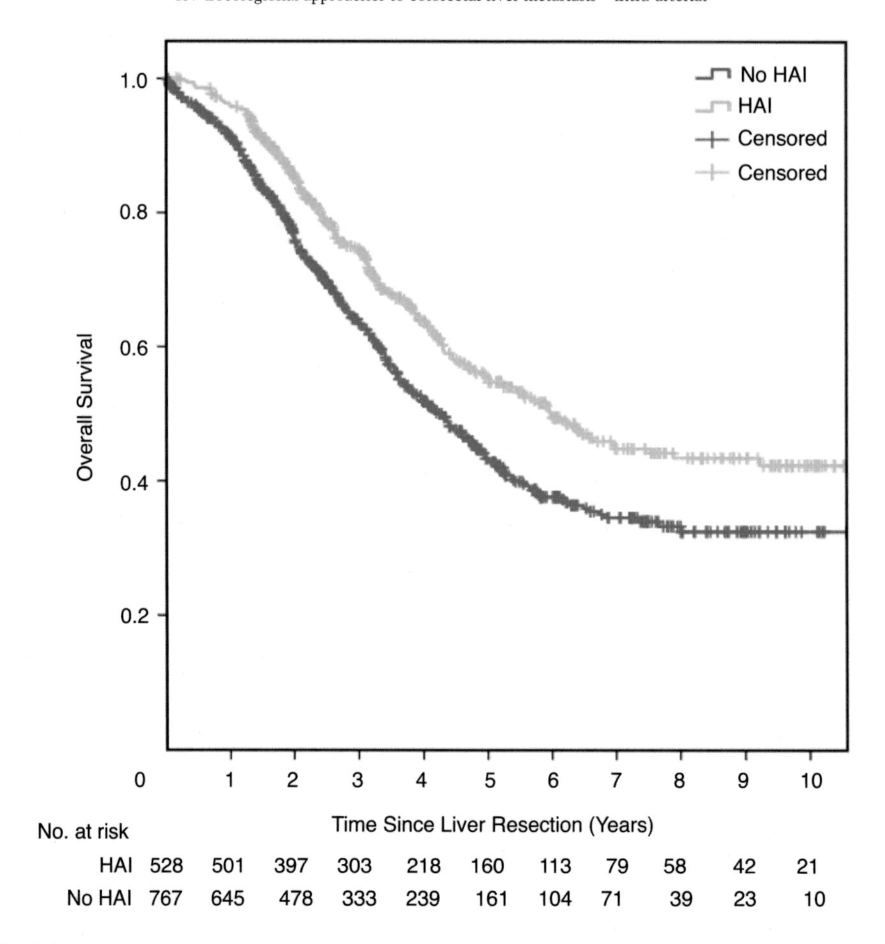

FIGURE 13.1 Kaplan-Meier analysis of overall survival in a retrospective analysis of 1,442 patients receiving systemic chemotherapy with or without hepatic artery infusion (HAI) chemotherapy. *From Koerkamp, BG, Sadot, E., Kemeny, NE, Gönen, M., Leal, JN, Allen, PJ, Cercek, A., DeMatteo, RP, Kingham, TP, Jarnagin, W. R. & D'Angelica, M. I. (2017). Perioperative Hepatic Arterial Infusion Pump Chemotherapy Is Associated With Longer Survival After Resection of Colorectal Liver Metastases: A Propensity Score Analysis. Journal of Clinical Oncology, 35(17), JCO.2016.71.834.* https://doi.org/10.1200/jco.2016.71.8346. Patients receiving adjuvant HAI chemotherapy with systemic chemotherapy had longer overall survival compared to those receiving systemic chemotherapy alone. Median overall survival 72 months in the HAI arm versus 51 months without HAI ($p < 0.01$).

should not be considered an absoluate contraindication to HAIC. In a series from MSKCC, patients with extrahepatic disease controlled on systemic therapy had significantly shorter overall survival after pump placement compared to patients with hepatic-only disease (16 vs 32 months, $p < 0.001$) (Ammori et al., 2012). Patients with extrahepatic disease in this series were younger and had already received more systemic therapy, suggesting that these patients have few, if any, alternative treatment options. HAIC may be considered in these cases but should be preceded by an extensive discussion between the patient and multidisciplinary team regarding the risks of treatment and the expected outcomes.

TABLE 13.2 Fong Clinical Risk Score variables, point totals, and disease-specific survival from the original (Fong et al., 1999) and updated (House et al., 2010) cohorts.

Variable	Point	Point total	Median disease-specific survival after hepatic metastectomy	
			Fong et al. (1999)	**House et al. (2010)**
Node-positive colorectal primary tumor	1	0	74 months	90 months
Disease-free interval from primary tumor to hepatic disease < 12 months	1	1	51 months	68 months
Number of tumors > 1	1	2	47 months	53 months
CEA level ≥ 200 ng/mL at time of presentation of hepatic disease	1	3	33 months	33 months
Largest hepatic tumor ≥ 5 cm	1	4	20 months	28 months
		5	22 months	22 months

Summary of hepatic arterial infusion chemotherapy

In summary, HAIC is a data-driven treatment option for patients with CRLM in multiple clinical scenarios and is a component of national guidelines for this disease. It is an active therapy for both patients with unresectable CRLM and in the adjuvant setting after complete resection. The future of HAIC has several directions. Direct comparison to modern systemic chemotherapy regimens is a priority as well as the development of biomarkers to help identify patients most likely to benefit from this therapy, and multiple trials are ongoing or in development.

HAIC outcomes relative to other intra-arterial therapies

Comparing outcomes of HAIC to those for other arterially-directed regional therapies for CRLM is complicated by a lack of randomized trials directly comparing these therapies, a lack of standardization in comparators arms in existing trials, and significant heterogeneity between treatment arms. A meta-analysis of HAIC, TACE, and TARE demonstrated that response rates were high for all modalities, particularly for patients who had not previously been treated with systemic therapy (Zacharias et al., 2015). No approach showed a statistically significant advantage in overall survival compared to the others. HAIC in combination with systemic therapy resulted in the longest median survival, 23 months vs 20 for TARE and 16 for TACE. HAIC was the only arterial therapy with any meaningful rate of conversion to complete resection: 15 percent versus 4 percent for TACE and 2 percent for TARE. Grade 3 or 4 complications were reported in 55 percent of patients undergoing HAIC, which is more than twice as high as the other approaches, and 11 percent had HAIC termination due to technical complications related to the pump such as catheter displacement, catheter or pump thrombosis, or hepatic artery thrombosis.

TABLE 13.3 Patients with variables commonly associated with lower risk of recurrence have better overall survival with HAI chemotherapy in this retrospective analysis. HAI: hepatic artery infusion. OS: overall survival. From Koerkamp BG et al., J Clin Oncol 2017 35(17):1938–45.

		Median OS (months)		
Variable	**n**	**HAI**	**No HAI**	**p**
Node Status of Primary Tumor				
N0	908	129	51	< 0.01
N1	882	57	43	< 0.01
N2	557	46	38	< 0.01
Disease-Free Interval				
< 12 months	864	63	43	< 0.01
≥ 12 months	1,504	72	45	< 0.01
Number of Resected Tumors				
1	1,010	83	53	< 0.01
2	462	86	42	< 0.01
3	308	68	39	< 0.01
4	172	66	43	< 0.01
5 - 9	347	47	33	0.01
≥ 10	69	36	20	0.05
CEA				
< 200 ng/mL	714	39	34	0.02
> 200 ng/mL	1,654	67	48	< 0.01
Clinical Risk Score				
Low (0–2)	1,252	89	53	< 0.01
High (3–5)	868	50	37	< 0.01

Conclusions

Overall, arterially-directed therapies are important treatment options for patients with CRLM. The data for TACE and TARE is limited in this disease and, as such, these interventions are not routinely incorporated into the multimodal management of patients with CRLM and are not included in national guidelines. Alternatively, HAIC is well-supported by data and can be applied in a number of clinical scenarios to offer prolonged survival or even cure in combination with curative-intent resection.

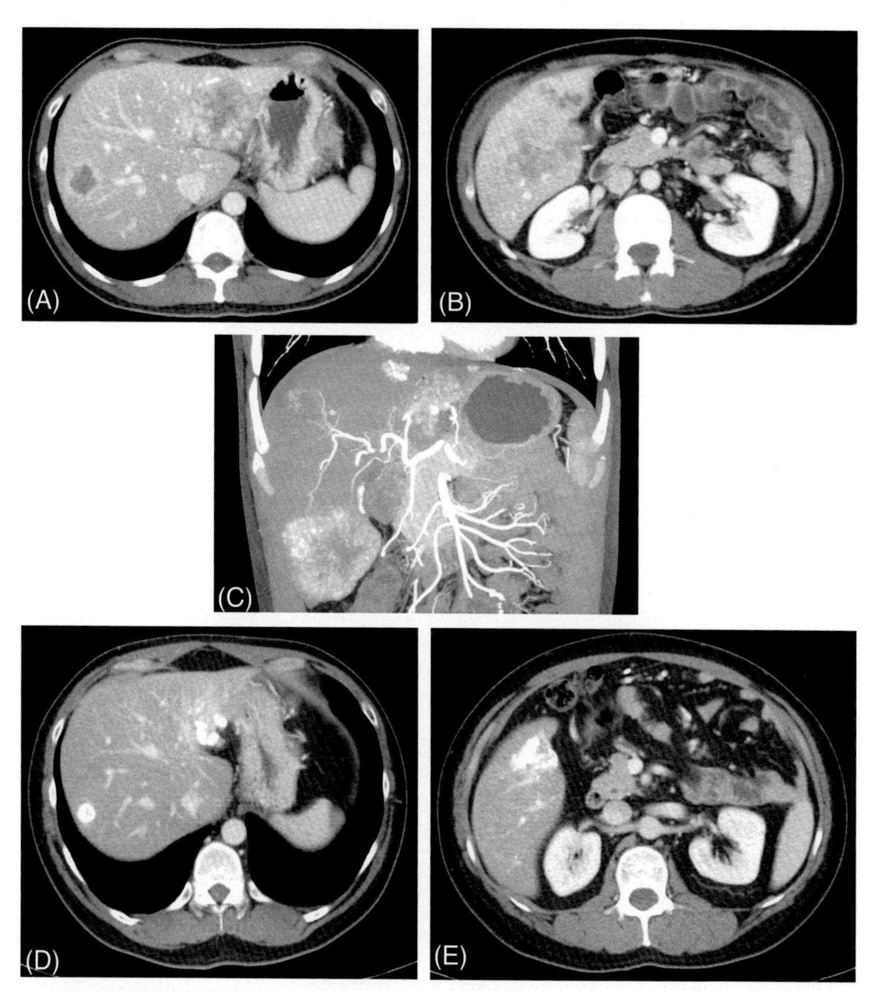

FIGURE 13.2 Imaging showing a patient who underwent hepatic artery infusion pump chemotherapy. Representative images from pretreatment (A, B), pre-operative CT angiogram (C), and post-hepatic artery infusion chemotherapy (D, E) demonstrate impressive response to therapy that allowed the patient to undergo complete surgical resection.

Case stem

A male patient (age withheld to preserve privacy) presented to our clinic 3 months after initiation of systemic chemotherapy for synchronous presentation of bilateral unresectable colorectal liver metastases. His primary tumor in the descending colon was resected due to obstructive symptoms prior to the initiation of FOLFOX chemotherapy; pathology was T4N1, microsatellite stable. After 6 cycles of systemic therapy, his bulky bilateral liver disease remained unresectable (Fig. 13.2A, 13.2B). He was referred for consideration of HAIC. Fig. 13.2C shows his preoperative CT angiogram, showing normal hepatic arterial anatomy with the exception of an accessory left hepatic artery. He underwent successful HAIP placement and was started on FUDR with systemic therapy. His systemic therapy included 6 cycles of FOLFOX before switching to FOLFIRI for 3 months due to neuropathy. He had an excellent response to the combination of systemic and HAIP chemotherapy (Figs. 13.2D, 13.2E) and was converted to resectable disease, eventually undergoing a combination of segmentectomies, wedge resections, and ablations in a single-stage procedure. He is currently undergoing surveillance. Images shared with patient permisison.

References

Allard, M. A., Sebagh, M., Baillie, G., Lemoine, A., Dartigues, P., Faitot, F., et al. (2015). Comparison of complete pathologic response and hepatic injuries between hepatic arterial infusion and systemic administration of oxaliplatin in patients with colorectal liver metastases. *Annals of Surgical Oncology, 22*(6), 1925–1932. https://doi.org/10.1245/s10434-014-4272-7.

Allen, P. J., Nissan, A., Picon, A. I., Kemeny, N., Dudrick, P., Ben-Porat, L., et al. (2005). Technical Complications and Durability of Hepatic Artery Infusion Pumps for Unresectable Colorectal Liver Metastases: an Institutional Experience of 544 Consecutive Cases. *Journal of the American College of Surgeons, 201*(1), 57–65. https://doi.org/10.1016/j.jamcollsurg.2005.03.019.

Allen-Mersh, T. G., Earlam, S., Fordy, C., Abrams, K., & Houghton, J. (1994). Quality of life and survival with continuous hepatic-artery floxuridine infusion for colorectal liver metastases. *Lancet, 344*(8932), 1255–1260. doi:10.1016/s0140-6736(94)90750-1.

Ammori, J. B., D'Angelica, M. I., Fong, Y., Cercek, A., Dematteo, R. P., Allen, P. J., et al. (2012). Hepatic artery infusional chemotherapy in patients with unresectable colorectal liver metastases and extrahepatic disease. *Journal of Surgical Oncology, 106*(8), 953–958. https://doi.org/10.1002/jso.23204.

Breedis, C., & Young, G. (1954). The blood supply of neoplasms in the liver. *American Journal of Pathology, 30*(5), 969–977. https://pubmed.ncbi.nlm.nih.gov/13197542.

Buchwald, H., Grage, T. B., Vassilopoulos, P. P., Rohde, T. D., Varco, R. L., & Blackshear, P. J. (1980). Intraarterial infusion chemotherapy for hepatic carcinoma using a totally implantable infusion pump. *Cancer, 45*(5), 866–869. https://doi.org/10.1002/1097-0142(19800301)45:5<866::aid-cncr2820450507>3.0.co;2-3.

Buisman, F. E., Grünhagen, D. J., Homs, M. Y. V., Grootscholten, C., Filipe, W. F., Kemeny, N. E., et al. (2019). Adjuvant Hepatic Arterial Infusion Pump Chemotherapy After Resection of Colorectal Liver Metastases: results of a Safety and Feasibility Study in The Netherlands. *Annals of Surgical Oncology, 26*(13), 4599–4607. https://doi.org/10.1245/s10434-019-07973-w.

Carmeliet, P. (2000). Mechanisms of angiogenesis and arteriogenesis. *Nature Medicine, 6*(4), 389–395. https://doi.org/10.1038/74651.

Cercek, A., Boucher, T. M., Gluskin, J. S., Aguiló, A., Chou, J. F., Connell, L. C., et al. (2016). Response rates of hepatic arterial infusion pump therapy in patients with metastatic colorectal cancer liver metastases refractory to all standard chemotherapies. *Journal of Surgical Oncology, 114*(6), 655–663. https://doi.org/10.1002/jso.24399.

Chang, A. E., Schneider, P. D., Sugarbaker, P. H., Simpson, C., Culnane,M., & Steinberg, S. M. (1987). Aprospective randomized trial of regional versus systemic continuous 5-fluorodeoxyuridine chemotherapy in the treatment of colorectal liver metastases. *Ann Surg, 206*(6), 685–693. 2961314. doi:10.1097/00000658-198712000-00001.

Chen, H. S., & Gross, J. F. (1980). Intra-arterial infusion of anticancer drugs: theoretic aspects of drug delivery and review of responses. *Cancer Treatment Reports, 64*(1), 31–40.

Chuang, V. P., & Wallace, S. (1981). Hepatic artery embolization in the treatment of hepatic neoplasms. *Radiology, 140*(1), 51–58. https://doi.org/10.1148/radiology.140.1.7244243.

Creasy, J. M., Sadot, E., Koerkamp, B. G., Chou, J. F., Gonen, M., Kemeny, N. E., et al. (2018). Actual 10-year survival after hepatic resection of colorectal liver metastases: what factors preclude cure? *Surgery, 163*(6), 1238–1244. https://doi.org/10.1016/j.surg.2018.01.004.

Ensminger, W. D., & Gyves, J. W. (1983). Clinical pharmacology of hepatic arterial chemotherapy. *Seminars in Oncology, 10*(2), 176–182.

Engstrand, J., Nilsson, H., Stromberg, C., Jonas, E., Freedman, J. (2018). Colorectal cancer liver metastases – a population-based study on incidence, management and survival. BMC cancer, 18(1), 78. https://doi.org/10.1186/s12885-017-3925-x.

Ensminger, W. D., Rosowsky, A., Raso, V., Levin, D. C., Glode, M., Come, S., et al. (1978). A clinical-pharmacological evaluation of hepatic arterial infusions of 5-fluoro-2'-deoxyuridine and 5-fluorouracil. *Cancer Research, 38*(11 Pt 1), 3784–3792.

Fiorentini, G., Aliberti, C., Tilli, M., Mulazzani, L., Graziano, F., Giordani, P., et al. (2012). Intra-arterial infusion of irinotecan-loaded drug-eluting beads (DEBIRI) versus intravenous therapy (FOLFIRI) for hepatic metastases from colorectal cancer: final results of a phase III study. *Anticancer Research, 32*(4), 1387–1395.

Fong, Y., Fortner, J., Sun, R. L., Brennan, M. F., & Blumgart, L. H. (1999). Clinical score for predicting recurrence after hepatic resection for metastatic colorectal cancer: analysis of 1001 consecutive cases. *Annals of Surgery, 230*(3), 309–318 discussion 318-21.

Gaba, R. C., Lokken, R. P., Hickey, R. M., Lipnik, A. J., Lewandowski, R. J., Salem, R., et al. (2017). Quality Improvement Guidelines for Transarterial Chemoembolization and Embolization of Hepatic Malignancy. *Journal of Vascular and Interventional Radiology, 28*(9), 1210–1223.e3. https://doi.org/10.1016/j.jvir.2017.04.025.

Goéré, D., Benhaim, L., Bonnet, S., Malka, D., Faron, M., Elias, D., et al. (2013). Adjuvant chemotherapy after resection of colorectal liver metastases in patients at high risk of hepatic recurrence: a comparative study between hepatic arterial infusion of oxaliplatin and modern systemic chemotherapy. *Annals of Surgery, 257*(1), 114–120. https://doi.org/10.1097/sla.0b013e31827b9005.

Hanahan, D., & Folkman, J. (1996). Patterns and emerging mechanisms of the angiogenic switch during tumorigenesis. *Cell, 86*(3), 353–364. https://doi.org/10.1016/s0092-8674(00)80108-7.

Hohn, D. C., Stagg, R. J., Friedman, M. A., Hannigan, J. F., Jr., Rayner, A., Ignoffo, R. J.,... Lewis, B. J. (1989). A randomized trial of continuous intravenous versus hepatic intraarterial floxuridine in patients with colorectal cancer metastatic to the liver: the Northern California Oncology Group trial. *J Clin Oncol, 7*(11), 1646–1654. 2530317. doi:10.1200/JCO.1989.7.11.1646.

House, M. G., Ito, H., Gönen, M., Fong, Y., Allen, P. J., DeMatteo, R. P., et al. (2010). Survival after hepatic resection for metastatic colorectal cancer: trends in outcomes for 1,600 patients during two decades at a single institution. *Journal of the American College of Surgeons, 210*(5), 744–752. https://doi.org/10.1016/j.jamcollsurg.2009.12.040.

Hunt, T. M., Flowerdew, A. D., Birch, S. J., Williams, J. D., Mullee, M. A., & Taylor, I. (1990). Prospective randomized controlled trial of hepatic arterial embolization or infusion chemotherapy with 5-fluorouracil and degradable starch microspheres for colorectal liver metastases. *British Journal of Surgery, 77*(7), 779–782. https://doi.org/10.1002/bjs.1800770720.

Ito, K., Ito, H., Kemeny, N. E., Gonen, M., Allen, P. J., Paty, P. B., et al. (2012). Biliary sclerosis after hepatic arterial infusion pump chemotherapy for patients with colorectal cancer liver metastasis: incidence, clinical features, and risk factors. *Annals of Surgical Oncology, 19*(5), 1609–1617. https://doi.org/10.1245/s10434-011-2102-8.

Kemeny, N., Conti, J. A., Sigurdson, E., Cohen, A., Seiter, K., Lincer, R., et al. (1993). A pilot study of hepatic artery floxuridine combined with systemic 5-fluorouracil and leucovorin. A potential adjuvant program after resection of colorectal hepatic metastases. *Cancer, 71*(6), 1964–1971. https://doi.org/10.1002/1097-0142(19930315)71:6<1964::aid-cncr2820710607>3.0.co;2-t.

Kemeny, N., Daly, J., Reichman, B., Geller, N., Botet, J., & Oderman, P. (1987). Intrahepatic or systemic infusion of fluorodeoxyuridine in patients with liver metastases from colorectal carcinoma. A randomized trial. Ann Intern Med, 107(4), 459–465. 2957943. doi:10.7326/0003-4819-107-4-459.

Kemeny, N., Gonen, M., Sullivan, D., Schwartz, L., Benedetti, F., Saltz, L., et al. (2001). Phase I Study of Hepatic Arterial Infusion of Floxuridine and Dexamethasone With Systemic Irinotecan for Unresectable Hepatic Metastases From Colorectal Cancer. *Journal of Clinical Oncology, 19*(10), 2687–2695. https://doi.org/10.1200/jco.2001.19.10.2687.

Kemeny, N., Huang, Y., Cohen, A. M., Shi, W., Conti, J. A., Brennan, M. F., et al. (1999). Hepatic arterial infusion of chemotherapy after resection of hepatic metastases from colorectal cancer. *New England Journal of Medicine, 341*(27), 2039–2048.

Kemeny, N. E., Melendez, F. D. H., Capanu, M., Paty, P. B., Fong, Y., Schwartz, L. H., et al. (2009). Conversion to resectability using hepatic artery infusion plus systemic chemotherapy for the treatment of unresectable liver metastases from colorectal carcinoma. *Journal of Clinical Oncology : Official Journal of the American Society of Clinical Oncology,, 27*(21), 3465–3471. https://doi.org/10.1200/JCO.2008.20.1301.

Kemeny, N. E., Niedzwiecki, D., Hollis, D. R., Lenz, H.-J., Warren, R. S., Naughton, M. J., et al. (2006). Hepatic arterial infusion versus systemic therapy for hepatic metastases from colorectal cancer: a randomized trial of efficacy, quality of life, and molecular markers (CALGB 9481). *Journal of Clinical Oncology, 24*(9), 1395–1403. https://doi.org/10.1200/jco.2005.03.8166.

Kerr, D. J., McArdle, C. S., Ledermann, J., Taylor, I., Sherlock, D. J., Schlag, P. M.,... Stephens, R. J. (2003). European Organisation for Research and Treatment of Cancer colorectal cancer study group. Intrahepatic arterial versus intravenous fluorouracil and folinic acid for colorectal cancer liver metastases: a multicentre randomised trial. *Lancet, 361*(9355), 368–373. 12573372. doi:10.1016/S0140-6736(03)12388-4.

Kim, H.-C., Chung, J. W., Lee, W., Jae, H. J., & Park, J. H. (2005). Recognizing extrahepatic collateral vessels that supply hepatocellular carcinoma to avoid complications of transcatheter arterial chemoembolization. *Radiographics, 25*(suppl_1), S25–S39. https://doi.org/10.1148/rg.25si055508.

Klopp, C. T., Alford, T. C., Bateman, J., Berry, G. N., & Winship, T. (1950). Fractionated intra-arterial cancer; chemotherapy with methyl bis amine hydrochloride; a preliminary report. *Annals of Surgery, 132*(4), 811–832. https://doi.org/10.1097/00000658-195010000-00018.

Koerkamp, B. G., Sadot, E., Kemeny, N. E., Gönen, M., Leal, J. N., Allen, P. J., et al. (2017). Perioperative Hepatic Arterial Infusion Pump Chemotherapy Is Associated With Longer Survival After Resection of Colorectal Liver Metastases: a Propensity Score Analysis. *Journal of Clinical Oncology, 35*(17). JCO.2016.71.834 https://doi.org/10.1200/jco.2016.71.8346 .

Leung, D. A., Goin, J. E., Sickles, C., Raskay, B. J., & Soulen, M. C. (2001). Determinants of postembolization syndrome after hepatic chemoembolization. *Journal of Vascular and Interventional Radiology, 12*(3), 321–326. https://doi.org/10.1016/s1051-0443(07)61911-3.

Lévi, F. A., Boige, V., Hebbar, M., Smith, D., Lepère, C., Focan, C., et al. (2016). Conversion to resection of liver metastases from colorectal cancer with hepatic artery infusion of combined chemotherapy and systemic cetuximab in multicenter trial OPTILIV. *Annals of Oncology, 27*(2), 267–274. https://doi.org/10.1093/annonc/mdv548.

Levy, J., Zuckerman, J., Garfinkle, R., Acuna, S. A., Touchette, J., Vanounou, T., et al. (2018). Intra-arterial therapies for unresectable and chemorefractory colorectal cancer liver metastases: a systematic review and meta-analysis. *HPB, 20*(10), 905–915. https://doi.org/10.1016/j.hpb.2018.04.001.

Lewis, A. L., Gonzalez, M. V., Lloyd, A. W., Hall, B., Tang, Y., Willis, S. L., et al. (2006). DC bead: in vitro characterization of a drug-delivery device for transarterial chemoembolization. *Journal of Vascular and Interventional Radiology, 17*(2), 335–342. https://doi.org/10.1097/01.rvi.0000195323.46152.b3.

Liu, Y., Chang, W., Zhou, B., Wei, Y., Tang, W., Liang, F., et al. (2021). Conventional transarterial chemoembolization combined with systemic therapy versus systemic therapy alone as second-line treatment for unresectable colorectal liver metastases: randomized clinical trial. *British Journal of Surgery, 108*(4), 373–379. https://doi.org/10.1093/bjs/znaa155.

Lorenz, M., & Müller, H. H. (2000). Randomized, multicenter trial of fluorouracil plus leucovorin administered either via hepatic arterial or intravenous infusion versus fluorodeoxyuridine administered via hepatic arterial infusion in patients with nonresectable liver metastases from colorectal carcinoma. *J Clin Oncol, 18*(2), 243–254. 10637236. doi:10.1001/archsurg.1990.01410200086013.

Martin, J. K., Jr., O'Connell, M. J.,Wieand, H. S., Fitzgibbons, R. J., Jr. Mailliard, J.A., Rubin, J.,... Krook, J.E. (1990). Intra-arterial floxuridine vs systemic fluorouracil for hepatic metastases from colorectal cancer. A randomized trial. *Arch Surg, 125*(8), 1022–1027. 2143063. doi:10.1001/archsurg.1990.01410200086013.

Martin, R. C. G., Scoggins, C. R., Schreeder, M., Rilling, W. S., Laing, C. J., Tatum, C. M., et al. (2015). Randomized controlled trial of irinotecan drug-eluting beads with simultaneous FOLFOX and bevacizumab for patients with unresectable colorectal liver-limited metastasis. *Cancer, 121*(20), 3649–3658. https://doi.org/10.1002/cncr.29534.

Martinelli, D. J., Wadler, S., Bakal, C. W., Cynamon, J., Rozenblit, A., Haynes, H., et al. (1994). Utility of embolization or chemoembolization as second-line treatment in patients with advanced or recurrent colorectal carcinoma. *Cancer, 74*(6), 1706–1712. https://doi.org/10.1002/1097-0142(19940915)74:6: <1706:aid–cncr2820740611>3.0.co;2-j.

Mocellin, S., Pilati, P., Lise, M., & Nitti, D. (2007). Meta-analysis of hepatic arterial infusion for unresectable liver metastases from colorectal cancer: the end of an era? *Journal of Clinical Oncology, 25*(35), 5649–5654. https://doi.org/10.1200/jco.2007.12.1764.

Mori, W., Masuda, M., & Miyanaga, T. (1966). Hepatic artery ligation and tumor necrosis in the liver. *Surgery, 59*(3), 359–363.

Moustafa, A. S., Aal, A., A. , K., Ertel, N., Saad, N., DuBay, D., et al. (2017). Chemoembolization of Hepatocellular Carcinoma with Extrahepatic Collateral Blood Supply: anatomic and Technical Considerations. *Radiographics : A Review Publication of the Radiological Society of North America, Inc,, 37*(3), 963–977. https://doi.org/10.1148/rg.2017160122.

Mulcahy, M. F., Mahvash, A., Pracht, M., Montazeri, A. H., Bandula, S., Martin, R. C. G., et al. (2021). Radioembolization With Chemotherapy for Colorectal Liver Metastases: a Randomized, Open-Label, International, Multicenter, Phase III Trial. *Journal of Clinical Oncology, JCO, 21*, 01839. https://doi.org/10.1200/jco.21.01839.

Noussios, G., Dimitriou, I., Chatzis, I., & Katsourakis, A. (2017). The Main Anatomic Variations of the Hepatic Artery and Their Importance in Surgical Practice: review of the Literature. *J Clin Med Res, 9*(4), 248–252. https://doi.org/10.14740/jocmr2902w.

Pak, L. M., Kemeny, N. E., Capanu, M., Chou, J. F., Boucher, T., Cercek, A., et al. (2018). Prospective phase II trial of combination hepatic artery infusion and systemic chemotherapy for unresectable colorectal liver metastases: long term results and curative potential. *Journal of Surgical Oncology, 117*(4), 634–643. https://doi.org/10.1002/jso.24898.

Qadan, M., D'Angelica, M. I., Kemeny, N. E., Cercek, A., & Kingham, T. P. (2017). Robotic hepatic arterial infusion pump placement. *HPB, 19*(5), 429–435. https://doi.org/10.1016/j.hpb.2016.12.015.

Richardson, A. J., Laurence, J. M., & Lam, V. W. T. (2013). Transarterial chemoembolization with irinotecan beads in the treatment of colorectal liver metastases: systematic review. *Journal of Vascular and Interventional Radiology, 24*(8), 1209–1217. https://doi.org/10.1016/j.jvir.2013.05.055.

Rougier, P., Laplanche, A.,Huguier,M., Hay, J.M., Ollivier, J.M., Escat, J.,... Gallot, D. (1992).Hepatic arterial infusion of floxuridine in patients with liver metastases from colorectal carcinoma: long-term results of a prospective randomized trial. *J Clin Oncol, 10*(7), 1112-1118. 1296590. doi:10.1200/JCO.1992.10.7.1112.

Rudroff, C., Altendorf-Hoffmann, A., Stangl, R., & Scheele, J. (1999). Prospective randomised trial on adjuvant hepatic-artery infusion chemotherapy after R0 resection of colorectal liver metastases. *Langenbeck's Archives of Surgery, 384*(3), 243–249. https://doi.org/10.1007/s004230050199.

Segall, H. N. (1923). An experimental anatomical investigation of the blood and bile channels of the liver. *Surgery, Gynecology & Obstetrics, 37*, 152–178. https://archive.org/details/surgerygynecolog37ameruoft/page/178/mode/2up.

Thiels, C. A., & D'Angelica, M. I. (2020). Hepatic artery infusion pumps. *Journal of Surgical Oncology, 122*(1), 70–77. https://doi.org/10.1002/jso.25913.

Wagman, L.D., Kemeny,M.M., Leong, L., Terz, J.J.,Hill, L.R., Beatty, J.D.,... Riihimaki, D.U. (1990). Aprospective, randomized evaluation of the treatment of colorectal cancer metastatic to the liver. *J Clin Oncol, 8*(11), 1885–1893. 2146370. doi:10.1200/JCO.1990.8.11.1885.

Wasan, H. S., Gibbs, P., Sharma, N. K., Taieb, J., Heinemann, V., Ricke, J., et al. (2017). First-line selective internal radiotherapy plus chemotherapy versus chemotherapy alone in patients with liver metastases from colorectal cancer (FOXFIRE, SIRFLOX, and FOXFIRE-Global): a combined analysis of three multicentre, randomised, phase 3 trials. *The Lancet Oncology, 18*(9), 1159–1171. https://doi.org/10.1016/s1470-2045(17)30457-6.

Watkins, E., Khazei, A. M., & Nahra, K. S. (1970). Surgical basis for arterial infusion chemotherapy of disseminated carcinoma of the liver. *Surgery, Gynecology & Obstetrics, 130*(4), 581–605.

Zacharias, A. J., Jayakrishnan, T. T., Rajeev, R., Rilling, W. S., Thomas, J. P., George, B., et al. (2015). Comparative Effectiveness of Hepatic Artery Based Therapies for Unresectable Colorectal Liver Metastases: a Meta-Analysis. *Plos One, 10*(10), e0139940. https://doi.org/10.1371/journal.pone.0139940.

CHAPTER

14

Locoregional Approaches to Colorectal Liver Metastasis – Radiation Options

Colin S. Hill[a], *Eugene J. Koay*[b] *and Joseph M. Herman*[c]

[a]Department of Radiation Oncology & Molecular Radiation Sciences, Johns Hopkins University School of Medicine, Baltimore, MD, United States [b]Department of GI Radiation Oncology, The University of Texas MD Anderson Cancer Center, Houston, TX, United States [c]Department of Radiation Medicine, Zucker School of Medicine at Hofstra/Northwell, Lake Success, New York, United States

Introduction: external beam radiation therapy (EBRT) for colorectal liver metastases

With the introduction of the oligometastatic concept in the 1990s, interest in metastasis directed therapy in the radiation oncology setting grew exponentially with evidence that patients so affected could be amenable to a curative therapeutic strategy (Hellman and Weichselbaum, 1995; Høyer et al., 2012; Palma et al., 2019). Although surgical management of colorectal cancer (CRC) liver metastases offers the potential for long-term control and survival, only a limited proportion of patients with liver metastases are candidates for a curative metastasectomy (Cummings et al., 2007; Misiakos et al., 2011). Liver failure from hepatic disease progression in CRC is common and may preclude the administration of systemic therapy in severe cases (Helling and Martin, 2014). Although integral to management, chemotherapy can be hepatotoxic in about 20–30 percent of patients with documented cases of injury including steatosis, steatohepatitis, and hepatic sinusoidal injury (Maor and Malnick, 2013; Pawlik et al., 2007). In addition, a limited number of metastases may emerge or progress despite control of the disease with systemic therapy elsewhere. However, utilizing external beam radiation to

Contemporary Management of Metastatic Colorectal Cancer: A Precision Medicine Approach
DOI: https://doi.org/10.1016/B978-0-323-91706-3.00007-2

provide local therapy for CRC liver metastases, especially in non-operable candidates, was historically limited by the use of older technology.

The use of radiation for liver malignancies date back to at least the 1920s but understanding of the acute and chronic effects of radiation on the liver were limited at the time (Case, 1924). A seminal paper by Stanford in the 1960s analyzed the liver specimens of patients treated with whole liver irradiation (WLI) to 30–59 Gy over 6 weeks for metastatic disease (Hellman and Weichselbaum, 1995). The predominant mode of hepatic injury was primarily vaso-occlusive around the central veins with decreased hepatic arterial and porto-venous perfusion, leading to fibrosis (Reed and Cox, 1966). Classic radiation-induced liver disease (RILD), as such, is a dose-limiting complication, and can occur 2–4 weeks after treatment and compromises anicteric hepatomegaly, ascites, and elevated liver enzymes, especially alkaline phosphatase (Reed and Cox, 1966; Koay et al., 2018). Subsequent trials by the Radiation Therapy Oncology Group (RTOG) in the 1970s and 1980s with whole liver irradiation (WLI) demonstrated that patients who received 30 Gy or lower to the whole liver did not develop classic RILD but 10 percent of patients who received more than 33 Gy developed RILD (Russell et al., 1993). As radiation techniques improved, more focal treatments with delivered doses limited only to partial volumes of the liver became possible. Subsequent studies with partial liver irradiation using a normal tissue complication probability (NTCP) model identified the mean liver dose an important predictor for classic RILD (Dawson et al., 2002). When the mean liver dose was kept lower than 32 Gy in 2 Gy fractions, the risk of classic RILD was estimated to only be $\sim$5 percent (Dawson et al., 2002).

Given such constraints, the use of older techniques with conventional doses of radiation (1.8 to 2 Gy per fraction, that is) were not able to deliver the ablative doses required to effectively eradicate metastatic disease due to the low tolerance of the liver to high-dose irradiation. This limited the use of radiation mainly to the palliative setting (Soliman et al., 2013). However, the 1990s and 2000s brought more sophisticated 3-dimensional treatment planning systems with image guidance, which allowed for the delivery of radiation in a truly conformal manner.

When radiation is delivered in high doses per fraction in $\leq$5 fractions or ultra-hypofractionated regimens ($\geq$6 Gy per fraction) with the use of image guidance and prescribed in a manner that allows for a steep dose gradient beyond the target volume, this is known as stereotactic body radiation therapy (SBRT). When ablative doses are used, it may be referred to as stereotactic ablative radiation therapy (SABR). With the emergence of SBRT/SABR, the ablative doses required for long-term disease control with CRC liver metastases in well-selected patients can now be delivered in a manner that mitigates the risk of significant injury to the liver, namely, RILD (Koay et al., 2018; Russell et al., 1993; Dawson et al., 2002; Soliman et al., 2013; Rusthoven et al., 2009). SBRT has fewer restrictions than surgery in the treatment of liver metastases, and, as such, has emerged as an appealing alternative option for aggressive treatment to oligometastatic disease in this setting (Fig. 14.1). However, delivery of ultra-hypofractionated regimens with SBRT can be challenging to administer in certain scenarios, and, in such situations, more moderate hypofractionated regimens with a longer overall treatment courses can be administered (4–5 Gy per fraction). In addition to photon-based treatments, proton beam radiation has also emerged as an effective treatment modality for liver metastases, and can also be prescribed in a stereotactic manner (Hong et al., 2017).

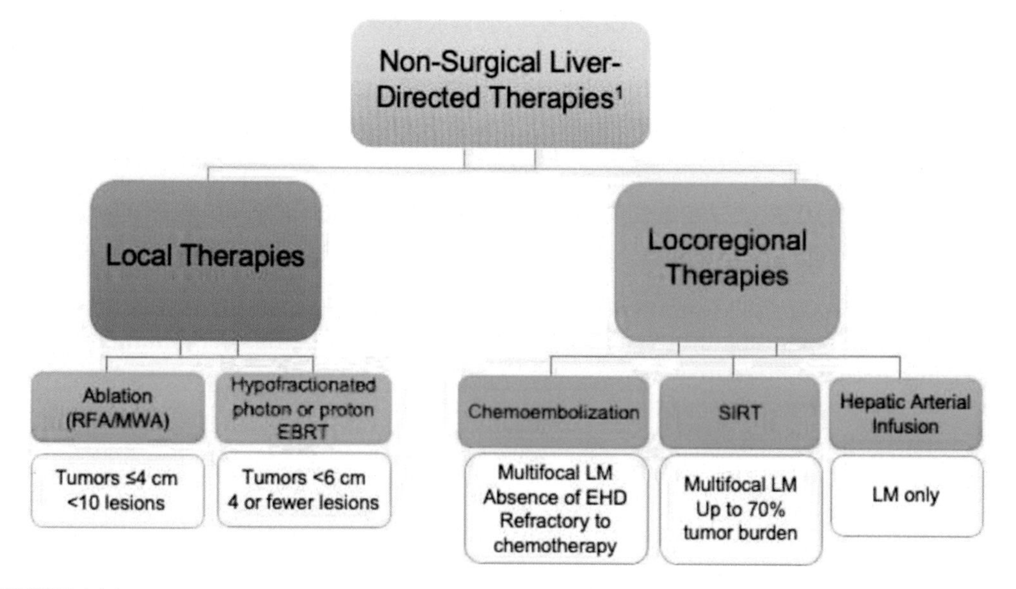

FIGURE 14.1 Proposed multidisciplinary treatment algorithm for unresectable disease.

TABLE 14.1 Definition of biologically effective dose (BED).

BED is a measure of the true ***biological*** dose delivered by a particular combination of ***dose per fraction*** and ***total dose*** to a particular tissue characterized by a specific **α/β ratio**
BED formula $= nd\,[1 + d/(\alpha/\beta)]$

- n: number of fractions
- **d:** dose per fraction
- α/β ratio: intrinsic sensitivity of tumor based on histology and tumor site to dose per fraction

External beam radiation: rationale for ablative dosing

In the initial applications with SBRT for liver metastases, there was no clear consensus regarding the optimal prescription dose in this setting and a wide variety of regimens were investigated in early trials with impressive outcomes at escalated radiation doses (Høyer et al., 2012; Rusthoven et al., 2009; Petrelli et al., 2018). In an effort to further elucidate the dose-response relationship, a multi-center study between Stanford, Princess Margaret Hospital, and the University of Colorado pooled patients treated with SBRT for liver metastases from CRC with varying prescription doses from 1–6 fractions to total doses ranging between 22–60 Gy (Chang et al., 2011). Interestingly, they determined that higher biological effective doses (BED) and higher total doses were significantly correlated with local control on multivariable analysis (MVA) (Chang et al., 2011). Tumor control probability (TCP) models demonstrated that estimated doses required for 90 percent local control at 1 year would require a BED_{10} of approximately 117 Gy which converted into a 3-fraction SBRT regimen required doses between 46 – 52 Gy in 3 fractions (Table 14.1) (Chang et al., 2011).

Given that comparable local control rates with SBRT for medically inoperable early-stage lung cancer were achieved with a BED of ≥100 Gy, the higher BED doses required for liver metastases from CRC suggested a more radioresistant histology was in play (Onishi et al., 2004). A retrospective SBRT series from Korea for liver metastases from CRC also confirmed that higher BEDs were necessary with 2-year local control rates of 52 percent, 83 percent, and 89 percent if the BED was ≤80 Gy, 100–112 Gy, or ≥132 Gy, respectively (Joo et al., 2017). An analysis by Memorial Sloan Kettering also demonstrated gastrointestinal (GI) histology was associated with a higher risk of local failure after SBRT to a liver metastasis compared to non-GI histologies (Katsoulakis et al., 2014). Mutational analysis has revealed that potential drivers of radioresistance may be the presence of KRAS and TP53 mutations, which are associated with a higher likelihood of local failure (Hong et al., 2017). However, in the era of immunotherapy, a higher mutational burden may increase the likelihood of a response to immunotherapeutic agents, and studies are underway exploring the combinatory role of SBRT with such agents (Le et al., 2015; Parikh et al., 2019).

External beam radiation: patient selection

Careful patient selection to identify which patients are ideal candidates for external beam radiation therapy requires consideration of multiple variables including liver tumor burden in the form of size, number, and volume of metastases; proximity to radiosensitive organs at risk, quality of liver function and functional liver reserve (FLR), extent of extrahepatic disease, vascular involvement; and the need for motion management. Ideally, a multidisciplinary team comprised of medical, radiation, surgical oncologists as well as radiologists and pathologists should be involved in the decision-making process on whether radiation should be offered over other options (surgery, radiofrequency ablation, radioembolization) and which EBRT technique may provide the most clinical utility such as SBRT.

Patients with lesions that are smaller in size may be amenable to liver-directed therapies other than EBRT for local control in this setting, such as microwave or radiofrequency ablation (RFA) (Ruers et al., 2012). Although randomized trials comparing RFA to SBRT or protons for metastatic liver disease are lacking, retrospective series inform us that tumors greater than 2–3 cm in size may be at a higher risk of local failure with RFA compared to SBRT (Jackson et al., 2018). In addition, RFA may be difficult to administer because of anatomical considerations (proximity to the biliary tree, major vascular structures, liver capsule, luminal GI structures, or tumors located on the dome) and, in some situations, may be technically challenging due to an inability to visualize the tumor well with ultrasound (Künzli et al., 2011). RFA and SBRT should be viewed as complementary techniques. Larger tumors may be more likely to derive a greater benefit from SBRT and the use of SBRT in tumors close to major vascular structures and the biliary tree may be preferred given the risk of a "heat sink" effect or biliary tree leak with RFA in such scenarios (Jackson et al., 2018). Ideally, combinations of therapy (RFA for small peripheral tumors and SBRT for larger centralized tumors, i.e.) may provide the best therapeutic benefit of maximizing control and limiting treatment related toxicities.

Delivering ablative doses to large liver lesions (≥ 7 cm) with SBRT can be challenging. In a report of sequential phase I and II trials of SBRT for 102 patients with hepatocellular carcinoma (HCC) with a median tumor size of 7 cm and not eligible for other liver directed therapies, locoregional control rate was 87 percent at 1 year but the risk of grade ≥3 toxicity was significant (30 percent) (Bujold et al., 2013). 7 deaths may have been related to treatment related complications but in 5 of these cases liver failure was involved with invasion of the common bile duct by HCC in one and massive tumor vascular thrombus in 2 (Bujold et al., 2013). In such situations, where the extent of the tumor burden is extensive, patients often have poorer baseline liver reserve, and this represents a significant challenge to safe and effective radiation treatment. Tumor-related dysfunction due to biliary or vascular compromise is more common with larger tumors, especially those near the confluence of the hepatic veins and inferior vena cava or the hilum (Tao et al., 2019). However, patients may also have limited reserve due to previous resection, hepatotoxic chemotherapy, or underlying liver disease such as cirrhosis. Patients with advanced cirrhosis (more common with hepatocellular carcinoma) may be at a higher risk of radiation-induced liver disease and, indeed, the threshold dose for the liver has been shown to be different in patients with primary vs metastatic liver disease (Lawrence et al., 1992).

Building on earlier studies demonstrating the importance of liver sparing with mean-liver dose metrics and extrapolating the functional liver reserve concept from the surgical literature, a landmark phase I/II trial of 3-fraction SBRT for liver metastases safely dose escalated from 36 Gy to 60 Gy total dose by requiring at least a minimum volume of 700 cc (DC700) of the normal liver to receive no more 15 Gy (Rusthoven et al., 2009). Out of 47 patients, only one patient (2 percent) experienced a dose limiting toxicity with this constraint (Rusthoven et al., 2009). A series from Princess Margaret, including 81 non-cirrhotic patients post-SBRT for liver metastases, showed that if the DC700 constraint was not violated acute transaminitis post-SBRT was associated with very little long-term toxicity (Barry et al., 2017). Higher doses for DC700, mean liver dose, and effective volume are associated with post-SBRT decompensation, and, as such, patients selected for radiation must be evaluated for the adequacy of their liver reserve upfront. In addition to the risk of RILD, patients with tumors located in close proximity to the biliary tree may be at risk of central hepatobiliary toxicity with radiation therapy, including central biliary obstruction and hepatobiliary infection (Toesca et al., 2017). The risk of central hepatobiliary toxicity appears correlated to the dose to the central biliary tract instead of the liver as a whole. For that reason, even tumors with a smaller size may not be amenable to radiation if ablative doses cannot be safely achieved (Toesca et al., 2017).

For patients with liver cirrhosis, scoring systems such as the Child-Pugh system are commonly utilized as another tool to evaluate a patient's candidacy for radiation. Generally speaking, patients with Child-Pugh (CP) Class A function may safely receive radiation if dose constraints can be met whereas CP class B or C patients are generally not considered candidates except in very select cases (Lasley et al., 2015). However, clinical judgment must be applied with utilization of the CP scoring system due to subjective variability in scoring encephalopathy and ascites, and its inability to distinguish between tumor-related dysfunction and underlying cirrhosis. More objective scoring systems have been proposed using serum markers, but these grading systems have yet to be applied to radiotherapy. In addition to underlying clinical factors and dose, acquiring measurements of indocyanine green (ICG) clearance can help increase the sensitivity of predicting post-SBRT liver function (Suresh et al., 2018).

For the cohort of patients that are not amenable to surgical resection, ablation, or radiotherapy, radioembolization or chemoembolization may represent a potential strategy for

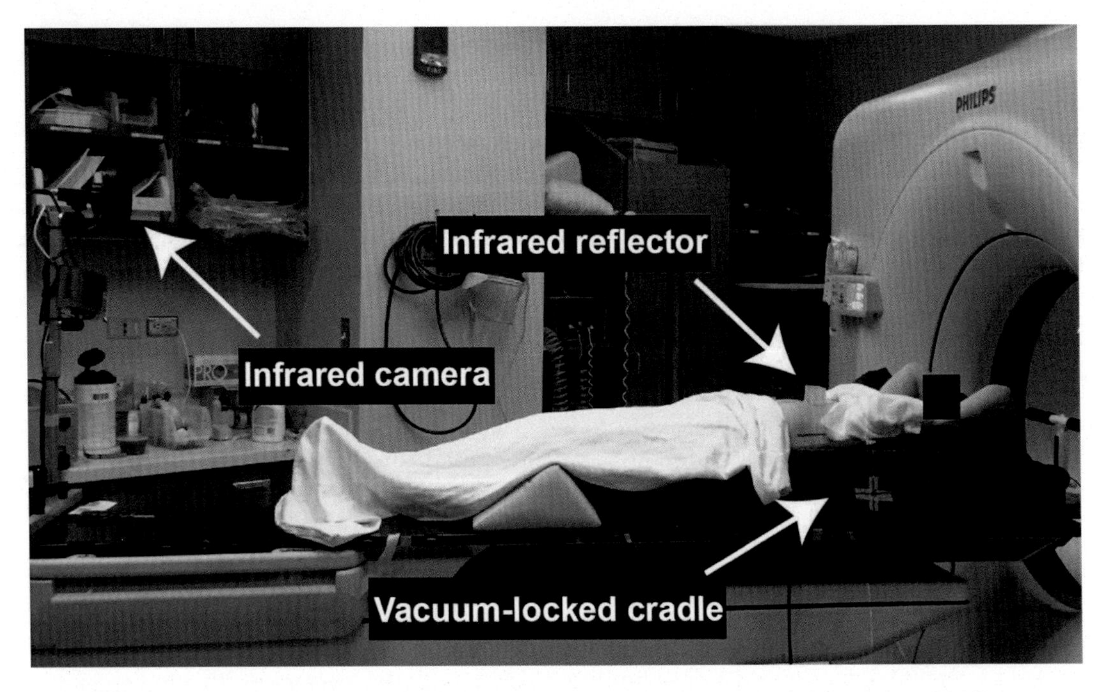

FIGURE 14.2 Non-surgical Directed Liver Therapies Abbreviations: EHD, extrahepatic disease; LM, liver metastases; MWA, microwave ablation; RFA, radiofrequency ablation; SBRT, stereotactic body radiation therapy; SIRT, selective internal radiation therapy (Koay et al., 2018).

locoregional control often in cases of very advanced disease with inadequate liver reserve or extremely large sizes. Further discussion of these techniques are beyond the purview of this chapter. However, it is important to acknowledge that several studies have investigated the safety of combined radioembolization with Yttrium-90 (Y-90) microspheres and external beam irradiation (Lam et al., 2013; Wang et al., 2018). Strong predictors for post-treatment hepatotoxicity include combined doses delivering ≥30 Gy to ≥13 percent (V30 ≥13 percent) and the volume of the liver receiving a combined dose of 100 – 140 Gy (V100 – V140) (Wang et al., 2018). Commercial software modules are now available that can help estimate the dose delivered to the liver with Y-90 but do have their limitations.

External beam radiation: treatment planning considerations

Patients that are deemed good candidates for external beam radiation therapy undergo a treatment planning session, otherwise known as a simulation, in the radiation oncology department with a computed tomography (CT) scan in the treatment position. This involves immobilizing the patient with a body mold and placing surface marks on the patient that allow for accurate daily set-up with infrared technology (Fig. 14.2). In certain departments, patients may also undergo simulation with positron emission topography (PET) or magnetic resonance imaging (MRI), which provides functional imaging in addition to anatomic imaging that can help with target delineation and motion management. After simulation, target volumes and organs at risk (OAR) are contoured by the radiation oncologist and treatment planning commences with the help of a dosimetrist and physicist until the desired dose objectives for the tumor and surrounding OAR are met.

Immobilization and infrared technology help with daily set-up but further strategies are needed for motion control. Suboptimal motion control increases the risk of a marginal miss and increases the risk of dose delivery to radiosensitive organs at risk such as the bowel. The liver is susceptible to motion by the diaphragm during respiration and the range of motion is greatest in the cranio-caudal direction, with amplitude exceeding 2 cm in some cases (Schuppan and Afdhal, 2008). In addition, day-to-day differences in luminal structures such as variability in stomach, bowel, and gallbladder filling can affect tumor positioning during treatment (Schiedermaier et al., 1997; Crane and Koay, 2016). To minimize stomach and bowel variability, patients are often instructed to be nil per os (NPO) for at least 3–5 h prior to radiation therapy. Medication management with simethicone may be utilized in cases with significant gaseous volume in the bowel.

Image-guided radiotherapy has made considerable advancements in the last few decades and accounting for organ-induced motion of tumors during treatment can now be achieved with a high degree of fidelity. Several strategies for motion management include real-time respiratory gating, active breathing control (ABC), and abdominal compression. Real-time respiratory gating during treatment can be done with continuous monitoring of endoscopic or percutaneous peritumoral placement of fiducials, often gold or carbon, with automated shifting guided by the ExacTrac or CyberKnife systems (Wurm et al., 2006). Orthogonal films or on-board imaging with cone-beam CT allow for fiducial-based alignment for target positioning but will not provide motion control alone (Fig. 14.3). In addition to continuous monitoring with fiducial-based systems, the Active Breathing Control (ABC) or Varian RPM systems allows for patients to be treated only during a certain phase of the respiratory cycle, often either in the expiratory or inspiratory breath hold phases. However, intra-fractional variation is not completely minimized with the breath hold technique and daily image guidance with orthogonal or 3D imaging using metallic fiducials or a soft tissue surrogate, such as the liver contour, is still required (Stick et al., 2020). In contrast to continuous monitoring or treatment with a breath hold, respiratory gating can trigger treatment only when the surface surrogate for breathing motion, such as a fiducial on the patient's abdomen tracked by a couch-mounted camera or the use of infrared technology with VisionRT, is within a certain phase of the respiratory cycle during the patients normal breathing cycle (phase-based gating) (Crane and Koay, 2016). When the breathing pattern is irregular, amplitude-based gating may be used instead (beam only at expiration) (Crane and Koay, 2016). In addition to the aforementioned strategies, some centers will use an abdominal compression device to restrict the movement of the abdomen, but this only minimizes rather than controls motion, and can push luminal structures closer to the liver, especially with metastases in the left liver lobe which are in close proximity to the stomach, and thereby may increase radiation dose delivered to these structures (Heinzerling et al., 2022).

For image guidance, on-board cone-beam CT is widely available at most centers (Fig. 14.4). However, motion artifact can be significant, and a 3-D breath hold or 4-D cone-beam CT can help improve image quality in tumors susceptible to organ-induced motion. Cone-beam CT can allow for treatment alignment using radiopaque markers such as peritumoral fiducials

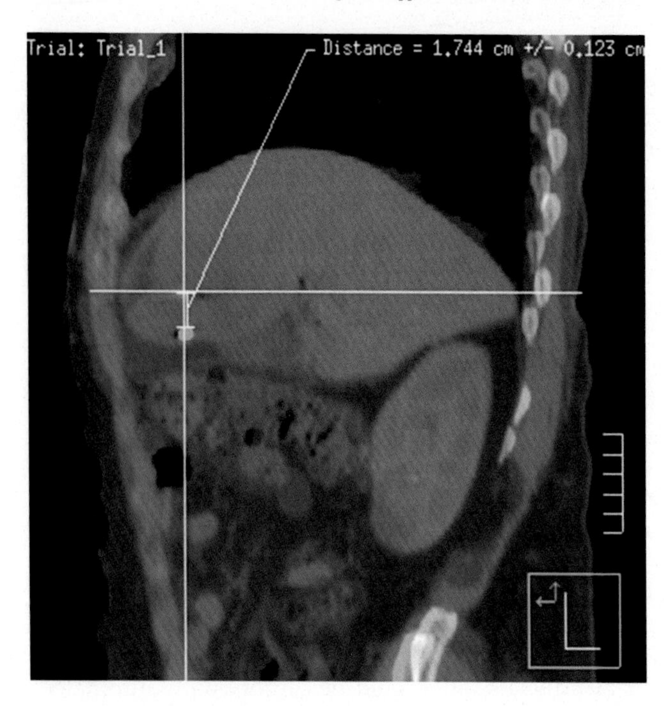

FIGURE 14.3 Example setup at Simulation with a Vacuum-locked cradle for immobilization and a thoracic wingboard to keep arms out of the radiation field and infared technology for positional alignment.

or soft tissue surrogates like the contour of the liver. In a limited number of centers, a CT-on-rails allows for diagnostic quality CT scans to be captured, providing improved visualization of the target and surrounding organs at risk compared to cone-beam CT. In recent years, linear accelerators with on-board MR imaging allows for even better soft tissue visualization for daily image guidance and adaptive replanning based on tumor and OAR positioning variability to maintain desired dose objectives achieved during planning (Rosenberg et al., 2018; Romesser et al., 2021). Dynamic MR based tumor tracking and gating of the tumor, which allow for monitoring of the tumor position in real-time with delivery of radiation and can reduce variability, will allow tighter margins to be used and, thus, increase sparing of healthy tissue (Sahin et al., 2019). Adaptive replanning with on-board MR imaging allows for changes to the radiation plan to be made on a daily basis to ensure optimal tumor target coverage and normal tissue sparing (Winkel et al., 2019). Such strategies will allow us to overcome limitations with SABR treatment using CT-based planning such as fiducial-less treatments and improved ability to meet dose-limiting constraints (Romesser et al., 2021).

External beam radiation: target volume design and treatment objectives

After simulation, target volumes are contoured by the radiation oncologist and used for treatment planning. In tumors that are amenable to 3–5 fraction SBRT and ablative doses, a gross tumor volume plus an institutional margin, generally 5 mm, serves as the target volume. Based on prospective clinical trials and multi-institutional studies, a prescription starting point that achieves a BED of $\geq$100 Gy to the target volume is preferred, such as 50 Gy in 5 fractions

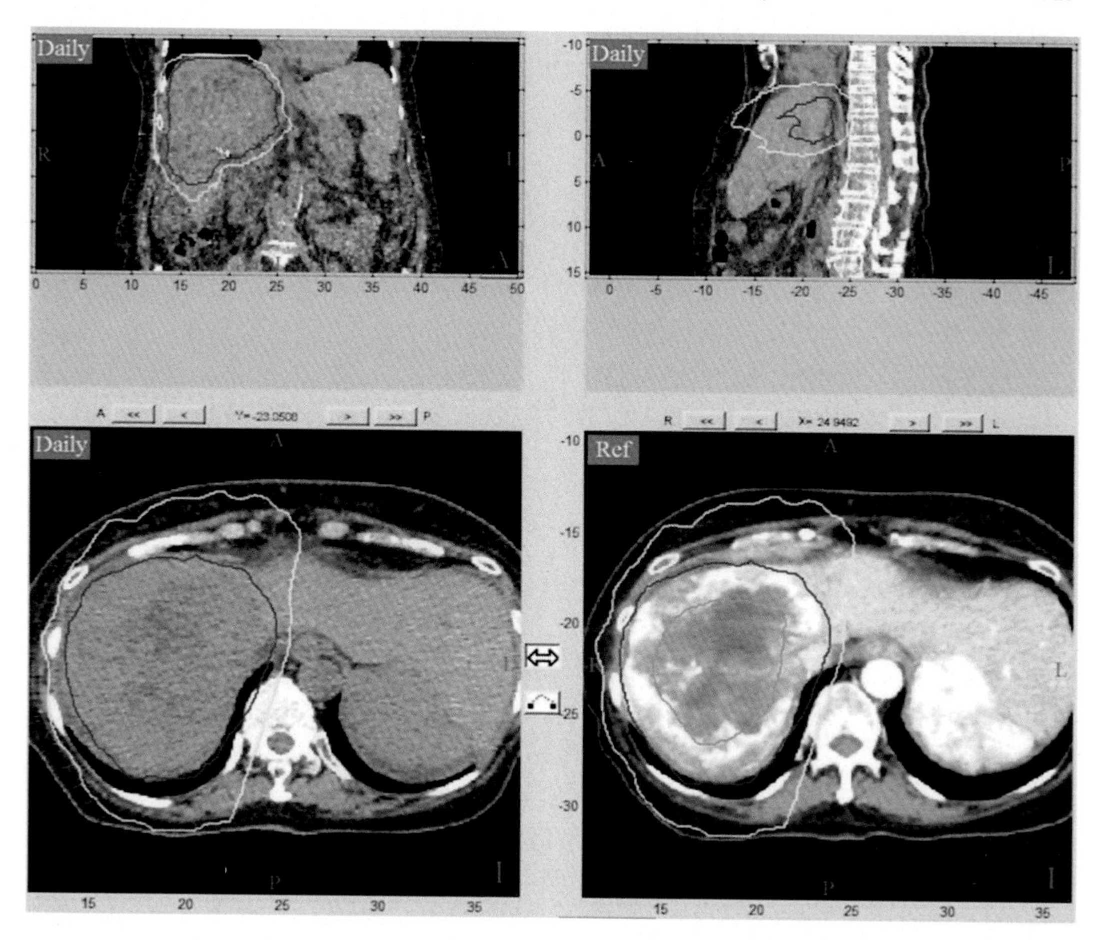

FIGURE 14.4 Peritumor Fiducial Surrogate for Daily Image Guidance with On-Board Imaging (Crane and Koay, 2016).

or 36–45 Gy in 3 (Table 14.2). In tumors that are large in size (≥6 cm) or have radiosensitive structures located within 1–2 cm of the tumor nearby (luminal organs, central biliary, that is), SBRT is not always the technique of choice. The principle of stereotactic treatment lends itself to significant heterogeneity, which means hotspots can be 110–150 percent hotter than the prescription dose may be allowed to achieve the sharp fall-off gradient around the tumor. This principle can prove prohibitive to the use of SBRT in the aforementioned situations, and will require significant under-coverage to areas of the target volume that abut significant structures at risk. To improve coverage in such situations and minimize treatment-related toxicity, IMRT regimens of 15 – 25 fractions in 67.5 – 75 Gy fractions may be utilized instead. Often, such plans, will require the creation of a simultaneous integrated boost (SIB) volume, whereby the high-dose target volume is constrained by an expansion off organs at risk (Fig. 14.5).

Where available, protons can serve as a potential alternative to photon-based treatments especially in cases where inadequate amounts of the normal liver can be spared with SBRT

TABLE 14.2 Dosing regimens explored with SBRT for liver metastases.

Study	Study type	Patients	Primary histology	Dose (Gy)/ Fraction number	BED (a/b = 10)
Herfarth et al. (Herfarth et al., 2001)	Phase I/II	37	Mixed	14–26 /1	33–94
Mendez-Romero et al. (Romero et al., 2006)	Phase I/II	17	Mixed	37.5/3	84
Rusthoven et al. (Rusthoven et al., 2009)	Phase I/II	47	Mixed	36–60/3	79–180
Lee et al. (Lee et al., 2009)	Dose escalation, phase I	68	Mixed	28–60/6	41–120
Rule et al. (Rule et al., 2010)	Dose escalation, Phase I	27	Mixed	30/3–50–60/5	60–132
Comito et al. (Comito et al., 2014)	Observational	42	Colorectal	75/3	263
Scorsetti et al. (Scorsetti et al., 2015)	Phase II	42	Colorectal	75/3	263
Goodman et al. (Goodman et al., 2010)	Dose escalation, phase I	26	Mixed	18–30/1	50–120
Meyer et al. (Meyer et al., 2016)	Dose escalation, Phase I	14	Mixed	35–40/1	158–200
Hong et al. (Hong et al., 2017)	Phase II	14	Mixed	30–50/5	48–100
Scorsetti et al. (Scorsetti et al., 2018)	Phase II	61	Mixed	75/3	263
Kang et al. (Kang et al., 2019)	Phase I	9	Mixed	36–60/3	79–180
Dawson et al. (Dawson et al., 2019)	Dose escalation, phase I, multicenter	26	Mixed	35–50/10	47–75

or IMRT photon-based techniques, such as in bi-lobar cases or with large liver tumors, and re-irradiation scenarios (Hong et al., 2017; Fukumitsu et al., 2015). The physical interactions of proton beams with normal tissue differs from that of photons and provides the rationale for proton beam radiotherapy (PBT). After a brief build-up zone, photons reach their maximum dose deposition in superficial tissue and deposit additional dose along the entire beam path until they exit the body which means non-target normal tissues are exposed to dose along the "entrance" and "exit" of the photon beam's path in front of and behind the target. In contrast, protons, deposit a lower dose in front of the target prior to entering tissue, and do not deposit most of their dose until a narrow peak at the end of the treatment range, known as the Bragg's Peak, and deliver almost no "exit dose" beyond the peak. Manipulation of the Bragg's peak

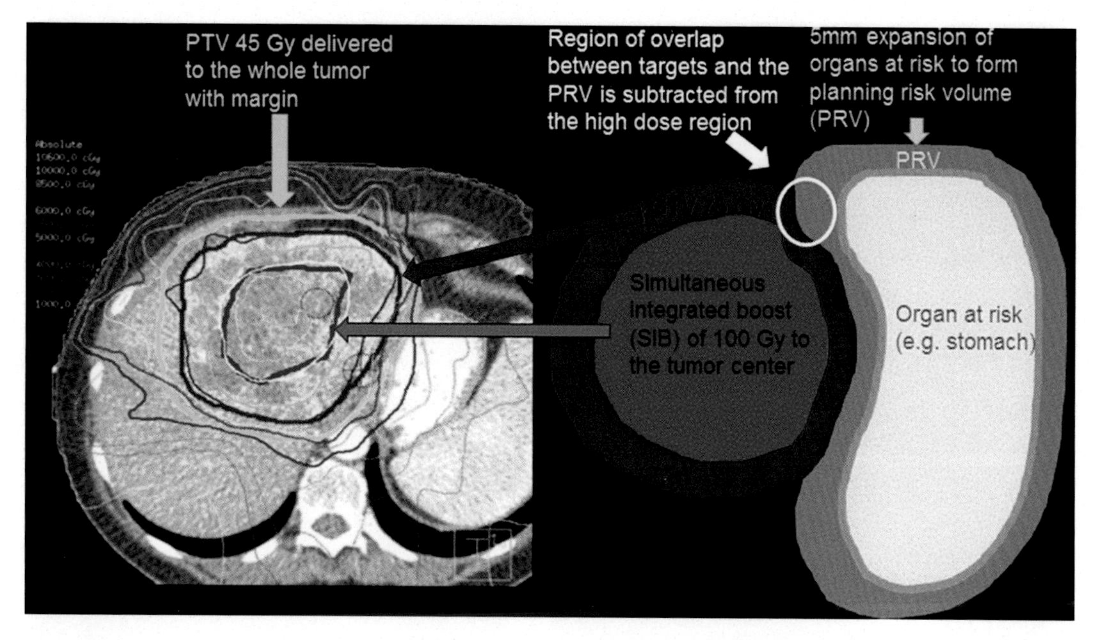

FIGURE 14.5 Daily Image Guidance for Liver SBRT with On-Board Cone-Beam CT Reference: Crane et al. (Crane and Koay, 2016).

with scattering and scanning techniques can significantly reduce the volume of liver irradiated compared to photons (Fig. 14.6) (Wang et al., 2008; Hallemeier et al., 2020).

With the advent of more conformal photon-based plans such as SBRT or IMRT, classic RILD is uncommonly seen in patients today and it is more common for patients to develop non-classic RILD. In such scenarios, a markedly elevated serum transaminase level (>5x upper limit of normal) and jaundice is seen, and the most vulnerable populations are those with underlying liver dysfunction from cirrhosis or viral hepatitis (Koay et al., 2018). The mechanism of injury is not well understood but may involve damage to regenerating hepatocytes or reactivation of viral hepatitis (Guha and Kavanagh, 2011). In such patients, protons may be useful to minimize the risk of non-classic RILD. However, proton beam ranges are susceptible to significantly more uncertainty and are less robust to variation in anatomic factors and motion management which can make protons challenging to deliver with high fidelity (Tryggestad et al., 2020). The uncertainty with the path of the beam and the potentially increased penumbra due to lateral scatter means protons are not a good choice if a critical structure is abutting the tumor at the end of the beam's path (Tryggestad et al., 2020). A summary of treatment planning considerations including technique of choice, target volume design, and treatment objectives are summarized in Table 14.3.

Generally, chemotherapy is held during SBRT for several weeks before and after treatment to minimize potential toxicity. Particular attention should be given to patients on antiangiogenic therapy as reports of unanticipated late luminal GI toxicities have emerged in patients treated with high-dose SBRT to GI structures while on such therapy. In theory, antiangiogenic therapy can impair the wound healing process from damage to GI structures

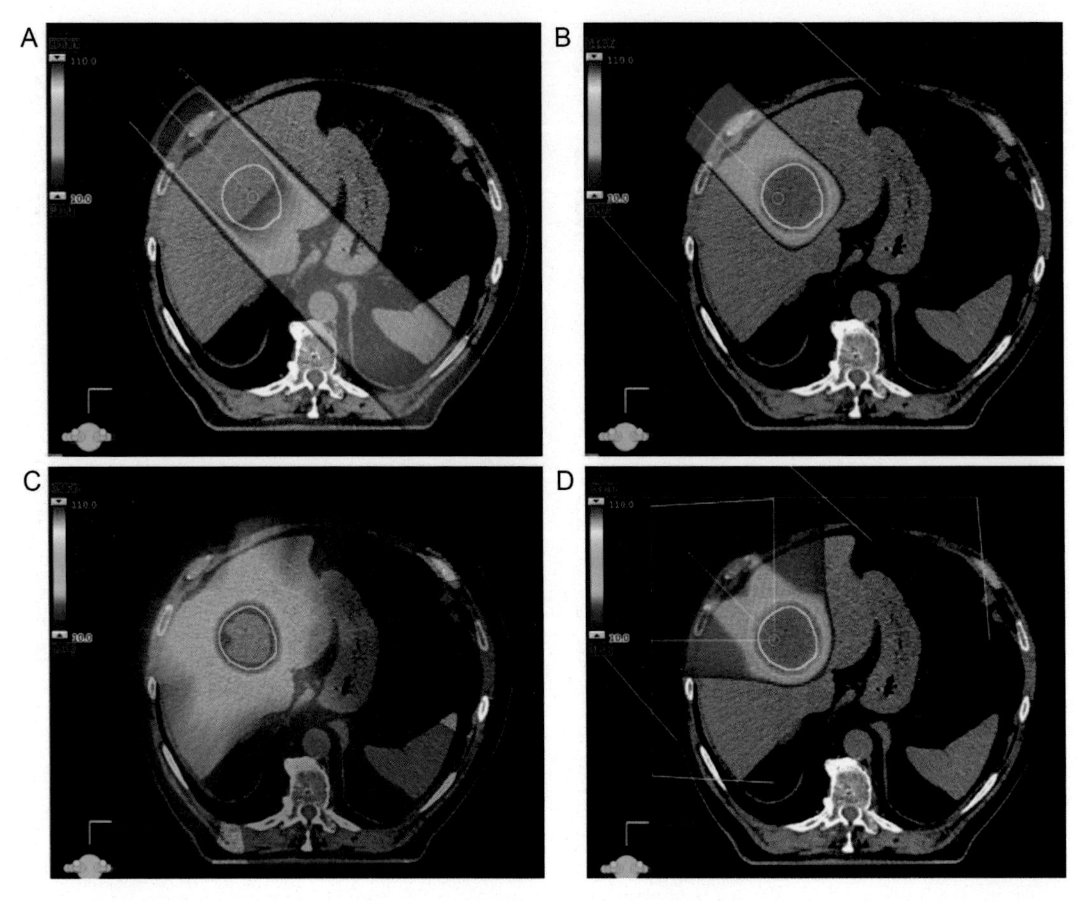

FIGURE 14.6 Simultaneous Integrated Boost (SIB) Volume Design for Target Volume Coverage and Organ at Risk (OAR) Sparing with moderately hypofractionated IMRT (3–4 Gy per fraction) Reference: Hallemeier et al. (Hallemeier et al., 2020).

inflicted by SBRT (Pollom et al., 2015). Until more robust data emerges to guide decision making with such therapy, caution should be employed in the concurrent or sequential use of radiation with such agents.

External beam radiation: outcomes and surveillance considerations

A systematic review of retrospective series and prospective studies with a total of 656 patients with heavily pre-treated oligometastatic hepatic CRC (1–2 lesions in most cases) with heterogenous dosing regimens report a pooled one- and two-year overall survival (OS) outcomes of 67 percent and 57 percent, respectively, and a median OS of 31 months (Petrelli et al., 2018). Median PFS was 11 months with pooled one-year and two-year LC outcomes of 67 percent and 59 percent, respectively. However, a correlation with BED was identified and

TABLE 14.3 Treatment planning summary and dose objectives.

Technique	Dose	Constraints
SBRT preferred for lesions ≤6 cm and limited in number (1–4 as a general rule) IMRT For large tumors or tumors close to sensitive structures (stomach, central hepatobiliary tract) where ablative doses are not possible, moderate hypofractionated IMRT courses may be preferred Protons preferred for re-irradiation, large liver tumors, or bilobar-cases or to spare critical structures located 1–2 cm behind the target	Generally prefer ablative doses that achieve a BED of 100 Gy: 50 Gy in 5 fractions 36–45 Gy in 3 fractions Moderately hypofractionated courses if ablative doses cannot be delivered: 67.5 in 15 fractions 75 Gy in 25 fractions	Liver For 3–5 fractions: 13–15 Gy mean liver dose with 700 cc normal liver no more than 15 Gy For moderately hypofractionated courses (3–4.5 Gy per fraction): 24 Gy mean liver dose and 700 cc of liver receiving no more than 24 Gy Stomach and Small bowel 22–30 Gy max dose if 3–5 fractions 40 Gy max dose if 10 fractions 45 Gy max dose if 15 fractions 54 Gy max dose if 25–28 fractions Large Bowel: 30 Gy max dose if 3–5 fractions 40 Gy max dose if 10 fractions 45 Gy max dose if 15 fractions 60 Gy max dose if 25–28 fractions Central biliary tree: 45 Gy max dose if 3–5 fractions 60 Gy max dose if 10 fractions 70 Gy max dose if 15 fractions 80 Gy max dose if 25–28 fractions Chest wall: 30 Gy to no more than 30 cc if 3–5 fractions

2-year LC and OS would be expected to increase by 21 percent and 11 percent, respectively, with a BED increase up to 100 Gy. In an international registry of 427 patients with 568 liver metastases with the CRC being the most common histology (44 percent), and a median SBRT dose of 45 Gy (range: 12 – 60 Gy) in a median of 3 fractions (range: 1–5 fractions), the median OS was 14 months for all histologies but greater for CRC at 27 months (Mahadevan et al., 2018). Smaller tumor volumes (<40 cm^3) correlated with a significantly improved mOS (25 months vs 15 months) and BED ≥100 Gy was also associated with improved OS rates (27 months vs 15 months) (Mahadevan et al., 2018). 2-year LC rates were improved with BED ≥100 Gy (78 percent vs 60 percent) and for tumors <40 cm^3 (52 vs 39 months) (Mahadevan et al., 2018). A summary of OS and LC outcomes from historical phase 1 and phase II trials are summarized in Table 14.4.

Regarding surveillance post-treatment, several considerations include the nature of imaging changes that can be associated with a treatment response and volumetric changes because of treatment. The University of Colorado reported a maximum total liver volume decrease of ~20 percent (the result of liver shrinkage) at 3 to 6 months after SBRT, followed by a recovery to ~10 percent less than the pretreatment volume at 12 months after SBRT, which suggests hepatic cell regeneration is possible after SBRT due to the parallel vascular supply of the liver (Stinauer et al., 2012). This has important implications in considering the potential for

TABLE 14.4 Historical outcomes with SBRT for liver metastases.

Study	Study type	Patients	Primary histology	Overall survival	Local tumor control	Toxicity
Herfarth et al. (Herfarth et al., 2001)	Phase I/II	37	Mixed	72 percent @ 1 year	71 percent @ 1 year	NR
Mendez-Romero et al. (Romero et al., 2006)	Phase I/II	17	Mixed	85 percent @ 1 year, 62 percent @ 2 years	100 percent @ 1 year, 86 percent @ 2 years	12 percent G3 liver
Rusthoven et al. (Rusthoven et al., 2009)	Phase I/II	47	Mixed	30 percent @ 2 years	95 percent @ 1 year, 92 percent @ 2 years	1.5 percent G3 (dermatitis)
Lee et al. (Lee et al., 2009)	Dose escalation, phase I	68	Mixed	47 percent @ 1.5 years	71 percent @ 1 year	10 percent G3+
Rule et al. (Rule et al., 2010)	Dose escalation, Phase I	27	Mixed	50 percent, 67 percent, 56 percent* @ 2 years	100 percent, 89 percent, 56 percent * @ 2 years	4 percent G3 Liver
Comito et al. (Comito et al., 2014)	Observational	42	Colorectal	85 percent @ 1 year, 65 percent @ 2 years	95 percent @ 1 year, 85 percent @ 2 years	60^ G2, 0 percent G3
Scorsetti et al. (Scorsetti et al., 2015)	Phase II	42	Colorectal	65 percent @ 2 years	95 percent @ 1 year, 91 percent @ 2 years, 85 percent @ 3 years	25 percent G2 Liver, 0 percent G3
Goodman et al. (Goodman et al., 2010)	Dose escalation, phase I	26	Mixed	50 percent @ 2 years	77 percent @ 1 year	8 percent GI Bleeding
Meyer et al. (Meyer et al., 2016)	Dose escalation, Phase I	14	Mixed	78 percent @ 2 years	100 percent @ 2.5 years	6 percent G2

(continued on next page)

TABLE 14.4 Historical outcomes with SBRT for liver metastases—cont'd

Study	Study type	Patients	Primary histology	Overall survival	Local tumor control	Toxicity
Hong et al. (Hong et al., 2017)	Phase II	14	Mixed	66 percent @ 1 year, 21 percent @ 3 years	72 percent @ 1 year, 61 percent @ 3 years	No G3+
Scorsetti et al. (Scorsetti et al., 2018)	Phase II	61	Mixed	85 percent @ 1 year, 31 percent @ 3 years, 18 percent @ 5 years	94 percent @ 1 year, 78 percent @ 3 years, 78 percent @ 5 years	2 percent G3 chest wall pain
Kang et al. (Kang et al., 2019)	Phase I	9	Mixed	NR	NR	No G3+
Dawson et al. (Dawson et al., 2019)	Dose escalation, phase I, multicenter	26	Mixed	NR	NR	7.7 percent G3 GI

retreatment with locoregional therapies such as radiation and other modalities like surgery, for example. In addition, early reorganizations of the irradiated volume due to ablative doses make evaluation of treatment response per RECIST criteria problematic (Tétreau et al., 2017). The response of liver metastases after SBRT can be more reliably assessed based on a combination of size and enhancement pattern, especially a lobulated pattern (Tétreau et al., 2017).

Future directions

The role of radiation continues to revolve at a rapid pace with new techniques yet on the horizon. Functional imaging with PET tracers may allow for biology-guided radiotherapy with improved target volume design to guide dose escalation approaches in the future (Shirvani et al., 2021). In addition, preclinical studies have reported that ultrahigh dose rates with FLASH radiation may lead to reduced radiation induced gastrointestinal toxicity (Levy et al., 2020). Precision medicine with radiation therapy biomarkers and liquid biopsies may allow for better patient stratification and improved monitoring of treatment response (De Michino et al., 2020). In addition, SBRT can potentially increase the immunogenicity of the tumor microenvironment and studies are current underway that are exploring the utility of combining SBRT with immunotherapeutic agents for hepatic metastases for colorectal cancer (Deming et al., 2020). In a recent report, patients with oligometastatic pancreatic and CRC received dual checkpoint inhibition with SBRT to 24 Gy in 3 fractions every other day (Parikh et al., 2019). Overall, 40 patients with CRC had a median disease control rate (DCR) of 25 percent with a median OS of 7.1 months but DCR improved to 37 percent with a median OS of 10.9 months if patients were able to receive radiation in the trial (Parikh et al., 2019). Pretreatment biopsies revealed low tumor mutational burden for all samples, but higher numbers of natural killer (NK) cells and expression of the HERVK repeat RNA in patients with disease control (Parikh et al., 2019). Future trials will need to incorporate patient-specific imaging, tissue, and serum biomarkers to improve patient stratification and treatment customization as we move towards making personalized medicine a reality for all.

References

Barry, A., McPartlin, A., & Lindsay, P. (2017). Dosimetric analysis of liver toxicity after liver metastasis stereotactic body radiation therapy. *Practice Radiation Oncology, 7*, e331–e337.

Bujold, A., Massey, C. A., Kim, J. J., Brierley, J., Cho, C., Wong, R. K., et al. (2013). Sequential phase I and II trials of stereotactic body radiotherapy for locally advanced hepatocellular carcinoma. *Journal of Clinical Oncology, 31*(13), 1631–1639. May 1 http://doi.org/10.1200/JCO.2012.44.1659. Epub 2013 Apr 1. PMID: 23547075.

Case, J. T. (1924). The occurence of hepatic lesions in patients treated by intensive deep roentgen irradiation. *American Journal of Roentgenology, Radium Therapy and Nuclear Medicine, 12*(27).

Chang, D. T., Swaminath, A., Kozak, M., Weintraub, J., Koong, A. C., Kim, J., et al. (2011). Stereotactic body radiotherapy for colorectal liver metastases: a pooled analysis. *Cancer, 117*(17), 4060–4069. Sep 1 http://doi.org/10.1002/cncr.25997. Epub 2011 Mar 22. Erratum in: Cancer. 2012 May 15;118(10):2776. PMID: 21432842.

Comito, T., Cozzi, L., Clerici, E., Campisi, M. C., Liardo, R. L., Navarria, P., et al. (2014). Stereotactic Ablative Radiotherapy (SABR) in inoperable oligometastatic disease from colorectal cancer: a safe and effective approach. *BMC cancer, 14*, 619. http://doi.org/10.1186/1471-2407-14-619.

Crane, C. H., & Koay, E. J. (2016). Solutions that enable ablative radiotherapy for large liver tumors: fractionated dose painting, simultaneous integrated protection, motion management, and computed tomography image guidance. *Cancer, 122*(13), 1974–1986. http://doi.org/10.1002/cncr.29878.

Cummings, L. C., Payes, J. D., & Cooper, G. S. (2007). Survival after hepatic resection in metastatic colorectal cancer: a population-based study. *Cancer, 109*, 718–726.

Dawson, L. A., Normolle, D., & Balter, J. M. (2002). Analysis of radiation-induced liver disease using the Lyman NTCP model. *International Journal of Radiation and Oncology in Biology and Physics, 53*, 810–821.

Dawson, L. A., Winter, K. A., Katz, A. W., Schell, M. C., Brierley, J., Chen, Y., et al. (2019). NRG Oncology/RTOG 0438: a Phase 1 Trial of Highly Conformal Radiation Therapy for Liver Metastases. *Pract. Radiat. Oncol., 9*, e386–e393. http://doi.org/10.1016/j.prro.2019.02.013.

De Michino, S., Aparnathi, M., Rostami, A., Lok, B. H., & Bratman, S. V. (2020). The Utility of Liquid Biopsies in Radiation Oncology. *International Journal of Radiation and Oncology in Biology and Physics, 107*(5), 873–886. Aug 1 http://doi.org/10.1016/j.ijrobp.2020.05.008. Epub 2020 May 14. PMID: 32417410.

Deming, D. A., Emmerich, P., Turk, A. A., Lubner, S. J., Volodymyrivna Uboha, N., LoConte, N. K., et al. (2020). Pembrolizumab (Pem) in combination with stereotactic body radiotherapy (SBRT) for resectable liver oligometastatic MSS/MMR proficient colorectal cancer (CRC). *Journal of Clinical Oncology, 38*(15_suppl), 4046.

Fukumitsu, N., Okumura, T., Takizawa, D., Makishima, H., Numajiri, H., Murofushi, K., et al. (2015). Proton beam therapy for metastatic liver tumors. *Radiotherapy and Oncology, 117*(2), 322–327. Nov http://doi.org/10.1016/j.radonc.2015.09.011. Epub 2015 Sep 15. PMID: 26385268.

Goodman, K. A., Wiegner, E. A., Maturen, K. E., Zhang, Z., Mo, Q., Yang, G., et al. (2010). Dose-Escalation Study of Single-Fraction Stereotactic Body Radiotherapy for Liver Malignancies. *International Journal of Radiation and Oncology in Biology and Physics, 78*, 486–493. http://doi.org/10.1016/j.ijrobp.2009.08.020.

Guha, C., & Kavanagh, B. D. (2011). Hepatic radiation toxicity: avoidance and amelioration. *Seminars in Radiation Oncology, 21*, 256–263.

Hallemeier, C. L., Ashman, J. B., & Haddock, M. G. (2020). Haddock MG. A brief overview of the use of proton beam radiotherapy for gastrointestinal cancers. *Journal of Gastrointestinal Oncology, 11*(1), 139–143. http://doi.org/10.21037/jgo.2019.07.06.

Heinzerling, J. H., Anderson, J. F., Papiez, L., Boike, T., Chien, S., Zhang, G., et al. (2022). Four-dimensional computed tomography scan analysis of tumor and organ motion at varying levels of abdominal compression during stereotactic treatment of lung and liver. *International Journal of Radiation and Oncology in Biology and Physics*.

Helling, T. S., & Martin, M. (2014). Cause of Death from Liver Metastases in Colorectal Cancer. *Annals of Surgical Oncology, 21*, 501–506. https://doi.org/10.1245/s10434-013-3297-7.

Hellman, S., & Weichselbaum, R. R. (1995). Oligometastases. *Journal of Clinical Oncology, 13*(1), 8–10. Jan http://doi.org/10.1200/JCO.1995.13.1.8. PMID: 7799047.

Herfarth, K. K., Debus, J., Lohr, F., Bahner, M. L., Rhein, B., Fritz, P., et al. (2001). Single-Dose Radiation Therapy of Liver Tumors: results of a Phase I/II Trial. *Journal of Clinical Oncology, 19*, 164–170. http://doi.org/10.1200/JCO.2001.19.1.164.

Hong, T. S., Wo, J. Y., Borger, D. R., Yeap, B. Y., McDonnell, E. I., Willers, H., et al. (2017). Phase II Study of Proton-Based Stereotactic Body Radiation Therapy for Liver Metastases: importance of Tumor Genotype. *JNCI: Journal of the National Cancer Institute, 109*(9). September, djx031. https://doi.org/10.1093/jnci/djx031.

Høyer, M., Swaminath, A., Bydder, S., Lock, M., Méndez, R. A., Kavanagh, B., et al. (2012). Radiotherapy for liver metastases: a review of evidence. *International Journal of Radiation and Oncology in Biology and Physics, 82*(3), 1047–1057. Mar 1 http://doi.org/10.1016/j.ijrobp.2011.07.020. PMID: 22284028.

Jackson, W. C., Tao, Y., Mendiratta-Lala, M., et al. (2018). Comparison of Stereotactic Body Radiation Therapy and Radiofrequency Ablation in the Treatment of Intrahepatic Metastases. *International Journal of Radiation and Oncology in Biology and Physics, 100*(4), 950–958. http://doi.org/10.1016/j.ijrobp.2017.12.014.

Joo, J. H., Park, J. H., Kim, J. C., Yu, C. S., Lim, S. B., Park, I. J., et al. (2017). Local Control Outcomes Using Stereotactic Body Radiation Therapy for Liver Metastases From Colorectal Cancer. *International Journal of Radiation and Oncology in Biology and Physics, 99*(4), 876–883. Nov 15 http://doi.org/10.1016/j.ijrobp.2017.07.030. Epub 2017 Jul 31. PMID: 29063852.

Kang, J. I., Sufficool, D. C., Hsueh, C.-T., Wroe, A. J., Patyal, B., Reeves, M. E., et al. (2019). A phase I trial of Proton stereotactic body radiation therapy for liver metastases. *Journal of Gastrointestinal Oncology, 10*, 112–117. http://doi.org/10.21037/jgo.2018.08.17.

Katsoulakis, E., Riaz, N., Cannon, D. M., Goodman, K., Spratt, D. E., Lovelock, M., et al. (2014). Image-guided Radiation Therapy for Liver Tumors. *American Journal of Clinical Oncology, 37*(6), 561–567. http://doi.org/10.1097/COC.0b013e318282a86b.

Koay, E. J., Owen, D., & Das, P. (2018). Radiation-Induced Liver Disease and Modern Radiotherapy. *Seminars in Radiation Oncology, 28*(4), 321–331. 10.1016/j.semradonc.2018.06.007. PMID: 30309642; PMCID: PMC6402843.

Künzli, B. M., Abitabile, P., & Maurer, C. A. (2011). Radiofrequency ablation of liver tumors: actual limitations and potential solutions in the future. *World Journal of Hepatology, 3*(1), 8–14. http://doi.org/10.4254/wjh.v3.i1.8.

Lam, M. G., Abdelmaksoud, M. H., Chang, D. T., Eclov, N. C., Chung, M. P., Koong, A. C., et al. (2013). Safety of 90Y radioembolization in patients who have undergone previous external beam radiation therapy. *International Journal of Radiation and Oncology in Biology and Physics, 87*(2), 323–329. Oct 1 http://doi.org/10.1016/j.ijrobp.2013.05.041. Epub 2013 Jul 9. PMID: 23849697.

Lasley, F. D., Mannina, E. M., Johnson, C. S., Perkins, S. M., Althouse, S., Maluccio, M., et al. (2015). Treatment variables related to liver toxicity in patients with hepatocellular carcinoma, Child-Pugh class A and B enrolled in a phase 1-2 trial of stereotactic body radiation therapy. *Practice Radiation Oncology, 5*(5), e443–e449. Sep-Oct http://doi.org/10.1016/j.prro.2015.02.007. Epub 2015 Apr 18. PMID: 25899219.

Lawrence, T. S., Ten Haken, R. K., Kessler, M. L., et al. (1992). The use of 3-D dose volume analysis to predict radiation hepatitis. *International Journal of Radiation and Oncology in Biology and Physics, 23*, 781–788.

Le, D. T., Uram, J. N., Wang, H., et al. (2015). PD-1 Blockade in Tumors with Mismatch-Repair Deficiency. *New England Journal of Medicine, 372*(26), 2509–2520. http://doi.org/10.1056/NEJMoa1500596.

Lee, M. T., Kim, J. J., Dinniwell, R., Brierley, J., Lockwood, G., Wong, R., et al. (2009). Phase I Study of Individualized Stereotactic Body Radiotherapy of Liver Metastases. *Journal of Clinical Oncology, 27*, 1585–1591. http://doi.org/10.1200/JCO.2008.20.0600.

Levy, K., Natarajan, S., Wang, J., et al. (2020). Abdominal FLASH irradiation reduces radiation-induced gastrointestinal toxicity for the treatment of ovarian cancer in mice. *Science Reports, 10*, 21600. https://doi.org/10.1038/s41598-020-78017-7.

Mahadevan, A., Blanck, O., Lanciano, R., et al. (2018). Stereotactic Body Radiotherapy (SBRT) for liver metastasis - clinical outcomes from the international multi-institutional RSSearch® Patient Registry. *Radiation oncology, 13*(1), 26. Published 2018 Feb 13 http://doi.org/10.1186/s13014-018-0969-2.

Maor, Y., & Malnick, S. (2013). Liver injury induced by anticancer chemotherapy and radiation therapy. *Int J Hepatol, 2013*, 815105.

Meyer, J. J., Foster, R. D., Lev-Cohain, N., Yokoo, T., Dong, Y., Schwarz, R. E., et al. (2016). A Phase I Dose-Escalation Trial of Single-Fraction Stereotactic Radiation Therapy for Liver Metastases. *Annals of Surgical Oncology, 23*, 218–224. http://doi.org/10.1245/s10434-015-4579-z.

Misiakos, E. P., Karidis, N. P., & Kouraklis, G. (2011). Current treatment for colorectal liver metastases. *World Journal of Gastroenterology, 17*(36), 4067–4075. Sep 28 http://doi.org/10.3748/wjg.v17.i36.4067. PMID: 22039320; PMCID: PMC3203357.

Onishi, H., Araki, T., Shirato, H., et al. (2004). Stereotactic hypofractionated high-dose irradiation for stage I nonsmall cell lung carcinoma: clinical outcomes in 245 subjects in a Japanese multiinstitutional study. *Cancer, 101*, 1623–1631.

Palma, D. A., Olson, R., Harrow, S., Gaede, S., Louie, A. V., Haasbeek, C., et al. (2019). Stereotactic ablative radiotherapy versus standard of care palliative treatment in patients with oligometastatic cancers (SABR-COMET): a randomised, phase 2, open-label trial. *Lancet, 393*(10185), 2051–2058. May 18 http://doi.org/10.1016/S0140-6736(18)32487-5. Epub 2019 Apr 11. PMID: 30982687.

Parikh, A. R., Clark, J. W., Wo, J. Y.-L., Yeap, B. Y., Allen, J. N., Blaszkowsky, L. S., et al. (2019). A phase II study of ipilimumab and nivolumab with radiation in microsatellite stable (MSS) metastatic colorectal adenocarcinoma (mCRC). *Journal of Clinical Oncology, 37*(15), 3514–3551 suppl.

Pawlik, T. M., Olino, K., Gleisner, A. L., Torbenson, M., Schulick, R., & Choti, M. A. (2007). Preoperative chemotherapy for colorectal liver metastases: impact on hepatic histology and postoperative outcome. *Journal of Gastrointestinal Surgery, 11*(7), 860–868. Jul http://doi.org/10.1007/s11605-007-0149-4. PMID: 17492335.

Petrelli, F., Comito, T., Barni, S., Pancera, G., Scorsetti, M., & Ghidini, A. (2018). SBRT for CRC liver metastases. Stereotactic body radiotherapy for colorectal cancer liver metastases: a systematic review. *Radiotherapy and Oncology, 129*(3), 427–434. Dec http://doi.org/10.1016/j.radonc.2018.06.035. Epub 2018 Jul 9. PMID: 29997034.

Pollom, E. L., Deng, L., Pai, R. K., et al. (2015). Gastrointestinal Toxicities With Combined Antiangiogenic and Stereotactic Body Radiation Therapy. *International Journal of Radiation and Oncology in Biology and Physics, 92*(3), 568–576. http://doi.org/10.1016/j.ijrobp.2015.02.016.

Reed, G. B. J., & Cox, A. J. J. (1966). The human liver after radiation injury. A form of veno-occlusive disease. *American Journal of Pathology, 48*(4), 597–611.

Romero, A. M., Wunderink, W., Hussain, S. M., De Pooter, J. A., Heijmen, B. J., Nowak, P. C., et al. (2006). Stereotactic body radiation therapy for primary and metastatic liver tumors: a single institution phase i–ii study. *Acta Oncol, 45*, 831–837. http://doi.org/10.1080/02841860600897934.

Romesser, P. B., Tyagi, N., & Crane, C. H. (2021). Magnetic Resonance Imaging-Guided Adaptive Radiotherapy for Colorectal Liver Metastases. *Cancers (Basel), 13*(7), 1636. Apr 1 http://doi.org/10.3390/cancers13071636. PMID: 33915810; PMCID: PMC8036824.

Rosenberg, S. A., Henke, L. E., Shaverdian, N., Mittauer, K., Wojcieszynski, A. P., Hullett, C. R., et al. (2018). A Multi-Institutional Experience of MR-Guided Liver Stereotactic Body Radiation Therapy. *Adv Radiat Oncol, 4*(1), 142–149. Aug 23 http://doi.org/10.1016/j.adro.2018.08.005. PMID: 30706022; PMCID: PMC6349638.

Ruers, T., et al. (2012). Radiofrequency ablation combined with systemic treatment versus systemic treatment alone in patients with non-resectable colorectal liver metastases: a randomized EORTC Intergroup phase II study (EORTC 40004)." Annals of oncology: official journal of the. *European Society for Medical Oncology, 23*(10), 2619–2626. http://doi.org/10.1093/annonc/mds053.

Rule, W., Timmerman, R., Tong, L., Abdulrahman, R., Meyer, J., Boike, T., et al. (2010). Chinsoo Cho L. Phase I Dose-Escalation Study of Stereotactic Body Radiotherapy in Patients with Hepatic Metastases. *Annals of Surgical Oncology, 18*, 1081–1087. http://doi.org/10.1245/s10434-010-1405-5.

Russell, A. H., Clyde, C., & Wasserman, T. H. (1993). Accelerated hyperfractionated hepatic irradiation in the management of patients with liver metastases: results of the RTOG dose escalating protocol. *International Journal of Radiation and Oncology in Biology and Physics, 27*, 117–123.

Rusthoven, K. E., Kavanagh, B. D., Cardenes, H., Stieber, V. W., Burri, S. H., Feigenberg, S. J., et al. (2009). Multi-institutional phase I/II trial of stereotactic body radiation therapy for liver metastases. *Journal of Clinical Oncology, 27*(10), 1572–1578. Apr 1 http://doi.org/10.1200/JCO.2008.19.6329. Epub 2009 Mar 2. PMID: 19255321.

Sahin, B., Mustafayev, T. Z., Gungor, G., Aydin, G., Yapici, B., Atalar, B., et al. (2019). First 500 Fractions Delivered with a Magnetic Resonance-guided Radiotherapy System: initial Experience. *Cureus, 11*, e6457. http://doi.org/10.7759/cureus.6457.

Schiedermaier, P., Neubrand, M., Hansen, S., & Sauerbruch, T. (1997). Variability of gallbladder emptying after oral stimulation. *Scandinavian Journal of Gastroenterology, 32*(7), 719–724. Jul http://doi.org/10.3109/00365529708996524. PMID: 9246714.

Schuppan, D., & Afdhal, N. H. (2008). Liver cirrhosis. *Lancet, 371*, 838–851.

Scorsetti, M., Comito, T., Clerici, E., Franzese, C., Tozzi, A., Iftode, C., et al. (2018). Phase II trial on SBRT for unresectable liver metastases: long-term outcome and prognostic factors of survival after 5 years of follow-up. *Radiation oncology, 13*, 234. http://doi.org/10.1186/s13014-018-1185-9.

Scorsetti, M., Comito, T., Tozzi, A., Navarria, P., Fogliata, A., Clerici, E., et al. (2015). Final results of a phase II trial for stereotactic body radiation therapy for patients with inoperable liver metastases from colorectal cancer. *Journal of Cancer Research and Clinical Oncology, 141*, 543–553. http://doi.org/10.1007/s00432-014-1833-x.

Shirvani, S. M., Huntzinger, C. J., Melcher, T., Olcott, P. D., Voronenko, Y., Bartlett-Roberto, J., et al. (2021). Biologyguided radiotherapy: redefining the role of radiotherapy in metastatic cancer. *British Journal of Radiology*, 2021 Jan 1;*94*(1117):20200873. doi:10.1259/bjr.20200873. Epub 2020 Oct 30. PMID: 33112685; PMCID: PMC7774706.

Soliman, H., Ringash, J., Jiang, H., Singh, K., Kim, J., Dinniwell, R., et al. (2013). Phase II trial of palliative radiotherapy for hepatocellular carcinoma and liver metastases. *J Clin Oncol Off J Am Soc Clin Oncol, 31*(31), 3980–3986. http://doi.org/10.1200/JCO.2013.49.9202.

Stick, L. B., Vogelius, I. R., Risum, S., & Josipovic, M. (2020). Intrafractional fiducial marker position variations in stereotactic liver radiotherapy during voluntary deep inspiration breath-hold. *British Journal of Radiology, 93*(1116), 20200859. Dec 1 http://doi.org/10.1259/bjr.20200859. Epub 2020 Sep 11. PMID: 32915653; PMCID: PMC7716004.

Stinauer, M. A., Diot, Q., Westerly, D. C., Schefter, T. E., & Kavanagh, B. D. (2012). Fluorodeoxyglucose positron emission tomography response and normal tissue regeneration after stereotactic body radiotherapy to liver metastases. *International Journal of Radiation and Oncology in Biology and Physics, 83*(5), e613–e618. Aug 1 http://doi.org/10.1016/j.ijrobp.2012.02.008. Epub 2012 Apr 10. PMID: 22494588.

Suresh, K., Owen, D., Bazzi, L., et al. (2018). Using Indocyanine Green Extraction to Predict Liver Function After Stereotactic Body Radiation Therapy for Hepatocellular Carcinoma. *International Journal of Radiation and Oncology in Biology and Physics, 100*(1), 131–137. http://doi.org/10.1016/j.ijrobp.2017.09.032.

Tao R., Krishnan S., Bhosale P. R., Javle M. M., Aloia T. A., Shroff R. T., et al. (2019). Ablative Radiotherapy Doses Lead to a Substantial Prolongation of Survival in Patients With Inoperable Intrahepatic Cholangiocarcinoma: A Retrospective Dose Response Analysis. *J Clin Oncol. 2016 Jan 20;34*(3):219–226. doi:10.1200/JCO.2015.61.3778. Epub 2015 Oct 26. Erratum in: J Clin Oncol. 2019 Apr 10;37(11):942. PMID: 26503201; PMCID: PMC4980564.

Tétreau, R., Llacer, C., Riou, O., & Deshayes, E. (2017). Evaluation of response after SBRT for liver tumors. *Reports of Practical Oncology and Radiotherapy, 22*(2), 170–175. http://doi.org/10.1016/j.rpor.2015.12.004.

Toesca, D. A., Osmundson, E. C., & Eyben, R. V. (2017). Central liver toxicity after SBRT: an expanded analysis and predictive nomogram. *Radiotherapy and Oncology, 122*, 130–136.

Tryggestad, E. J., Liu, W., Pepin, M. D., Hallemeier, C. L., & Sio, T. T. (2020). Managing treatment-related uncertainties in proton beam radiotherapy for gastrointestinal cancers. *Journal of Gastrointestinal Oncology, 11*(1), 212–224. http://doi.org/10.21037/jgo.2019.11.07.

Wang, T. H., Huang, P. I., Hu, Y. W., Lin, K. H., Liu, C. S., Lin, Y. Y., et al. (2018). Combined Yttrium-90 microsphere selective internal radiation therapy and external beam radiotherapy in patients with hepatocellular carcinoma: from clinical aspects to dosimetry. *Plos One, 13*(1), e0190098. Jan 2. http://doi.org/10.1371/journal.pone.0190098. PMID: 29293557; PMCID: PMC5749761.

Wang, X., Krishnan, S., Zhang, X., Dong, L., Briere, T., Crane, C. H., et al. (2008). Proton radiotherapy for liver tumors: dosimetric advantages over photon plans. *Medical Dosimetry, 33*(4), 259–267. Winter. http://doi.org/10.1016/j.meddos.2007.04.008. PMID: 18973852.

Winkel, D., Bol, G. H., Kroon, P. S., Van Asselen, B., Hackett, S. S., Werensteijn-Honingh, A. M., et al. (2019). Adaptive radiotherapy: the Elekta Unity MR-linac concept. *Clinical and translational radiation oncology, 18*, 54–59. http://doi.org/10.1016/j.ctro.2019.04.001.

Wurm, R. E., Gum, F., Erbel, S., et al. (2006). Image guided respiratory gated hypofractionated Stereotactic Body Radiation Therapy (H-SBRT) for liver and lung tumors: initial experience. *Acta Oncol, 45*, 881–889.

CHAPTER

15

Immunotherapy and targeted therapies for colorectal liver metastasis

Ashish Manne, MBBS and Anne Noonan, MBBCh

The Ohio State University, Internal Medicine Department, Medical Oncology Division, Columbus, OH, United States

Hepatic metastatic disease from colorectal cancer or colorectal liver metastasis (CLM) occurs in almost half of patients with primary colorectal cancer (CRC) (Van Der et al., 2012). Management of CLM depends on its resectability (synchronous metastasis or recurrence) and often involves a multidisciplinary approach. For liver metastases that are unresectable upfront, chemotherapy, known as conversion therapy (CT) is given. The size (diameter < 6 cms vs ≥ 6 cms) and the number (≤ 4 vs > 4) of CLM are independent factors associated with successful CT (Ma and Li, 2021). In this chapter, we focus on targeted therapy and immunotherapy in the management of CRC with specific emphasis on CLM.

Targeted therapy in CRC with CLM

The backbone of cytotoxic chemotherapies used in metastatic colorectal cancer are FOLFOX (5FU, leucovorin, and oxaliplatin) and FOLFIRI (5FU, leucovorin, irinotecan). The two major classes of drugs currently added to these chemotherapy regimens are anti-VEGF (bevacizumab) and EGFR inhibitors (EGFRi) for RAS wild-type tumors (RAS-WT) (cetuximab and panitumumab).

Resectable CLM at diagnosis with no extra-hepatic metastatic disease

The addition of bevacizumab (Bev) or cetuximab (Cet) to FOLFOX or FOLFIRI is acceptable in resectable liver metastases though some controversy exists on the benefit of adding a

Contemporary Management of Metastatic Colorectal Cancer: A Precision Medicine Approach
DOI: https://doi.org/10.1016/B978-0-323-91706-3.00005-9

targeted therapy. However, the addition of Bev to capecitabine and oxaliplatin combination or CAPEOX (six cycles and no Bev on last for the last cycle) before surgery in high-risk CRC had an impressive objective response rate or ORR (73 percent) in a single-arm Phase II trial (Gruenberger et al., 2008). In this trial, CRC with synchronous liver metastases, metastatic disease developed within one year after primary resection, lymph node-positive primary tumors, CLMs, >1 or > 5 cm, and positive carcinoembryonic antigen level were considered high-risk. Alternatively, cet did not significantly impact when added to perioperative therapy (POT) (Primrose et al., 2014; Bridgewater et al., 2020). When the interim-analysis was first published in 2014 with a median follow up of 20.7 m, the median progression free survival (mPFS) difference was significant (14.1 m without Cet vs. 20.5 m with Cet, hazard ratio or HR of 1.48, $p = 0.030$). The survival advantage was not significant on the updated results published in 2020 with a median follow-up of 66.7 m (22.2 m without Cet vs. 15.5 m, HR of 1.17, $p = 0.304$). Notably, the median overall survival (mOS) was significantly worse with cetuximab (81 m without Cet vs. 55.4 m with Cet, HR of 1.45, $p = 0.036$). Therefore, targeted therapy is not typically used in CRC with resectable CLM, but there is some evidence of bevacizumab's benefit in high-risk disease. After resection, adjuvant therapy is recommended with 5-Fluorouracil/Leucovorin (5FU/LV) and oxaliplatin (FOLFOX).

Unresectable CLM at diagnosis with a potential for resection with no extra-hepatic metastatic disease

Neoadjuvant therapy (NAT) with CAPEOX + Bev in high-risk CRC (>4, >5 cm in diameter, unlikely R0 resection or inadequate viable liver function if undergoing upfront resection, or inability to retain liver vascular supply) had an ORR of 78 percent (Wong et al., 2011). Out of 46 patients enrolled, 40 percent of the patients with unresectable disease at diagnosis had a resection. Four patients had such a good response that they were placed on observation without surgery when the trial results were published. Bev with FOLFOXIRI (combination of 5FU/LV, oxaliplatin and irinotecan) has a higher resection rate (61 percent vs 49 percent), R0 resection rate (49%percent vs 29 percent), ORR (81 percent vs 62 percent), mPFS (18.6 vs 11.5 m) compared to FOLFOX (Gruenberger et al., 2015). The addition of Bev to chemotherapy does not have any survival advantage after hepatic artery infusion chemotherapy (HAIC) pump placement (Kemeny et al., 2011). Alternatively, it increases liver toxicity (hyperbilirubinemia > 3 mg/dL) and is not recommended.

In the POCHER trial, when Cet administration was followed by chronomodulated irinotecan (Iri), 5FU/LV on days 2–6 every two weeks as NAT for 43 patients with unresectable CLM, 60 percent (25/43) had complete resections (Garufi et al., 2010). The study population included nine patients with >5 cm lesions and 29 patients with > 4 lesions. The 2-year survival rate was 68 percent for the entire population. In resected patients, it was as high as 80 percent. This led to studies that assessed the utility of EGFRi in NAT or POT. The CELIM study published in 2014 showed a long-term survival advantage when Cet was added to FOLFOX or FOLFIRI in patients with inoperable CLM at diagnosis in eligible patients (with K-RAS codon 12/13/61 WT) (Folprecht et al., 2014). In summary, for patients with unresectable CLM at diagnosis but with the potential for resection with POT or NAT, there is no clear winner between anti-VEGF therapy and EGFRi therapy (in the eligible patients).

CLM with no potential for resection and/or unresectable extra-hepatic disease

First-line therapy- in combination with chemotherapy

In mCRC with CLM and no surgical consideration, Bev is recommended in the first-line in RAS-mutated (RAS-MT) tumors. In RAS-WT tumors, a metanalysis of two randomized control studies and three observational studies reported better OS, ORR, and complete response (CR) rate with Cet over Bev (with chemotherapy backbone) (Zheng et al., 2019). The same study reported no significant differences in PFS, disease control rate (DCR), and partial response (PR) rate between two drugs. Similarly, Pan improved PFS with no difference in OS when compared to Bev in the PEAK trial (Rivera et al., 2017). The role of the primary tumor side (right vs. left) was studied extensively in the last 5 years. Two metanalyses have clearly shown that left-sided tumors respond well to EGFRi than Bev irrespective of the CLM-status (Arnold et al., 2017; Holch et al., 2017).

On the other hand, there was no statistically significant OS and PFS difference between Bev and EGFRis in right-sided tumors. In the PEAK trial and FIRE-3 trial, the depth of response (the percentage of tumor shrinkage observed at the nadir compared with baseline) was more with EGFRi than Bev (with chemotherapy) in RAS-WT tumors (Rivera et al., 2017; Mansmann et al., 2013; Stintzing et al., 2016). Another essential factor in deciding the drugs is tolerability. Anti-VEGF therapy is not preferred in patients with the history of thromboembolic disease, uncontrolled hypertension, proteinuria, high-risk for bleeding, and gastrointestinal perforation (Piawah and Venook, 2019). Therefore, in RAS-WT mCRC with CLM, EGFRi (Cet or Pan) is preferred over Bev (with chemotherapy) in left-sided tumors, while either of them can be used in right-sided tumors.

Currently, biosimilars such as bevacizumab-awwb can be used instead of Bev, but other VEGF inhibitors (Ramcurimab or Ram and Ziv-aflibercept or Ziv) are reserved for second-line therapy. Between Pan and Cet, there is no clear evidence of one being better than the other. As Pan is a humanized monoclonal antibody (mab), it is often preferred in patients who have allergic reactions to Cet, a mouse-based mab.

Table 15.1 below describes the approved targeted therapies and the chemotherapy pairings in metastatic colorectal cancer in addition to the ongoing trials adding newer targeted agents.

Subsequent lines of therapy

When Bev is used in first-line, prospective and retrospective studies showed that continuing Bev in the second line improves PFS and OS with no increase in adverse events (Masi et al., 2015; Bennouna et al., 2013; Grothey et al., 2008; Cartwright et al., 2012). There is no conclusive evidence suggesting any benefit in switching Bev to Cet or Pan in eligible patients after disease progression. Switching Bev to other VEGF inhibitors has no advantage either. Ziv-aflibercept or Ramucirumab is beneficial in patients who progress on oxaliplatin-based therapy (FOLIRI-naïve) and when given in combination with FOLFIRI (Van Cutsem et al., 2012; Tabernero et al., 2015). Bev can be used with TAS-102 (trifluridine and tipiracil hydrochloride) in the third or fourth line, too (Pfeiffer et al., 2020).

TABLE 15.1 Targeted therapy in the management of colorectal cancers.

Targeted therapy	Approved	Ongoing trials
EGFRi inKRAS/NRAS/BRAF WT mCRC	Cetuximab or Cet + FOLFOX or FOLFIRI* (Zheng et al., 2019) Cet + Irinotecan (Iri)** (Kopetz et al., 2021) Panitumumab or Pan + FOLFOX or FOLFIR* (Rivera et al., 2017)	Cet + Pembrolizumab (Pembro) in mCRC (NCT02713373)$^{I/II}$ Cet + Encorafenib, + Nivolumab (Nivo) in MSS, BRAFV600E-MT mCRC(NCT04017650)$^{I/II}$ Cet or Pan + Regorafenib (Reg) in mCRC (NCT04117945)^{II} Cet + Utomilumab + Iri in mCRC (NCT03290937)^{I} Vemurafenib + Cet + Irinotecan in mST (NCT01787500)^{I} Tepotinib + Cet in RAS/BRAF – WT (NCT04515394)^{IIX} Cet + Avelumumab (Ave) in mCRC EGFRi-Refractory (Troiani et al., 2019) Pan, alone or with Trametinib (MEK-inhibitor) in EGFRi-Refractory mCRC (NCT03087071)^{II} Pan + Niraparib in mCRC NCT03983993^{II}
Adagrasib in KRAS 12C Mutated CRC		Monotherapy vs. with Pembro, Afatinib or Cet (NCT03785249)$^{I/II}$
BRAF inhibitor KRAS/NRAS/ WTBRAFV600E MT	Encorafenib + Cet+ (± Binimetinib)** (Van Geel et al., 2017)	Vemurafenib (Vem) + Cet + FOLFIRI in mCRC (NCT03727763)^{II} Vem + Cet + Camrelizumab (ICI) in MSS mCRC (NCT05019534)^{I} Dabrafenib + Tramatenib PDR001 in mCRC (NCT04294160)^{II}
Neurotrophic tyrosine receptor kinase (NTRK) inhibitors (in NTRK positive tumors)	Entrectanib** (Doebele et al., 2020) Larotectinib** (Drilon et al., 2018)	Entrectanib in mST (NCT02568267)^{II} Larotectinib in mST (NCT02576431)^{II}
HER2 inhibitors HER2 amplified withKRAS/NRAS/BRAFWT	Trastuzumab (Traz) + Pertuzumab (Per)** (Meric-Bernstam et al., 2019) Traz + Laptinib** (Sartore-Bianchi et al., 2016)Trastuzumab deruxtecan (T-dx)** (Siena et al., 2021)	Neratinib + Traz vs Neratinib + Cet (Need PIK3CA WT too) mCRC (NCT03457896)^{II} Traz + Per vs Cet + Iri in mCRC (NCT03365882)^{II} Pyrotinib Maleate ± Traz in mCRC (NCT04380012)^{IIT}-DXd in mCRC (NCT04744831)^{II} T-Dx in mST (NCT04639219)^{II} Tucatinib + Traz in mCRC (NCT03043313)^{II} Tucatinib + Tras + Oxaliplatin-based mGI (NCT04430738)$^{Ib/II}$ BDC-1001 ± Pembro in mST (NCT04278144) $^{I/II}$
Anti Vascular Endothelial Growth Factor Receptor (VEGF)	Bevacizumab* or Bev + FOLFOX or FOLFIRI or FOLFOXIRI (Cremolini et al., 2015; Emmanouilides et al., 2007; Heinemann et al., 2014) Bev + TAS-102** (trifluridine and tipiracil hydrochloride) [29] Ziv-aflibercept**^{Y} (Van Cutsem et al., 2012) Ramucirumab**^{Y} (Tabernero et al., 2015)	Atezolizumab (Az)+ FOLFOXIRI + Bev vs FOLFOXIRI + Bev^{II*} (NCT03721653)FOLFOX + Bev + Az vs Az in MSI-H mCRC (NCT02997228)^{III} *Az + Bev + FOLFOX in CLM (NCT03698461)$^{II\ Neoadjuvant}$ Pembro + Ziv-aflibercept in mST (NCT02298959)^{I}
Tyrosine Kinase Inhibitor	Regorafenib (Reg) (Grothey et al., 2013)	Reg + Ipi/Nivo^{IR} (NCT04362839) Reg+ Avelumab in mST (NCT03475953)$^{I/II}$ Reg + Pembro (NCT03657641)$^{I/IIR}$ Reg followed by Irinotecan + Cet or Pan (NCT04117945)^{IIR} Pan vs Reg or TAS-02 mCRC (NCT03992456)^{II}

X – Wild-Type Left-Sided mCRC Patients Having Acquired Resistance to Anti-EGFR Antibody Targeting Therapy Due to MET Amplification Y – In combination with FOLFIRI in FOLFIRI naïve patients after progression on Bev; EGFRi – Epidermal growth factor receptor inhibitors. mCRC – metastatic colorectal cancer, mST – mestastaic solid tumors (basket trials); WT – wild type, MT-mutated; I – phase I trial, II – phase 2 trial; R – in resected tumors; *Approved for the first line or secondline; **Approved subsequent lines, Neoadjuvant – therapy in the neoajuvant setting.

If Cet or Pan is used the first-line, continuing EGFRi does not have OS benefit (Cremolini et al., 2018; Cremolini et al., 2019). Acquired resistance that can develop in a few patients can be detected in circulating tumor DNA (Siravegna et al., 2015; Misale et al., 2012; Sartore-Bianchi et al., 2021). This resistance is expected to wear off with time (Parseghian et al., 2019). Therefore, switching to Bev is recommended. Switching from Cet to Pan or vice versa is not beneficial after disease progression. If not used in the first-line, EGFRi can be given alone (monotherapy in patients who cannot tolerate chemotherapy) or with Iri, FOLFIRI, or FOLFOX, but not with CAPEOX (Karapetis et al., 2008; Au et al., 2009; Van Cutsem et al., 2007; Sobrero et al., 2008; Cunningham et al., 2004; Peeters et al., 2010). Current trials are studying them in combination with other drugs such as ICI, BRAF inhibitors, and tyrosine kinase inhibitors (TKI), as summarized in Table 15.1. MRTX849 (adagrasib) is a molecular inhibitor against $KRAS^{G12C}$. It has shown the potential to treat cancers in preclinical studies and is being studied as a single-agent and in combination with Cet, Afatinib, Pembrolizumab (KRYSTAL-1, NCT03785249) (Hallin et al., 2020; Janes et al., 2018).

In refractory mCRC, patients with BRAF mutation, specifically, BRAF V600E and KRAS-WT, can be treated with doublet, including BRAF inhibitors (such as Encorafenib) and Cet or Pan (Kopetz et al., 2021; Kopetz et al., 2019). Triplet therapy with MEK inhibitor (Binimetinib) showed survival advantage over the control group (Cet with Iri or FOLFIRI) and the doublet therapy in the interim-analysis of BEACON trial (Kopetz et al., 2019). However, an updated analysis published in 2021 showed no advantage of triplet therapy over doublet compared to the control group (Tabernero et al., 2021). Other BRAF inhibitors, Dabrafenib and Vemurafenib, with/without MEK inhibitors (Trametinib), showed encouraging results in the early trials with Pan (Corcoran et al., 2018; Yaeger et al., 2015).

About 6 percent of CRCs have HER2 amplification or overexpression (Ross et al., 2018; Seo et al., 2014). In refractory mCRC patients with HER2 amplification and RAS/BRAFWT, Trastuzumab (Traz), a HER2 inhibitor, with Pertuzumab (a mab that prevents dimerization of HER2 and HER3) or Lapatinib (inhibitor of that binds to the cytoplasmic ATP-binding site inhibitor EGFR/HER1 and HER2 receptors) (Meric-Bernstam et al., 2019; Sartore-Bianchi et al., 2016). Trastuzumab deruxtecan (T-dx), an antibody-drug conjugate of humanized anti-HER2 antibody with topoisomerase I inhibitor, showed good ORR (24 percent) in refractory mCRC that earned its approval in May 2021 (Siena et al., 2021). T-dx showed activity in the patients who were refractory to HER2 inhibitors also. Neurotrophic tyrosine receptor kinase (NTRK) genes code tyrosine kinase receptors that regulate cell proliferation, and rearrangements in them lead to uncontrolled cell growth (Lange and Lo, 2018). Its prevalent in just 0.3 percent of solid tumors and was initially identified in CRC (Pulciani et al., 1982). The trials that gave NTRK inhibitors such as Entrectanib and Larotectinib in solid tumors had 7 percent of CRC (Doebele et al., 2020; Drilon et al., 2018). This can be an option in patients with NTRK mutations.

The CORRECT trial, which gave us Regorafenib (Reg), a multikinase tyrosine kinase inhibitor, is a multicenter, randomized placebo-controlled, phase 3 trial (Grothey et al., 2013). Reg had a 1.4-m survival advantage over placebo (mOS is 6.4 for Reg vs. 5 m for Placebo, $p = 0.0052$). Reg was associated with higher treatment-related toxicity (93 percent in Reg vs 61 percent in placebo). Hand-foot skin reactions were the most frequent (83 percent) adverse reaction reported, followed by fatigue (48 percent) and hypertension (36 percent). It is currently being studied in combination with ICIs such as pembrolizumab (Pembro), ipilimumab

(Ipi)/nivolumab (Nivo), and EGFRis (NCT04117945, NCT03844620, & NCT03657641). Its use is often compared with TAS-102 that included the improved OS by 1.8 m over placebo (Mayer et al., 2015). It is under investigation with ICI and EGFRi combinations (Table 15.1).

Immunotherapy

In the current clinical practice, immunotherapy in CRC is synonymous with ICI such as PD-1 inhibitors such as Pembro and Nivo; PDL-1 inhibitors such as Atezoliuzumab (Az), Avelumab (Ave), and Durvalumab (D); CTLA4 inhibitors such as Ipilumimab (Ipi) and Tremelimumab (T). Microsatelliote intsability-high (MSI-H) mCRC patients with no potential for resection or in patients with CLM (or lung metastasis) who are inoperable at presentation but have a potential for resection are treated with Pembro or Nivo (± Ipi) (Le et al., 2017; Overman et al., 2018; Overman et al., 2017; André et al., 2020). We summarized the current ICI status in managing mCRC in Table 15.2 below. ICI is not approved for treating resectable CRC as NAT or AT. It can be used in POT for unresectable CLM with a potential for resection.

In a randomized phase III study (KEYNOTE-177), Pembro was superior to chemotherapy (5FU based ± Bev or Cet) in the first line for PFS (16.5 vs. 8.2 m; HR, 0.60; 95 percent confidence interval [CI], 0.45 to 0.80; $P = 0.0002$) at the second interim-analysis published in 2020 with a median follow-up of 32.4 m (André et al., 2020). Nivo (± Ipi) approval was based on the success of CHECKMATE-142, a phase II, non-randomized trial in MSI-H mCRC who progressed on at least one line of chemotherapy (Overman et al., 2018; Overman et al., 2017). Early clinical trials with Ave (in MSI-H and POLE positive mCRC) and $D + T$ (MSI-H mCRC) are encouraging (Kim et al., 2020; Chen et al., 2020). The former is a single-arm study, while in the latter, the comparative arm was best supportive care. Using T alone (irrespective of MSI-H status) did not significantly improve ORR in refractory CRC (Chung et al., 2010). Similarly, Az did not have success as maintenance therapy (with 5FU/Bev in mCRC stable after 16 weeks of FOLFOX) or third-line setting (± Cometinib vs. Reg) (Eng et al., 2019; Grothey et al., 2018).

Adoptive cell therapy (ACT) and vaccines are other types of immunotherapy that are not approved for CRC management yet. There has been some success in early trials, as discussed in Table 15.3 (below) and Table 15.4.

ACT comes in many forms, and it can be a) genetically engineered (chimeric antigen receptors or CARs) autologous T cells or NK cells directed against proteins such as carcinoembryonic antigen (CEA) and tumor-associated glycoprotein (TAG)−72), b) Tumor-infiltrating lymphocytes (TIL), and c) dendric cells (DC) (Parkhurst et al., 2011; Hege et al., 2017; Xiao et al., 2019; Tran et al., 2016). One of the first trials with CAR-T in mCRC was directed against CEA (Parkhurst et al., 2011). In that trial, 1/3 patients showed an objective response in the lung and liver metastatic disease while all the patients showed a significant decrease in the CEA level (74–99 percent). All three patients had dose-limiting colitis though. A similar trial (NCT04513431) is currently going on in an adjuvant setting, including the patients with resected CLM. In another phase one trial, CAR-T against TAG-72 showed relative safety when administered intravenously (C-9701) or into CLM via hepatic artery infusion (Hege et al., 2017). The response was promising when messenger RNA (mRNA) CAR-modified NK cells were injected intraperitoneally or into CLM in mCRC patients (Xiao et al., 2019). Metastatic

TABLE 15.2 Immune-checkpoint inhibitors in management of colorectal cancers.

Immune-check point inhibitor	Approved	Early success	Ongoing trials
Pembrolizumab (Pembro)	In MSI-H mCRC* (André et al., 2020)	Pembro+ Napabucasin (STAT3 inhibitor)$^{I/II}$ in mCRC (MSS and MSI-H)	XmAb®22,841 Monotherapy & in Combination w/ Pembrolizumab in mST (NCT03849469)^{I} Cet + Pembro in mCRC (NCT02713373)$^{I/II}$ Adagrasib monotherapy vs with Pembro, Afatinib or Cet (NCT03785249)$^{I/IIBDC}$-1001 +/- Pembro in mST (NCT04278144)$^{I/II}$ Pembro + Ziv-aflibercept in mST (NCT02298959)^{I} Reg + Pembro (NCT03657641)$^{I/IIR}$
Nivolumab (Nivo) and Ipilumimab (Ipi)	In MSI-H mCRC* (Overman et al., 2018)	Nivo + Regorafenib (Reg) in mCRC (and GC)^{Ib} (Fukuoka et al., 2020)	FOLFOXIRI + Bev + Nivo in RAS-MT/BRAF-MT (NCT04072198)^{II}*SX-682 + Nivo for MSS /RAS-WT (NCT04599140)$^{Ib/II}$ Reg + Nivo in MSS mCRC (NCT04030260)^{II} Cet + Encorafenib, + Nivo in MSS, BRAFV600E-MT mCRC (NCT04017650)$^{I/II}$ Reg + Ipi/Nivo^{IR} (NCT04362839)
Avelumab (Ave)		Ave in MSI-H and POLE positive mCRC^{II} [65]	Ave + second-line chemo in MSI-H mCRC (NCT03186326)^{II}**Avelumab + chemotherapy in MSI-H/POLE Stage III CRC (NCT03827044)$^{III\ Adjuvant}$ Reg+ Avelumab in mST (NCT03475953)$^{I/II}$
Durvalumab (D)+ Tremelimumab (T)		*D* + T^{II} in MSI-H mCRC[66]	*D* + *T* + FOLFOX (NCT03202758)$^{I/II}$**D* + T in resected CLM (NCT02754856)^{I}
Atezolizumab (Az)			Az+ FOLFOXIRI + Bev vs FOLFOXIRI + Bev^{II}* (NCT03721653)mFOLFOX6 + Bev + Az vs Az in MSI-H mCRC (NCT02997228)^{III} *Az + Bev + FOLFOX in CLM (NCT03698461)$^{II\ Neoadjuvant}$

GC – gastric cancer. Bev – Bevacizumab; MSI-H – MicroSatellite Instability-High; mCRC – metastatic colorectal cancers; mST – metastatic solid tumors (baslet trial); I – phase I trial, II – phase 2 trial; R – in resected tumors; *Approved for the first line or secondline; **Approved subsequent lines, Neoadjuvant – drugs used for neoadjuvant therapy.

TABLE 15.3 Adoptive cell therapy in refractory colorectal cancer.

	Early success	Ongoing trials
Chimeric antigen receptor (CAR)-T cell	Against Carcinoembryonic antigen (CEA) in mCRC[Pilot] (Parkhurst et al., 2011)Against Tumor-associated glycoprotein (TAG)−72 (CART72 cells) intravenously in mCRC or directly into CLM[I] (Hege et al., 2017)	Against CEA in high-risk Stage IIICRC (T4/N2) or resected CLM (NCT04513431)[I adj] CAR targeting EpCAM (EPCAMCAR-T) in mGIC (NCT05028933)[I] αPD1-MSLN– CAR T Cells in MSLN-positive mST (NCT04503980)[I] UniCAR02-T Cells and PSMA Target Module (TMpPSMA) in PSMA-Positive (NCT04633148)[I] CAR against Various Antigens to mST (NCT04842812)[IX] Binary Oncolytic Adenovirus + HER2-Specific autologous CAR-T, in HER+ mST (NCT03740256)[I]
CAR-NK	CAR with fusion of NKG2D to DAP12 in mCRC[Pilot] (Xiao et al., 2019)	CYAD-101 (allogeneic NKG2D-based CAR)+ FOLFOX/FOLFIRI in mCRC (NCT03692429)[I]CYAD-101 + FOLFOX + Pembro in mCRC (NCT04991948)[I]
TIL	CD8 + targeting KRAS G12D and HLA-C*08:02 in mCRC[Pilot] (Tran et al., 2016)	PD-1 Monoclonal Antibody-activated Autologous Peripheral Blood T- lymphocyte (PD1-T) + XELOX + Bev in mCRC (NCT03950154)*[III]PD1-*T* + XELOX in Stage III CRC (NCT03904537)[I/II adj] Autologous TIL in mST (NCT03935893)[II]
DC	Recombinant CEA-pulsed DCs + tetanus toxoid + low dose IL-2 in mCRC[I] (Liu et al., 2016)	mCRC s/p resection (NCT02919644)[II adj]

NK – natural killer cells; TIL – tumor-infiltrating lymphocytes; DC – dendritic cells; X – HER2, Mesothelin, PSCA, MUC1, Lewis-Y, GPC3, AXL, EGFR, Claudin 18.2/6, ROR1, GD1, or B7-H3; adj – adjuvant therapy; EPCAM – Epithelial Cell Adhesion Molecule; mCRC – metastatic colorectal cancer; mST – metastatic solid tumors (basket trials). WT – wild type, MT-mutated; I – phase I trial, II – phase 2 trial; Pilot – pilot trial.

lung lesions responded well to TILs targeting KRAS G12D in mCRC patients (Tran et al., 2016). Other ACTs are discussed in Table 15.3.

The proposed vaccines proposed are, i) T-cell or DC based; ii) against proteins such as CEA, MUC1, frame-shift proteins, tumor-associated antigen (TAA), and p53 synthetic long peptide; iii) can be used in combination with chemotherapy, and/or Granulocyte-colony-stimulating factor G-CSF; iv) used in palliative or adjuvant setting (Speetjens et al., 2009; Balint et al., 2015; Morse et al., 2010; Crosby et al., 2020; Morse et al., 2013; Gatti-Mays et al., 2019; Gulley et al., 2008; Kloor et al., 2020; Scurr et al., 2017; Kaufman et al., 2008; Harrop et al., 2008; Kawamura et al., 2018; Murahashi et al., 2016; Morse et al., 2013; Rodriguez et al., 2018; Caballero-Baños et al., 2016; Barth et al., 2010). One of the important trials is a randomized clinical trial with modified vaccinia Ankara–5T4 (MVA-5T4) published in 2017, where mCRC patients who are stable on standard chemotherapy for > 4 weeks were randomized into four groups, a) wait and watch group – patients were given treatment breaks, b) MVA-5T4 vaccine alone, c) MVA-5T4 vaccine plus cyclophosphamide (to deplete the T cells before the vaccine), d) cyclophosphamide only (Scurr et al., 2017). Patients who received the vaccine had better

TABLE 15.4 Experimental vaccines in colorectal cancer.

	Early success	Ongoing trials
T lymphocyte –mediated	p53 synthetic long peptide (p53-SLP)[I/II] (Speetjens et al., 2009)Virus-like replicon particle (VRP)-CEA (Morse et al., 2010; Crosby et al., 2020) Ad5 [E1-, E2b-]-CEA(6D)[I/II] (Balint et al., 2015; Morse et al., 2013) Against CEA/MUC1 (Gatti-Mays et al., 2019; Gulley et al., 2008) Frame shift proteins in MMR colon cancer[I/II] (Kloor et al., 2020) Modified vaccinia Ankara–5T4 (MVA-5T4)[I/II] in mCRC (Scurr et al., 2017) TAA in mST[IA] (Murahashi et al., 2016)	Ad5.F35-hGCC-PADRE in mGIC (NCT04111172)[II] Arginase-1 (ARG-1) peptide in mST(NCT03689192)[I] Recombinant human IL-7-hyFc (NT-I7) in mST (NCT04054752)[I] ELI-002 in KRAS mST (NCT04853017)[I/II B Adj]
Dendric cell (DC)-mediated	Resectable CLM after POT – autologous DC loaded with tumor lysate[II] (Rodriguez et al., 2018) mCRC[II RCT BSc terminated] (Caballero-Baños et al., 2016) With vs without CD40L activation in Resected CRC (Barth et al., 2010) Modified CEA and MUC1 in resected mCRC[II] vs Pox vectors (Morse et al., 2013)	Stage I/II CRC (NCT03730948)[I/II adj]
In combination with chemotherapy	ALVAC–CEA/B7.1 + FOLFIRI in mCRC[84][II] Modified vaccinia Ankara (MVA) encoding the tumor antigen 5T4 (TroVax®) + FOLFIRI mCRC[II] (Harrop et al., 2008) MVA 5T4 + Cyclophosphamide (Scurr et al., 2017)RF + *T* + UFT/LV[II] (Kawamura et al., 2018) G-CSF + IL-2 + G/FOLFOX (Correale et al., 2008; Correale et al., 2005; Caraglia et al., 2019; Correale et al., 2014)	KRAS peptide vaccine + Ipi/Nivo (NCT04117087) in MSS mCRC (and resected PDA)[I] Personalized vaccine with Pembro in mCRC or PDA (NCT02600949)[I] Or with Ipi/Nivo in mST (NCT03953235)[I/II Z] Neoantigen DC vaccine + Nivo in HCC and CLM s/p resection (NCT04912765)[II Adj] V941(mRNA-5671/V941) ± Pembro (NCT03948763)[I] CV301+ M7824 (PD-L1 inhibitor) in mSBC and mCRC (NCT04491955)[II] DSP-7888 + Nivo or Pembro in mST (NCT03311334)[I/II] ATP128 ± BI 754,091 (PD-1 inhibitor) in MSS CRC (NCT04046445)[I/II] TAEK-VAC–HerBy vaccine + HER2 inhibitor +/- ICI in mST (NCT04246671)[I/II] A personalized vaccine with Pembro in mCRC or PDA (NCT02600949)[I] Or with Ipi/Nivo (NCT03953235)[I/IIC]
Tumor cells and Virus	Recombinant vaccina virus (JX-594) in mCRC (NCT01394939)[I/II]	Intratumoral influenza vaccine in early-stage resectable CRC (NCT04591379)[II]Autologous and Allogeneic Whole-Cell Cancer Vaccines (NCT00722228)[I/II D] Autologous tumor cells - with adenoviral-mediated gene transfer to secrete GM CSF (NCT01952730)[ID]

A – tumor-associated antigen (TAA) epitope peptides from KOC1, TTK, URLC10, DEPDC1 and MPHOSPH1; B – ELI-002 – a lipid-conjugated immune-stimulatory oligonucleotide [Amph-CpG-7909] plus a mixture of lipid-conjugated peptide-based antigens [Amph-Peptides]; C – With neoantigens, GRT-C903 + GRT-R904, a neoantigen-based therapeutic cancer vaccine + Ipi/Nivo; D – Cancer cells are irradiated; RF – Ring finger protein 43; T – translocase of the outer mitochondrial membrane; UFT/LV – Uracil-tegafur/leucovorin; mCRC – metastaic colorectal cancer; mST – metastaic solid tumor; GIC – gastrointestinal cancers; Nivo – Nivolumab; Ipi – Ipilimumab; Pembro – Pembrolizumab; PDA – pancreatic ductal adenocarcinoma; mSBC – metastatic small bowel cancers; DSP-7888 – Ombipepimut-S dosing emulsion. ATP128 – self adjuvanted chimeric recombinant protein vaccine.

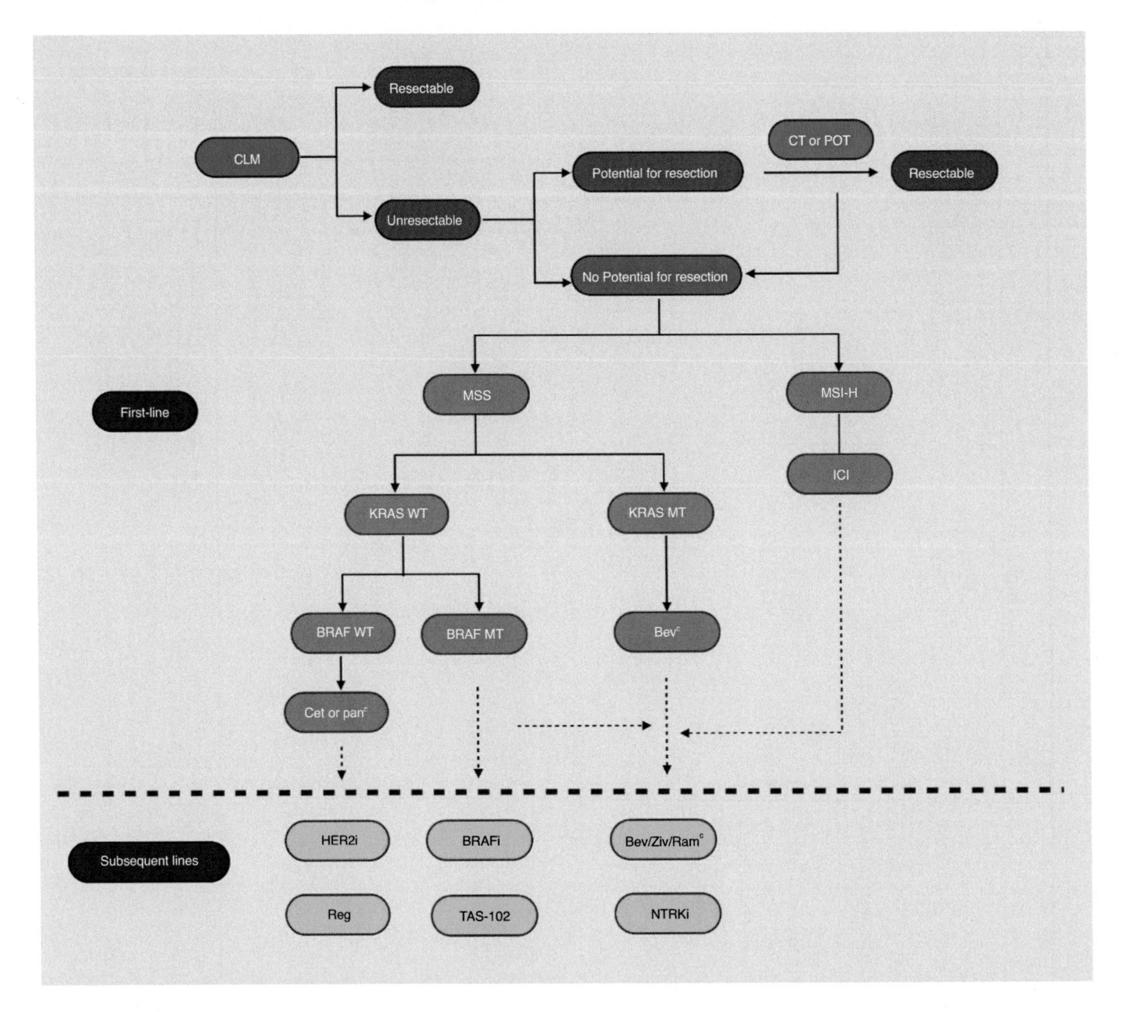

FIGURE 15.1 Approved therapy in the management of colorectal liver metastasis. CLM-colorectal liver metastasis; CT-conversion therapy; POT- perioperative therapy; MSS- microsatellite stable; MSI-H – microsatellite instability – high; MT-mutated; WT- wild type; Cet- Cetuxumab; Pan-Panutumumab; Bev-Bevacizumab; C-along with chemotherapy; HERi-HER2 inhibitors; BRAFi-BRAF inhibitor; Ziv - Ziv-aflibercept; Ram- Ramucirumab; NTRKi - Neurotrophic tyrosine receptor kinase inhibitor; Reg- Reforafenib; TAS-102 - Trifluridine and tipiracil hydrochloride; ICI – immune-checkpoint inhibitor, Pembrolizumab or Nivolumab (± Ipilumimab). Dotted arrow – progression.

survival, and cyclophosphamide did not improve the immune response. Other vaccine trials are discussed in Table 15.4 below.

The future in the immunotherapy space is exciting, and there is preliminary evidence (clinical and preclinical) that suggests improved susceptibility of CRCs to ICI with chemotherapy, targeted therapy (Cet), or drugs such as captopril or novel nanoliposomal lipopolysaccharides trapping proteins (Song et al., 2018; Inoue et al., 2017, 98; Roselli et al., 2016; Scurr et al., 2017; Dosset et al., 2018; Huang et al., 2020; Dagenborg et al., 2020; Vallejo Ardila et al., 2020). The current management of the CLM can be summarized in Fig. 15.1.

References

André, T., et al. (2020). Pembrolizumab in Microsatellite-Instability–High Advanced Colorectal Cancer. *New England Journal of Medicine, 383*(23), 2207–2218.

Arnold, D., et al. (2017). Prognostic and predictive value of primary tumour side in patients with RAS wild-type metastatic colorectal cancer treated with chemotherapy and EGFR directed antibodies in six randomized trials. *Annals of Oncology, 28*(8), 1713–1729.

Au, H.-J., et al. (2009). Health-Related Quality of Life in Patients With Advanced Colorectal Cancer Treated With Cetuximab: overall and KRAS-Specific Results of the NCIC CTG and AGITG CO.17 Trial. *Journal of Clinical Oncology, 27*(11), 1822–1828.

Balint, J. P., et al. (2015). Extended evaluation of a phase 1/2 trial on dosing, safety, immunogenicity, and overall survival after immunizations with an advanced-generation Ad5 [E1-, E2b-]-CEA(6D) vaccine in late-stage colorectal cancer. *Cancer Immunology, Immunotherapy,, 64*(8), 977–987.

Barth, R. J., et al. (2010). A Randomized Trial of Ex vivo CD40L Activation of a Dendritic Cell Vaccine in Colorectal Cancer Patients: tumor-Specific Immune Responses Are Associated with Improved Survival. *Clinical Cancer Research, 16*(22), 5548–5556.

Bennouna, J., et al. (2013). Continuation of bevacizumab after first progression in metastatic colorectal cancer (ML18147): a randomised phase 3 trial. *The Lancet Oncology, 14*(1), 29–37.

Bridgewater, J. A., et al. (2020). Systemic chemotherapy with or without cetuximab in patients with resectable colorectal liver metastasis (New EPOC): long-term results of a multicentre, randomised, controlled, phase 3 trial. *The Lancet Oncology, 21*(3), 398–411.

Caballero-Baños, M., et al. (2016). Phase II randomised trial of autologous tumour lysate dendritic cell plus best supportive care compared with best supportive care in pre-treated advanced colorectal cancer patients. *European Journal of Cancer, 64*, 167–174.

Caraglia, M., et al. (2019). GOLFIG Chemo-Immunotherapy in Metastatic Colorectal Cancer Patients. A Critical Review on a Long-Lasting Follow-Up. *Frontiers in oncology, 9*, 1102.

Cartwright, T. H., et al. (2012). Survival Outcomes of Bevacizumab Beyond Progression in Metastatic Colorectal Cancer Patients Treated in US Community Oncology. *Clinical Colorectal Cancer, 11*(4), 238–246.

Chen, E. X., et al. (2020). Effect of Combined Immune Checkpoint Inhibition vs Best Supportive Care Alone in Patients With Advanced Colorectal Cancer. *JAMA oncology, 6*(6), 831.

Chung, K. Y., et al. (2010). Phase II Study of the Anti-Cytotoxic T-Lymphocyte–Associated Antigen 4 Monoclonal Antibody, Tremelimumab, in Patients With Refractory Metastatic Colorectal Cancer. *Journal of Clinical Oncology, 28*(21), 3485–3490.

Corcoran, R. B., et al. (2018). Combined BRAF, EGFR, and MEK Inhibition in Patients with BRAFV600E-Mutant Colorectal Cancer. *Cancer discovery, 8*(4), 428–443.

Correale, P., et al. (2005). Chemo-Immunotherapy of Metastatic Colorectal Carcinoma With Gemcitabine Plus FOLFOX 4 Followed by Subcutaneous Granulocyte Macrophage Colony-Stimulating Factor and Interleukin-2 Induces Strong Immunologic and Antitumor Activity in Metastatic Colon Cancer. *Journal of Clinical Oncology, 23*(35), 8950–8958.

Correale, P., et al. (2008). Immunity Feedback and Clinical Outcome in Colon Cancer Patients Undergoing Chemoimmunotherapy with Gemcitabine + FOLFOX followed by Subcutaneous Granulocyte Macrophage Colony-Stimulating Factor and Aldesleukin (GOLFIG-1 Trial). *Clinical Cancer Research, 14*(13), 4192–4199.

Correale, P., et al. (2014). Gemcitabine, Oxaliplatin, Levofolinate, 5-Fluorouracil, Granulocyte-Macrophage Colony-Stimulating Factor, and Interleukin-2 (GOLFIG) Versus FOLFOX Chemotherapy in Metastatic Colorectal Cancer Patients: the GOLFIG-2 Multicentric Open-label Randomized Phase III Trial. *Journal of Immunotherapy, 37*(1), 26–35.

Cremolini, C., et al. (2015). FOLFOXIRI plus bevacizumab versus FOLFIRI plus bevacizumab as first-line treatment of patients with metastatic colorectal cancer: updated overall survival and molecular subgroup analyses of the open-label, phase 3 TRIBE study. *The Lancet Oncology, 16*(13), 1306–1315.

Cremolini, C., et al. (2018). Activity and Safety of Cetuximab Plus Modified FOLFOXIRI Followed by Maintenance With Cetuximab or Bevacizumab for RAS and BRAF Wild-type Metastatic Colorectal Cancer. *JAMA oncology, 4*(4), 529.

Cremolini, C., et al. (2019). Rechallenge for Patients With RAS and BRAF Wild-Type Metastatic Colorectal Cancer With Acquired Resistance to First-line Cetuximab and Irinotecan. *JAMA oncology, 5*(3), 343.

Crosby, E. J., et al. (2020). Long-term survival of patients with stage III colon cancer treated with VRP-CEA(6D), an alphavirus vector that increases the CD8+ effector memory T cell to Treg ratio. *Journal for ImmunoTherapy of Cancer, 8*(2), e001662.

Cunningham, D., et al. (2004). Cetuximab Monotherapy and Cetuximab plus Irinotecan in Irinotecan-Refractory Metastatic Colorectal Cancer. *New England Journal of Medicine, 351*(4), 337–345.

Dagenborg, V. J., et al. (2020). Neoadjuvant chemotherapy is associated with a transient increase of intratumoral T-cell density in microsatellite stable colorectal liver metastases. *Cancer Biology & Therapy, 21*(5), 432–440.

Doebele, R. C., et al. (2020). Entrectinib in patients with advanced or metastatic NTRK fusion-positive solid tumours: integrated analysis of three phase 1-2 trials. *The Lancet Oncology, 21*(2), 271–282.

Dosset, M., et al. (2018). PD-1/PD-L1 pathway: an adaptive immune resistance mechanism to immunogenic chemotherapy in colorectal cancer. *Oncoimmunology, 7*(6), e1433981.

Drilon, A., et al. (2018). Efficacy of Larotrectinib inTRKFusion–Positive Cancers in Adults and Children. *New England Journal of Medicine, 378*(8), 731–739.

Emmanouilides, C., et al. (2007). Front-line Bevacizumab in combination with Oxaliplatin, Leucovorin and 5-Fluorouracil (FOLFOX) in patients with metastatic colorectal cancer: a multicenter phase II study. *BMC cancer, 7*(1), 91.

Eng, C., et al. (2019). Atezolizumab with or without cobimetinib versus regorafenib in previously treated metastatic colorectal cancer (IMblaze370): a multicentre, open-label, phase 3, randomised, controlled trial. *The Lancet Oncology, 20*(6), 849–861.

Folprecht, G., et al. (2014). Survival of patients with initially unresectable colorectal liver metastases treated with FOLFOX/cetuximab or FOLFIRI/cetuximab in a multidisciplinary concept (CELIM study). *Annals of Oncology, 25*(5), 1018–1025.

Fukuoka, S., et al. (2020). Regorafenib Plus Nivolumab in Patients With Advanced Gastric or Colorectal Cancer: an Open-Label, Dose-Escalation, and Dose-Expansion Phase Ib Trial (REGONIVO, EPOC1603). *Journal of Clinical Oncology, 38*(18), 2053–2061.

Garufi, C., et al. (2010). Cetuximab plus chronomodulated irinotecan, 5-fluorouracil, leucovorin and oxaliplatin as neoadjuvant chemotherapy in colorectal liver metastases: POCHER trial. *British Journal of Cancer, 103*(10), 1542–1547.

Gatti-Mays, M. E., et al. (2019). A Phase I Dose-Escalation Trial of BN-CV301, a Recombinant Poxviral Vaccine Targeting MUC1 and CEA with Costimulatory Molecules. *Clinical Cancer Research, 25*(16), 4933–4944.

Grothey, A., et al. (2008). Bevacizumab Beyond First Progression Is Associated With Prolonged Overall Survival in Metastatic Colorectal Cancer: results From a Large Observational Cohort Study (BRiTE). *Journal of Clinical Oncology, 26*(33), 5326–5334.

Grothey, A., et al. (2013). Regorafenib monotherapy for previously treated metastatic colorectal cancer (CORRECT): an international, multicentre, randomised, placebo-controlled, phase 3 trial. *Lancet, 381*(9863), 303–312.

Grothey, A., et al. (2018). Fluoropyrimidine (FP) + bevacizumab (BEV) + atezolizumab vs FP/BEV in BRAFwt metastatic colorectal cancer (mCRC): findings from Cohort 2 of MODUL – a multicentre, randomized trial of biomarker-driven maintenance treatment following first-line induction therapy. *Annals of Oncology, 29*, viii714–viii715.

Gruenberger, B., et al. (2008). Bevacizumab, Capecitabine, and Oxaliplatin As Neoadjuvant Therapy for Patients With Potentially Curable Metastatic Colorectal Cancer. *Journal of Clinical Oncology, 26*(11), 1830–1835.

Gruenberger, T., et al. (2015). Bevacizumab plus mFOLFOX-6 or FOLFOXIRI in patients with initially unresectable liver metastases from colorectal cancer: the OLIVIA multinational randomised phase II trial. *Annals of Oncology, 26*(4), 702–708.

Gulley, J. L., et al. (2008). Pilot Study of Vaccination with Recombinant CEA-MUC-1-TRICOM Poxviral-Based Vaccines in Patients with Metastatic Carcinoma. *Clinical Cancer Research, 14*(10), 3060–3069.

Hallin, J., et al. (2020). The KRASG12C Inhibitor MRTX849 Provides Insight toward Therapeutic Susceptibility of KRAS-Mutant Cancers in Mouse Models and Patients. *Cancer discovery, 10*(1), 54–71.

Harrop, R., et al. (2008). Vaccination of colorectal cancer patients with TroVax given alongside chemotherapy (5-fluorouracil, leukovorin and irinotecan) is safe and induces potent immune responses. *Cancer Immunology, Immunotherapy,, 57*(7), 977–986.

Hege, K. M., et al. (2017). Safety, tumor trafficking and immunogenicity of chimeric antigen receptor (CAR)-T cells specific for TAG-72 in colorectal cancer. *Journal for ImmunoTherapy of Cancer, 5*, 22.

Heinemann, V., et al. (2014). FOLFIRI plus cetuximab versus FOLFIRI plus bevacizumab as first-line treatment for patients with metastatic colorectal cancer (FIRE-3): a randomised, open-label, phase 3 trial. *The Lancet Oncology, 15*(10), 1065–1075.

Holch, J. W., et al. (2017). The relevance of primary tumour location in patients with metastatic colorectal cancer: a meta-analysis of first-line clinical trials. *European Journal of Cancer, 70*, 87–98.

Huang, K. C.-Y., et al. (2020). Decitabine Augments Chemotherapy-Induced PD-L1 Upregulation for PD-L1 Blockade in Colorectal Cancer. *Cancers (Basel), 12*(2), 462.

Inoue, Y., et al. (2017). Cetuximab strongly enhances immune cell infiltration into liver metastatic sites in colorectal cancer. *Cancer Science, 108*(3), 455–460.

Jabbari, N., et al. (2022). Modulation of Immune Checkpoints by Chemotherapy in Human Colorectal Liver Metastases. *Cell Rep Med, 2020, 1*(9), 100160.

Janes, M. R., et al. (2018). Targeting KRAS Mutant Cancers with a Covalent G12C-Specific Inhibitor. *Cell, 172*(3), 578–589.e17.

Karapetis, C. S., et al. (2008). K-rasMutations and Benefit from Cetuximab in Advanced Colorectal Cancer. *New England Journal of Medicine, 359*(17), 1757–1765.

Kaufman, H. L., et al. (2008). Combination Chemotherapy and ALVAC-CEA/B7.1 Vaccine in Patients with Metastatic Colorectal Cancer. *Clinical Cancer Research, 14*(15), 4843–4849.

Kawamura, J., et al. (2018). Multicenter, phase II clinical trial of peptide vaccination with oral chemotherapy following curative resection for stageï¿½III colorectal cancer. *Oncology letters.*

Kemeny, N. E., et al. (2011). Randomized Phase II Trial of Adjuvant Hepatic Arterial Infusion and Systemic Chemotherapy With or Without Bevacizumab in Patients With Resected Hepatic Metastases From Colorectal Cancer. *Journal of Clinical Oncology, 29*(7), 884–889.

Kim, J. H., et al. (2020). A Phase II Study of Avelumab Monotherapy in Patients with Mismatch Repair-Deficient/Microsatellite Instability-High or *POLE*-Mutated Metastatic or Unresectable Colorectal Cancer. *Cancer Research and Treatment.*

Kloor, M., et al. (2020). A Frameshift Peptide Neoantigen-Based Vaccine for Mismatch Repair-Deficient Cancers: a Phase I/IIa Clinical Trial. *Clinical Cancer Research, 26*(17), 4503–4510.

Kopetz, S., et al. (2019). Encorafenib, Binimetinib, and Cetuximab in BRAF V600E–Mutated Colorectal Cancer. *New England Journal of Medicine, 381*(17), 1632–1643.

Kopetz, S., et al. (2021). Randomized Trial of Irinotecan and Cetuximab With or Without Vemurafenib in BRAF-Mutant Metastatic Colorectal Cancer (SWOG S1406). *Journal of Clinical Oncology, 39*(4), 285–294.

Lange, A., & Lo, H.-W. (2018). Inhibiting TRK Proteins in Clinical Cancer Therapy. *Cancers (Basel), 10*(4), 105.

Le, D. T., et al. (2017). Mismatch repair deficiency predicts response of solid tumors to PD-1 blockade. *Science, 357*(6349), 409–413.

Liu, K.-J., et al. (2016). A phase I clinical study of immunotherapy for advanced colorectal cancers using carcinoembryonic antigen-pulsed dendritic cells mixed with tetanus toxoid and subsequent IL-2 treatment. *Journal of Biomedical Science, 23*(1).

Ma, R., & Li, T. (2021). Conversion therapy combined with individualized surgical treatment strategy improves survival in patients with colorectal cancer liver metastases. *Int J Clin Exp Pathol, 14*(3), 314–321.

Mansmann, U., et al. (2013). Quantitative Analysis of the Impact of Deepness of Response on Post-Progression Survival Time Following First-Line Treatment in Patients with Mcrc. *Annals of Oncology, 24*, iv14.

Masi, G., et al. (2015). Continuation or reintroduction of bevacizumab beyond progression to first-line therapy in metastatic colorectal cancer: final results of the randomized BEBYP trial. *Annals of Oncology, 26*(4), 724–730.

Mayer, R. J., et al. (2015). Randomized Trial of TAS-102 for Refractory Metastatic Colorectal Cancer. *New England Journal of Medicine, 372*(20), 1909–1919.

Meric-Bernstam, F., et al. (2019). Pertuzumab plus trastuzumab for HER2-amplified metastatic colorectal cancer (MyPathway): an updated report from a multicentre, open-label, phase 2a, multiple basket study. *The Lancet Oncology, 20*(4), 518–530.

Misale, S., et al. (2012). Emergence of KRAS mutations and acquired resistance to anti-EGFR therapy in colorectal cancer. *Nature, 486*(7404), 532–536.

Morse, M. A., et al. (2010). An alphavirus vector overcomes the presence of neutralizing antibodies and elevated numbers of Tregs to induce immune responses in humans with advanced cancer. *Journal of Clinical Investigation, 120*(9), 3234–3241.

Morse, M. A., et al. (2013). A Randomized Phase II Study of Immunization With Dendritic Cells Modified With Poxvectors Encoding CEA and MUC1 Compared With the Same Poxvectors Plus GM-CSF for Resected Metastatic Colorectal Cancer. *Annals of Surgery, 258*(6), 879–886.

Morse, M. A., et al. (2013). Novel adenoviral vector induces T-cell responses despite anti-adenoviral neutralizing antibodies in colorectal cancer patients. *Cancer Immunology, Immunotherapy,, 62*(8), 1293–1301.

Murahashi, M., et al. (2016). Phase I clinical trial of a five-peptide cancer vaccine combined with cyclophosphamide in advanced solid tumors. *Clinical Immunology, 166-167*, 48–58.

Overman, M. J., et al. (2017). Nivolumab in patients with metastatic DNA mismatch repair-deficient or microsatellite instability-high colorectal cancer (CheckMate 142): an open-label, multicentre, phase 2 study. *The Lancet Oncology, 18*(9), 1182–1191.

Overman, M. J., et al. (2018). Durable Clinical Benefit With Nivolumab Plus Ipilimumab in DNA Mismatch Repair–Deficient/Microsatellite Instability–High Metastatic Colorectal Cancer. *Journal of Clinical Oncology, 36*(8), 773–779.

Parkhurst, M. R., et al. (2011). T Cells Targeting Carcinoembryonic Antigen Can Mediate Regression of Metastatic Colorectal Cancer but Induce Severe Transient Colitis. *Molecular Therapy, 19*(3), 620–626.

Parseghian, C. M., et al. (2019). Anti-EGFR-resistant clones decay exponentially after progression: implications for anti-EGFR re-challenge. *Annals of Oncology, 30*(2), 243–249.

Peeters, M., et al. (2010). Randomized Phase III Study of Panitumumab With Fluorouracil, Leucovorin, and Irinotecan (FOLFIRI) Compared With FOLFIRI Alone As Second-Line Treatment in Patients With Metastatic Colorectal Cancer. *Journal of Clinical Oncology, 28*(31), 4706–4713.

Pfeiffer, P., et al. (2020). TAS-102 with or without bevacizumab in patients with chemorefractory metastatic colorectal cancer: an investigator-initiated, open-label, randomised, phase 2 trial. *The Lancet Oncology, 21*(3), 412–420.

Piawah, S., & Venook, A. P. (2019). Targeted therapy for colorectal cancer metastases: a review of current methods of molecularly targeted therapy and the use of tumor biomarkers in the treatment of metastatic colorectal cancer. *Cancer, 125*(23), 4139–4147.

Primrose, J., et al. (2014). Systemic chemotherapy with or without cetuximab in patients with resectable colorectal liver metastasis: the New EPOC randomised controlled trial. *The Lancet Oncology, 15*(6), 601–611.

Pulciani, S., et al. (1982). Oncogenes in solid human tumours. *Nature, 300*(5892), 539–542.

Rivera, F., et al. (2017). Final analysis of the randomised PEAK trial: overall survival and tumour responses during first-line treatment with mFOLFOX6 plus either panitumumab or bevacizumab in patients with metastatic colorectal carcinoma. *International Journal of Colorectal Disease, 32*(8), 1179–1190.

Rodriguez, J., et al. (2018). A randomized phase II clinical trial of dendritic cell vaccination following complete resection of colon cancer liver metastasis. *Journal for ImmunoTherapy of Cancer, 6*(1).

Roselli, M., et al. (2016). The association of clinical outcome and peripheral T-cell subsets in metastatic colorectal cancer patients receiving first-line FOLFIRI plus bevacizumab therapy. *Oncoimmunology, 5*(7), e1188243.

Ross, J. S., et al. (2018). Targeting HER2 in colorectal cancer: the landscape of amplification and short variant mutations inERBB2andERBB3. *Cancer, 124*(7), 1358–1373.

Sartore-Bianchi, A., et al. (2016). Dual-targeted therapy with trastuzumab and lapatinib in treatment-refractory, KRAS codon 12/13 wild-type, HER2-positive metastatic colorectal cancer (HERACLES): a proof-of-concept, multicentre, open-label, phase 2 trial. *The Lancet Oncology, 17*(6), 738–746.

Sartore-Bianchi, A., et al. (2021). Phase II study of anti-EGFR rechallenge therapy with panitumumab driven by circulating tumor DNA molecular selection in metastatic colorectal cancer: the CHRONOS trial. *Journal of Clinical Oncology, 39*(15_suppl), 3506.

Scurr, M., et al. (2017). Low-Dose Cyclophosphamide Induces Antitumor T-Cell Responses, which Associate with Survival in Metastatic Colorectal Cancer. *Clinical Cancer Research, 23*(22), 6771–6780.

Scurr, M., et al. (2017). Effect of Modified Vaccinia Ankara–5T4 and Low-Dose Cyclophosphamide on Antitumor Immunity in Metastatic Colorectal Cancer. *JAMA oncology, 3*(10), e172579.

Seo, A. N., et al. (2014). HER2 Status in Colorectal Cancer: its Clinical Significance and the Relationship between HER2 Gene Amplification and Expression. *Plos One, 9*(5), e98528.

Siena, S., et al. (2021). Trastuzumab deruxtecan (DS-8201) in patients with HER2-expressing metastatic colorectal cancer (DESTINY-CRC01): a multicentre, open-label, phase 2 trial. *The Lancet Oncology, 22*(6), 779–789.

Siravegna, G., et al. (2015). Clonal evolution and resistance to EGFR blockade in the blood of colorectal cancer patients. *Nature Medicine, 21*(7), 795–801.

Sobrero, A. F., et al. (2008). EPIC: phase III Trial of Cetuximab Plus Irinotecan After Fluoropyrimidine and Oxaliplatin Failure in Patients With Metastatic Colorectal Cancer. *Journal of Clinical Oncology, 26*(14), 2311–2319.

Song, W., et al. (2018). Trapping of Lipopolysaccharide to Promote Immunotherapy against Colorectal Cancer and Attenuate Liver Metastasis. *Advanced Materials, 30*(52), 1805007.

Speetjens, F. M., et al. (2009). Induction of p53-Specific Immunity by a p53 Synthetic Long Peptide Vaccine in Patients Treated for Metastatic Colorectal Cancer. *Clinical Cancer Research, 15*(3), 1086–1095.

Stintzing, S., et al. (2016). FOLFIRI plus cetuximab versus FOLFIRI plus bevacizumab for metastatic colorectal cancer (FIRE-3): a post-hoc analysis of tumour dynamics in the final RAS wild-type subgroup of this randomised open-label phase 3 trial. *The Lancet Oncology, 17*(10), 1426–1434.

Tabernero, J., et al. (2015). Ramucirumab versus placebo in combination with second-line FOLFIRI in patients with metastatic colorectal carcinoma that progressed during or after first-line therapy with bevacizumab, oxaliplatin, and a fluoropyrimidine (RAISE): a randomised, double-blind, multicentre, phase 3 study. *The Lancet Oncology, 16*(5), 499–508.

Tabernero, J., et al. (2021). Encorafenib Plus Cetuximab as a New Standard of Care for Previously Treated BRAF V600E–Mutant Metastatic Colorectal Cancer: updated Survival Results and Subgroup Analyses from the BEACON Study. *Journal of Clinical Oncology, 39*(4), 273–284.

Tran, E., et al. (2016). T-Cell Transfer Therapy Targeting Mutant KRAS in Cancer. *New England Journal of Medicine, 375*(23), 2255–2262.

Troiani, T., et al. (2019). Phase II study of avelumab in combination with cetuximab in pre-treated RAS wild-type metastatic colorectal cancer patients: CAVE (cetuximab-avelumab) Colon. *Journal of Clinical Oncology, 37*(4_suppl), TPS731.

Vallejo Ardila, D. L., et al. (2020). Immunomodulatory effects of renin–angiotensin system inhibitors on T lymphocytes in mice with colorectal liver metastases. *Journal for ImmunoTherapy of Cancer, 8*(1), e000487.

Van Cutsem, E., et al. (2007). Open-Label Phase III Trial of Panitumumab Plus Best Supportive Care Compared With Best Supportive Care Alone in Patients With Chemotherapy-Refractory Metastatic Colorectal Cancer. *Journal of Clinical Oncology, 25*(13), 1658–1664.

Van Cutsem, E., et al. (2012). Addition of Aflibercept to Fluorouracil, Leucovorin, and Irinotecan Improves Survival in a Phase III Randomized Trial in Patients With Metastatic Colorectal Cancer Previously Treated With an Oxaliplatin-Based Regimen. *Journal of Clinical Oncology, 30*(28), 3499–3506.

Van Der, P. A. E. M., et al. (2012). Trends in incidence, treatment and survival of patients with stage IV colorectal cancer: a population-based series. *Colorectal Disease, 14*(1), 56–61.

Van Geel, R. M. J. M., et al. (2017). A Phase Ib Dose-Escalation Study of Encorafenib and Cetuximab with or without Alpelisib in Metastatic BRAF-Mutant Colorectal Cancer. *Cancer discovery, 7*(6), 610–619.

Wong, R., et al. (2011). A multicentre study of capecitabine, oxaliplatin plus bevacizumab as perioperative treatment of patients with poor-risk colorectal liver-only metastases not selected for upfront resection. *Annals of Oncology, 22*(9), 2042–2048.

Xiao, L., et al. (2019). Adoptive Transfer of NKG2D CAR mRNA-Engineered Natural Killer Cells in Colorectal Cancer Patients. *Molecular Therapy, 27*(6), 1114–1125.

Yaeger, R., et al. (2015). Pilot Trial of Combined BRAF and EGFR Inhibition in BRAF-Mutant Metastatic Colorectal Cancer Patients. *Clinical Cancer Research, 21*(6), 1313–1320.

Zheng, B., et al. (2019). First-line cetuximab versus bevacizumab for RAS and BRAF wild-type metastatic colorectal cancer: a systematic review and meta-analysis. *BMC cancer, 19*(1).

CHAPTER

16

Adjuvant therapy following resection of colorectal liver metastases

Jaime Arthur Pirolla Kruger, Gilton Marques Fonseca and Paulo Herman

Servico de Cirurgia do Figado, Departamento de Gastroenterologia, Hospital das Clinicas HCFMUSP, Faculdade de Medicina Universidade de Sao Paulo

Introduction

Liver resection is considered the mainstay treatment for colorectal cancer liver metastases, playing a central role in long-term disease control and cure (Adam et al., 2012). Metastatic colorectal cancer management is complex, and optimal patient selection for hepatectomy is achieved through a multidisciplinary approach in which diagnostic radiology, interventional radiology, liver surgeons, and medical oncologists all take part (Kruger et al., 2018).

Best oncological outcomes are achieved in patients bearing favorable clinical and biological risk factors. Clinical risk scores are useful in patients selection and include easy to use information routinely obtained in preoperative staging, such as primary tumor nodal status, timing of liver metastasis (whether synchronic or metachronic), number and size of hepatic nodules, uni or bilobar liver disease, carcinoembryonic antigen serum levels and the presence of additional extra-hepatic metastases (Fong et al., 1999). Information such as RAS and BRAF mutational status along with microsatellite stability profile provides further information on patient prognosis and guidance on management but are more applicable to selecting chemotherapy regimens rather than the indication for surgery (Afrăsânie et al., 2019).

Systemic treatment is another relevant part of the management of metastatic patients and response to chemotherapy is widely accepted as a marker of biological behavior, as good responders will present better survival after hepatectomy (Adam et al., 2004).

Contemporary Management of Metastatic Colorectal Cancer: A Precision Medicine Approach

DOI: https://doi.org/10.1016/B978-0-323-91706-3.00017-5

Although considered as the best treatment for CRLM, liver resection is followed by high recurrence rates, as up to two-thirds of patients will recur on the first two years after hepatectomy (de Jong et al., 2009). Recurrence will be either hepatic or extra-hepatic, implying that locoregional control is needed as much as systemic control. Strategies to reduce the recurrence rate are highly appreciated and adjuvant chemotherapy is arguably part of such strategy.

The rationale for providing adjuvant treatment after hepatectomy mirrors the management of the colorectal primary tumor. After colonic resection adjuvant therapy has proven to be beneficial in stage III cancers or stage II bearing risk factors such as adjacent organ invasion (T stage 4b), differentiation grade 3, inadequate lymphadenectomy (under 12 lymph nodes sampled), lymphatic or perineural invasion, presentation with obstruction or perforation undergoing emergency operation. In such cases adjuvant treatment with 5FU + leucovorin + oxaliplatin has proven to be beneficial in reducing recurrence rates, increasing disease-free and overall survival (André et al., 2004). The benefit on overall survival comes as the ultimate goal after curative-intent resection, as disease-free survival can be biased by subjectivity and intervals or length of follow up (i.e. according to the timing of staging) and will not reflect whether the benefit of additional chemotherapy exceeds its implications on tolerance and quality of life during treatment (Khoo et al., 2016).

Timing of systemic treatment

The timing of systemic treatment on the management of CRLM is variable depending on the clinical scenario and treatment can be offered as neoadjuvant (preoperative), perioperative (before and after hepatectomy), or adjuvant.

Neoadjuvant therapy is analyzed in detail elsewhere in this book. Briefly, it can be performed before liver resection in unresectable disease, aiming optimal response in order to downstage tumor with conversion into resectable disease (Bismuth et al., 1996). It has also a major contribution in resectable patients who otherwise present with negative prognostic factors, such as synchronic disease, large and multiple nodules, raised CEA levels, where the response to chemotherapy will indicate better survival chances after hepatectomy (Ayez et al., 2015). The major concern on preoperative treatment is its duration since chemotherapy will increase the risk of hepatic parenchymal injury (oxaliplatin-induced sinusoidal obstruction syndrome and irinotecan-induced chemotherapy-associated steatohepatitis). Extensive preoperative chemotherapy will increase surgical complication rates and should be restricted to 1 or 2 cycles (about 3 months) of treatment (Abdalla and Vauthey, 2008).

Limited preoperative treatment will lead to a need for the completion of systemic therapy after hepatectomy, comprising the perioperative approach (Nordlinger et al., 2008), which is likely the most frequently employed regimen for CRLM patients. The completion of postoperative treatment will use the same drug scheme employed before resection, which should have led to responding disease as an in vivo test of treatment efficacy.

When there is no clear indication for preoperative systemic treatment and the liver resection is feasible upfront, with technically resectable tumor(s) and expected remnant liver volume adequate to cope with postoperative liver function, chemotherapy can be performed solely as adjuvant treatment.

Role of adjuvant treatment

Major national institutional guidelines (13 Mohamed et al., 2020) as well expert consensus (Van Cutsem et al., 2016) suggest the application of systemic treatment after the resection of CRLM.

Few randomized trials have attempted to address the benefits of chemotherapy after successful resection of colorectal metastases.

The study from Portier et al. in 200,6[16] was the first randomized trial comparing adjuvant treatment after hepatectomy versus observation. This multicentric French study recruited 173 patients from December 1991 to December 2001 in 47 different hospitals; patient inclusion was then stopped due to the low rate of accrual rhythm. Patients randomized to the adjuvant chemotherapy arm had longer 5-year disease-free survival (33.5 percent vs 26.7 percent $p = 0.028$) and longer but not significant 5-year overall survival (51.1 percent vs 41.1 percent $p = 0.13$). It is important to mention that during the study period the therapeutic regimen employed was 5-FU and leucovorin (FULV) in the intervention arm, drugs that are less effective than oxaliplatin and irinotecan that came into practice as first-choice treatment in the early 2000s.

A pooled analysis from two randomized trials was made public in 2008. Mitry et al. (Mitry et al., 2008) analyzed data from phase III studies prematurely closed due to the slow accrual rate. One study was the above-mentioned French study from Portier et al. (Portier et al., 2006) and the other study population came from the ENG Trial (Langer et al., 2002) that recruited 129 patients from 67 centers in Canada and Europe from February 1994 to January 1998. Once again, the intervention arm was composed of patients receiving FULV. The results showed improved survivals in absolute numbers, but no significant increase in disease-free survival (27.9 months vs. 18.8 months $p = 0.058$) or overall survival (62.2 months vs. 47.3 months $p = 0.095$).

In 2009 a prospective randomized trial employed adjuvant FOLFIRI (fluorouracil, leucovorin, and irinotecan) as the intervention arm (Ychou et al., 2009). The more effective regimen was expected to extend overall survival in comparison to FULV. Three hundred and twenty-one patients were included from 66 centers in 15 countries from December 2001 to July 2006. One arm received postoperative FOLFIRI and the other arm received FULV as adjuvant therapy. Despite receiving a theoretically more effective drug regimen, median disease-free survival did not show any benefit of one treatment over another (21.6 months FULV versus 24.7 months FOLFIRI $p = 0.44$) and 3-year overall survival was similar between study groups (72 percent FULV versus 73 percent FOLFIRI $p = 0.69$).

Another randomized trial (the New EPOC study) (Primrose et al., 2014) evaluated the benefit of adding cetuximab to perioperative chemotherapy with oxaliplatin and 5FU (12 weeks prior plus 12 weeks after liver resection). The group that received cetuximab had a significantly worse progression-free survival.

A recently published Japanese phase III trial randomized patients into two groups, comparing adjuvant FOLFOX (fluorouracil, leucovorin, and oxaliplatin) to observation after hepatectomy (Kanemitsu et al., 2021). Accrual started in March 2007 and was finished in January 2019, including 300 patients. Five-year disease-free survival was 38.7 percent for the hepatectomy alone group versus 49.8 percent for the hepatectomy followed by chemotherapy group ($p = 0.006$). The improved disease-free survival did not translate into better 5-overall survival, which was 83.1 percent in the hepatectomy alone group versus 71.2 percent in the hepatectomy plus adjuvant chemotherapy group.

It is interesting to analyze the above-mentioned trials, which were created with excellent design but failed to accrue patients in a prevalent disease such as metastatic colorectal cancer. It is arguable that physicians were prone to giving adjuvant chemotherapy and patients were willing to receive treatment instead of engaging in clinical trials in which they might not receive postoperative chemotherapy. Although expected to increase overall survival, adjuvant chemotherapy has never proven to be beneficial in such outcomes in prospective and randomized studies. Those studies were limited by low accrual rates, application of outdated chemotherapy regimens, and short follow-up.

Different from prospective trials, retrospective studies have brought another view on the effect of adjuvant treatment after CRLM resection.

Parks et al. (Parks et al., 2007) gathered data from two tertiary centers, one in the United States and another in Europe, including 792 liver resections performed from 1991 to 1998. There were 518 patients treated with no chemotherapy after hepatectomy and 274 patients that received post-operative 5-fluorouracil based regimens. Patients receiving chemotherapy tended to be younger, had a shorter disease-free interval, and had more multiple tumors. Despite the apparent worse prognostic factors, the authors found adjuvant therapy to be beneficial to the whole cohort, with the probability of survival increasing from 1.3 to 2.0 times according to the clinical risk score stratification. The adjuvant chemotherapy group had 47 months median survival, with 37 percent of patients living 5 years after resection. In the surgery alone group, median survival reached 36 months and 5-year survival was 31 percent. Despite the improved outcomes, this large cohort study was impaired by its retrospective nature and the employment of less effective chemotherapy.

In 2014 a nice study employed modern chemotherapy regimens and stratified patients according to the Memorial Sloan Kettering Cancer Center Clinical Risk Score (Rahbari et al., 2014). Differently from previously mentioned studies, patients were included only if they did not receive neoadjuvant treatment, had no extra-hepatic disease, and had free resection margins. Two hundred and ninety-seven patients were analyzed, 137 (43 percent) of them bearing high CRS (score greater than 2). One hundred and sixteen patients (39 percent) received adjuvant treatment, of those 53 percent received oxaliplatin, 14 percent irinotecan, and 33 percent FULV. Adjuvant treatment emerged as an independent prognostic factor for survival in multivariable analysis for patients with high CRS, significantly improving survival in this subgroup of patients. The same effect was not observed on low CRS patients. Fig. 16.1 depicts the influence of adjuvant therapy on overall survival according to the patients' risk status (Rahbari et al., 2014).

Another interesting study sought to investigate the role of adjuvant treatment in patients with metachronous CRLM. Kelm et al. (Kelm et al., 2021) analyzed the results of adjuvant effective chemotherapy in patients with early metachronous disease (detection of liver metastasis within the first year of follow up) and late metachronous metastasis (> 1 year). Additive chemotherapy was identified as an independent factor for overall survival in both groups, with patients receiving adjuvant treatment having longer mean overall survival (62 vs 57 months, $p = 0.023$) and 10-year survival (42 percent vs 0 percent $p = 0.023$), underscoring the importance of long-term follow up to reach cure in CRLM.

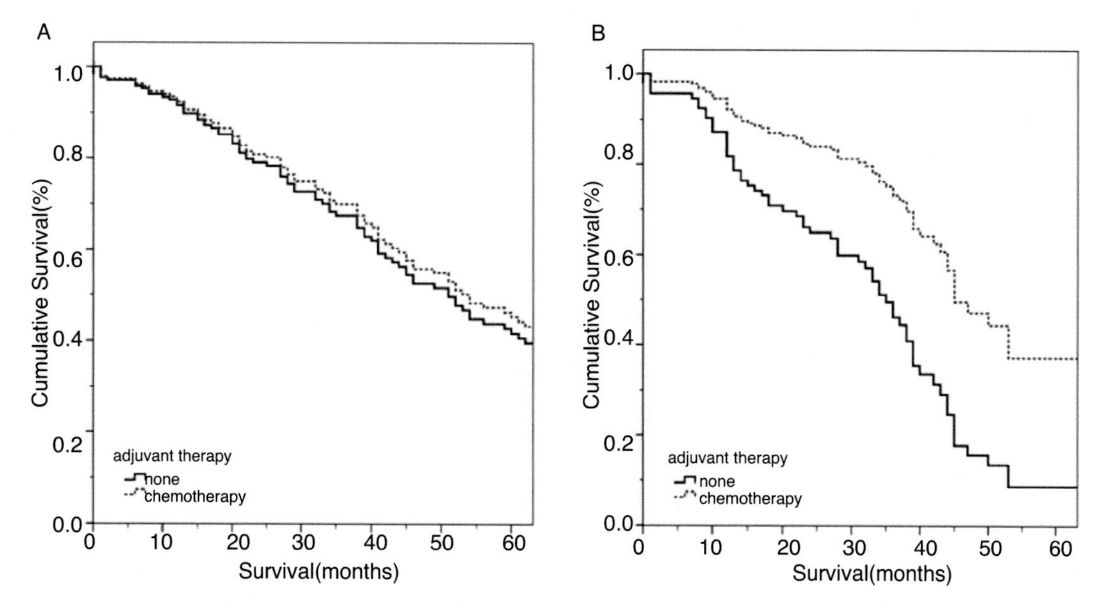

FIGURE 16.1 Influence of adjuvant chemotherapy on overall survival after potentially curative resection of colorectal liver metastases depending on patients' risk status. A) Overall survival of patients with a MSKCC-CRS $<= 2$ stratified for the type of adjuvant therapy ($p = 0.53$). B) Overall survival of patients with a MSKCC-CRS > 2 stratified for the type of adjuvant therapy ($p = 0.007$). Data are presented as Cox proportional hazards.

A large cohort of patients analyzed 6,025 subjects with synchronous CRLM to investigate the factors associated with early recurrence (in less than 6 months) after hepatectomy. The study was motivated by the deeply detrimental impact on survival induced by early recurrence and included patients that had undergone complete liver resection between 1998 and 2009. At some point during follow up 2,734 had recurred and of those 639 (10.6 percent) were considered early recurrences. In the multivariable analysis, the response to chemotherapy (partial or complete) and the administration of adjuvant chemotherapy were independently protective factors against early recurrence. Such information is another way to identify the favorable impact of adjuvant treatment on disease-free survival. Moreover, the overall outcome was affected by early recurrences, as 5-year survival rates were 49.4 percent on the late recurrence group versus 26.9 percent on the early recurrence ($p < 0{,}001$).

Araujo et al. (Araujo et al., 2015), in a systematic review and meta-analysis comparing surgery plus systemic chemotherapy, regardless of the timing of administration, with surgery alone, analyzing long-term outcomes for patients with CRLM who underwent liver resection, showed that the association relatively improved overall survival rates for 23 percent of the patients when compared to surgery alone (HR, 0.77; 95%percent confidence interval [CI] 0.67–0.88; $p < 0.001$) and relatively improved recurrence-free survival for 29 percent of the patients when compared to surgery alone (HR, 0.71; 95%percent CI 0.61–0.83; $p < 0.001$). The authors concluded that the use of chemotherapy for patients with CRLM who underwent resection with curative intent is a worthwhile strategy for improving both recurrence-free and overall survival.

Adjuvant intra-arterial chemotherapy following resection of colorectal liver metastases

Hepatic arterial infusion chemotherapy (HAIC) has been developed at the Memorial Sloan Kettering Cancer Center (MSKCC, New York, USA) in the 1980s, with the biological rationale that most of the blood supply for liver tumors is determined by hepatic artery branches rather than the portal vein. In this therapy, chemotherapeutic drugs are delivered directly into the hepatic artery through a surgically implanted catheter connected to an external pump. This technique allows an exposition of the metastatic tumor or cells to a high concentration of chemotherapeutic agents, limiting systemic toxic effects and sparing the background liver parenchyma (Kwan and Pua, 2021). Thus, floxuridine, a prodrug of 5-fluorouracil and the widest agent used in HAIC pumps, allows a tumor exposure 400-fold higher when compared with systemic chemotherapy with minimum systemic side effects. Modern chemotherapy drugs such as oxaliplatin and irinotecan have also been used for HAIC therapy (Buisman et al., 2021).

The rationale for using HAIC as adjuvant therapy after resection of CRLM is that in half of the patients the liver is the initial site of recurrence. HAIC has the potential to target residual hepatic micro metastases, reducing the risk of hepatic recurrence and improving survival. The outcomes reported on studies evaluating its adjuvant role vary according to different intra-arterial agents, methods of drug infusion (surgical or percutaneous catheter insertion), and the combination or not with systemic treatment.

A recent meta-analysis evaluated quantitatively the overall survival in 15 studies with 1391 patients treated with adjuvant HAIC versus 2193 patients without adjuvant HAIC after resection of CRLM (Buisman et al., 2021). Eight of them were randomized clinical trials (RCT). The results favored patients that received adjuvant HAIC in the pooled analysis (HR: 0.77; 95 percent CI: 0.64–0.93), with a benefit when floxuridine was used (pooled HR 0.76; 95 percent CI: 0.62–0.94), the catheter was surgically inserted (pooled HR 0.71, 95 percent CI: 0.61–0.84), and adjuvant systemic chemotherapy was associated (pooled HR 0.75, 95 percent CI: 0.59–0.96). However, when only RCTs were evaluated, results did not show the benefit of HAIC on OS (HR 0.91 95 percent CI 0.72–1.14), mainly due to heterogeneity of treatment, relatively small sample size, and early closing of 4 RCT due to lack of effectiveness or low accrual. The largest RCT (total 156 patients) used floxuridine in 74 patients. The median progression-free survival in patients who underwent HAIC was 31.3 months versus 17.2 months in patients without adjuvant HAIC ($p = 0.02$). The 10-year OS was 41.1 percent in the HAIC group versus 27.3 percent in the non-HAIC group.

The largest study about the impact of adjuvant HAIC in CRLM evaluated 2358 consecutive patients who underwent hepatectomy for colorectal metastases in MSKCC from 1992 to 2012 (Groot Koerkamp et al., 2017). The HAIC group (785 patients), despite a significantly higher tumor burden, had a longer median OS of 67 months when compared to 44 months for the group treated with exclusive adjuvant systemic chemotherapy ($p < 0.01$). The benefits of HAIC were demonstrated even in a subgroup analysis with patients receiving modern systemic chemotherapy.

Beyond the limitations of RCT mentioned previously, there are other limitations in the studies regarding the adjuvant role of HAIC after resection of CRLM. Most retrospective studies have poor quality and abroad patients treated before 2012. Finally, the actual standard of chemotherapy regimens based on oxaliplatin or irinotecan was not used in most of the studies (Buisman et al., 2021).

Despite systemic toxicity with HAIC is very low due to high drugs extraction rates, there are complications related to the catheter (arterial bleeding, arterial wall dissection, thrombosis, pump pocket hematoma or infection), and to chemotherapy toxicity (elevation of liver enzymes, hyperbilirubinemia, biliary sclerosis, gastric ulceration, gastrointestinal symptoms). Dexamethasone has been used in combination with floxuridine to decrease the risk of biliary toxicity (Connell and Kemeny, 2021).

HAIC is available only in a few centers around the world. The likely reasons are studies showing the benefits of HAIC were overshadowed because they were published at the same period when oxaliplatin and irinotecan were introduced; floxuridine and the required pump were not registered in Europe; and HAIC requires experience, skills, and a dedicated multidisciplinary team (Buisman et al., 2021).

There are currently 2 ongoing RCT evaluating the adjuvant impact of HAIC plus systemic chemotherapy. PACHA-01 (Goéré et al., 2018) is a phase II/III trial in Europe with an estimated ending in 2028 comparing adjuvant systemic FOLFOX versus HAIC oxaliplatin plus systemic 5-FU in patients with a high risk for recurrence (4 or more resected CRLM). The second one is called the PUMP trial (Buisman et al., 2019), a phase III multi-center study in the Netherlands that compares adjuvant HAIC plus systemic 5-FU versus no systemic adjuvant therapy in patients with low risk for recurrence (up to 2 factors of worse prognosis according to Fong et al. (Fong et al., 1999)).

Conclusion

Hepatic resection is considered the standard of care for patients with resectable colorectal liver metastases; however, 60–70 percent of patients will recur. The rationale for the use of systemic chemotherapy in association with surgery is to decrease recurrence rates. There is strong data showing that systemic chemotherapy is likely to improve recurrence-free survival, but its' impact on overall survival has not been clearly demonstrated.

Despite the paucity of data justifying the routine use of adjuvant treatment following CRLM resection, systemic treatment might play a role in CRLM due to the systemic nature of the disease and the wider availability in most oncologic centers. Thus, almost all specialized centers associate systemic chemotherapy with surgery for patients with CRLM.

The preferred adjuvant regimens are based on oxaliplatin and FULV. The regimens based on irinotecan, cetuximab, or bevacizumab did not show any benefit in an adjuvant scenario.

In some institutions where the infusion pump is available, there is a dedicated team to deal with patients submitted to this therapeutic strategy, and for selected patients, especially those with multinodular metastatic disease, HAIC may be a useful tool as an adjuvant treatment.

Clinical case

Men, 63-years-old.
Sigmoid colon cancer resected elsewhere.

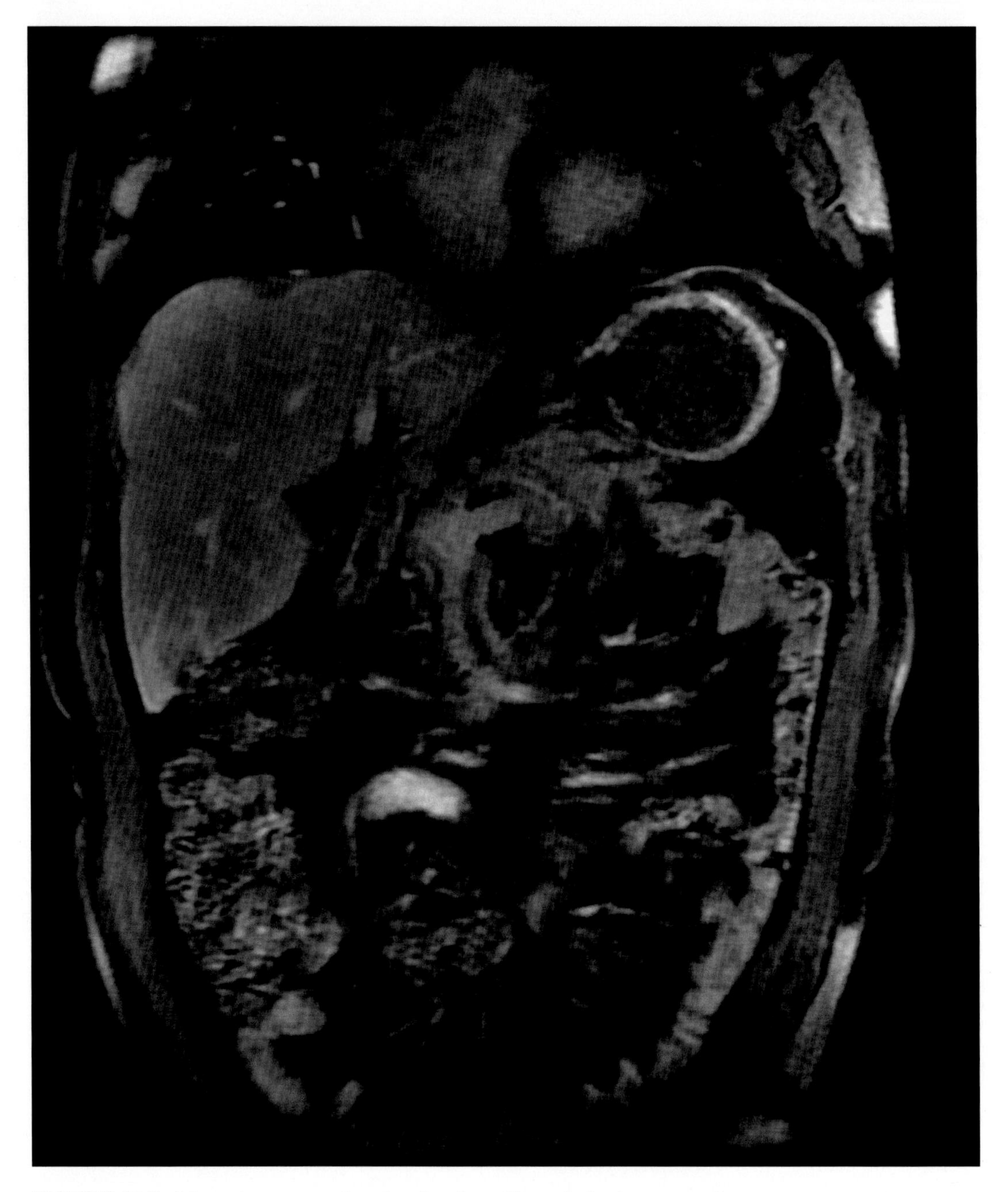

FIGURE 16.2 Magnetic resonance imaging showing a 25 mm lesion in segment 6.

Pathology report: moderately differentiated adenocarcinoma with 4cm in diameter (T3); no positive lymph nodes in 19 evaluated (0/19 = N0). Non-mutated KRAS and BRAF; proficient DNA repair enzymes.

Considered as low risk by the oncologist, no adjuvant treatment.

Referred to our institution after 6 months due to the appearance of a single metastatic nodule.

CEA 3.4ng/ml.

MRI = single liver nodule (25 mm) segment 6 (Fig. 16.2).

After multidisciplinary meeting discussion: Fong´s Critical Risk Score = 1 (synchronic < 1 year metastasis); Good prognosis. Upfront resection; adjuvant systemic treatment.

Uneventful laparoscopic wedge resection; Hospital discharge on day 3.

Adjuvant treatment with FLOX x 3.

Alive and free of disease after 97 months.

References

https://www.nice.org.uk/guidance/ng151/resources/colorectal-cancer-pdf-66141835244485, 2022.

Abdalla, E. K., & Vauthey, J. N. (2008). Chemotherapy prior to hepatic resection for colorectal liver metastases: helpful until harmful? *Digestive Surgery, 25*(6), 421–429.

Adam, R., De Gramont, A., Figueras, J., et al. (2012). The oncosurgery approach to managing liver metastases from colorectal cancer: a multidisciplinary international consensus. *The Oncologist, 17*(10), 1225–1239.

Adam, R., Pascal, G., Castaing, D., et al. (2004). Tumor progression while on chemotherapy: a contraindication to liver resection for multiple colorectal metastases? *Annals of Surgery, 240*(6), 1052–1061 discussion 1061-1054.

Afrăsânie, V. A., Marinca, M. V., Alexa, S. T., et al. (2019). KRAS, NRAS, BRAF, HER2 and microsatellite instability in metastatic colorectal cancer - practical implications for the clinician. *Radiology and Oncology, 53*(3), 265–274.

André, T., Boni, C., Mounedji-Boudiaf, L., et al. (2004). Oxaliplatin, fluorouracil, and leucovorin as adjuvant treatment for colon cancer. *New England Journal of Medicine, 350*(23), 2343–2351.

Araujo, R. L., Gonen, M., & Herman, P. (2015). Chemotherapy for patients with colorectal liver metastases who underwent curative resection improves long-term outcomes: systematic review and meta-analysis. *Annals of Surgical Oncology, 22*(9), 3070–3078.

Ayez, N., van der Stok, E. P., Grünhagen, D. J., et al. (2015). The use of neo-adjuvant chemotherapy in patients with resectable colorectal liver metastases: clinical risk score as possible discriminator. *European Journal of Surgical Oncology, 41*(7), 859–867.

Bismuth, H., Adam, R., Levi, F., et al. (1996). Resection of nonresectable liver metastases from colorectal cancer after neoadjuvant chemotherapy. *Annals of Surgery, 224*(4), 509–520 discussion 520-502.

Buisman, F. E., Filipe, W. F., Galjart, B., et al. (2021). Adjuvant intra-arterial chemotherapy for patients with resected colorectal liver metastases: a systematic review and meta-analysis. *HPB (Oxford).*

Buisman, F. E., Homs, M. Y. V., Grünhagen, D. J., et al. (2019). Adjuvant hepatic arterial infusion pump chemotherapy and resection versus resection alone in patients with low-risk resectable colorectal liver metastases - the multicenter randomized controlled PUMP trial. *BMC cancer, 19*(1), 327.

Connell, L. C., & Kemeny, N. E. (2021). Intraarterial Chemotherapy for Liver Metastases. *Surgical Oncology Clinics of North America, 30*(1), 143–158.

de Jong, M. C., Pulitano, C., Ribero, D., et al. (2009). Rates and patterns of recurrence following curative intent surgery for colorectal liver metastasis: an international multi-institutional analysis of 1669 patients. *Annals of Surgery, 250*(3), 440–448.

Fong, Y., Fortner, J., Sun, R. L., Brennan, M. F., & Blumgart, L. H. (1999). Clinical score for predicting recurrence after hepatic resection for metastatic colorectal cancer: analysis of 1001 consecutive cases. *Annals of Surgery, 230*(3), 309–318 discussion 318-321.

Goéré, D., Pignon, J. P., Gelli, M., et al. (2018). Postoperative hepatic arterial chemotherapy in high-risk patients as adjuvant treatment after resection of colorectal liver metastases - a randomized phase II/III trial - PACHA-01 (NCT02494973). *BMC cancer, 18*(1), 787.

Groot Koerkamp, B., Sadot, E., Kemeny, N. E., et al. (2017). Perioperative Hepatic Arterial Infusion Pump Chemotherapy Is Associated With Longer Survival After Resection of Colorectal Liver Metastases: a Propensity Score Analysis. *Journal of Clinical Oncology, 35*(17), 1938–1944.

Kanemitsu, Y., Shimizu, Y., Mizusawa, J., et al. (2021). Hepatectomy Followed by mFOLFOX6 Versus Hepatectomy Alone for Liver-Only Metastatic Colorectal Cancer (JCOG0603): a Phase II or III Randomized Controlled Trial. *Journal of Clinical Oncology, 39*(34), 3789–3799.

Kelm, M., Schollbach, J., Anger, F., et al. (2021). Prognostic impact of additive chemotherapy after curative resection of metachronous colorectal liver metastasis: a single-centre retrospective study. *BMC cancer, 21*(1), 490.

Khoo, E., O'Neill, S., Brown, E., Wigmore, S. J., & Harrison, E. M. (2016). Systematic review of systemic adjuvant, neoadjuvant and perioperative chemotherapy for resectable colorectal-liver metastases. *HPB (Oxford), 18*(6), 485–493.

Kruger, J. A. P., Fonseca, G. M., Makdissi, F. F., Jeismann, V. B., Coelho, F. F., & Herman, P. (2018). Evolution in the surgical management of colorectal liver metastases: propensity score matching analysis (PSM) on the impact of specialized multidisciplinary care across two institutional eras. *Journal of Surgical Oncology, 118*(1), 50–60.

Kwan, J., & Pua, U. (2021). Review of Intra-Arterial Therapies for Colorectal Cancer Liver Metastasis. *Cancers (Basel), 13*(6).

Langer, B., Bleiberg, H., Labianca, R., et al. (2002). Fluorouracil (FU) plus L-leucovorin (l-LV) versus observation after potentially curative resection of liver or lung metastases from colorectal cancer (CRC): results of the ENG (EORTC/NCIC CTG/GIVIO) randomized trial. *Proceedings American Society of Clinical Oncology, 21*(149a), 592 abstract.

Mitry, E., Fields, A. L., Bleiberg, H., et al. (2008). Adjuvant chemotherapy after potentially curative resection of metastases from colorectal cancer: a pooled analysis of two randomized trials. *Journal of Clinical Oncology, 26*(30), 4906–4911.

Mohamed, F., Kallioinen, M., Braun, M., et al. (2020). Management of colorectal cancer metastases to the liver, lung or peritoneum suitable for curative intent: summary of NICE guidance. *British Journal of Surgery, 107*(8), 943–945.

Nordlinger, B., Sorbye, H., Glimelius, B., et al. (2008). Perioperative chemotherapy with FOLFOX4 and surgery versus surgery alone for resectable liver metastases from colorectal cancer (EORTC Intergroup trial 40983): a randomised controlled trial. *Lancet, 371*(9617), 1007–1016.

Parks, R., Gonen, M., Kemeny, N., et al. (2007). Adjuvant chemotherapy improves survival after resection of hepatic colorectal metastases: analysis of data from two continents. *Journal of the American College of Surgeons, 204*(5), 753–761 discussion 761-753.

Portier, G., Elias, D., Bouche, O., et al. (2006). Multicenter randomized trial of adjuvant fluorouracil and folinic acid compared with surgery alone after resection of colorectal liver metastases: FFCD ACHBTH AURC 9002 trial. *Journal of Clinical Oncology, 24*(31), 4976–4982.

Primrose, J., Falk, S., Finch-Jones, M., et al. (2014). Systemic chemotherapy with or without cetuximab in patients with resectable colorectal liver metastasis: the New EPOC randomised controlled trial. *The Lancet Oncology, 15*(6), 601–611.

Rahbari, N. N., Reissfelder, C., Schulze-Bergkamen, H., et al. (2014). Adjuvant therapy after resection of colorectal liver metastases: the predictive value of the MSKCC clinical risk score in the era of modern chemotherapy. *BMC cancer, 14*, 174.

Van Cutsem, E., Cervantes, A., Adam, R., et al. (2016). ESMO consensus guidelines for the management of patients with metastatic colorectal cancer. *Annals of Oncology, 27*(8), 1386–1422.

Ychou, M., Hohenberger, W., Thezenas, S., et al. (2009). A randomized phase III study comparing adjuvant 5-fluorouracil/folinic acid with FOLFIRI in patients following complete resection of liver metastases from colorectal cancer. *Annals of Oncology, 20*(12), 1964–1970.

CHAPTER

17

Long-term prognosis and surveillance of patients with resected colorectal liver metastasis

Monica M. Dua, MD and Raja R. Narayan, MD

Department of Surgery, Stanford University School of Medicine, Palo Alto, CA, USA

Introduction

The treatment of colorectal liver metastases (CRLM) has evolved over the last decades with improvements in all aspects of management. Advancements in radiographic imaging, developed roles of tumor biology, increased utility of perioperative chemotherapy, and numerous surgical strategies have changed our ability to expand indications for hepatectomy and safely remove larger burdens of liver disease to improve long-term survival. Although a large proportion of patients with CRLM present with unresectable disease, in the modern era, patients with complete resection now have an associated 5-year survival ranging from 50 to 60 percent (Tzeng and Aloia, 2013) and a long-term 10-year survival of approximately 20 percent in well-selected patients (Margonis et al., 2016; Tomlinson et al., 2007). Despite this progress, this population of patients is still the minority and up to two-thirds of patients will develop either intra- or extra-hepatic recurrence within the first 5 years following hepatectomy. Given this varied long-term outcome for patients with CRLM, several tools to better prognosticate patient outcomes and select patients for these aggressive surgical approaches have been developed to maximize therapeutic benefit. Critical assessment of these prognostic risk factors in patients who undergo curative-intent resection of CRLM is also essential to develop improved surveillance algorithms to detect early manifestations of recurrence (Kawaguchi et al., 2020).

Contemporary Management of Metastatic Colorectal Cancer: A Precision Medicine Approach
DOI: https://doi.org/10.1016/B978-0-323-91706-3.00004-7

Clinical risk scores

Previously, many retrospective series of patients undergoing hepatic resection for CRLM have reported on individual predictors of survival. Common predictors of shorter survival were based on preoperative carcinoembryonic antigen (CEA) level, hepatic tumor size, number of tumors, shorter disease-free interval to liver metastases, primary tumor node positivity and stage of tumor, positive margins, and presence of extra-hepatic disease (Pawlik and Choti, 2007; Smith and D'Angelica, 2015). However, despite numerous studies correlating patient and tumor factors to survival, many of these vary among different institutions and reliable predictors remain inconsistent. To refine patient selection for resection and adjuvant therapy, several prognostic scoring systems have been proposed to stratify patients into risk categories for treatment.

In 1999, a Clinical Risk Score (CRS) that predicts recurrence after hepatic resection for CRLM was developed by Fong, Blumgart and colleagues (Fong et al., 1999) using 1001 patients treated from 1985 to 1998 at Memorial Sloan Kettering Cancer Center. The CRS was developed on the basis of five criteria: metastatic nodes associated with the primary tumor, disease-free interval from primary to metastases less than 12 months, more than one hepatic tumor, size of the largest hepatic tumor greater than 5 cm, and a CEA level greater than 200 ng/ml. When these five criteria were used in a preoperative scoring system assigning one point for each criterion and six defined risk groups, the total score was highly predictive of long-term outcome. The 5-year survival rate for patients with 0 points was 60 percent whereas that for patients with 5 points was 14 percent (Fong et al., 1999). Although this CRS from a single institution was broadly adopted over time, its generalizability across heterogeneous patient populations has been an area of debate (Mann et al., 2004; Zakaria et al., 2007). Specifically, Zarakria et al. examined a cohort from the Mayo Clinic to validate several existing large population scoring models (in addition to the Fong CRS). These included the model by Nordlinger et al. (Nordlinger et al., 1996) which was a prognostic scoring system from a national collective registry of 1568 patients based on 7 identified risk factors and another model by Iwatsuki et al., which was a large single institution study based on 4 risk factors which were all characteristics of hepatic metastases (number, size, time to metastasis, and bilobar disease) (Iwatsuki et al., 1999). A comparison of these larger representative CRS models is shown in Table 17.1. The authors concluded that neither disease-specific survival nor recurrence among their cohort was stratified discretely by any of the scoring systems and all models were only marginally better than chance alone in predicting both.

Currently the overall utility of the CRS has been questioned in the modern age of neoadjuvant chemotherapy and genetic data (Ayez et al., 2011). There has been increasing interest in the prognostic role of molecular factors as biomarkers of cancer biology. As a result, Brudvik and Vauthey proposed a modified CRS based on the incorporation of the rat sarcoma viral oncogene homolog (RAS) mutational status (Brudvik et al., 2019) given its potential to serve as a marker to provide an accurate predication of survival after hepatic resection for CRLM (Nash et al., 2010). The resulting risk score from these authors was therefore based on 3 factors (using two from the traditional Fong-Blumgart CRS): one point for positive nodes associated with the primary tumor, one point for the diameter of the largest liver metastatsis > 5 cm, and then including one point for having a mutation in either the KRAS or NRAS codons (Table 17.1).

TABLE 17.1 Representative clinical risk scoring systems for patients with CRLM.

Author	Date range	N	Factors used for CRS	Grading system	Outcome
Nordlinger et al	1968-1990	1568	**1.** Age > 60 **2.** Present extension into serosa of primary tumor **3.** Present lymphatic spread of primary **4.** Time interval from time primary to metastases <2 yrs **5.** Size of largest metastases ≥ 5 cm **6.** Number of metastases (4+) **7.** Margin clearance < 1 cm	Each factor = 1 point Low risk: 0-2 Intermediate risk: 3-4 High Risk: 5-7	2-year Survival Low: 79% Intermediate: 60% High: 43%
Fong et al	1995-1998	1001	**1.** Nodal postive primary **2.** Disease-free interval to liver metastases <12 months **3.** Number of tumors >1 **4.** Preoperative CEA >200 ng/ml **5.** Size of largest metastases > 5 cm	Each factor = 1 point Score range 0-5	5-year Survival 0: 60% 1: 44% 2: 40% 3: 20% 4: 25% 5: 14%
Iwatsuki et al	1981-1996	305	**1.** Number of tumors > 2 **2.** Size of largest metastases >8 cm **3.** Disease-free nterval to liver metastases ≤30 months **4.** Bilobar tumors	Each factor = 1 point Grade 1-5 based on number of risk factors	5 -year Survival 1: 48.3% 2: 33.7% 3: 17.9% 4: 6.4% 5: 1.1%
Zakaria et al	1960-1995	662	**1.** Metastasis ≤30 months **2.** Metastasis diameter >8 cm **3.** Transfusions **4.** Hepatoduodenal lymph node	3 Groups based on combo of 4 factors: Group I, II, and III	5-year Survival I: 55% II: 39% III: 20%
Brudvik et al	2005-2013	564	**1.** Nodal positive primary **2.** Size of Largest metastases >5 cm **3.** RAS mutation status	Each factor = 1 point Score range 0-3	5-year Survival 0: 67% 1: 44% 2: 24% 3: 17%

This modified CRS outperformed the traditional Fong score at stratifying patients by overall survival in both the MD Anderson Cancer Center cohort and an International Multicenter Validation Cohort. They concluded that adding the RAS mutation status also indirectly accounted for important postoperative predictors of survival given the previous RAS associations with both resection margin status and pathologic response to chemotherapy (Brudvik et al., 2019).

Other prognostic tools

Another prognostic tool that has been used to predict outcomes among patients undergoing hepatic resection for CRLM are nomograms. Nomograms take the specific value of multiple factors into consideration rather than just the inclusion of a certain number of clinical criteria like the CRS. One of the earlier nomograms developed was based off of 1,477 patients who underwent resection for CRLM during a study period of 1986 to 1999 to predict 96-month disease-specific survival (Kattan et al., 2008). The factors used were gender, age, primary tumor site (colon and rectum), nodal status of the primary tumor, disease-free interval, preoperative CEA (ng/ml), number of hepatic tumors, largest metastasis size, bilateral resection, and extent of resection (lobectomy or more). This nomogram achieved a concordance index of 0.61 with good calibration. Predictions from this model were also compared with those of the Fong score when both were applied to future patients and the nomogram was found to be more accurate in predicting survival, implying that not all clinical risk factors carry the same weight in predictions. An example the authors provided was that continuous variables like CEA or tumor size may results in considerable information loss if they are only considered as binary counts (yes/no) rather than an actual value. Another nomogram designed by Kanemitsu et al. was based on a study of 578 patients who underwent hepatectomy for CRLM treated at 18 major Japanese medical centers between 1990 and 1998 (Kanemitsu and Kato, 2008). Their model incorporated five significant preoperative predictors including primary histology, nodal status of primary tumor, number of hepatic tumors, presence of extrahepatic disease, and pre-hepatectomy CEA level (ng/ml). They demonstrated good calibration of this preoperative nomogram by comparison of the nomogram predicted probability of survival compared with the actual survival estimated at 3 years by Kaplan-Meier method. Both of these larger nomograms were externally validated by another cohort of patients undergoing hepatic resection for CRLM with high predictive accuracy, but nomograms can also be susceptible to the general limitations of selection bias (those already selected to undergoing hepatectomy) and institutional variability related to local referral patterns and treatment approaches (Takakura et al., 2011).

Another limitation of both clinical risk scoring systems and nomograms is that both have not consistently predicted outcomes well enough to effect clinical practice or guide individualized treatment decisions. The next wave of biological markers to predict long-term outcomes after treatment for various cancers are gene expression profiles of tumors. Ito and colleagues analyzed RNA samples from the liver samples of 96 patients with CRLM at Memorial Sloan Kettering Cancer Center who underwent a microscopically-negative (R0) liver resection (Ito et al., 2013). The genes associated with disease-specific survival and liver-recurrence-free survival were identified and selected to construct a molecular risk score (MRS) to predict long-term outcomes after surgery. The MRS predicted survival independently of the CRS, and when combined with the CRS, stratified subgroups of patients with extremely high- and low-risk for liver recurrence and death. Among the entire cohort, 90 percent of the patients classified as high-risk by both CRS and MRS developed liver recurrence and more than 65 percent died within 3 years. Conversely, more than 85 percent of those classified as low-risk both by CRS and MRS were liver-recurrence-free and 90 percent were alive at 3 years.

Inflammatory and immune predictors of survival

Other studies have focused on the immune response to neoplastic cells as a means for predicting survival in patients with malignancies including primary colon cancer (Mlecnik et al., 2011). Specifically, tumor-infiltrating lymphocyte (TIL) counts have been shown to predict outcome in a selected group of short- and long-term survivors following resection of CRLM (Katz et al., 2013). By characterizing the T-cell infiltrate within tumor tissue of 162 patients who underwent liver resection, independent correlates of 10-year survival following resection included a high number of cytotoxic CD8+ T cells, a low number of helper CD4+ T cells and a CRS less than or equal to 2. Authors from the same institution again confirmed in a larger and more recent study that CRLM CD8 T-cell infiltration correlates with survival, suggesting that these cytotoxic T-cells play a role in direct mediators of tumor cell lysis and an enhanced activation status of TILs in livers with metastases compared to non-tumor bearing liver (Galon et al., 2007; Katz et al., 2013). This subsequent study also reported on role of other immunologic factors including regulatory T-cells and demonstrated that a high number of these Treg cells (which prevent the other cells from mounting an effective tumor immune response) in relation to cytotoxic and helper T-cells leads to a more suppressive tumor microenvironment and therefore, decreased survival.

Besides cellular immunity, several investigators have also attempted to identify other prognostic inflammatory mediators and comprehend the nature of pro-inflammatory pathways associated with poorer clinical outcomes in CRLM (Hamilton et al., 2014). Many papers have reported on elevations in inflammatory markers such as C-reactive protein (Wong et al., 2007), IL-8 and PDGF-AB/BB (Hamilton et al., 2014), albumin (Wong et al., 2007), or the neutrophil-to-lymphocyte ratio (Giakoustidis et al., 2015; Halazun et al., 2008) as associated with worse survival in CRLM. The Glascow Prognostic Score (GPS), an inflammation-based prognostic score that is based on C-reactive protein and serum albumin levels has also been described to prognosticate for colorectal cancer and CRLM (Hamilton et al., 2014; Kobayashi et al., 2010). Kobayashi and colleagues divided 63 consecutive patients who underwent curative resection for CRLM into three different scores for the GPS where patients with both an elevated C-reactive protein (>10 mg/l) and hypoalbuminemia (<35 g/l) were allocated a GPS score of 2, those with one biochemical abnormality had a score of 1, and those with both normal levels of C-reactive protein and albumin received a score of 0. The authors showed in a multivariate analysis that the GPS score measured prior to the operation was reliable as a prognostic variable after hepatic resection for CRLM. The 5-year survival rates of patients with GPS 0, 1, and 2 were 56.2 percent, 25.0 percent, and 0 percent, respectively. These results highlighted a subgroup of patients with resectable CRLM who are eligible for curative resection but ultimately show poor prognosis (Kobayashi et al., 2010).

Predicting recurrence

A novel machine-learning statistical approach to develop a weighted recurrence prediction model was recently reported as the Paredes-Pawlik clinical score. Using an international, multi-institutional database, 1,406 patients with CRLM who underwent hepatectomy between 2001 and 2018 were identified, of which 842 (59.9 percent) had recurrence. The full predictive model was based on age, sex, primary tumor location, T stage, receipt of chemotherapy before hepatectomy, lymph node metastases, number of metastatic lesions in the liver, size of the largest hepatic metastases, CEA level, and KRAS status. The authors demonstrated the model to have good discriminative ability to predict 1-year, 3-year, and 5-year risk of recurrence assessed by area under the receiver operative curve. In the model design and validation cohorts with the incorporation of KRAS status, the Paredes-Pawlik clinical score performed better than the traditional Fong-Blumgart CRS and Brudvik-Vauthey CRS in predicting recurrence; specifically, the AUC for predicting 1-year recurrence was 0.693, (95 percent CI 0.684–0.704) versus 0.527 (95 percent CI 0.514–0.538) and 0.524 (95 percent CI 0.514–0.533), respectively, with similar trends also noted for 3- and 5-year recurrence (Paredes et al., 2020).

Surveillance and recurrence

Within the first two years after hepatectomy, 70 percent of patients will recur making it imperative to follow these patients to identify and manage these recurrences (de Jong et al., 2009). A report from Gomez et al. showed that repeat resection for liver or lung recurrence within the first year after hepatectomy for CRLM results in improved survival over those managed non-operatively (Gomez et al., 2010). In addition to systemic chemotherapy, patients with disease recurrence may be eligible for repeat hepatectomy (Butte et al., 2015) (Petrowsky et al., 2002), ablation (Schullian et al., 2021), or hepatic artery infusion chemotherapy (Buisman et al., 2021) for liver lesions, lung resection for pulmonary metastases (Suzuki et al., 2015), and cytoreductive surgery with or without hyperthermic intraperitoneal chemotherapy for peritoneal surface recurrences (Adileh et al., 2021).

The current guidelines on how to best follow patients after hepatectomy for CRLM are surprisingly limited. The only level I evidence to guide surveillance include clinical trials comparing low and high intensity screening strategies, albeit in stage II and III colorectal cancer patients (Rosati et al., 2016; Wille-Jørgensen et al., 2018). Although these trials reported that high intensity strategies discovered recurrences sooner, survival did not differ from the low intensity arms. As a result, it remains unclear whether more intensive surveillance strategies improve oncologic outcomes. Only the National Comprehensive Cancer Network (NCCN) and the American Society of Colon and Rectal Surgeons (ASCRS) provide guidance on how follow stage IV colorectal cancer patients, as summarized in Table 17.2 (Benson et al., 2021; Hardiman et al., 2021).

A retrospective cohort study of 1,070 stage IV colorectal cancer patients undergoing curative resection reported by Kishiki et al. in 2018 provides some guidance on how best to follow these patients (Kishiki et al., 2018). Multivariate analysis found that early recurrence (within

TABLE 17.2 Existing surveillance recommendations following resection of stage IV colorectal cancer.

Parameter	NCCN (2021)	ASCRS (2021)
History and Physical Examination		
0–2 years	Every 3–6 months	Every 3–12 months
2–5 years	Every 6 months	Every 6–12 months
CEA measurement		
0–2 years	Every 3–6 months	Every 3–12 months
2–5 years	Every 6 months	Every 6–12 months
Axial imaging		
0–2 years	Every 3–6 months	Every 6–12 months
2–5 years	Every 6–12 months	Every 6–12 months

NCCN = National comprehensive cancer network, ASCRS = American society of colon and rectal surgeons, CEA = Carcinoembryonic antigen.

one year of resection) was associated with primary tumors arising in the rectum, advanced T stage, advanced N stage, venous invasion, and hepatic metastasis; late recurrence (over 2 years following resection), however, was associated with largest tumor size less than 5 cm and peritoneal metastases. Since varying features are associated with early or late recurrence, some groups have sought to define risk factors for recurrence to help guide surveillance. Although the Fong CRS was described to predict risk for recurrence after hepatectomy, surveillance strategies have not been built to incorporate it into personalized follow-up strategies for patients (Fong et al., 1999). Galjart et al. studied a cohort of Dutch patients from their center that underwent curative resection of CRLM to determine risk factors for recurrence after three years of disease-free survival (Galjart et al., 2016). Although their report found no difference in clinicopathologic features associated with early (within three years) or late recurrence, this study defined patients with primary node-negative disease and disease-free interval >12 months as low-risk for recurrence after 3 years; all others were defined as high risk for recurrence. With only 4 percent of low risk patients having recurrence detected after three years of follow-up, the authors showed that this risk stratification could predict late recurrences with a c-index of 0.71 and sensitivity of 92 percent. This report and others with similar intent suggest that tailored follow up can be established based on the specific disease pattern.

A recent report on 1,221 CRLM patients that underwent hepatectomy at MD Anderson Cancer Center expanded on this by investigating recurrence rates at different time points in relation to various clinicopathologic markers and RAS mutation status (Kawaguchi et al., 2020). Therein, the risk for recurrence was highest within the first two years after hepatectomy and rare once disease-free for four years. After two years disease-free, RAS alteration was found to be the only factor associated with recurrence detection thereafter. Integrating these findings, the authors recommended a new surveillance strategy with a tailored approach based on RAS status to monitor altered patients more frequently between 2 and 4 years after hepatectomy as depicted in Fig. 17.1. Future work should seek to identify other factors that

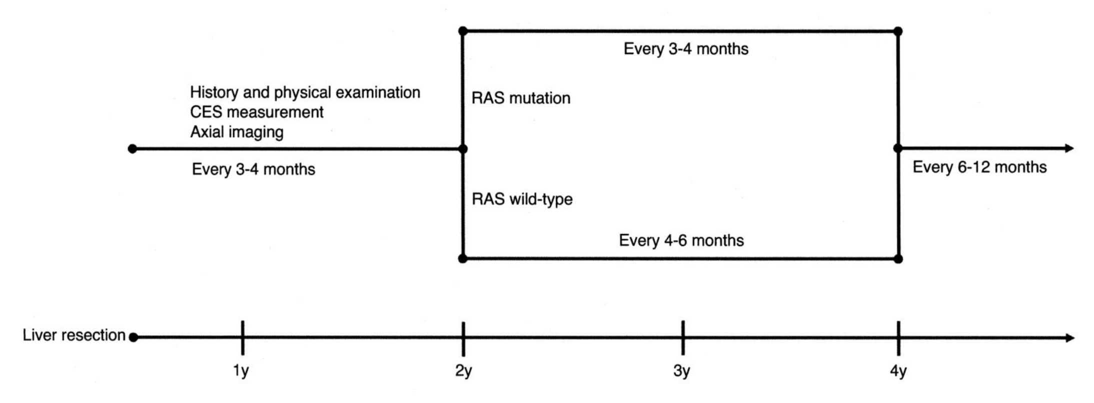

FIGURE 17.1 Integrating Tumor RAS Status into Surveillance Strategy Following Hepatectomy for Colorectal Liver Metastasis From Kawaguchi, Y., Kopetz, S., Lillemoe, HA, Hwang, H., Wang, X., Tzeng, C.-WD, Chun, YS, Aloia, T. A. & Vauthey, J.-N. (2020). A New Surveillance Algorithm After Resection of Colorectal Liver Metastases Based on Changes in Recurrence Risk and RAS Mutation Status. Journal of the National Comprehensive Cancer Network : JNCCN, 18(11), 1500–08. https://doi.org/10.6004/jnccn.2020.7596 CEA = carcinoembryonic antigen.

can tailor surveillance strategies for CRLM patients based on their tumor biology.

In addition to predictors of recurrence, the utility of disease detection must be considered especially in aging CRLM patients. Surveillance imaging is not without its consequences, especially since elderly patients are at increased risk of contrast-induced nephropathy (Moos et al., 2013). If recurrent disease is identified, elderly patients above 75 years old have also been reported to have more evident cognitive decline following oncologic surgery (Plas et al., 2017). Alabraba et al. conducted a systematic review of salvage therapies rendered in elderly patients after detection of recurrent disease noting that despite undergoing less extensive liver resections compared to patients younger than 75 years old, worse morbidity, mortality, and long-term survival outcomes occur in older patients after salvage hepatectomy (Alabraba and Gomez, 2021). Moreover, elderly patients were found to receive less targeted therapies, more systemic monotherapy, and experience more toxicity compared to patients under 75 years old. Conversely, elderly patients were found to have similar morbidity, mortality, and long-term survival outcomes after lung resection for recurrent disease. The authors recommended that patients 75 years and older take a Comprehensive Geriatric Assessment to help determine their cognitive and physical fitness for an intervention if a recurrence is found (Extermann et al., 2005; Hurria et al., 2014). Ultimately, the decision to stop surveillance must be a decision made in conjunction with the patient after considering the risks of continued imaging, the options for intervention if recurrence is found, and whether these interventions are feasible given the fitness of the patient, reasonably safe, or even desired by the patient.

Conclusion

Despite multiple modifications to various prognostic scoring systems throughout the decades to refine patient selection for hepatic resection, the ideal prognostic method for the clinical management of patients with CRLM still does not exist. Many of these models incorporate factors that are proven significant by rigorous statistical analyses to be predictors of survival, but these do not always exclude patients from resection given the possibility of a long-term disease free interval in the presence of poor prognostic factors. In addition, molecular and immunologic markers have also played a role in improving patient selection for resection. As further studies uncover the implications of various markers on tumor biology, surveillance strategies for patients following resection for CRLM must be tailored to specific disease burden and characteristics. Although evidence-based guidelines are essential to guide providers on how to follow patients, their fitness for intervention if a recurrence is detected, and their willingness to undergo the necessary procedure, must be weighed in when personalizing a surveillance program.

References

Adileh, M., Mor, E., Assaf, D., Benvenisti, H., Laks, S., Ben-Yaacov, A., et al. (2021). Perioperative and Oncological Outcomes of Combined Hepatectomy with Complete Cytoreduction and Hyperthermic Intraperitoneal Chemotherapy for Metastatic Colorectal Cancer. *Annals of Surgical Oncology, 28*(6), 3320–3329. https://doi.org/10.1245/s10434-020-09165-3.

Alabraba, E., & Gomez, D. (2021). Systematic Review of Treatments for Colorectal Metastases in Elderly Patients to Guide Surveillance Cessation Following Hepatic Resection for Colorectal Liver Metastases. *American Journal of Clinical Oncology, 44*(5), 210–223. https://doi.org/10.1097/COC.0000000000000803.

Ayez, N., Lalmahomed, Z. S., van der Pool, A. E. M., Vergouwe, Y., van Montfort, K., de Jonge, J., et al. (2011). Is the clinical risk score for patients with colorectal liver metastases still useable in the era of effective neoadjuvant chemotherapy? *Annals of Surgical Oncology, 18*(10), 2757–2763. https://doi.org/10.1245/s10434-011-1819-8.

Benson, A. B., Venook, A. P., Al-Hawary, M. M., Arain, M. A., Chen, Y.-J., Ciombor, K. K., et al. (2021). Colon Cancer, Version 2.2021, NCCN Clinical Practice Guidelines in Oncology. *Journal of the National Comprehensive Cancer Network : JNCCN,, 19*(3), 329–359. https://doi.org/10.6004/jnccn.2021.0012.

Brudvik, K. W., Jones, R. P., Giuliante, F., Shindoh, J., Passot, G., Chung, M. H., et al. (2019). RAS Mutation Clinical Risk Score to Predict Survival After Resection of Colorectal Liver Metastases. *Annals of Surgery, 269*(1), 120–126. https://doi.org/10.1097/SLA.0000000000002319.

Buisman, F. E., Filipe, W. F., Kemeny, N. E., Narayan, R. R., Srouji, R. M., Balachandran, V. P., et al. (2021). Recurrence After Liver Resection of Colorectal Liver Metastases: repeat Resection or Ablation Followed by Hepatic Arterial Infusion Pump Chemotherapy. *Annals of Surgical Oncology, 28*(2), 808–816. https://doi.org/10.1245/s10434-020-08776-0.

Butte, J. M., Gönen, M., Allen, P. J., Kingham, P., T. , S., C. , T., et al. (2015). Recurrence After Partial Hepatectomy for Metastatic Colorectal Cancer: potentially Curative Role of Salvage Repeat Resection. *Annals of Surgical Oncology, 22*(8), 2761–2771. https://doi.org/10.1245/s10434-015-4370-1.

de Jong, M. C., Pulitano, C., Ribero, D., Strub, J., Mentha, G., Schulick, R. D., et al. (2009). Rates and patterns of recurrence following curative intent surgery for colorectal liver metastasis: an international multi-institutional analysis of 1669 patients. *Annals of Surgery, 250*(3), 440–448. https://doi.org/10.1097/SLA.0b013e3181b4539b.

Extermann, M., Aapro, M., Bernabei, R., Cohen, H. J., Droz, J.-P., Lichtman, S., et al. (2005). Use of comprehensive geriatric assessment in older cancer patients: recommendations from the task force on CGA of the International Society of Geriatric Oncology (SIOG). *Critical Reviews in Oncology/Hematology,, 55*(3), 241–252.

Fong, Y., Fortner, J., Sun, R. L., Brennan, M. F., & Blumgart, L. H. (1999). Clinical score for predicting recurrence after hepatic resection for metastatic colorectal cancer: analysis of 1001 consecutive cases. *Annals of Surgery, 230*(3), 309–318 discussion 318-21.

Galjart, B., van der Stok, E. P., Rothbarth, J., Grünhagen, D. J., & Verhoef, C. (2016). Posttreatment Surveillance in Patients with Prolonged Disease-Free Survival After Resection of Colorectal Liver Metastasis. *Annals of Surgical Oncology, 23*(12), 3999–4007.

Galon, J., Fridman, W.-H., & Pagès, F. (2007). The adaptive immunologic microenvironment in colorectal cancer: a novel perspective. *Cancer Research, 67*(5), 1883–1886.

Giakoustidis, A., Neofytou, K., Khan, A. Z., & Mudan, S. (2015). Neutrophil to lymphocyte ratio predicts pattern of recurrence in patients undergoing liver resection for colorectal liver metastasis and thus the overall survival. *Journal of Surgical Oncology, 111*(4), 445–450. https://doi.org/10.1002/jso.23845.

Gomez, D., Sangha, V. K., Morris-Stiff, G., Malik, H. Z., Guthrie, A. J., Toogood, G. J., et al. (2010). Outcomes of intensive surveillance after resection of hepatic colorectal metastases. *British Journal of Surgery, 97*(10), 1552–1560. https://doi.org/10.1002/bjs.7136.

Halazun, K. J., Aldoori, A., Malik, H. Z., Al-Mukhtar, A., Prasad, K. R., Toogood, G. J., et al. (2008). Elevated preoperative neutrophil to lymphocyte ratio predicts survival following hepatic resection for colorectal liver metastases. *European Journal of Surgical Oncology : The Journal of the European Society of Surgical Oncology and the British Association of Surgical Oncology,, 34*(1), 55–60.

Hamilton, T. D., Leugner, D., Kopciuk, K., Dixon, E., Sutherland, F. R., & Bathe, O. F. (2014). Identification of prognostic inflammatory factors in colorectal liver metastases. *BMC cancer, 14*, 542. https://doi.org/10.1186/1471-2407-14-542.

Hardiman, K. M., Felder, S. I., Friedman, G., Migaly, J., Paquette, I. M., & Feingold, D. L. (2021). The American Society of Colon and Rectal Surgeons Clinical Practice Guidelines for the Surveillance and Survivorship Care of Patients After Curative Treatment of Colon and Rectal Cancer. *Diseases of the Colon and Rectum, 64*(5), 517–533. https://doi.org/10.1097/DCR.0000000000001984.

Hurria, A., Wildes, T., Blair, S. L., Browner, I. S., Cohen, H. J., Deshazo, M., et al. (2014). Senior adult oncology, version 2.2014: clinical practice guidelines in oncology. *Journal of the National Comprehensive Cancer Network : JNCCN, 12*(1), 82–126.

Ito, H., Mo, Q., Qin, L.-X., Viale, A., Maithel, S. K., Maker, A. V., et al. (2013). Gene expression profiles accurately predict outcome following liver resection in patients with metastatic colorectal cancer. *Plos One, 8*(12), e81680. https://doi.org/10.1371/journal.pone.0081680.

Iwatsuki, S., Dvorchik, I., Madariaga, J. R., Marsh, J. W., Dodson, F., Bonham, A. C., et al. (1999). Hepatic resection for metastatic colorectal adenocarcinoma: a proposal of a prognostic scoring system. *Journal of the American College of Surgeons, 189*(3), 291–299.

Kanemitsu, Y., & Kato, T. (2008). Prognostic models for predicting death after hepatectomy in individuals with hepatic metastases from colorectal cancer. *World Journal of Surgery, 32*(6), 1097–1107. https://doi.org/10.1007/s00268-007-9348-0.

Kattan, M. W., Gönen, M., Jarnagin, W. R., DeMatteo, R., D'Angelica, M., Weiser, M., et al. (2008). A nomogram for predicting disease-specific survival after hepatic resection for metastatic colorectal cancer. *Annals of Surgery, 247*(2), 282–287. https://doi.org/10.1097/SLA.0b013e31815ed67b.

Katz, S. C., Bamboat, Z. M., Maker, A. V., Shia, J., Pillarisetty, V. G., Yopp, A. C., et al. (2013). Regulatory T cell infiltration predicts outcome following resection of colorectal cancer liver metastases. *Annals of Surgical Oncology, 20*(3), 946–955. https://doi.org/10.1245/s10434-012-2668-9.

Kawaguchi, Y., Kopetz, S., Lillemoe, H. A., Hwang, H., Wang, X., Tzeng, C.-W. D., et al. (2020). A New Surveillance Algorithm After Resection of Colorectal Liver Metastases Based on Changes in Recurrence Risk and RAS Mutation Status. *Journal of the National Comprehensive Cancer Network : JNCCN,, 18*(11), 1500–1508. https://doi.org/10.6004/jnccn.2020.7596.

Kishiki, T., Lapin, B., Matsuoka, H., Watanabe, T., Takayasu, K., Kojima, K., et al. (2018). Optimal Surveillance Protocols After Curative Resection in Patients With Stage IV Colorectal Cancer: a Multicenter Retrospective Study. *Diseases of the Colon and Rectum, 61*(1), 51–57. https://doi.org/10.1097/DCR.0000000000000950.

Kobayashi, T., Teruya, M., Kishiki, T., Endo, D., Takenaka, Y., Miki, K., et al. (2010). Elevated C-reactive protein and hypoalbuminemia measured before resection of colorectal liver metastases predict postoperative survival. *Digestive Surgery, 27*(4), 285–290. https://doi.org/10.1159/000280021.

Mann, C. D., Metcalfe, M. S., Leopardi, L. N., & Maddern, G. J. (2004). The clinical risk score: emerging as a reliable preoperative prognostic index in hepatectomy for colorectal metastases. *Archives of Surgery (Chicago, Ill. : 1960), 139*(11), 1168–1172.

Margonis, G. A., Sasaki, K., Kim, Y., Samaha, M., Buettner, S., Amini, N., et al. (2016). Tumor Biology Rather Than Surgical Technique Dictates Prognosis in Colorectal Cancer Liver Metastases. *Journal of Gastrointestinal Surgery : Official Journal of the Society for Surgery of the Alimentary Tract,, 20*(11), 1821–1829.

Mlecnik, B., Tosolini, M., Kirilovsky, A., Berger, A., Bindea, G., Meatchi, T., et al. (2011). Histopathologic-based prognostic factors of colorectal cancers are associated with the state of the local immune reaction. *Journal of Clinical*

Oncology : Official Journal of the American Society of Clinical Oncology,, 29(6), 610–618. https://doi.org/10.1200/JCO.2010.30.5425.

Moos, S. I., van Vemde, D. N. H., Stoker, J., & Bipat, S. (2013). Contrast induced nephropathy in patients undergoing intravenous (IV) contrast enhanced computed tomography (CECT) and the relationship with risk factors: a meta-analysis. *European Journal of Radiology, 82*(9), e387–e399. https://doi.org/10.1016/j.ejrad.2013.04.029.

Nash, G. M., Gimbel, M., Shia, J., Nathanson, D. R., Ndubuisi, M. I., Zeng, Z.-S., et al. (2010). KRAS mutation correlates with accelerated metastatic progression in patients with colorectal liver metastases. *Annals of Surgical Oncology, 17*(2), 572–578. https://doi.org/10.1245/s10434-009-0605-3.

Nordlinger, B., Guiguet, M., Vaillant, J. C., Balladur, P., Boudjema, K., Bachellier, P., et al. (1996). Surgical resection of colorectal carcinoma metastases to the liver. A prognostic scoring system to improve case selection, based on 1568 patients. Association Française de Chirurgie. *Cancer, 77*(7), 1254–1262.

Paredes, A. Z., Hyer, J. M., Tsilimigras, D. I., Moro, A., Bagante, F., Guglielmi, A., et al. (2020). A Novel Machine-Learning Approach to Predict Recurrence After Resection of Colorectal Liver Metastases. *Annals of Surgical Oncology, 27*(13), 5139–5147. https://doi.org/10.1245/s10434-020-08991-9.

Pawlik, T. M., & Choti, M. A. (2007). Shifting from clinical to biologic indicators of prognosis after resection of hepatic colorectal metastases. *Current Oncology Reports, 9*(3), 193–201.

Petrowsky, H., Gonen, M., Jarnagin, W., Lorenz, M., DeMatteo, R., Heinrich, S., et al. (2002). Second liver resections are safe and effective treatment for recurrent hepatic metastases from colorectal cancer: a bi-institutional analysis. *Annals of Surgery, 235*(6), 863–871.

Plas, M., Rotteveel, E., Izaks, G. J., Spikman, J. M., van der Wal-Huisman, H., van Etten, B., et al. (2017). Cognitive decline after major oncological surgery in the elderly. *European Journal of Cancer (Oxford, England : 1990), 86*, 394–402. https://doi.org/10.1016/j.ejca.2017.09.024.

Rosati, G., Ambrosini, G., Barni, S., Andreoni, B., Corradini, G., Luchena, G., et al. (2016). A randomized trial of intensive versus minimal surveillance of patients with resected Dukes B2-C colorectal carcinoma. *Annals of Oncology : Official Journal of the European Society for Medical Oncology,, 27*(2), 274–280. https://doi.org/10.1093/annonc/mdv541.

Schullian, P., Johnston, E. W., Putzer, D., Laimer, G., Waroschitz, G., Braunwarth, E., et al. (2021). Stereotactic radiofrequency ablation (SRFA) for recurrent colorectal liver metastases after hepatic resection. *European Journal of Surgical Oncology : The Journal of the European Society of Surgical Oncology and the British Association of Surgical Oncology,, 47*(4), 866–873. https://doi.org/10.1016/j.ejso.2020.09.034.

Smith, J. J., & D'Angelica, M. I. (2015). Surgical management of hepatic metastases of colorectal cancer. *Hematology Oncology Clinics of North America, 29*(1), 61–84. https://doi.org/10.1016/j.hoc.2014.09.003.

Suzuki, H., Kiyoshima, M., Kitahara, M., Asato, Y., & Amemiya, R. (2015). Long-term outcomes after surgical resection of pulmonary metastases from colorectal cancer. *Annals of Thoracic Surgery, 99*(2), 435–440. https://doi.org/10.1016/j.athoracsur.2014.09.027.

Takakura, Y., Okajima, M., Kanemitsu, Y., Kuroda, S., Egi, H., Hinoi, T., et al. (2011). External validation of two nomograms for predicting patient survival after hepatic resection for metastatic colorectal cancer. *World Journal of Surgery, 35*(10), 2275–2282. https://doi.org/10.1007/s00268-011-1194-4.

Tomlinson, J. S., Jarnagin, W. R., DeMatteo, R. P., Fong, Y., Kornprat, P., Gonen, M., et al. (2007). Actual 10-year survival after resection of colorectal liver metastases defines cure. *Journal of Clinical Oncology : Official Journal of the American Society of Clinical Oncology,, 25*(29), 4575–4580.

Tzeng, C.-W. D., & Aloia, T. A. (2013). Colorectal liver metastases. *Journal of Gastrointestinal Surgery : Official Journal of the Society for Surgery of the Alimentary Tract,, 17*(1), 195–201. quiz p.201-2 https://doi.org/10.1007/s11605-012-2022-3 .

Wille-Jørgensen, P., Syk, I., Smedh, K., Laurberg, S., Nielsen, D. T., Petersen, S. H., et al. (2018). Effect of More vs Less Frequent Follow-up Testing on Overall and Colorectal Cancer-Specific Mortality in Patients With Stage II or III Colorectal Cancer: the COLOFOL Randomized Clinical Trial. *Jama, 319*(20), 2095–2103. https://doi.org/10.1001/jama.2018.5623.

Wong, V. K. H., Malik, H. Z., Hamady, Z. Z. R., Al-Mukhtar, A., Gomez, D., Prasad, K. R., et al. (2007). C-reactive protein as a predictor of prognosis following curative resection for colorectal liver metastases. *British Journal of Cancer, 96*(2), 222–225.

Zakaria, S., Donohue, J. H., Que, F. G., Farnell, M. B., Schleck, C. D., Ilstrup, D. M., et al. (2007). Hepatic resection for colorectal metastases: value for risk scoring systems? *Annals of Surgery, 246*(2), 183–191.

CHAPTER

18

Management of secondary recurrence of intra-hepatic colorectal liver metastasis following initial hepatic resection

Guillaume Martel and Kimberly Bertens

Department of Surgery, Liver and Pancreas Unit, The Ottawa Hospital, University of Ottawa, 501 Smyth Rd, CCW 1667, Ottawa, ON, K1H 8L6, Canada

Introduction

Approximately 50 percent of patients with colorectal cancer will develop liver metastases during the course of their disease. Complete surgical resection of all colorectal liver metastases (CRLM) remains the only potentially curative option for these patients. Following liver resection for CRLM, approximately 20–25 percent of patients will become actual 10-year survivors (Creasy et al., 2018; Pulitanò et al., 2010). The vast majority of the remainder of patients treated surgically will develop disease recurrence, which will eventually lead to their demise. It is likely that most patients who experience recurrence had occult disease at the time of their initial hepatectomy, which eventually progressed and led to measurable evidence of cancer on traditional imaging modalities. Among those with recurrence, 43–46 percent have liver-only metastases, 21–22 percent have liver and extra-hepatic metastases, and 32–36 percent have extra-hepatic metastases alone (Hallet et al., 2016; De Jong et al., 2009). Within the subset of patients with limited liver disease and possibly extra-hepatic disease, repeat liver resection with curative intent may be considered. Alternatively, patients with recurrent CRLM may be treated with one of several other loco-regional modalities or systemic chemotherapy options.

Contemporary Management of Metastatic Colorectal Cancer: A Precision Medicine Approach
DOI: https://doi.org/10.1016/B978-0-323-91706-3.00010-2

Surveillance following initial hepatectomy

As discussed in chapter 17, it is necessary to reflect on what purpose post-treatment surveillance serves when framing the discussion of surveillance following liver resection for CRLM. The intention of surveillance in colorectal cancer is two-fold; to identify new metachronous primary neoplasms at a precancerous stage (polyps) and to discover cancer recurrence when it is potentially curable. For the purpose of this chapter on recurrent CRLM, the focus will be on the latter.

Frequency of testing

Liver metastases are common in patients with colorectal cancer. Approximately 15–20 percent of patients will present with synchronous CRLM, and another 30 percent will develop metachronous CRLM following curative intent therapy for the primary cancer (Manfredi et al., 2006). Furthermore, although liver resection is standard therapy for resectable CRLM, more than half of patients that undergo hepatic metastectomy will experience a recurrence. Despite this, there is a paucity of evidence relating to surveillance of patients with Stage IV disease. Multiple randomized control trials (RTC) have set out to examine the proposed benefit of high versus low intensity surveillance in Stage II and III disease (Rosati et al., 2016; Wille-Jørgensen et al., 2018; Kjeldsen, Thorsen, Whalley, and Kronborg, 1999; Pietra et al., 1998; Secco et al., 2002; Rodríguez-Moranta et al., 2006). Some organizations (Benson, Venook, and Al-Hawary, 2021a; Benson, Venook, and Al-Hawary, 2021b; Steele et al., 2015) have published guidelines extrapolating these data to Stage IV patients, while others (Meyerhardt et al., 2013) (E. Kennedy, Zwaal, and Asmis, 2021) have refrained from including metastatic patients in surveillance guidelines due to a lack of data. Both the NCCN and the ASCRS recommend surveillance of Stage IV patients with isolated metastases that were resected for cure (Benson et al., 2021a; Benson et al., 2021b; Steele et al., 2015). However, the recommended surveillance intervals vary.

The COLOFOL trial looked at treated stage II-III colorectal cancer patients and randomized them to high and low-intensity follow-up (Wille-Jørgensen et al., 2018). Patients were randomized to computed tomography (CT) of the chest, abdomen and pelvis and serum carcinoembryonic antigen (CEA) at 6, 12, 18, 24, and 36 months after surgery (high-frequency) or at 12 and 36 months after surgery (low-frequency). This large, multi-national trial randomized 2,509 patients and found no difference in the 5-year disease-specific mortality rate in the high (10.6 percent) or low-frequency (11.4 percent) groups ($p = 0.52$). Other RCTs have demonstrated a higher likelihood of reoperation for cure, and improved OS with higher-intensity surveillance (Kjeldsen et al., 1999; Pietra et al., 1998; Secco et al., 2002; Rodríguez-Moranta et al., 2006). A recently published Cochrane Review that includes 15 RTCs and 12,528 patients failed to show a survival benefit for intensifying the follow-up schedule (Jeffery, Hickey, and Hider, 2019). There was no difference in detection of recurrence in those undergoing high-intensity surveillance, yet significantly more surgical procedures for recurrence were performed in this group (Jeffery et al., 2019).

Specific to patients with Stage IV disease, Hyder et al. studied the Surveillance, Epidemiology and End Results (SEER) dataset for colorectal cancer patients that had liver resection and/or ablation (Hyder et al., 2013). The authors concluded that intensity of imaging did not

TABLE 18.1 Surveillance guidelines for colorectal cancer with relation to liver metastases*.

	NCCN Stage IVa (Benson et al., 2021a,b)	ASCRS Stages Ib-III and Stage IVc (Steele et al., 2015)	ASCO Stages II-III (Meyerhardt et al., 2013)	CCO Stages I-IIIf (Kennedy et al., 2021)
History and physician exam				
0–2 years	Every 3–6 mo	Every 3–6 mo	Every 3–6 mo	Every 6 mo
2–5 years	Every 6 mo	Every 6 mo	Every 3–6 mo	Every 6 mo[e]
CEA				
0–2 years	Every 3–6 mo	Every 3–6 mo	Every 3–6 mo	Discretion of MD
2–5 years	Every 6 mo	Every 6 mo	Every 3–6 mo	Discretion of MD
CT scan (chest/abdomen/pelvis)				
0–2 years	Every 3–6 mo	Every 12 mo	Every 12 mo[d]	At 12 and 24 mo OR at 18 mo[e]
2–5 years	Every 6–12 mo	Every 12 mo	Every 12 mo[d,e]	

*Please note that colonoscopy is also recommended to assess for local recurrence (a) After curative intent surgery for liver and/or lung metastases (b) High-risk Stage I patients only (c) Isolated metastases, resected for cure (d) For high-risk patients it is reasonable to consider imaging every 6–12 mos for first 3years (e) For 3 years after surgery, following this at discretion of treating MD (f) Does not apply to rectal cancer Abbreviations: ASCO- American Society of Clinical Oncology; ASCRS- American Society of Colorectal Surgeons; CEA: carcinoembryonic antigen; CCO- Cancer Care Ontario; mo: months; CT: computed tomography; NCCN- National Comprehensive Cancer Network.

influence time to second procedure or median survival, and as such annual surveillance may be sufficient. Conversely, Kawaguchi et al. advocated for an enhanced surveillance schedule for treated Stage IV colorectal cancer patients based on RAS status (Kawaguchi et al., 2020). The authors retrospectively followed more than a thousand patients who underwent resection for CRLM. They reported a recurrence risk of 62.7 percent at 2 years and in those that were disease free at 2 years, the recurrence rate was 23.2 percent at 4 years. The authors argue that increased surveillance is justified in resected stage IV patients since they have a recurrence rate at 2 years that is nearly 3 times that of Stage II and III patients. The authors propose surveillance every 3–4 months during years 0–2. For the subsequent 2 years those with RAS mutation would continue to have surveillance every 3–4 months and those that are RAS wild-type would have their interval lengthened to every 4–6 months. Following this, if patients are recurrence-free at 4 years, imaging is recommended every 6–12 months (Kawaguchi et al., 2020).

Length of surveillance

Traditionally patients with colorectal cancer have been enrolled in survivorship programs for 5 years. The risk of recurrence after 5 years has been reported as less than 1.5 percent per year, and less than 5 percent recur after 5 years (Sargent et al., 2009; Seo et al., 2013). More recently, both the COLOFOL and FACS trials demonstrated no clear benefit of surveillance beyond 3 years in Stage II/III and Dukes' stage A-C colorectal cancer respectively (Wille-Jørgensen et al., 2018; Mant et al., 2017). The aforementioned Cochrane review showed that 90 percent of recurrences were found within 36 months of follow-up (Jeffery et al., 2019). Yet, again, this systematic review did not include resected Stage IV patients. It is plausible that the recurrence patterns of Stage IV colorectal cancer patients following resection of CRLM are not comparable to those patients with stage I-III disease. In fact, Kawaguchi et al. demonstrated that nearly one quarter of patients will recur between 2 and 4 years following liver resection, and this is even higher in patients with a RAS mutation (Kawaguchi et al., 2020). In another observational study, 28 percent of patients were disease-free after 3 years post CRLM resection (Galjart, van der Stok, Rothbarth, Grünhagen, and Verhoef, 2016). In these 152 patients, the recurrence risk at 10 years was 27 percent. The authors demonstrated that those with a node negative primary and disease-free interval of <12 months between primary resection and liver resection had a low risk of recurrence after 3 years, and may not require ongoing surveillance. Currently the optimal duration of surveillance post liver resection of CRLM remains undefined.

Testing parameters

The published guidelines pertaining to colorectal cancer all recommend at minimum twice annual history and physical examination. The additive benefit of routine CEA testing was brought into question in the FACS trial (Mant et al., 2017). This study randomized patients to minimal follow-up (CT at 12 and 18 months), CEA only, CT only or CT and CEA. The study failed to demonstrate a survival advantage to CEA and CT over CT alone. The accepted cross-sectional imaging modality for surveillance of colorectal cancer is CT of the chest, abdomen and pelvis. There is no role for positron emission tomography (PET) imaging in routine surveillance of patients with colorectal cancer, although it can be considered as further work up in patients with an unexplained elevation of CEA. Colonoscopy is also required; however the details of this are beyond the scope of this chapter.

Repeat liver resection

The first series of repeat liver resection for recurrent malignant tumors of the liver was published in 1989, which included 10 cases of CRLM (Lange, Leese, Castaing, and Bismuth, 1989). Since then, numerous investigators have reported on their experience with repeat liver resection as a potentially curative modality for recurrent CRLM

Technical considerations

Repeat (or "redo") liver resection is widely considered more challenging than the initial hepatectomy carried out for CRLM. The functional status of the patient must carefully be reviewed prior to surgery. Hepatic reserve and predicted future liver remnant volume must also be examined. Formal volumetric assessment of the future liver remnant can be carried out when planning segmental or lobar resections. This can be accomplished using radiologic software, understanding that the total volume of the hypertrophied remnant should be used as the current denominator, rather than the patient's original liver volume prior to the initial hepatectomy (i.e. [FLR_{redo} = remnant $volume_{redo}$ / total liver $volume_{redo}$] x100). As discussed in chapter 3, formulae used to generate estimates of the total liver volume based on body surface area should be avoided (Vauthey et al., 2002), as they cannot be considered accurate following initial hepatectomy and subsequent hypertrophy of the remnant. Criteria for technical resectability are no different for repeat hepatectomies than for the patient's initial liver resection. The surgeon must preserve adequate portal and arterial inflow, hepatic venous outflow, and biliary drainage. The magnitude of the initial hepatectomy may in fact limit repeat resection options, owing to the loss of vascular and biliary pedicles in major resections. As patients can now routinely undergo two, three, or sometimes more than three liver resections over the course of their disease, a greater emphasis has recently been placed on parenchymal-sparring techniques to save healthy residual parenchyma, increase salvageability, and consequently improve overall survival following CRLM recurrence within the liver (Mise et al., 2016).

When the initial hepatectomy was done in an open fashion, it is most probable that the repeat operation will also be done open. If the initial hepatectomy was performed laparoscopically or robotically, it may then be reasonable to consider a repeat minimally invasive hepatectomy, based on surgeon preference and expertise. Van der Poel and colleagues have recently reported on 271 repeat liver resections that were done laparoscopically at 7 high-volume European centers, within a greater cohort of 425 (64 percent) repeat resections (Poel et al., n.d.). Importantly, among the laparoscopic cases, only 31 percent were previously done in an open fashion, and 84 percent of repeat laparoscopic cases had a minor hepatectomy at the initial operation. The authors compared the laparoscopic and open cohorts using propensity score-matching and concluded that laparoscopy for repeat liver resection was safe in selected patients, and was associated with similar morbidity and mortality rates, as well as decreased operative time (56 min), blood loss (100 mL), and length of stay in hospital (1 day).

The conduct of a repeat hepatectomy can be very challenging (Adam et al., 1997). Intraabdominal and peri–hepatic adhesions can be complex to manage. Adhesiolysis at repeat hepatectomy is likely to significantly increase operative time, even for liver resections that may otherwise have been minor. Great care should be taken around the central liver, where porta hepatis structures are more prone to misidentification and could be injured in the process. Challenges in dissecting and correctly identifying porta hepatis structures is compounded by the rotation of the liver that occurs following an initial major liver resection, as well as the associated hypertrophy of the remnant that can make intra-operative interpretation more difficult (Fig. 18.1). Adhesions to the liver capsule, as well as cautery artifact, can also obscure intra-operative ultrasound identification of small intra-parenchymal tumors and thus make their resection more challenging. In this context, data from the SEPRA-C2T trial can be informative (Dupré et al., 2013). In this small phase 2 trial, 54 patients undergoing two-stage hepatectomy were randomized (3:1 ratio) to the use of a bioresorbable hyaluronic acid/carboxymethylcellulose membrane after the first procedure or to standard care. Patients underwent their second stage resection after a median of 2.1 months in the intervention arm. Application of the bioresorbable membrane resulted in a 33 percent decrease in time to complete liver mobilization (25 min difference) and the risk of grade 3–4 adhesions was 31 percent in the intervention arm compared to 55 percent in the control group. Observational data in repeat liver surgery (Kobayashi et al., 2021), as well as a broader systematic review of 28 abdominal surgery trials (Ten Broek et al., 2014), further support the use of bioresorbable membranes to reduce adhesions in repeat liver surgery.

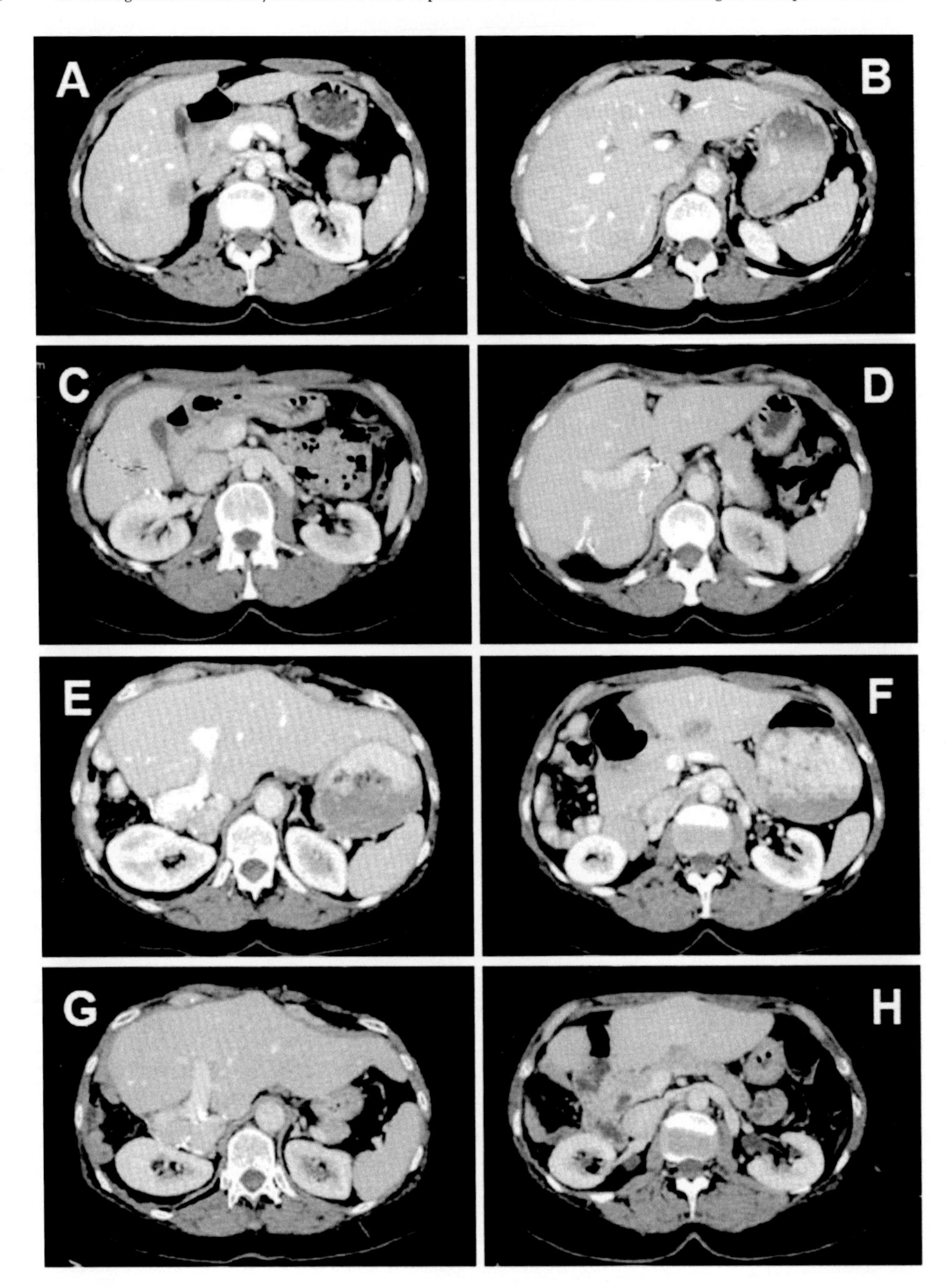

FIGURE 18.1 Evolution of CT appearance of a 57 year old woman's recurrent colorectal liver metastases. A/B: Initial presentation with lesions in segments 1, 5, and 6. C/D: Scan prior to second liver resection with lesions in segments 5 and 7. E/F: Scan prior to third liver resection with a single lesion in segment 3. Note hypertrophy of the left lobe and rotation of the liver hilum to the right post right hepatectomy. G/H: Surveillance scan after third liver resection demonstrating no evidence of disease.

Published experience with repeat hepatectomy

Several groups have reported on repeat liver resection for CRLM. At least 10 series with samples sizes greater than 100 patients can be identified in the contemporary literature (Table 18.2) (Hallet et al., 2016; De Jong et al., 2009; Poel et al., n.d.; Petrowsky et al., 2002; Adam et al., 2003; Ishiguro et al., 2006; Adair et al., 2012; Wicherts et al., 2013; Butte et al., 2015; Schmidt et al., n.d.). Wicherts and colleagues have reported on a cohort of 933 patients who underwent consecutive liver resections for CRLM at a single high-volume center in France (1990–2010) (Wicherts et al., 2013). Among those, 288 patients (31 percent) underwent repeat hepatectomy for recurrent disease. A total of 63 and 11 went on to have a third and fourth liver resection, respectively. Major resections were more common at the initial hepatectomy compared to the second and third operations (34 percent vs 17 percent vs 5 percent, $p < 0.001$). Peri-operative morbidity following a second hepatectomy was 34 percent compared to 27 percent ($p = 0.069$) after the initial resection. Similarly, mortality was 3.1 percent after repeat resection compared to 1.6 percent at the initial operation. Perhaps most importantly, the overall survival of patients who underwent two hepatectomies were significantly greater than those who underwent a single resection (5-year OS 54 percent vs 45 percent, $p = 0.003$). This finding appears to be driven primarily by those who had one resection, but did not undergo resection for their recurrence (5-year OS 29 percent). Five-year OS following a second hepatectomy and third hepatectomy were 41 percent and 45 percent, respectively, which compare very favorably to the survival outcomes achieved among those who had only one resection. On multivariate analysis, only having a repeat hepatectomy was found to be significantly associated with overall survival.

More recently, Butte and colleagues have presented data on 952 patients who had a liver resection for CRLM (10 years, single center, 1994–2004), of which 694 experienced recurrence (median 13 months) (Butte et al., 2015). Among those, potential salvage therapy with complete resection of all recurrent disease was carried out in 160 (17 percent), most typically for a single site of disease recurrence in 93 percent. Among those patients 25 percent were described as having achieved effective salvage therapy, remaining disease-free for at least 36 months post-resection. Median survival among those patients who had potential salvage resection was 84 months, compared to 34 months among those treated with a palliative intent. Factors associated with longer recurrence-free survival included having a node-negative primary, single initial metastasis, and low Clinical Risk Score.

A number of systematic reviews examining the role of repeat hepatectomy for CRLM have been published over the last several years (Lam et al., 2013; Luo, Yu, Huang, and Wu, 2014; Wurster et al., 2017; Wang, Si, Cai, and Zhou, 2019; Hellingman et al., 2021). The most up to date and comprehensive of these reviews included 34 studies and 3,039 patients by Wang et al. (Wang et al., 2019). Across included papers, the authors described a median overall morbidity rate of 23 percent after repeat hepatectomy, a mortality range of 0–6 percent, and a 5-year OS of 42 percent (range 17–73 percent). Clearly, the wide range of reported outcomes highlights the heterogeneity of patients selected for repeat hepatectomy across published series. Meta-analysis identified several factors associated with OS at initial hepatectomy (primary T3/T4 stage, number of lesions >1, largest tumor ≥ 5 cm, and R1 margin) and at repeat hepatectomy (high CEA, disease-free interval >12 months, number of lesions >1, largest tumor ≥ 5 cm, R1 margin, bilobar disease, extrahepatic disease).

TABLE 18.2 Selected series of repeat liver resection for colorectal cancer liver metastases ($n \geq 100$) published since 2000.

Studies	Country	RH	R0 margin	Major rxn	Mortality	Morbidity	Median OS	3-yr OS	5-yr OS	Factors associated with survival
Petrowsky et al., 2002 [33]	USA/Ger	126	79 percent	29 percent	1.6 percent	28 percent	37 months	51 percent	34 percent	Tumor >5 cm and >1 tumor at repeat resection associated with OS
Adam et al., 2003 [34]	France	199	88 percent	59 percent	3 percent	23 percent		54 percent	35 percent	Tumor >3 cm at initial liver resection, extrahepatic disease at second resection, and non-curative pattern of third resection associated with OS
Ishiguro et al., 2006 [35]	Japan	111	84 percent	12 percent	0	14 percent	43 months	74 percent	41 percent	Synchronous primary, hepatic/portal vein involvement at initial liver resection, and >3 tumors at repeat resection associated with OS
De Jong et al., 2009 [5]	USA/It/Sw/Be	246	90 percent	21 percent	0.4 percent	21 percent	42 months	52 percent	33 percent	–

(*continued on next page*)

TABLE 18.2 Selected series of repeat liver resection for colorectal cancer liver metastases ($n \geq 100$) published since 2000—cont'd

Studies	Country	RH	R0 margin	Major rxn	Mortality	Morbidity	Median OS	3-yr OS	5-yr OS	Factors associated with survival
Adair et al., 2012 [36]	UK	195	48 percent	17 percent	1.5 percent	20 percent	25 months	44 percent	29 percent	Tumor size ≥5 cm at repeat resection associated with OS
Wicherts et al., 2013 [37]	France	288	61 percent	17 percent	2.4 percent	34 percent	44 months	58 percent	41 percent	Having a repeat hepatectomy associated with OS
Butte et al., 2015 [38]	USA	160	86 percent	–	–	–	87 months	–	65 percent	N-negative primary, single initial tumor, and low CRS associated with RFS
Hallet et al., 2016 [4]	France	447	–	26 percent	1 percent	29 percent	–	78 percent	57 percent	–
Schmidt et al. 2018 [39]	Germany	169	65 percent	30 percent	–	28 percent	–	–	57 percent	Unilobar, metachronous, N-negative, and no medical complications associated with OS
van der Poel, et al. 2019 [28]	UK/Neth/Nor/Fr/Be/It/Sp	425	87 percent	24 percent	0.9 percent	–	–	–	–	–

Another recent meta-analysis was published by Wurster and colleagues (Wurster et al., 2017). In this work, the authors included only 8 observational studies ($n = 450$), where cases of liver resections for recurrent CRLM were compared to 2,669 cases of single hepatic resections. These studies had to include patients from independent collectives, such that many other studies were not included. Median time from the colorectal resection to first/single hepatectomy was 10–13 months in the recurrent group and 12–20 months in the single group. The median interval between the first and repeat hepatectomy was 15–16 months. There was no significant difference between single and repeat resections in terms of peri–operative complications, including hepatic insufficiency, bile leak, and blood loss. Similarly, peri–operative mortality was not significantly different between the groups, as was overall survival when measured from the time of the first or single hepatectomy. Importantly, one paper noted that those patients who underwent repeat resection had significantly longer survival than those who did not have repeat surgery following recurrence.

In summary, repeat hepatectomy for recurrent liver-only CRLM appears safe and associated with a degree of peri–operative morbidity and mortality that is comparable to initial liver resections. This finding is likely related to careful patient selection within published observational series. Finally, repeat liver resection appears associated with a cancer survival advantage over and above palliation following disease recurrence and is likely associated with cancer outcomes that are similar to that of the initial liver resection. In short, repeat liver resection can be considered the standard of care, where it can be accomplished safely and effectively.

Early recurrence

It is sometimes very difficult for liver surgeons and members of the multidisciplinary tumor board to determine the optimal course of treatment for patients who experience early liver recurrence following hepatectomy. There is no uniform consensus on the definition of early recurrence (Imai et al., 2016), but time intervals in the first 12 months after surgery have been most commonly considered (Hellingman et al., 2021).

Several investigators have considered this question of early recurrence. Vigano and colleagues have reported on 6,025 patients from the LiverMetSurvey, an international registry of patients undergoing surgery for CRLM between 1998 and 2009 (Viganò et al., 2014). Among those, 2,734 (45 percent) experienced disease recurrence and 639 (11 percent) had an early recurrence defined as the first 6 months after initial hepatectomy. Among those with early recurrence, 234 (37 percent) underwent repeat hepatectomy. The repeat hepatectomy rate was lower among those with early recurrence than among those with recurrence after 6 months (47 percent vs 60 percent, $p < 0.0001$). Patients who underwent liver resection for early recurrence had a far superior survival compared to those who did not undergo re-resection (5-year OS 47 percent vs 8.9 percent, $p < 0.0001$; liver-only disease 51 percent vs 8.3 percent, $p < 0.0001$). Importantly, the survival of patients with early recurrence was not significantly different from those with recurrence after 6 months (liver-only 5-year OS 51 percent vs 49 percent, p=NS).

A more recent meta-analysis by Hellingman and colleagues included 28 observational studies, of which 15 were pooled in a meta-analysis ($n = 1{,}039$ patients) (Hellingman et al., 2021). This paper specifically examined whether repeat resection for early recurrence (<6 months) was appropriate and associated with survival. The authors reported that repeat resection for

CRLM was associated with a median OS of 54 months in those with recurrence after 3–6 months, 53 months in those with recurrence after 7–12 months (HR 0.89, 95 percent CI 0.66–1.18, $p = 0.410$), and 60 months among those with recurrence after 12 months (adjusted HR 0.70, 95 percent CI 0.53–0.92, $p = 0.012$). The authors concluded that while disease-free interval was associated with overall survival, it could not be utilized as a selection criterion for repeat resection, given the generally good outcomes achieved with all recurrence categories after 3 months. Although this paper supports the conduct of repeat resection for early recurrence of CRLM, it should be noted that included studies had a relatively short median follow-up of 29 months and none of the pooled survival estimates were adjusted for confounders.

Liver surgeons are keen to provide patients with treatment options that are most likely to improve their survival, while also minimizing impairment to quality of life by avoiding futile re-operations. For this reason, many favor the administration of systemic chemotherapy prior repeat hepatectomy for early recurrence. This strategy is can provide a "test of time" or a "test of biology" by selecting patients for repeat resection who do not progress with additional liver or extra-hepatic lesions while on chemotherapy (Wicherts et al., 2013). Vigano and colleagues have specifically recommended that surgeons consider administering chemotherapy prior to repeat resection for early CRLM recurrence, as the latter was associated with improved 5-year OS (61.5 percent vs. 43.7 percent, $p = 0.028$) and was also significantly associated with improved survival on multivariable analysis after accounting for other prognostic variables (Viganò et al., 2014). While intuitively appealing, the role of chemotherapy prior to repeat re-section remains unclear, as other groups did not identify it as a relevant prognostic factor (Butte et al., 2015). The potential confounding role of chemotherapy prior to repeat hepatectomy was acknowledged by Hellingman et al. in their systematic review addressing the survival impact of early recurrence (Hellingman et al., 2021).

Other treatment modalities

A significant number of patients with recurrent CRLM will not be candidates for re-resection. In such situations, it is imperative that patient-defined goals of care are utilized to help select future treatment modalities. Very little of the published literature on various loco-regional treatment options for CRLM is specific to patients experiencing recurrent CLM after resection. Therefore, recommendations have been generalized from the existing literature which predominately includes patients who have not underwent previous hepatic resection.

Systemic therapy

The backbone of treatment for patients with unresectable recurrent CRLM is systemic chemotherapy. Although chemotherapy can be utilized as a multimodal therapy to attempt to downstage CRLM to resectability, the vast majority of patients with unresectable liver recurrence are being treated with palliative intent. In phase III trials of CRLM patients being treated with chemotherapeutics and biologics, the median reported OS was as high as 37 months; however real-life estimates, outside of clinical trials are closer to 15 months (Hamers et al., 2021). The role of targeted therapy has become more prominent in colorectal cancer, and all patients should undergo testing for KRAS/NRAS and BRAF mutations, HER2 amplification and MSI/MMR status.

Ablation therapy

Tumor ablation is an umbrella term encompassing radiofrequency ablation (RFA), microwave ablation (MWA), irreversible electroporation (IRE) and cryoablation. Patients may be selected for ablation for a variety of reasons including inadequate liver volume for resection, tumor proximity to vasculobiliary structures rendering them unresectable, or patient condition/comorbidities that make surgery undesirable or ill-advised. For patients with recurrent CRLM that are not surgical candidates, ablation is a reasonable treatment option as long as tumors are small (<3 cm) and can be ablated with clear margins (Wang et al., 2013; Sofocleous et al., 2011; Shady et al., 2016). There are no randomized studies in CRLM comparing ablation to resection, however observational data suggest that ablation is inferior to resection with higher risk of local recurrence and shorter OS (Weng et al., 2012; Otto et al., 2010). Given the observational nature of this data, selection bias may be at play. A phase II trial that randomized patients to receive systemic therapy alone versus systemic therapy and RFA (+/- resection) demonstrated improved progression free survival (PFS) at 3 years in the RFA group (10.6 percent vs. 27.6 percent, $p = 0.025$) (Ruers et al., 2012), as well as OS at 3-, 5- and 8-years (Ruers, Coevorden, and Punt, 2017). While most data exist for RFA, MWA has similar outcomes with regards to local recurrence, and has been shown to have improved efficacy for perivascular tumors (Shady et al., 2018). Current evidence dictates that resection is preferable to ablation. However, when resection is not feasible, ablation has an established role in the treatment of CRLM tumor recurrence <3 cm, where a 1 cm ablation margin can be obtained.

Ablative radiation

Stereotactic body radiotherapy (SBRT) enables the delivery of high-dose, focused radiation with fewer treatments than traditional external beam radiation. In the case of primary non-small cell lung cancer (NSCLC), SBRT has been shown to yield favorable local control and low treatment-related toxicity (Badra, Baumgartl, Fabiano, Jongen, and Guckenberger, 2021). Further, in oligometastatic NSCLC, a multi-center randomized phase II study demonstrated improved PFS over patients on chemotherapy alone (Gomez et al., 2016). In contrast, the data supporting its use in CRLM is not yet as robust. Outcomes of SBRT in a 388 patient colorectal cancer cohort with 500 liver or pulmonary metastases (liver $n = 291$) demonstrated a median OS of 27.9 months, with local recurrence reported in 31.3 percent of treated liver metastases (Klement et al., 2019). Most importantly, the authors reported a risk-adjusted survival benefit in patients where local control was achieved. In another 60-patient CRLM cohort, local control was reported as 50 percent at one year and 26 percent at 4 years, emphasizing a high recurrence risk post treatment (McPartlin et al., 2017). Risk of recurrence is associated with tumor site (liver > lung), tumor size, and dose regimen (Klement et al., 2019; Rule et al., 2011). When optimized, local control rates of 80 percent for CRLM have been reported (Rule et al., 2011). Despite the potential benefits of a short treatment course and low toxicity, high-quality prospective trials are needed to define the role of SBRT in patients with CRLM. It should be reserved for use in unresectable patients without other optimal ablative options or in the setting of a clinical trial.

Transarterial chemoembolization (TACE)

TACE is delivered via the hepatic artery and works by inducing both tumor ischemia as well as the local delivery of chemotherapy. Although TACE is a mainstay of treatment for hepatocellular carcinoma, the data pertaining to its efficacy in CRLM is less robust. Observational data exist on the use of both bland embolization, as well as various chemotherapeutics in CRLM. To date, 2 RTCs have examined the use of irinotecan-coated drug-eluding beads (DEBIRI) in patients with CRLM. Fiorentini et al. randomized 74 patients with CRLM to DEBIRI versus FOLFIRI and demonstrated improved overall survival (22 vs. 15 months, $p = 0.03$) and improved response rate (69 percent vs. 20 percent) (Fiorentini et al., 2012). Similarly, Martin and colleagues randomized 70 patients to modified FOLFOX and bevacizumab with or without DEBIRI (Martin et al., 2015). They demonstrated a significantly greater overall response rate and improved median PFS (15.3 vs 7.6 months) in the DEBIRI group. TACE with DEBIRI can be considered in the setting of unresectable recurrent CRLM, particularly when there has been failure of other modalities. Further studies are needed to assess the role of DEBIRI in the first line setting.

Transarterial radioembolization (TARE)

TARE, also known as selective internal radiation therapy, is a selective radioembolization with yttrium-90 bonded to resin or glass microspheres. The majority of data pertaining to the use of TARE in CRLM is as a salvage therapy for chemo-refractory disease. An RTC of 44 patients with CRLM who had progressed on initial therapy demonstrated improved PFS for radioembolization combined with chemotherapy (2.1 vs. 4.5 months, $p = 0.03$) (Hendlisz et al., 2010). Multiple large case series on TARE in the chemo-refractory setting report a median OS of 10.5–13 months (Kurilova et al., 2019) (A. S. Kennedy et al., 2015; Saxena et al., 2015). The presence of extra-hepatic disease is a particularly poor prognostic indicator, as is large tumor burden, high number of previous chemotherapy lines and high CEA (Kurilova et al., 2019). Importantly, a combined analysis of three prominent phase III RTCs (SIREFLOX, FOXFIRE, and FOXFIRE-Global) examining the additive benefit of TARE to first-line chemotherapy for liver-only or liver-dominant CRLM failed to demonstrate improvement in OS for with TARE (Wasan et al., 2017). Interestingly, in a subgroup analysis limited to right-sided tumors, improved OS was noted in patients treated with Y90 and chemotherapy (22.0 vs. 17.1 months, $p = 0.008$) (Gibbs, Heinemann, and Sharma, 2018). As such, currently there is little role for TARE in the early treatment for CRLM, although more studies are needed to define its possible role in right-sided tumors. TARE can be considered in select patients with recurrent chemo-refractory disease and preferably hepatic-only disease.

Hepatic artery infusion chemotherapy (HAIC)

A surgically-implanted, subcutaneous pump attached to a catheter placed into the gastroduodenal artery can be used to give hepatic artery-directed floxuridine (FUDR) chemotherapy. Both the surgical and oncologic aspects of management of HAIC can be complex, and this has limited the general uptake to select high-volume institutions. The potential for biliary toxicity can also limit treatment duration. Following liver resection, HAIC has been shown to have superior disease-free survival to chemotherapy alone in the adjuvant at 2 years (Kemeny et al., 1999). Additional trials are needed to see whether this benefit will persist in the modern era of systemic chemotherapy. In unresectable CRLM, both treatment response and time to liver-related progression have favored HAIC when compared to systemic chemotherapy alone, although there has yet to be a demonstrable clear survival benefit. HAIC may be useful in the conversion of unresectable CRLM to resectable disease. Conversion rates as high as 47 percent have been reported (D'Angelica et al., 2015). Currently, HAIC should be used selectively in patients with liver only disease who have progressed on first line chemotherapy, and only at institutions with experience in the placement and management of pumps.

Transplant

Liver transplantation (LT) as a treatment for liver metastases has historically been avoided due to concerns that systemic metastases would respond poorly to post-transplant immunosuppressive therapy, resulting in early recurrence. In 2013, the first prospective study examining LT for unresectable CRLM was published (Hagness et al., 2013). This Norwegian SECA-1 study consisted of a relatively heterogeneous group of 21 patients with liver-only metastases, an excised primary tumor and at least 6 weeks of chemotherapy. The authors reported a 5-year OS of 60 percent, with the majority experiencing pulmonary metastatic recurrence. The subsequent SECA-II study, which used more stringent inclusion criteria demonstrated an improved 5-year OS of 83 percent (Dueland et al., 2020). Given the significant impact on organ allocation, clear criteria for when LT is appropriate for CRLM were needed. The International Hepato-Pancreato-Biliary Association recently published expert consensus guidelines for LT for patients with unresectable CRLM (Bonney et al., 2021). The guidelines heavily emphasize the need for appropriate biologic selection of patients most likely to benefit, setting the bar that LT should aim to achieve a 5-year OS of greater than 50 percent (Bonney et al., 2021). As such, tumor histology of undifferentiated adenocarcinoma or signet ring carcinoma, BRAF V600E mutation, MSI-H, and progression during bridging systemic therapy were all considered contraindications to LT. Given that there is concern for high risk of allograft rejection if immunotherapy is given post solid organ transplant, patients with MSI-H tumors were excluded as it was felt that they would not be candidates for palliative immunotherapy. Furthermore, the guidelines recommend bridging systemic therapy of at least one line of 5-FU-bassed, oxaliplatin-based or irinotecan-based chemotherapy with observed, sustained response for at least six-months, and a minimal 1 year interval between diagnosis of CRLM and LT (Bonney et al., 2021). These guidelines can presumably be extrapolated to patients with recurrent CRLM who have previously had a partial hepatectomy. The type of graft used should be decided upon within a national organ allocation system, and may differ between countries.

References

Adair, R. A., Young, A. L., Cockbain, A. J., et al. (2012). Repeat hepatic resection for colorectal liver metastases. *British Journal of Surgery, 99*, 1278–1283.

Adam, R., Waechter, F., & Engerran, L. (1997). Repeat hepatectomy for colorectal liver metastases. *Annals of Surgery, 225*, 51–62.

Adam, R., Pascal, G., Azoulay, D., Tanaka, K., Castaing, D., & Bismuth, H. (2003). Liver resection for colorectal metastases: the third hepatectomy. *Annals of Surgery, 238*, 871–884.

Badra, E. V., Baumgartl, M., Fabano, S., et al. (2021). Stereotactic radiotherapy for early stage non-small cell lung cancer: current standards and ongoing research. *Translational lung cancer research, 10*, 1930–1940.

Benson, A. B., III, Venook, A. P., Al-Hawary, M. M., et al. (2021a). Colon Cancer, version 2.2021, NCCN clinical practice guidelines in oncology. *Journal of the National Comprehensive Cancer Network, 19*, 329–359.

Benson, A. B., III, Venook, A. P., Al-Hawary, M. M., et al. (2021b). NCCN clinical practice guidelines in oncology: rectal cancer, version 2.2021. *Accessed Sept, 13*. https://www.nccn.org/professionals/physician_gls/pdf/rectal.pdf.

Bonney, G. K., Chew, C. A., Lodge, P., et al. (2021). Liver transplantation for non-resectable colorectal liver metastases: the International Hepato-Pancreato-Biliary Association consensus guidelines. *Lancet Gastroenterology & Hepatology, 6*, 933–946.

Butte, J. M., Gönen, M., Allen, P. J., et al. (2015). Recurrence after partial hepatectomy for metastatic colorectal cancer: potentially curative role of salvage repeat resection. *Annals of Surgical Oncology, 22*, 2761–2771.

Creasy, J. M., Sadot, E., Koerkamp, B. G., et al. (2018). Actual 10-year survival after hepatic resection of colorectal liver metastases: what factors preclude cure? *Surgery, 163*, 1238–1244.

D'Angelica, M., Correa-Gallego, C., Paty, P. B., et al. (2015). Phase II trial of hepatic artery infusional and systemic chemotherapy for patients with unresectable hepatic metastases from colorectal cancer: conversion to resection and long-term outcomes. *Annals of Surgery, 261*, 353–360.

de Jong, M. C., Pulitano, C., Ribero, D., et al. (2009). Rates and patterns of recurrence following curative intent surgery for colorectal liver metastasis: an international multi-institutional analysis of 1669 patients. *Annals of Surgery, 250*, 440–448.

Dueland, S., Syversveen, T., Solheim, J. M., et al. (2020). Survival following liver transplantation for patients with nonresectable liver-only colorectal metastases. *Annals of Surgery, 271*, 212–218.

Dupré, A., Lefranc, A., Buc, E., et al. (2013). Use of bioresorbable membranes to reduce abdominal and perihepatic adhesions in 2-stage hepatectomy of liver metastases from colorectal cancer: results of a prospective, randomized controlled phase II trial. *Annals of Surgery, 258*, 30–36.

Fiorentini, G., Aliberti, C., Tilli, M., et al. (2012). Intra-arterial infusion of irinotecan-loaded drug-eluting beads (DEBIRI) versus intravenous therapy (FOLFIRI) for hepatic metastases from colorectal cancer: final results of a phase III study. *Anticancer Research, 32*, 1387–1395.

Galjart, B., van der Stok, E. P., Rothbarth, J., et al. (2016). Posttreatment surveillance in patients with prolonged disease-free survival after resection of colorectal liver metastasis. *Annals of Surgical Oncology, 23*, 3999–4007.

Gibbs, P., Heinemann, V., Sharma, N. K., et al. (2018). Effect of primary tumor side on survival outcomes in untreated patients with metastatic colorectal cancer when selective internal radiation therapy is added to chemotherapy: combined analysis of two randomized controlled studies. *Clinical Colorectal Cancer, 17*, e617–e629.

Gomez, D. R., Blumenschein, G. R., Lee, J. J, et al. (2016). Local consolidative therapy versus maintenance therapy or observation for patients with oligometastatic non-small-cell lung cancer without progression after first-line systemic therapy: a multicentre, randomised, controlled, phase 2 study. *Lancet Oncol, 17*, 1672–1682.

Hagness, M., Foss, A., Line, P. D., et al. (2013). Liver transplantation for nonresectable liver metastases from colorectal cancer. *Annals of Surgery, 257*, 800–806.

Hallet, J., Sa Cunha, A., Adam, R., et al. (2016). Factors influencing recurrence following initial hepatectomy for colorectal liver metastases. *British Journal of Surgery, 103*, 1366–1376.

Hamers, P. A. H., Elferink, M. A. G., Stellato, R. K., et al. (2021). Informing metastatic colorectal cancer patients by quantifying multiple scenarios for survival time based on real-life data. *International Journal of Cancer, 148*, 296–306.

Hellingman, T., de Swart, M. E., Haymans, M. W., Jansma, E. P., van der Vliet, H. J., & Kazemier, G. (2021). Repeat hepatectomy justified in patients with early recurrence of colorectal cancer liver metastases: a systematic review and meta-analysis. *Cancer Epidemiology, 74*, 101977.

Hendlisz, A., Van den Eynde, M., Peeters, M., et al. (2010). Phase III trial comparing protracted intravenous fluorouracil infusion alone or with yttrium-90 resin microspheres radioembolization for liver-limited metastatic colorectal cancer refractory to standard chemotherapy. *Journal of Clinical Oncology, 28*, 3687–3694.

Hyder, O., Dodson, R. M., Mayo, S. C., et al. (2013). Post-treatment surveillance of patients with colorectal cancer with surgically treated liver metastases. *Surgery, 154*, 256–265.

Imai, K., Allard, M. A., Benitez, C. C., et al. (2016). Early recurrence after hepatectomy for colorectal liver metastases: what optimal definition and what predictive factors? *The Oncologist, 21*, 887–894.

Ishiguro, S., Akasu, T., Fujimoto, Y., et al. (2006). Second hepatectomy for recurrent colorectal liver metastasis: analysis of preoperative prognostic factors. *Annals of Surgical Oncology, 13*, 1579–1587.

Jeffery, M., Hickey, B. E., & Hider, P. N. (2019). Follow-up strategies for patients treated for non-metastatic colorectal cancer. *Cochrane Database of Systematic Reviews (Online), 9*, CD002200.

Kawaguchi, Y., Kopetz, S., Lillemoe, H. A., et al. (2020). A new surveillance algorithm after resection of colorectal liver metastases based on changes in recurrence risk and RAS mutation status. *Journal of the National Comprehensive Cancer Network: JNCCN, 18*, 1500–1508.

Kemeny, N., Huang, Y., Cohen, A. M., et al. (1999). Hepatic arterial infusion of chemotherapy after resection of hepatic metastases from colorectal cancer. *New England Journal of Medicine, 341*, 2039–2048.

Kennedy, A. S., Ball, D., Cohen, S. J., et al. (2015). Multicenter evaluation of the safety and efficacy of radioembolization in patients with unresectable colorectal liver metastases selected as candidates for (90)Y resin microspheres. *Journal of gastrointestinal oncology, 6*, 134–142.

Kennedy, E., Zwaa, C., Asmis, T., et al. (2021). Follow-up care, surveillance protocol, and secondary prevention measures for survivors of colorectal cancer. *Ontario Health: Cancer Care Ontario*. accessed Sept 13, 2021 https://www.cancercareontario.ca/en/file/64251/download?token=PlQYi3eJ .

Kjeldsen, B. J., Thorsen, H., Whalley, D., et al. (1999). Influence of follow-up on health-related quality of life after radical surgery for colorectal cancer. *Scandinavian Journal of Gastroenterology, 34*, 509–515.

Klement, R. J., Abbasi-Senger, N., Adebahr, S., et al. (2019). The impact of local control on overall survival after stereotactic body radiotherapy for liver and lung metastases from colorectal cancer: a combined analysis of 388 patients with 500 metastases. *BMC cancer, 19*, 173.

Kobayashi, Y., Shindoh, J., Okubo, S., et al. (2021). Hyaluronic acid/carboxymethyl cellulose-based adhesion barrier reduces surgical difficulty and complication in repeat hepatectomy. *HPB, 23*, 907–914.

Kurilova, I., Beets-Tan, R. G. H., Flynn, J., et al. (2019). Factors affecting oncologic outcomes of 90Y radioembolization of heavily pre-treated Patients with colon cancer liver metastases. *Clinical Colorectal Cancer, 18*, 8–18.

Lam, V. W. T., Pang, T., Laurence, J. M., et al. (2013). A systematic review of repeat hepatectomy for recurrent colorectal liver metastases. *Journal of Gastrointestinal Surgery, 17*, 1312–1321.

Lange, J. F., Leese, T., Casting, D., & Bismuth, H. (1989). Repeat hepatectomy for recurrent malignant tumors of the liver. *Surgery, Gynecology & Obstetrics, 169*, 119–126.

Luo, L. X., Yu, Z. Y., Huang, J. W., & Wu, H. (2014). Selecting patients for a second hepatectomy for colorectal metastases: an systemic review and meta-analysis. *European Journal of Surgical Oncology, 40*, 1036–1048.

Manfredi, S., Lepage, C., Hatem, C., et al. (2006). Epidemiology and management of liver metastases from colorectal cancer. *Annals of Surgery, 244*, 254–259.

Mant, D., Gray, A., Pugh, S., et al. (2017). A randomised controlled trial to assess the cost-effectiveness of intensive versus no scheduled follow-up in patients who have undergone resection for colorectal cancer with curative intent. *Health Technology Assessment (Winchester, England), 21*, 1–86.

Martin 2nd, R. C., Scoggins, C. R., Schreeder, M., et al. (2015). Randomized controlled trial of irinotecan drug-eluting beads with simultaneous FOLFOX and bevacizumab for patients with unresectable colorectal liver-limited metastasis. *Cancer, 121*, 3649–3658.

McPartlin, A., Swaminath, A., Wang, R., et al. (2017). Long-term outcomes of phase 1 and 2 studies of SBRT for hepatic colorectal metastases. *International Journal of Radiation and Oncology in Biology and Physics, 99*, 388–395.

Meyerhardt, J. A., Mangu, P. B., Flynn PJ, P. J., et al. (2013). Follow-up care, surveillance protocol, and secondary prevention measures for survivors of colorectal cancer: American Society of Clinical Oncology clinical practice guideline endorsement. *Journal of Clinical Oncology, 31*, 4465–4470.

Mise, Y., Aloia, T. A., Brudvik, K. W., Schwarz, L., Vauthey, J. N., & Conrad, C. (2016). Parenchymal-sparing hepatectomy in colorectal liver metastasis improves salvageability and survival. *Annals of Surgery, 263*, 146–152.

Otto, G., Duber, C., Hoppe-Lotichius, M., et al. (2011). Radiofrequency ablation as a first-line treatment in patients with early colorectal liver metastases amenable to surgery. *Annals of Surgery, 251*, 796–803.

Petrowsky, H., Gonen, M., Jarnagin, W., et al. (2002). Second liver resections are safe and effective treatment for recurrent hepatic metastases from colorectal cancer: a bi-institutional analysis. *Annals of Surgery, 235*, 863–871.

Pietra, N., Sarli, L., Costi, R., et al. (1998). Role of follow-up in management of local recurrences of colorectal cancer. *Diseases of the Colon and Rectum, 41*, 1127–1133.

Pulitanò, C., Castillo, F., Aldrighetti, L., et al. (2010). What defines 'cure' after liver resection for colorectal metastases? Results after 10 years of follow-up. *HPB, 12*, 244–249.

Rodríguez-Moranta, F., Saló, J., Arcusa, A., et al. (2006). Postoperative surveillance in patients with colorectal cancer who have undergone curative resection: a prospective, multicenter, randomized, controlled trial. *Journal of Clinical Oncology, 24*, 386–393.

Rosat, G., Ambrosin, G., Barni, S., et al. (2016). A randomized trial of intensive versus minimal surveillance of patients with resected Dukes B2-C colorectal carcinoma. *Annals of Oncology, 27*, 274–280.

Ruers, T., Punt, C., Van Coevorden, F., et al. (2012). Radiofrequency ablation combined with systemic treatment versus systemic treatment alone in patients with non-resectable colorectal liver metastases: a randomized EORTC Intergroup phase II study (EORTC 40004). *Annals of Oncology, 23*, 2619–2626.

Ruers, T., Van Coevorden, F., Punt, C. J., et al. (2017). Local treatment of unresectable colorectal liver metastases: results of a randomized phase II trial. *JNCI: Journal of the National Cancer Institute, 109*, djx015.

Rule, W., Timmerman, R., Tong, L., et al. (2011). Phase I dose-escalation study of stereotactic body radiotherapy in patients with hepatic metastases. *Annals of Surgical Oncology, 18*, 1081–1087.

Sargent, D., Sobrero, A., Grothey, A., et al. (2009). Evidence for cure by adjuvant therapy in colon cancer: observations based on individual patient data from 20,898 patients on 18 randomized trials. *Journal of Clinical Oncology, 27*, 872–877.

Saxena, A., Meteling, B., Kapoor, J., et al. (2015). Is yttrium-90 radioembolization a viable treatment option for unresectable, chemorefractory colorectal cancer liver metastases? A large single-center experience of 302 patients. *Annals of Surgical Oncology, 22*, 794–802.

Schmidt, T., Nienhüser, H., Kuna, C., et al. (2018). Prognostic indicators lose their value with repeated resection of colorectal liver metastases. *European Journal of Surgical Oncology, 44*, 1610–1618. doi:10.1016/j.ejso.2018.07.051.

Secco, G. B., Fardelli, R., Gianquinto, D., et al. (2002). Efficacy and cost of risk-adapted follow-up in patients after colorectal cancer surgery: a prospective, randomized and controlled trial. *European Journal of Surgical Oncology, 28*, 418–423.

Seo, S. I., Lim, S. B., Yoon, Y. S., et al. (2013). Comparison of recurrence patterns between ≤5 years and >5 years after curative operations in colorectal cancer patients. *Journal of Surgical Oncology, 108*, 9–13.

Siegel, R. L., Miller, K. D., & Jemal, A. (2020). Cancer statistics, 2020. *CA: A Cancer Journal for Clinicians, 70*, 7–30.

Shady, W., Petre, E. N., Gonen, M., et al. (2016). Percutaneous radiofrequency ablation of colorectal cancer liver metastases: factors affecting outcomes - a 10-year experience at a single center. *Radiology, 278*, 601–611.

Shady, W., Petre, E. N., Do, K. G., et al. (2018). Percutaneous microwave versus radiofrequency ablation of colorectal liver metastases: ablation with clear margins (A0) provides the best local tumor control. *Journal of Vascular and Interventional Radiology, 29*, 268–275.

Sofocleous, C. T., Petre, E. N., Gonen, M., et al. (2011). CT-guided radiofrequency ablation as a salvage treatment of colorectal cancer hepatic metastases developing after hepatectomy. *Journal of Vascular and Interventional Radiology, 22*, 755–761.

Steele, S. R., Chang, G. J., Hendren, S., et al. (2015). Practice guideline for the surveillance of patients after curative treatment of colon and rectal cancer. *Diseases of the Colon and Rectum, 58*, 713–725.

ten Broek, R. P. G., Stommel, M. W. J., Strik, C., van Laarhoven, C. J. H. M., Keus, F., & van Goor, H. (2014). Benefits and harms of adhesion barriers for abdominal surgery: a systematic review and meta-analysis. *Lancet, 383*, 48–59.

van der Poel, M. J., Barkhatov, L., Fuks, D., et al. (2019). Multicentre propensity score-matched study of laparoscopic versus open repeat liver resection for colorectal liver metastases. *British Journal of Surgery, 106*, 783–789.

Vauthey, J. N., Abdalla, E. K., Doherty, D. A., et al. (2002). Body surface area and body weight predict total liver volume in Western adults. *Liver Transplantation, 8*, 233–240.

Vigano, L., Capussotti, L., Lapointe, R., et al. (2014). Early recurrence after liver resection for colorectal metastases: risk factors, prognosis, and treatment: a LiverMetSurvey-based study of 6,025 patients. *Annals of Surgical Oncology, 21*, 1276–1286.

Wang, S. J., Si, X. Y., Cai, Z. B., & Zhou, Y. M. (2019). Survival after repeat hepatectomy for recurrent colorectal liver metastasis: a review and meta-analysis of prognostic factors. *Hepatobiliary & Pancreatic Diseases International, 18*, 313–320.

Wang, X., Sofocleous, C. T., Erinjeri, J. P., et al. (2013). Margin size is an independent predictor of local tumor progression after ablation of colon cancer liver metastases Cardiovasc. *Interventional Radiology, 36*, 166–175.

Wasan, H. S., Gibbs, P., Sharma, N. K., et al. (2017). First-line selective internal radiotherapy plus chemotherapy versus chemotherapy alone in patients with liver metastases from colorectal cancer (FOXFIRE, SIRFLOX, and FOXFIRE-Global): a combined analysis of three multicentre, randomised, phase 3 trials. *Lancet Oncology, 18*, 1159–1171.

Weng, M., Zhang, Y., Zhou, D., et al. (2012). Radiofrequency ablation versus resection for colorectal cancer liver metastases: a meta-analysis. *PLos One, 7*, e45493.

Wicherts, D. A., de Haas, R. J., Salloum, C., et al. (2013). Repeat hepatectomy for recurrent colorectal metastases. *British Journal of Surgery, 100*, 808–818.

Wille-Jørgensen, P., Syk, I., Smedh, K., et al. (2018). Effect of more vs less frequent follow-up testing on overall and colorectal cancer-specific mortality in patients with stage II or III colorectal Cancer: the COLOFOL randomized clinical trial. *Journal of the American Medical Association, 319*, 2095–2103.

Wurster, E. F., Tenckhoff, S., Probst, P., et al. (2017). A systematic review and meta-analysis of the utility of repeated versus single hepatic resection for colorectal cancer liver metastases. *HPB, 19*, 491–497.

CHAPTER

19

Colorectal liver metastasis: survivorship

Shannon Radomski, MD[a], *Kimberly Kopecky, MD*[b] *and Fabian Johnston, MD*[b]

[a]Department of Surgery, Johns Hopkins Hospital, Baltimore, MD, USA [b]Division of Surgical Oncology, Department of Surgery, Johns Hopkins Hospital, Baltimore, MD, USA

Introduction

The number of cancer survivors increases yearly due to the aging population, advances in treatment prolonging survival and improvement in supportive care. It was estimated that in 2019 alone, seventeen million cancer survivors were living in the United States, with projections to be around twenty-two million by the year 2030 (Cancer Treatment and Survivorship Facts and Figs., 2019). Widespread emphasis on the importance of survivorship care followed a 2006 report by the Institute of Medicine entitled "From Cancer Patient to Cancer Survivor: Lost in Transition" (Council, 2005). The report highlighted four essential components for the care of these patients Fig. 19.1:

1. Surveillance for Recurrence and Screening for Second Primary Cancers
2. Assessment and Management of the Physical and Psychosocial Effects of Cancer and Treatment
3. Routine Health Promotion Needs
4. Coordination of Care Among Specialists and Primary Care Clinicians

What is a cancer survivor?

This chapter focuses on the essential components of care for cancer survivors. Historically, the term cancer survivor has been used to refer to any person with a history of cancer (Shapiro et al., 2016). This includes the period from initial diagnosis to the end of life. For

Contemporary Management of Metastatic Colorectal Cancer: A Precision Medicine Approach
DOI: https://doi.org/10.1016/B978-0-323-91706-3.00016-3

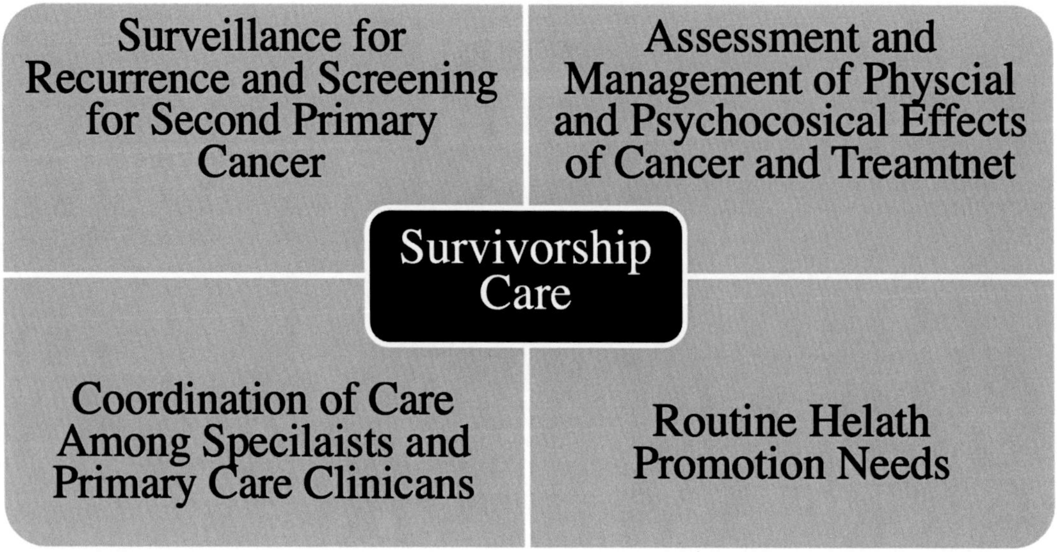

Surveillance for Recurrence and Screening for Second Primary Cancer

Assessment and Management of Physcial and Psychocosical Effects of Cancer and Treamtnet

Survivorship Care

Coordination of Care Among Specilaists and Primary Care Clinicans

Routine Helath Promotion Needs

FIGURE 19.1 From Council, NR. (2005). From Cancer Patient to Cancer Survivor: Lost in Transition. Four essential components of survivorship care.

the cancer survivor, survivorship therefore is a term used to describe both the state of being a survivor as well as the experiences of this group of individuals. Cancer survivorship can be divided into three distinct stages following diagnosis. The first is from diagnosis to the end of initial treatment, then the transition from treatment to extended survival, and the last is long-term survival (Shapiro et al., 2016). Long-term survival is often used to describe patients who are five years or greater from initial diagnosis. One important limitation to this term is that it often refers to patients who have no evidence of active disease or recurrence. As a result, some patients who have been living with a diagnosis of metastatic cancer are not commonly grouped in this category and instead their cancer is treated as a chronic condition. For this reason, some patients do not identify with the term cancer survivor at all. For the purpose of clarity in this chapter, we will use the term cancer survivor to describe patients at any stage of survivorship who have been diagnosed with colorectal liver metastasis (CRLM) regardless of the presence of chronically active disease.

Colorectal cancer survivors with liver metastases

Colorectal cancer (CRC) is the third most common cancer in the United States, with approximately 146,000 new diagnoses per year (Cancer Treatment and Survivorship Facts and Figs., 2019). Approximately 1.5 million people in the United States are living with a prior or current diagnosis of colorectal cancer. For all stages, the distribution of years since diagnosis is shown in Fig. 19.2, with 35 percent having the diagnosis for less than 5 years and 16 percent

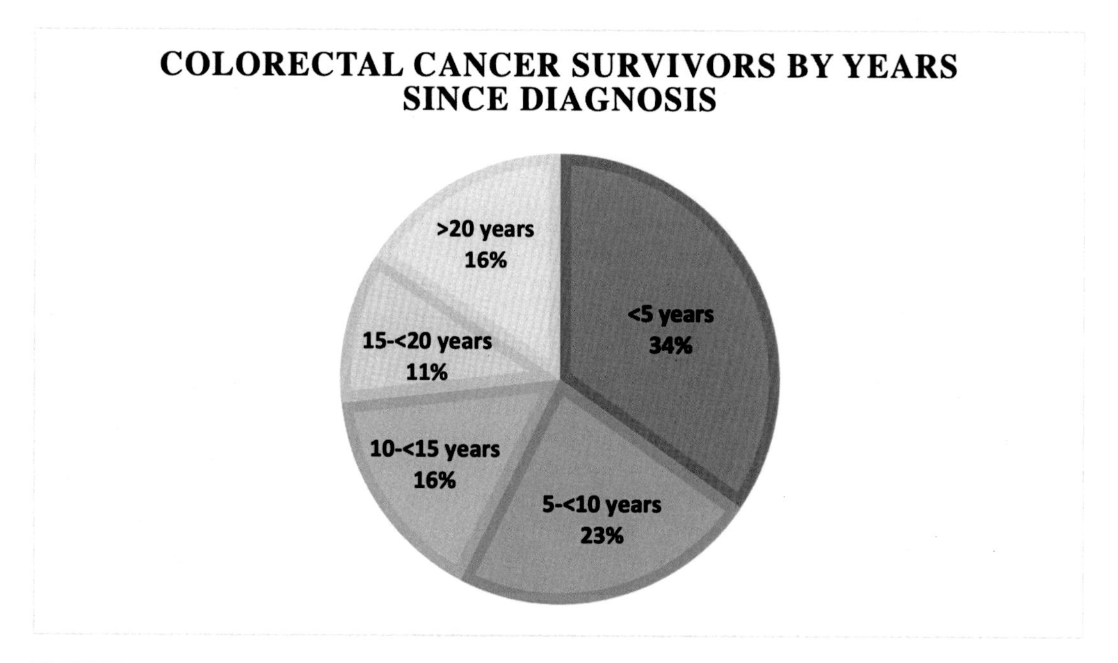

FIGURE 19.2 From Cancer Treatment & Survivorship Facts & Figs. (2019). Estimation of the Distribution of Survivors of Colorectal Cancer by Years since Diagnosis as of January first 2019.

living with the diagnosis for greater than 20 years (Cancer Treatment and Survivorship Facts and Figs., 2019). Up to a quarter of these patients were found to have liver metastasis at the time of diagnosis and another 50 percent of patients will be diagnosed with liver metastasis over the course of their disease (Welten et al., 2021). Overall CRC incidence rates have decreased over the past few decades due to preventative screening measures, early detection, and removal of precancerous polyps. One notable exception is found among younger patients (<50) in whom the rates have been increasing for unknown reasons. In the following chapter we aim to summarize current research on the four essential components of survivorship care in patients with CRLM, describe limitations of current research, and offer insights for future directions to continue to best serve this vulnerable group of patients.

Surveillance for recurrence and screening for second primary cancers

Prognosis

Predicting prognosis in metastatic cancer is a challenge. For patients, having a realistic understanding of prognosis helps frame conversations about end-of-life planning and enables patients to prioritize what matters most when survival is limited. The range of potential outcomes in metastatic colorectal cancer (mCRC) continues to expand due to the availability of novel treatment approaches that offer the potential for long-term survival and even cure.

TABLE 19.1 Summary of published clinical prognostic factors for colorectal cancer.

Age
Sex
Medical comorbidities
ECOG Performance status
Depth of invasion
Tumor diameter
Positive LNs
Margin status
Histologic grade
metastases: diameter of largest hepatic metastasis
Peritoneal involvment
Laboratory values: CEA, LDH, LFTs, albumin
Surgical resection
# of different chemotherapy agents administered
Response to systemic therapy
Recurrence

Data from Mahar AL, Compton C, Halabi S, Hess KR, Weiser MR, Groome PA. Personalizing prognosis in colorectal cancer: A systematic review of the quality and nature of clinical prognostic tools for survival outcomes. J Surg Oncol. 2017;116(8):969–982. doi:10.1002/jso.24774.

As a result, there is almost an endless algorithm of survival outcomes for these patients as highlighted in prior chapters. The widespread acceptance and practice of treatments such as hepatic metastasectomy, radiofrequency ablation, chemoembolization with hepatic artery infusion pumps, new chemotherapeutics, and novel immunotherapies has improved the median survival to >40 months with a five-year survival of 30–55 percent for patients with liver-limited disease that is amenable to complete surgical resection (Hamers et al., 2021; Raoof, Haye, Ituarte, and Fong, 2019). This is in stark contrast to the prognostic estimates of 20 years ago, when mCRC conferred a prognosis of 6–9 months. Because of this wide range of potential and ever-shifting outcomes, a staging system for stage IV colorectal cancer has been suggested, however, robust data supporting its development and use is not yet available. A summary of important patient and tumor related prognostic variables is found in Table 19.1 (Mahar et al., 2017). Several molecular, genetic, and anatomic prognostic indicators have been identified in small patient samples but have not been tested at a population level, and/or are not currently therapeutically actionable (Datta et al., 2020). A greater symptom burden, including worsening pain, fatigue, and drowsiness, has been repeatedly shown to correlate with worse overall survival and increased incidence of major post-operative morbidity (Subbiah et al., 2021).

Disparities in metastatic colorectal cancer survival

Racial, geographic, and socioeconomic disparities impact patients diagnosed with and treated for CRC, and these disparities influence cancer-related prognosis. In one study of over 33,000 patients with mCRC, one-and five-year overall adjusted survival was shown to be statistically different for patients treated at academic versus community hospitals (Welten et al., 2021). Patient-level data was limited, but the observed survival differences were hypothesized to be related, in part, to disparities in practice and referral patterns at academic versus community facilities. A population-based study out of the Netherlands revealed similar findings- that over an eight year period from 2008 to 2016, median overall survival remained unchanged except for patients who had undergone metastasectomy (which is usually performed at tertiary referral centers), and for whom the median overall survival increased within the study timeframe (Hamers et al., 2021).

Systemic racism, historical mistrust, lack of education, knowledge gaps, provider-level factors, insurance coverage, national practice guidelines, and medical comorbidities all collectively contribute to observed outcome differences among patients of different races and ethnicities diagnosed with CRC (Johnston, Yeo, Clark, and Stewart, 2021). For example, African Americans (AA) are more commonly diagnosed with CRC at an advanced stage and have a 35 percent disproportionately higher overall mortality compared to non-Hispanic Whites (NHWs) (Cancer Treatment and Survivorship Facts and Figs., 2019). Relative to NHWs, AA patients are less likely to have health insurance and to have completed a high-school or college education, both of which impact access to health care and knowledge of screening recommendations. Other factors such as differential perception of risk, misunderstanding of the utility of screening, and altered referral patterns also negatively impact the survival of AA patients with mCRC compared to their peers (Johnston et al., 2021). Other factors hypothesized to contribute to the observed racial disparities amongst AA include an increased prevalence of right-sided tumors, increased incidence of obesity and other medical comorbidities, and increased incidence of microsatellite instability, all of which are independent factors for worse prognosis. (Elizabeth Hamers et al., 2021; McCracken et al., 2019).

Surveillance and screening

Several cancer societies, including the American Society of Clinical Oncology, the American Cancer Society, and the National Comprehensive Cancer Network have published guidelines for post-treatment surveillance for resected CRC. These recommendations guide the care of patients diagnosed with Stage I-III disease. Many practitioners follow a similar approach for patients with Stage IV disease who have responded well to therapies. The recommendations generally include:

1. A physical exam every 3–6 months for the first five years
2. Carcinoembryonic antigen (CEA) testing every 3–6 months for the first five years
3. CT imaging every 6–12 months for the first five years
4. Repeat colonoscopy one year after resection

For patients, this means frequent contact with the healthcare system which can contribute to time lost from work, increased costs related to travel, and continued reminders of ones'

TABLE 19.2 Dimensions of health-related quality of life.

Physcial	Social	Emotional	Economic	Family	Medical Aspects
Physcial health	Distress management	Anxiety	Transportation/ medical costs	Concerns about future parenting abilities	Diarrhea
Pain/discomfort	Inability to socialize	Depression	Missed employment	Inability to provide appropiate support	Fatigue
General health perception		Low self esteem		Fertility perservation	Impaired body image
					Sexual problems

From Bonnetain, F., Borg, C., Adams, RR, Ajani, JA, Benson, A., Bleiberg, H., Chibaudel, B., Diaz-Rubio, E., Douillard, JY, Fuchs, CS, Giantonio, BJ, Goldberg, R., Heinemann, V., Koopman, M., Labianca, R., Larsen, AK, Maughan, T., Mitchell, E., Peeters, M., ... de Gramont, A. (2017). How health-related quality of life assessment should be used in advanced colorectal cancer clinical trials. Annals of Oncology, 28(9), 2077–85. https://doi.org/10.1093/annonc/mdx191.

cancer diagnosis. Additionally, many patients experience fear and dread in the days or weeks leading up to surveillance scans and for some patients these scans can trigger fears of cancer recurrence (Bui et al., 2021).

Patients with CRC have a small increased risk of developing a subsequent cancer compared to the rest of the population (odds ratio 1.01 in males, 1.11 in females) (Cancer Treatment and Survivorship Facts and Figs., 2019). As a result, the American Cancer Society recommends concurrent screening for breast, cervical, endometrial, lung, and prostate cancers based on age, gender, and other risk factors.

Assessment and management of physical and psychosocial effects of colorectal cancer and treatment

There are numerous studies which report on health-related quality of life (HRQoL) and patient report outcomes (PROs) in patients with CRC. These studies often include patients at all stages of disease and do not specifically comment on patients with liver metastases. Below we describe PROs in specific domains of quality of life and then review in depth the few studies that specifically studied patients with CRLM.

Methods of assessment

The assessment of the physical and psychosocial effects of CRC and its treatment is often through PROs on HRQoL questionnaires. These scales capture an individual's or group's perceived physical and mental health over time. Examples of the concepts included in these scales are shown in Table 19.2 (Bonnetain et al., 2017). There are a wide range of scales that are used for quality of life assessment including generic and disease and/or cancer specific versions that have been developed and validated. In CRC, the most widely used scales are the European Organization for Research Treatment of Cancer Quality of Life Core Questionnaire (EORTCQOL-C30), the Functional Assessment of Cancer Therapy (both the general version

(FACT-G) and the colorectal version (FACT-C)), the EuroQoL-5D (EQ-5D), and the generic 36-item short form health survey (SF-36) (Ganesh et al., 2016; Jenkinson, Coulter, and Wright, 1993; Wiering et al., 2011). Recently a version of the EORTC QOL questionnaire was developed specifically for use in patients with liver metastases from colorectal cancer (EORTCQOL-LMC21) (Blazeby et al., 2009). A brief comparison of these scales in shown in Table 19.3.

Post-Diagnosis pain

Few analyses have been done to identify specific pain concerns of CRC patients in the immediate post-operative period. One study from Taiwan followed post-operative pain trajectories for five days among CRC patients. Of these patients 70 percent started with mild pain that dropped to low pain, 20 percent had moderate/severe pain that improved to mild pain, and 10 percent had moderate pain that worsened to severe pain. In a study of the 4–6 week post-operative timeframe for patients with CRC pain, "being poorly prepared to manage pain" was described as the most frequently reported stressful event (Smith, Öhlén, Persson, and Carlsson, 2018).

In studies of long-term CRC survivors, pain is not frequently characterized; situation-specific discomforts such as skin issues around ostomies, allergic reactions to adhesives, irritated and excoriated perineal areas from frequent diarrhea, and peripheral neuropathy from prescribed chemotherapeutic regimens are discussed with diminished precedence compared to other concerns. Survey studies reveal that low-income (≤$30,000/year) survivors of CRC reported higher pain scores up to six-years post-diagnosis compared to CRC survivors with a yearly income ≥$70,000 (McDougall et al., 2019).

Fatigue and physical activity

In CRC survivors surveyed five years after diagnosis, higher physical activity was strongly associated with lower physical, cognitive, and affective fatigue (Eyl et al., 2020). Being female, single, living in a more populated area, having a lower level of education, receiving chemotherapy, having medical comorbidities, being a current smoker, being obese, and having a stoma were all associated with increased levels of fatigue and/or physical inactivity (Eyl, Xie, Koch-Gallenkamp, Brenner, and Arndt, 2018). In one study of patients undergoing surveillance after curative-intent resection, 20 percent reported needing help with healthy living/exercise (Vu, Matusko, Hendren, Regenbogen, and Hardiman, 2019).

Mood/Mental health/depression/fear

Greater than 30 percent of CRC survivors report anxiety and depression; females and those with additional medical co-morbidities are at higher risk (Braamse et al., 2016). Fear of cancer recurrence is common and associated with increased physical symptoms even when surveillance studies were reassuring. Among advanced cancer patients, recurrence was described as "shocking" and many patients had existential concerns regarding whether or not they had done something wrong to contribute to the recurrence (Lim et al., 2021). When patients' outcomes were different than their expectations, existential suffering increased (Lim et al., 2021). Responses from low-income survey respondents indicate that this population has

TABLE 19.3 Comparison of characteristics of HRQoL scales.

Characteristics	EORTCQLQ-C30	EORTCQLQ-LMC21	FACT-G	EQ-5D	SF-36
Response options	4-point Likert scale 7-point Likert scale for global QoL	4-point Likert scale	5-point Likert scale	3 options: no problems, some problems, severe problems	Variety: 3–6 point Likert scales, Yes/No items
Interpretation of score	Higher scores=worse QoL	Higher scores=worse QoL	Higher scores=better QoL	Higher scores=worse QoL	Higher scores=worse QoL
# items	30	21	28	31	36
Layout/main domains	Functional scales: physical, role, emotional, cognitive, social functions, global QoL	Functional scales: nutritional problems, activity/vigor problems, pain, emotional function	Physical, social/family, emotional, function wellbeing	Mobility, self-care, usual activities, pain and discomfort, anxiety, and depression	Domains: Physical functioning, bodily pain, role limitation due to health problems, role limitation due to personal or emotional problems, emotional well-being, social function, energy/fatigue, health perceptions
	Symptom scales: fatigue, pain, nausea/vomiting	Single items: Jaundice, peripheral neuropathy, sore mouth/tongue, dry mouth weight loss, contact with friends, talking about feelings, sex life			Single item: perception of change in health

(*continued on next page*)

TABLE 19.3 Comparison of characteristics of HRQoL scales—cont'd

Characteristics	EORTCQLQ-C30	EORTCQLQ-LMC21	FACT-G	EQ-5D	SF-36
	Single items: dyspnea, sleep disturbance, appetite loss, diarrhea, constipation, financial impact				
Cancer specific versions of the scale	EORTCQLQ-C38: Functional scale: body image, sexual functioning, sexual enjoyment, future perspective, 8 symptom items: micturition problems, GI symptoms, chemotherapy side effects, defecation problems, stoma-related problems, male sexual problems, female sexual problems, weight loss		FACT-C (colorectal) (9 items) includes questions specific to stomach swelling/cramping, bowel control, digestion, diarrhea, appetite, weight loss, body image, ostomy-related questions		
	EORTQLQ-C29: Functional Scales; urinary frequency, blood/mucous in stool, stool frequency, body image, 19 single item: urinary incontinence, dysuria, abdominal pain, buttock pain, bloating, dry mouth, hair loss, tase, anxiety, weight, flatulence, fecal incontinence, sore skin, embarrassment, stoma care problems, sexual interest for men/women, impotence, dyspareunia				

higher reported rates of post-diagnosis depression, similar to the pattern found for reports of post-operative pain.

Bowel function

Many survivors of CRC experience issues with diarrhea and/or constipation after surgery. These symptoms persist even after ostomy reversal for most patients. Low anterior resection (LAR) syndrome is common in patients with rectal cancer who undergo this procedure. This syndrome, which effects 60–90 percent of these patients, is characterized by increased frequency of bowel movements, increased urgency, clustering of stools, and incontinence in some extreme situations. This syndrome has been shown to negatively impact QoL. Even in patients who do not have a rectal resection, a LAR type syndrome has been described to impact 21 percent of patients (Heinsbergen et al., 2019). For many patients, bowel dysfunction (frequency, urgency, unexpected bowel movements) impacts social functioning and contributes to decreased outings and alterations of routine activities due to worries about locating a bathroom (Rutherford, Müller, Faiz, King, and White, 2020). Many patients modify their dietary intake according to their bowel function which can further contribute to social isolation. Increased frequency of bowel movements also impacts quality of sleep and, in some patients, can contribute to tension between partners (Rutherford et al., 2020). Anxiety, uncertainty, fear, embarrassment, and frustration are predominantly featured in qualitative studies that examine bowel functioning in CRC survivors (Lim et al., 2021; Rutherford et al., 2020).

Ostomy-Specific concerns

Embarrassing smells, noises, leakage around an ostomy appliance, stool consistency, skin problems, and parastomal bulges/hernias are all ostomy-specific concerns raised by patients (Elfeki et al., 2018). Similar to patients who have changes in bowel function, patients with an ostomy may be uncomfortable managing their ostomy outside of home and/or require increased bathroom utilization. Many patients, especially those with baseline caregiver needs, require partner and/or family support to empty and change the ostomy appliance which can be met with negative judgements (family member disgust; feeling like a burden) (Rutherford et al., 2020). For many, having an ostomy impacts body image, sleep, and sexual wellness. Patients with stomas report interferences in daily activities including worries about physical contact, such as hugging, and routine activities, such as wearing a seat belt. For many patients, the presence of a stoma is an additional persistent reminder of having had cancer (Lim et al., 2021).

Sexual wellness

Sexual dysfunction is a common, multifactorial, sequela of treatment from CRC that is infrequently addressed in both the pre-operative and post-operative settings. The type of cancer and surgical resection required (i.e. rectal cancer versus colon cancer, segmental resection versus abdominoperineal resection) and need for pelvic radiation or ostomy impact post-treatment sexual wellness and function (Donovan, Thompson, and Hoffe, 2010). For men, the most common post-operative complaints include erectile and ejaculatory dysfunction whereas for women pain, poor lubrication, and alterations in orgasm are the most commonly reported symptoms (Donovan et al., 2010). Unpartnered survivors feared future sexual rejection, and both genders describe reduced sexual desire (Donovan et al., 2010; Lim et al., 2021). Studies show that approximately 40–70 percent of sexually active female patients with CRC became sexually inactive after diagnosis, and women with pre-operative sexual difficulties more commonly report sexual difficulties post-operatively (Rutherford et al., 2020). Some patients change their usual sexual practices to accommodate their new post-cancer needs, and others describe a decreased requirement for sexual engagement (Rutherford et al., 2020).

Financial burden

Recent literature has categorized financial hardship for cancer patients into three main conceptual domains: material, psychological, and behavioral.at (Altice, Banegas, Tucker-Seeley, and Yabroff, 2017). Material hardship includes out-of-pocket expenses, missed work/lost income, and medical debt; psychological financial consequences relate to feelings of distress and concern about the expenses associated with required procedures and treatments; and behavioral consequences of financial distress include actions such as purposefully skipping medications, treatments, or clinician visits to save money. CRC patients with increasingly lengthening prognoses face the financial burdens that fall under these three domains.

Specific HRQoL outcomes in patients with colorectal cancer liver metastases

Few studies have looked at HRQoL specifically in patients with CRLM who underwent surgical resection. Langenhoff et al. was the first to report on this in 97 patients with CRLM (Langenhoff, Krabbe, Peerenboom, Wobbes, and Ruers, 2006). These patients were divided into three groups: surgical treatment ($n = 59$), inoperable disease at laparotomy ($n = 12$), and inoperable disease at outpatient visit ($n = 16$). Patients answered the EORTCQLQ-C30 and EQ-5D questionnaire at baseline, 2 weeks, 3, 6, 12 months after operation or at routine follow up. In the surgery group there was a clear decrease in global health status and functional scales, but at 3 months most scores had returned towards baseline and at 6 months almost all values were the same as baseline. In the patients who underwent aborted laparotomy, there was a clear decrease on the global health status and functional scales which persisted at 6 months. Those who underwent no operation experienced no large changes at 2 weeks or 3 months, but by 6 months scores had declined on global health and functional scales. This report was the first to show that there is a short period of decreased HRQoL related to hepatic resection which mostly recovers by 3–6 months after surgery. This also illustrated the importance of perioperative planning to prevent aborted laparotomies as there appeared to be an ongoing detrimental effect on HRQoL in these patients.

A similar study by Wiering et al. utilized the generic EQ-5D questionnaire in a sample of 145 patients with CRLM (Wiering et al., 2011). The patients were followed after surgery for 3 years at intervals of 3 months. A similar result was found in that patients who underwent curative surgery experienced a decline in HRQoL which recovered to baseline levels at 3 months. In a group of patients whose initial surgery was aborted, or palliative chemotherapy was started, a sustained decline was noted with no improvement post-operatively. At three years, patients who experienced recurrence had deterioration in HRQoL compared with their counterparts with no recurrence.

Rees et al. reported on a cohort of 203 patients who completed the EROTCQLQ-LMC21 and the EORTCQLQ-C30 scales at baseline (prior to surgery) and at 3, 6, and 12 months after hepatic resection of CRLM (Rees et al., 2012). Similar to prior reports, PROs at 3 months after surgery declined for the majority of scales and items, most significantly in role function. There was an increase in patients experiencing severe problems with almost all symptoms (ex. fatigue, nausea, vomiting, pain, dyspnea, insomnia, constipation, diarrhea), with one third of patients reporting severe problems with activity/vigor and sexual functioning. By 6 months, mean scores for functional aspects returned to baseline levels, an effect that was maintained at 12 months. The exception, as noted in other studies, is that patients continued to report severe problems with sexual function (31 percent), tingling in fingers (17 percent), anxiety (18 percent), and problems with activity/vigor (21 percent).

A long term follow up study of this cohort was published for patients who survived for 5 years or more after liver surgery (Rees et al., 2014). This report included 68 patients with a median follow up time of 8 years (range 6.9–9.2 years). For this cohort, patients reported good function/global health and few symptoms. Compared to baseline, the survivors had improvements in emotional, social, and role function. Regarding individual symptoms, the percentage of patients reporting insomnia, issues talking about feelings, and severe anxiety decreased over time, while severe constipation and diarrhea increased, and peripheral neuropathy and problems with sexual function - although high at baseline (29 percent) - remained stable. Although performed in a small sample size, this study provides important information for clinicians when counseling patients about long term outcomes 5–8 years after surgery.

Tohme et al. published on HRQoL in patients who underwent resection of hepatic malignancies (Tohme et al., 2020). Fifty percent of the sample group included patients undergoing resection for mCRC ($n = 62$). The patients were administered FACT-G and a sub-scale for hepatobiliary cancer and fatigue in addition to the Center for Epidemiologic Studies Depression scale. The patients were administered the scales before surgery and then 4,8, and 12 months after surgery. Overall, based on the FACT-G score, the patients experienced a decline in HRQoL at 4 months post-operatively which improved back to baseline by 8 months after surgery. More importantly this study found that better preoperative HRQoL was significantly associated with overall survival.

Although the recurrence rate of CRLM after initial resection is estimated to be 57 percent, there are few studies which report on HRQoL in these patients. The one study which did report on patient who underwent repeat liver resections used the EORTCQLQ-C30 and QLQ-LMC21 questionnaires (Heise et al., 2017). In this sample, 65 patients in the initial resection group and 21 patients in the repeat resection group completed the study. Patients were administered questionnaires at a median of 21 months after initial hepatectomy. Although limited by sample size, there were no differences between groups concerning overall QoL functional scores, or GI symptoms during the postoperative course. This study highlights the possibilities of patients to undergo aggressive repeated treatments without substantial impact on QoL at close to 2 years after initial surgery.

Routine health promotion needs

Health promotion refers to the process of encouraging people to increase control, and improve, their own health (Cancer Treatment and Survivorship Facts and Figs., 2019). This includes counseling related to obesity prevention, physical activity, healthy diets, and tobacco cessation. There are no large, randomized trials on the effect of these interventions on the progression of mCRC or mortality. Prospective and retrospective reports suggest obesity may increase the risk of second primary cancers, but the role of post cancer diagnosis weight on recurrence and disease free survival has not been clearly determined (Gibson et al., 2014). In regards to physical activity, it has been reported in the general population that increased physical activity levels are associated with better HRQoL and better performance on physical functioning scales (El-Shami et al., 2015). Diets high in red and processed meat, refined grains, and sugary desserts have also been posited to contribute to CRC recurrence (Meyerhardt et al., 2012). However, strict diets and those high in vegetables can be difficult for those with new ostomies. Lastly, smoking cessation has obvious health benefits. Smoking cessation should be emphasized in pre-treatment counseling as it has been shown in non-metastatic CRC patients to increase all cause and cancer specific morality (Yang, Jacobs, Gapstur, Stevens, and Campbell, 2015). Smoking can also contribute to the risk of developing second primary cancers.

In general, numerous studies have reported on the importance of health promotion in the general population and on subgroups of patients. These guidelines are applicable to all people including cancer survivors. The more important issue, especially in patients with mCRC, is the promotion of these guidelines and encouragement of healthy behaviors by primary care physicians (PCPs) during survivorship care.

Coordination of care among specialists and primary care clinicians

The last essential component of survivorship care is the management of care after diagnosis and treatment. Open and frequent communication between the various oncology teams (medical, radiation, and surgical) and the PCP is essential. The current recommendation is that patients who have completed primary treatment be provided with a comprehensive treatment summary and survivorship care plan (SCP) for review with their PCPs. Although cited as time consuming to complete (1–4 h), this is key for a smooth transition and execution of long-term care of the patient (El-Shami et al., 2015).

Experience with healthcare providers

A small number of studies have examined CRC survivors' interactions with their medical providers. These studies show that survivors often felt guilty for having unmet needs and frequently tried to navigate difficulties without the help of a healthcare provider. Patients describe feeling both supported and unsupported by their healthcare team, while others felt dismay regarding the level of communication and lack of perceived empathy from their providers (Lim et al., 2021). Many survivors report that during their treatment course they received conflicting information from various care providers that often lead to confusion (Lim et al., 2021).

Progressive disease

For patients who have already survived several years with metastatic cancer, it is important for providers to explain the clinical significance of disease progression. Isolated sites of metastasis and local tumor progression may potentially be addressed with repeat metastasectomy or non-surgical options including radiofrequency ablation and second-line chemotherapeutics. Other presentations of recurrence, such as extrahepatic and wide-spread metastases have fewer treatment options. In a study of 483 patients on palliative chemotherapy for mCRC, 81 percent were under the impression that the chemotherapy would cure them of disease. This finding- that patient's overestimate their prognosis and have unrealistic expectations from treatment- was corroborated in a review of twenty articles dedicated to this topic (Young et al., 2018). Disclosure of progressive disease should be balanced with hope and expectation setting for the future. Initiating a referral to a palliative care specialist is often appropriate if pain or symptoms are poorly controlled.

Palliative care involvement

The American Society of Clinical Oncology recommends the integration of palliative care for all patients with metastatic cancer at time of diagnosis. As such, palliative care principles are an essential component to the SCP. Although often thought of as an intervention for those with poor prognosis and high symptom burden, involvement of palliative care providers early in diagnosis can allow for the development of a longitudinal relationship between the patient and provider. One randomized controlled trial evaluated the effect of palliative care visits on HRQoL and PROs about end-of-life planning. Although patients in the treatment group had similar HRQoL metrics to the control group, these patients were more realistic about their likelihood of cure, more likely to have a surrogate documented, an advance directive completed, and a non-full code status (Bischoff et al., 2020). All patients and primary care givers also expressed high satisfaction with the program and would recommend to others diagnosed with cancer.

Limitations and future directions

The limitations in the research related to each of the four essential domains of survivorship care originate from the fact that patients with Stage IV CRC are excluded from most original research papers, reviews, and even guidelines. For example, in the American Cancer Society's survivorship guidelines for colorectal cancer, the systematic review used to identify papers to guide recommendations omitted those regarding patients with stage IV disease (El-Shami et al., 2015). Another example is a recent review that summarized the current research on interventions aimed at the essential components of survivorship care. The study found 5 reviews and 25 individual trials, only 9 of which included patients with stage IV disease, and no study was focused solely on patients with CRLM or widespread metastatic disease

(Luo et al., 2021). Below we critically evaluate the limitations of current research by essential domain of survivorship care.

Surveillance for recurrence and screening for second primary cancers

The surveillance guidelines in CRC are clear for patients with Stage I-III disease. For practical purposes these guidelines are frequently extrapolated to surveil patients with resected mCRC (Stage IV), but currently there is no robust data to support this practice. CRC survivors with metastases to the liver, as well as providers who take care of these patients, deserve consensus guidelines for surveillance.

Assessment and management of physical and psychosocial effects of colorectal cancer and treatment

There are several limitations with the assessment of HRQoL in general. Logistic issues with these studies are frequent as the questionnaires must be administered at various time points, must be easy to understand and not be overly lengthy. Other issues arise due to validity and reliability of these measures, particularly those that are developed for specific sub populations of patients. For longitudinal studies, the selection of appropriate time-points for measurement and the frequency of these measures must be optimized. Standardization of results is also difficult as studies use different scales that range from generic to cancer specific, making comparisons between populations difficult.

The subgroup of patients with CRLM is understudied. The limited number of studies which report on specific issues related to QoL in these patients are performed in a small set of patients after treatment. As a result, all patients that are studied are not living with CRLM at the time of study. Frequent changes in disease status and the implementation of treatments, some approved and others as part of clinical trials, can affect patient's HRQoL. The time points of questionnaire administration vary significantly and very rarely are patients followed longitudinally to capture the effect of treatment on QoL. Additionally, it is difficult to measure changes in HRQoL with smaller sample sizes and to define changes in measurements as clinically significant. Qualitative studies in this population are also needed to identify if there are symptom items and issues that are omitted from standardized questionnaires.

A major gap in the literature exists regarding the impact on both fertility and reproductive planning in patients with mCRC. One reason for the lack of studies about fertility is that most patients who are diagnosed with CRC are considered outside of their reproductive years. However, with the rising incidence in the younger population this will become of increasing importance, particularly in rectal cancer patients who might receive radiotherapy as part of their treatment plan. Reproductive planning and referrals to specialists should be a part of comprehensive care plan of any young patient diagnosed with disease.

In summary, measurements of HRQoL have limitations in any population in which they are used. Specific to patients with CRLM, there are few papers which directly report on HRQoL, as described above. The issue is that these studies are neglecting large groups of patients with CRLM. There is no information about those that have undergone treatments other than surgery for CRLM, patients who might have undergone surgery many years ago and are now undergoing second- or third-line therapies, and patients that had surgery and did not survive to the first or second follow up questionnaire. A future direction would be robust prospective studies that include both qualitative and quantitative patient specific time point measurements of HRQoL along a patient's entire cancer history. This would enable capture of HRQoL at diagnosis, at times related to various treatment approaches, and at the time of progression of disease. Dedication to the study of HRQoL should be included in all SCPs.

Coordination of care among specialists and primary care clinicians

There are no high-level studies on the use of SCPs in patients with mCRC. Challenges cited to the development of SCPs include feelings of inadequacy from PCPs to serve in the role of the primary physician to a complex patient, time constrictions, and confusion about roles on the survivorship care team. In patients with metastatic disease, it is essential to have a SCP at the conclusion of treatment, or if there is no treatment, at the conclusion of consultation with a medical, radiation, or surgical oncologist. The concepts of living with stable stage IV disease and not receiving treatment can cause confusion for health care providers who might not be accustomed to caring for these patients. This can lead to unnecessary scans and laboratory tests and anxiety for the patient with interpretations of those diagnostics. A solution at some institutions has been the establishment of cancer specific survivorship clinics. Research on the impact of this interdisciplinary care team model on patient survival, satisfaction, and HRQoL in CRLM patients will be essential to support the use of resources for this type of clinic at other institutions.

Lastly, an important limitation about the coordination of care in cancer survivors, and particularly those with metastatic disease, is the lack of focus on the primary care giver as a member of the care team. Those with metastatic disease often require inordinate amounts of care if they present at the late stages of disease, and those with stable metastatic disease require medical care and emotional support for long periods of time. Research and interventional studies focused on the integration of the primary care giver to SCPs are needed, as are recommendations for ensuring the health of these individuals is also prioritized.

Summary

The importance of survivorship care cannot be understated. As the number of cancer survivors continues to rise and providers follow society guidelines, the topic becomes even more critical to ensuring that these patients' needs are met. Although many of the same concerns that exist in the non-metastatic CRC population exist in patients with CRLM there are important differences that add a layer of complexity. More research in this arena is needed, and future interventions aimed at improving the coordination of this complex and comprehensive care will have an immense impact on the lives of these survivors.

References

Altice, C. K., Banegas, M. P., Tucker-Seeley, R. D., & Yabroff, K. R. (2017). Financial hardships experienced by cancer survivors: a systematic review. *JNCI: Journal of the National Cancer Institute, 109*(2), 1–17. https://doi.org/10.1093/jnci/djw205.

Bischoff, K. E., Zapata, C., Sedki, S., Ursem, C., O'Riordan, D. L., England, A. E., et al. (2020). Embedded palliative care for patients with metastatic colorectal cancer: a mixed-methods pilot study. *Supportive Care in Cancer, 28*(12), 5995–6010. https://doi.org/10.1007/s00520-020-05437-6.

Blazeby, J. M., Fayers, P., Conroy, T., Sezer, O., Ramage, J., & Rees, M. (2009). Validation of the European Organization for Research and Treatment of Cancer QLQ-LMC21 questionnaire for assessment of patient-reported outcomes during treatment of colorectal liver metastases. *British Journal of Surgery, 96*(3), 291–298. https://doi.org/10.1002/bjs.6471.

Bonnetain, F., Borg, C., Adams, R. R., Ajani, J. A., Benson, A., Bleiberg, H., et al. (2017). How health-related quality of life assessment should be used in advanced colorectal cancer clinical trials. *Annals of Oncology, 28*(9), 2077–2085. https://doi.org/10.1093/annonc/mdx191.

Braamse, A. M. J., Van Turenhout, S. T., Terhaar Sive Droste, J. S., De Groot, G. H., Van Der Hulst, R. W. M., Klemt-Kropp, M., et al. (2016). Factors associated with anxiety and depressive symptoms in colorectal cancer survivors. *European Journal of Gastroenterology & Hepatology, 28*(7), 831–835. https://doi.org/10.1097/MEG.0000000000000615.

Bui, K. T., Liang, R., Kiely, B. E., Brown, C., Dhillon, H. M., & Blinman, P. (2021). Scanxiety: a scoping review about scan-associated anxiety. *BMJ Open, 11*(5), 1–22. e043215, https://doi.org/10.1136/bmjopen-2020-043215 .

Cancer Treatment & Survivorship Facts & Figs. (2019).

Council, N.R. (2005). From Cancer Patient to Cancer Survivor: lost in Transition.

Datta, J., Smith, J. J., Chatila, W. K., McAuliffe, J. C., Kandoth, C., Vakiani, E., et al. (2020). Coaltered Ras/B-raf and TP53 Is Associated with Extremes of Survivorship and Distinct Patterns of Metastasis in Patients with Metastatic Colorectal Cancer. *Clinical Cancer Research, 26*(5), 1077–1085. https://doi.org/10.1158/1078-0432.ccr-19-2390.

Donovan, K. A., Thompson, L. M. A., & Hoffe, S. E. (2010). Sexual function in colorectal cancer survivors. *Cancer Control, 17*(1), 44–51. https://doi.org/10.1177/107327481001700106.

Elfeki, H., Thyø, A., Nepogodiev, D., Pinkney, T. D., White, M., Laurberg, S., et al. (2018). Patient and healthcare professional perceptions of colostomy-related problems and their impact on quality of life following rectal cancer surgery. *BJS Open, 2*(5), 336–344. https://doi.org/10.1002/bjs5.69.

El-Shami, K., Oeffinger, K. C., Erb, N. L., Willis, A., Bretsch, J. K., Pratt-Chapman, M. L., et al. (2015). American Cancer Society Colorectal Cancer Survivorship Care Guidelines. *CA Cancer Journal for Clinicians, 65*(6), 427–455. https://doi.org/10.3322/caac.21286.

Eyl, R. E., Thong, M. S. Y., Carr, P. R., Jansen, L., Koch-Gallenkamp, L., Hoffmeister, M., et al. (2020). Physical activity and long-term fatigue among colorectal cancer survivors - A population-based prospective study. *BMC cancer, 20*(1), 1–11. https://doi.org/10.1186/s12885-020-06918-x.

Eyl, R. E., Xie, K., Koch-Gallenkamp, L., Brenner, H., & Arndt, V. (2018). Quality of life and physical activity in long-term (≥5 years post-diagnosis) colorectal cancer survivors - systematic review. *Health and Quality of Life Outcomes [Electronic Resource], 16*(1), 1–13. https://doi.org/10.1186/s12955-018-0934-7.

Ganesh, V., Agarwal, A., Popovic, M., Cella, D., McDonald, R., Vuong, S., et al. (2016). Comparison of the FACT-C, EORTC QLQ-CR38, and QLQ-CR29 quality of life questionnaires for patients with colorectal cancer: a literature review. *Supportive Care in Cancer, 24*(8), 3661–3668. https://doi.org/10.1007/s00520-016-3270-7.

Gibson, T. M., Park, Y., Robien, K., Shiels, M. S., Black, A., Sampson, J. N., et al. (2014). Body mass index and risk of second obesity-associated cancers after colorectal cancer: a pooled analysis of prospective cohort studies. *Journal of Clinical Oncology, 32*(35), 4004–4011. https://doi.org/10.1200/JCO.2014.56.8444.

Hamers, P. A. H., Elferink, M. A. G., Stellato, R. K., Punt, C. J. A., May, A. M., Koopman, M., et al. (2021). Informing metastatic colorectal cancer patients by quantifying multiple scenarios for survival time based on real-life data. *International Journal of Cancer, 148*(2), 296–306. https://doi.org/10.1002/ijc.33200.

Heinsbergen, M., Haan, N., Maaskant-Braat, A. J., Melenhorst, J., Belgers, E. H., Leijtens, J. W., et al. (2019). Functional bowel complaints and quality of life after surgery for colon cancer: prevalence and predictive factors. *Colorectal Disease, 22*(2), 136–145. https://doi.org/10.1111/codi.14818.

Heise, D., Bayings, W., Tuinhof, A., Eickhoff, R., Kroh, A., Ulmer, F., et al. (2017). Long-term outcome and quality of life after initial and repeat resection of colorectal liver metastasis: a retrospective analysis. *International Journal of Surgery, 48*, 281–285. https://doi.org/10.1016/j.ijsu.2017.11.032.

Jenkinson, C., Coulter, A., & Wright, L. (1993). Short form 36 (SF 36) health survey questionnaire: normative data for adults of working age. *British Medical Journal, 306*(6890), 1437–1440. https://doi.org/10.1136/bmj.306.6890.1437.

Johnston, F. M., Yeo, H. L., Clark, C., & Stewart, J. H. (2021). Bias Issues in Colorectal Cancer Management: a Review. *Annals of Surgical Oncology*, 1–8. https://doi.org/10.1245/s10434-021-10232-6.

Langenhoff, B. S., Krabbe, P. F. M., Peerenboom, L., Wobbes, T., & Ruers, T. J. M. (2006). Quality of life after surgical treatment of colorectal liver metastases. *British Journal of Surgery, 93*(8), 1007–1014. https://doi.org/10.1002/bjs.5387.

Lim, C.Y.S., Laidsaar-Powell, R.C., Young, J.M., Kao, S.C.H., Zhang, Y., & Butow, P. (2021). Colorectal cancer survivorship: a systematic review and thematic synthesis of qualitative research. *European Journal of Cancer Care*, 30(4), 1–18. e13421, https://doi.org/10.1111/ecc.13421.

Luo, X., Li, J., Chen, M., Gong, J., Xu, Y., & Li, Q. (2021). A literature review of post-treatment survivorship interventions for colorectal cancer survivors and/or their caregivers. *Psycho-Oncology, 30*(6), 807–817. https://doi.org/10.1002/pon.5657.

Mahar, A. L., Compton, C., Halabi, S., Hess, K. R., Weiser, M. R., & Groome, P. A. (2017). Personalizing prognosis in colorectal cancer: a systematic review of the quality and nature of clinical prognostic tools for survival outcomes. *Journal of Surgical Oncology, 116*(8), 969–982. https://doi.org/10.1002/jso.24774.

McCracken, E., K. , E., Samsa, G. P., Fisher, D. A., Farrow, N. E., Landa, K., et al. (2019). Prognostic significance of primary tumor sidedness in patients undergoing liver resection for metastatic colorectal cancer. *HPB, 21*(12), 1667–1675. https://doi.org/10.1016/j.hpb.2019.03.365.

McDougall, J. A., Blair, C. K., Wiggins, C. L., Goodwin, M. B., Chiu, V. K., Rajput, A., et al. (2019). Socioeconomic disparities in health-related quality of life among colorectal cancer survivors. *Journal of Cancer Survivorship, 13*(3), 459–467. https://doi.org/10.1007/s11764-019-00767-9.

Meyerhardt, J. A., Sato, K., Niedzwiecki, D., Ye, C., Saltz, L. B., Mayer, R. J., et al. (2012). Dietary glycemic load and cancer recurrence and survival in patients with stage III colon cancer: findings from CALGB 89803. *JNCI: Journal of the National Cancer Institute, 104*(22), 1702–1711. https://doi.org/10.1093/jnci/djs399.

Raoof, M., Haye, S., Ituarte, P. H. G., & Fong, Y. (2019). Liver Resection Improves Survival in Colorectal Cancer Patients: causal-effects From Population-level Instrumental Variable Analysis. *Annals of Surgery, 270*(4), 692–700. https://doi.org/10.1097/SLA.0000000000003485.

Rees, J. R., Blazeby, J. M., Brookes, S. T., John, T., Welsh, F. K., & Rees, M. (2014). Patient-reported outcomes in long-term survivors of metastatic colorectal cancer needing liver resection. *British Journal of Surgery, 101*(11), 1468–1474. https://doi.org/10.1002/bjs.9620.

Rees, J. R., Blazeby, J. M., Fayers, P., Friend, E. A., Welsh, F. K. S., John, T. G., et al. (2012). Patient-reported outcomes after hepatic resection of colorectal cancer metastases. *Journal of Clinical Oncology, 30*(12), 1364–1370. https://doi.org/10.1200/JCO.2011.38.6177.

Rutherford, C., Müller, F., Faiz, N., King, M. T., & White, K. (2020). Patient-reported outcomes and experiences from the perspective of colorectal cancer survivors: meta-synthesis of qualitative studies. *Journal of Patient-Reported Outcomes, 4*(1), 1–19. https://doi.org/10.1186/s41687-020-00195-9.

Shapiro, C. L., Jacobsen, P. B., Henderson, T., Hurria, A., Nekhlyudov, L., Ng, A., et al. (2016). ReCAP: ASCO Core Curriculum for Cancer Survivorship Education. *Journal of Oncology Practice, 12*(2), 145. https://doi.org/10.1200/JOP.2015.009449.

Smith, F., Öhlén, J., Persson, L.-O., & Carlsson, E. (2018). Daily Assessment of Stressful events and Coping in early post-operative recovery after colorectal cancer surgery. *European Journal of Cancer Care, 27*(2), 1–10. https://doi.org/10.1111/ecc.12829.

Subbiah, I.M., Charone, M.M., Roszik, J., Haider, A., Vidal, M., Wong, A., et al. (2021). Association of Edmonton Symptom Assessment System Global Distress Score With Overall Survival in Patients With Advanced Cancer. *JAMA Network Open*, 4(7), e2117295, https://doi.org/10.1001/jamanetworkopen.2021.17295.

Tohme, S., Sanin, G. D., Patel, V., Bess, K., Ahmed, N., Krane, A., et al. (2020). Health-Related Quality of Life as a Prognostic Factor in Patients After Resection of Hepatic Malignancies. *Journal of Surgical Research, 245*, 257–264. https://doi.org/10.1016/j.jss.2019.07.061.

Vu, J. V. T., Matusko, N., Hendren, S., Regenbogen, S. E., & Hardiman, K. M. (2019). Patient-Reported Unmet Needs in Colorectal Cancer Survivors After Treatment for Curative Intent. *Diseases of the Colon and Rectum, 62*(7), 815–822. https://doi.org/10.1097/DCR.0000000000001326.

Welten, V.M., Fields, A.C., Yoo, J., Irani, J.L., Goldberg, J.E., Bleday, R., et al. (2021). Survival Outcomes for Colorectal Cancer with Isolated Liver Metastases at Academic Versus Community Hospitals. *Journal of Gastrointestinal Surgery*, 26(1), 209–213. https://doi.org/10.1007/s11605-021-05062-6.

Wiering, B., Oyen, W. J. G., Adang, E. M. M., Van Der Sijp, J. R. M., Roumen, R. M., De Jong, K. P., et al. (2011). Long-term global quality of life in patients treated for colorectal liver metastases. *British Journal of Surgery, 98*(4), 565–571. https://doi.org/10.1002/bjs.7365.

Yang, B., Jacobs, E. J., Gapstur, S. M., Stevens, V., & Campbell, P. T. (2015). Active smoking and mortality among colorectal cancer survivors: the cancer prevention study II nutrition cohort. *Journal of Clinical Oncology, 33*(8), 885–893. https://doi.org/10.1200/JCO.2014.58.3831.

Young, A. L., Lee, E., Absolom, K., Baxter, H., Christophi, C., Lodge, J. P. A., et al. (2018). Expectations of outcomes in patients with colorectal cancer. *BJS Open, 2*(5), 285–292. https://doi.org/10.1002/bjs5.73.

Index

Page numbers followed by "*f*" and "*t*" indicate, figures and tables respectively.

Printed in the United States
by Baker & Taylor Publisher Services